AMERICA'S LOST PLAYS

VII

The Early Plays of
JAMES A. HERNE

VIII

THE GREAT DIAMOND ROBBERY
and Other Recent Melodramas

A series in twenty volumes of hitherto unpublished
plays collected with the aid of the Rockefeller
Foundation, under the auspices of the Dramatists'
Guild of the Authors' League of America, edited
with historical and bibliographical notes.

BARRETT H. CLARK

GENERAL EDITOR

Advisory Board

ROBERT HAMILTON BALL, QUEENS COLLEGE

HOYT H. HUDSON, PRINCETON UNIVERSITY

GLENN HUGHES, UNIVERSITY OF WASHINGTON

GARRETT H. LEVERTON, FORMERLY OF NORTHWEST-
ERN UNIVERSITY

E. C. MABIE, UNIVERSITY OF IOWA

ALLARDYCE NICOLL, YALE UNIVERSITY

ARTHUR HOBSON QUINN, UNIVERSITY OF
PENNSYLVANIA

NAPIER WILT, UNIVERSITY OF CHICAGO

The Early Plays of

James A. Herne

WITH ACT IV OF

GRIFFITH DAVENPORT

EDITED WITH AN INTRODUCTION BY

ARTHUR HOBSON QUINN

INDIANA UNIVERSITY PRESS

BLOOMINGTON

Requests for authorization of the use of any of the plays in this volume on the stage, the screen, or for radio or television broadcasting, or for any purpose of reproduction, will be forwarded by Princeton University Press to the proper persons.

Second printing April 1964

CONTENTS

INTRODUCTION

THESE plays of James A. Herne, now printed for the first time, represent him in the earlier stages of his career, with the exception of the fragment of *The Reverend Griffith Davenport*. He was born February 1, 1839, at Cohoes, N.Y., and made his stage début as George Shelby in *Uncle Tom's Cabin* at the Adelphi Theatre in Troy, in 1859. After playing several seasons with stock companies in Baltimore, Philadelphia and Washington, he became the leading man for Lucille Western, and his first visit to California, in 1868, was with her company. It was in the 'seventies, however, when he became the stage manager at Maguire's New Theatre in San Francisco, that he began to write plays. His great admiration for Dickens is reflected not only in some of these adaptations, which have perished, but also in his acting parts such as Caleb Plummer, Dan'l Peggotty and Captain Cuttle. Herne preferred to represent real life upon the stage, but he had also the actor's inherent love of romance and his first adaptation to survive in manuscript represents an interesting example of his collaboration with David Belasco, at all times a romantic artist.

Of even more importance for Herne's future career was his marriage with Katharine Corcoran, to whom he gave her first opportunity as an actress in 1877 and who, after their marriage in 1878, joined the Baldwin Theatre Stock Company. Her encouragement and her understanding of dramatic values were of inestimable advantage to Herne in his playwriting, and in his most important plays the leading part was interpreted by her with a skill which was amply recognized by contemporary dramatic criticism.

Within an Inch of His Life is a free adaptation of Emile Gaboriau's novel, *La Corde au Cou*. Miss Julie Herne is of the opinion that her father worked from an English translation, as his study of French began only in 1896. The relative shares of Herne and Belasco it is not possible now to assign accurately. Belasco's representation of the fire scene through red and yellow silk slips was one of his early successful bits of stage mechanics. The manuscript is not in the handwriting of either, but it remained in the possession of Herne and certain marginal notes are clearly in his script. The dramatization of *La Corde au Cou,* while it accentuated certain of the melodramatic elements of the original and even created new ones, is not on the whole unskilful. The painstaking details which French legal customs forced Gaboriau to insert, are done away with with a cheerful disregard of facts, amply justified by the directness of the play. While Herne and Belasco might have made a good scene out of the trial, the omission of the detective, Goudar, and his investigation of the illicit relations of Jacques de Boiscoran with the Comtesse de Claudieuse, as they are called in the novel, is a distinct improvement. The playwrights establish the relations of these two in Act I, Scene 2, which is not in the novel, but which is described much later by Jacques to his attorney. In the play the audience is put at once into possession of a knowledge of these relations, and suspicion is directed against the Comtesse. Her denunciation of Jacques is made the climax of the act. This greater emphasis makes Jacques' revelation of their relations more consistent with his rôle of hero. Another change was made by having Dionysia Chandore overhear the confession of Jacques to his counsel, and yet assert her love for him still. In the novel, she discovered his relation to the Comtesse by a slip of the attorney's tongue. The play thus carries over from the novel the strong motive of her devotion to her lover, but it establishes this motive earlier, and, in the hands of Katharine Corcoran, she was evidently an appealing figure on the stage.

In the novel, Jacques is condemned not to death but to twenty years' imprisonment, and his release is secured not only through Cocoleu's confession, but also through the Comte's dying statement that he believes Jacques innocent.

The most effective change came in the character of Cocoleu. In the novel he is simply an imbecile, devoted to his mistress, who reveals his crime to the detective under the influence of liquor. In the last scene of the play, however, his devotion is an active, not merely a passive force, and he comes of his own accord to the prison, and establishes much more convincingly the motive for the murder.

The Minute Men of 1774-1775 is the first surviving play of Herne's which may be considered entirely original. It represents a transitional stage in his development. The plot is conventional, and the historical background is not convincingly worked into the dramatic movement. Herne anticipated later writers, however, in making Lieutenant Smollet a natural, likable gentleman instead of the caricature which the British officer so often became in our drama of the Revolution. Ann Campbell may seem exaggerated for purposes of low comedy, but she was not unlike the pioneer type whose services to the Revolution are matters of record. The achievement of Herne in this play lay in the character of Dorothy Foxglove, written for Mrs. Herne. Whenever she appears, the stage takes on life. Instead of being merely receptive, like the usual romantic heroine, she is an active force, dominating the scene, but ruling it through her charm and spontaneity, which are reflected even in the manuscript. In the hands of Katharine Corcoran, they must have been irresistible.

The criticisms in the *Philadelphia Ledger* and the *Philadelphia Press* of April 7 speak of the effectiveness of the production, which was enthusiastically received by the audience.

Herne's next step in the progress toward realism is represented in *Drifting Apart*. The manuscript of this play has disappeared and the early form here printed under its first title, *Mary the Fishermen's Child,* underwent much revision before it saw the stage. It is hardly fair to judge Herne by this preliminary draft. The low-comedy scenes which he himself stigmatizes as "weak" are certainly overstressed.

What makes the play of especial interest, however, is the early use of the dream scene in Acts III and IV. Any competent dreamer will recognize the confusion of motivation in the third Act, especially in the relations of Mary and Percy, as quite in keeping with a dream in Jack's state of mind. Also quite natural, in a dream, was the transition to stark tragedy in the fourth Act. Such a scene as that which closed the fourth Act seems quite in keeping with modern stage technique. But in 1888 it was daring, for audiences still felt called upon to be shocked by such death scenes, unless they were placed in the past, and dignified by the glamour of poetry.

Drifting Apart, though it ran for two hundred and fifty performances, was not considered a financial success. According to Mrs. Herne, audiences disliked having their feelings harrowed by what turned out to be a dream. But the play attracted the attention of realists like William Dean Howells and Hamlin Garland, and Herne was encouraged to write his epoch making play, *Margaret Fleming. Shore Acres* followed and after a romantic play, *My Colleen,* which has been lost, came *The Reverend Griffith Davenport.* This was based upon a novel, *An Unofficial Patriot,* by Helen H. Gardener. Herne moulded this loosely constructed story into a unified drama to which contemporary criticism gave a high place for its sweep and color and for its character portrayal.

The unique manuscript of *Griffith Davenport* was burned in the fire which destroyed Herne Oaks. When the late Brander Matthews was in London in 1925, he was presented with the manuscript of the fourth Act, which is here printed. It had been found among the papers of the critic, William Archer, and his executors, knowing Archer's high opinion of Herne's work, felt it should be preserved in the United States. In a recent letter of C. Archer, he speaks of his late brother's attitude:

"In his [William Archer's] article on *The Development of American Drama* (*Harper's Monthly Magazine,* December 1920), speaking of the state of the drama in 1899, he says: 'In *Shore Acres* and *Sag Harbour* James A. Herne was producing delicately faithful pictures of rural life; while in *Griffith Davenport* (an unappreciated and now lost work) he had created an exquisitely true and beautiful drama of American history.'"

Brander Matthews loaned me the manuscript on his return and I had copies made for Mrs. Herne, for the collection of manuscripts in the Library of the University of Pennsylvania, and for Dr. Matthews. He stated to me at that time that it was his intention to deposit the original manuscript in the Brander Matthews Dramatic Museum at Columbia University. The manuscript has not been found, however, either at Columbia or among his papers. It would have again been lost if the copies had not been made. For the scenario of the other Acts, which is printed as an introduction to Act IV, I am indebted to Mrs. Herne and to Miss Julie Herne, who acted Emma West in the play.

I have deemed it best to print the plays, so far as possible, exactly as Herne wrote them. Students of the drama will be interested to have the stage directions reproduced just as a practical playwright of that era indicated them for his actors. Obvious mistakes in spelling and punctuation made by copyists have, however, been corrected.

It has not been possible to give complete casts of those who acted in the first productions of the plays. Information derived from T. Allston Brown's *History of the New York Stage,* from William Winter's *Life of Belasco,* from the newspapers and from Miss Julie Herne, has been incorporated in the casts as given. Unfortunately, no programs remain in Mrs. Herne's possession. The cast of *The Minute Men* was furnished by the courtesy of Mrs. Charles Wesley Phy, from the notes of her late husband, who at the time of his death had almost brought to completion his *History of the Philadelphia Stage from 1878 to 1890.*

WITHIN AN INCH OF HIS LIFE

CAST OF CHARACTERS

(Grand Opera House, San Francisco, February 17, 1879)

JULES DE DARDEVILLE	JAMES O'NEILL
DR. SEIGNEBOS	J. W. JENNINGS
COUNT DE CLAIRNOT	JAMES A. HERNE
COCOLEAU	LEWIS MORRISON
GALPIN	A. D. BRADLEY
SENESCHAL	
MECHINET	
FOLGAT	
MAGLOIRE	
BLANGIN	
RIBOT	WILLIAM SEYMOUR
GAUDRY	JOHN N. LONG
PIERRE	
GENEVIEVE, *Countess de Clairnot*	ROSE WOOD
DIONYSIA CHANDORE	KATHARINE CORCORAN
COLLETTE	
GENDARMES, PEASANTS, ETC.	

ACT I.

SCENE 1: *Forest of Rochpommier. Time: Night. Enter Gaudry, a ragged poacher, R.1.E.*

GAU. A good night for poaching! Dark as pitch, and every keeper snug in bed! My traps are set and before morning will catch game enough to keep me a week. Hark! Some one comes. [*Looks off R.1.E.*] Who can it be? He who walks the forest of Rochpommier at this hour has business of more importance than gathering chestnuts. [*Enter Jules de Dardeville, hurriedly, R.1.E., with gun. See description in Act II.*]

JUL. A good path:—deserted, and not a soul stirring. So far, so good.

GAU. [*Aside, from concealment*] It is Jules de Dardeville, who is going to be married to the heiress, Miss Dionysia. I'd better be off! Poaching's dangerous business. [*Sneaks off L.1.E.*]

RIB. [*Outside R.1.E.*] Hello, there!

JUL. [*Starting*] Some one coming! It is too late to hide myself.

RIB. [*Entering R.1.E.*] Who's there?

JUL. A stranger; on his way to Brechy.

RIB. [*Aside, eyeing Jules closely*] On his way to Brechy? Well, he has taken a rather roundabout way to go to Brechy! [*Aloud*] Why, the high road would fetch you there in half the time.

JUL. [*Quickly*] I—I did not mean Brechy. I meant Seille.

RIB. Ha! Ha! Seille! Come, that's good! The nearest road to Seille is by the cross-road.

JUL. True! True!

RIB. True! Come, confess; confess at once! There's a woman in it. You're good-looking, like me! There's some one in the woods dying to see you; and you are dying to see some one. That's me! I don't deny it; I glory in it. Only I'm not so spooney as to get bothered and mixed up when I'm caught, eh? Ha! Ha! [*Laughing and poking Jules*]

JUL. [*Affecting a laugh*] Really, my friend, you mistake me! I am going to shoot tomorrow at Seille. You see! Here's my gun!

RIB. Yes. Ha! Ha! And so am I! Only it isn't exactly that kind of game. [*Bell strikes eleven*] Eleven o'clock! I must be off. I wish you luck anyhow; only, stranger, look out. It's dangerous business. [*Going L., aside*] That's

Jules de Dardeville. The sly dog don't know Ribot, but Ribot knows him. [*Exits chuckling*]

JUL. Dangerous business? Yes. Too true, too true! I have been observed, but not recognized. [*Examining gun*] One barrel empty. It's best to be prepared for an emergency. [*Takes curtridge box from pocket and puts cartridges in gun*] There! Thank Heaven tonight will decide this ugly affair and, I hope, forever. [*Exits L.1.E.*]

SCENE 2: *Valpinson by moonlight. Chateau with large massive doors. Balcony, steps, etc., C. Private entrance concealed by shrubbery, etc., etc. For full description of scene, see diagram.*[1] *Enter Countess Clairnot, hurriedly, from private entrance R.3.E. She looks around to see that she is not observed.*

COUNTESS. [*Coming C.*] Another hour and the dream of my life is broken. Yes, one short hour will end it all. Oh, Count Clairnot, you were cruel to forget that you were thirty years older than your wretched bride! I sacrificed myself to save my father's honor. But the restoration of that honor has been the ruin of a life! From that moment, I have hated and despised you! My father owes his life to you and your gold—and I—I, all my shame and despair. [*Turning towards R.3.E.*] He comes! Jules de Dardeville; the lover of Countess Clairnot. [*Laughs*] What would the world say, did they hear that? The world—[*Enter Jules R.3.E.*]

JUL. Genevieve.

COUNTESS. [*Coldly*] You have come. Jules de Dardeville, let us understand each other. You have proposed the mutual return of our correspondence. You say your mother wants you to marry. And you—what do you want?

JUL. I? [*Laughs*] I want nothing just now. But the thing will have to be done, sooner or later! A man must have a home—must have domestic relations, which the world acknowledges—

COUNTESS. And I—what am I to you?

JUL. You—you, Genevieve! I love you with all the strength of my heart! But we are separated by a gulf. You are married.

COUNTESS. Married. In other words, you have loved me as a toy. I have been the amusement of your idle hours;—that love, that romance, which every man must have. Now you are getting serious, and you leave me.

JUL. You—you have your home, your husband, your child—

COUNTESS. [*Bitterly*] Yes. I shall live here at Valpinson—when every place recalls to me your presence. I shall live here with my husband, whom I have betrayed; with my child, who is—[*Turning to him expressively*]

[1] No diagram was discovered with the manuscript.

JUL. Genevieve! This cannot last forever. Through my mother's earnest desire—not mine—I am betrothed to Dionysia Chandore. Shortly she will become my wife.

COUNTESS. [*Fiercely*] Your wife! No, Jules, no! That shall never be!

JUL. [*Quickly*] What would you do?

COUNTESS. Do? [*Slowly and deliberately*] I should give your letters to my husband.

JUL. You would not do that!

COUNTESS. [*Calmly*] Do not try me too far. [*Looking at him with a smile*] You are surprised at my determination, Jules de Dardeville. Hitherto, wives who have deceived their husbands have not held their lovers responsible. They have been betrayed but dared not cry aloud;—abandoned, only to submit and hide their tears—for who would pity them? But what no one dares, I dare! It shall not be said that in our common fault there are two parties, and that you shall have all the advantages and I must bear all the disgrace. What? You would be free, that you might console yourself with a new love! And I—I should have to sink under my shame and remorse. No! No! Such bonds as ours are not broken so easily. You belong to me! You are mine; and I shall defend you with such arms as I possess. I told you I valued my reputation more than my life—that my life was nothing. But now my reputation is less than my life. Go, marry Dionysia Chandore; and, as the priest joins your hands, my husband shall know all!

JUL. Madness!

COUNTESS. Aye, madness! Call it what you will. Call it love—to you a whim—a toy to be cast aside and trampled on—to me, life, death, desperation! Madness! Yes, madness that would sacrifice your life, your honor, with a smile on my lips, even though my heart should break.

JUL. Genevieve, we *must* part—it is for the best.

COUNTESS. Part! I inspire you with horror, do I? You would be free? Free! Beware! Beware!

JUL. Not so loud!—

COUNTESS. What do I care? What does it matter? Happiness awaits you, a new life, full of intoxicating hope. It is quite natural that *you* should dread discovery. *I,* whose life is ended, and who have nothing to look for—I, in whom you have killed every hope—I am not afraid.

JUL. [*Aside*] She is determined. But Jules de Dardeville never was afraid of an enemy; not even the Count Clairnot! [*Clutching his gun. Aloud*] You say you love me?

COUNTESS. Madly! Passionately!

JUL. Then in the name of that love, I appeal to you to release me.

COUNTESS. To wed another? Never! Never!

JUL. If I had foreseen this, our acquaintance never would have existed.

COUNTESS. Acquaintance? You confess then that you have never loved me!

JUL. You know the contrary.

COUNTESS. Still you think of abandoning me for another—for this Dionysia.

JUL. You are married. You cannot be mine!

COUNTESS. [*Quickly*] Then if I were free—

JUL. Free? You would be my wife.

COUNTESS. [*Aside, taking stage*] His wife! If I were free, I would be his wife! God! Luckily that thought never occurred to me before. Murder!

JUL. Calm yourself, Genevieve. This marriage which I mentioned is not my doing but that of my family. I have had no hand in it. My father called on M. de Chandore and asked him for the hand of his daughter. I have been publicly acknowledged as her betrothed and they themselves have fixed the wedding day.

COUNTESS. Is this true?

JUL. I swear it!

COUNTESS. You are not deceiving me, Jules?

JUL. Deceiving you? Why should I? I have loved you always—I love you still.

COUNTESS. But she—Dionysia—loves you. That love which is my disgrace is her honor.

JUL. But my love is, and always shall be, yours.

COUNTESS. [*With joy*] Oh, Jules! [*Recovering herself*] I believe you! I must believe you!

JUL. [*Aside*] At any price, I must have those letters.

COUNTESS. Jules, promise me one thing—till I of my own free will release you, you will never, never marry this Dionysia Chandore.

JUL. I promise! Where is the Count Clairnot?

COUNTESS. Confined to his room. He thinks I am sitting up with my child. But now to the business that brings you here. You think it best that we destroy our letters?

JUL. Yes. We cannot foresee events. The Count may discover them.

COUNTESS. True! Where are mine?

JUL. Here they are. [*Takes packet from pocket*]

COUNTESS. And here are yours. [*Produces them*]

JUL. [*Quickly*] We'll burn them!

COUNTESS. [*Gives them to him*] You see, Jules, I trust you. [*Jules goes to shrubbery R. lights both packets and then throws them out of sight*]

COUNTESS. [*As he comes down*] And that is all—all that remains of five years of our life, of our love, and of our vows—ashes!

JUL. Genevieve, forgive me all this bitterness. I, too, am unhappy—unhappy as yourself. But remember we are separated by an impassable gulf—society, family, marriage. In a word, the world stands between our loves. My family decides I must marry. Prudence compels it. I must go my way, and you yours. But till you of your own free will release me and break the chains that bind us I will remain faithful to my promise. Calm yourself. Do not grieve me more. Genevieve, promise me.

COUNTESS. [*Turns from him*] Spare me! I promise nothing! Go! Go! [*Crosses L.*]

JUL. Good-bye! Let us part friends. [*Offers his hand*]

COUNTESS. [*Taking it*] Good-bye.

JUL. [*Going R. turns and looks at Countess for a moment. She stands as immovable as a statue*] Genevieve! Farewell! [*Exits quickly through private entrance R.3. A slight pause. The Countess then suddenly realizes that she is alone*]

COUNTESS. [*With a cry*] His wife! [*Rising*] If I were free, I would be his wife. What terrible thought is darkly hidden in those words! [*In a hoarse whisper*] Murder! Murder! [*Exits greatly agitated R.3.E. A fire starts up from the place where Jules fired the letters and reaches to the house; and spreads till the whole building is in flames. Slight hurry inside. Cries of "fire" heard within. Count Clairnot rushes from doors C. and stands on steps*]

COUNT. Fire! Fire! Help! Help! [*At the same moment a shot is fired from shrubbery of private entrance.* NOTE: *The gun-barrel must be pushed forward enough to let the audience see the discharge, but not who discharges it. The Count staggers forward*]

COUNT. I am murdered! Assassin! [*He staggers towards shrubbery. Just before he reaches it, another shot is fired from the same place. The Count reels and falls C.*] Help! Murder! Help! [*Hurry within. Loud cries of "fire," general commotion and conflagration. Servants enter from house, and peasantry, citizens, etc., from all directions*]

PIERRE. [*Seeing Count*] What! The Count murdered!

OMNES. Murdered? [*Enter Countess from R.3.E.*]

COUNTESS. My husband! Murdered! The house in flames! [*The screams of a child heard in house*]

COUNTESS. My God! My child! Save her!

OMNES. It is impossible!

COUNTESS. [*Sinking on her knees*] Oh, wretched, wretched Genevieve! My child! She is lost! [*Suddenly the C. doors which are enveloped in flames are burst open and the idiot, Cocoleau, appears half blinded with smoke and fire carrying the child of the Countess*]

COCO. [*Coming down*] No! No! Ha! Ha! Ha! Saved, saved! [*Laughs idiotically. House falls with a crash*]

ACT II.

SCENE: *Chamber in the house of M. Seneschal, the mayor of Valpinson. Time: Night. Large C. doors. Doors R. and L.2.E. Count Clairnot on sofa R.H. Doctor Seignebos standing near table, arranging bandages, etc. Countess at foot of sofa kneeling. Mechinet standing at table with writing materials down L. Galpin at rear C. Two Gendarmes at C. doors. Gendarmes at door R. and L.*

COUNT. [*With effort*] My friends, you see the year 1871 is a fatal year. It has left me nothing but a handful of ashes.

SEN. Thank Heaven, you are safe.

COUNT. Who knows? I am suffering terribly!

COUNTESS. Courage, husband, courage!

COUNT. Pardon me, dear Genevieve, pardon me, if I show any want of fortitude.

DR. S. [*Addressing Omnes*] You see, gentlemen, he's in a bad plight! Wounds of this kind, although apparently not of a serious nature at first, often prove fatal.

GAL. [*Coming forward, to Doctor*] Therefore, Doctor, I am here. A crime has been committed. The criminal must be tracked, discovered, convicted, and punished! [*With great authority*] Therefore, I request your assistance and the assistance of those around me, in the name of the *Law!* [*Turning to Doctor*] Have you any objection to my questioning your patient?

DR. S. It would certainly be better for him to be left alone. I have made him suffer quite enough already. But if it must be—

GAL. It must be.

DR. S. Well, then, make haste.

GAL. [*Takes seat, beside the Count, at sofa*] Are you strong enough to answer my questions?

COUNT. Yes, yes, quite.

GAL. Then tell me all you know of the events of last night.

COUNT. I know but little. Shortly after the bell had struck eleven, a bright blaze flashed upon my window. Amazed, yet half-asleep, I was quickly aroused by the crash of something falling and the cry of "Fire." I rushed down stairs, but had hardly made a step, when I felt a fierce pain in my right side and heard a shot. I remembered I had that very evening left my gun in the shrubbery on the right of the steps. I endeavored, as best I could, to reach it and defend myself from the assassin, when directly from the shrubbery the assassin fired again, and after that all is blank.

GAL. [*Interestedly*] You did not see the assassin then?

COUNT. [*Shakes his head*] No.

GAL. Who can tell us what happened after you fell?

COUNT. Probably my wife, the Countess.

GAL. True! The Countess, no doubt, got up when you rose.

COUNT. My wife had not gone to bed. [*Galpin turns quickly to Countess, who avoids his glance*] Bertha, our little child, has been very ill. My wife was sitting up with her.

GAL. [*Suspiciously*] Exactly. [*To Countess*] When, and how did *you* become aware of the situation?

COUNTESS. My husband has told you I was sitting up with little Bertha. I was tired, for I had not gone to bed the night before, and had fallen into a doze when a sudden noise and light aroused me. Just then I heard a shot, quickly followed by another, and then cries for help! I hurried down in great haste. The front door was open and by the light of the flames I beheld my husband lying on the ground! Remembering my child, I beseeched the people to save it, but none would dare to venture, for the flames had enveloped everything. Then Cocoleau rushed from amidst the burning mass, bearing my child from the very jaws of death!

COUNT. Brave fellow!

GAL. Cocoleau—and who is Cocoleau?

DR. S. An idiot! An imbecile!

COUNTESS. This fire will probably ruin us! But what matters that so long as my husband and my child are safe!

DR. S. [*Rising*] Now sir, I hope you'll let me have my patient again.

GAL. Sir, I appreciate your duties, but mine are no less important.

DR. S. [*Sitting down*] Fudge!

GAL. Consequently, you will be pleased, sir, to grant me five minutes more.

DR. S. Ten, if it must be, sir. Only, I warn you that every minute henceforth may endanger the life of my patient.

GAL. I have only one more question to ask. [*To Count*] Where were you standing, and where do you think the murderer was standing, at the moment when the crime was committed?

COUNT. I was standing, as I told you, on the threshold of my door facing the courtyard. The murderer must have been standing some twenty yards off, on my right, behind a pile of wood.

GAL. [*Turning to Doctor*] You heard what he said, sir. It is for you now to aid justice by telling us at what distance the murderer must have been when he fired.

DR. S. I don't pretend to solve riddles.

GAL. Oh, have a care, sir! Justice, whom I here represent, has the right and the means to enforce respect. You are a physician, sir, and your medical science enables you to answer this question with almost mathematical accuracy.

DR. S. [*Aside*] Mathematical fiddlesticks!

GAL. What distance was the assassin from the Count when he fired?

DR. S. A conundrum! I give it up!

GAL. Have a care, sir! I can enforce the law.

DR. S. Then to answer you plainly, sir, it all depends upon the species of weapon used; whether it be a cannon, a gun, or a pistol. [*Sitting down*]

GAL. [*Enraged*] Remember, sir, that—

OMNES. [*Outside*] Death to the incendiary! Death to the assassin! [*Enter Pierre C. L.*]

PIERRE. [*Hurriedly*] A citizen and one of the firemen have been missing since the fall of the north wall. We have just discovered their remains among the ruins.

COUNT. Great Heavens! And I was complaining of my losses! Two men killed! Murdered! Poor men! Their bravery has cost them dear!

OMNES. [*Outside*] Death to the incendiary! Death to the assassin!

GAL. [*To Gendarmes at C. D.*] Admit the people. [*Gendarmes open doors C. Enter Peasants*]

OMNES. Death to the incendiary! Death to the assassin!

GAL. [*To Peasants*] You are right, good people! But we must first discover the criminal. Some one among you probably knows something. [*Pierre exits quickly C. Noise off C. Enter Pierre and a Peasant pushing Cocoleau in front of them. Cocoleau slightly resists*]

PIERRE. [*Pushing Cocoleau forward*] He knows something!

PEASANTS. Make him tell! Make him tell! [*Cocoleau stares around half-frightened, then suddenly starts to go off door C. Pierre, with Peasants, stops Cocoleau and pushes him down C. again*]

GAL. [*To Pierre*] Who is this, my good fellow?

PIERRE. Cocoleau.

GAL. Oh! So this is Cocoleau?

PIERRE. He knows something. He said so himself.

PEASANTS. Make him tell! Make him tell!

GAL. Aha! That is what we want. [*To Cocoleau*] Cocoleau?

COCO. [*Glances from one person to another idiotically, then looks at Galpin*] Eh?

DR. S. Stay, sir. You don't really mean to examine this fellow as a witness?

GAL. And why not?

DR. S. Because he cannot possibly understand your questions. He's a fool! An ass! And an ass is a fool; and a fool is a natural born ass!

GAL. [*Decidedly*] I know *my* duty, sir!

DR. S. [*Pompously*] And I know *my* duty, sir! Consider, sir, if this fellow should make a formal charge against any one! [*Cocoleau looks frightened at Dr. Seignebos*]

COUNT. At all events it was he who saved our child. Come nearer, Cocoleau. [*Cocoleau first hesitates, then finally steps nearer Count*] Come nearer. No one here would harm you. See, here is the Countess. She has been very kind to you.

COCO. [*Looks at Countess tenderly*] Good—dear—dear—lady!

GAL. Madam, request him to speak. He knows something. [*Countess starts*]

GAL. He seems attached to you and perhaps, if you will ask him, will tell us—

COUNTESS. [*Recovering herself*] Cocoleau, do not be afraid. Tell us what you know.

COCO. [*Reassured, stutters*] I—am—not—afraid.

DR. S. [*Rising*] Once more, I protest!

GAL. [*To Dr. Seignebos*] Sit down, sir!

DR. S. Fudge! [*Takes seat*]

COUNT. [*To Galpin*] It may be dangerous to question an irresponsible party.

GAL. [*Decidedly*] Gentlemen, I must beg to proceed in my own way. You will be silent. [*To Cocoleau*] Cocoleau, my boy, listen, and try to understand what I am going to say. [*Cocoleau nods head and looks stupidly*]

GAL. There has been a fire—

COCO. [*Knowingly*] Fire!

GAL. Yes, fire—which has burned down the house of your benefactor—fire which has killed two good men.

Coco. [*Repeats*] Killed—two—men.

GAL. But that is not all! They have tried to murder! Do you see him there in his bed, wounded and covered with blood? [*Cocoleau turns his face slowly to Count*]

GAL. Do you see the Countess, how she suffers?

Coco. [*Turning and looking at Countess with a look of pity and love*] Yes.

GAL. All these misfortunes are the work of a wicked man, a vile assassin! You hate him, don't you? You hate him?

Coco. [*Savagely, through his teeth*] Ye—yes!

GAL. You want him to be punished?

Coco. Yes! Yes!

GAL. Well then, you must help us to find him out so that the Gendarmes may catch him and put him in jail. [*Cocoleau hangs down his head, then glances from under his shaggy hair and looks furtively around the room, finally resting his eyes on the Countess*]

GAL. Do you hear me, my good boy?

Coco. Ye—yes!

GAL. And you will speak? [*Cocoleau slowly eyeing Countess, nods his head*]

GAL. [*With satisfaction*] Good! Then where did you spend last night?

Coco. [*Repeats the question, then answers*] In—the—courtyard.

GAL. Were you asleep when the fire broke out?

Coco. [*Quickly*] No!

GAL. Did you see it commence?

Coco. [*Long pause. He thinks, then answers suddenly*] Yes!

GAL. How did it commence? [*Cocoleau shakes his head; won't answer. Looks towards Countess with the timid expression of a dog who tries to read something in his master's eyes*]

COUNTESS. Yes, Cocoleau, tell us how it commenced.

Coco. [*With a flash of intelligence*] They—they set it afire!

GAL. On purpose?

Coco. Yes!

GAL. Who?

Coco. A—gentleman.

DR. S. [*Rising*] I protest! Such an examination is sheer folly!

GAL. [*Loudly to Dr. Seignebos*] Sit down, sir!

DR. S. [*Sitting*] Fudge!

GAL. Did you see the gentleman?

Coco. Yes!

GAL. Do you know who he is?

Coco. Very—very—well!

GAL. What is his name? [*General interest manifested*]

Coco. [*Slight pause*] Jules—Jules—de—de—Dardeville!

COUNT. Absurd!

DR. S. [*Keeping seat, triumphantly*] There! I told you so!

SENE. [*To Galpin*] If I were you, I'd attach no importance to the answer and consider it not given.

GAL. No. I shall proceed.

DR. S. [*Rising*] Proceed to what, sir? To array this idiot against your friend, Jules de Dardeville? Why the thing is ridiculous! You know that such a crime in him is actually impossible! And yet, without any evidence except the ravings of this idiot, you would publicly disgrace the man whom you pretend to be your friend, and whom you have dined with a hundred times, and who is universally respected by us all!

GAL. [*Sternly*] Nevertheless, gentlemen, I know my duty and shall proceed. [*To Cocoleau*] Do you know, my boy, what you say? Do you know that you are accusing a man of a horrible crime?

Coco. I—I—am—telling the—truth.

GAL. Jules de Dardeville set Valpinson on fire?

Coco. [*With conviction*] Yes.

GAL. How did he do it? [*Cocoleau pauses*]

GAL. Speak!

Coco. [*With countless contortions and painful efforts to speak commences*] I saw Jules de Dardeville—pull out—some—papers from his—pocket—light them—put them in—in shrubbery—near château!

COUNTESS. [*Aside, with a cry*] Oh!

[NOTE: *The actor playing the part of Cocoleau should study the business of Jules in Act I and go through same business here*]

GAL. [*To Cocoleau*] Now, good Cocoleau, since you have told us that Jules de Dardeville set the château on fire, tell us who fired upon the Count.

Coco. Who fired? [*Looks around, eyes the Countess, smiles with assurance*] Why—Jules de Dardeville—after—he—set—the—house—on—fire. Master—came—out—at—the—door—and—he—fired—from—the—trees. Master—fell! [*Laughs idiotically*] Ha! Ha! I saw it all! I saw it all! Yes! Ha! Ha!

GAL. If you saw it all, why didn't you seize the assassin?

Coco. [*Shakes his head*] Ha! Ha! Might get shot myself! Yes! Ha! Ha! Might get shot myself!

GAL. Since you saw it was Jules de Dardeville, tell us how he was dressed.

COCO. [*Looks at his own clothes, laughs*] Straw hat—short jacket—boots up here—[*Motioning*]—and gun.

DR. S. This is monstrous! To listen to the ravings of an idiot!

COUNT. Yes, I think myself, it's somewhat ridiculous to allow an honest man to be arraigned by this Cocoleau, who can scarcely remember from one hour to the other. Jules de Dardeville and myself had once a landsuit that culminated in a deadly quarrel. Still he is an honorable man and, although we once came near exchanging shots, I would as soon vouch for his honor as my own.

GAL. [*To Cocoleau*] Enough. [*Motions Cocoleau away. Cocoleau draws back and laughs meaninglessly, looking at Countess*]

DR. S. [*To Galpin*] What are you going to do?

GAL. I am going to prosecute. [*Noise outside center*] What is that? [*Enter Ribot and Gaudry C.*]

RIB. [*To Galpin, enquiringly*] The magistrate?

GAL. Yes. Can you throw any light upon this affair?

RIB. Yes. There was something suspicious happened to me last night.

GAL. [*To Mechinet*] Mechinet, here is another statement. [*To Ribot*] Well, sir, proceed.

RIB. Last night I was going through the forest of Rochpommier and, as I came near Valpinson, just as the bell struck eleven, I met a man hurrying along and acting as though he didn't want anyone to know much about him. He said he was going to Brechy, but when I told him he wasn't on the Brechy road, he looked confused and said he meant Seille. And I knew he lied, for if he was going to Seille he'd have taken the cross-roads—

GAL. Did you notice his dress?

RIB. Yes. He wore a straw hat, hunting jacket, and over-boots. He had a gun in his hand.

GAL. [*Interestedly*] Indeed! Could you swear to this?

RIB. Yes.

GAL. Did you recognize him as anyone you had seen before?

RIB. Yes—Jules de Dardeville. [*General movement*]

GAL. Jules de Dardeville! [*With satisfaction, to Mechinet*] Mechinet, have you taken down this witness's statement carefully?

MECH. Yes.

GAL. [*To Ribot*] That will do. [*Ribot bows and draws back*]

GAL. Now then, the next witness. [*Gaudry comes down*] Now then, my man, tell us what *you* know.

GAU. Last night I was in the forest of Rochpommier—

GAL. [*Interrupting*] Ah! You rascal! What were you doing there?

GAU. That's where I sleep, sir, on the leaves among the brushwood, for the sake of the fresh air.

GAL. Why do you sleep there?

GAU. So as to get up in the morning early. I pick chestnuts, sir, for the market.

GAL. Yes, I see. Go on.

GAU. Well, sir, I heard a noise, sir, and looking around, I saw a man coming along with a gun, talking to himself excited like, and going towards Valpinson. Shortly afterwards, I sees a blaze there and who should come back but the same man, going on just as before, only hurrying more and never looking back, but walking faster than a man could run.

GAL. You recognized him both times?

GAU. Yes.

GAL. Are you sure?

GAU. I would stake my life.

GAL. Then state in the presence of all, his name.

GAU. Jules de Dardeville.

GAL. Enough. Is there anyone else who knows anything. [*Pause*] None. Then we shall close the examination. You see, gentlemen, I was right. What, at first, was merely a doubt, gathered into a suspicion and then, at last facts. Cold, stern facts, promising actual proof, point in the direction of Jules de Dardeville! [*Noise off C. Enter Jacques*][1]

JAC. We have just discovered something, sir. [*Showing cartridge to Galpin*]

GAL. [*Taking cartridge from Jacques*] Why it is a cartridge! Where did you find this?

JAC. We found it near the shrubbery where the assassin concealed himself. He, no doubt, dropped it there last night.

COUNT. [*To Galpin*] Let me see it. [*Galpin gives cartridge to Count*] I can tell, at least, if the weapon used against me was my own, or that of another. [*Examines it*] No such cartridge as this belonged to me. [*Hands cartridge to Galpin*]

SENE. That cartridge was evidently the property of the assassin. He dropped it providentially as an evidence of his guilt. The weapon Jules de Dardeville used was the Remington and the only one of that make in the district. Examine the cartridge. If it is not a Remington it proves his innocence.

---

[1] There is no character given in the cast as "Jacques."

GAL. [*Examines cartridge. Starts triumphantly. To Seneschal*]   There! Read for yourself! [*Hands cartridge to Seneschal*]

SENE. [*Examines cartridge. Starts*]   Heavens! It is so! He is guilty!

DR. S.   Guilty? Impossible! What would be his motive for such a crime? M. Jules de Dardeville has nothing to lose. Do you know among all your friends a happier man than he is? Young, handsome, rich, esteemed! Besides there is another fact which will at once remove all suspicion. M. Jules de Dardeville is desperately in love with the beautiful Dionysia Chandore.

COUNTESS. [*Aside, starting*]   In love with Dionysia Chandore?

DR. S.   And she returns his love. [*Countess clutches her hands*]

DR. S.   And tomorrow is the day fixed for his marriage. He told me so himself last night.

COUNTESS. [*Aside, unable to control herself*]   Wretch! He has lied to me!

DR. S.   Gentlemen, I tell you it is impossible!

COUNTESS. [*Rising quickly, full of hate and anger*]   Impossible? And why impossible? Did he not hate my husband? Has he not in a quarrel threatened his life? Does not a chain of indisputable evidence wind itself, link by link, around him? You think it nothing if he had robbed me of my husband, yet you melt at the thoughts of tearing him from his *beautiful Dionysia Chandore!* Yes, I believe him guilty! May Heaven bring down on his head the misery he has inflicted on mine!

GAL.[2]   Calm yourself, madam! Calm yourself! Justice shall be done!

ACT III.

SCENE: *The prison at Sauveterre, overlooking courtyard. Large grated window C. with balcony exterior. Door L.3.E. with steps to stage. Balcony runs from door to window, exterior C. Jules seated at table L.H. Noise of unlocking door.* [*Enter Blangin*]

BLAN.   Prisoner!

JUL. [*Raising his head*] Well?

BLAN.   The magistrate. [*Admits Galpin, Seneschal and Mechinet*]

JUL. [*Approaching and offering his hand to Seneschal*]   Ah! My old friend! [*Seneschal takes Jules' hand and shakes it heartily*] And you, too, Galpin! [*Offering his hand*]

GAL. [*Sternly refusing hand*]   Wait, sir.

JUL.   What? You do not know me? I do not understand all this! Probably you can explain. As for myself, I know nothing! Not even the cause

[2] This speech is crossed out in the manuscript and was evidently not used in the acting version.

of my arrest—thanks to the gendarmes who brought me so quietly here. Not a word could I get from them, only that I should know all soon enough. Perhaps you have come to enlighten me?

GAL. I have. Jules de Dardeville, a terrible charge has been brought against you! Unfortunately, I am a magistrate, sir. It is on your answers to my questions that your honor, your liberty, perhaps your very life, depend.

JUL. [*Surprised*] My life?

GAL. Yes, sir—your life. First, you are charged with setting fire to the Château of Valpinson.

JUL. What! I? Come, come, Galpin! You know me better than that!

SENE. [*Aside, to Galpin*] That man is certainly innocent. [*Aloud*] But not only are you charged with setting fire to the château, but also with murder!

JUL. [*Intensely surprised*] Murder?

GAL. Yes, murder.

JUL. And you, my old friend, Galpin, are my prosecutor? Impossible!

GAL. We shall have to forget our relations, sir. It is not as a friend I have come to see you, but as a magistrate.

JUL. If anyone, in my presence, had dared to accuse you of a crime, I should have defended you till absolutely undeniable evidence had proved your guilt, and even then I should have pitied you. But *you!* I am accused falsely, wrongfully—and you, my friend, not only believe the charge, but hasten to become my judge! Well, Galpin, I know you now.

GAL. [*Motions Mechinet to table*] Enough, sir! You forget our present positions.

JUL. I shall forget them no longer. Proceed. I am at your service. [*Mechinet goes to table L., takes seat, places writing materials on table, and proceeds to take down the examination*]

GAL. You were out last night?

JUL. Yes.

GAL. You took your gun—a Remington?

JUL. I did.

GAL. The only Remington in this district?

JUL. I believe so. I ordered it directly from the maker.

GAL. So you must have been on the spot where such a cartridge as this was found?

JUL. [*Takes cartridge and examines it*] Not of necessity. [*Aside*] Heavens! It is mine! How did it come there? Ah! I must have dropped it in taking the letters from my pocket. [*Handing back the cartridge*] Yes, it is a Remington. I cannot explain it.

GAL. You cannot? Now then, I beg you will give us an account of how you spent last night, between eight and eleven o'clock. [*Pause. Jules becomes greatly agitated, but quickly recovers himself*] Consider! Take your time and answer frankly, for remember, your life depends upon the question.

JUL. How do I know? I walked about.

GAL. That is no answer. You went through the forest of Rochpommier?

JUL. No, I did not.

GAL. Jules de Dardeville, you are not telling the truth.

JUL. Sir!

GAL. Do not attempt to deny it. Two witnesses will swear to what I say.

JUL. Two witnesses?

GAL. Yes. You told one of them you were going to Brechy, then corrected yourself and said to Seille. Jules de Dardeville, you went neither to Brechy or to Seille. You went to Valpinson. Last night, between eleven and twelve, Valpinson was burned to the ground!

JUL. Ah!

GAL. A private individual and a fireman perished in the flames; the Count Clairnot was shot by an assassin; and strong reasons point to you, Jules de Dardeville, as the incendiary and murderer!

JUL. Horrible!

GAL. You are charged with these crimes. It is for you to exculpate yourself.

JUL. [*In despair*] How can I? How can I?

GAL. Humph! If you are innocent, nothing is easier. Tell us where you were between eight and twelve o'clock last night.

JUL. [*Firmly*] I've told you all I can.

GAL. Then I must commit you for trial.

JUL. As you please.

GAL. Then you confess?

JUL. What?

GAL. That you are guilty?

JUL. No! I am innocent!

GAL. Prove it.

JUL. [*Turning away*] I can prove nothing.

GAL. [*Aside*] The greatest criminal case in the calendar! I'm sure of promotion! My fortune's made! On the other hand, if I should fail, his powerful and wealthy friends would ruin me. But nothing can save him! He will have to go to the guillotine, or to the galleys. [*Goes up*]

JUL. [*To Galpin*] A word before you go. Do you believe me guilty?

GAL. [*Coldly*]   That is not for me to say. You have refused to answer my questions. I am but the representative of the law. [*Exits through door*]

JUL.   And you, good Seneschal? [*Taking his hand*]

SENE.   No! Never! Courage! Courage, my boy! In spite of appearances, I am still your friend. [*Exit Mechinet and Seneschal through door*]

JUL. [*Sinking into seat at table*]   There is one, at least, who believes me innocent. [*Enter Blangin*]

BLAN.   Prisoner, a lady to see you.

JUL.   A lady? Who? [*Enter Dionysia*] Dionysia!

DION.   Jules! [*They embrace. Exit Blangin and locks door*]

JUL.   You here! You here? You have come to see Jules de Dardeville, even in a felon's cell?

DION.   Why should I hesitate? Your honor is at stake, and your honor is my honor, as your life is my life!

JUL.   And do you look upon me as the guilty wretch that some would deem me?

DION.   No, Jules! By the sacred memory of my mother, I assure you that I have never doubted your innocence, even for a moment!

JUL. [*Embraces her*]   Dear, dear Dionysia!

DION.   They say that you will only have to prove that you were elsewhere at the time and all will be well.

JUL.   Alas, I cannot!

DION.   You cannot?

JUL.   No, Dionysia, it is impossible!

DION.   Ah, Jules, I am sure you could if you would. You are not aware of the danger you run, you do not know—

JUL.   Yes, Dionysia, I know! I know that the guillotine or the galleys are at the end, and yet I must keep silent.

DION.   You have not considered—

JUL.   Considered? What do you think I have been doing all these dreadful hours since my arrest?

DION.   Then why do you not speak? I, your Dionysia, your betrothed, beseech you—Jules de Dardeville, speak!

JUL.   I dare not!

DION.   Why not?

JUL.   Because it would not establish my innocence if I did.

DION.   My God! What do you say?

JUL.   I say that there are circumstances which upset our reason—unheard of circumstances—which makes one even doubt one's very self. Everything accuses me, everything overwhelms me! I am neither a child, nor a coward, but I have measured the danger and I know it is fearful!

DION. And cannot you even confide it to me—your betrothed—your Dionysia?

JUL. To you less than to anyone else! Your mind is too pure. I would not have it stained by the slime into which fate has thrown me! [*Steps back from her. Then with uplifted hands*] Oh, Dionysia, leave me! Leave me! You do not know me!

DION. [*Springing towards him, terrified*] I do not know you? What do you mean?

JUL. Nothing! Nothing! Do not ask me!

DION. Why? Have I not the right? Am I not your betrothed? Have you not said you loved me, and have I not accepted your love?

JUL. Yes—yes!

DION. And when I have thus willingly placed my life in your care, have I not proved my trust?

JUL. You have—you have!

DION. Then why can you not place an equal confidence in me?

JUL. Oh, Dionysia!

DION. Why, standing here today, innocent, yet charged with crime, do you not dare speak? Not even to me? Do you think I am a child, from whom the truth must be concealed? Am I in your eyes of such a trivial nature as not to comprehend the importance of a secret that seals your lips and holds your life in jeopardy? Jules, Jules, you have no faith in me! You do not really love me! [*Sinking at his feet*]

JUL. [*Raising her*] If you knew what seals my lips, it would make you wretched! I have given you pain enough! I would not make your young life more unhappy! Were I to speak, it would make you *hate* me!

DION. What could you have done to make me hate you?

JUL. Do not ask me!

DION. Is it then such a secret?

JUL. Yes! And should you know it, I should lose the last prop of my strength and courage, Dionysia—my love! [*Embraces her. Enter Blangin*]

BLAN. Madam, your time's up. Prisoner, your counsel, M. Folgat and M. Magloire, awaits you. [*Exit. Jules gazes into Dionysia's face and smiles sadly*]

DION. You smile, Jules. You must have hope.

JUL. Yes, we all have hope! A crime has been committed, lives lost, Valpinson laid in ashes, the Count Clairnot fired upon! I am innocent! I swear it! I know the assassin! The world bids me speak—and yet, to speak would but proclaim me an accomplice and lead me to the guillotine!

DION. No, no! It must not—shall not be!

JUL. But how?

DION. [*Looking around. Then in a whisper*] You must escape!

JUL. Escape!

DION. Yes. Nothing easier! We have gold and can bribe your jailors. They will open the doors for you. In four hours you can reach Rochelle. Then a pilot boat will take you to England. Once there you are free! Jules de Dardeville, you are free!

JUL. And abandon you?

DION. No! I will follow you!

JUL. You would follow me?

DION. Yes! Do you think me base enough to abandon you, when all the world betrays you? No! We will meet in England. There we will change our name—go to some distant country. Once there, we shall be happy, happy!

JUL. [*Overcome*] Dionysia!

DION. [*Quickly*] Let us fix the day.

JUL. The day?

DION. Yes. The day for our flight.

JUL. The dream is too beautiful! [*After a pause*] No, Dionysia! No, I must not escape!

DION. You refuse me then, when I will join you and share your exile? Do you doubt my word? How can I bend you? What must I say? For my sake, if not for your own, let us fly! You escape disgrace! You secure liberty! Can nothing move you? What do you want? Must I throw myself at your feet?

JUL. I am innocent! To escape would be to confess that I am guilty!

DION. [*Clasping her hands over head, exclaims hopelessly*] I can say no more! I can say no more! [*Going up slowly, sobbing*]

JUL. [*Looking tearfully towards her, exclaims hysterically*] Dionysia! [*They embrace. He kisses her, then disengages her, and goes slowly towards seat near table*]

DION. [*Goes slowly up to door, stops, looks towards Jules*] Good-bye! Good-bye! [*Exits*]

JUL. [*Sinking in seat*] Good-bye! [*Then starting up*] No, no! To escape would be easy, but what then? To be a refugee trembling, day and night, lest a confessed murderer and incendiary should be detected! No, no! My dungeon walls would be a Heaven to such a life as that! Here I can sleep in quiet consciousness that I am innocent. Yes! I'll meet my fate and defend my honor to the last! [*Enter Blangin*]

BLAN. Prisoner, your counsel. [*Enter Folgat and Magloire. Jules receives them. Aside, down right*] A wonderful little woman, that Miss Dionysia! When I says here are the lawyers, ma'am, coming to hear what he has to say, says she to me, slipping me a whole napoleon, says she, "Let me hear what he says to the lawyers and I make it a hundred." [*Scratching his head*] Blangin, there's money in this case for you! [*Goes up and exits*]

FOL. Why, Jules, my boy, what a change has come over you!

MAG. Never fear, it will be all right. The commitment has not been made out. An alibi will free you tomorrow.

JUL. An alibi? That, my friends, I cannot prove. [*Dionysia appears at window-bars*]

FOL. and MAG. What?

JUL. An alibi, I cannot prove. For I was there.

FOL. and MAG. You were there?

JUL. Yes. Though, nevertheless, I am innocent.

FOL. Yet the world, even the Countess, believes you guilty.

JUL. [*Surprised*] The Countess Clairnot?

FOL. Yes, the Countess Clairnot! She has publicly and positively denounced you as the incendiary and assassin and demands justice!

JUL. [*Aside*] Traitress!

MAG. How do you explain it?

JUL. In a word—I was the *lover* of the Countess Clairnot!

DION. [*Aside*] Lover of the Countess Clairnot!

MAG. That is improbable!

FOL. Absurd!

JUL. Yes, but nevertheless the truth!

MAG. Are there any proofs of the fact?

JUL. None. We destroyed the letters a few moments before the fire.

FOL. Then you were at Valpinson a few minutes previous to the fire?

JUL. Yes.

FOL. If so, you probably may have heard or seen something to raise a suspicion in your mind as to who really was the incendiary?

JUL. I did.

FOL. Who?

JUL. The Countess Clairnot.

DION. [*Starts*] Ah!

FOL. and MAG. The Countess?

JUL. Yes. Her unjust accusation compels me to the confession. Had she never denounced me, knowing me to be innocent, I would have remained silent forever.

Mag. Speak! Who fired upon the Count?

Jul. Herself. [*General movement*]

Mag. But her object?

Fol. Yes, what could have been her object?

Jul. [*Bitterly*] To get rid of her husband, so that she could be free to claim her lover.

Fol. Did you see her in the act?

Jul. Is it likely that I would be accessory to such an act?

Fol. No! And yet you confess to having been a partner in the cause that impelled her to the crime—this secret and criminal alliance between herself and you. State to us the facts of the interview.

Jul. We had met at Valpinson, for the purpose of destroying our correspondence. She was very angry. I gave as a reason for my action that she was married and could never be mine. She asked me excitedly if I would have married her, had she been free. And to appease her, I weakly answered yes. Then she exclaimed "Oh, God! Luckily that thought never entered my brain before! Murder!" We parted. Shortly afterwards I heard a couple of shots. I thought it was poachers in the forest of Rochpommier and, looking back, beheld a conflagration. I thought it was the cathedral—then, the village. I hurried home, was arrested today, and charged with the crime!

Mag. To expose this assignation at Valpinson would avail you nothing.

Fol. No! It would, on the contrary, prove a motive for the crime, and be a confession that you were her accomplice.

Mag. Better keep the secret.

Fol. It is plain, that unless she confesses her entire guilt and, at the same time, avows your innocence—Jules de Dardeville, there is no escape for you!

Jul. That she will never do!

Dion. [*Aside*] But she shall! And to me—and to me! [*Disappears from window*]

Mag. [*To Folgat*] Why not one of us visit her and question her?

Fol. Right! I, or Magloire, shall go tomorrow and, if we do not succeed—

Jul. Then I will go myself!

Fol. But how?

Jul. How? I have a fortune! What is that to life, liberty and honor? Gold shall purchase me the freedom of a night. And, if she has concluded to sacrifice me for her crime, in the presence of her husband, I will brand her with infamy!

Fol. Jules, my boy, this is terrible!

Jul. It is indeed! But I place my trust in Providence! Tell me—my father —my mother—do they believe me guilty?

Fol. No. They still have faith in a de Dardeville and, should all the world abandon you, believe you innocent.

Dion. [*Appears at door*] And so would I!

Jul. [*Surprised*] Dionysia! Still here?

Dion. Yes! I could not rest, knowing that you kept a secret so terrible in its character as to close your lips even to me. I listened there at the bars and, now that I know all—have heard all—I have come to forgive you. For I believe you innocent and, more than ever, I love you still! [*They embrace*]

ACT IV.

Scene: *Chamber salon in the château of Count Clairnot. Doors R. and L.3.E. Large C. windows overlooking garden. Windows curtained. Large massive fireplace L.2.E. with fire. The whole appearance of the room elegant and massive. Large armchair L. Sofa R. Other articles of furniture around the room. Collette discovered arranging furniture, etc.*

Col. [*Coming C.*] Oh, how dreadful! How terrible! The Count Clairnot given up by the doctor and little Bertha dying! Yet madame, herself, goes about attending to everything just as calm, as cool and as kind as an angel! Ah, what a wonderful woman! [*Enter Dr. Seignebos L.3.E., coming down, unobserved by Collette and slapping her on the back*]

Dr. S. Well, I'm going.

Col. [*With a startled scream*] How you frightened me!

Dr. S. I say I'm going.

Col. Any one can tell that.

Dr. S. Fudge!

Col. Indeed they can! Whether you are going or coming, you do everything with such a fuss and such a bounce that, really, I sometimes think it's an earthquake.

Dr. S. What a girl—what a girl!

Col. How has the Count slept?

Dr. S. Hasn't slept a wink. And as for poor little Bertha, she's wasted to a skeleton! I don't think she'll last much longer.

Col. And to think of all these dreadful things happening at once!

Dr. S. Fate! [*Shaking his head*] But bad—bad! I've done all I can for them. There is no hope, Collette, no hope! [*Abruptly*] The Countess—how does she bear up?

Col. Ah, poor madame, she watches like an angel! She never leaves them. I don't think she has touched food, or closed her eyes, since the fire.

DR. S. [*Moved*] Poor Countess—poor Countess! I pity her! Pity her! [*Suddenly*] Well, I'm going. [*Slaps his hands, then slaps Collette on the shoulder*] Good-night. [*Exits quickly R.3.E.*]

COL. Bless me! He nearly broke my back! [*She turns down the gas. The moonlight falls through windows and illuminates the room*] I never saw such a man—comes and goes like a whirlpool—whirlwind—I mean. [*Going towards door R.3.E. Jules suddenly appears at door. Collette starts back and screams slightly*]

JUL. Silence! Is the Countess Clairnot in?

COL. The Countess cannot see anyone.

JUL. Cannot? Where is she? [*Coming down*]

COL. She's with her husband and her child. They are both very ill.

JUL. I must see her.

COL. Impossible!

JUL. Tell her that a gentleman who has been sent by Galpin, the prosecutor of Jules de Dardeville, desires to see her for a moment.

COL. Sent by Galpin, the prosecutor of the assassin! Certainly. Take a seat [*Points to sofa*] if you please, sir—and I'll tell her immediately. [*Exits R.3.E.*]

JUL. Ah, Countess Clairnot, we did not part forever! Fate brings us face to face once more! [*Places himself behind curtain C. Enter Countess Clairnot, hurriedly, L.3.E.*]

COUNTESS. A gentleman from M. Galpin to see me! Who can it be? [*Looking around*] I see no one. [*Jules steps from behind curtains*]

JUL. At last!

COUNTESS. [*Frightened*] Ah! [*Recognizing him*] Jules de Dardeville! [*She starts to door L. Jules quickly closes it and places himself before it*]

JUL. Stay, madam! Do not attempt to escape me. For if you do, I will pursue you to the very bedside of your husband!

COUNTESS. You—you, here! [*Leans against armchair L.*]

JUL. Yes, I am here. You are astonished, are you? You thought I was in prison, safe under lock and key. You said to yourself "No evidence can be found. Jules dare not speak. I have committed the crime. He will be punished for it! I am guilty, but I shall escape! He is innocent—yet he shall be sacrificed!" Is it not so? Speak! Is it not so?

COUNTESS. [*Alarmed*] I do not understand—

JUL. How I am here? Well, gold has purchased me the freedom of an hour. And I have come to brand you with the crime for which you would send me to the galleys.

COUNTESS. This is monstrous!

JUL. Aye! Monstrous, indeed!

COUNTESS. Murderer! Incendiary!

JUL. [*Laughs*] Ha! Ha! Ha! And you—*you* call *me* so?

COUNTESS. Yes! Yes! *I* call you so! You cannot deny your crime to me. I know the motives which the authorities do not even guess. You thought I would carry out my threat and you were frightened!

JUL. Frightened?

COUNTESS. Yes, frightened! All your promises and protestations were false —false as you are! You thought to yourself "Poor deluded woman—if I can but prevail upon her to destroy those letters, all proofs of our past intimacy will be ended! I'll then be free—*free* to marry this Dionysia Chandore! She will confess all to her husband! I will prevent that!" Aha! You see, you cannot deceive me! You kindled that fire in order to draw my husband out of the house. You incendiary! And then fired at him! You coward! [*Count appears at door L.3.E. He is very pale*]

JUL. Ha! Ha! Ha! Ha! And this is *your* plan? Who will believe this absurd story? Our letters were burnt. And, if you deny having been my mistress, I can just as well deny having been your lover. And, as to my being afraid of the Count Clairnot, your husband, it is well known that I am afraid of no one. When we were concealing our loves, at our secret place of meeting, I might have been afraid. For, had he surprised us there and availed himself of that just and righteous law which makes the husband both judge and executioner of his own case, [*The Count with fierce determination raises his pistol*] he could have shot me down like a dog. [*Count about to shoot*] Or, as I had tarnished his honor, he could abide his time to stain mine and avenge himself. [*Count, with a cry, lowers his pistol*] Except for this, what cared I for the Count Clairnot? What cared I for your threats or his hatred?

COUNTESS. If you are innocent, who, then, could be guilty?

JUL. [*Seizes both her hands and hisses in her ear*] You! Wretched woman —you!

COUNTESS. [*With a cry of horror*] Me? Great Heaven!

JUL. You wanted to be free that you might prevent me from breaking the chains in which you held me. At our last meeting, when I thought you were crushed by grief, and was softened by your hypocritical tears—your anger, which I mistook for love—I was weak enough to say "I marry Dionysia only because you are not free." Then you cried "Oh, God! How lucky it is that thought never entered my brain before!" What thought? Come! Answer me! Confess!

COUNTESS. Confess?

JUL. Aye! That thought was murder!

COUNTESS. I was mad—mad—I tell you, with jealousy and anger! I have outraged and destroyed my husband's honor! But to murder him! Bah! You accuse me of what you know to be a lie!

JUL. Then, madam, as you say—if you are innocent, who could be guilty? [*Countess sinks in chair with horror*]

JUL. [*Bitterly*] You act your part well!

COUNTESS. You believe I am the guilty one?

JUL. [*Ironically*] Perhaps you only planned the crime and ordered some one else to execute it.

COUNTESS. Great Heavens! [*They stand for a few moments staring at each other silently*] Well, sir, what is to be done?

JUL. The truth must be told.

COUNTESS. Which truth?

JUL. That I have been your lover; that I went to Valpinson, by appointment with you; that I came for the purpose of destroying our letters; and that the cartridge found there was accidentally dropped by me when I drew your letters from my pocket.

COUNTESS. You want me to say this?

JUL. Yes.

COUNTESS. You want me to bear half the guilt?

JUL. The truth must be told.

COUNTESS. Never!

JUL. It shall be told!

COUNTESS. Never! Never! Do you not see that the truth cannot be told—that it would prove that we were accomplices and convict us both?

JUL. Never mind. I am not willing to die.

COUNTESS. Rather say, that you do not want to die alone—that you want to drag me down with you!

JUL. Be it so.

COUNTESS. To confess, would be to ruin me! Is that what you want? Would your fate be less cruel if there were two victims instead of one?

JUL. You calculate—you bargain!

COUNTESS. Yes. Because I love you. Remember, Jules, you are the father of my child. [*Drawing closely to him, her voice losing its intensity and speaking in a soft, pleading way*] One word from you, and I leave them all! Country, friends, husband, *child!* Speak that word, Jules, and I follow you, without turning my head, without a regret, without a tear. Why do you hesitate? Do you not see that I cannot part from you? Why, man, man, do you not see that I am ready to sacrifice my very soul for you? [*She throws herself at his feet*] Speak! Speak! [*Jules throws her off. She reels and falls on sofa R.*]

JUL. No! No! [*Following her*] Murderess! Rather the scaffold! [*Pause*]

COUNTESS. [*Recovering and speaking slowly*]   Then what do you want of me?

JUL. The truth.

COUNTESS. To what purpose? [*Jules turns from her*] That you may be free to marry Dionysia Chandore! I am the past to you! She is the future! The old love must be made a footstool for the new! I must be disgraced, that she be honored! I must weep, that she may smile! No! No! [Note: *The actor playing the Count is the best creator of his business and by-play during this scene*]

JUL. Wretch!

COUNTESS. [*Savagely*]   You do not know me yet! You shall never be hers! You belong either to the scaffold or to me! Either your life, or my love! [*Holding out her hands in supplication*]

JUL. We shall see! [*Starts towards door L.3.E.*]

COUNTESS. Where would you go?

JUL. To your husband.

COUNTESS. [*Defiantly*]   Go! Speak! Denounce me! M. Folgat no doubt has told you how well I can defend myself. Your word would not be worth that! [*Snaps her fingers defiantly*]

JUL. Fiend! [*Rushes towards her as though to strike her. The Count comes C. from his place of concealment*]

COUNT. Do not strike that woman! [*Pointing pistol*]

JUL. The Count!

COUNTESS. My husband!

COUNT. I have heard all! [*Looking at them both with disgust and scorn*] Miserable wretches! [*Countess sinks into armchair L.*]

JUL. I have insulted you, sir. Avenge yourself!

COUNT. [*With a cold, hard laugh, lowering his pistol*]   No, no! The law will avenge me.

JUL. What! Would you permit me to be condemned for a crime of which I am innocent? Ah! That would be cowardly!

COUNT. [*Supporting himself by back of chair*]   Cowardly? What do you call the act of him who, meanly, disgracefully, robs another of his wife, and palms his own child upon him? What is the fire in my house compared with the ruin of my faith? What are the wounds in my body in comparison with that in my heart? Go! Go! Miserable wretch! You cannot escape! I leave you to the law!

JUL. Rather death, death! [*Baring his breast*] Why do you not fire? Are you afraid of blood? Shoot! I have been the lover of your wife! Your daughter is my child! [*Count with a cry of rage, raises his pistol*] Kill me and avenge your honor!

COUNT. [*Lowering pistol*] No! The arm of the law is more certain than mine—its aim more unerring!

JUL. [*In despair*] You will not kill me?

COUNT. No! Remember your own words, "As I had tarnished his honor, he could abide his time to stain mine and avenge himself."

JUL. My God!

COUNT. Now you know why I will not kill you. You have robbed me of my honor and I must have yours. And, if you cannot be condemned without it, in my dying deposition I shall say—I shall swear—that I recognized you as the assassin. [*With a cry of horror, Jules crouches on sofa R. Countess stands as immovable as a statue L. Count, overcome with passion, stands with almost superhuman strength, then totters and falls*]

ACT V.

SCENE: *Elegant salon in the château of the Countess Clairnot. C. doors. Door R.3.E. Large bay-window opening on porch L. Fireplace R.2.E. Elegant furniture and decorations in room. Armchair R.1.E. Armchair L.2.E. Sofa L., etc. Collette discovered on porch, arranging flowers, etc. Dr. Seignebos enters R.3.E.*

DR. S. [*Loudly*] Well?

COL. [*Startled*] Oh! [*Coming forward*] Goodness, how you startled me! I thought the roof had fallen in!

DR. S. [*Feeling her pulse*] Nervousness! Nervousness!

COL. No, sir! Allow me to say I am not nervous. I have courage enough to stand anything in reason.

DR. S. Fudge! How is the Countess since yesterday?

COL. Very quiet, sir.

DR. S. And little Bertha?

COL. Worse than when you left her.

DR. S. I am afraid she will soon follow her father.

COL. Poor Count!

DR. S. Where did you find him the night he died?

COL. In the library, pale and rigid, his features fearfully distorted. He was unconscious and never spoke.

DR. S.[3] He became delirious, no doubt, with fever brought on by his wounds and, wandering from his apartment, his bandages came off, occasioning his immediate death.

COL. Poor master! Poor master!

DR. S. Yes, yes! [*Abruptly, but very quiet*] Now then, Collette, I will attend to Bertha. [*Exits C. and L.*]

COL. [*Surprised*] Why, what has come over the doctor? I never saw him go out so quiet before! [*Dionysia appears at door R.3.E. Turning and seeing her*] Madame—

DION. [*Coming down*] Is your mistress in?

COL. Yes, madame.

DION. Tell her a lady wishes to see her.

COL. [*Going, then stops*] Shall I say whom, madame?

DION. It is unnecessary. Merely say that it is important. [*Collette bows and exits C. and L.*]

DION. Yes, I shall speak to her! I shall ask her how she dares to rob him of life and honor, knowing him to be innocent and herself the criminal! He is innocent! He is innocent! And if I cannot move her to pity they will murder him! His best friends acknowledge him no longer! No hand will grasp his! And even those who were most proud of his friendship pretend to have forgotten his name! Great Heaven! And they call this human justice! But she can save him! She can save him! But will she—will she? [*Collette re-enters C. and L.*]

COL. Madame, the Countess sends word she cannot see you.

DION. Cannot? She must! She shall! Go back. Tell the Countess that it is *I*, Dionysia Chandore! That if she does not come to me, I shall go to her. That I will arouse the neighborhood and publicly accuse her of the infamy for which another now innocently suffers!

COL. But madame—

DION. Go. [*Pointing*] It is a question of life and death! [*Collette bows and exits*] Yes, of life and death! And all depends on me, on me! But if I fail? Fail! I cannot—I must not fail! [*Enter Countess C., pale but very calm*]

COUNTESS. Since you insist upon it, madame, I have come to tell you myself that I cannot listen to you. Are you not aware that I am standing near the grave of my poor child? [*Going*]

DION. If you leave me without listening to me, I will follow you and shall speak in the presence of the dying.

COUNTESS. Indeed! Is your business of so much importance then?

---

[3] This speech is crossed out in the manuscript and was evidently omitted in the acting version.

DION. [*Tearfully*] It is, madame.

COUNTESS. [*Immovable*] Then be seated. [*Dionysia sits R. Countess sits L.*] Proceed. I hear you.

DION. It is unnecessary to tell you my name.

COUNTESS. It is. I know! [*Half looking up*] You are Dionysia Chandore.

DION. You know that Jules de Dardeville has been put on his trial?

COUNTESS. I do.

DION. And that you—you—can save him—

COUNTESS. [*Calmly looking up*] I?

DION. You seemed surprised, madame.

COUNTESS. And why should I not be? What do I know of Jules de Dardeville? How could I save him?

DION. He asserts that you know a great deal. Your past intimacy—

COUNTESS. [*Affecting great surprise*] My past intimacy?

DION. Yes. He states that he left you only a few moments before the fire took place—that you know his innocence and can prove it.

COUNTESS. [*Starting up*] This is infamous! Infamous! What? Jules de Dardeville has dared to tell you that?

DION. Do not misunderstand me. Jules de Dardeville was your lover. He deserted you. You would now have your revenge by making him suffer for a crime of which he is innocent!

COUNTESS. Innocent? Has he the audacity to assert this? Has he the audacity to charge me with having been his mistress? And to *you*?

DION. No. He told me nothing. He simply confided it to his counsel. I listened and overheard all!

COUNTESS. Then what do you want of me?

DION. To testify in his behalf—to confess enough to save him!

COUNTESS. To confess *enough*? I do not understand you!

DION. Yes, you do understand me, madame. Why will you deny it? Do you not see that I know all?

COUNTESS. [*Controlling herself*] Oh, this is too much! This is too much!

DION. Can you not see that his love for you has brought him to destruction? That he suffers wrongfully and you stand coldly by? Oh, what a woman you must be, not to cry out in open court and proclaim his innocence! How can you live and see the man you love go down to shame and infamy?

COUNTESS. [*Rising*] No, no! It is not so! Only a week ago, he came here and I offered to fly with him. He had only to say the word and I would have given up everything for him!

DION. [*Quickly*] And he answered?

COUNTESS. Rather the scaffold! [*Approaching her*] Did this look as though I cared to see him go to shame and infamy? He refused me! He condemned himself! [*Dionysia sinks down, burying her face in her hands. Over her*] I was quite willing to ruin myself for him. But I am certainly not willing to do so for another woman!

DION. [*Supplicating*] Pity!

COUNTESS. For you? *You*, for whose sake he abandoned me! *You*, whom he was going to marry! *You*, with whom he hoped to enjoy long, happy years!

DION. Pity! Pity!

COUNTESS. [*Through her teeth*] To you? *You*, to whom I owe all my misery and sorrow?

DION. Not for me—for him! I have come to offer you a bargain.

COUNTESS. [*Recovering herself*] A bargain? What bargain can *you* have to offer *me*?

DION. Save Jules and, by all that is sacred to me in the world, I promise that I will enter a convent! I will renounce the world and you shall never hear of me again.

COUNTESS. [*Seated L., ironically*] You would really do that?

DION. Unhesitatingly!

COUNTESS. *You* would make this great sacrifice for me?

DION. For you—for Jules!

COUNTESS. You love him then so dearly, do you?

DION. I love him dearly enough to prefer his happiness a thousand times to my own! Even when buried in a convent, I should have the consolation of knowing I had saved him.

COUNTESS. And would this make him love me? No! You know that he loves you alone. Heroism with such conditions is easy enough! What have you to fear? Buried in a convent, he would love you none the less, and hate me all the more!

DION. But he shall never know—

COUNTESS. What would that matter? He loves me no longer. My love, to him, is a heavier load than the cannonball that's fastened to his chains!

DION. [*In despair*] Oh, this is horrible!

COUNTESS. [*With force*] Horrible? Yes! [*Dionysia looks up*] You look amazed! You have, as yet, only seen the morning of your love. Wait till the dark evening comes on! Then you will understand me—

DION. [*Pleading*] Oh, pity me, madame, pity me! [*Falls on sofa*]

COUNTESS. [*Following her up*] Our stories are the same. I have seen Jules at my feet. *You* have him now at yours. The vows of love he swore to me, he now swears to *you*. You *have* his promises—so *had* I!

DION. Oh, madame, spare me—spare me!

COUNTESS. But you think you will be his wife? And I never was! What does that matter? What does he tell you? That he will love you forever, because his love is under the protection of God and man? He told me, because our love was not thus protected, that we should be united by an indissoluble bond—a bond stronger than all others—Death! You have his promise! So have I! It is time for one of us to claim it.

DION. [*Overcome, falls at her feet*] My God! Mercy! Mercy! No more!

COUNTESS. You—you have sacrificed nothing for him—I, everything—the world! I gave him all and, if there had been more to give, he should have had it! Aye, even my very soul! And now, to be betrayed, forsaken, despised! And then to allow myself to be moved by your tears! No, no! Do not think I'll let the vengeance I hold in my hands slip from me at your bidding! Go! Go! [*Pointing*] Expect nothing from me.

DION. No, no, I cannot go! I will not go, till you proclaim his innocence. Save him! Save him! [*At her feet*] Here at your feet, I beg, I implore, I supplicate, for mercy! Save him! My God! Would you see me die? Would you see me go mad—mad? [*Dionysia drags herself up to Countess. Countess throws her off. Dionysia falls and catches back of armchair L. and supports herself*]

COUNTESS. Girl, girl, you plead in vain! Let him expiate his crime by the law. He is an incendiary, a murderer!

DION. [*Suddenly raising herself upright and turning to the Countess*] Countess Clairnot, you lie!

COUNTESS. [*Triumphantly*] Who then is?

DION. You! Murderess! You!

COUNTESS. [*Starts, clutches back of chair R.*] Me? Have a care! Have a care!

DION. Oh, I fear you no longer! I supplicate no longer! We have proof! Absolute, overwhelming proof!

COUNTESS. [*Laughs*] Then produce your proof! We shall see if the vile calumnies of an incendiary can stain the reputation of an honest woman!

DION. [*Mockingly*] An honest woman!

COUNTESS. Yes. We shall see if a single speck of this mud in which you wallow can reach up to me! Go! Go, I tell you!

DION. [*Rushing to Countess*] Woman, woman, you must! You shall! [*Collette enters quickly C.*]

COL. Madame, little Bertha is sinking fast, and asks for you.

COUNTESS. [*With great impatience, waving her off fiercely*] In a moment! In a moment! Go! [*Exit Collette*]

COUNTESS. [*Turning to Dionysia*] I *must*, I *shall*, what?

DION. Save Jules's life!

COUNTESS. [*Through her teeth*] Never! Never!

DION. By the memory of your dying child, in its name, in its love, forgive Jules—forgive me—and save him!

COUNTESS. [*Throwing her off*] Never! Never! Never! [*Enter Dr. Seignebos and Collette C.*]

DR. S. Madame, your child is dead.

COUNTESS. [*Stunned*] Dead? Dead! [*Pause*] The last tie that bound me to him is severed. My life has passed away! My heart is stone! Go, go to your lover, girl, and tell him this for me—that the Countess Clairnot confesses before these witnesses that she was the assassin of her husband, and Jules de Dardeville her accomplice. [*Dionysia shrieks and falls*]

ACT VI.

SCENE: *Reception room in the prison of Sauveterre. C. doors opening on corridor and view of a portion of prison. Large marble steps leading to room. Door R.3.E. with steps. Door L.2.E. leading to private room. Grated window L. Chant heard as curtain rises. Prison bell strikes seven. Blangin discovered looking off C. towards L.*

BLAN. Another hour and Jules de Dardeville will be no more. [*Enter Dr. Seignebos R.3.E. He comes down steps and approaches Blangin, unobserved*]

DR. S. [*Loud and suddenly*] Well?

BLAN. [*Starting*] The devil! I thought the prisoner had escaped!

DR. S. Fudge! [*Aside*] I wish he had!

BLAN. But he's all right. His death will be painless.

DR. S. How do you know? Did you ever try it?

BLAN. Me? No, I never had that pleasure. [*Noise of hammering heard off L.*]

DR. S. What's that?

BLAN. Oh, they're only putting up the scaffold.

DR. S. *Only?* Does the prisoner hear it?

BLAN. Certainly. It must be a great consolation for him to know his troubles will soon be over.

DR. S. *Great* consolation indeed!

BLAN. It was an awful crime, sir, and the prisoner deserves his fate.

DR. S. [*Aside*] Deserves a fiddlestick!

BLAN. The poor Countess has never recovered from the shock.

DR. S. No! Nor perhaps she never will. I was at her house the night she lost her wits.

BLAN. [*Interested*] Tell me about it.

DR. S. It was caused by overexcitement. The condemned's betrothed had called to ask the Countess to intercede in his behalf. The previous events— the fire—the death of her husband—followed so suddenly by that of her child —all combined, were too much for her mind to bear. She became delirious, hysterical, actually insane, began to rave, and declared herself the assassin of her husband, and Jules de Dardeville only her accomplice!

BLAN. Ridiculous!

DR. S. Yes. No notice was taken of her ravings, for we all knew she was *non compos mentis.*

BLAN. Poor woman!

DR. S. She hasn't recovered from the shock since. The only thing that interests her is the trial and conviction of Jules de Dardeville.

BLAN. [*Looking off L.*] Hush! Here is the magistrate. [*Enter Galpin and Seneschal R.3.E. and come down steps*]

GAL. [*Bows stiffly to Doctor, then turns to Blangin*] How has the prisoner spent the night?

BLAN. Very quietly, sir.

GAL. Are the good fathers with him still?

BLAN. Yes, sir.

GAL. He is reconciled, then, to meet his fate?

BLAN. Yes. So I heard him tell them.

GAL. That will do. [*Blangin bows and exits C. off L.*]

DR. S. [*Crossing to Galpin, ironically*] M. Galpin, allow me to compliment you upon your admirable prosecution of the case. You will no doubt some day become a very great man.

GAL. I did my duty, sir. Had he been my brother, it would have been all the same.

DR. S. [*Aside, going L.*] Yes, or your grandmother! [*Enter Folgat and Magloire R.3.E. Bows exchanged*]

FOL. [*To Galpin*] I was seeking you. Has the petition for delay been received?

GAL. No.

FOL. [*In despair*] No?

GAL. No! You may expect no mercy from the Emperor. The condemned was an avowed Republican.

FOL. There is then no hope?

GAL. None. [*Bell strikes one, a quarter past. To Blangin, who walks up and down corridor*] Admit the prisoner. [*Blangin exits L. Sound of unlocking prison bolts. Two Gendarmes enter and place themselves R. and L. of C. doors, followed by Jules de Dardeville. He is pale but very calm. Blangin continues his walk up and down the corridor. Jules comes down and grasps the hands of Folgat and Magloire, then the Doctor. He turns around and bows to Galpin and Seneschal*]

FOL. Ah, Jules, this is hard, very hard!

JUL. Bear up my friend! Do not unman me. I am innocent and can face death like a man. [*Grasping his hand*] You have done all that you could for me, but fate has ordained it otherwise. [*Turns to Magloire*] You, too, have been my friend. Good-bye! [*Magloire shakes hands with Jules, then retires up stage, greatly moved. To Doctor, who comes down*] Ah, Doctor, friendship's a word that's easily said, but you have proved a true friend indeed. [*Shakes his hand*] Farewell!

DR. S. [*Overcome*] Fif-fif-fer—well! [*Goes up, wiping his eyes with handkerchief*]

GAL. [*Crosses to Jules*] You will, I am sure, pardon me for the unpleasant part I have taken in your prosecution. You know law is law.

DR. S. [*Aside, at back*] D-da-damn the law!

JUL. M. Galpin, life is too short to waste in enmity. Standing, as I am, upon the verge of eternity, I would not deprive you of whatever satisfaction you may have in life. You have done your duty, such as you consider it! Farewell! [*Offers his hand*]

GAL. [*Taking it*] Farewell! [*Aside, going R.*] The greatest execution on the calendar! My fortune's made! [*Bell strikes two*]

JUL. [*Struggling with his feelings, overcomes them and continues calmly*] Now comes the worst of all. Dionysia. [*To Blangin*] Admit her. [*Blangin exits L.2.E. and enters immediately with Dionysia. She rushes to Jules. He opens his arms*] Dionysia!

DION. [*Sobbing*] Jules! Jules! [*Enter Countess Clairnot R.3.E. in deep mourning and heavily veiled. She remains at back unobserved*]

JUL. Dionysia, do not unman me.

DION. [*Sobs*] Oh, my heart, my heart is breaking!

JUL. Dionysia! Dionysia! Let me meet my fate calmly. See! I am not afraid. I never was more resigned to anything in my life. Nothing but the sight of your grief could unman me.

DION. Jules! Jules!

JUL. Your sweet and innocent love for me has turned and stung you like a serpent! If it were not for this, I could go to my grave without a pang, without a sorrow.

DION. Oh, Jules, Jules, would that I could die with you!

GAL. [*Coming to her*] Calm yourself. [*Dionysia turns away from him without noticing his remark*] I am the magistrate, yet I can sympathize.

DION. [*Turning to him*] You—you sympathize? Yes, as the serpent sympathizes with the victim it fascinates! He was your friend! In his noble and generous nature, he cherished you. Misfortune came and you turned upon him like a viper! May the memory of his headless corpse be to you an accursed phantom, hideous as the image of your own soul, cruel as your miserable ambition!

DR. S. [*At back, aside*] Bravo! Bravo!

GAL. [*Annoyed*] Were it not for the situation, miss, I should teach you to respect the magistrate, if you did not the man. [*Goes up. Bell strikes three*]

DION. [*Screams and clings to Jules*] Oh, Jules, Jules, must you die?

JUL. [*Embracing her quickly*] Dionysia! My love! My love! I cannot struggle! I cannot fight with fate! My end is drawing near. [*Kisses her, then disengages himself from her*] Farewell! Farewell! [*Dionysia, screaming, is taken from his arms by Folgat and led off L.2.E. Jules for the first time is overcome and bursts into tears, and sinks on chair L.*] This is terrible! Thank Heaven, I am spared another meeting with my parents!

GAL. [*Comes down and touches him on shoulder*] M. Jules de Dardeville, you have but a few moments left. Prepare yourself. [*Jules rises quickly and stands erect and calm. Folgat enters L.2.E.*]

JUL. [*To Folgat*] To you, I entrust my fortune, to be divided among such charitable institutions as you think fit. Comfort my poor parents—and— [*Mastering himself*]—and—Dionysia! Farewell! [*Turning to Galpin*] Sir, I am ready. [*They move up slowly to C. The Guard appears in corridor and stands in file. Enter Cocoleau, quickly, R.3.E. He is pale and wild looking, his eyes almost staring out of his head. He sees Countess, who comes down R. corner unobserved, as others move up C.*]

COUNTESS. [*Seeing him, seizes him by the arm and brings him to her*] The vial! Quick, Cocoleau! The vial!

COCO. [*Laughs*] He! He! He! Here it is. [*Takes it from his breast*] I found it just where you told me—in the little back drawer. I got it! I got it! Here it is. [*Gives it to her and, putting his hands to his head, laughs idiotically*]

COUNTESS. In life he has been mine! Death shall not part us. [*Snatches vial from Cocoleau and throws off her veil*] Jules de Dardeville, we die together! [*General movement*]

OMNES. Countess Clairnot!

COUNTESS. Aye! The Countess Clairnot! [*Raises the vial quickly, then starts*] It is empty! [*To Cocoleau*] Wretch! Fool! What have you done with the contents?

COCO. [*Almost reeling, places his hand to his head, and starts as if in great pain*] Done—with—contents? [*Laughs*] He! He! He! I drank it.

COUNTESS. You drank it?

COCO. [*Laughing and smiling knowingly*] Ye—yes!

COUNTESS. Idiot! You are poisoned!

OMNES. Poisoned?

COCO. [*Staggers C. and stands in great suffering, showing the symptoms of a poisoned man, and in spite of all, looking at Countess with an expression of profound love and devotion, smiles*] I—I—I know it.

COUNTESS. You knew it? And still you drank it? [*Characters all drop down, interested*]

COCO. [*Knowingly*] Ye—yes—for if I hadn't—*you* would—and—and—Cocoleau didn't want that! Cocoleau didn't want—that.

COUNTESS. [*Turns away*] Fool! [*Cocoleau reels and falls C.*]

GAL. [*Impatiently*] We are wasting time.

FOL. We still have five minutes. I crave your indulgence—

GAL. I regret it deeply, but—

FOL. The ravings of this idiot convicted my client. His ravings now may clear him. I *insist!*

GAL. [*Impatiently*] As you please.

FOL. [*Bows*] Thank you. [*Cocoleau recovering and looking in a sort of dazed manner, his eyes finally resting on the Countess, then on Jules. He then bursts into a flood of tears*] There is something he wants to tell.

DR. S. [*Going to Cocoleau*] He is sinking fast. In a few moments all will be over.

FOL. [*Kneeling by Cocoleau*] My boy, is there anything I can do for you?

COCO. [*Looking at him*] Ye—yes!

FOL. What? Speak.

COCO. Raise—raise me up! I—I—want—to say something.

FOL. [*Raises his head*] Now say it, my boy. [*Cocoleau turns and looks at Countess with expression of "May I?"*]

COUNTESS. Speak!

Coco. [*With effort*] Yes—I—want—to—say—it—so bad. [*To Countess*] You—won't—be angry—with—poor Cocoleau—will you? I—I—can't keep—it—any longer. I—I—must speak—or I—shall choke—choke! [*Tears open his collar; after a slight pause*] You—sent—me for the poison. You—wanted to—drink it—because—you—were so—unhappy—and—when—you—were—unhappy—Cocoleau was—unhappy too! I love you—I love you—oh, so much! You—wanted—to—drink it—because—he—he—[*Pointing to Jules*]—was—going to die—and you—wanted—to die—with him! [*Laughs*] But I—can save—him! I can—save—him! And—you can live—live—and poor Cocoleau—will die for—both—both! [*Falls back*]

Fol. Go on, my boy! Go on!

Dr. S. Hush!

Coco. [*After effort, painfully*] He—he—[*Pointing to Jules*] didn't—kill master. No—no—no! [*Laughs idiotically*]

Fol. No? Then who did?

Coco. [*Triumphantly*] I—I—I! [*Laughs. Magloire exits L.2.E. and enters immediately with Dionysia. Dionysia, with a cry, rushes to Jules*]

Countess. You?

Jul. You?

Omnes. You? [*Countess and Jules stare at each other*]

Coco. Yes—I—shot—Count Clairnot—and—Jules—de—Dardeville—is—innocent!

Gal. *You* shot Count Clairnot? Why?

Coco. [*Crawling to feet of Countess and kissing her dress*] To—to please—my pretty lady. [*Looking up in her face with the love and devotion of a dog*] She loved—him—[*Pointing to Jules*] and—she—didn't love—the Count! She—she used—to cry—much—much—to herself—and say—if she—was free—Jules de Dardeville would—marry her. She was—always—so good—and—kind—to—poor Cocoleau—and Cocoleau—loved her—loved her—and puzzled—his poor—brain—[*Feels his burning temples*] to find out—how he—could—save her. So—when—he—came—the—night of—the fire—I was—hid—in—the shrubbery—and—heard what—they said. And—when—he burnt the letters—I threw—them under—the house with—some—shavings—just to—draw—master out. [*Looking up*] It—was—not—my fault if the—whole house—went afire. And—when—master came—out—I shot—him! [*Sinks back exhausted*]

Countess. [*Aside*] Jules de Dardeville innocent!

Jul. [*Aside*] She, guiltless!

GAL. This confession, to have weight, must be corroborated by something more than a simple self-accusation. The law is very clear on this point. [*To Cocoleau, as he slowly raises himself up*] Have you anything more to say? [*Cocoleau shakes his head painfully*]

FOL. Can you think of nothing? [*Cocoleau shakes his head. Suddenly*] The weapon? What did you do with the weapon?

COCO. [*After effort*] The gun—the gun—[*Suddenly remembering*] Ah! It's there—there—under—the steps—of the prison. I hid—it—there—last night. [*Folgat exits quickly R.3.E. Delirious, crawling to Countess*] Good-bye —good-bye! Don't curse poor Cocoleau. He did—it—all for you—all—for— you—dear—dear—lady! [*Dies. During the last of Cocoleau's death scene, he rises and staggers towards L.2.E. and when he dies, he is caught in the arms of two Gendarmes and dragged off L.2.E. Enter Folgat with gun. He hands it to Galpin*]

GAL. [*Takes gun and examines it*] Yes, this was the property of the Count Clairnot. His name is on the stock. It now rests on the Countess Clairnot to substantiate the dying statement of Cocoleau. [*All eyes are turned on the Countess Clairnot. To Jules*] Your life is in her hands. It is a trying moment. For her honor, her reputation hangs in the balance.

JUL.[5] What will she do? [*Pause*]

COUNTESS. [*Slowly, without raising her eyes*] Jules de Dardeville, inno- cent myself, I believed you guilty. I *hated* her. I *hated* her so, that I could have seen you expiate the crime with which you were charged with joy. Had I known you to be innocent, I should have spoken before this. I do not ask forgiveness. I do not even want your pity. You have wronged me more deeply than I have wronged you. Your wound will heal. Mine never will—for it has left its poison here! [*Clasps her hand over her heart and turns away for a sec- ond, deeply affected*]

JUL.[6] Genevieve—for her sake—

COUNTESS. What little reparation I can make, I make to her. [*To Dio- nysia*] You are too good and noble, your love too innocent and pure, to be shadowed by the darkness that broods over mine. My sacrifice is great, very great—for it leaves me nothing—not even my good name. [*Turning to Gal- pin*] M. Galpin, what M. Jules de Dardeville has stated before is true, every word of it. [*To Dionysia*] Forgive me!

DION. [*Goes and kisses Countess*] Freely.

[5] This speech was added to the manuscript in revision in Herne's handwriting.
[6] This speech was also added to the manuscript in revision in Herne's handwriting.

COUNTESS. [*Patting her head*] He loves you, and you were ready to sacrifice your life for his sake! He forsakes me, but I sacrificed my name, my honor, for him. Farewell! Jules! [*Jules embraces Dionysia*] Let my great and overwhelming love for you be my excuse. [*Kisses his hand*] Farewell! You will never see me again. [*Turns to Dionysia*] From my convent cell I will pray that you may be happy! God bless you! [*Overcome, covers her face with her hands. Jules kisses Dionysia. Bell strikes eight*]

CURTAIN

"THE MINUTE MEN"
OF
1774-1775

CAST OF CHARACTERS

[*Chestnut Street Theatre, Philadelphia, April 6, 1886*]

SIR FREDERICK SHELTON, *Colonel in His Majesty's
18th British Grenadiers*   HENRY TALBOT

CAPTAIN HENRY WINSLOW, *Retired officer
of the old French War*   THOMAS J. HERNDON

REUBEN FOXGLOVE, *"Minute Man"*   JAMES A. HERNE

NED FARNSWORTH, *Captain of the Minute Men*   CHARLES G. CRAIG

ROANOKE, *An Indian*   CHARLES W. VANDENHOFF

DYKE HAMPTON, *Cousin of, and affianced to Rachel*   M. J. JORDAN

MORTON HANDY, *In service of Hampton*   J. C. WALSH

LIEUTENANT SMOLLET, *Of the 18th Grenadiers*   HARRY M. PITT

DOROTHY FOXGLOVE, *Adopted daughter of Reuben*   KATHARINE CORCORAN

RACHEL WINSLOW, *Daughter of Captain Henry Winslow*   MARY WILKES

ANN CAMPBELL, *A woman of the period*   JENNIE REIFFERTH

JOE ALLEN   ⎫
                     ⎬ *Minute Men*
ROBERT HERRICK   ⎭

AN ORDERLY, *English*

A SERGEANT, *English*

COLONEL SMITH, *English*

MINUTE MEN, ENGLISH AND AMERICAN SOLDIERS, DRUMMERS, FIFERS, INDIANS,
ETC., ETC.

ACT I.

SCENE 1: *Dorchester Heights with Bay of Massachusetts seen in distance R.H. The scene at opening represents a summer afternoon after a heavy thunderstorm, and must have that grand effect the sun gives shining through a peculiar sky after a rain, rendering one portion of the scene nearly dark, the other lighted by a peculiar but very effective brightness—the entire effect very picturesque and true to history. During the Act the sun sets and twilight appears—the sky and entire scene must change with the setting sun. On the left is an old-fashioned farm house and dairy. The house is built after the manner of the better houses of its period—say 1740 or thereabouts: viz. logs or timbers so exactly squared and joined as to make smooth compact walls, has long low porch and low verandah, the whole neatly whitewashed; vines clamber over porch and flower garden surrounds the R.H. end and corner. Old-fashioned plow R.3.E. Rustic seat R. of dairy. Rustic chair down R. The dairy is open to the audience and contains churn of the period and dairy implements, all of which are scrupulously clean, a pail partly filled with clean water and a gourd for dipping it out. The R.H. is shrubbery and foliage—the back looking on to the arm and away to the Bay on the R. and distant hills on the L.H. Discovered: Ann Campbell in dairy churning. She is dressed in homespun old-fashioned gown, hair plainly done in style of time; is a good natured, determined woman. British Soldiers in fatigue dress are seen occasionally passing to and fro at back during scene, but paying no attention to dialogue or action. "Music" very bright and characteristic at rise—opens ff., becomes piano as curtain goes up and dies gradually away as Hampton speaks. Enter from U.E.R. Dyke Hampton, a dark, sinister man about forty-five years of age. He is dressed in riding habit of well-to-do man of period, carries a whip.*

DYKE. [*Speaking as he enters*]   Good-day, Mrs. Campbell. I hope I see you well!

ANN. [*Looking up but not ceasing work and evincing no pleasure at seeing him*]   Why, Mr. Hampton! Who'd a'thought a'seein' yeou, this day of all days!

DYKE. [*Coming towards dairy*]   Well, you see, like the hunter in the chase, I thought I'd be in at the death! [*Music ceases*]

ANN. Yes! An' as Rachel writes, ef it hadn't a'been for the all merciful hand o'Providence, it might a'been in at the death indeed! [*Pours water into churn*]

DYKE. [*Taking seat R. of dairy*] The accident was serious then!

ANN. [*Churning*] Wa'll it wa'ant no jokin' matter—but where was yeou that yeou didn't know?

DYKE. Absent at York. Trying to recover some of my Hampshire land grants.

ANN. Ya'as—lands, some folks about here say you never lost!

DYKE. Indeed—who are the some folks—pray?

ANN. [*Looking at him curiously, then taking off churn cover, looking into churn, replacing. cover and churning furiously*] I disremember they're names jist now; but you was atalkin' about the Captain and Rachel!

DYKE. Yes—I am anxious to obtain the particulars of the accident. Will you be good enough to relate them?

ANN. Sartin! Sartin! Unless you'd prefer to hear 'em from the lips of Rachel herself, which of course you've a right to, seein' as how you're engaged—eh? They say you be engaged! Be you?

DYKE. Pardon me, Mrs. Campbell, but will you oblige me with the information I came to seek?

ANN. Sartin! Sartin! Well, yeou see, about a month ago the Captain an' Rachel was a'returnin' hum from they're visit to Albany, when in descendin' a mountainious rud the hosses took fright an' gettin' the better of the Captain, who ain't as young as he was once, dashed down the mountain like all possessed. The carriage was overturned an' the Captain was purty badly shook up besides a' sprainin' of what he calls his fightin' leg—cos it wouldn't run away when the other one wanted to at the battle of Quebec—an'—

DYKE. Yes—yes—I know!

ANN. Exactly! Well, Rachel, she screams an' then faints—as any other brave woman'd a'done—an' out o' the forest comes a tall, handsome man— jist for all the world like a page out'n a story book, an' manages to carry 'em to his cabin nearby—an' bein' half hunter—half docter—good Samaritan, Balm O'Gillead an' ministerin' angel all rolled into one—he sets to work a'nussin' an' a'docterin' 'em with harbs an' simples till they're strong enough to resume journey hum, where if nothing further happens they'll all three arrive afore dusk!

DYKE. Oh! Then this hunter-doctor is expected too?

ANN. Sartin! Rachel wouldn't take no for an answer. She said she was afeared to travel without her physician, an' the Captain swears in good sound cuss words that his nuss shall make his hum here for a year at least!

DYKE. Rachel writes in glowing terms of her new friend, then?

ANN. Glowin'? Well—she jist glows all over—she says he's the tallest, strongest, handsomest, self-sacrificin'st man she ever see. Ahem!

DYKE. I trust a further acquaintance will give her no cause to change her sentiments, I'm sure. And as any service rendered her is fully appreciated by me, I shall avail myself of an early opportunity to thank this handsome stranger for his care and attention to my fair cousin.

ANN. Yes—I'd so advise, as your fair cousin looks to see Mr. Wynthrop well received by all who call themselves her friends!

DYKE. [*Bows as if to satisfy her of his sincere intentions*] And now—tell me, Mrs. Campbell, how do you like active service?

ANN. What d'ye mean by active service? [*Stops churning*]

DYKE. Is not Sir Frederick Shelton quartered here?

ANN. Oh! Yes, ef that's what you mean—but I want yeou to understand that I hain't in his active service, nor in the active service of any Britisher that ever wore scarlet.

DYKE. Captain Winslow and he were brother officers in the Old French War, I believe?

ANN. Yes. An' when the Captain heard of Sir Frederick's rigimint bein' camped near here, he writ to hev Sir Frederick an' his staff make themselves to hum in this house till he returned. They've done so—an' while I've too much respect for the old Captain to disrespect any guest o' his'n, when it comes to active service, you'll find me on the other side o' the fence tooth an' nail. America's my country! An' if it comes to a fight, I can carry a musket an' use it too as well as the next man. Active service indeed! [*Takes butter out of churn and slaps it into wooden bowl with a bang. Characteristic music to take Dyke off and bring Reuben[1] and Roanoke on*]

DYKE. Dear Mrs. Campbell, neither your courage nor your skill are to be doubted! I thank you for your cheerfully given information and will endeavor to be present at the reception of our expected guests. Good-day to you!

ANN. Good-day—an' don't forgit that I'm allus ready for active service, but it must be in a righteous cause! [*Takes butter and exits through rear of dairy*]

DYKE. [*Turning to go R.1.E.*] So! So! a new found friend who may prove a rival! This must be looked to. I must press the Captain to a speedy fulfillment of his promise. Delays are dangerous—to lose the girl were to lose all! All? No—should I not still hold her fortune? Fortune? Jove! Dyke

---

[1] In the manuscript this character's name is spelt "Rueben," evidently through an error of the copyist.

Hampton, would you deceive yourself? The fortune of a monarch would not content you without her. Your passionate love for her burns in your veins and swells your heart till you pant and thirst like the tracking bloodhound, and, like him, you will not be balked of your prey. Faugh! It may be but a scare after all. Forewarned is forearmed—and I start with the advantage on my side! [*Exit slowly R.1.E. Music increases and Reuben enters followed by Roanoke, U.E.R. Reuben quaintly dressed in hunting costume but carries no gun. A man of 55 years or thereabouts. Iron gray hair which he wears long, no beard—face weatherbeaten and grizzled, but bearing the stamp of perpetual good-nature and generosity. He carries a bundle of herbs. Roanoke, a tall, handsome young Indian, of 25 years or so, face as light as a man heavily tanned and sunburned. He must be straight as an arrow and lithe as a willow. He is fully and picturesquely costumed (see plate), carries a rifle and game, consisting of squirrels, pigeons and small birds. Music drops as they begin dialogue and finally dies away*]

REU. Roanoke, you've begun the week well, as the feller said who was to be hanged on a Monday. Pigeons, plover, squirrels! You're airly on the wing, as the worm said to the robin! [*Reuben L., Roanoke R.*]

ROAN. Roanoke is never lighter of heart, fleeter of limb, stronger of arm or surer of aim, than when serving a friend. He would fret like a wounded deer could he not bring his share of the feast that is to welcome home the White Captain and his beautiful daughter!

REU. Right you are. It's more blessed to give than to receive, as the mate said when he flogged the cabin boy—an' you're allus a'givin' an' a'doin' suthin' for the Captain, Rachel or my Dorothy!

ROAN. Dorothy—the Little Primrose—voice like the matin' song of the lark—laugh like the rippling water—eyes like the liquid dew-drop—step like the bounding fawn—shedding life and joy on every living thing blessed by the sunlight of her presence! Roanoke like all else loves her. The Great Spirit watch over and protect her—and the vengeance of Roanoke on him who wounds her even by a look!

REU. That's Injun all over, that is. Let an Injun love anything an' he's—all—Injun. Let him hate anything an' he's—well—he's all Injun too! [*Music pp. till Roanoke off*]

ROAN. Why should not the Indian love the sweet Primrose? Has she not taught him all he knows beyond the ways of his tribe? Has she not brought light to his darkened mind—taught him to read the grand books—told him tales of the brave warriors and mighty hunters, who have gone before—taught him to shrink from the cruelties of his race—to love only that that is good and beautiful—to hope that he might one day be something more than a mere Indian—and be worthy to pluck the pretty Primrose, plant it in his heart, there to blossom and bloom forever?

REU. Roanoke—there's a good deal o' man in yeou—as Jonah said to the whale's belly—an' when that little Primrose makes up her mind just where she wants to be transplanted, I ain't a'goin' to say a word agin' her choice, so long's the soil's fresh 'n sweet 'a kep well watered by truth, honesty 'n manhood. I can't expect to keep her allus. When the time comes I'll give her up—with an achin' heart meb'be, but I'll give her up all the same. An' now let's find Mrs. Campbell an' hand over our plunder. That's a great woman, Roanoke—Mrs. Campbell is—she ain't no primrose an' they ain't much boundin' fawn left in her, but fur fryin' doughnuts, darnin' a feller's stockin's, nussin' a sick baby, or smoothin' a dyin' woman's piller—I'll put her agin' any woman in Massachusetts!

ROAN. Give her these, Father Reuben. [*Gives game*] Say Roanoke sends them with his best love, and will return to greet the White Captain and bid him welcome home!

REU. [*Taking game*] Be sure yeou do git back. Yeour face'd be one o' the fust to be missed by the Captain ye know.

ROAN. Roanoke will return—fear not! [*Exit through trees at back, looking around house and at windows in hope of getting a glimpse of Dorothy. At same time enter from house C., Ann Campbell. Music ceases. Reuben turns from looking after Roanoke and meets her*]

REU. Ah! Mrs. Campbell!

ANN. Hello! Reuben! That yeou?

REU. Yes. I was jist goin' to look you up. Me'n Roanoke's been a'huntin'. I dunno's Roanoke's hunted any more'n I hev, but he found more—them's his'n. [*Gives game*] An' them's mine! [*Gives herbs*]

ANN. [*Smelling them*] Sassafras! How good it does smell! Thank ye— I was afeared you'd forgit it!

REU. Forgitten ain't one o' my strong points—but—say—Ann—er, Mrs. Campbell—what on airth be ye agoin' to do with all them 'ere yarbs?

ANN. Experimint—don't intend to drink no chiny tea till the tax's took off. Mean to try fust one thing an' then another an' sometime I'll hit on suthin'll make as good tea if not better'n chiny tea. This is a great country an' everything ain't found out yit. There's checkerberry now—it makes good tea 'f tain't allowed to bile. Bile checkerberry an' it loses its vartue.

REU. I've e'en a'most forgot the taste o' chiny tea myself. I ain't drinked no checkerberry—but I've swallered enough Balm o' Gillead—sage—mountain mint—sweet fern an' catnip to start a pothecary in bizzness.

ANN. I love 'em—every one on 'em! There's a flavor of freedom in 'em all!

REU. Freedom's all very well, but what's the use o' lyin' when the truth kin be proved agin' ye—an' I say I'd give a good deal for a cup o' good ole-fashioned chiny tea, all the same!

ANN. Well—ef yeou wait for Ann Campbell to brew it for ye—ye'll hev checkerberry a sproutin' out all over ye, an' catnip juice a'oozin' out'n yer finer e'ends! What's the news over in Boston?

REU. There was a big meetin' in ole Tunnel last night. Sam Adams an' Dr. Warren made some purty strong speechifyin'—they say there's no way out'n it 'cept fight!

ANN. Fight! That's it! Fight! That's the way out'n it—an' the sooner it comes the better say I!

REU. It'll make purty hard times! [*Looking at her slyly*]

ANN. Hard times ain't a'goin' to skeer me, nor hard blows—nuthin' if it comes to that!

REU. Talkin' o' fightin', what's come o' Dorothy? [*Dorothy's music begins pp., swells as she enters and dies away during her scene*]

ANN. Cleanin' house! She wouldn't let me lay a finger on a blessed thing in Rachel's room. She's been as busy as a bee all day, and she hed that English *Imitation* soldier a'runnin' around like mad—luggin' water an' a'sweepin' an' a'dustin', an' the sweat a'runnin' off'n him like rain off from a duck's back. The last I see on 'em, she hed an apron on him an' he was a settin' on the winder lidge, cleanin' winders!

REU. Well, she couldn't put the British Army to better use, I'm sure! [*Dorothy laughs in house*] Hello—talk o' the ole boy—

DOR. [*In house*] What, an officer, and can't pare apples! Where's your military education?

SMOL. [*In house*] Dear Miss Foxglove, paring apples does not come under the head of military tactics!

DOR. [*In house*] Oh! Nonsense! Soldiers should know everything! [*Laughs*]

REU. It seems to be gineral trainin' day with her. I'll make myself scurse or she'll want to press me into the service! [*Exit U.E.R. laughing and looking back at house. At same time Ann exits with game and herbs, through dairy. Music swells with Dorothy's laughter till it becomes a perfect burst as she enters and then quiets down and gradually dies away. She has knife and wooden bowl; dressed handsomely and has large apron over all; locket on slender chain around neck. She is immediately followed by Smollet, who has coat sleeves rolled up, English Lieutenant's Undress Uniform, a woman's*] *apron on and carries a pan of apples. Smollet is an elegant English gentle-man, full of humor, and gallantry. Dorothy, the quintessence of roguish and witching comedy. Smollet protests and she will not listen till they are well on the stage]*

Dor. [*Laughing*] There! There! Don't talk! Let us get to work! Or there will be no pie for supper. I declare you've done nothing but talk this blessed day!

Smol. [*R. protesting good-naturedly*] But dear Miss Foxglove, suppose Sir Frederick were to surprise me?

Dor. He will never surprise you in better company, nor in a more useful occupation!

Smol. Do let us retire to the kitchen, the proper place for—

Dor. The kitchen is too hot! *I'm* hot!

Smol. Warm!

Dor. No! Hot! When I'm warm, I'm warm; and when I'm hot, I'm hot. And now I'm *hot!* [*Looking at him decidedly*]

Smol. Yes! Hot! [*Eyeing her with a smile. She bows as if satisfied*] The rear porch, then!

Dor. Lieutenant Smollet—

Smol. [*Correcting her*] *Smollet*, please!

Dor. Smullet!

Smol. Smollet!

Dor. Smallet!

Smol. Smollet! S-m-o-l-l-e-t—permit me to know my own name, please!

Dor. Smollet! Excuse me—I—you are ashamed to be found in my company and engaged in the useful occupation of paring apples. Why—[*Attempts to take apples from him*]

Smol. Oh! Good gracious—no! Only too happy to be near you under any circumstances—I assure you!

Dor. Then sit down and let us get to work: [*Seats him on steps of porch. Sits near him. Business of arranging the apples and getting closer and closer to him until she is quite snug and comfortable. Looks at him archly during all this. He plays this entire scene with extreme good nature, but is at no time the slightest particle silly. She now begins to pare apples. Finds knife dull and after one or two attempts stops*] Oh! Pshaw! What a knife! It's as dull as a hoe! It wouldn't cut butter if it were hot! I'll run and get another! [*Attempts to rise*]

Smol. [*Preventing*] Oh! No! No! No! Don't do that—here, take my pen-knife! [*Offering it*]

DOR. That will never do, Lieutenant! They say that to give a person a knife is a sure sign of a quarrel! [*Archly*]

SMOL. But I don't intend to give it—only lend it to you!

DOR. Oh! [*Simply*] That's a different thing altogether. Thank you. [*Takes his knife; gives him hers*] You can use this—strop it a little on your belt. [*Both begin work*] Now we are all right. You can talk. We'll both work. Be sure you say pretty things to me. [*Laughs*] And I'll keep a look out for my boy. He generally needs his mother about this time, so he's sure to be along presently to hunt me up!

SMOL. Boy! Good gracious! Miss Foxglove, do you mean to say that you are a mother?

DOR. [*Without looking up*] Umps.

SMOL. Where's your husband?

DOR. Never had one!

SMOL. Miss Foxglove!

DOR. Fact, I assure you!

SMOL. And you are a mother?

DOR. Yes!

SMOL. How long have you been a mother?

DOR. Ever since I can remember!

SMOL. Good gracious! How old is your boy, pray?

DOR. About fifty.

SMOL. Most extraordinary! May I ask how you call him?

DOR. Whistle for him! Or blow the horn!

SMOL. [*Laughing*] No! No! What's his name?

DOR. Reuben Foxglove!

SMOL. [*Laughs heartily*] Oh! I see! And *you* are *his* mother?

DOR. The only one he has—and a precious trouble he is too, I can tell you—always losing his buttons!

SMOL. You Colonists!

DOR. Americans, please!

SMOL. Beg pardon. Americans are singular people!

DOR. Strange! That's exactly what we think of you English!

SMOL. I dare say, but I have failed to find in England the case of a daughter being mother to her own father!

DOR. Quite a common thing in America!

SMOL. Really?

DOR. Really!

SMOL. Humph! Miss Foxglove, I'm an orphan!

DOR. You look it!

SMOL. Do I really?

DOR. You do, really!

SMOL. Would you mind twins?

DOR. Lieutenant!

SMOL. [*Quickly*] No! No! No! I don't mean that that—but would you mind being a mother to me? I never thought of it before but now that you've put it into my head I believe I need a mother!

DOR. I believe you do!

SMOL. I'm *sure* I do. And then think what a large circle of relatives we should have and all within ourselves, as I may say! You would be your husband's mother and I'd be my wife's son and my father-in-law's father and he'd be his son-in-law's son and father-in-law's son's mother—sisters—e —e—at all events we should be quite a snug family party, don't you think so?

DOR. And when you were naughty boys, I could punish you both and put you to bed, eh?

SMOL. That would be charming, I'm sure!

DOR. But Lieutenant! Won't it be rather awkward when this war breaks out, to have my two children fight against each other?

SMOL. Dear Miss Foxglove, there will be no war!

DOR. What makes you think so?

SMOL. The Colonists.

DOR. Americans! [*Looking at him correctingly*]

SMOL. Americans [*Bowing*] will never think of resisting when the powerful armies of England are sent against them. It would be a useless slaughter of brave men. Your leaders will think better of it. Fight? What for?

DOR. Liberty! The grandest word ever uttered by the tongue of man! I tell you, Lieutenant, you have to fight for everything you get in this world. We Colonists, as you call us, have fought the savages for our land, the land inch by inch for our crops—the hungry wolves and prowling bears for our bleating sheep and their innocent lambs—and now we'll fight the King's soldiers for that most priceless of God's gifts—Liberty—and think it cheaply purchased by the best blood of our country!

SMOL. [*Amazed*] Good gracious, Miss Foxglove, I had no intention of wounding your feelings. I assure you I am extremely sorry. I was wrong to—

DOR. And I, Lieutenant—pardon *me*. I should not allow my feelings to carry me away. I am thoroughly American—that must be my excuse for this breach of politeness, to say the least. You are an Englishman and our guest. [*He bows. She changes her manner and breaks into a laugh*] But it's all the fault of that jackknife! Take it back. I never wish to see it again. [*He takes it*] Am I forgiven?

SMOL. Freely! Dear Miss Foxglove!

DOR. And now let us dismiss a subject that never should have been broached between us!

SMOL. With all my heart! What an unique medallion that is you have! [*Points to locket*] English, is it not?

DOR. [*Hastily, covering it with both hands and rising*] I do not know. It was, I believe, my mother's. In it is all I have ever known of her. I prize it so dearly, that I seldom wear it. [*The chain has broken as she clutched it and comes off her neck*]

SMOL. There! You've broken the chain—all my fault—how stupid of me!

DOR. Oh! that's nothing. The chain is very slight. I'll put it on a ribbon presently! [*Puts it in pocket*] Speaking of ribbons, reminds me that I have not decorated you yet!

SMOL. Oh! I am to be decorated? What for, pray?

DOR. Gallant conduct in the field! [*Pinning apple paring on his left breast*] That's for polishing the silver. [*Puts one on right breast*] That's for cleaning the windows so nicely!

SMOL. You are too good! [*Dubiously*]

DOR. [*Putting one on left ear*] That's for being the *dear, good-natured, courteous gentleman that you are.*

SMOL. [*Pleased*] Thank you!

DOR. [*Putting one on right ear*] And this, wear as the colors of your lady, whose beauty you are to defend against all comers!

SMOL. Believe me, I will prize the last beyond all else in life!

DOR. There! Now stand up! [*He does so*] And let me see how you look on dress parade! [*He has the pan of apples. She puts him in position*] Attention! Heads up! [*Reuben comes on at back*] Forward—march! [*They march down stairs*] File left! [*They do so*] File left! [*They do so*]

REU. [*At back*] Halt! [*They stop suddenly and all laugh*] Dorothy, you was a filin' left with the wrong foot!

SMOL. I dare say I look quite ridiculous, Mr. Foxglove!

REU. Yes, quite—but I've been there myself!

DOR. Reuben Foxglove, don't you interfere with my army! We are just going to make the pies, aren't we, Lieutenant?

SMOL. Yes, certainly, anything to oblige!

DOR. And the Lieutenant is going to help me with the crust. So please don't bother us now. [*About to go, looks at Reuben, sees button off his coat*] Oh! Good gracious! Oh! Dear me! [*Thrusts her bowl hastily into Smollet's pan*] Hold that! [*Runs to Reuben*] Now, Reuben Foxglove, where's that button? [*Talks breathlessly, shaking her head at him. At same time takes threaded needle and thimble from quaint bag at her side*] Oh! Dear! Dear! What a boy you are for losing buttons! When you left home this morning, every button was in its place, and you come to me now with the most prominent one gone, for gone I'm sure it is. You're never on speaking terms with any of them. They leave you—

REU. [*Who has quietly taken button from pocket*] On the slightest provocation. Only this one [*Handing it*] I managed to ketch jest as he was a'sneakin' off the last thread!

DOR. Give it to me, stupid boy! [*Dorothy's music pp. till Sir Frederick on and off, then change to lively to bring Winslow's party on*] Sit down. [*Seats him on old plow. Kneels in front of him and sews button playing scene over shoulder at Lieutenant*] Tired, Lieutenant?

SMOL. Not at all. Quite a recreation, I assure you.

REU. Say, Dorothy, hain't yeou an' him rather chummy for a rebel and a Britisher?

DOR. He's perfectly harmless, aren't you, Lieutenant?

SMOL. [*Who has not heard what she said*] Yes! Yes! Certainly! [*All laugh. Sir Frederick Shelton, a fine-looking, middle-aged English gentleman, very elegant, very dignified, in undress of Colonel of Grenadiers, strolls on quietly; stops; views the position of the parties in some amazement. By this time Dorothy has finished button and rises*]

DOR. [*Putting things in bag*] There you are—all right—and tight, once more! Now, Lieutenant—[*Going towards him, sees Sir Frederick. Stops and curtseys very low*] Sir Frederick, your most obedient! [*Sir Frederick acknowledges salute*]

SMOL. Sir Frederick—who—what? [*Turns and sees him*] The Devil! I beg pardon, sir. The fact is—I—she—you—[*Confusedly endeavoring to salute, etc.*]

DOR. There, there! Don't stammer. [*Goes to him, rights the bowl and pan*] The fact is, Sir Frederick, I've enlisted him in the domestic brigade till roll call, when I'll return him to you right side up with care. Attention! [*Slips arm through Smollet's arm*] Forward! [*Marches him into house and off L.H. laughing heartily, in which Reuben joins. Sir Frederick follows, looking after them good-naturedly, then comes down C.*]

SIR F. [*To Reuben, who has dropped down R. After a pause, slowly*] Your daughter?

REU. [*Looking at him suspiciously*] Ye-e-s!

SIR F. May I ask her age?

Reu. [*Same manner*] Nineteen!

Sir F. Her mother—

Reu. Died when she was a baby.

Sir F. And you have brought her up?

Reu. [*As before*] Ye-e-s!

Sir F. She has attended school? [*Smollet with dress arranged enters and remains respectfully at back*]

Reu. Ye-e-s—somewhat.

Sir F. She seems a charming girl!

Reu. She *is!*

Sir F. She must be a blessing to you!

Reu. She is!

Sir F. A very charming girl!

Reu. Ye-e-s! [*Sir Frederick bows very proudly and goes down stage. Reuben bows politely and strolls off at back R., looking at Sir Frederick as if some dread haunted him. Smollet drops down L. of Sir Frederick*]

Sir F. Strange how that girl affects me. Her age—her likeness to—Pshaw! Impossible! Poor wronged Agnes—[*Sadly, then changing to half anger*] why will that woman always haunt me? She must be—she *is* dead—both dead—no trace of either for nearly twenty years. [*Sadly*] Dead! But does her death atone for the wrong I did her? Alas! No! That can never *be* atoned.

Smol. Miss Foxglove always seems to affect you strangely, Sir Frederick.

Sir F. [*Starting, as if from a reverie*] Yes! In my daily intercourse with her, I seem to live the past over again; to catch a glimpse of that Heaven which might have been mine, had I not wantonly closed my doors against an angel's love!

Dor. [*From house, running on backwards, speaking as she enters. Runs against Sir Frederick and Smollet, and off at back R.H. Jumping and clapping hands with glee*] Here they come! Here they come! Mrs. Campbell! Father! Where are you? I'm so happy I can't contain myself! They're coming, I tell you! I must be the first to meet them! Rachel! Rachel! Don't speak to anyone till I've kissed you. [*Runs off*]

Ann. [*Who has hurried on through dairy*] Mercy on us! That gal's enough to give one the hystericks!

Sir F. Who is coming, may I ask?

Ann. The Captain and Rachel, I suppose, by the way *she* goes on! [*Goes up; looks off R.*] Yes, there they be, sure as a gun!

Sir F. [*To Smollet*] I shall be glad to shake the hand of my old comrade and thank him for his hospitality. Let us retire for the present, however, lest we mar the welcome these good people have prepared. [*They exeunt*

R.1 E. Music changes to lively air. Enter from R. at back, Captain Winslow, leaning on the arm of Roanoke, the Captain a dark, little old man, with white military whiskers; semi-military in dress and wholly so in manner; lame in right leg; carries a cane. Ann Campbell wipes old-fashioned chair and places it R.C. for him. Rachel and Dorothy come, arms around each other's waists, drop L.C. Reuben and Ned follow—Ned in handsome hunting costume. They join ladies. The entrance all animation. All talk together till Captain is seated and stage dressed]

CAPT. *[As he enters]* Thank ye. Thank ye. I'm as glad to get home as you are to see me, I'm sure!

ANN. *[As they enter]* Well, well, sakes alive, if they ain't jest as nat'ral as life!

DOR. *[As she enters]* Oh, Rachel, I'm so happy! I've got so much to tell you!

RACH. *[As she enters]* Dear old Dorothy, it seems as if I had not seen you for an age!

REU. *[As he enters]* Well, I hope you'll make yourself to hum. No ceremony wanted here!

NED. *[As he enters]* Thank you! Thank you! I'm sure!

CAPT. What a demonstration to be sure! One would think we had returned from a trip to the Antipodes! Well, I must say it is pleasant to be welcome even in one's own home. *[Taking chair and Ann's hand]* Mrs. Campbell, I hope Reuben has been civil to you during my absence!

ANN. Civil! I'd like to catch him bein' anything else to me! Captain, the sight on ye is good for sore eyes! *[Goes to place and is introduced to Ned. Curtseys]*

CAPT. Reuben, old friend, how go things with you?

REU. I jog along about the same old sixpence, Captain, sometimes walking on the balance on foot!

CAPT. And Roanoke! My faithful Roanoke! I've missed you sadly, boy— I don't know why—only that I love to look on your bright, manly face— and the day seemed to lack something without it. I hope Dorothy has been behaving herself. Here, Dorothy, you mischievous puss, come and give me another kiss. *[She does so]* I hope you have not been breaking poor Roanoke's heart!

DOR. Roanoke knows me too well to mind my idle pranks. *[Crosses to Roanoke and, giving him her hand, seriously]* I could not wound the thing I love—and I love—*[Checking herself]*—we *all* love Roanoke!

ROAN. White Captain, the little Primrose grows in the path of Roanoke. Its scent fills the air of his life. He is happy. *[He has taken her right hand in his right, placed his left arm around her waist and almost drawn her to his breast. She yields, then suddenly but not urgently checks the impulse*]

DOR. Isn't Mr. Wynthrop handsome? [*Military music behind scenes, distant, kept up till cue to cease. Roanoke looks into her face for a moment, drops her hand, she crosses to her former position. At same instant an orderly enters from R.1.E. and salutes*]

ORDERLY. Captain Winslow?

CAPT. [*Saluting*] I have that honor. [*Orderly marches up to him, salutes, gives paper, faces about. Marches back to place, faces about, awaits orders. Captain reads written letter*] "Sir Frederick Shelton presents his compliments to Captain Winslow and politely requests him, if not too fatigued, to witness regimental drill of His Majesty's Grenadiers, after which Sir Frederick will do himself the honor of dining with his old comrade and friend." [*To Orderly*] I shall attend Sir Frederick's pleasure—say so. [*Orderly salutes, faces and marches off*] Reuben and Roanoke, I shall need your assistance. This infernal fighting leg of mine, you know! Mr. Wynthrop, will you accompany us?

NED. Thank you, Captain! No! His Majesty's soldiers have no charm for me at present, though they may have later on!

CAPT. Ah, Rebel, take care! I leave Rachel and Dorothy to entertain you till I return. [*Bows and exits, E.R. leaning on Roanoke and accompanied by Reuben*]

ANN. Ef you'll excuse me, I'll give the finishin' touches to the table. [*Exit through dairy*]

DOR. And my pies forgotten in the oven. I'll bet a cookie they're burnt to a cinder. [*Goes up to door, then down to Rachel. Aside*] He's handsomer than Mr. Hampton. I *love* a handsome man. You go right ahead. If anyone comes, I'll cough. Ahem! See? [*By-play between her and Rachel. She chuckles and exits into house and off L.*]

NED. This is indeed a charming spot, Miss Winslow. [*He offers arm. She takes it. They stroll and finally Rachel seats herself on rustic seat L.H.*] I can now understand your glowing eulogisms on your Massachusetts home. Were you born here, may I ask?

RACH. Yes—beneath that roof my brother Harry and I entered and our dear mother left, this world. I have known and wish to know no other home.

NED. Your brother was your elder, I believe?

RACH. Three years.

NED. He suddenly and mysteriously disappeared, your father told me.

RACH. Yes. My father was absent with his regiment at the time, my mother an invalid, and I a baby by her side.

NED. Was his fate never learned?

RACH. Oh, yes! Mr. Hampton, who made the most strenuous exertions in our behalf, brought incontestable proofs that he had been stolen and murdered by a band of Mohawk Indians who committed many depredations in this vicinity about that time. My poor mother never spoke after the news was broken to her. She passed silently away, I hope, to join the boy she loved so dearly.

NED. Mr. Hampton! Humph! It is he, I think your father also told me, who by your uncle's will inherits the estate which should have been your brother's had he lived.

RACH. Yes. He is my father's cousin.

NED. And a claimant for your hand?

RACH. [*Hanging her head*] He has asked my *father* for my hand.

NED. And you?

RACH. Have promised to marry him.

NED. May I ask if you love him?

RACH. [*Rising*] Mr. Wynthrop!

NED. Pardon. Did it never occur to you that Mr. Hampton might be interested in your brother's death?

RACH. You go too far, sir.

NED. Again your pardon. Stranger things have been known.

RACH. I must not listen to you, sir!

NED. I crave one moment. I have thought that were there a way out of this marriage you would avail yourself of it. Is it so?

RACH. By what right do you ask?

NED. The right an honest man has to undo a wrong. Listen to a little romance. [*Seats her*] Once upon a time there lived two children, a boy and a girl, both motherless, who, thrown much together, learned to love each other as only children can, and in the impulses of their fresh young hearts plighted their youthful troths, vowing that nothing but death should separate them— that if they lived they should become man and wife. The boy's father died, and cruel fate bound him to a crueller master in the form of one Dyke Hampton. One outrage succeeded another, until at last, stung beyond endurance, the boy dared to resent an infamous wrong and was, for his bravery, felled to the earth by a blow from his brutal master. Crushed, bleeding, but not subdued, the boy crept silently away into the shadows of the night and was seen no more, but before he went he sent a message to his baby bride telling her that if he lived he would sure return.

RACH. [*Who has slowly risen, having drunk in every word he uttered, with a wild cry*] Man! Man! Who are you?

NED. Ned Farnsworth. [*She shrieks and falls into his arms*] Your boy lover! [*Military music ceases*]

RACH. Ned! My Ned!

DOR. [*Entering hurriedly from house*] What's the matter? Doctor pulling your tooth? [*Takes in the situation*] Excuse me—my pies are burning! [*Exit hurriedly into house again*]

RACH. Ned, why did you not tell?

NED. Because the time had not come. Nor must I now be known by any here save as Mr. Wynthrop, your accidental friend. But Rachel, the day is far distant when Dyke Hampton calls wife the woman who pledged her baby troth to Ned Farnsworth. [*Enter Sergeant and file of Soldiers. When they are in position*]

SERG. Halt! [*They do so*] Front! [*They do so*] Present! [*Enter Sir Frederick in full dress and Winslow, arm in arm, followed by Smollet in full dress, Reuben and Roanake as they pass on*] Recover! [*They do so*] Right face! [*They do so*] Forward, by file right, march! [*Men march off*]

CAPT. Wynthrop, you missed a grand sight! It does an old soldier's heart good to witness such discipline and precision. Rachel, girl, welcome my old friend, Sir Frederick Shelton. My daughter, Sir Frederick. [*They bow. Dorothy's music till end of act, very piano at first, works with scene*]

RACH. [*Crossing, taking Sir Frederick's hand*] Proud to meet any friend of my father's, sir.

CAPT. [*Introducing*] Mr. Wynthrop, my Galen of the forest. [*They bow*] Daughter, Lieutenant Smollet. [*They bow*] Mr. Wynthrop. [*Smollet and Ned bow*] Rachel, give your arm to Sir Frederick. The Lieutenant will follow. Wynthrop and myself will bring up the rear—and so far—

DOR. [*Appearing on steps, locket on neck on ribbon*] Supper! [*All laugh. Rachel gives arm to Sir Frederick. Ned passes over to Winslow. Smollet crosses up behind Winslow. General movement. As Sir Frederick goes up he keeps his eyes on Dorothy. As he nears her he sees locket, stands transfixed, then slowly retreats with back to audience—seems to half faint. Smollet rushes to him, placing chair. He sinks into it. Ned goes to Rachel. All advance*]

SIR F. [*Recovering himself, speaking slowly and in hoarse whisper*] In God's name, girl—how came you by that locket?

DOR. It was clasped around my neck when Reuben found me—placed there, as I believe and hope, by my mother before she died.

SIR F. [*Same tone*] Why have I not seen it before?

Dor. I never wear it but on holidays and Sundays. It is too sacred for every day. [*Half frightened by his manner*] Why do you look at me so strangely? You frighten me! Reuben! Roanoke! [*Roanoke springs down R. She crosses quickly to him and shelters herself in his arms. Reuben drops down also*]

Sir F. Found—Reuben—found. Are you not then his child?

Reu. In all that makes her so cept'n blood—an' that's better done a'thout sometimes.

Sir F. If not your child, whose is she?

Reu. God's, I reckon. Leastwise, he give her to me!

Sir F. [*In whisper as before*] Her story!

Reu. One terrible snowy night, eighteen years ago, after buildin' a big fire on my hearth, I went as usual to bait and set my traps. When I got back I found my cabin door open—the wind, I reckon, had undid the latch. I entered an' right on the hearth afore the fire I see suthin' a'shinin' bright an' yaller—jest like gold. I stooped to pick it up, an' it was hair—bright, golden, shiny hair—an' there was this child—this angel baby—a'lyin' on my cabin floor an' sleepin' as gently an' as peacefully as if she was a nussin' from her mother's breast.

Sir F. [*Almost overcome with grief and excitement, as before*] Go on!

Reu. I will. [*Wipes eyes*] At fust I kinder conjured as how some one must a'left her there, an' I stepped to the door to look around. It had stopped snowin' an' the moon was a'shinin' bright as day—not a sound 'cept the howlin' o' the wolves. I was about to close the door agin when I see the baby's footsteps in the snow. I follered 'em, an' a thin ten paces came on the form of a woman lyin' in the snow. She was dead. Then I see it all. The woman had got lost in the storm. She tried to reach my cabin—fell exhausted—the child must a' rolled from her arms an', baby like, attracted by the light, toddled to my door. Heaven opened it for her—she crept in—the warm fire lulled her to sleep—an' there I found her! [*During this scene, Dorothy has crept to him, sobbing and almost buried herself in his bosom*]

Sir F. [*As before*] And that locket was clasped around her neck?

Reu. Yes!

Sir F. Have you ever opened it?

Reu. Tried to, but couldn't. Allus thought there wan't no openin' to it.

Sir F. Let me see it!

Dor. [*Clasping it with both hands*] No—no—you shall not!

Sir F. [*Gently*] Fear nothing, child. I will restore it.

REU. [*Half afraid*]   Let him see it, Dorothy. No harm can come to it. [*He gently unties it from her neck and passes it to Sir Frederick, who rolls it over in his hand and it opens*]

SIR F. [*Springing up with a wild scream*]   See! My marriage certificate! Her mother's likeness! She is my child!

ALL.   Your child!

DOR. [*Screams and clings to Reuben*]   No! No! Don't listen, Reuben! He's mad! *Here* is my father! You'll break his heart—you'll kill me. Give me back my locket. Shut it up! [*Springs towards Sir Frederick*] Reuben! Roanoke! Don't let him take me! I—Oh! Ha—ha—ha! [*Screams—laughs hysterically and falls in Reuben's arms as curtain descends*]

PICTURE AND END OF ACT I.

ACT II.

("Descriptive music" to take up curtain)

TIME: *April 1775.*

SCENE I: *Dorchester Heights. Interior of old-fashioned kitchen, roofed; with large old-fashioned fireplace, crane, log fire, etc. Heavy beams or rafters on which are hung dried apples, tufts of herbs, bunches of onions, crook-neck squash, bell peppers, etc. Everything about this scene—furniture, pots, pans, dishes, etc., must be historically correct. Same backing as Act I. At Rise: Evening. Scene lighted wholly by fire-log. Towards end of Act it grows dark outside and moon rises. Ann Campbell discovered washing dishes in (smoking) hot water. She pays no attention to scene. After she has finished the dishes she carries them off R. door. Returns, wipes up table, takes dishpan, etc. and exits R.D. Returns after a bit with lighted candle and exits up the stairs as if to go to bed. Rachel is spinning. Captain Winslow smoking pipe. He is very careworn and smokes slowly and thoughtfully. Dyke Hampton is seated cross-legged on chair with its back in front of him—he is dressed as before—with addition of top coat. He is in the act of receiving papers from Captain Winslow.*

DYKE.   I am glad the accounts are correct. My father, during his life, left undone nothing that in his judgment would enhance your interests; and I as his successor, have, I trust, been fully as vigilant. Yet, in spite of all, we have not succeeded so well as we could have wished.

CAPT.   You have succeeded in leaving me a beggar!

DYKE.   Captain—I—

CAPT. You say the Van Orten suit has been decided against me?

DYKE. [*Slowly, as if loathe to admit it*] Y-e-s!

CAPT. And that tomorrow he will claim this, my last bit of property?

DYKE. Unless certain conditions can be met!

CAPT. Which you know I cannot meet!

DYKE. Not without assistance—I am aware.

CAPT. Dyke—I don't say that my property has been wrongfully managed. It is too late for that now. But it is singular that while I have grown steadily poor, you have grown *as* steadily rich.

DYKE. Do you blame me for having prospered?

CAPT. I blame no one—I say it's strange, that's all.

DYKE. You forget that my cousin, your brother, added materially to my worldly store!

CAPT. Poor Edward—basely deceived by the only woman he ever loved, he could not forgive my daughter's birth. Had he ever looked into her face, he had not been so cruel in his will.

DYKE. I will not say that he was altogether just. The fact remains nevertheless—that—your son dead—the property comes to me. I, therefore, should be wrong to quarrel with the memory of the giver. I can, however, correct his error. Let this marriage between Rachel and myself take place at once and half your brother's estate is yours. [*Weird pathetic music now till Dyke off and Reuben on*]

CAPT. You ask me to sell my own flesh and blood?

DYKE. No! Your word and hers are both pledged to the union—and— [*Humbly*] am I not worthy of her? [*With passionate intensity*] I tell you I love your daughter with a passion beyond the conception of other men—I would for her sake—

RACH. [*Looking up, smiling sadly, with cheek on hand, leaning on the knee of her father*] Be generous?

DYKE. [*As if avoiding a trap*] How—generous?

RACH. Give—me—up! [*Same tone*]

DYKE. Do—you—love another? [*Slowly, passionately, almost between his teeth*]

RACH. [*Droops head and says quietly*] We are never masters of our own hearts!

DYKE. [*Springing up with violent passion—overturning chair and raising aloft clenched hand in which he holds whip*] Then—by God—I'll kill him! [*Rachel, who has sprung up and clung about her father's neck, utters a smothered scream and hides her face*]

CAPT. [*Who has risen at same time, says sternly and with his old dignity and fire*] Hampton—you forget yourself!

DYKE. [*Recovering and trembling with excitement*] Yes—I—my feelings —forgive me—I'll leave you—a gallop across the hills will compose me. [*Crosses to L.H. door*] I'm unstrung. [*Turns and speaks moodily*] Rachel— you are a woman and I ask you to pity me from a woman's heart. For something tells me that my love for you is the chain that will yet drag me down to infamy and eternal damnation. Don't judge me wrongfully. I value wealth only as it serves to bind you to me—with you—I might be—[*Almost tempted to betray all he knows, then checks himself*] I cannot say—without you, I *know* I shall be a *Devil*. You ask me to give you up. Well, what then, to another? [*Through teeth*] No! Never! [*Change*] That is—I'm afraid I could not. [*With moody ferocity*] Don't tempt me. I tremble for you. I tremble for him. I tremble for myself. I'll go now—pardon me. [*Gets near door, then turns*] I love you, Rachel. [*Looks earnestly at her*] Good-night. [*Exit. Rachel pale and calm on her father's breast. He looking after Dyke. Picture. Pause*]

RACH. [*Coldly*] Father—I'll marry Dyke.

CAPT. Do you love him?

RACH. No! But I fear him—I must save him—I must save you—I must save—

CAPT. [*Reading her thoughts*] Wynthrop?

RACH. [*Same tone*] Yes.

CAPT. You love Wynthrop?

RACH. Else I'd never marry Hampton!

CAPT. Will Wynthrop consent to this?

RACH. He must—he will. He loves me!

CAPT. [*Bitterly*] And yet he deserts you! Disappears in the dead of night, leaving no word, no token, and is as utterly lost to you as if the earth had opened and swallowed him!

RACH. He will return—and if not—it were better so.

CAPT. My poor child—I fear I have been much to blame in all this. I never should—

RACH. There, father—let us talk no more tonight. I am weary. Tomorrow, perhaps—

CAPT. Perhaps—

RACH. Good-night. [*Kisses him tenderly*]

CAPT. Good-night. [*Kissing her. She goes to door, turns, looks at him, smiles*]

RACH. Good-night! [*She exits. Captain looks after her, thinks a moment, goes to fireplace, throws pipe into fire, puts hands into breeches pockets.*

Crosses down to R.H. corner, turns and meets Reuben and Roanoke, who have entered from L.H. door. Reuben throws himself on settee; Roanoke crosses and throws himself into upper seat in chimney corner. Reuben and Roanoke very dejected. Music dies away]

CAPT. Been to the city again, eh, Reuben? You quite live there now!

REU. Well, what's the use'n a feller distributin' himself around in pieces. My heart's over there—an' I dunno's I care much what comes o' the rest o' me!

CAPT. Seen Dorothy?

REU. Yesterday. Shouldn't a' come back ef I hadn't.

CAPT. Well?

REU. Well—they'r goin' to send her to England to be eddicated.

CAPT. Sir Frederick has established his claim, then?

REU. Yes. All the papers have arrove from England, an' they've settled that he is her father and entitled to her custody. [*Dorothy's music begins*]

CAPT. Was the mystery of the mother cleared up?

REU. Yes! It appears that Sir Frederick fell in love with her mother who was what they call over there, of low birth, for her purty face. After they was married he was ashamed of her—his family refused to hev anything to do with her—and so he pensioned her off in a leetle seaport town, an' then neglected her. After Dorothy's birth, failin' to get any satisfaction even for her baby, she concluded to leave him and England forever, sellin' what few trinkets she had. She managed to get to America, an' after sufferin' God knows what, died, as we all know. An' now they'r a'goin' to send Dorothy over for some other Lord knows who—to do the same by her! Dorothy says I must be patient an' it'll come out all right in the end. I try to be—an' I hope I shell be, but I tell ye, Captain, it's pretty hard to ring a hog's nose a'thout the hog's a'squalin'!

DOR. [*Putting head in R. door*] Anybody at home? May I come in? [*Enters with a clear ringing laugh*]

ALL. [*Rising*] Dorothy!

DOR. [*Entering like a sunbeam*] Yes, the same old Dorothy. [*She is elegantly attired, wears locket*] In a little handsomer frame, perhaps, but I hope that doesn't alter the picture. They wanted to change my name as well as my dress, but I told them that Dorothy I was and Dorothy I would remain to the end of the chapter! [*They all stand silent*] Why, what's the matter with you all? [*Laughs*] Not afraid I've brought the plague with me, are you? Captain, aren't you glad to see me?

CAPT. Why, Lady Shelton! [*Half jesting*]

Dor. [*Laughing*] Lady Fiddlesticks. Here—[*Shakes hands*] call me Dorothy and say you are glad to see me if you don't want to be cashiered for neglect of duty!

Capt. [*Laughing and shaking hands*] Dorothy, I *am* glad to see you!

Dor. That is a little more like it! [*He is about to drop her hand*] Here! Here! Here! [*Puts up lips to be kissed. He kisses her. They both laugh*] Now, Roanoke—[*Her manner changing to Roanoke, who has crossed down R.H., offering his hand, which she takes*] What have you to say?

Roan. Only that the heart of Roanoke is sad, for he knows that another land than that which gave him birth claims the Little Primrose for its own, and that the tall ship will soon spread its white wings to bear her afar over the bosom of the mighty water, where she will be lost to him forever.

Dor. [*Looks at him sadly—tries to speak—she cannot. Her eyes fill with tears. She drops his hand and her head, surreptitiously brushes a tear from her eye, then quickly turns, all smiles, to Reuben. Roanoke goes back to fireplace*] And there's my boy—looking as if he'd lost *every* friend he had in the world! [*Laughs*] Here, Reuben—kiss your mother! [*He does so*] Do you call that a kiss—you naughty boy! There! [*Kissing him*] And there! [*Kissing him*] And there! [*Kissing him—laughs*] Now let me see if your buttons are all right. [*Looks him over*] Yes, for once—I declare—all right! Who will take care of you when I'm gone, I wonder? I'm afraid you'll go buttonless to bed many a night, my poor boy—with no Dorothy to—[*Tries to laugh. Looks up at him, sees a tear on his cheek, takes his face in both her hands, kisses the tear away and nestles to him in the old, old way*] Reuben, don't—don't cry— speak to me! Hold me in your arms as you used to do when I was a little child and there was no *other* father to come between us. Help me to be brave. Reuben, don't you see that I am trying so hard—that I am not happy? That I am only pretending? That my heart is breaking? [*Bursts into tears—gives up entirely and sobs on his breast. Enter Sir Frederick in military cloak. Stops at door*]

Sir F. You forget, child, that you are my daughter!

Reu. [*Still holding her*] Forgettin' seems to run into the family, Sir Frederick. You forgot her mother was your wife.

Sir F. [*Wincing*] I committed a grievous sin! I have never ceased to repent it! I shall do my best to repair the wrong I did the mother by justice to the child.

Reu. It's a kind o' pity ye can't repair one wrong a'thout doin' another, hain't it? Pity it couldn't a been done years ago, afore the little tender vine had twined itself in an' out around the limbs an' branches of the old oak till they became one. Ye must chop down the oak now to free the vine.

Sir F. [*Abashed*] I shall settle a fine allowance on you. You shall be well paid for all your care and trouble.

Reu. There's some things that can't *be* paid for, an' love's one on 'em.

Sir F. [*Trying to excuse himself*] It is for the girl's good—wealth, station, name—would you deprive her of all these?

Reu. No. You have the right to take her, an' it's for her good that she goes. The last's the argyment that silences me. I hain't a'goin' to stand agin that.

Sir F. 'Tis useless to prolong a scene painful to us all. To me, whose sin has been its cause, more painful than to any here! Captain Winslow—[*Taking his hand*] pardon me. I leave my daughter with you till the morrow, when I will either call or send for her. Duty demands my immediate departure. Good-night.

Capt. Good-night.

Sir F. [*Going, turns, looks sadly at Reuben and Dorothy, says kindly but with much dignity*] Good-night, Mr. Foxglove. [*Exit. The moon has slowly risen by this time. It lights the exterior; the fire, the interior*]

Rach. [*Entering from R.D.*] Father, there is—[*Sees the group. Her eyes catch a glimpse of Dorothy. She springs forward*] Dorothy!

Reu. [*Staying her*] Hush! She's sobbed herself to sleep! Ef you don't mind, I'll set here an' hold her awhile. She's dreamin', mebbe, an'll be glad to find herself in my arms when she wakes. [*Takes her in arms and sits on settee with her head on his breast. Music changes. Enter Dyke Hampton, pale and haggard, his dress awry, hair dishevelled. Has the appearance of a man who has ridden hard and had a terrible struggle with himself. He does not notice Reuben, Roanoke or Dorothy. Rachel looks frightened; Captain surprised. Dyke stops at door as if afraid she would not be there*]

Dyke. [*Speaks hurriedly and with passionate effort to be calm*] Rachel Winslow, I rode from this spot resolved never to see you again. I rode hard. I struggled fearfully with myself. But as I spurred my panting horse into the thickness of the night, I seemed to see you in another's arms. At the sight all the fiends of darkness seized my struggling soul. I struggled longer, in vain. I turned my horse's head and lashed him on. He lies dying at your door. I entered fearful lest I should find my vision true. I cannot—I *will* not, give you up!

Capt. Dyke Hampton, listen to me!

Dyke. Captain Winslow—listen to me! [*Furiously*] She loves this Wynthrop! I know it now, and so do you! [*The Captain is taken aback at this*] Your word is pledged to me. Keep it. Give her to me—or tomorrow sees her homeless and you a beggar! [*As Dyke comes down, Reuben lays Dorothy on settee—motions to Roanoke, who comes down noiselessly. Reuben commits Dorothy to his care and quietly exits*]

CAPT. [*Almost paralyzed, doubting how to act or what to say*] I—I—

RACH. [*Calmly*] Father, let me speak. [*Crosses to Dyke*] Dyke Hampton, I do love Mr. Wynthrop. You, I never can love! Take me but as I am and I will become your wife.

DYKE. [*Amazed, springs towards her*] Rachel!

CAPT. [*Turning her around*] No! I'll be damned if you do! I am an old man, worn out, it may be, with hard service, but hand in hand we'll go forth into the world. You shall not give your hand to one man while your heart is wedded to another.

DYKE. [*Worked up to a paroxysm of rage and disappointment*] Then go forth to beg—to starve—for, by my soul, you sleep not another night under this roof. I might have guessed as much when that canting, hypocritical scoundrel became your guest! A man of whom no one knows aught—who is, if the truth were known, a fugitive before the law—hiding in the dark, afraid to show his face in the broad light of day!

NED. [*Springing through door*] You lie, you hound—you lie!

RACH. [*Rushing to him*] Ned!

CAPT. and DYKE. [*Astonished*] Ned?

NED. Yes! Ned Farnsworth! [*Dyke staggers back, thunderstruck*] Do you know me now, you craven cur? The boy your coward hand struck to the earth—from whom has sprung the avenging man to pay you back ten-fold the blow you gave, and who will not rest till your foul carcass swings from the gallows tree! Murderer!

ALL. Murderer?

DYKE. [*Livid with rage*] Take care—

NED. Yes, murderer—the murderer of this old man's son!

CAPT. Merciful Heaven, can this be true? [*About to fall. Ned and Rachel run to him*]

NED. Look to your father. [*As Ned turns his back, Dyke quickly draws pistol and fires at Ned. Roanoke, who has been watching him, seizes his arm, the pistol is discharged in the air. Dorothy awakes—is dazed. Reuben enters hastily, carrying gun—speaks in loud whisper. Change music and keep up till end of scene*]

REU. Silence, every one an' ye! Eight hundred British soldiers under Pitcairn are a'marchin' to seize the stores an' ammunition at Concord—see— [*Points. All the characters, who have stopped in exactly the positions they were in when he entered, now crane forward without moving their bodies, to see. The moon is now very bright, and the British soldiers are seen marching silently past window from R. to L. Instant's pause*] The hour for action has come at last. Ned, where's your horse?

NED. Fastened under the shadow of the great oak.

REU. Mount like litenin'! Rouse the Minute Men as you go! We must be there afore 'em.

CAPT. Rachel! My gun! [*She exits—re-enters with gun and powder horn —gives them*]

DYKE. [*Who has been watching his chance, makes rush for the door*] Ah! Rebels! Not yet! Ho! There rebels!

REU. [*Seizes him by the throat*] Silence, or ye'll never speak that word again! [*Thrusts him back*] Roanoke, take charge of that yelpin' wolf! If he moves, strangle him! [*Roanoke stands guard with folded arms*] The Committee of Safety's assembled at the house of Jonas Hundel in West Cambridge. If surprised they're lost. Who will warn them?

DOR. [*Springing down*] I will!

REU. Brave girl! Mount Brown Winnie. [*She starts off R.*] Don't spare the lash! Ride for your life!

DOR. [*As she exits*] I will!

REU. [*Arms aloft*] And now, God of Battles, inspire this, the first blow for *American Independence*. [*All kneel except Roanoke and Dyke. At same moment Ann Campbell appears on stairs with gun*]

PICTURE

Second picture: Dyke and Roanoke in same position—Ann back to audience, guarding door with gun, ready—Rachel kneeling and clinging to her, but on her R.H. Close in with SCENE 2—*"The Stand at Lexington." Lexington Green in 1775. See historical picture. Enter Reuben marching on twenty men in double column, followed by Ned and twenty men in same manner. As they reach positions.*

REU. Halt! [*They do so*]

NED. Halt! [*They do so*]

REU. Ned! Talk to 'em.

NED. [*Stepping to the front*] Comrades! The hireling soldiers of an obstinate and audacious King are at last marching through the peaceful villages of Massachusetts to seize by force of arms, confiscate and destroy, our property, invade and lay waste our homes! Not content with depriving us of every right granted us by charter, with taxing the very air we breathe, with closing our ports, removing our seats of government, quartering his soldiers on our people, he has, in a speech to his corrupt ministers in Parliament, declared us rebels—outlaws—and set a price upon the heads of those who dare to resist his mandates! To us will belong the imperishable, the priceless honor of repelling the first advance of those armed marauders, of striking the first blow for a *Nation's* life!—a blow that will resound from Ocean to Ocean—find a welcoming echo in every true American heart—heal discord—cement our cause—encourage the timid—strengthen the brave—till the nation, rising as one man, will fight while a single arm remains—fight till the glorious cause is won and the last invading soldier has left our shores! Be firm—be true—be brave—and we cannot fail!

REU. Here they come. Steady! Steady! There's a heap on 'em, but don't be skeered! Let them shoot first! Wait for the word—but when you do shoot, shoot to kill! Steady, I say! [*Enter L.1.E. British Grenadiers and Light Infantry, all bayonets fixed. They form L. of stage.* NOTE: *The Americans have all sorts of guns, and not above five with bayonets*]

COL. SMITH. Disperse, ye rebels! Disperse! Throw down your arms and disperse! [*Dead silence*] Fire! [*First platoon fires—retire. Second takes its place. No one falls*] Rebels! My soldiers fired over your heads. The next volley will be at your hearts! Again I say disperse! [*Silence*] Ready! [*His men get ready*] Lay down your arms and disperse! [*No answer*] Fire! [*They do so and several Americans fall, among them Reuben, who at once springs to his feet*]

REU. Fire! [*The Americans fire. Several British fall. The Americans retreat, carrying off their dead*]

COL. SMITH. Load! [*The men, who have discharged their pieces, now load with great precision*] I think that's given the Yankees all they care to have. About! [*They do so*] March! [*They exeunt L.1.E. The church bells now begin to ring an alarm. Men, Women and Boys, in all manner of costume, some just from the plow, a Blacksmith, etc., etc.—some without coats, some without hats. Some have guns. Blacksmith has sledge, Farmer has axe, etc., etc. One Old Man hobbles on, on crutches. An Old Woman gives him a gun and powder horn. He hobbles off R. Boy runs on—gives Man a gun. Wives and Husbands embrace, kiss, etc. Some of the Women go off crying—others cling to their Husbands—others go on to the fight with them—all silent and determined. No confusion. This scene must be dressed, rehearsed and acted from pictures. Enter R.H. Dorothy. She has the appearance of having ridden all night*]

DOR. Men! Men! For the love of God—hasten! There—there—[*To a Woman who has a Baby in her arms and who is clinging about her Husband's neck*] Woman, is this a time to stay your husband? Brave men! Brave men! Quick! Quick! On to Concord! Every arm is needed now! [*To a Boy who rushes past with a gun*] Well done, young hero! Oh, no—King George, you'll never conquer iron hearts like these! [*Distant cannonading*] Hark! Artillery! They are reinforced. Haste, or all is lost! [*Cannonading—booming —bells—fife and drum—distant musketry, etc., etc.*] Quick! To a peerless victory or a glorious death! [*Hurries them all off and exit R.H. See all ready for*]

BATTLE OF CONCORD

[*When in full blast, change to* SCENE 3—*"The Concord Fight." To be rehearsed and arranged from plates and as will prove most acceptable; practicable and effective, and*]

ACT III.

TIME: *June 1775.*

SCENE 1: *Mystic River. This scene represents a regular log fort. Supposed to have been built during the French War as a protection against Indian surprises. Large logs well chinked with mud. It is roofed and is set so as to show exterior action on L.H. of stage and is built to burn—fall to pieces and blow up during action of play. Long rifle over chimney place. Reuben discovered in rocking chair, head bandaged. Ann Campbell setting cooking things to rights. Characteristic music at rise.*

ANN.   There! I think that'll do agin the Captain and Rachel comes!

REU.   Hes the skins arrove?

ANN.   Yes. This mornin'. Mr. Farnsworth ses there's commissary stores for a month. He's gone now to fetch the folks. How in the name of Ephriam did you find this 'ere place anyhow?

REU.   Didn't find it. It found us. Ned and me's hed to do consid'able skirmishin' o' late an' one night found us in a dense pine wood—it was so dark you could scursely see yer hand afore ye. We darsn't build no fire afear o' Injuns, so we laid down at the foot o' what we supposed was a huge rock to wait for daylight. It rained cats an' dogs in the night. In the mornin' we found that we'd been a'makin' a dam of ourselves to keep the water from runnin' under this 'ere cabin. After cussin' ourselves for a couple o' natural born suckers an' findin' the place was deserted, we took possession on't in the name of the Continental Congress.

ANN.   I've heard o' folks that didn't know enough to go in out'n the rain, but I didn't think you was one on 'em.

REU. [*Laughing*]   We named it Fort Farnsworth. We've made good use of it since. It's a safe place to hide sich ammunition an' stores as we come across. We've got a bar'l o' gunpowder an' about a ton o' lead under this floor now!

ANN.   Mercy on us! Where?

REU. [*Laughing*]   I thought you wan't a'feared o' powder?

ANN.   No more I hain't, when it comes straight agin me from the inside of a gun! But I don't keer to cook my vittals with it.

REU.   There ain't no danger. This 'ere powder's too well brought up not to know when to go off! It can tell a Red Coat or a mean Injun as far as you can smell a skunk! You can't make it kill a Yankee no how!

ANN.   I wasn't born in the woods to be skeered by an owl—but I'll whistle Yankee Doodle everytime I sweep this floor—for all that!

REU. [*Slyly*]   I wouldn't do that ef I was you—the British whistled that tune marchin' to Concord an' they run so all-fired fast gittin' back that they hadn't breath enough left to whistle fer a dog!

ANN.   Concord! Ef I'd only been there to see it! It's jist like showin' a red flag to a mad bull to talk to me about them British! [*Thinks to herself a minute, then suddenly with both hands on hips*] Say, Reuben, I'd like to 'list.

REU.   'List?

ANN.   Yes—'list! They've called for men—hain't they?

REU.   Thirty thousand's got to be riz' in New England—13,000's Massachusetts' share—I'm one o' *them!*

ANN.   An' I'm another!

REU.   You! [*Laughs*]

ANN.   Yes, me! It won't be the fust time a woman's wore the breeches!

REU. [*Slyly*]   Did you ever wear 'em, Mrs. Campbell?

ANN.   No! But I kin—an' I hain't the only woman that kin an' will ef her country's to be served by doin' it! Jist let Congress call for women, an' ef I don't raise a rigiment on 'em that'll lick Satan out'n the same number o' Red Coats an' make 'em wear petticoats arterwards, my name hain't Ann Campbell! That's all. [*Dorothy's music*]

REU. [*Smiling*]   I'll mention it to Colonel Ward the next time I see him. [*Dorothy heard singing off stage L.*] There's a recruit for yeou! Now I'd like to command a rigiment o' them! Handsome as a picter on dress parade an' truer'n steel in action! [*During this Dorothy has sung herself on stage so that she is at the door by the end of Reuben's speech. She carries a pail of water*]

DOR. [*Outside door, laughing*]   Pull your chairs away! I'm coming. Quick! [*Puts head in—laughs*] Ah—I caught you! [*Enters with clear ringing laugh. Reuben chuckles. Ann pretends to be angry*] What makes you blush so? [*Laughs*]

ANN. Dorothy Foxglove! D'ye mean to say I'm a'blushin'? Why, I'd think no more a'settin' up clus to Reuben then a hen would a'layin' a egg! [*Dorothy's music ceases*]

REU. What d'ye want to deny it fur? Ye know ye had yer arms around my neck! [*Chuckles*]

ANN. Reuben Foxglove, ef that was the fust lie ye ever told it'd a'choked ye! [*Smiling at the thought of the past*] It's a good long time sense I had my arms around a man's neck, and I dunno's I'll ever git 'em there agin—but if I *do*, they'll *stay* there for the balance o' my nat'ral existence. So put that in yer pipe an' smoke it fur tobaccy! [*Exit a la militaire, R.D.*]

DOR. [*Who has placed the pail on bench and has been listening with a pleased expression—fills a gourd with water and comes to Reuben with a laugh*] Here, take a drink of water to rinse that down with. [*They both laugh*] And how is your poor head today?

REU. On my shoulders, thanks to you, Dorothy! [*Drinks water. Dorothy replaces gourd. Music to bring on Ned, Rachel, Roanoke and the Captain*]

DOR. Nonsense! I only did what any other mother would have done for her sick boy. [*Laughing*] Once you were so helpless, Reuben, you didn't have ambition enough to even lose your buttons. [*Laughs*] And now, sir, I'm going to make you a nice pan of hot biscuit for your supper. [*Going to R.D.*]

NED. [*Off stage L.*] Yes, rather difficult, but all the safer for it!

DOR. [*Stopping*] Hark! Mr. Farnsworth's voice. It's Rachel! [*Runs to L. door and throws it open. Rachel enters. They embrace*] Rachel—dear Rachel! [*They retire up R.H. Dorothy relieves Rachel of things and gives them to Ann, who has come on R. door. Ann takes the things off R. Captain Winslow enters. Reuben rises and shakes him by the hand. Takes Captain's gun and places it against chimney. Roanoke enters and after placing gun against wall U.L. corner, turns to talk to Ann, who has entered and crossed over to table with materials for mixing bread. Ned enters and leans his gun against wall L.H.* NOTE: *All Ann's entrances and exits in this Act must be a la militaire— all her movements and actions the same*]

REU. [*As if continuing conversation with Captain*] Yes, thank'er, Captain, 'bout as good as new, I reckon. [*Cease music*]

NED. There, Captain! And you, Miss Rachel, welcome to Fort Farnsworth. [*To the Captain*] We thought this would be the safest place for you till matters cleared up a bit!

CAPT. [*Bowing his head and then taking a survey of the premises*] Comfortable enough and capable of resisting quite a siege!

NED. Built during the French War, I should judge, as a protection against Indians. You see, we have the loops and all the requisites—[*Pointing to them*] of a first-class fort.·[*Laughing*]

CAPT. If these old logs could speak they might tell strange tales of the past. Who knows?

NED. Reuben, are you able to report for duty?

REU. Able an' willin', Ned. My ole legs's been idle so long, they're twisted up like a skein o' yarn.

NED. Then come along! [*Reuben gets up*] There's glorious work afoot. We meet a few friends at the old place. Roanoke, it is important that we are not surprised! You understand?

ROAN. The dog is not more faithful—the fox more cunning—the eagle more vigilant! [*Takes up gun*] Fear nothing.

NED. Ladies, are you afraid to be left alone till evening?

DOR. We are soldiers' daughters, Mr. Farnsworth!

ANN. [*From table*] An' I'm a soldier—don't yeou forget *that!*

NED. There is not much danger of our retreat being discovered—still caution is never to be despised. I would advise barring the doors and shutters and not stirring abroad till we return.

DOR. [*Laughing*] Ah, you'll find us safe and sound. Never fear! [*The men all exit L., carrying their guns—Roanoke last. As he gets to the door he casts a long, lingering, hungry look at Dorothy. Their eyes meet. She smiles and inclines her head to him. His face lights up and he exits joyously. Music dies gradually away and changes to distant march, which is kept up now working with scene till Lieutenant Smollet is on stage and scene with Dorothy well begun, when it dies away*] Now, Rachel, you sit there—[*Places her in rocking chair*] and tell me all the news, while I—[*Turns and sees Ann getting dough ready*] Now, Mrs. Campbell, I thought I was to make those biscuits! Here, now—you just give me that apron. [*Takes apron off her*] And if you've anything else to do, go and do it! [*Laughs*]

ANN. Well, as you'rn my superior officer I reckon my duty is to obey. [*Salutes and marches off L. Rachel and Dorothy laugh*]

RACH. Our home has been seized and, at the instigation of Dyke Hampton, an order has been issued for the arrest of my father on a charge of treason. The soldiers are now in search of him. If he should be taken, I tremble for life!

DOR. They'll not find him. Mr. Farnsworth is a match for twenty Hamptons!

RACH. I pray for his safety but a little while longer. Congress has appointed George Washington, Commander-in-Chief of our armies. He is expected in Cambridge within a month to take command. My father, who fought with him under Braddock, will seek a position on his staff.

Dor. And you—[*Rolling dough*]

Rach. I'll remain where Ned thinks safest and best till his duty permits him to call me wife!

Dor. He's handsome, isn't he? I love to look at a handsome man. That's why I'm so fond of looking at Reuben. [*Laughs. Six Soldiers, "British," headed by Smollet march on from L. and range behind house*] Well—if I were a man—Hush!

Smol. [*Outside*] Halt! Two of you guard the right hand. [*Two do so*] Two the left. [*Two do so*] And two this window. If any person attempts to enter or leave the premises, arrest them. If they resist—fire!

Dor. Lieutenant Smollet! [*Startled*] They've tracked your father. If he sees you, all is lost—in there—and leave me to try and baffle him! [*Rachel exits R. Dorothy sings and busies herself with the biscuits as if nothing had occurred. Smollet puts head in at window*]

Smol. Beg pardon! I'm in search of—[*She looks up*] Lady Shelton!

Dor. [*As if surprised*] Lieutenant Smollet! [*Laughs*] You are just in time to help me with the biscuits! Come in. [*He does so*] Sit down. [*He does so*] I'm delighted to see you! Excuse my not shaking hands. [*Showing hands—all flour*] Now, make yourself perfectly at home. Well, well, this is a surprise! [*Smollet is a trifle weary*]

Smol. Lady Shelton!

Dor. Dorothy Foxglove—if you please!

Smol. Miss Foxglove—[*Bowing*] I cannot say how delighted and pained I am to meet you again—pained because I come on an unpleasant duty. [*Placing hat on bench*]

Dor. Indeed! Does it concern me? [*Working—not looking*]

Smol. It does! I am ordered to arrest and convey you to your father. [*She stares, but instantly recovers*] Also, to arrest Mr. Foxglove on the charge of abducting one of his Majesty's subjects.

Dor. [*Furtively looking around as if for means of escape—then changing to laughing manner*] But he did not abduct me—I abducted myself!

Smol. Beg pardon! I have my orders.

Dor. What if I refuse to accompany you?

Smol. You will compel me to use—[*Very respectfully*] force!

Dor. [*Must show that she is thoroughly frightened and only trying to find a way out of the dilemma*] What? Carry me off? Wouldn't that be romantic! Well, I must get these biscuits ready for supper before I go, at all events!

Smol. Where is Mr. Foxglove?

Dor. I do not know.

Smol. On your honor?

Dor. On my honor.

Smol. [*Bowing*] Are you alone here?

Dor. No. My friend Rachel Winslow and Mrs. Campbell are in that room. [*Points to R. door*]

Smol. No one else?

Dor. If you doubt me, order your men to search.

Smol. Miss Foxglove, I will subject you to no indignity I can avoid, believe me! [*Bowing*]

Dor. [*Bowing*] Thank you! [*Aside*] If I could but detain him till the men return!

Smol. [*Who has been taking a survey of the premises*] I wish this duty had been assigned to another!

Dor. [*Coquettishly*] Do you—really?

Smol. [*Embarrassed*] Well, that is—I don't exactly—

Dor. Since I must be *carried*—[*Coquettishly*] off by some one, I know of no one I'd prefer to you.

Smol. [*Amazed*] Thank you!

Dor. [*Who has gotten a pan of biscuits ready*] Please put this on the hearth. [*Giving him pan. He obeys without thinking what he is doing*] Thank you. Do you know you used to say a great many pretty things to me?

Smol. Did I?

Dor. Did you mean them?

Smol. Well—I—

Dor. Oh, dear! I forgot to cover the pan. Please put this over those biscuits—[*Giving cloth. He takes it, same manner*]

Smol. [*Very much in love and showing it*] I was going to say—

Dor. [*Simply*] You once told me you loved me.

Smol. [*Confirmatively*] I did.

Dor. Here. This is ready. [*Giving him another pan. He takes it as before*] Did you mean it? [*Hands him another cloth*]

Smol. [*Covering the bread*] From the bottom of my heart!

Dor. [*Finishing work at table—wiping hands clean*] Do you love me still? [*Coming down—Dorothy L.—Smollet R.*]

Smol. Yes!

Dor. Prove it!

Smol. How—by getting down on my knees? [*Laughs*] My men! [*Points to window*] Rather an undignified action under the circumstances—don't you think so?

Dor. I'll close the shutter. [*Does so*]

Smol. Ask something else—I beg!

Dor. [*Getting close to him—finally drawing his arm around her waist and toying with his hand*] Go back to Sir Frederick and say your search was unsuccessful.

Smol. Miss Foxglove, you were never more charming. It breaks my heart to refuse you—but—

Dor. You *do* refuse?

Smol. Positively! [*Decidedly*]

Dor. I think I like you better—I certainly respect you more—for it.

Smol. I'm sure you do.

Dor. Then I presume I must go with you. But I shall need close watching! If I can escape, I will. [*Laughing*]

Smol. Decidedly! All's fair in love and in war, you know!

Dor. [*Laughing*] Do you remember the day I decorated you with apple parings?

Smol. I shall never forget it! [*Laughs*]

Dor. [*Coquettishly*] You used to call me your little Captain.

Smol. And shall be proud to do so still!

Dor. Does it become me? [*Putting on his hat*]

Smol. Everything becomes you! It is a pleasure even to be the object of your sport! [*Music till picture formed by Ann and Rachel*]

Dor. I wonder if you have forgotten our drill. Let me have your sword. [*He gives it*] Now! Attention! [*He stands in position*] Heads up! [*Coming close to him*] Lieutenant Smollet—[*Laughing*] You are my prisoner! [*He laughs. She at once changes her manner and says in low quick decisive tones*] If you attempt to move but as I dictate, I'll send a bullet through your brain. [*Throwing away sword and quickly snatching pistol from his belt, cocking it and pointing it at his head*]

Smol. [*Realizing*] My dear Miss Foxglove—

Dor. Attention! [*He does so. She speaks in hurried whisper*] Order your men to stack arms and enter. And remember, the slightest sign and you are a dead man.

Smol. [*Deeply chagrined—hesitates—then concludes to obey*] Corporal, call in your men! Stack arms and enter. There is a mistake here! [*The two Men on guard L.H. go behind house. All are heard to stack arms. Then they enter, single file—range across back of stage and face audience*]

Dor. Bar the shutter! [*Smollet does so*] Take your place there. [*Places him C., facing audience. He folds his arms. She takes position in front of him, back to audience. Pistol aimed*] And remember, I am a determined and desperate woman! [*To Soldiers who are now on*] Soldiers, as your officer tells you, there *has* been a slight mistake here. He came to take me prisoner. I have turned the tables on him—that's all! [*Soldiers look at each other an instant—then at the Lieutenant—and realizing the situation, start R. and L. as if to recover their guns. At the same instant enter Ann R.D. with soldier's gun and fixed bayonet, and Rachel same way from L. They rush down and form a line in front with Dorothy. Aim at Soldiers. Picture. Cease music*]

ANN. I'm 'listed at last! Three cheers for the first regimint of American women!

DOR. Lieutenant, order your men to remove that trap and go below!

SMOL. [*Without looking*] Corporal! Obey! [*Corporal directs men—they remove trap and go below—the Corporal last. He makes a dart at Ann. She presents the gun*]

ANN. I know a trick worth two of that. Go below! Go below! [*He finally does so*] Now shut up the shop! [*He closes the trap*]

DOR. Lieutenant, give me your word not to attempt to escape or release your men, and you are at liberty!

SMOL. You have it!

DOR. Guard's relieved! [*Rachel puts up gun*] Forgive me, Lieutenant— [*Offering hand cordially*] But all's fair in love and war, you know! [*Music till Reuben and party on*]

SMOL. [*Hesitates—then laughs—takes hand*] You've fairly won, Miss Foxglove, and, upon my word, I'm not half sorry either! [*Dorothy, Rachel and Smollet retire. Ann marches on to trap—goes rapidly through the manual of arms—then marches up to C., puts down gun—marches off R.—returns with guns—places them beside hers, and continues quickly till all the guns on—keep last gun and stand sentry on trap door. This business will be new and very fine if done right. Enter Reuben, Ned, Captain Winslow, Roanoke and two Woodmen—all armed*]

REU. Well, Dorothy, how about them 'ere? [*Sees Lieutenant—aims gun quickly. The others act also, but in different positions*] Ah! A surprise!

DOR. Yes!

REU. Ah! [*Movement*]

DOR. [*Quickly and springing in front of Smollet*] B—but for the Lieutenant, father—not for us!

REU. What in the name of Satan—[*Ned has crossed to Rachel, U.1.R. She is telling him. He laughs*]

DOR. You shall see. Sergeant Campbell!

ANN. Private, if you please! High private's good enough for me!

DOR. Private Campbell—[*Ann presents*] Bring forth the prisoners.

ANN. [*Throwing up trap*]   Rats! Come out'n yer holes! [*Soldiers come up. She points. They range down R.*]

DOR.   You see, father—Lieutenant Smollet was detailed to take you and me prisoner.

REU.   Well! Be we took?

DOR.   No! I relieved him of the disagreeable duty!

REU.   Wa'al b'gosh! [*The Soldiers look at each other and smile. The Woodmen slap each other on the back and shake hands*] How in natur—

DOR.   You shall know all—in good time. [*During this scene Ann has paced up and down in front of Men as sentry*] The question now is the disposal of these men!

REU.   Ned! What'll we do with the critters?

ANN.   Give 'em to me for target practice!

NED. [*To Lieutenant*]   How did you discover our retreat?

SMOL.   Mr. Hampton gave the information to Sir Frederick on condition that he would use it to secure Mr. Foxglove and his daughter only. [*Reuben's party all look at each other*]

NED.   Captain—[*To Winslow*] there's more in this. What do you advise?

CAPT.   Bind them! [*Reuben, Ned, Roanoke and the two Men bind the Soldiers with withes*] Allen, you two take them by the circuitous route to the place from whence we have just come. Use caution. Report at once to Colonel Ward. [*Smollet comes down to him and holds out hands. Captain smiles*] No! No! Lieutenant, you will remain with us and make yourself as comfortable as circumstances will permit!

SMOL.   Thank you! [*Bows. Over, joins Ladies*]

CAPT. [*To the Men*]   Forward! [*Allen stands at door and points off. The Soldiers exit and off followed by Allen and Herrick as they are going*]

ANN.   Let me go with 'em, Captain. They may need another man!

REU. [*Coming down to her*]   Say, don't yer forgit this regimint's got to eat! An' you're cook!

ANN.   Cook! That settles it! No use'n a feller tryin' to win martial glory here! I see that! [*Puts gun against wall and exits R. door very dejectedly*]

REU.   Captain! Ned! There's danger ahead! [*Music till end of act*] Dyke Hampton's tracked us out.

CAPT.   Well, what then?

REU.   Don't you see? First git rid o' me'n Dorothy—then secure Rachel, murder Ned an' kill you if necessary—or I'm a double-headed Dutchman!

NED. [*With decision*]   Reuben is right. We must not remain here! [*It has gradually grown dark outside and in. Ann re-enters as if to set table*]

ROAN. [*Who has been listening*]   Silence. Stir not till Roanoke returns.

[*All stand in exactly the positions they were in, as if straining to catch the slightest sound. Roanoke exits noiselessly, but swiftly. Listens with ear to ground and suddenly but silently darts into the woods and disappears. He is gone about ten seconds when he as silently and swiftly re-enters—bounds into the cabin and bars the door. Reuben quickly bars the other*] The White Panther and his Renegades!

REU. Dyke an' his Injuns—by thunder!

NED. Quick, let us escape before we are surrounded!

ROAN. And fall into the ambush of the cunning Panther! Hark! [*Indian heads are now seen darting from all parts of the scene. They are hideously painted*]

REU. Ned! [*Aside to him, but so as to impress the audience*] How's the tide?

NED. [*Same manner*] Full.

REU. Then we're in for it. There'll be fightin' enough now, I reckon! [*At the word fighting, Ann, who has been listening, springs and gets her gun*] How many ar'em, Roanoke?

ROAN. The Renegade is a coward! He will not attack an equal foe. The ear of Roanoke deceives him not. He outnumbers us ten fold!

REU. Let's draw the Panther's claws a bit!

ALL. How?

REU. I'll show ye an' all Indian fighter's trick! [*Takes off coat—stuffs blanket in it to make dummy—breaks broom handles for arms. All in cabin busy themselves in this so as not to notice action outside of cabin. Reuben gets long poker from chimney place. During this enter cautiously from behind house Dyke and Morton Handy, a renegade white man in Indian dress. It is quite dark now*]

DYKE. You got the barrel of rum I sent?

HANDY. Yes, or I wouldn't 'a been here.

DYKE. The soldiers have doubtless gone with Foxglove and his daughter. That leaves but the Captain, the old woman Campbell, the girl and—[*Between his teeth as if he could not bring himself to speak the word*] her lover. Batter down the door. Fire upon the men. Do as you will the women. But the girl—harm not a hair of her head. Place her alive—alive, within my arms —[*Passionately*] and then ask of me what you will!

HANDY. Trust me! I'll do my best!

DYKE. Good! Remember—Rachel alive to me! [*They retire*]

REU. [*All being ready*] Here, Dorothy. You work this Fandango—go— Rachel, you open the shutters. Boys, yer muzzles to your loops and wait for the word! Now!

Smol. Mr. Foxglove, I am an Englishman and your prisoner. But I am also a soldier. Will you permit me to assist in protecting these ladies? [*Spoken quietly and with dignity*]

Reu. Lieutenant, you're—a—man! Give him a gun!

Smol. I have one, thank you. [*Quietly, as if it were an every day occurrence. Dorothy looks gratitude. Smollet knows it, but seems not to*]

Reu. Silence all! Ready! [*Rachel opens half the shutter. Dorothy works dummy out of window. At same instant a volley from all sides followed by the Indians who rush out to scalp body*] Fire! [*Ann, Captain, Reuben, Ned, Roanoke, fire. Three Indians on L. fall dead. The others disappear. Dorothy hastily withdraws dummy. Rachel blockades window*] Well done, my beauties! Load quick, lads! Dorothy, tend to Trusty while I reconnoiter. That kinder staggered 'em, I reckon! [*They all load. Dorothy loads Reuben's rifle. Ann and Smollet take Soldiers' guns. Reuben at loop*] They're goin' to batter down the door. All on this side! [*Men do so and get ready*] Study-y-[*Twelve Indians appear bearing large pine trunk as a ram—it is very heavy. Two others creep around from behind house placing brush, etc. When the ram is near enough, the men swing it backwards and forwards several times to give it an impetus*] Fire! [*Six Indians fall. The balance drop the ram and disappear. Four are killed of the six who fall, the other two regain their feet and stagger off badly wounded*] Good boys—load! Here, Dorothy—[*Gives her gun. Places eye to loop*] Give me a gun! Quick! [*She gives him Soldier's gun. At that instant an Indian darts out from L. with pine knot lighted. Reuben fires. The Indian falls*] Another gun! Quick! [*Before they can get it to him, another Indian rushes on, snatches torch from dead one and fires the house. A tremendous yell and the Indians swarm around the fire*] They have fired the fort! We're lost! [*All stand aghast*]

Smol. Throw open the doors—[*Very coolly*] and let us fight our way through them!

Capt. That were certain death to us—and to these poor *girls* a fate *more* terrible!

Reu. [*In hoarse whisper*] There's one chance for us—an' but one! Ned! Quick! [*Ned disappears down trap. All seem to exclaim "Thank God"*] There's an underground passage that fills an' empties with the tide! If the tide's out—we're safe. If not—[*Ned appears*] How is it, Ned?

Ned. On the turn! There's a chance! [*All faces light up*]

Reu. Quick, then! [*Ladies are passed down first. Captain, Roanoke, Smollet and Ned follow. Reuben keeps guard till the last. As he is going*] If that fails—the gunpowder! [*Descends and closes trap. Meantime the Indians have gathered around the house with guns ready to shoot when the people*] *shall be forced to appear. The house falls in with a crash. The Indians fire a volley and yell. Dyke Hampton and Handy appear. Picture*]

DYKE. Damnation! They have escaped! [*Terrific explosion. The scene is blown to pieces and amid the din, smoke and yells, and groans of the dying and wounded Indians, the Curtain descends*]

ACT IV.

TIME: *June 1775.*

SCENE 1: *On Mystic River. Picturesque landscape at daybreak. Distant hilly country very fair and beautiful on R. Water of creek supposed to flow in from river—sort of cove L. The sun rises during action of scene and must be very fine or not done at all. Two boats moored on beach. Camp fire and kettle R.1.E. at which are seated Reuben and Ned. They are in tatters. Reuben no coat or hat. Ned part of coat and hat. The idea to be conveyed is that the explosion had almost stripped them. Ann Campbell with man's coat and hat on, gun between knees, asleep against large rock R.C. Dorothy and Rachel asleep on blanket spread on stage L.C. Rachel covered with an old skin—wolf; Dorothy, by what is left of Smollet's coat. Smollet in shirt sleeves, shirt torn, no hat, hair and beard awry—one boot, this very much the worse for wear, is seated L., tying up other foot in colored silk handkerchief. Roanoke on ground C. Allen with Reuben. Allen no coat or hat. Ann has them. Captain asleep L.1.E. Music at rise. Dies out as scene well open.*

REU. [*As if continuing conversation*] Wa'al, ye see the dumed thing went off sooner'n I kalkelated!

NED. Why didn't you tell us you were going to fire the powder?

REU. There wa'ant no time to talk. Allus stretch yer legs accordin' to the length o' yer coverlet. Dyke wanted a bonefire 'n I thought I'd give him one. I laid the train from my powder horn as I went along an' soon's I see the Captain 'n Roanoke 'n the wimmen in the boat I let'r rip!

NED. You took a desperate chance, Reuben!

REU. Got to when the odd's agin ye. Ye can't ketch no trout a'thout wettin' yer feet. I wa'ant a goin' to hev them cut-throats foller us if I could help it!

SMOL. They will never again follow anyone in the world.

REU. There's no danger o' our meetin' 'em in the next. I giv 'em a ticket clean through to the other side, I reckon. Come—[*Rising*] all rise. Let's see how breakfast's progressin', Lieutenant. After breakfast you are at liberty to depart. Tom Allen'll show ye the nearest way to your command.

To-night yer men'll be sent to join ye. An' if ever ye get into trouble an' we kin help ye out, call on us an' ye'll find us there. [*Offers hand*]

SMOL. Thank ye, Mr. Foxglove. [*Taking hand*] I shall regret to leave you all, however.

ANN. [*Asleep*] That's it! Giv it to 'em! Second section—forward!

REU. [*Smiling*] The Brigadier's at it agin! [*All listen*]

ANN. Ready! Present!

REU. [*In her ear*] Fire!

ANN. [*Jumping up and pointing gun first at one and then the other*] Come on, durn ye! I ken lick a regimint on ye! [*All laugh. She realizes the situation. Joins in laughter*] What'n thunder'd ye want to wake a feller up for? I'd a captured the hull British army'n another minit!

REU. We kind o' hed pity on 'em, ye see! [*Reuben, Ned, Roanoke and Allen, carrying their guns with them, start off L.1.E.*] Come along, boys. [*Exeunt*]

ANN. [*To Smollet*] Where be they a-goin'?

SMOL. To look after breakfast.

ANN. Oh! I was afeared they was a skirmish afoot an' they wanted to leave me behind! I'll be glad when we git inter the reglar army. I'm sick a'cookin'! [*Going off carrying gun. Looking back and talking to Smollet, stumbles across the Captain*] Mercy on us! [*Sees who it is*] Beg pardon, Captain! [*Exit L.1.E.*]

CAPT. Don't mention it. [*Gets up quite stiffly. Stretches and yawns*] Hello, Smollet, that you?

SMOL. Minus a boot and other articles!

CAPT. [*Seeing girls asleep*] Girls not up yet, eh?

SMOL. Heard them snoring as I passed their room just now.

DOR. [*From the blanket*] *Never* snored in my life! [*Sits up laughing*]

SMOL. Beg pardon. Meant figuratively, of course! [*Laughs*]

DOR. Rachel—let's get up!

SMOL. [*Naïvely*] Shall I retire?

DOR. If you're sleepy.

SMOL. I mean—to permit you ladies to rise.

DOR. [*Laughing*] We can rise without your permission. Here, give me your hand! [*He does so. She jumps up*]

SMOL. Shall I assist you, Miss Winslow?

RACH. No—thank you. [*Jumps up laughing. Sees Captain. Goes to him*] Good-morning, father.

CAPT. Good-morning, my daughter.

DOR. Excuse me. Good-morning, Captain.

CAPT. Good-morning, Dorothy, child. [*Rachel and Captain L. Dorothy at blanket. Smollet R. of her. Rachel and Captain talk together and finally saunter off L.1.E.*]

DOR. Lieutenant, come and help me make this bed!

SMOL. With pleasure. [*They fold up blankets*]

DOR. Allow me. [*Offers to help him on with his coat*] That's the first red coat I ever wore.

SMOL. Did you find it comfortable?

DOR. Extremely so!

SMOL. Continue to wear it.

DOR. [*Archly*] The colors might run.

SMOL. Warranted fast.

DOR. [*Archly*] *How* fast?

SMOL. [*Same way*] *Stead*-fast! [*Turning and offering his arm*]

DOR. [*Singing and putting the coat on him*]
    Steadfast and true
    I'll prove to you
    If you'll follow me, over the sea! [*Laughs*]

SMOL. I return to my regiment today.

DOR. Do you? [*Half seriously*]

SMOL. [*Sadly*] Yes. What shall I say to Sir Frederick?

DOR. [*Archly*] Tell the truth! [*He looks at her. Their eyes meet. Both laugh*]

SMOL. I mean—concerning you!

DOR. [*Laughing*] Say that I am all right!

SMOL. You are relinquishing a grand position.

DOR. I am retaining my liberty—and the wealth of honest hearts that love me!

SMOL. Your title is—

DOR. One of which I am very proud—an American Girl! [*Smiling and bowing*]

SMOL. [*Resignedly and offering hand*] Perhaps we may meet again.

DOR. I hope so. [*Seriously*] Believe me! [*Takes his hand*]

SMOL. We're friends. [*Smiling*]

DOR. [*Looking him fairly in the face, as if to undeceive him as to any hope beyond*] Yes—friends. True, honest friends! [*They look at each other a moment, then drop hands*]

SMOL. [*Quickly*] I wish I could find my other boot. [*Limps. Enter from L.1.E. Reuben*]

REU. Now then, Lieutenant. Hello! Dorothy, up and dressed!

Dor. Not much dressing to do, father. [*Looks at him comically*] Whatever will you do now, child! You've no buttons to lose!

Reu. Borry some o' the Brigadier's! Come along to breakfast. Lieutenant, escort her to the dinin' hall. [*Exit Reuben, L.1.E. Music very lively till Smollet and Dorothy off, then change to bring Dyke and Handy on and off, then change to bring Roanoke on. Keep up through his scene and change again and keep up till end of Act*]

Smol. [*Limps over to her—places hand on heart, bows very low and offers arm. She accepts with great ceremony. He limps off, steps on pebble, business and exit. Music changes. Enter Dyke Hampton, Morton Handy and Two Indians from U.E.L. Dyke is bruised and wounded almost beyond recognition. They have no guns*]

Dyke. You must be mistaken.

Handy. No! How did ye say he came here? [*Laughs outside L. by Reuben and Party. Not too loud*]

Dyke. With a band of Mohawks. About ten years ago. When they left he went with them, but one day suddenly returned. He seemed fascinated with the place, as a strange dog will sometimes be—disappearing one day—returning the next. They all took kindly to him, and so he's lived among them ever since.

Handy. Then, I'm not mistaken. I've not seen him for eighteen years, but I'll swear to his face.

Dyke. So—you lied to me!

Reu. [*Outside*] Three cheers for the Brigadier! [*All laugh*]

Handy. [*Avoiding the question*] I told you I'd put him out o'way, and I believed I'd done it. I give him to a Mohawk chief who for a portion of the money you give me promised I'd never hear of him agin—but it's him. The fates seem agin ye, Dyke! Best give this thing up.

Dyke. Never!

Smol. [*Outside*] No! No! No!

Dor. [*Outside*] Yes! Yes! Yes! [*All laugh*]

Handy. It's cost a good many lives already.

Dyke. What's a few Indians? I live and while I live I'll not give her up. I love her. [*Handy laughs*] Yes, love her. And I hate that man. I'll kill him and have her, if all Hell stood between us! Once in my possession I'm her Master! [*Dorothy sings a line and ends with a merry laugh. Handy's eyes light up with passion*]

Handy. Dyke! I've got a cage that'd just fit that singin' bird. I want her!

Dyke. [*Appalled*] That's dangerous. She's an English Colonel's daughter.

Dor. [*Outside*] No! I'm not!

HANDY. [*Lecherously*] I must have her! [*They look at each other*]

DYKE. Take her. Now to our places. This time we'll *not* fail! [*Exeunt from whence they came, Dyke last. Music changes. Enter Roanoke, gloomy and despondent. Seats himself on rock R.C.*]

SMOL. [*Outside*] What I mean to say is—

DOR. [*Outside. Laughing*] You've said quite enough! I'll not hear another word. [*Runs on laughing*] I'll—[*Sees Roanoke. Runs to him*] Why, Roanoke—are you ill?

ROAN. No. Roanoke is not ill. He is sad. [*She coils herself down at his feet and leaning on his knees, looks up into his face*] Very sad! He must say farewell.

DOR. [*Alarmed*] And why?

ROAN. The English officer loves the Primrose.

DOR. [*Looking at him half laughing, half frightened, trying to draw away*] Why, Roanoke, you're jealous!

ROAN. [*Seizing her fiercely and restraining her*] As the Tiger of his mate! Roanoke loves—but his skin is dark! His race wild, untutored, savage! His birth unknown. His very tribe a question!

DOR. But safe and gentle of nature—strong of arm and brave of heart. He is a Man! All are not such who wear a fairer skin.

ROAN. The English officer is brave.

DOR. As a lion!

ROAN. And noble!

DOR. As a Prince!

ROAN. Does the Primrose love him?

DOR. I—[*Casting down eyes*] I—you—

ROAN. Does the Primrose love him? [*Fiercely*]

DOR. You frighten me! [*Springs up. Gets away from him*]

ROAN. [*Going up stage to R.*] Forgive. Roanoke will not harm. He will wander away into the depths of the silent forest from whence he never should have emerged. He will seek the tribe from which he never should have strayed—and never shall the shadow of his life fall athwart the sunlight of your path again.

DOR. [*Going to him and almost unconsciously drawing him back to his seat and resuming her position*] All sunshine and no shadow would wither and kill the sturdiest flower. How then could the fragile Primrose hope to survive its fierce rays?

ROAN. Other forms will shelter, other arms protect, other eyes bedew it!

DOR. Roanoke will not leave us—[*He looks at her*]

ROAN. He must!

Dor. His country?

Roan. He has no country.

Dor. His friends?

Roan. He has no friends.

Dor. [*Half laughing—half crying*] What! No Reuben, who has loved him as a son?

Roan. [*Impatiently rising as if not to acknowledge it*] No!

Dor. For—[*With wild cry*] my sake—[*Frightened the moment she has spoken. Change music*]

Roan. [*Catches her in his arms like a whirlwind. She tries to resist. All useless*] You love Roanoke—[*At that instant enter Herrick U.E.R. Carries gun. Speaks like lightning as he enters. Distant cannonading which continues all through scene*]

Her. Reuben! Farnsworth! Quick! Quick! [*All enter from L.1.E.*] Prescott and Putnam are fortified on Bunker's Hill and Howe with all his force is marching to dislodge them! [*Ann rushes off L.1.E.*]

Reu. Dorothy, a kiss—[*She rushes to him, is clasped a second in his arms. Captain and Ned have kissed Rachel*] Come, Ned! [*Going R.U.E.*] Concord and Bunker's Hill!—

Ned. [*Following*] Will leave a record to the world! [*Exeunt Captain and Herrick, follow quickly*]

Roan. [*Quick as lightning to Dorothy*] Roanoke protects you!

Dor. Protect our country first. If you live, return to me. [*Roanoke stares—bethinks him of his gun. Starts L.1.E. to get it. Meets Ann, who has rushed on with hat, coat and gun. Seizes her gun—quick struggle. He throws her off. She almost falls as he exits R.U.E. with gun. Distant rumbling of cannon all the time. The scene must be played with lightning's rapidity. Rachel and Dorothy have gone up R. to look after men*]

Ann. Well, durn your copper colored carcass! [*Enter at same time Dyke, Handy and Two Indians—no guns. Dyke has large knife in belt. Dyke seizes Rachel from behind and pinions her in his arms. Handy seizes Dorothy same way. An Indian seizes Ann same way and bears her to left corner. Other Indian strikes Smollet on head with tomahawk and fells him, then rushes to assist Indian with Ann. As he nears her she kicks him in the stomach. He turns a complete somersault—recovers quickly. Women scream*]

Dor. Help! Father! Roanoke!

Rich. Help! Help!

Dor. Roanoke!

Roan. Here. [*Bounds on like a panther. Snaps gun at Handy. It misses fire. Throws away gun and springs for Handy's throat. Handy lets go*

Dorothy. Indian drops Ann and seizes Dorothy. Handy and Roanoke meet C. A terrific struggle for the supremacy—a la Lorna Doone. During it Smollet recovers and is seen to steal off. Handy has Roanoke by the throat and is strangling him]

DOR. Roanoke! [*Seeing him nearly overpowered*] I love you! [*At the sound of her voice Roanoke gathers superhuman strength and is in the act of overpowering Handy, whom he now has by the throat, when Rachel, scarce knowing what she does, breaks from Dyke, seizes knife from his belt, rushes down to stab Handy. He adroitly turns Roanoke so that she stabs him. With a cry he relinquishes his hold on Handy and falls. Dorothy breaks from Indian, runs to Roanoke and takes his head on breast, passionately kissing and calling on him to speak. Rachel stands transfixed with horror*]

HANDY. [*Quickly recovering himself*] Rachel Winslow! You have killed your brother. [*Rachel shrieks, stands like one mad, then faints. Indian catches her*]

DYKE. [*Springing down, catches Handy by the throat, as if to choke the words back*] You lie! You lie!

PICTURE AND CURTAIN

[*Change music to Yankee Doodle. Boom the cannon. Discharge musketry, etc., etc., and ring up when all is ready on*]

SECOND PICTURE

YANKEE DOODLE

[*See Plate. When all ready they march to R. Change music and change to*]

THIRD PICTURE

BATTLE OF BUNKER'S HILL

[*See Plate. Part action, part tableau. Reuben, Ned, Captain on promenade. All the cannons, guns and drums and*]

RING ACT DROPS

ACT V.

TIME: *1776.*

SCENE: *Dorchester Heights. Same scene as Act I—except to have house further off stage to give more room for tableau at end. Discovered: Captain Winslow smoking and seated on rustic seat L. Rachel in low rocker sewing. Music at rise.*

CAPT. Yes—my dear daughter—this is indeed a glorious day for us and for our cause. The British at last compelled to evacuate our city and leave our people once more to the enjoyment of life, liberty and happiness!

RACH. And you, dear father, restored to the wealth of which you had been so willfully deprived—blest by the discovery of a son, long mourned as dead—

CAPT. Possessing the love of a daughter whose courage and devotion have never faltered! It needs but the success of my country's arms to make a peaceful ending to an eventful, active life!

RACH. You have positively reconsidered your determination of entering the Army?

CAPT. Yes. I am old—and a cripple. You will be alone. I don't know how a piece of an old soldier like myself can better serve his country than by protecting one of her fairest and bravest daughters!

RACH. Oh, father!

CAPT. No word from Ned yet, eh?

RACH. No, father. He said he would not return till he brought undoubted proofs of dear Harry's identity—and Hampton's villainy.

CAPT. Oh! I've no doubt of Roanoke's identity at all. There was always a something that seemed to draw me towards him! Handy's story—the scar over the right eye caused by the fall he received when a baby—the unmistakable likeness to his dead mother—are all proofs positive that he is my son. Still, I presume that for the Law's sake, it is right to establish the fact beyond question.

RACH. What a strange fatality was that—that impelled me to rush to his aid—and so nearly made me the instrument of his death! [*Peculiar strain for Roanoke's entrance—kept up till his exit*]

CAPT. Fatality, indeed! 'Twas that blow—struck as he believed fatally— that caused Handy to cry out in his savage joy, "You have killed your brother!"

RACH. The Hand of Heaven, father! Let us acknowledge its wisdom and power. [*Enter U.E.L. Roanoke in full Continental uniform—"Private"— followed by Reuben dressed as Continental Sergeant*]

REU. Well, Captain—here we be! How d'ye think the boy looks in his regimintals?

CAPT. Look! [*Enthusiastically*] Like the hero he is sure to prove himself—like the soldier it gladdens the old man's eyes to look upon! God bless you, my boy! [*Embraces Roanoke, crosses to Reuben wiping eyes*] God bless you, my boy!

RACH. [*Embracing Roanoke*] My dear—dear *brother!*

ROAN. Sister! Father! [*Taking hand of each. Then looking up reverently*] *Mother!* Strange—sweet words to the Indian's tongue! Had Roanoke known them sooner—he might 'perhaps have prized them more! But now there is another and a dearer—*Wife*—the great spirit has no gift to equal that!

REU. Look here—if Dorothy loves you—

ROAN. Roanoke knows she loves him! [*Crosses to Reuben*]

REU. Then, all's I got to say is—it'll be purty durned hard work to keep ye apart. She's little, but by Mighty—she's slicker'n a fox. I allus found out —that ef she would—she would—an' ef she wouldn't all Natin couldn't make her!

ROAN. Her father—

REU. See here—don't yeou go to stealin' a feller's privileges! I'm her father a good deal more'n he is!

ROAN. Keeps her prisoner!

REU. There ain't no more prisoners in Boston—that is evacuation day— an' ef she don't give 'em a slip I miss my guess!

CAPT. Come, my son. Calm yourself. All will yet be well! Come into the house.

ROAN. Roanoke cannot dwell within walls like a caged animal! He must be free to come and go at will! He will wander toward the great city. He may meet her. Should he do so and they deny her to him—let them beware the Indian's fury! [*Strides out majestically, raising himself to his full height, 1.E.R.*]

RACH. [*Clinging to the Captain*] How fierce he looked, father! He terrifies me. Can this be my brother? [*Music dies out gradually*]

CAPT. I almost doubt—myself—I never saw him so before. Perhaps his wound—[*Offers arm to Rachel*]

REU. That's it—his wound—not the one Rachel give him though. Dorothy's wounded him her—[*Points to heart*] an' he's cut deep too—he is!

CAPT. I fear he will never learn—never be able to accustom himself to our ways. [*Going L.2.E. with Rachel*]

REU. Give him a chance—ye can't expect to make a white man out'n an Injun in a day! Time'll fetch him around all right.

CAPT. I hope so!

REU. I know so! I know Injuns—I do! [*Captain and Rachel exit. Ann enters from house. Stops on steps at seeing Reuben and holds up both hands in delight*]

ANN. Well, Reuben Foxglove! An'—*in*—yer *new rig-i-mintles,* as I'm a sinner! [*Comes down*] Turn around an' lets hev a look at ye. [*Turns him around*] Well, ef you hain't stunnin'! I'd give the hull balance o' my life to wear that suit jist five minutes by the watch!

Reu. [*Slyly*] Come into the Dairy 'n I let ye try 'em on!

Ann. [*Paying no attention to that*] Them's the kind o' clothes for a feller to fight in! No petticoats a'flappin' round a man's legs to trip him up! *So—that's* the new uniform, eh? [*Her eyes fairly dancing with admiration*]

Reu. Yes! We've took the swaddlin' clothes off'n the child Independence and dressed him in Continentals—no more creepin' for him. He's got to walk alone now! An' afore King George knows it he'll walk clean through the British Armies—ownin' *and controlin'* every foot of this—*the Land that give him birth!*

Ann. Ef a feller wa'ant a woman what fun he could hev'n them clothes!

Reu. Ye got a leetle the wust b' the last skirmish didn't ye, Brigadier?

Ann. 'Twa'ant no fair fight—no how!

Reu. What was it the Injun said to ye?

Ann. Wanted me to go to his wigwam an' be his squaw!

Reu. Did ye go?

Ann. I hain't yit! I'm a'waitin' till he comes round agin!

Reu. An' so Lieutenant Smollet got ye all out'n the scrape—eh?

Ann. Yes—he managed to crawl off unobserved—an' jest as Hampton thought he had us all in a hornet's nest—he surrounded us with a party of his own soldiers an' took us all prisoners!

Reu. All on ye?

Ann. All but Dyke! He jumped into the river'n by swimmin' under water escaped. Smullet marched us all afore Sir Frederick who give orders to have Roanoke's wounds seen to—an' all on us released except Dorothy. The Injuns an' Handy he turned over to a guard! I tell ye, Reuben, that Smullet's a good 'un! If ever I do go to a wigwam to be a squaw, it'll be with a man like Smullet! [*Dorothy's music*]

Reu. Say, Brigadier! I've been a'thinkin'—that ef you'n me—that is, ef we was to form ourselves into a platoon—[*She looks at him in perfect amazement*] ef we was to—[*Tittering laugh heard from bushes R.*]

Ann. [*Hearing it*] What's that?

Reu. Woodchuck, I reckon. Here, take my arm ef ye're skeered! [*She does so*] I was a'thinkin'—[*Laugh heard again*]

Ann. [*Stopping*] Reuben, that wa'ant no woodchuck!

Reu. 'Twas a squirrel a'chatterin', then—[*Listens*] I was a'thinkin'—[*Laugh heard again*]

Ann. There it is agin! [*In loud whisper*] Reuben Foxglove, there's somebody a' listenin' to ye!

REU. [*In loud whisper*] There hain't!

ANN. [*Same manner*] There is too! I'm so shamed—I'm blushin' all up an' down my back. Hark! [*Music swells*]

DOR. [*Unable longer to restrain—bursts into a loud peal of laughter and appears from behind shrubbery, followed by Smollet. Ann gathers her clothes up around her and makes a comic exit. Reuben stands shame-faced. Dorothy rushes to him and clasps him around the neck and kisses him. Smollet enjoys the scene*] Oh! You dear darling old dad—and so you've been and gone and done it! How delightful! Would you believe it, Lieutenant—that boy—that child—actually in love and never let his mother know a word about it! [*Laughs*] But I'll pay you up for it, sir! [*Shaking finger at him*] But I'll take you away from her. [*Laughs*] She shan't have you—there! She's a designing minx—that's what she is! She has taken advantage of my absence to lead you away! I always told you to beware of the female sex! Here—hold up your head—[*Laughs*] Now, tell me the truth. What was she saying to you? [*Music dies away*]

REU. She wanted me to go to her wigwam an' be her squaw! [*Dorothy and Smollet laugh*] Dorothy—don't say anything about it, will ye? [*She laughs*] Ye needn't laugh. You know how it is yerself!

DOR. Well, I shan't. [*Patting his cheeks*] It shall fall in love if it wants to —and its mother won't plague it—a dear—darling—old popsey-wopsey! [*Laughs*]

REU. [*Looking kind of sheepish*] It was kind o' mean to sneak in on a feller. [*Laughs*] Lieutenant, I thought you—

SMOL. Don't blame me, Mr. Foxglove. I only obeyed orders!

DOR. [*Turning Reuben around*] Let us look at you! What a lot of buttons! What fun you will have losing them! [*Seriously and nestling up to him*] You won't let anyone but Dorothy sew them on, will you father?

REU. My darling—there's nothin' on this earth'll ever take your place in old Reuben's heart—be sure o' that. [*Lifting her face between his hands and kissing it*]

DOR. [*Nestling*] I like that! [*Then quickly changing*] Where's Rachel? I'm dying to see her. Lieutenant, please find her for me.

SMOL. Certainly. [*Crosses to house and exits. Roanoke's music*]

DOR. Father—[*Smiling and hesitating*] I want to tell you something. [*Clasps her hands and hesitates*] It's a great secret—but, oh, such a sweet— happy secret! I'm—[*Roanoke enters R.2.E.*]

ROAN. Primrose!

DOR. [*With a scream of joy rushes to his arms*] Roanoke!

REU. [*Smiles to himself*] Ya-a-s—a great secret! [*Exits into house*]

ROAN. Roanoke feared he had lost his sweet Primrose forever—

DOR. She told him she would come. Did he doubt her?

ROAN. He doubted those who took her from him—but he holds her in his arms once more. [*Fiercely*] They shall never tear her from them again. [*Music dies out*]

DOR. Tut! Tut! Tut! You must not look so fierce—[*Laughs*] Remember you are not an Indian any more—and your name is not Roanoke—it is Harry! [*Laughs*]

ROAN. [*With disgust*] Laugh! The name of a baby! Roanoke is a mighty name.

DOR. [*Repeating as if to taste the words*] Roanoke is a mighty name. [*Half to herself*] I love it. Let me look at you. How handsome you do look in your fine uniform—and yet I do not know but that you were grander in your old savage dress!

ROAN. [*Starting to go*] Roanoke will put it on again!

DOR. No! No! No! [*Laughs*]

ROAN. Roanoke, too, loves it best. It was for her he put on this. [*Dorothy's music*]

DOR. And for her must he wear it to the end! It is this uniform—covering hearts like his—brave, honest hearts—that is destined to give the world its mightiest Nation. Bring—[*Laying hand on coat. Then sadly*] or send this back to me—stained—worn—bloody—if need be—and I will worship it and you—my Indian—soldier—hero—husband in life or death!

ROAN. Roanoke hears! [*Proudly*] His heart beats! His veins swell! His breath comes thick and fast! He pants to show the Primrose what brave deeds he'll dare for her sake!

DOR. And now Harry—[*Laughs. He gives her a look. She corrects*] Roanoke—sit down. [*Seats him on old plow—comes around and seats herself between his knees. Throws head back and arms around his neck*] I am going to introduce you to a person you have hitherto ignored but whose close acquaintance and friendship it will be very necessary for you to court in the future—I am going to—[*Laughs*] introduce you to the first pronoun—I— [*He looks as if he could not comprehend*]—say—I—love—you!

ROAN. The Primrose loves Roanoke!

DOR. No! No! No! [*Laughs*] You—love—me!

ROAN. Roanoke loves the Primrose!

DOR. [*Laughs*] How stupid! Here! Repeat—just what I say. Understand? [*He tries to comprehend*] Say—I understand!

ROAN. [*Face lighting up*] I understand! [*Pleased*]

DOR. That's right. [*Delighted*] Now say after me—I—

ROAN. I—[*Pleased with himself*]

DOR. Love—

ROAN. Love—

DOR. You—

ROAN. You—

DOR. Capital! And I will—

ROAN. Capital! And I will—

DOR. [*Laughs and continues*] Obey you in all things!

ROAN. Obey you in all things!

DOR. Good!

ROAN. Good!

DOR. Hush! [*Puts hand over his mouth*] Now listen and do not speak. [*Changes her whole manner*] My father will be here today.

ROAN. [*Fiercely—jumping up as if comprehending the meaning of the visit*] No! No! He shall not—

DOR. [*Soothing him*] Hush! [*Smiling in his face*] You promised to obey. [*Changes manner again*] He is my father—and during these past few months that I have lived with him, he has been so kind—so good—so gentle—he suffers so terribly for the wrong he did my mother—he loves me so dearly and he is so sad and lonely—that I have grown to pity—to love him.

ROAN. I understand! [*He must change here to broken-hearted submission, all his Indian fire gone*]

DOR. And so—at last I have come to think—that perhaps it is my duty not to leave him to himself. That my mother would be happier in Heaven, were I to help him atone for his sin. That she would look down and even smile—to see us together—father and daughter!

ROAN. [*As before*] I understand.

DOR. We are all called upon at some time to make sacrifices in this world —and I believe we are purer—nobler—holier—for having made them bravely—heroically!

ROAN. I understand. [*As before*] Your father will take you from me.

DOR. If it is his will that I accompany him—

ROAN. You will obey? [*Same tone*]

DOR. He is my father!

ROAN. You will obey? [*Same tone*]

DOR. [*Slowly and sadly—but firmly*] I—will—obey.

ROAN. [*Looks at her a moment—then raises his hands to heaven—and in a sudden heart-broken burst—cries—*] My God! My God! My God! [*Bursts into tears and his head falls on his breast*]

DOR. [*Awe stricken, almost afraid to break in on his grief*] Roanoke!

ROAN. [*Without looking up*] Roanoke no more! [*Hoarse whisper*] That name is lost to him forever!

DOR. [*Winding arm around him*] Roanoke!

ROAN. [*Without looking*] Silence—pity—silence!

DOR. Are you then the only sufferer—have I no heart to surge, to break, to part? Do I not love you? And must I not give you up? [*Bursts into tears on his breast. He takes her in his arms*]

ROAN. Does your father know you love me?

DOR. He does!

ROAN. I understand. The Indian's love would stain.

DOR. Not Indian—you are—

ROAN. Indian by nature if not by birth. He would wed you to one of his own proud people!

DOR. [*With decision*] That—shall he *never* do!

ROAN. [*Quickly, taking both her hands, holding her at arm's length, looking steadily into her eyes*] Promise that!

DOR. [*Firmly*] I swear it!

ROAN. Let me then seek him. I'll not rave. [*Fiercely*] I'll not kill him. I'll beseech—[*Soft*] I'll plead—I'll fall upon my knees and implore him not to part us!

DOR. And if he will not listen?

ROAN. I, too, will obey!

DOR. My brave—lionhearted Roanoke! [*He gazes into her face a moment, then pulls her to his breast and gives her a long passionate kiss. Music changes to lively air. At the same moment enter Smollet from house. She hears his step and turns all smiles*] Lieutenant, I was just telling Roanoke how cleverly you succeeded in bringing me before my father after all! Ha! Ha! Ha! [*Laughs heartily*]

SMOL. [*Laughs*] Ah, it was quite an accident. Hampton really had more to do with bringing it about than I after all. I was going to remark that I've searched the whole house and the only female I could find was Mrs. Campbell and she seemed endeavoring to escape to the roof by way of the kitchen chimney! [*Laughs heartily in which Dorothy joins. Music swells. Enter R.1.E. Sir Frederick, Rachel and Captain L.3.E. Dorothy runs to Sir Frederick. Roanoke retires R. Captain comes C. meeting Sir Frederick. Dorothy after embracing Sir Frederick goes to Rachel. They kiss, etc. Smollet salutes, as Sir Frederick enters and, after they take positions, Sir Frederick eyes Roanoke sternly. Roanoke endeavors to read his fate in Sir Frederick's face and fails*]

CAPT. Sir Frederick welcome once more. Allow me to present my long lost son! [*Roanoke advances and bows respectfully; Sir Frederick with much ceremony and dignity. Dorothy watches eagerly and is telling Rachel*]

SIR F. [*To both*] I congratulate you both. [*Then to the Captain—Roanoke turns away disappointed*] My regiment will be the last to leave the city. I obtained through the kind courtesy of your commanding general—permission to pay my respects to you before departing. [*Music changes*]

NED. [*Outside R.2.E.*] No violence, boys! Bring him before the Captain— that's all! [*Enter Ned as Continental Captain—followed by Two Continental Soldiers forcing on Dyke who has on a British soldier's coat and belt, etc.*] Captain, here's a gentleman to see you! [*Ned has bundle of papers*]

CAPT. Dyke Hampton! Look at me! [*Dyke does not*] Ah! You dare not! Your cowardice does you credit. You *should* be ashamed to look upon the man you have so deeply wronged! [*To Ned*] Where did you find him?

NED. We were searching his house and unearthed him trying to burn these papers. He had traded coats with a soldier and was endeavoring to escape that way. But my men were too quick for him. Here are the complete proofs of his villainy—your brother's will—the identity of your son—in the dying confession of the savage to whom he was sold—and the statement of his father acknowledging the misappropriation of your property during your absence! [*Gives papers*]

CAPT. [*To Dyke*] What have you to say? [*Looking over papers*]

DYKE. Only this—I love your daughter. To force her to my arms I did it all. No punishment you can inflict will equal the torture of losing her. Do with me as you will. I'll speak no more.

NED. What shall be done with him, Captain?

CAPT. [*To Sir Frederick*] He wears your uniform, Sir Frederick.

SIR F. [*Shaking his head with contempt*] No! We hold no league with cut-throats and murderers!

NED. I have it—Allen—[*To one of the men*] strip that coat off his back. Give him the blue and buff. If he attempts to shirk the slightest duty belonging to it, shoot him on the spot! [*Music changes. They take Dyke off. Ned goes to Rachel and Dorothy. Sir Frederick and Captain retire. Reuben and Ann enter from L.2.E. not noticing balance of characters*]

REU. What I was a'goin' to say—when we was interrupted that time was —[*She looks stolidly into his face*] that is I've been a'thinkin' that is—now that—[*Desperately*] Say, what's the use a'lyin' when the truth ken be proved agin ye. Ann Campbell I'm—say, be ye ever troubled with cold feet? [*She remains immovable. He puts his arms around her waist and kisses her on cheek. She turns and falls on his breast. Business of Reuben. Drum corps heard in distance. Sees party. Tries to rouse her. She is immovable*] Say—Ann—[*Then to party apologizing, not realizing what he says*] Ann's busted her gallusses an' I'm a'fixin' 'em for her—[*To her*] Say, Ann—they're all a'lookin' at ye!

ANN. [*Recovering, half fainting—half crying*] Let 'em look! I don't care a continental cuss! It's been many a year since I've hed my arms around a man's neck—an' now I hain't a'goin' to let nothin' choke me off! Reuben, I'm yourn, an' I'll stick to ye like death to a nigger an' don't ye *forgit* that! [*Reuben and Ann retire to Dorothy as Sir Frederick speaks. Dorothy's music*]

SIR F. [*To the Captain speaking with severity*] I am determined and it shall not be otherwise. [*Gently*] Dorothy, my child, come here. [*She comes tremblingly. Rachel and Ned to L.U.E. To Roanoke—sternly*] Approach, sir! [*Roanoke does so*] Captain Winslow, I am called to battle for my King and country. To your care I commit my child. Should I fall, here—[*Giving paper*] is that will secure her my name and fortune. [*To Roanoke*] You, sir, love my daughter. Go forth. Fight as bravely in your cause—as be sure I shall in mine. She will watch and pray for your return. Dorothy—[*Taking her to his breast*] be happy! I give you *freely*—give you to the man you love! [*Kisses her, passes her to Roanoke, then looks up and says as if to himself*] Am I forgiven?

DOR. [*After embracing Roanoke, returns weeping for joy, to hide herself on her father's breast*] Oh, father! For now you are indeed my father! [*Half laughing—half crying*] Roanoke—why don't you say something? [*Goes up to Reuben. He takes her in his arms—kisses her*]

ROAN. [*Who has been spellbound*] Roanoke has no words! His voice is in his heart. The silent water is ever the deepest. So be his love and gratitude. Let his eyes speak. Awed by the sublimity of the gift, let him stand dumb in the majestic presence of the giver. [*Dorothy brings Reuben down. Roanoke retires. She has Reuben's left hand—takes Sir Frederick's right. They look at each other a moment. She looks into the faces of both. They look at her, then at each other. They smile. She joins, then kisses both their hands, laughs through her tears and runs up to Roanoke. They go to and receive the congratulations of the rest of the party*]

SIR F. Mr. Foxglove—what shall I—what can I say to such a man as you have proved yourself to be! Take this. [*Offers pocketbook. Reuben shakes head*] Not as a reward—but as a token of my sincere and honest love—[*Reuben still hesitates*] for my daughter!

REU. Sir Frederick, I know ye mean well—but what's the use'n lyin'—when the truth ken be proved agin ye. I love that child. Ef it hain't askin' too much, I'd like to hear ye say *our daughter!*

SIR F. [*Extending both hands. They look steadily into each other's eyes—both affected*] For our daughter's sake!

REU. [*Shaking him heartily by the hand—wiping eyes*] Then, I'll take it. [*Takes pocketbook*] It'll help Ann an' me set up shop! [*They go up arm in arm and join party*] Say, Captain, you ken pay Ann's wages to me hereafter! [*Dorothy and Smollet come down*]

SMOL. I certainly congratulate you, Miss—Miss—[*Smilingly*] What shall I say, Foxglove or Shelton?

DOR. [*Laughing and pointing to Sir Frederick and Reuben who are still arm in arm*] Both! See! [*They both laugh*]

SMOL. Well, really you have the most extraordinary family complications! When I first met you you were the mother of one father and now you are the daughter of two! [*Both laugh*]

DOR. Lieutenant—I am indebted to you for many acts of kindness. How shall I thank you for them?

SMOL. [*Lightly, but with a strata of deep feeling underneath*] Pshaw! I've done nothing any other fellow wouldn't have had himself cashiered for the privilege of doing! The society of a charming lady—[*Bows. She smiles*] is not so often thrown in the way of a poor devil of a soldier that he can afford not to be civil! True—I did at one time hope that you—[*She looks at him appealingly*] Well—no matter. [*Seriously*] I've passed the happiest hours of my life in your company. If I, in return, have afforded you any amusement—

DOR. [*Supplicatingly and smiling*] Pleasure—let us call it pleasure, Lieutenant!

SMOL. [*Looking at her curiously*] Pleasure! Why, I'm content—and if circumstances will only permit—I will dance as merrily at your wedding as if it were my own. [*Bows very ceremoniously. She curtseys very low. Bugle calls "Five" heard in distance*]

SIR F. Hark! That bugle warns me to depart. Farewell! [*Takes Dorothy in his arms, kisses her fervently*]

DOR. [*Clinging to him*] Father! [*Calmly*] Is it right that you go—*now?* Right that you should sever every earthly tie—[*With a desperate effort brings herself to say*] Right that you [*Looking at Roanoke and Reuben, then back to him*] should fight against him [*To Reuben*]—against the husband of your child?

SIR F. Hush! A soldier has no choice. Love is strong, but honor and duty are impregnable. I go. But if I live I will return to pass my days among you—and ask no sweeter resting spot than in a land hallowed by a mother's sufferings—blessed by a daughter's love. [*Drums have constantly increased, are now quite loud. Calcium lights on. All the characters retire L.H. Enter L.U.*

E. Drum Corps playing. They march off R.1.E. Then a company of soldiers with their officers. They march off R.1.E. Cannons boom. Bells ring. Second Company. Same. Drum Corps. Third Company. Yankee Doodle. All the ladies, handsomely dressed, strewing flowers. General Washington on horseback—accompanied by his Generals all made up in character and on horseback. More soldiers. The stage is completely filled. Characters shout. Ladies wave their handkerchiefs. Soldiers all shout. Washington lifts hat. Grand Tableau and]

END OF PLAY

CAST OF CHARACTERS

*[First performance on any stage, The People's Theatre, New York,
May 7, 1888]*

JACK HEPBURNE, *skipper o' the "Dolphin"—rough
but honest, with a "failin'"* — JAMES A. HERNE

PERCY SEWARD, *son of a rich mother whom he loves;
a good fellow but a trifle sentimental* — H. M. PITT

SILAS CUMMINGS, *"Dep'ty Sheriff, Farmacuterist
and Clarinettist"* — C. W. BUTLER

HARRY MERTON, *of Percy's set*

ALECK SAUNDERS ⎫ — PHINEAS LEACH
JOSH WHILBECK ⎭ *two of Mary's fathers* — ROBERT ALEXANDER

MARY MILLER, *belongs to the village, the fishermen's
child* — KATHARINE C. HERNE

MARGARET HEPBURNE, *Jack's mother* — MRS. CHARLES RAE

MRS. SEWARD, *Percy's mother* — HENRIETTA BERT

HESTER BARTON, *stage struck, wants patronage and
endorsement* — VIC REYNOLDS

MISS STANLEY ⎫ — MAUDE JEFFRIES
MISS FAIRCHILD ⎬ *of Percy's set* — ADELAIDE NELSON
MISS EASTERBROOK ⎭ — LUCILLE PEARSON

LITTLE MARGARET, *Mary's child* — LITTLE DOT WINTERS

FISHERMEN, VILLAGE GIRLS, LADIES, GENTLEMEN, ETC., ETC.

TIME: PRESENT DAY.

ACT I. NEAR GLOUCESTER, MASS.

ACT II. JACK'S CABIN, GLOUCESTER.

ACT III.   HOME OF PERCY SEWARD, BOSTON.

ACT IV.   ATTIC IN TENEMENT HOUSE, NORTH END, BOSTON.

ACT V.   JACK'S CABIN AS BEFORE.

ACT I.

Scene 1: *Near Gloucester, Mass. Fishing village on beach. Wharves, shipping warehouses, etc. on R. Gloucester in distance on R.*
Time: *August, present day. Sea with fishing fleet at anchor in distance supposed to have arrived before the calm fell. The horizon that hazy gray that betokens extreme heat; heat lightning at intervals. Sea is dead calm. The set is a fisherman's hut R., a little better than its fellows; it is built of the hull of a vessel, has a low porch and step; overhung vines; bench beneath window. On L. old wreck to work and work lights behind. A piece or two of wreckage on shore; bead cloth down.*
Thunder; lightning; clouds and rain all to work during act. Wind and sea to move schooner, three master, to work on, go about, tack, drop anchor. Men to go aloft, furl and take in sail. Boat with men to leave schooner. Row towards shore. Sun shines brightly at rise.

Music.

Aleck and Josh discovered removing bars, etc., from dory, which is beached C.R.; they are rough fishermen about 50, with weather-beaten faces and brown hands. Aleck smokes clay pipe. There is a laugh outside R. by Mary and Hester; they run on, arms about each other's waist. They are followed by Percy Seward, a tall, handsome young man about twenty-three, dressed in elegant yachting costume. Hester leaves Mary, goes to Aleck and Josh, slaps them familiarly on the back; they turn and greet her smilingly, she is a rollicking good-natured girl, dressed plainly but picturesquely and coquettishly. She and the men converse in dumb show; the men point off to the fleet; look at the sea, sky, etc.; she sits on the edge of dory, and swings her heels, Nick sits on hunkers, Josh stands leaning on oar; Nick is spinning a yarn to Hester, Josh listening. They enjoy the scene without interfering with that of Percy and Mary.

Percy.   Really, Miss Mary, I think it quite unreasonable, to say the least, to laugh at my protestations of lo—
Mary. [*Laughing and holding up her finger*]   Ah! Ah!
Percy.   Respect, I'm sure I see nothing in my infatuation to laugh at. I do lo—[*She looks at him, he checks himself*]—admire you, and why not? Everyone here loves you.

MARY. [*Seriously*] And that is the very reason *you* should not. I am an orphan—poor—ignorant—

PERCY. [*Interrupting*] No! Not ignorant.

MARY. Well, unlearned, except for such learning as one gets from these rough, honest people, among whom it has been my fortune to be born. You say you are rich—I have been taught that the rich are proud—are you proud?

PERCY. Yes—in the just pride that always accompanies wealth when tempered with refinement and good breeding—there are different kinds of pride.

MARY. Well, I too am proud! You say you have a dear mother—who loves you and whom you love. [*Taking his hand*] I honor you for that—I can only love the *memory* of mine—her I have never known—neither father nor mother; my father they say was lost at sea. The shock killed my mother—and I was launched—as I may say tempest tossed, upon the sea of life—an orphan. The fisher folks cared for me, first one and then the other—I was known as "the fishermen's child"; at the age of three years Mrs. Hepburne took me as her own. I have lived here [*Points to cabin*] with her and [*Blushes*] Jack ever since.

PERCY. Yes, I have heard that story and will confess that it was that that first awakened a feeling of lo—[*She looks at him*] I see nothing in it to prevent your listening to me.

MARY. Everything—the fact of my being what I am and your being what [*Hesitates*] you say you are—prevents—say that you are honest and would make me your wife, which—[*Hesitates*]

PERCY. You have no right to doubt.

MARY. [*Avoiding that*] Would it not break the heart of that mother you love—to see you married to the "fishermen's child"—would she be willing to receive me as a daughter?

PERCY. Well—[*Hesitates*] she might not at first—but eventually her love for me—

MARY. There—you see that with all your learning I am wiser than you, in that wisdom born of instinct, and which none possess to such a degree as the child of nature—granting even that your mother—how I love that name! with that holy mother love—before which all other love palls as the dew melts before the sun's hot rays, should cast aside all pride of birth, all thought of station and for her *"boy's"* sake clasp me to her breast in loving welcome— how would it be with you after the first flush of fancied bliss had passed? Would you not tire of your fisher bride—would you not shame to present her to your fashionable friends—blush at her awkward ways and country manners—would you not soon learn to draw comparisons between her and the proud and cultured ladies of your class?

PERCY. No! Never—I swe—

MARY. Hush! Yes—In spite of yourself would come the doubt as to the wisdom of your choice—you would learn to ponder on what *might* have been —the caresses you once so eagerly sought would gradually grow irksome— following this would come coldness—neglect—and finally abandonment—for you perhaps remorse—for me the blankness of despair. Ah! No, best leave the daisy of the field in the field, where the hand of God hath sown it! Transplant it to the hothouse—it will wither—fade, fall and die.

PERCY. You have painted a gloomy picture.

MARY. Let us say a true one. There, let us be friends, you know but little of me—*I* nothing of you save that you have flattered me with your attentions —that you are a gentleman I feel—and as such there is my hand—go back to your city friends, choose from among them one more worthy to share your life than I—and you will one day thank me for having saved you from a step you would have regretted to your dying day. [*Hangs her head silently, brushes away a tear, looks up smilingly, laughs*] Besides, do you not know I am not free, that I am already promised to another?

PERCY. Yes—to Jack Hepburne. Mary—may I call you so?

MARY. Yes, my name is Mary.

PERCY. Is he worthy of *you*—you have drawn a picture of your fancied life with me—have you ever drawn one of your life with him?

MARY. Yes—to live always here, among the rough, kind hearts that have known me from birth—to be the staff of his aged mother's declining years and perhaps to close her gentle eyes in sleep at last—to be a fisherman's wife, true and loyal, to make his home bright and happy with my smiles and cheer him with my love—to bid him godspeed on his departure and welcome home on his return. Perhaps one day to place within his arms a fragile image of himself, to kneel with him and thank the giver of all good for the boon of his bestowal—the greatest in his gifts, the blessing of motherhood.

PERCY. But do you not fear that he—

MARY. May *one* day not return—[*Sadly*] Yes—I have thought of that, not with fear, however, for we fisher folks are not much given to fear—but with a sort of dread—but we are a pious people here—the fisherman's life is a hazardous one at best, and we are taught that "He that giveth also taketh away," and to say "Thy will be done." There are worse things than death in this world.

PERCY. I do not mean sea faring dangers, I mean, pardon me—his love for—

MARY. What he calls a social glass?

PERCY. Yes, I have seen—

MARY. So have I. All our people here drink more or less, they seem to inherit it from their cradles. It is as natural for a fisherman to drink as it is for the fish they risk their lives to catch—

PERCY. Have you then no fears that this pernicious habit may grow upon him and one day wreck his life and yours—yes—even that of the unborn babe of which you just now spoke?

MARY. Hush—please—don't, please don't. I dare not look so far as that. Jack is young, and thoughtless, he is rough, but he is honest as he is rough, he loves me [*Hastily*] that I know, and he has promised me that on the day I become his wife—he will give up drink forever. I believe him, I trust him. I must do so, for do I not love him? But, [*Drying her eyes*] there, there, here I stand chatting with you while his vessel lies in the offing waiting only for the breeze to freshen to bring her safely to anchor, and *him* to his mother's arms. I must in and help prepare his welcome, so good-bye for the present. [*Gives her hand*] Forget all that has passed between us, and please do not refer to it again. Believe me you will find *your life* elsewhere.

PERCY. Mary. [*Seriously, respectfully, and with deep feeling*] I can never forget, I accept the sacred title of friend. Let me think of you in my own odd way, I believe I'm better for having known you, and I hope—[*Corrects himself*] I know Jack will be, *must* be nobler for becoming your husband. And now let me exact one promise, and that is, should the day ever come—which God forbid—that you need a friend, you will seek, as you will surely find, that friend, in Percy Seward.

MARY. [*Deeply affected*] I promise. [*He raises her hand respectfully to his lips; she blushes, bows her head and exits into cottage; he raises his hat; as she is off, he turns away with a sigh*]

PERCY. Heigho! Percy, old fellow, you had best order the *Sybil* to weigh anchor and resume her cruise. I'm afraid this is a bad case. You've met pretty girls before and got away scot free, but I'm afraid the fisher girl has unwittingly meshed you in her net. By George! what a brainy creature she is, and what wisdom for one who knows nothing of this bright, beautiful world, save what is found here in this fishiest of fishing villages. She is a gem, and only needs proper setting to be of great price. After all she may be right. You might tire of her; in trying to polish the diamond we might destroy its lustre. She is happy here, she loves this Jack, and I daresay he loves her in his rough way. Far be it from you, Percy Seward, to cast one shadow across her path. No! No! You are her *friend*, let that content you, and the province of a friend is to stand by when danger threatens, and that you'll do Percy, for you're a pretty good sort of a fellow, although a bit sentimental. [*During this speech Nick and Josh have finished their story and gone off R.U.E. At*

"shadow across her path" Hester *has gone with them as far as the entrance,
then returning comes R. of Percy who has crossed L. in meditation; she gets
in front of him, stoops, looks up into his face*]

Hes. A penny for your thoughts!

Percy. [*Laughs*] I don't know that they are worth a penny.

Hes. Not worth a penny! Of who ever could you be thinking then?

Percy. [*Laughingly*] Of a very idle, purposeless sort of gentlemanly vaga-
bond—myself.

Hes. Oh, Mr. Seward! You're in love, hain't you—ha! Ha! Ha!

Percy. A natural consequence—with a rich-only-to-please himself in the
world young fellow, on the one side, and the sweetest, prettiest girl in the
world on the other side.

Hes. [*With a low courtesy*] Oh! Mist-e-r-Seward—

Percy. [*Alarmed*] Good gracious, Miss Barton, I didn't mean you.

Hes. Why, you said a rich young fellow on one side and the sweetest,
prettiest girl in the world on the other, didn't ye?

Percy. Yes—I confess I—

Hes. Well! Hain't you on the one side and hain't I on tother?

Percy. Yes—there's no denying that—but—I—I—

Hes. There, there—don't stammer, it always puts me in a perspiration to
hear anyone stammer—ha! ha! ha! I forgive ye—it's only another image *scattered*.

Percy. [*Correcting her*] Idol shattered!

Hes. Eh?

Percy. Idol shattered!

Hes. Oh! Yes—Idol shattered. I knew it was some kind of a image—I
only heard it once—it was in the theater up at the Town Hall, Lampey's Un-
equalled Dramatic Alliance from the Boston Museum, every member a star,
in a carefully selected repature.

Percy. Repertoire!

Hes. I guess so. Six days only, three grand performances daily, mornings
at ten, afternoons at two, evenings at eight, admission ten cents, a few very
choice seats reserved at five cents extra, change of bill at each performance—
special provisions for families from the country desiring to eat lunch in the
theater—

Percy. Why! Of course, they could not eat lunch without provisions—
see?

Hes. [*Looks at him*] Don't interrupt me—lemonade, popcorn, candies
and peanuts, served by gentlemanly attendants—no whistling, stamping or
catcalls allowed—did you ever see Lampey's Constellation?

PERCY. Never heard of it before.

HES. Why, you live in Boston, don't ye?

PERCY. Yes—born there.

HES. And—ye—*never—heard—of—Lampey's—*Constellation?

PERCY. *Never!*

HES. Don't ye ever go to the Museum?

PERCY. Oh yes! Frequently.

HES. Well—They're from the Museum.

PERCY. I dare say—a very long way from it. [*Laughs*]

HES. You needn't laugh. Lampey's great. I've seen all the constellations that come here—I've seen *Peck's Bad Boy, Uncle Tom, Ten Nights in a Barroom, Alvin Joslyn* and all of them and I like Lampey's in "Alonzo the Brave" better than any of them—but then mebbe you see more actin' in Boston then we do down here.

PERCY. Very likely.

HES. I wish I was an actor. I wish some rich man would fall in love with me and put me on the stage. [*Looks at him archly, laughs*] Lampey says I only needs patronage—what's that?

PERCY. Why, when some person high in position, such as the Governor or President in this country, or the Prince of Wales in England, endorses you and introduces you into his set.

HES. Is the Prince of Wales coming to Gloucester?

PERCY. Not that I've heard.

HES. Because he might endorse *me*—Lampey says the more patronage, good clothes and less talent you have nowadays, the better you'll draw. Si! he won't hear of my going on the stage.

PERCY. Si?

HES. Yes, Si Cummins keeps the drugstore up on the corner yonder, haven't you seen his sign? Silas Cummins, Depity Sherff and Farmacuterist, Manifacter'r, Cummins' Bloodroot, Anti-appetite pills, Cummins' Corn Salve, Cummins' Liver Expander, e-t-c., e-t-c., e-t-c.

PERCY. Oh! Yes, I've met the gentleman.

HES. Well, him and me's engaged, but he's got no soul for high art. Lampey says he's of the world, worldly, but he plays the clarinet beautiful and he could lead the band waggin splendid—who leads the band waggin of the Boston Museum?

PERCY. I don't know. [*Laughingly*] I don't think they have one.

HES. No band waggin! Why how on earth do they let 'em know there's goin' to be a show. [*Silas heard off R. playing clarinet: "The Girl I Left*

Behind Me." Hester hears him, with delight, claps her hands] There's Si! Ain't he splendid!

PERCY. Magnificent! [*Silas plays away quite absorbed, gets down between them, finally sees them, blows a terrific blast in Percy's ear, Percy gives a start, claps his hand to his ears*] Mercy on us!

HES. [*Without moving, smiles complacently*] Oh! Couldn't he lead a band waggin though?

SI. I beg pardon Mr. Seward, jest practisin'.

PERCY. Yes, so I perceive—don't mention it, I beg.

SI. Didn't startle you, did it?

PERCY. Oh! No! Not at all.

SI. [*Patronizingly*] But pshaw! I suppose you've heard musicianers afore?

PERCY. Well, yes, some few.

SI. Ever heer Baily Cross?

PERCY. Never.

SI. He was a powerful musicianer, I've seen him play the trombone and Macbeth the same night. He's dead!

PERCY. [*Aside*] He ought to be. [*Aloud*] Is he?

SI. Yes—Trombone busted in the last act an' blowed the top of his head off. Somebody loaded it while he was on the stage "a ministerin' to a mind deseased."

PERCY. Rather sad!

SI. Yes—it ended the piece! Musicianers are scurcer now. [*Plays*]

PERCY. I wonder, Mr. Cummings.

SI. Cummi*ns*.

PERCY. Isn't there a final *G* to you name?

SI. Not as I've heerd on—say, Hester, is there a final *G* to Cummins?

HES. [*Who has been sitting on bench R.*] Yes! G.R.

SI. Oh, yes, *Gr.* that means gunior—see, my father was old Si Cummins, and of course I'm Si Cummins Gr.

PERCY. Yes, I see. Well, I wonder you don't go to the city. Such talent is wasted here, that is to a certain extent.

SI. Well, I've hed a good many offers, but I'm kind o' tied here. [*Plays*] Think I'd kinder astonish 'em up there—don't you?

PERCY. Oh, I've no doubt of it at all.

SI. [*Playing*] The've hed nothing like me up there.

PrRCY. Not just exactly like you—you would be a novelty.

SI. Well, you might speak to 'em when you get hum—I might be in-dooced, jest for a short while, though I couldn't stop long.

PERCY. No—I think a short engagement *would* be best!

HES. [*Who has been acting to herself now crosses to Percy in an abstracted manner*] "Two souls with but a single thought, two hearts that beat as one." [*Throws herself on Percy's breast, Percy folds her in his arms and kisses her. Silas turns her quickly around to L.*]

SI. Say look a here, ef you've got any more soul than you want you jest give it to me. [*Percy laughs*]

HES. [*Pouting*] Oh Silas, you're jealous.

SI. No, I hain't jealous.

HES. It was only a bit of stage business that I was practising anyhow.

SI. Well, you just practise it on me, I can stand it.

NICK. [*Outside R.*] There she comes mates, see her creepin' on over to the westward. [*Enter Nick, Josh, fisherman and female villagers. Nick has ship's glass, all group in semicircle on R. of stage*]

```
 - - - - -      Josh              Silas
   - - - - -        *    Nick       *
     - - -        Hester     *     Percy
                     *               *
```

[*Breeze is now seen to freshen and move the sea, gradually growing stronger. Enter from cottage Mrs. Hepburne and Mary. Mary leads Mrs. Hepburne to seat on bench and stands beside her*]

MARY. There mother, sit there, his first thought is sure to be of you, and I wish your face to be the first to greet his eyes.

MARG. Heaven bless you, my child!

NICK. [*As breeze freshens*] There she comes, isn't that a glorious sight! What can cheer the heart of the homeward bound sailor like the breeze that bears him to the mother he honors . . . [*Looks at Margaret*] and the girl he loves [*Looks at Mary, who smiles and bows, glass to eye*] Ha-ah—see—up go the sails, how gloriously they fill, now she weighs, see her stretch her arms like a huge giant after his sleep, she yawns, she struggles, she trembles like a schoolgirl over her first loveletter, now she starts. [*The stage has been all excitement during this—people peering over each other to catch a glimpse, Silas running from one spot to another, and getting ready to shout at every exclamation of Nick's; Mary's face radiant; Hester stands on tiptoe, two of the men make a chair of their hands, seat her in it and raise her up—it doesn't suit—she beckons Silas to come and stoop down—he does so, the men take her hands, she jumps on Silas' back, the men holding her hands, and settles herself to comfortably enjoy the scene*] She's off, here she comes. [*Schooner now works on from L., tacks, goes about, lowers sail, drops anchor*] Huzza! [*All shout. Men on schooner man yards; lower boat. Five men get into boat and row away, finally disappearing behind wreck. All shout and wave hats. Hes-*]

ter jumps up shouting, Silas falls, she jumps to stage, all laugh] And now, Hester, clear your pipes for a song of welcome to Jack Hepburne, the best skipper and truest mate that ever trod a deck.

HES. [*Sailor fashion*]   Aye! Aye! My hearties, and clear your pipes for the chorus. [*Song and Chorus: as it ends glee is taken up off L., very distant. All listen; it comes nearer and nearer, the sound of oars is heard and the scene is worked up, till at end of glee, the boat touches beach, and Jack jumps ashore. Men in boat cast painter ashore, men ashore grasp it and make it fast to toggle, four men follow Jack. Girls and men all crowd around and grasp hands. Girls kiss their sweethearts. Jack goes directly to his mother, kneels, embraces her*]

JACK.   Mother! [*Rises*] Mary! [*Clasps her to his heart and gives her a long passionate kiss. Note: Jack must be tall and manly, handsome, about thirty, reddish brown hair and eyes, must be picturesquely dressed in half sailor, half fishing garb, clothes must be clean and fit him perfectly, supposed to be his holiday suit. He sees Percy, who has crossed down L.*]

<pre>
                                Sea

          - - - - -
              - - - - - Group
          - - - - ,
              - - - Mary, Jack
    Margaret   *   *
       *   Percy   *
R.   Footlights   L.
</pre>

JACK.   Hello, a stranger! [*Mary is about to speak. Percy checks her*]

PERCY.   Permit me to introduce myself—Percy Seward, of Boston, on a yachting cruise. I dropped anchor in your charming bay, and drifted ashore some weeks since. I have been fortunate enough to make the acquaintance of Miss Miller and your mother as well as these other good people.

SI.   Hester, we're the good people. [*Hester nods*]

PERCY.   And have found them so entertaining that to tell the truth I have no desire to continue my cruise further. My yacht—

SI.   I allus thought that was *yatch*.

PERCY.   The *Sybil* lies yonder and is at the service of yourself and friends during my stay.

JACK. [*Offering hand*]   Glad to see you, Mr. Seward, and thank ye kindly for your invitation, but after a fellow has had months of the geniwine article he don't hanker much arter playin' sailor. No offense and thank ye all the same. [*Percy goes up, sees Silas and Hester, crosses to them*] Hello Si! [*Shakes hands*] and Hester! [*Kisses her*] Gone play actin' yet?

Hes.   No, Jack, I'm waiting to be endorsed.

Jack.   [*Crosses C.*]   Well, mother, and you Mary, you'll be glad to hear that we've had a glorious trip, the finest of weather, the biggest catch of the year, and better than all, to learn that I'm to go no more to sea.

Mary.   [*Springing to him*]   Oh! Jack!

Marg.   [*Tries to rise, cannot*]   My boy! My boy! [*Jack goes hastily to her, assists her and holds her in his arms. Mary leans on his shoulder*]

Jack.   True mother, my father lost his life in the service of Hemingway & Son—I have labored faithfully for them since I have been able to tell a mackerel from a cod, and for all this I've been given charge of the warehouses here, and there's $300 to be placed in the village bank for me the day that I'm married, and here's the letter that tells the good news. [*Shows letter to Margaret and Mary, they eagerly look over it*]

Hes.   [*To Silas*]   Why ain't you given in charge of something?

Si.   I have been, ain't I Depity Sherff of this deestrict? [*During this clouds have gradually darkened the horizon although the sun shines brightly on the stage. Horizon quite dark*]

Jack.   So now, Mary, my darling, here in the presence of these, my honest shipmates, whose dangers on the sea I shall no longer share I ask you to name the day that I may call you wife, and—

Si.   Collar the $300, don't forget that Jack. [*Omnes laugh*]

Mary.   Jack, you have always had my heart, there's my hand. [*Gives it*] Let the day be when you will.

Jack.   [*Snatching her to his heart and kissing her. Silas does same to Hester. All the men upstage do same to their sweethearts*]   No time like the present —let it be now, send for the parson, [*Boy runs off R.*] run for the fiddler—

Hes.   No! No! Here's the clarinette. [*Points to Silas*]

Jack.   We'll have such a jollification as never was. [*All shout*] Oh, mother, [*Goes to her, kisses her*] Mary, my own, my wife. [*Goes to embrace her. The horizon has become black by this. At the word "wife" a terrific flash of lightning and a crash of thunder. At its sound all the characters who had their hats in hand in act of shouting, pause. Picture of alarm and fear; Margaret springs up in alarm, Mary shrieks and hides her head on Jack's breast; Jack looks alarmed but defiant. Hester alone faces the sea and looks boldly at the storm. Silas hides himself behind her*]

Mary.   Oh, Jack, if that should be an evil omen!

Jack.   Nonsense. [*Half superstitious himself*] It's but a summer storm, and see how brightly the sun shines on us—what matter the storm, it cannot harm the sea—look up, there is no danger. [*A terrific flash of lightning and crash of thunder, a bolt descends and fires Jack's ship*]

NICK. The *Dolphin's* struck! Jack, your ship's on fire! [*Jack is panic-stricken. Clouds move on, rain descends in torrents in the distant horizon. Sun shines brighter than ever on shore. Margaret staggers to C.*]

MARG. [*With a superhuman effort*] Kneel my children. [*Jack and Mary kneel. Margaret raises hands aloft*] Father, we are in Thy hands, "Thy will be done."

(Chorus "Rock of Ages")

PICTURE AND END OF ACT

Percy
*

- - - -
- - - - -
- - - -
- - -

Margaret
*   *   *   Hester
Jack   Mary   *   Silas
                                        *

ACT II.

TIME: *Fifteen months elapse. It is Christmas Eve. The interior of cabin represents an old ship's cabin; no plaster or whitewash, all oak timber with heads of wooden pegs, iron bolts, nuts, etc., seen. Good thickness of pieces on all doors and windows, borders represent roof or deck, everything very clean. Oblong window C. with white muslin curtain on drawing string, curtain drawn back so as to show distant sea and snow storm without. Oaken shutters outside windows to close and bar, oaken door L.U.E.; recess with curtains L.I.E. back by continuation of cabin bed with patch work quilt, in recess, arch with curtain. R.U.E. there is shown the continuation of cabin furnished; fireplace R.2.E. ship's locker against L. side of cabin, washstand with pitcher of water, bowl, soap, etc., etc., R.I.E., roller towel at stand, clothes rack, pegs, with southwestern coat, etc., R. of window, rubber boots beneath ship's glass on peg, old fashioned leaf table at window, dresser with dishes in R. arch, large photo of Jack, Mother and Mary over and at sides of window. Clock and ornaments on mantel, kettle steaming and singing on hob, cricket chirping on hearth. Within all warm and cozy, without storm howling; candles on mantel, lamp holly branches ready for Jack, dog and cat lying on hearth.*

Music.

Sleigh bells heard ever and anon during scene. This carefully rehearsed. Low rocker for Mother, wooden chairs, flower stands with flowers R. and L.U. corners, small C. table, singing bird hanging in recess L., rag carpet, rugs, two oars, blades uppermost in corners behind flower stands. Snow to drift in at door and for characters, large watch, bundles, goose, etc., etc., for Jack, amber calciums R. and L. through window, red ditto through fireplace, fire log burning. Stage, semi-dark at rise to get effect of lights then gradually but imperceptibly light up, till full on, except borders behind window. Small mirror over washstand, beach and sea backing. 1st, act. drop.

DISCOVERED: *Margaret discovered in rocker knitting; Mary at table cutting out baby clothes; Jack at glass by washstand shaving; clean white shirt on bed in recess, stockings ready L.*

JACK. [*Washing his face and neck thoroughly in water and singing all the time, and drying himself on the towel. Sings "Oh! There was a jolly miller once, lived happy on the river Dee"*] There, that's over. Now Mary, where's my clean shirt?

MARY.   There, Jack, on mother's bed, and your collar and handkerchief all ready.

JACK.   Oh, Lord—Lord—what a little wife you are—eh mother! ain't she just the blessedest little wife in the world? [*Goes off L.1.*]

MARG.   That she is, Jack, and you see that you prove the best of husbands to her.

JACK. [*Outside*] Oh! Never fear me—say, mother, don't you forget to hang up the stockings. Will ye?

MARY. [*Laughing*]   Oh Jack! What nonsense!

JACK. [*Outside*]   No nonsense about it; Christmas is Christmas! It comes but once a year—I'm goin' to have the stockings hung up—and I'm going to have lots of holly—and mince pie and goose and a regular New England jollification, there now: [*Coming out*] So, for fear you might forget it, I'll just hang them up myself. [*Comes out with stockings, one long black one, one long gray one, and one man's blue woolen sock*] Say, Mary hain't you got no better stocking than this? [*Shows black one*]

MARY. [*Going to him and trying to take the stockings from him*]   Why, Jack, what ever are you going to do?

JACK.   Hang up the stockings I tell you—[*She tries to get them; he puts them behind his back*] Now, it's no use little woman, ain't agoin' to give old Santa Claus any excuse. Ha! Ha! Ha! So, mother, you just give me some pins. [*Margaret feels in her breast, laughs, and gives him the pins. He puts them in his mouth*] Then Mother, first. [*Pins long gray one on line left of fire*] You next, Mary. [*Pins black one on line right of fire*] And me in the middle; there we be all in a row. [*Margaret has enjoyed this. Mary now comes down L. of stage, Jack stands C., admiring the stockings. Mary goes to him, she has baby's garment in her hand, places hand on his shoulder. Music*]

MARY. Jack, did you ever think that perhaps next Christmas there might be another stocking, a tiny one, Jack, to hang in the chimney corner?

JACK. Why, Mary child, there's tears in your eyes. [*Goes to wipe her eyes with the work she has, sees it's a baby's dress*] Why, bless my soul, what's this?

MARY. Do you remember Bella and John in *Our Mutual Friend*—that I read to you?

JACK. Yes, perfectly.

MARY. Well, there are sails Jack—sails for the little ship that's coming across the unknown sea—to you and me, Jack. [*Falls weeping in his arms. Margaret silently wipes her eyes. Jack is deeply affected, kisses Mary fervently. Silence and moment's pause*] Jack, have I been any comfort to you—have I made your life any happier by becoming your wife?

JACK. Happier! don't talk like that, Mary—why I couldn't live without you—now—

MARY. Then if anything should ever come between us—

JACK. Come between us—[*Fiercely*]

MARY. [*Placing hand over his mouth*] No! No! I don't mean that—I mean—if ever you should be tempted to—

JACK. [*Soothingly*] Oh! there I see now. [*Kisses her*] Bless you why didn't you say that before? There, I'll not go out at all—

MARY. [*Recovering herself*] Oh! yes, you must, your men expect you; it would be selfish of me to keep you here—don't mind me Jack—you know we women are apt to be moody and capricious when—

JACK. [*Stops her with a kiss*] Yes, yes, I know—I was only going because the men want to present me with a span new silver watch. Ho! Ho! Ho! and it says on it "to Jack Hepburne as a token of respect from his fellow workmen"—but I won't go.

MARY. [*Getting his coat*] Yes, yes—you must—there, now, see I'm all smiles again—now don't forget the holly—

JACK. [*Dressing*] No—nor the things for the stockings—nor the goose—mind, mother, that you put plenty of onions in the stuffin'—[*By this time he is dressed, kisses mother*] Good-bye. [*Kisses Mary*] I'll not be long away. [*Dog rises to follow*] No! No! Caesar, we mustn't both be absent at once; you stay here and take care of them till I come back, with my new silver watch. Mary you must keep asking me what time it is every hour in the day. Ho! Ho! Ho! [*Goes out; as he passes door, snow drifts in; Mary goes to window, as he passes, watches him, throws kiss, bursts into tears, rushes to Margaret and throws herself into her lap, weeping*]

MARG. Why, child alive—what's ever come over you? [*Smooths Mary's hair*]

MARY. I don't know, mother, it seems as if some great evil was about to fall upon us—try as I will I cannot shake it off. [*With fear*] Oh! Mother, if Jack should—

MARG. But he won't—you have been married now better than a good year —and has he not faithfully kept his promise?

MARY. [*Music changes; sleigh bells, etc.*] Yes.

MARG. Then trust him further, there dry your eyes—now and—[*Sleigh bells have become more distinct*]

SI. [*Outside*] Whoa, Deuteronomy! Whoa—boy! whoa! [*Bells stop*]

HES. [*Outside*] Help me out, Si Cummins, my legs is all twisted up in this horse blanket.

MARY. Hello! Visitors. [*Dries her eyes, looks through window and off L.*]

SI. Hold on till I hitch old Deuteronomy.

HES. Get me out I tell you—do you want me to freeze before I make my daybu?

SI. All right. All right. Gin us yer pump handles here—there ye are steady now. [*As they are heard approaching door, Mary goes to let them in. Silas stamps his feet and kicks his toes against door step. Mary opens door, snow drifts in; Silas enters carrying Hester. She is wrapped up in large old fashioned cloak and hood, heavy blue stockings over shoes; muffler on neck and mittens on hands; Silas in fur cap, long overcoat, with large white bone buttons, heavy boots, comforter around neck, mittens; they are covered in snow; he plumps Hester down before fire, starts to go off*]

MARY. Why, Silas, won't you warm yourself before you go?

SI. Oh!—Yes—I'll be back—I jist want to hitch Deuteronomy that's all.

MARY. Afraid he'll run away, Silas.

SI. Oh, no'm—afeard he'll fall down ef he hain't tied to suthin'. [*Goes off, all laugh*]

HES. [*Who has taken off her wraps, goes to Mrs. H.; kisses her*] Well, mother. [*Kisses Mary*] Merry Christmas.

MARY. [*Smiling*] Aren't you a little early?

HES. Well, you see I shan't have time tomorrow—I'll be awful busy tomorrow. Have you seen the bills?

MARY. Bills! What bills?

HES.   The play bills, of course—what other bills are there? Lampey's—you know he's here for the holidays. [*Silas enters, shakes snow off coat, cap, and feet; takes off great coat, comforter, cap and mittens, lays them on locker*]

MARY.   Yes—I know that—we are all going—Jack is to take us tomorrow night.

HES.   [*Clapping her hands*]   Is he—ah—good—ain't that splendid—got your seats?

MARY.   I don't know, I presume so, however.

HES.   If you ain't you better get 'em, there'll be a jam.

SI.   Ye kin get 'em at my store—got a few choice reserves at five cents extra.

HES.   Do you think ye'll know me?

MARY.   Know you!

HES.   Yes—I'm going to make my *day*-bu—

SI.   An so'mi—

MARY.   [*In surprise, but with a pleased expression*]   What?

HES.   Yes—Lampey says he will waive patronage—and try talent.

SI.   Yes—he's gin us a chance—though he says he don't think talent's much yuse.

MARY.   Well—I'm sure I'm *d*elighted—tomorrow evening—eh!

HES.   [*Grandiloquently*]   Tomorrow evening. [*Waves her hand*]

SI.   I lead the band waggin twicet—morning and afternoon—but Hester stars in the evening.

HES.   Show her the bill, Silas.

SI.   I will. [*Gets out play bill*]

MARY.   [*Takes it, reads*]   Town Hall, Gloucester, extraordinary attraction. Engagement at enormous expense of the young, beautiful and talented comedienne, Miss Hester Barton, assisted by the incomparable musician and pharmacoepeist, Mr. Silas Cummings, who will appear for one night only, Thursday, Dec. 25th, in conjunction with Lampey's Dramatic Constellation in a monster programme. Secure your seats at Cumming's drug store and avoid the rush at the doors. N.B. weather permitting band chariot, drawn by six snow white Arabian steeds will parade the principal streets at nine A.M. and one P.M.

SI.   The band's chariot's Aleck Pearce's ice cart with flags over it.

HES.   S—I—L—A—S—

MARY.   And Silas Cummings will lead Lampey's Metropolitan Band of forty pieces and perform several popular solos on the clarionet. Well—well— that is splendid—but why do you only play one night?

SI.   Lampey thinks one night's enuff.

Mary. But the bill don't say what you do, what do you do?

Si. Lampey'll announce that from the stage. I think it's safest.

Mary. Safest? In what way?

Si. Cos ef any eggs is fired, Lampey'll git 'em.

Hes. Oh! Silas ain't you awful? Why Mary, I sing a ballad and for an encore Silas and me do a double song and dance.

Si. Say—s'pose there hain't no encore.

Hes. Oh, there's sure to be—we rehearsed it this morning and Lampey said it would paralyze 'em.

Si. Or they'll paralyze us.

Hes. Would you like to hear us rehearse?

Mary. Should be delighted.

Hes. Come along Silas. [*Getting ready to sing and dance*] Mary'll play for us. [*Gives roll of music; Mary goes to piano*]

Si. I hain't thawed 'eout yet.

Hes. You just come along—you mean thing. [*Pulls him up*]

Si. I got a corn on my heel.

Hes. Ready, Mary.

Mary. All ready?

Si. Let 'er go, Gallagher. [*Song and dance*]

Mary. Bravo—Bravo—why Silas you're quite an actor. [*It has grown quite dark outside by this*]

Hes. Oh, he's got to act if he wants to marry me—I'll never marry anyone but an actor. [*Silas and Hester get ready to go*]

Si. Oh! I'll act—I'll act—only let the audience keep their claws off—an' I'll act.

Mary. Won't you stay to tea—Jack'll be back soon—he'd like you to stay to tea, I know.

Hes. No, thank you—I've got my wardrobe to look after and my *theatre trunk,* ahem! to pack.

Si. Yes—an' I've got to give Deuteronomy a coat of whitewash and git him ready for one of the six snow white Arabian steeds. [*By this time they're ready to go*] So I guess we'd best be off—goodnight.

Hes. [*Kissing Margaret and Mary*] Good night and a happy Christmas to you, as for me this'll be the happiest Christmas of my life—be sure you come early—so as not to miss any of me—and get good seats—good night—[*Talking as she goes off*]

Mary. Good night. [*They are off now*]

Si. Whoa,—Deuteronomy—[*Sleigh bells tinkle as Silas removes blanket and gets into sleigh, and chirks merrily as they ride off. Mary watches them through the window till they disappear, kissing hand to them, then lights candles and lamp, opens window, as it is now quite dark, closes shutters, draws curtain*]

MARY. [*As she works*] Ah! dear, light hearted little Hester—I hope her début will be a success, I'm sure—it will break her heart to fail—I must ask Jack to get me some flowers to throw to her.

MARG. Well—for my part, I never set much store by play actors—though they may be as good as any one else for all I know.

MARY. Yes, mother, there are good and bad in all lines of life—the player I presume is no exception to the rule. [*She now wheels the C. table away, the big table C. and prepares to set the supper table*] Hark! I thought that was Jack's step—[*Laughs*] Poor fellow, how proud he'll be of his watch and how like a great boy he insisted on hanging the stockings. [*Kettle begins to sing*] Why, even the kettle is merry tonight. [*Cricket chirps*] And the cricket, too, bless me, quite a happy family, come puss—[*To cat*] haven't you a note to add to the chorus and you Caesar—[*To dog*] Come sir, get ready to welcome your master. [*By this time she has finished the table*] There we are all ready now, I'll just put the tea to draw—[*Does so*] Now for Jack's favorite preserves—[*Goes into recess R., brings cake dish with cake in it and glass dish of preserves—Christmas carol heard in the distance—she stops and listens—it grows gradually nearer—passes window*] Hark! Mother! Is not that sweet— Ah! blessed, happy—happy Christmas—[*Resumes work—brings meat and bread from dresser—cuts bread, etc., etc., Christmas carol dies gradually away —and "we won't go home till morning" begins in the distance—she stops— listens—staggers—leans on table—singing comes nearer—nearer—ends near door. There is a loud laugh—door bursts open—Jack staggers in very drunk —laden with bundles. He wears a watch and has holly branches and wreathes. He drops them all on floor, staggers to locker, falls full length on it in drunken stupor—Mary shrieks—and falls senseless on floor. Margaret rises, falls on knees in prayer. Percy appears at door in handsome winter suit, snow drifts in through door—wind howls—sleigh bells in distance, chorus outside "Rock of Ages."*]

PICTURE AND END OF ACT

ACT III.

SCENE I: *The City. Night. Five years have elapsed. Residence of the Seward's. A grand hop in preparation. Carpets down all through covered with drugget; everything very elegant. Flowers, statuary, chandeliers, side lights, etc., etc.*

Magnificent garden illuminated by electricity. Balustrade of second story balcony overlooking garden.

Music.

At rise, as curtain ascends, male servant in livery, descends staircase carrying a large vase of flowers. This servant a tall, fat man, very particular for business with Silas at end of Act. Crosses to folding doors R., enters apartment, exits, after a moment's elapse returns without flowers, crosses and exits C. and L. At same time female servant with cap, apron, collar, cuffs, etc., etc., dressed in new stiff dress, supposed to be her best, enters from R.H. arch and crosses to apartment L.1.E. and exits passing male servant in livery who enters R.1.E., and exits up staircase as the female servants enter from R.C. and exits up staircase. These four servants stand ready for Act, to cross and re-cross as directed at rehearsal. There is music in the garden and laughter before and after curtain till the scene is well begun. Enter down staircase Mrs. Seward, a dark, dignified lady, with a stern but just face, elegantly and quietly dressed, and Mary, elegantly attired but wearing a saddened expression of face.

Mrs. S. [*Leading Mary to tête a tête R. and seating her*]   There my child, for you are now my child. My son has told me your story and although I am proud, and at first strongly opposed him in what I believed a mad infatuation, yet I could not permit my pride to stand as a barrier to his happiness. He—loves—you—you are his wife and I love you too. Percy tells me that your first husband has been dead four years.

Mary.   Dead four years! [*Aside*]—to me. To me. [*Aloud*] Yes madam.

Mrs. S.   Do not call me madam, call me mother.

Mary. [*Looks at her wistfully, hesitates, then suddenly falls on her knees, her head in Mrs. Seward's lap*]   Mother! [*She bursts into tears as Percy enters C.L.*]

Mrs. S. [*Kissing her*]   That's right—[*Smooths Mary's hair in the way Jack's mother did in Act II*] That's right, I must leave you now and show myself among your guests. [*Sees Percy*] Ah! my son, you come very apropos. Mary seems a little sad and downhearted, cheer her up—you can—for who can comfort and cheer a young wife like her young husband? [*Smiles very kindly yet with quiet dignity and exits C.L. At the word wife Percy seems a little embarrassed, slightly drops his head, not enough to be noticed by Mrs. Seward. As his mother goes, he crosses to Mary*]

Percy.   Why Mary darling, do not give way like this.

MARY. Percy, is this right?

PERCY. Is what right?

MARY. This deceit—this living lie—Oh! Percy I have never deceived a human being before. And to think that the first should be the one to whom you owe so much—your noble mother—Percy—think—she bade me call her *Mother*—and that sacred name—that I have so yearned—so *hungered* for—I uttered tonight with a lie in my heart—Shame! shame!! shame! [*Crosses L. and flings herself in chair*]

PERCY. You look only on the blackness of the clouds; you will not see the silver lining beyond.

MARY. Ah! Percy, I fear there is no silver lining for me.

PERCY. [*Continuing*] Besides—you are my wife in the sight of Heaven, you will soon be so in the face of man.

MARY. Yes, Percy! I believe you honestly intend all you say, and that you will, if permitted, perform all that you have promised, but the fact remains, that until that time I am but your—

PERCY. [*Alarmed*] Hush, my darling, hush!

MARY. Percy, have you never been haunted by the thought that *he* might still live?

PERCY. [*Decidedly*] Never! I tell you his death is almost certain. Four years and no word or sign from him. Four years since his ship was lost and never a soul left to tell the tale. There! There! Wait but the return of my messenger with the confirmation he is certain to bring, [*Cheerfully*] then for a quiet little marriage and I trust a long and happy life. [*Laughter outside L.C.*] Ah! Here are your eccentric friends, it will go hard if they do not bring the smiles back to your lips—I verily believe Miss Barton would chase away a fit of the blue imps itself. Ha! Ha! [*Exit through folding door R. At the same time enter C., from L., Hester, handsomely attired in what is supposed to be a stage dress, with a very long train, which is carried by Silas. He is in full evening dress, with very tight pantaloons. As Hester sees Mary, she makes a rush towards her. Silas, not starting quickly enough, almost falls, and the train comes off in his hands. Picture. Hester's dress is made so that it is complete even without the train, she does not know that it is off, but goes directly to Mary. Silas stands dismayed, looks at Hester, then at dress, tries to speak, his tongue cleaves to roof of his mouth. Keeps this business up just a moment. He must not over do this,—points to Hester, then to dress, then to himself in despair. A happy thought strikes him, he hastily folds up train, just then servant maid enters, down staircase, and crosses to R.C. He sees her, taps her on shoulder and presents her with train. She accepts, curtseys very low, he kisses her, she is pleased; curtseys again, he*] *bows, she exits. He comes down left, very highly pleased with himself as much as to say "I flatter myself that was decidedly neat." Meantime Hester has gone to Mary, shaken both hands, kissed her, and talks all through Silas' business*]

HES. Oh Mary! Ahem! I beg pardon, Mrs. Seward. [*Mary checks her*] Let me look at you. Well I declare if you ain't just beautiful—you look for all the world as if you were born here and had lived here all your life, and had never been within a thousand miles of old Gloucester.

MARY. Dear Old Gloucester, I fear I was happier there than I ever shall be here.

HES. Oh! How can you say so. For my part I hate the very name of the place. Paugh! I can smell it now.

SI. Kin ye? Well then ye've got a derned sight better smellin' factory than I hev, and I'm willin' to at that—I'd give suthin to jest poke my *oil* factory into Old Heminway's packin' shed this minit. [*Snuffs*] I jest love the smell. o' fish.

HES. I dare say,—you'd rather be stuck behind that dilapidated pill counter of yours, peddling blood root than gratifying a lofty ambition.

SI. Lofty ambition be blowed! Blood root is better than actin' enny day—blood root's ghost allus walks; that's one thing.

HES. Silas, that's a cowardly allusion to poor Mr. Lampey's misfortunes.

SI. I wish Mr. Lampey'd drink less and pay more salaries.

HES. [*To Mary*] You must know my dear that I'm Lampey's stock star now, and *such* a favorite. I have a carriage to and from—stop at all the best hotels.

SI. She don't know that I have to peddle appetite pills and corn salve on the Q.T. to pay the bills.

HES. And I *have* an *understudy*—and Silas, he's Juvenile Tragedy and leads the orchestra.

SI. [*Aside*] Orchestra! Clarionette and one fiddle.

HES. You just ought to see Silas play "Alonzo the Brave." Oh! my, but he is splendid and then at the end, in the great scene where he takes the poison, he crawls off L.H., in dying agony and plays the slow music to let the curtain down; he's great—Lampey says he's a better actor than Booth.

SI. I guess I am, but Booth gets more pay.

HES. Just play that poison scene for her Silas.

SI. I hain't got no pizen—'sides ef I fell deown in these ere pants, [*With significance*] I'd—well—ye'd have to ring deown that's all—

HES. Well then give a recitation.

SI. I hain't no good recitator.

Hes. You are, too.

Si. [*Yielding, wanting to be urged*] I *can't act.*

Hes. You can too.

Si. I tell ye I can't.

Hes. You can, too.

Si. Well I'll give you a recitation. [NOTE: *This must be delivered in dead earnest, with no attempt at burlesque except what the natural twang and character of the man gives it. Silas really thinks he's great*]

Mary and Hes. [*Clapping hands*] Bravo! Bravo!

Hes. Ain't he just splendid? I wish Mr. Field could hear him—he'd soon have Barron's place. Mary, why don't you go on the stage; Lampey could advertise you so now; you've got such notes. [*Sees that Mary is pained, checks herself*] No, I didn't mean that. [*Hastily changes the subject*] How do you like my dress?

Mary. It's beautiful, I'm sure.

Hes. Hain't too good, is it? [*Whispers*] It's one of my stage dresses—[*Laughs*] how do you like my train? [*Turning around*] Is it too long?

Si. Ahem! [*Begins to hum to himself and turns up stage*]

Mary. [*Not knowing anything about the train, thinking Hester joking, smiles*] Ah! no! I should say not a bit too long.

Si. [*Reassured*] No, I should say just about the right *lenth.*

Hes. But when is the dancing to begin! I love to dance.

Mary. [*Kissing her*] Hester dear, I believe you were born dancing and will leave this world singing your way into the next. [*Takes Hester's face between her hands and looks earnestly at her*] If there were only more like you, the world would be better for it; you are a ray of sunshine to me, so sing and dance to your heart's content: You merry—harmless—hopeful little cricket. [*Kisses her and exits R.*]

Hes. [*Who has been affected, looks after her, bursts into tears, crosses, throws herself on Silas' breast*] W-h-a-a-t—d-i-d—she—make me cry for?

Si. [*Wiping his eyes, in a hoarse whisper*] I don't know.

Hes. [*Drying her eyes*] I think it was real mean of her: Just as I wanted to look nice. Is my nose red?

Si. No, is mine?

Hes. No—wait—[*Takes powder, rag and small glass out of pocket, powders Silas' nose, then her own*] There now we are all right, let's go and find the company. [*Starts to go; waltz heard behind scenes; she stops*] Ah Silas, my waltz song. [*She listens, tries to restrain herself, but can't; gracefully begins to waltz and hum to herself. Silas does the same, and finally she seizes Silas and whirls him away in waltz. Waltz, song and dance by*

Silas and Hester. NOTE: *Very neat at the end, all the Guests waltz on through C. arches R.L.* NOTE: *If encore, guests waltz at back but do not sing. Hester utterly absorbed sees nothing—knows nothing. Mary enters R.H. takes her from Silas and they waltz off R. Waltz continued outside, Silas waltzes by himself. Miss Stanley enters R.C. from R., he waltzes against her*]

Si. Beg pardin'.

Miss S. Are you waiter here?

Si. Yes, been waitin' some time for the dancin' to begin.

Miss S. I don't mean that. How long have you been tender here. [*Inadvertently placing her hand over her heart*]

Si. [*Same business*] *Tender* here, wa'al I hain't been here long, but if you stand there looking at me that 'ere way—there's no knowing how tender I may git.

Miss S. Oh pshaw! I mean are you a hired domestic.

Si. *Me! No!* I'm one o' the company.

Miss S. I beg your pardon. [*Curtseys very low*]

Si. Don't mention it. [*Curtseys very absurdly*]

Miss S. I—dear me—how awkward—I—hope, [*Curtsying and getting toward C.R.*] You'll excuse—[*Exits, he following to entrance bowing and assuring her that there is no harm done; enter from C.L. Miss Fairchild, fanning herself, throws herself on ottoman L. quite exhausted*]

Miss F. Here—you! [*Silas, bowing after Miss S.*] Young man! [*He turns*]

Si. Mean me, Miss?

Miss F. Yes, get me a lemonade.

Si. Where'll I get it?

Miss F. On the sideboard there. Stupid! [*Points to R. arch*]

Si. In there?

Miss F. Yes—yes—be quick please.

Si. All right. [*Goes off, Miss Fairchild lies back and fans herself. Silas re-enters with lemonade with a straw in it*] Here ye are, Miss.

Miss F. Is it sweet?

Si. I guess so. [*Sucks through straw*] Yes, it's very sweet. [*Offers it*]

Miss F. You insolent—how dare—you—[*About to flounce off C.R., Silas following with lemonade*]

Si. Here's yer lemonade, don't you want it?

Miss F. I'll have you discharged for this. [*Exits very angry, C.R.*]

Si. Discharged! Goin' to tell Lampey on me, I don't care—this lemonade's all fired good though. [*Drinks it, places glass on stand L. Enter Miss Easter-*

brook C. from R. with wrap as if from garden; throws off wrap as she enters, sees Silas]

Miss E. Here young man, take this to the ladies' dressing room. [*Exits C.L.*]

Si. Ladies' dressin' room! [*Looks around, laughs*] Gosh! They won't let me into the Ladies' dressin' room. [*Same maid to whom he gave train now enters R. arch. Silas stops her, presents wrap;—same business as with train. She exits up staircase*] That's the second present I've gin that gal this evening, if I keep on she'll hev a regular Christmas. [*Enter all the guests R. and L.*]

Harry. Now then, partners and places for a quadrille.

Si. [*Calling him*] Mr.—[*Touching him on shoulder*] Mr.—

Harry. Merton, Sir.

Si. Merton sir—will you please to introduce me to a partner.

Harry. Certainly, your name?

Si. Cummins. Silas Cummins. [*During this time Miss Stanley, Miss Fairchild and Miss Easterbrook have been in the foreground, whispering and pointing to Silas. Miss Stanley is telling them that he is a guest; they laugh, blush, etc. Harry goes up to Miss Easterbrook, speaks to her, she assents, brings her down, etc., introduces her to Silas*]

Harry. Mr. Cummings, Miss Easterbrook. [*They bow, etc. Silas very awkwardly*]

Si. [*Aside*] That's the gal that gin me the shawl.

Miss E. Mr. Cummings, I believe I owe you an apology.

Si. Don't mention it. [*Aside*] I owe her a shawl.

Harry. All ready? [*Dance. This must be arranged to give Silas all the opportunity for fun; he must be careful not to exceed the bounds of propriety; at one portion of the dance, and at its end, Silas does some terrific leaps and steps; stops suddenly, all stop in amazement, he sides over to R.H.1E.*] What's the matter?

Si. Nothin' only you'll hev to excuse me, jist get some one else to take my place a minit. Will ye? [*At this a tall fat servant enters from L.1. Crosses to R.1E. Silas seizes him, whispers in his ear. He laughs and assents and exits R.1. as Silas sides off, keeping face towards company*] I knowed them blame trousers was too tight when I put 'em on. [*Exit R.1E. at same time servant enters R. arch*]

Servant. Supper. [*Music changes to march, all exit R.H. Music changes. Enter Jack L.C. gray hair, pale, aged, ill, but with an endeavor to present a cleanly appearance. He is clad in a sailor suit, very poor. At same time enter from R.1E. Mary and Hester. Mary now quite cheerful as through the influence of Hester*]

HES. [*Speaking as she enters*] My dear Mary what an elegant place you have here, to be sure; next to being on the stage, I know of nothing that would please me so well as living like this.

MARY. Ah, Hester dear, you must remember the old saw "All is not gold that glitters." [*By this time they have gotten quite close to Jack who has been staring at them. Mary, who has been looking squarely into Hester's face, and Hester into hers, now looks up and meets Jack's eyes*] Jack! [*Hester astonished, shrinks as if afraid*]

JACK. Yes.

MARY. [*Much moved*] We—[*Corrects herself*] I thought you dead.

JACK. The boon of death is not given to men like me.

MARY. Hester—run—keep—him—[*Corrects herself*] *Them* from coming here. [*Hester runs off R. arch*] What has brought you here?

JACK. To see you.

MARY. You have grown strangely considerate, after four years of silent absence.

JACK. After that fatal night four years ago—the night—that in my delirium—I—so far forgot myself as to—

MARY. [*As if ashamed to revert to it*] Hush!

JACK. Oh! Why was not my arm palsied first? I fled the cabin—and sought my refuge—the dram shop—I knew no more till I found myself at my old trade—bound on a fishing cruise aboard the "Sprite."

MARY. All this I know.

JACK. The "Sprite" was wrecked, as you must also know. All on board—save myself—went down. After sixty hours I was picked up by an outward bound brig—a trader in the China Seas. For weeks I lay between life and death—at last we were overhauled by a Chinese Pirate and I doomed to a living death—service aboard her. I escaped and I know not how I reached the old—old place; reached it to find the cabin ashes—you gone. To my inquiries I could only learn that you were in the city. I came here—watched—searched high and low—at last I bethought me of Mr. Seward and that possibly he could aid me—I inquired of a policeman where he could be found, "Why," said he, "there is his carriage now"—I looked, and in it saw you. You know the rest—they tell me you are—

MARY. [*Firmly, but not tauntingly*] I *am*—and who has made me what I am? [*He hangs his head*] Jack Hepburne—I loved you from the first hour in which I learned to lisp your name—I clambered upon your knees in childhood—walked hand in hand with you to church in girlhood, in maidenhood, watched, with tear dimmed eyes, each departing vessel as it bore you from me, and every night upon my knees sent forth the orphan's prayer to the

God of the fatherless for your speedy and safe return. At last what had been a seed—a blade—a leaf—a bud burst forth in blossom—and became a peerless flower—a priceless gem—a *woman's* pure and holy love—and *still* 'twas all your own—what did you with it? [NOTE: *this speech with all the firm decisive pathos possible, quiet but intensely strong*]

JACK. I know—I know—

MARY. [*Continuing*] After one year of bliss, the like of which my yearning soul never even pictured to itself—you forgot your promises—forgot your oath—cast aside my love and *became* a drunkard.

JACK. [*Groaning in shame*] Oh! My God! my God—

MARY. For still another year I bore it—I hoped against hope—I strove by every means in human power to save you—to reclaim you—to bring you back to manhood—and to self—in vain. Where I looked for loving words— I found neglect—where I sought happiness, I found poverty and despair. At last with my arms clasped fast about your neck in woman's weak endeavor to shield you from your demon—you struck me to your feet and fled—I who had loved you so—who became your wife—the mother of your child—

JACK. Enough! enough!

MARY. And now you seek me for what, to drag me back to the old life? *Never.* But do not think it is this luxury that binds me here—I would rather share one humble crust with Jack Hepburne than all the wealth a king could offer—but Jack Hepburne—*my* Jack Hepburne is dead—and I will not accept this semblance that has risen in his stead.

JACK. You wrong me, Mary—I do not come to ask you to share my lot— I have none to offer. The hospital and when strong enough, the sea is my only refuge now—I will not take from you the life within your grasp.

MARY. [*Struggling with her tears*] Ah! If you only knew.

JACK. But tell me, Mary, our child—our little Margaret—is she alive?

MARY. Yes.

JACK. [*Wiping eyes*] And well?

MARY. And well.

JACK. [*Almost afraid to ask*] Is—is—she here?

MARY. She is safe. Know that it is for her sake and hers alone that I am here—I would not have her meet my sad fate—and—so—[*Slowly almost vacantly*] I sold the mother to save the child.

JACK. [*With bowed head*] May—I—see her?

MARY. [*Looks at him almost as if she would go to him at this tearful request. He does not see the action, after an effort*] It is better not—the image of the father I have taught her to pray for night and morning is sacredly engraven on her young heart—best not destroy it—

JACK. Be it so—mother is I suppose—

MARY. Dead! Yes—her last thoughts were of you: Her last words "Jack!—poor Jack."

JACK. [*Raises his eyes to Heaven as if he saw her*] Mother! [*Breathes a silent prayer*] Well I will go now. Farewell.

MARY. [*Much moved*] Is there nothing I can do for you? Do you not need money?

JACK. [*Looks at her reproachfully*] Ah! Mary—not that—spare me that—no—not *his* money—[*Jack is going, Mary makes motion as if impelled to follow or stay him. At same time enter Mrs. Seward, Percy, R. and Hester backing on trying to stay them*]

HES. But I tell you, madam, she is not quite ready yet; I assure you I will bring her, I beg of you to return to the guests.

MRS. S. Nonsense child, I will know what detains my daughter; when courtesy demands her presence amongst her guests. [*Sees Jack*] Mercy on us, what is this!

PERCY. [*Aside startled*] He here!

HES. Now for the fifth act.

Mrs. S.

Percy

Hester   Jack

Mary

R.   L.

MRS. S. [*Sees the picture of alarm on all faces and suspects something wrong*] Who are you, sir? [*To Jack*]

JACK. A shipwrecked sailor.

MRS. S. What seek you here?

JACK. [*With meaning*] Charity!

MRS. S. Do you know this woman? [*Points to Mary*]

PERCY. Mother!

MRS. S. Silence! [*Repeating question*] Do you know this woman?

JACK. [*Raises head slowly, looks at Mary, deep struggle*] No. [*Percy breathes a long breath of relief. Mary makes no movement*]

MRS. S. Then leave this apartment—go below; the servants will see that your wants are met. How dare you intrude your presence here? [*Jack bows, silently turns to go, at same time little Margaret runs on from first entrance L. with doll, and runs directly to Mary*]

LITTLE M. Oh! Mama! See what a beautiful dress Louise has made for my doll. [*At the sound of her voice Jack stops at the word "mama." Unable to restrain himself he shrieks*]

JACK. My child! [*Checks himself, but sees it is too late. He is dazed. A picture of dismay on all faces, except Mary's, who has made no movement during scene; and Mrs. Seward's, who wears the expression of wounded pride*]

MRS. S. His child. Percy what is the meaning of this? [*All the guests quietly enter from R. Silas with large pantaloons enters R.1. Hester goes down to him, she is explaining in dumb show*]

PERCY. I cannot answer.

MRS. S. [*To Mary*] Speak you, madam, who is this man?

MARY. [*Calmly*] My husband.

MRS. S. [*To Percy*] And you have dared to insult me thus—

PERCY. Mother, hear me.

MRS. S. Silence! As for you madam—I—pity you—but—leave—my house —go—[*Mary makes no motion, slowly crosses, leading her child; she offers her hand, Jack takes it in act of moving off, Hester and Silas following*]

Guests			Servants
	Percy	Mrs. S.	
			Mary Jack
Silas			Little Margaret

ACT IV.

SCENE 1: *Garret in North End, very squalid; bed, wooden table and one chair, old stove in fireplace, no fire; door L., boxing attic window R.F., candle in old candlestick lighted on table. Backing, a dirty hall in tenement house.*

window		
	table	door
stove		
		chair
bed		

Little Margaret discovered in bed, Mary kneeling beside her. Mary is very poorly dressed, pale and thin. Jack enters slowly and despondently. Mary who has been intently listening to baby's breathing hears him, and motions to him to make no noise. He enters on tip-toe; he is very pale and haggard.

MARY. Hush! Step lightly, she is asleep. Well! [*Spoken in hoarse whisper*]

JACK. [*Despairingly, shaking head*] Nothing, no work, no bread.

MARY. Did you go to him?

JACK. Yes: Even to him. His mother has sent him abroad; she is pitiless. How is baby?

MARY. Worse Jack, I fear she is starving.

JACK. Starving! No! No! Not that, [*wild*] it cannot be—it shall not be—by God! I'll tear food from their—

MARY. [*Staying him*] Hush.

LITTLE M. [*Faintly*] Mama!

MARY. [*Goes quickly to her*] Yes, my darling.

LITTLE M. I'm *so* hungry. Are you hungry, mama?

MARY. [*Almost choking, Jack stands, wild*] No, my darling.

LITTLE M. It's dreadful to be hungry, ain't it, mama?

MARY [*Rushing to Jack, hoarsely but furiously*] Do you hear, Jack? Go, beg, steal, *murder,* but bring food to my starving child.

JACK. [*Desperately*] I will. [*Rushes out*]

LITTLE M. Mama. [*Mary goes to her*]

MARY. My baby.

LITTLE M. Is papa gone?

MARY. Yes dear, he has gone to get bread for my baby.

LITTLE M. Will he come back soon?

MARY. Yes dear, very soon.

LITTLE M. Oh! mama, I had such a beautiful dream.

MARY. Did you dear?

LITTLE M. Would you like to hear it?

MARY. Yes darling, tell mama your little dream.

LITTLE M. I dreamed that papa had never gone away, that we were all back in our own beautiful home; not that great big home, but our own little home by the bright, blue sea.

MARY. Yes, dear.

LITTLE M. And gran'ma was there, not that grand gran'ma, but my own beautiful gran'ma; and we were all *so* happy, and we went down to the sea and watched the ships sailing up and down, and they looked like great, white birds floating on the water.

MARY. Yes, dear.

LITTLE M. And the sea was so still and bright, and the sun so shiny and warm, and the sky was so blue; and pretty soon there came a great black cloud, and the sun went *out.*

MARY. My baby!

LITTLE M. And the sea began to roar, and the big waves threw the poor ships clear away up to the sky almost. And ah! such a dreadful storm as I never saw before.

MARY. Was my baby frightened?

LITTLE M. Ah! Yes mama, so frightened.

MARY. It was only a dream, my darling.

LITTLE M. I know mama, but it frightened me all the same, but the storm didn't stay long.

MARY. Didn't it, dear?

LITTLE M. No mama, it went away, and the sea got still again, and pretty soon I looked up and I saw such a beautiful ship, all gold and silver, coming right to us, and it came and took you and papa and gran'ma and me and dolly, and sailed away to the most beautiful land. It seemed like the fairy land you used to read to me about, and ah! mama, look! [*Raising up in bed; Mary holds her*] The ship—call papa—quick.

MARY. There is no ship darling, you are dreaming still.

LITTLE M. No mama, there—don't you see? Look! the angels, sailing over it, they're calling us mama. Come! [*She gets up in bed. Mary holds her and tries to calm her*]

MARY. There, there, my child, lie down. [*Almost frantic, she realizes that death has come, but dare not give way*]

LITTLE M. Don't you hear mama? They are calling you too. Come mama, or the beautiful ship will be gone. Quick! [*Makes a step*] Ah mama, [*Crying*] give me your hand, it's all dark now; I can't see the ship, it's all dark. Where are you, mama?

MARY. [*Holding her in her arms*] Here darling, here.

LITTLE M. Kiss me, mama. I wish papa would come, will he know that the ship took you and me? There it is again, I'm coming, I—goodbye papa, come mama, come! see! I—[*She dies. Mary lays her down, closes her eyes, takes her hand and hides her own head in the bed clothes. The door bursts open. Jack enters, followed by Hester and Silas, he is laden with food*]

JACK. See! Mary! *food! food!* at last.

MARY. Too late, Jack, she's dead. [*Jack drops food, stands transfixed, Hester and Silas get around to R. of bed*]

HES. Mary—see—we've found you at last.

MARY. Oh! Hester—she's gone—my beautiful baby, my little Margaret's gone—see—isn't she beautiful? See the smile upon her lips—she is waiting for me—she wants her mother. Yes—baby—I'll come to you—Jack—[*Half turning to Jack*]—I love you Jack—I forgive and love you—but I cannot stay —I must go with baby—don't blame me—and don't mourn, it was to be.

You remember the storm on our wedding day—well it has ended at last—don't drink Jack! Be brave—be my old, old Jack once more. Goodbye, Hester, dear kind Hester and Silas too. Ah Silas! I'll never ride Deuteronomy again. [*As if to baby*] Yes, yes I'm coming, good—bye—I'm coming. [*She turns and quietly dies, with her back against the bed and her head on the child's body*]

HES.   Jack—Jack—she's dead!

JACK. [*Who has not moved, stares wildly around and sees Mary's body and goes to her*] Why Mary girl, what is the matter with you, child? Oh I see—well—well—I'll not go out tonight; let the watch go. Come let's fill the stockin's, perhaps in a year there may be another stockin' hangin' here. Ha! ha! ha! there Caesar, you stop here with them—Mary be sure you keep askin' me the time o' day. Ha! ha! ha! Why, what place is this? I won't stay here, come Mary, let's go. [*He lifts her and supports her in his arms; her dead body is limp, but he is strong*] Let's go home, back to the old home in Gloucester—[*Kisses her*] Poor child—I have so loved—so wronged you. But I'll make amends—I'll drink no more, come. Mother, be sure you put plenty of onions in the stuffin'—Mother—see—here's Mary—she's not well, poor girl—quick, food. She's starvin', I tell you—come Mary, we'll go home—home—home—[*Moving towards door with dead body of Mary, Hester and Silas horrified but unable to stay him*]

PICTURE AND CURTAIN

ACT V.

SCENE: *Christmas Morning.*

MUSIC: *Same as Act II—early morning, the table cleared away, the shutters open and the sun streaming in. Holly wreaths hanging on each end of mother's picture, one on Mary's, one on Jack's: Holly branches over window and mantel; stockings filled. Mother discovered knitting by fire, Mary cutting dress, dog and cat on hearth; Jack asleep, as he had fallen. Sleigh bells heard in distance before curtain goes up and all through scene. Music kept up till Jack's scene well on.*

JACK. [*In his sleep*]   No—no—you shall not tear her away from me—I tell you she is not dead—let her go—[*Furiously*] I tell you let her go—I—do you hear? [*Springs up*] Let her go. [*Mary has stopped work at his first ravings and comes down L. as he gets C.*] Let her go—I'll brain the first man who—[*He sees Mary, then Margaret, then mother*] Mary, mother—[*With a wild *cry*] A dream! Thank God! A dream! [*Falls sobbing hysterically at his mother's knees*]

MARY. Why Jack, what ever has come over you?

JACK. [*Jumps up, takes her to his breast*] Ah! Mary, Mary, I've had such a horrid dream—but you're not dead, [*Almost smothering her with kisses*] and mother's not dead—and the bab—

MARY. Hush Jack, all in good time, Heaven willing. [*Taking off Jack's heavy coat, hanging it up. Christmas carol in distance*]

JACK. [*Catching her as she comes down and kissing her*] But you're sure you're not dead, Mary?

MARY. [*Smiling*] Quite sure Jack.

JACK. And mother—bless her dear old face. Are you quite sure you're not dead, mother?

MARG. I'm worth a dozen dead women yet, Jack. [*Jack kisses her*]

JACK. Ah Mary! I have had such a dream, but it's a lesson to me. [*Seriously*] Mary! will you trust poor Jack once more?

MARY. With all my heart—I trust you as I love you Jack.

JACK. [*Seriously*] I'll never break my word again—I swear it on the "Rock of Ages." [*Christmas carol has come nearer and nearer, finishes now; and Hester, Silas and fishermen and village girls all in holiday attire burst in with—*]

OMNES. Merry Christmas! Merry Christmas.

JACK. Merry Christmas! Merry Christmas.

MARY. Merry Christmas! Merry Christmas!

MARG. Merry Christmas! [*Mary and Hester kiss, Hester kisses Margaret. Silas goes down L. and shakes hands with Jack*] What time is it Jack?

JACK. Ah Silas! I've had such a dreadful dream.

SI. Hev ye, a few appetite pills or a little blood root'll cure them. [*Sleigh bells very heavy have approached door. The driver says "whoa!" Noise of stopping sleigh; enter Percy well wrapped and all smiles*]

PERCY. Merry Christmas to you all.

MARY. Thank you, Mr. Seward, the same to you and many of them. [*Silas goes up, Percy comes down, at the sound of his voice Jack starts as if he could not realize*]

PERCY. [*Giving hand*] Merry Christmas, Mr. Hepburne.

JACK. [*Sternly*] The last time I see you—you was—[*Checks himself, grasps hand heartily*] A thousand of 'em, sir, and there ain't no man that I'm gladder to see here this day than you.

PERCY. Thank you, and now my friends I have a proposition to make—I have outside a sleigh and six prancing horses—

SI.   I hope they hain't Lampey's six snow white Arabians.

PERCY.   The sleigh will just hold this party, so I invite you all to a jolly sleigh ride, a good old fashioned Christmas dinner, and a visit to Lampey's to do honor to our fair debutante and finish up the festivities in the evening. What say you?

ALL.   Yes, yes, three cheers for Mr. Seward, the Fisherman's Santa Claus. Huzza—huzza—huzza—

PERCY.   And long life and happiness to Jack Hepburne and Mary the
FISHERMEN'S CHILD.

[*Song. "Turn your glasses upside down"—temperance song and chorus to be written—song with inverted glasses. Picture*]

Mary			group at
Mother	Percy		back
Jack			Silas
			Hester

END OF PLAY

THE REVEREND GRIFFITH DAVENPORT

CAST OF CHARACTERS

Lafayette Square Theatre, Washington, D.C., January 16, 1899[1]

"Engagement of the Eminent Character Actor
JAMES A. HERNE
and production of his Latest American Play, entitled
REV. GRIFFITH DAVENPORT
(Circuit Preacher)
Founded on Helen H. Gardener's novel "An Unofficial Patriot."

ACT I.

GRIFFITH DAVENPORT		MR. JAMES A. HERNE
BEVERLY DAVENPORT	*his sons*	MR. SYDNEY BOOTH
ROY DAVENPORT		MR. BERT YOUNG
COLONEL ARMOUR, *a lawyer*		MR. NEWTON CHISNELL
HAMILTON BRADLEY		MR. FRANK M. CORNELL
SQUIRE NELSON		MR. LOGAN PAUL
LENGTHY PATTERSON		MR. ROBERT FISCHER
UNCLE NED	*slaves of the Davenports*	MR. LAWRENCE MERTON
PETE		MR. JOSEPH H. HAZLETON
JOHN, *property of Mr. Bradley*		MR. JOHN W. BANKSON
FREE JIM, *a free nigger*		MR. H. G. CARLETON
FREE JIM'S BOY		MASTER KENNETH BARNES
JACK, *a recent purchase of Mr. Nelson*		MR. E. P. SULLIVAN
KATHARINE DAVENPORT		MRS. HERNE
EMMA WEST, *a young Tennessean*		MISS JULIE A. HERNE

[1] This cast is derived from a program of February 13, 1899, at the Herald Square Theatre, New York. Miss Herne assures me, however, that there were no changes.

SUE HARDY, *a young Virginian*   MISS CHRYSTAL HERNE

LITTLE MARGARET, *Davenport's daughter*   GERTRUDE NELSON

SALLIE, *private property of Mrs. Davenport, and married to Mr. Bradley's John*   MISS HELEN ROBERTSON

MAMMY, *Margaret's nurse*   MISS MOLLIE REVEL

AUNT JUDY   MISS SADIE STRINGHAM

TILLY, *the cook*   MISS LUCY NELSON

DINAH   MISS DOROTHY THORNTON

LIPPY JANE   MISS RACHEL BLAKE

THE TWINS, *children of Pete and Tilly*   BY THE TWINS

SALLIE'S BABY   BY HERSELF

ACTS II AND III.

MAJOR HARDY, *father of Sue*   MR. THOMAS M. HUNTER

LEADER OF THE HORSEMEN   MR. H. G. CARLETON

And all of the characters of Act I excepting Free Jim and his son.

ACT IV.

OLIVER P. MORTON, *Governor of Indiana*   MR. WARREN CONLAN

And Griffith Davenport, Roy Davenport, Katharine Davenport, Pete, Uncle Ned, Mammy, Sallie, Aunt Judy, Tilly and little Margaret.

ACT V.

GENERAL LAMOINE, *U.S.A.*   MR. T. C. HAMILTON

SURGEON U.S.A.   MR. FRED JEROME

MAJOR HUNTER, *Chief of Engineer Corps*   MR. PIERRE YOUNG

ORDERLY   MR. ROWLAND EDWARDS

SERGEANT MORRIS   MR. C. C. QUIMBY

PRIVATE BATES	MR. THOMAS INCE
PRIVATE HOEY	MR. ROBERT GRAY
PRIVATE LANG	MR. GEORGE CULVER
PRIVATE STEVENS	MR. J. HANCOCK HERVEY
PRIVATE ALBERTS	MR. HOWARD RALEIGH
MR. MONROE ⎫ *two old Virginians*	MR. JOHN W. BANKSON
MR. SUTTON ⎭	MR. J. B. EARLY
A CONFEDERATE'S WIDOW	MISS SUSAN GOOLD
HER MOTHER	MRS. ISABELLA PRESTON
AN OLD SOUTHERN WOMAN	MRS. ROSE ATKINS

And Griffith Davenport, Beverly Davenport (now a Confederate captain), Bradley (now a Confederate lieutenant), Major Hardy, Lengthy Patterson, Katharine Davenport and Sue.

ACT I.—VIRGINIA, APRIL 1860.
"COMING EVENTS CAST THEIR SHADOWS"

ACT II.—VIRGINIA, MAY 1860.
THE NOMINATION OF ABRAHAM LINCOLN

ACT III.—VIRGINIA, NOVEMBER 1860.
THE ELECTION OF ABRAHAM LINCOLN

ACT IV.—WASHINGTON, MARCH 1862.
AN UNOFFICIAL PATRIOT

ACT V.—VIRGINIA, APRIL 1864.
FIRST SCENE—THE SHENANDOAH VALLEY. SECOND SCENE—THE NEXT EVENING.

SYNOPSIS OF SCENERY

ACT I. HOUSE AND GROUNDS OF THE DAVENPORTS IN VIRGINIA.

ACT II. AND III. GRIFFITH DAVENPORT'S STUDY AND LIBRARY.

THERE WILL BE AN INTERMISSION OF FOUR MINUTES ONLY BETWEEN ACTS II. AND III.

ACT IV. A ROOM IN THE DAVENPORTS' WASHINGTON HOME. TIME: MARCH 1862.

ACT V. IN THE VALLEY OF THE SHENANDOAH.

THE REVEREND GRIFFITH DAVENPORT

THE scenes of *Griffith Davenport* are laid in Virginia and in Washington, D.C., before and during the Civil War. Griffith Davenport is a Methodist circuit rider, who naturally has learned to know the roads in Virginia. He is a member of an old Virginia family and his communings with God and with nature have deepened the mysticism natural to him. He is opposed to slavery, but he owns a large plantation and a number of slaves, to which are added those that his wife, Katharine, brings him at their marriage. The conflict between them begins at this point for she can see nothing wrong in slavery. In the novel on which the play was based both sons of Griffith Davenport had been Union men, but in the play the eldest son, Beverly, is made a Confederate and Roy, the younger, enters the Union Army. This change adds to the conflict and the drama.

The first act shows the garden of the Davenport estate, with its iron gates, and on one side, the entrance to the fine old mansion. It is a scene of happiness, prosperity and peace. The negro servants, Judy, Pete and others, amble in and out, going about their household tasks in their lazy, easygoing, good-natured fashion, showing the almost ideal conditions under which they live. Most of them have grown up with "Marse and Mis'" and are indulged like a lot of children. They are merry, happy and devoted. Then enters Sally, Katharine's personal maid. She is in a state of helpless misery. She tells the others that the Davenports' neighbor, "Marse Bradley," is forced to sell his coachman, her husband John. If "Marse Grif" won't buy John, it means separation. And Sally and John have a little baby. A hush falls on the other servants as they listen to her. Then they comfort her. *Of course* "Marse Grif" will buy John.

A diversion is caused when the family nurse appears, searching for little Margaret, the Davenports' youngest child, who has run away. She is presently found and returned to her home by Free Jim's boy, the son of an outcast "free nigger," who lives with his father in a wretched cabin on a nearby marsh. When the poor little fellow appears with Margaret, he is almost mobbed by the infuriated Davenport slaves. In their eyes a freed negro, " 'thout no fam'ly nor nothin' " is the most despicable of all creatures, fit only for hatred and contempt. They surround the boy, reviling him, until his father, a huge savage in rags enters. With a simple, tragic dignity, he obliges the slaves to fall back, and carries off his boy.

Now another planter, Nelson, comes, and demands to see Griffith. This man is a stern and cruel taskmaster, and his slaves are overworked and rebellious. One of them, Sampson, has tried to run away, and Nelson has handcuffed him to another slave to prevent a second escape. He shows him now to the shocked and horrified Davenport, and tells Griffith that the easygoing ways of his own slaves are corrupting Nelson's establishment. He angrily requests Griffith to keep his "niggers" off the Nelson place. Sampson attempts to justify his action by pleading that he has always been a coachman, and cannot endure the hard labor in the fields which Nelson forces upon him. He begs to be allowed to return to the stables, but Nelson, obdurate, marches him away with an oath.

This scene deeply affects Griffith, and he has hardly recovered from it when Bradley, his neighbor, and John's owner arrives, and pleads with Griffith to buy John, whom he is forced, through gambling debts, to sell, so that husband and wife need not be separated. Katharine too, comes, to add her plea for the almost frantic Sally. But Griffith reminds her of his old resolution, never to buy or sell a human being. Bradley attempts to argue with him. To him, Griffith seems almost a fanatic. Even Katharine is hurt by his seeming hardness. But when Sally herself begs pitifully for her husband, and implores Griffith to buy him for her baby's sake, the man's big heart cannot hold out. He sacrifices his own conviction and buys John. To the others, it seems only that he is making a humanitarian concession. But in his own soul it brings about a climax. Slavery is no longer endurable. He will end it, so far as lies in his power. He will free his own slaves, and if she consents, those of his wife.

He talks it over with Katharine, and she, only half understanding the ethics of the question, but full of faith and love for him, consents. She has long felt that Griffith was not all hers. If it is this question of owning slaves that is dividing them, then, the slaves must be freed.

Act II takes place a few weeks later, in the stately drawing-room, on the evening upon which this momentous decision is to become a fact. Griffith has been to the city, and has returned with the manumission papers. Beverly, his older son, is infuriated at his father's action. He protests to his brother Roy, who sides with his father, and the two boys have their first real disagreement. Beverly feels this division in the family is ominous of larger issues.

"Roy, if this thing ever comes to a war between the North and the South, which side are you going to fight on?"

"On my side," replies Roy, laughing.

Beverly looks at him thoughtfully. "Roy, if I ever met you in a battle, I believe I'd kill you quicker than I would a real Yankee."

Roy takes a deep breath, and then, "I'm sorry, Bev," he says, "but I'm afraid I'll have to give you the chance!"

Presently Griffith assembles his household to hear the momentous announcement. A few curious neighbors are present to witness the strange proceeding. They are all dubious and disapproving, but Griffith is beaming, Katharine reflects his happiness, and Roy is bursting with pride in his father. Only Beverly remains apart. In troop the happy servants, singing and laughing in the anticipation of some sort of treat, for "Marse Grif" always brings them presents when he comes from town. They are counting on tobacco and new calico. And then Griffith Davenport makes them a little speech and shows them some papers. He tells them they are manumission papers, and that now everybody is free. But they do not understand him. They regard him stupidly, wistfully, like a lot of disappointed children. Griffith turns helplessly to his wife, and she tries to explain.

"You're free—you don't belong to us any more," she says.

There is a wail of protest. They, "free niggahs!" They, "not belong to nobody!" They repudiate the idea indignantly. Their pride as members of the family is deeply injured. It is all so different from what Davenport expected.

Suddenly Nelson's big Negro, Sampson, bursts into the room, a broken chain dangling from his ankle, a pruning knife in his hand. He has made another attempt to escape. But Nelson, with dogs and men is at his heels. Without even an apology to Mrs. Davenport Nelson rushes in, and orders his men to take Sampson. The men make a lunge, but Sampson holds up his knife. "Ef you come neah me I'll cut mah throat," he said quietly. Griffith, aghast, is impelled to cry, "I'll buy him from you, Nelson!" "I won't sell him!" replies the infuriated Nelson, and makes a move towards Sampson. But the Negro, with a quick movement, plunges the knife into his throat and falls dead before them all. There is a wail of horror from the assembled Negroes. Nelson gives Sampson's body a kick and says, "There goes fifteen hundred dollars!" Then bitterly to Davenport, "This is what your damn anti-slavery theories have come to!" Griffith stands dazed and speechless, and Katharine sinks beside him in a dead faint. Nelson's bitterness towards Davenport gradually communicates itself to the entire countryside, and his old friends and neighbors begin to view Griffith with hatred and alarm. Outwardly, though, all is calm, and life in the Davenport household runs on as before.

Act III shows the Davenport drawing-room on the evening of the Presidential election. The family is gathering for supper when Griffith returns from the polls and announces that he has cast his vote for Abraham Lincoln. Lengthy Patterson, a tall mountaineer, Griffith's devoted follower, appears and asks in his laconic fashion, "Kin I stay here tonight?" They gladly invite him to do so. He stands guard in the drawing-room while the unsuspecting family is at supper. Lengthy has heard that something is in the wind, and presently a mob of angry men storms the house and march into the room. Lengthy bars their way. The family hurries in from the dining-room. Nelson, who is in command, tells Davenport that his voting for Lincoln is the last straw, and commands him to quit the state. Griffith refuses. Someone threatens to burn the house over his head. Katharine says with quiet, bitter dignity, "We will go." A dusty rider hurries in. "Gentlemen," he cries breathlessly, "There is a possibility that Lincoln may be elected!" A groan goes up. The news seems to stun the men. They depart quietly.

Driven from his home, and persecuted for his opinions, something of the martyr's fervor seems now to seize upon Griffith. He gathers his little family about him and prays fervently to God for help and guidance in the new life which they must face, and for the safety of his beloved country in the hour of trial which he foresees must descend upon her.

In the novel Davenport went to Indiana after a brief stay in Washington. For the sake of unity Herne kept the scene of Act IV, here printed, in Washington. In the novel and in the first form of the play Lincoln had sent for Davenport and personally asked him to guide the Union forces through Virginia. This scene, while well written, seemed to be ineffective when the play was in its early rehearsals and then Mrs. Herne, who acted Katharine, saw the difficulty. It was an error in technique to bring to the most important scene a character who overshadowed the hero. Lincoln at once dominated the scene and reduced Griffith Davenport to a secondary position. It was therefore decided to indicate his influence through Governor Morton of Indiana, who as a matter of fact in real life had persuaded the father of the author of the novel to enter the service.

There are two scenes in Act V, in the first of which Griffith Davenport leads the Union troops through his native country until they approach his own home, when he declines to go further. In the play he is captured by the Confederates under his own son, Beverly, and is accused of being a spy. He is, however, searched and his commission being found on him, he becomes a prisoner of war. He is allowed to speak to Katharine before he is taken to prison and the play ends with husband and wife sitting together on the steps of the porch in the moonlight, renewing their vows of love and faith. Katharine asks him to sing an old song of their courtship days, and he begins: "Oh, if I were king of France—" as the curtain falls.

ACT IV.

"All quiet on the Potomac"

SCENE 1: *Interior of a room in a house in the suburbs of Washington in 1862. The house is on a supposed elevation and through the window—a large square old-fashioned window—in the center may be seen—over the landscape—the White House—and Washington Monument. There is real glass in the window panes—it is a regular March day—rain and sleet beat on the panes at intervals—the room is a sort of study, library and office combined—one or two of the most prominent pieces of furniture were seen in Act III in Virginia— but in the main the furniture is different, colder, more modern—the atmosphere of the place differs from that of the Virginia home.* [NOTE: *the Washington Monument was only partially built in '62.*] *During the entire act there is heard at intervals drum corps, bands, and the noise and movement of marching men—very distant—to suggest war times in Washington in '62. All trimmings are gloss white and ornamented.*

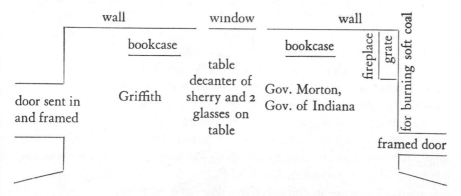

A fine large engraving of Mr. Lincoln—in 1861—in a plain walnut frame must hang so as to be seen by entire audience [NOTE: *Governor Morton must show that the first part of this scene has no interest for him, that he is here upon an important and delicate mission, and that he is puzzled just how to lead up to it successfully, but after he has led up to it he becomes very earnest.*]

Gov. M. [*Abstractedly*] So you've quite settled down here, eh Davenport?

Grif. [*Griffith is smoking and talks and stops and talks to show that he and Morton are intimate and stand upon no ceremony with each other*] Yes —my congregation is poor—my salary small, but I manage to make both ends meet.

Gov. M. [Let's] see, what is your church?

Grif. Calvary—Uncle Ned calls it "De Cavalry." [*Laughs. Morton laughs mechanically. Note: Little Margaret runs on from L. door laughing and jumping on her father's knee—he helps her up—but pays no particular attention to her. Mammy follows her on*]

Mammy. [*In loud whisper*] Heah, heah! [*Laughing*] Yo' paw doan wan fo' to be boddered wif yo' now—yo' come along o' yo' Mammy. [*Carries the child off*]

Gov. M. [*Gets up as child enters, talks through Mammy's scene*] Methodist of course.

Grif. [*Laughs*] Ah! Of course.

Gov. M. [*Walks up and down, stops occasionally—sometimes with his back to audience and talks*] Pity you couldn't have seen your way to taking the position I got for you—Indiana is getting to be a big state—and Professor of Theology at Asbury Institute is a fine position. The College is second to none in the country—and Greencastle is a very pleasant place to live.

Grif. [*Walks*] Yes, I know—but when I found that I couldn't take my black people into the state—not even as hired help, in my own house—I— kind of—[*Winks eye and shakes head*] and then I don't believe Katharine would ever have been satisfied to live so far North.

Gov. M. [*Stops and shows a little more interest*] I never knew a thing about that law in our state—until you brought it to my notice. I don't believe there's a half dozen men in the state who know it now.

Grif. Well, it's there just the same. It's more than a law—it's part of your Constitution. Your Constitution distinctly forbids any person to bring a free nigger into the state of Indiana—that is to live there. I presume it was done to protect labor in your state, I reckon!

Gov. M. I suppose so. Silly though—don't you think so?

Grif. I certainly do. [*Enter Sallie*]

Sal. Mas Grif—Cain Pete an Uncle Naid speak wid yo' fo' a minute?

Grif. Certainly. [*Griffith Davenport, Katharine Davenport, and Roy speak with a Southern accent. Sallie exits leaving the door open—the Parrot of Act I walks in—Judy follows. As Parrot enters, Governor Morton is slightly amused—stops—leans against a table or sits on arm of chair and listens*]

Judy. [*To Parrot*]   Yere—yo' walk yo'se'f outen yere. [*Laughs*] 'Scuse me, Mas Grif—but dis yeah bird—thinks he own dis house, des as ef he was in ol Virginny! [*Catches Parrot*] Come outen yere—What yo' wan' to do—study one o' Mas Grif sahmons? [*Laughs and talks herself off. Pete and Ned have entered in the meantime. Pete is all covered with lime—like a whitewasher. Ned is still a general servant*]

Grif.   Well, boys—what is it?

Pete. [*Grinning*]   Mas Grif, has yo' got change fo' dis yere shin-plaistah? [*Handing him a fifty-cent note*] Ah done got a job a-whitewashin'—and de lady gimme two dollahs. [*Has fifty-cent notes*] Uncle Naid he say he got ter hab a levee on a fip—an'

Grif. [*Giving him the change in two notes*]   What for?

Uncle Ned. [*Stammers*]   'Twas jes dis way, Mas Grif—Ah was a-comin' home from de market—day fo' yesaday—a—a—an a lady axes me ef Ah cain git her a boy fo' to whitewash—an—an—Ah tole her Ah could—an Ah s—s—sent Pete dar—das dess de whole trufe, Mas Grif.

Grif.   I think Uncle Ned is entitled to his commission, Pete. I'd give him a quarter if I were you. It will encourage him.

Pete. [*Grinning*]   Yes sah—all right—Ah des wan'ed to know—dat's all, [*Gives Ned one note*] kase Ah done all de wuk. [*They are going out when Tilly, who has been in the doorway, stops Pete*]

Tilly. [*To Pete*]   Heah—yo' gimme dem shin-plaistahs. I'll take car ob dem. [*Pete gives them to her ruefully and they all exit*] They won't buhn no hole in mah pocket!

Gov. M. [*Seating himself in his own chair. Laughing*]   Do you have much of that to do?

Grif. [*Laughing*]   Yes, sir! Yes, that's one of my perquisites. [*Laughs*]

Gov. M.   You took a pretty big contract when you undertook to free 'em all down there—didn't you?

Grif.   Yes, I freed the slaves—and now I own a lot of free niggers! [*Laughs*]

Gov. M.   Why don't you hire 'em out and make 'em earn their own living?

Grif. [*Cheerily*]   The young ones do in a measure—but the old ones own us—we never did own them—they think we'd go to the dogs if they left us—they're just like a lot of children. [*Laughs*]

Gov. M. [*Getting up*]   I suppose it'll take 'em some time to adapt themselves to the new condition.

Grif.   A generation or two, I reckon.

Gov. M. [*Going to window*]   Reg'lar March day!

GRIF. [*Cheerily*]   Yes—He's come in like a sure enough lion this time! [*Laughs*] But that's no reason you should keep walking about the room as if to keep warm. Isn't the room comfortable?

Gov. M. [*Quickly*]   Ah yes! Perfectly so—but I'm nervous today—I can't sit still. [*Coming down a little*]

GRIF.   Got something on your mind?

Gov. M.   Yes. Men in public office in time of war have always something on their minds.

GRIF.   Come here and sit down—and enjoy your cigar—and tell me all about it—perhaps I can help you out. [*Lighting his cigar which has gone out*] There are two things in this world I really enjoy—a fine horse and a fine cigar!

Gov. M.   Davenport, you can help me. And you are the only man who can. I've got an order to deliver and it is a very delicate one and I don't know just how it is going to be received. It may cost me the friendship of the man I must deliver it to.

GRIF.   Why don't you mail it with a fine letter?

Gov. M. [*Getting up and going to window*]   That won't do. It is from the President—it is confidential and it is to one of my very dear friends and I am ordered to deliver it in person.

GRIF.   From the President? I—I see nothing to do but to deliver it.

Gov. M. [*With his face to the window and his back directly on Griffith*] Did you ever see Mr. Lincoln?

GRIF.   Ah yes. I meet him occasionally.

Gov. M.   What do you think of him?

GRIF. [*Smiling*]   What a question—you know perfectly well what I think of Abraham Lincoln!

Gov. M. [*Turning around*]   He's a great man, isn't he?

GRIF. [*Writing*]   I thought so when I voted for him—I know so now.

Gov. M. [*Half to himself*]   Yes—he's a v-e-r-y g-r-e-a-t man—the South didn't know him or she never would have seceded—doesn't know him yet. [*Coming down*] Did you ever talk with him?

GRIF. [*Astonished*]   Gracious—no! He don't know me.

Gov. M. [*Sitting in his chair*]   Ah, yes he does! I've told him all about you —he's very much interested in you.

GRIF.   That was kind of you and it's good in him—but I can't see what interest the President of the United States can have in a simple citizen like me.

Gov. M. [*Takes his cigar out of his mouth*]   He wants to see you. He sent me to fetch you. [*Rises*] Come—I'll introduce you to him.

GRIF. [*Carelessly*]   What does he want to see me for?

Gov. M. He wants to offer you a position he has vacant.

GRIF. [*Cheerfully*] I don't want any position—I'm not in the political market.

Gov. M. It's not a political position—it's a military one.

GRIF. [*Smiling*] I'm not a soldier—I don't know a thing about—

Gov. M. Come along and see Mr. Lincoln—and let him explain himself—he may—

GRIF. I'll do that. I shall be very glad to meet Mr. Lincoln—but I don't want any position. [*Rises*] I'm satisfied as I am. [*Enter Roy in uniform of 2nd. Lieut. cavalry*]

Roy. [*Breathlessly*] Where is mother? [*Touches cap to Governor Morton. The Governor returns salute*] Morning, Governor!

Griffith   Gov. M.

Roy

GRIF. [*Putting table to rights. Without turning points to L.H. door*] Yonder, I reckon. [*To Governor Morton*] Yes, it's—

Roy. Well, father, I've done it!

GRIF. Done what? [*Sees him*] Enlisted!

Roy. Yes—19th Indiana—we are to join Grant in the West.

GRIF. [*To Governor Morton*] You knew this? [*Governor Morton nods*]

Roy. Are you angry, father?

GRIF. No—I'm not angry, my son—but I don't know what your mother will say. [*Calls*] Katharine!

Roy. Don't call her, father, let me tell her. [*Starts towards L. door when it opens and Katharine enters*]

KATH. Did you call me, Griffith? Good morning, Governor—here is a letter from—[*Sees Roy*] Why, Roy—

Roy. [*Trying to be cheery. Throwing his cap on a table*] I have enlisted, Mother.

KATH. Well—I don't know as I am surprised.

Gov. M. [*Enthusiastically*] That is the spirit that's going to save this Union, Mrs. Davenport!

KATH. That spirit is going to make women like me very bitter against the whole thing! To think of my two boys as babies [*Shakes her head*] and to see them now! [*Sighs*]

Roy. [*Tentatively*] I knew Beverly would call me a traitor—but I kind of hoped you would be proud of me.

KATH. [*Wearily*] I suppose I ought to be—proud of you, Roy—everybody else will be—but my boys are worth a good deal more to me—as my boys—

than as heroes. [*Takes a letter from her pocket*] I have a letter from Beverly. Read it. Excuse me, Governor. [*Gives him the letter and exits L. door*]

GRIF. [*To Governor Morton*] Beverly—our oldest boy is in the Confederate Army.

Gov. M. Yes—so you told me—that letter is from him? [*Seating himself*]

GRIF. Yes—read it, Roy.

ROY. Aloud, father?

GRIF. Yes.

ROY. [*Reading*] "Camp Fairfax, March 19, 1862. My own darling Mother: I don't know whether this letter will ever reach you, but I must write it. Jerry is going to try to get through the Yankee lines to post it. I must tell you that you are a grandmother—Jerry brought me the news this morning—we have a beautiful baby girl—the image of her mother, and you know how handsome Sue is. They are all at the old home. Sue sends word that she is very happy—and I'm very happy—happier than I thought I ever could be without you. Do you think that when this war is over, you may come back here and visit us? For I don't suppose you'll ever live South again. I still think father was wrong—but there—that's done. I'm Captain of a Company of Virginia sharp shooters, and we've done some excellent work, and have been personally complimented for bravery and skill—but mother dear, I wish now that the war had never been—not but what I still believe the South right—but I wish this thing could have been settled some other way—but of course it couldn't. I wish slavery had never been—for it cost me my *Mother*. Don't let *Roy* go into the Army, mother. He and I once had some talk about the war, and I said some things to him that I wish now I hadn't said. We are bound to win—for we have the advantage. The Yankees have got to fight us on our own ground all the time—the great decisive battles have got to be fought right here in Virginia—*in the Shenandoah Valley*. They don't know the Valley nor the Mountain passes—we do—we can ambuscade 'em at every turn just as we did at Bull Run—and they know it—that's why it's all quiet on the Potomac, as your newspapers put it—they daren't move—they are afraid of being let into a trap. The fact of their changing Army Commanders isn't going to help 'em. They've made McClellan General in Chief of all their forces —well—they'll never get an able General at the head of their Armies—what they need now are guides. I'm going to have Sue get some pictures taken of her and baby as soon as she's well enough to go out, and I'll try to get one to you. No use to ask you to write because your letters would probably never reach me. Good-bye, mother dear—give my love to father and to Roy—kiss little Madge for me—but keep the dearest and best of me for your own—own

—sweet self—won't you—my—mother. Beverly." [*Griffith is silent. The Governor is very thoughtful*]

GRIF. What *was* the talk you and he had about the war, Roy?

ROY. It was only talk, father—he was angry and so was I.

GOV. M. Come—let us go and see the President!

GRIF. No, I reckon Katharine will want to talk to me now. Excuse me to the President. I'll go with you tomorrow morning.

GOV. M. [*Emphatically*] Tomorrow morning won't do. You've *got* to see him today. [*Seating himself*] Davenport, that boy of yours has hit the nail on the head—our Generals *don't* know that country down there. It's been simply a slaughter of our men every time they've tried to move.

GRIF. Yes, Virginia certainly is a mighty poor country to move an army in, unless a fellow knows it.

GOV. M. *You* know it—every foot of it.

ROY. [*Smiling*] He ought to! He rode it day and night for thirty odd years.

GOV. M. Your knowledge of that country is simply invaluable to Mr. Lincoln just now—and he's got to have it, that's all there is about it. [*Rises and walks about*]

GRIF. [*Excitedly*] Hold on, Governor, hold on! When I first came here we talked that all over and agreed to hoe in our own corn fields.

GOV. M. You can see yourself what the Army is doing down there in Virginia—simply nothing at all! What do you suppose the rebs keep their strongest Generals and their best men right between Washington and Richmond for?

GRIF. Why, that country is the key to the whole situation.

GOV. M. Exactly, and they know that if they can get into Washington they're sure of foreign recognition. [*This sets Griffith to thinking*]

ROY. Gosh! They've come mighty close to Washington more than once.

GOV. M. Close—well, if their Generals had known as much as we did— they'd have walked right up to the Capitol steps. That's what's the matter— they don't know our position and we don't know their country—and there we both are—one's afraid and the other dassn't. If we knew that country—we'd go right into Richmond. You wouldn't like to see our cause lost, would you?

GRIF. I've told you time and again that I believe in the Union. I'm a Union man.

GOV. M. How much of a Union man are you?

GRIF. [*Almost resentfully*] What do you mean by that?

GOV. M. Are you enough of a Union man to help save her?

GRIF. How can I?

Gov. M. [*Drawing his chair in front of table and sitting down again close to Griffith*] I'll tell you something and I know what I'm talking about. If a move isn't made before long—and made right—the Union's gone up in a balloon. [*Pause. Draws chair closer to Griffith's chair, leans forward and whispers aloud*] I'll tell you something more—and this is in strict confidence —[*Slowly and emphatically*] The—President—knows—it—[*Lays his hand on Griffith's knee*] and he hasn't got a soul who knows that country that he dare trust. [*Leans back in his chair and looks steadily at Griffith*] And I've got that from his own lips not half an hour ago. [*Pause*] Now, that's a nice position for the President of the United States to be in—isn't it? [*Changing his whole manner to a determined one*] That's what brought me to Washington. That's what he wants to see you for. *You're* the man he needs—you're the *one* man and the *only* man—who can—

Grif. [*With much feeling, but with great firmness*] No—the South's my home—she's wrong, but I can't fight against her.

Gov. M. Nobody wants you to *fight*. You *voted* for Mr. Lincoln—you helped to put him in the position he is in, and by the Eternal—you've got to sustain him! You've got no right to desert him now when he needs you. It's *treason!*

Grif. No! I'm neutral—I—

Gov. M. [*Vehemently*] There is no neutral ground now. The man who is not *with* Mr. Lincoln now is *against* him.

Grif. [*Smiling*] That's what the fellows in Virginia said to me when I voted for Mr. Lincoln.

Roy. [*Enthused*] Ah! I wish I knew the country as well as father does. I'd—

Gov. M. [*Showing a map which he has carried in his hand. It is wrapped in a black oil cloth*] Here, I want you to run your eye over that and tell me how you would like to move an army by it?

Grif. What is it?

Gov. M. The map of the Shenandoah Valley—and of the mountains and passes of Virginia that General McClellan has been planning this campaign by.

Grif. Where'd you get it?

Gov. M. [*Slowly and impressively*] The President of the United States asked me to show it to *you.* [*The steady gaze of Governor Morton meets the eyes of Griffith, who has stared at him at the words "asked me to show it to you." They look fixedly at each other—Griffith feeling that if he takes that map he will yield, Morton determined he shall take it. After a pause Griffith takes the map and slowly unrolls it. Then Governor Morton changes his tone and becomes colloquial. Indicating place on the map*] There's a strip along there he can't make out. [*Pointing farther along*] That seems to be an opening in the mountains—but—[*Roy has drawn near and is interested in the map*]

GRIF. [*Who has scanned the map carefully, speaks in very positive tones*] No! No! The real opening, the road pass—let me see—what's the scale of miles here? Four—why the road pass is at least five miles farther on! [*He draws an imaginary line with lead pencil which he takes from table*] There! M-m-m—[*Thoughtfully, taking his chin in his hand*] No—n-o-o; this map's all wrong. The road—trends—along here—so. Then you cross the ridge at an angle—so. There ought to be a stream here—oh, pshaw! This map's—where did he get this map? It's no account at all! There are at least seven miles left out right here. Why, right here where they have got those little, insignificant foothills, is one of the most rugged and impassable places in this world! [*Draws several imaginary lines*] Right about here is the Bedolph estate, a splendid place—then as you go up here, you pass into a sort of a pocket. If they got you in there it'd be pretty hard work to get out. But you can cut all that off and go—so—see? There is a mill, and a fine old mill stream, pure water as you ever drank, right here. [*Throws down his pencil*] This map is no good! It would be absolute murder to move an army by that map.

Gov. M. [*Following up his advantage*] The President is aware of that and he is helpless. That's why he turns to you. Now you know why "All is quiet on the Potomac." We daren't move. The Army of the Potomac would mutiny if it knew the real state of affairs.

GRIF. [*Is dazed*] I never saw it in that light before. Just what does he want me to do?

Gov. M. He wants you to be an unofficial patriot.

GRIF. [*Slowly and almost sadly*] An—un—of—ficial—pa—triot—. Ah! [*Shakes his head*]

Gov. M. He's going to send a corps of engineers down there to make a new map of that country. He wants you to lead that corps. You can go in your character of chaplain or—

GRIF. No. If I do this thing, I'll do it outright! I've never seen it as you've made me see it today. If I go I'll ride in the lead, not as a chaplain nor as sutler, but as just what I shall be—God help me—a government guide.

Gov. M. All right. Now about your pay. How does a colonel's commission and pay strike you? [*He says this as if it were an extraordinary offer, one which no sane man would refuse*]

GRIF. [*Indignantly*] Commission? Pay? Am I to understand that he offers to pay me to—

Gov. M. [*Quickly and pacifically*] No! No! But you have got to be carried on the pay roll. You've got to have *grub-rations*. The commission is for your personal security. It is necessary, in case of—of—accident, it secures you the right of honorable exchange and fair treatment as a—a—prisoner of war.

Grif. I shall be a spy, all the same, in my own heart—I shall be a spy. I can't do it. I can *not* do it!

Gov. M. Faugh! I've no patience with you. Did you ever see a panic of wounded men after a battle?

Grif. [*Horrified*] Oh! My God—yes! I saw McDowell's army cross Long Bridge yonder [*Points*] on the 21st day of last July—young men and boys— [*Unconsciously embraces Roy*] singing, cheering, filled with the ecstasy of life and youth and joy. And I saw their retreat from Bull Run the next day. My God! I've seen nothing else since, day or night!

Gov. M. [*Sternly*] You could have prevented that disaster, and you will have yourself to blame if the President of the United States and the Generals of the Union Army have to account for another *like* it. And now I'm going to see the President. Will you come?

Grif. No. Not today. [*Rolls up the map and offers it to the Governor*]

Gov. M. [*Refuses to take it*] No, I want you to think it over, and I want you to read this. [*Takes official document, which is in an official envelope, from his breast pocket and hands it to Griffith, who takes it in a nerveless sort of way, as if he had no power to resist*]

Grif. What's this?

Gov. M. The order I was commanded by the President to deliver in person to a very dear friend. [*To Roy, while Griffith reads the paper*] I expect to hear good reports of you. [*Then goes down to Griffith; slowly*] That's a p-e-r-e-mptory order. [*Takes out watch*] I shall expect you to meet me at Willards at four o'clock. It is 3:15 now, and we will go over there together. [*Griffith is in a daze. The Governor starts to go, stops, comes back*] And by the way, you might as well make up your mind not to come back to the house for the present. You'll probably have to go into commission at once. Four o'clock, at Willards. Good-bye. [*To Roy, who shows him to the door*] Good-bye, my son. [*Shakes hands with Roy. Roy touches his forehead in military salute. The words of the Governor have inspired him with pride. Closes the door just in time to see his father, who has read the paper, fall into a chair with his head buried in his arms. The paper falls on the floor*]

Roy. What is it, father? [*Sees the paper, picks it up. Enthusiastically, with a smile, reads:*]

Executive Mansion,

March 16, 1862

Oliver P. Morton, Governor of Indiana:

Order your man, Davenport, to report to me immediately.

(Seal)   *A. Lincoln*

[*Pause*] You've got to obey *that* order, father.

GRIF. I can't, Roy. I can't!

ROY. [*Partly astonished and partly disappointed that his father does not respond to the order*] You must—you can't help yourself.

GRIF. What will your mother say? [*His head still buried in his arms*]

ROY. [*Decisively*] I don't know, but you have got to obey that order. [*Ends in fatalistic half whisper. Enter Katharine L. door. She is dressed for walking. She is intent on buttoning her gloves, and does not look up as she speaks*]

KATH. Griffith, I'm going out for a walk. Is there—

ROY. [*Cheerily*] Do you want me to go with you, mother?

KATH. No—I—[*Looks up, sees Griffith bowed down. Springs to him*] Why, Griffith! What's the matter? Has anything happened? [*Griffith merely shakes his head and swings his body*]

KATH. [*With more emphasis*] What's the matter? Can't you speak? Roy —what—[*Turns her head, sees the paper which Roy is turning over in his hands. She stops, turns pale and sick. Whispers*] Beverly—[*She can scarcely speak*] When—how—where—

ROY. [*Extending the paper. Shakes his head to indicate "No"*] Mother, the President orders father to report to him immediately.

KATH. [*With a long breath*] Oh! Mercy! Why didn't you say so? You gave me a dreadful shock. I thought Beverly had been killed. [*Takes the paper, tries to command herself. Reads*] Why—this is to Governor Morton. Oh! I see! "Order your man, Davenport, to report to me immediately, A. Lincoln." [*Indignantly*] Well—I—your *man*, Davenport—the presumption! [*To Griffith*] What are you going to do with this, Griffith? [*Holding the telegram towards him*]

GRIF. [*Hesitatingly*] I don't know—yet—

KATH. [*Surprised*] Don't *know*?

GRIF. I was trying to think what I ought to do—what would you do, if you were me?

KATH. I'd tear it to tatters! [*Attempting to suit the action to the word*]

ROY. Mother, don't—

KATH. [*Almost shrieks*] Let me alone! [*Then to Griffith in a quieter but still intense tone*] That's what I'd do with it.

GRIF. [*Rising and quietly taking the paper from her*] I wouldn't tear it, Katharine, if I were you. That won't help matters.

KATH. What does this—*man,* Lincoln, want with you, Griffith?

GRIF. [*Slowly*] I reckon he wants me to give him a key to the Shenandoah Valley.

KATH. A—key—to—the—Shenan—

GRIF. McClellan has 100,000 men down there in the Army of the Potomac, and he can't move 'em—without—

KATH. You don't mean to say—that he wants you to guide his Army?

GRIF. I reckon that's about what it amounts to. He wants me to map the Shenandoah Valley and mountain passes for him.

KATH. [*Indignant*] Oh, Griffith—what an insult!

ROY. [*Astonished*] Insult? Why, mother! It's an honor.

KATH. [*Indignantly*] Is it—well—I'd rather a man would horsewhip me— than to offer me such an honor!

ROY. Governor Morton says it's father's duty.

KATH. Governor Morton is not dictator in this family. [*Getting more and more excited as she goes on; tears off her right glove*] I'll answer this!

GRIF. Wait a minute—let us go slow—let us talk the thing over. Now as I look at it—this—[*Holding up the paper*] is a peremptory military order.

KATH. [*Still indignant*] But you are not one of this man's soldiers.

GRIF. [*Continuing*] And it is signed by the President of the United States.

KATH. [*Amazed*] Why, Griffith! You surely have no idea of obeying that order?

GRIF. I don't know that I've got the right to refuse.

KATH. [*Astounded*] Griffith!

GRIF. This is an extraordinary case. Here is a man at the head of a great nation—

KATH. [*Proudly*] The *North is not* the nation. I'm a Southern woman. Virginia is my home. The people there are my people. I did not leave it because I didn't love it, or because I was not happy there; I left it because *you* were not happy there. [*Begins to unconsciously, half angrily, excitedly, take off hat, shawl and coat, throwing them on chair or table as she gets them off*]

GRIF. Katharine—

KATH. I left refinement, all my old and congenial friends—and everything I had been accustomed to all my life. I have never pretended that it wasn't a sacrifice on my part—I am not a hypocrite—I realize the difference between my home and this house—I never will, never *can* love this place. [*Contemptuously*] These narrow, penurious, unsympathetic Northern people are as far from me as day is from night. I don't hate them, but I've nothing in common with them. But I do love *you* and I've been happy, *even here—with you.* I'll follow you into the frigid zone, if you ask me to—but when the President of the Yankee States orders you to leave me and guide his Army against *my country* and *my people,* I say *"No"!* You shall not do it.

GRIF. There are *times*—when patriotism—

KATH. Griffith, this is a *brutal* war. You have said so yourself a hundred times. It isn't a war against oppression; it hasn't the righteousness of *1776* to sanctify it. It's a *factional fight*—it's a *political war!* Patriotism! Think of our two brave boys with guns in their hands, ready to murder each other in the name of patriotism, and now you want to kill me [*Weeps*] under the same delusion.

GRIF. Katharine! This is the first time you and I have come to words on this question. I didn't believe we ever could have done so. I thought we understood each other too well for that. You are very bitter against the North. I can't blame you for that, but I—

KATH. [*Earnestly*] No, Griffith—it's not that—I pledge you my word, it's not that—it's *you,* my *husband.* I'm frightened—I've lost my two boys—I expected that—I was sort of prepared for that—but oh!—*you,* Griffith—I never expected to lose *you.* I've always sort of hoped that when the time came I might go first. I don't want you in this war on either side. Oh, Griffith—my husband, don't go—for God's sake, don't go—don't leave me here alone!

GRIF. Katharine, [*Pointing to picture*] that is Abraham Lincoln, the President of the United States, after his inauguration March 4, 1861. [*Taking cabinet photo of Lincoln from top of bookcase*] This is Abraham Lincoln March 1, 1862. Do you see the change in the face? No human being has ever suffered in a life time what this man has suffered in one short year. Men think it is a great thing to be the president of a great nation; and so it is, in time of peace; but ah, Katharine, in time of war! President Lincoln hasn't got a man he dare trust to map this country. [*Shows map*] Look at that. [*Getting excited*] He turns to me, and he says, "Davenport, I need *you.* I answered when you all needed me. Now, when I need you—" He points his accusing finger at me and says, "There is but one way to shorten this war, to lessen the awful slaughter, the carnage and suffering, on *both* sides. There is but one man who knows how to do this, and that man is" [*Pointing to himself*] "*you.* And you have not done your duty to your country. No sir, nor to your God, until you have done that." [*Falls into a chair overcome with his emotions, and buries his face in his arms*]

KATH. [*Almost heart-broken*] I know—I know—but ah—to think of you, my husband, guiding an army against—

GRIF. Look at that bridge. Do you remember that bridge on the 22d of last July? [*Points out of window in direction of Long Bridge*] Do you see young sons like yours dragging bleeding limbs across it? Do you see terror stricken horses trampling down those wounded boys?

KATH. [*Horrified*] Don't, Griffith! For God's sake, don't!

GRIF. It is for God's sake. I pray to my God that I may never see another such day in my life. If I knew how to prevent a railroad accident—what would you think of me if I did not prevent it?

KATH. You have sacrificed so much already, Griffith. You have impoverished yourself—

GRIF. I know, I know—

KATH. The people down there loved you so before. I hoped that after all perhaps we might some day go back there again, but now—[*Shakes her head*] every man, woman and child in Virginia will hate—and despise you—

GRIF. The people down there never understood me. But *you*—you do. Would you ever have loved me—had I been different?

KATH. [*Going to him. Firmly*] No.

GRIF. Will you respect me now, if I do not respect myself?

KATH. No.

GRIF. Then kiss me, and tell me to go.

KATH. Do you realize what you ask of me?

GRIF. Yes.

KATH. Is there no other way?

GRIF. I see none.

KATH. Ah, Griffith! How can I say it? Suppose anything should happen to you? That you should be taken? [*Breaking down*] I'd never forgive myself. I believe I'd kill myself. [*Recovering herself*] Griffith, I have made sacrifice after sacrifice for you. Now you come to me and ask me to make the supreme sacrifice of my life. I rebel. I cannot do it. [*Decisively*] I *will* not do it. [*Changing her tone*] Ah, Griffith, my husband, you are all I have! I love you —I tell you I love you. I cannot give you up!

GRIF. Katharine, this is not a question of your life or my life, or of our love for each other. The life of the nation is at stake. Abraham Lincoln calls out to me, "Help me to save the nation. Help me to save this nation." I can't shut my ears to his pitiful cry.

KATH. You solemnly believe it your duty to go, do you?

GRIF. Yes, Katharine. It is a duty I owe my fellow men on both sides of Mason and Dixon's line. It is a duty I owe to the man I helped to make responsible for this war. It is a duty I owe the government under which I live, and of which I am an infinitesimal part.

KATH. [*Seeing that argument is useless*] Well, then—go! [*This last with a supreme effort*]

GRIF. [*Relieved*] I knew I could depend on you. You are the bravest little woman in the world.

ROY. [*Going to her tenderly*] God bless you, my mother.

KATH. [*Smiling sadly*] Why! I'm quite a hero! Go, Griffith, but before you go, I want to tell you one thing. I will go too.

GRIF. [*Astonished*] Go—where?

KATH. Home. To my home. To Virginia.

GRIF. [*Horror-stricken*] Katharine—you will not do—

KATH. I will do just what you are going to do. Help the cause I believe in.

GRIF. You will not do this?

KATH. Why not? If the Army of the Potomac needs you, the Army of Virginia needs me.

GRIF. To think of you on a battle field or in a hospital—

KATH. Where can I be more useful now than among our sick and suffering soldiers?

GRIF. If I promise you—

KATH. Promises will not hold us together now. We have come to the fork in the road.

GRIF. I'm not going to fight, Katharine. [*Smiling*]

KATH. I believe I'd rather you were. I believe I'd rather see you with a sword or a gun in your hand than to see you guiding an Army against my country, against my people, against my son—

GRIF. [*Pleading*] Tell me that I shall find you here when I return.

KATH. No! When you return I'll come back, if you want me, but I must go now. I must do my duty as I see it—just as you do yours.

GRIF. You are right. Your heart is there. It is your duty to go.

KATH. When are you to see your president?

GRIF. [*As if talking from a dream or reverie. Looks at watch*] Now. I must go *now*.

KATH. Tell him he must send me and my household through the lines. I shall take Sallie and Judy, Mammy and Uncle Ned; the others must shift for themselves. [*Griffith's lips part as if to protest. She divines his thought*] I *forbid* you to accept any position under him, unless he agrees to do this for me. It is my right.

GRIF. He shall do this for you or do without me. Good-bye.

KATH. Good-bye, Griffith.

GRIF. Won't you kiss me?

KATH. Yes. [*Does so tenderly and lovingly*]

GRIF. Sometimes we come to a fork in a road, Katharine—and both branches meet again a few miles further on. Good-bye. [*Katharine totters after him to the door as if to recall him; then goes to table and leans against it in a heartbroken way, and is immersed in the thought of her loneliness and of how she is to get away from this place quickly. Griffith goes to Roy, takes him in his arms. They kiss each other on the cheek. Griffith pantomimes to Roy to comfort his mother. Roy signifies yes. Griffith goes slowly and silently out at street door, looking at watch as he goes*]

ROY. [*Going to her*] Mother! [*Softly, putting arms around her. Sallie enters. She is crying softly*]

SAL. Mis Kate, John wan's ter shake han's. He reg'men oddahed to de fron'.

KATH. Oh! Yes—John's a soldier too.

SAL. 'Es, Mis Kate. Kinder sojah—not reg'lah. He—

ROY. [*Enthusiastically*] Aren't you proud of him, Sallie?

SAL. I was proud at fust, Mas Roy, but seems des as ef Ah coulden be proud terday. [*Sees Roy's uniform for the first time*] Oh, Mas Roy—is yo'—[*Sort of horrified*]

KATH. When do you go, Roy?

ROY. Tomorrow, mother.

KATH. Sallie, we must get ready to leave this place. [*Picking up hat and walking things. Band, distant march*]

SAL. [*Stops crying, loses all interest in herself and her own trouble, frightened and anxious*] Leave heah, Mis Kate? Wha' fo'? Whar we all gwan ter *now*?

KATH. [*Tottering towards the door opposite from that which Davenport made his exit, speaks slowly, brokenly*] Back to Virginia. [*Goes slowly off L.2.E.*]

SAL. Oh! Mas' Roy, wha's happen—wha—

ROY. Hush! She's going back to Beverly, that's all. [*Motions her to follow her mistress. Sallie goes slowly out at door L.2.E., looking back at Roy, mystified and scared. Band music (march) nearer. Roy puts on his cap and goes to the window. March louder*]

CURTAIN

BIBLIOGRAPHY

JAMES A. HERNE

SHORE ACRES AND OTHER PLAYS. Revised by Mrs. James A. Herne. Biographical Note by Julie A. Herne, 1928. Contains *Shore Acres, Sag Harbor, Hearts of Oak*.

MARGARET FLEMING. In *Representative American Plays*, 1930 and later editions, edited by Arthur Hobson Quinn.

BIOGRAPHICAL AND CRITICAL

Herne, James A. "Old Stock Days in the Theatre," *Arena*, Vol. VI (Sept. 1892), pp. 401-16.

Herne, James A. "Art for Truth's Sake in the Drama," *Arena*, Vol. XVII (Feb. 1897), pp. 361-70.

Corbin, John. "Drama," *Harper's Weekly*, Vol. XLIII (Feb. 11 and March 4, 1899), pp. 139 and 213. [Griffith Davenport]

Flower, B. O. "Mask or Mirror," *Arena*, Vol. VIII (Aug. 1893), pp. 304-13.

Garland, Hamlin. "Mr. and Mrs. Herne," *Arena*, Vol. IV (Oct. 1891), pp. 543-60.

Garland, Hamlin. "On the Road with James A. Herne," *Century Magazine*, Vol. LXXXVIII, N.S. (Aug. 1914), pp. 574-81.

"An Appreciation: James A. Herne, Actor, Dramatist and Man," Articles by Hamlin Garland, J. J. Enneking and B. O. Flower. *Arena*, Vol. XXVI (Sept. 1901), pp. 282-91.

Hapgood, Norman. *The Stage in America*, pp. 61-9.

Howells, W. D. "Editor's Study," *Harper's Magazine*, Vol. LXXXIII (Aug. 1891), pp. 478-9. [Margaret Fleming]

Quinn, Arthur Hobson. *A History of the American Drama from the Civil War to the Present Day*, Vol. I, Chap. vi, "James A. Herne and the Realism of Character," pp. 125-62. Revised edition in one volume, 1936.

Tiempo, Marco. "James A. Herne in Griffith Davenport," *Arena*, Vol. XXII (Sept. 1899), pp. 375-82.

THE GREAT DIAMOND ROBBERY
& OTHER RECENT MELODRAMAS

A series in twenty volumes of hitherto unpublished
plays collected with the aid of the Rockefeller
Foundation, under the auspices of the Dramatists'
Guild of the Authors' League of America, edited
with historical and bibliographical notes.

BARRETT H. CLARK
GENERAL EDITOR

Advisory Board

ROBERT HAMILTON BALL, QUEENS COLLEGE
HOYT H. HUDSON, PRINCETON UNIVERSITY
GLENN HUGHES, UNIVERSITY OF WASHINGTON
GARRETT H. LEVERTON, FORMERLY OF NORTHWEST-
ERN UNIVERSITY
E. C. MABIE, UNIVERSITY OF IOWA
ALLARDYCE NICOLL, YALE UNIVERSITY
ARTHUR HOBSON QUINN, UNIVERSITY OF
PENNSYLVANIA
NAPIER WILT, UNIVERSITY OF CHICAGO

A complete list of volumes, with the names of
plays contained in each, will be found on pages
256-7 of this volume.

THE GREAT
DIAMOND ROBBERY

& Other Recent Melodramas

BY

EDWARD M. ALFRIEND & A. C. WHEELER
CLARENCE BENNETT · CHARLES A. TAYLOR
LILLIAN MORTIMER · WALTER WOODS

EDITED BY GARRETT H. LEVERTON

INDIANA UNIVERSITY PRESS

BLOOMINGTON

Requests for authorization of the use of any of the plays in this volume on the stage, the screen, or for radio or television broadcasting, or for any purpose of reproduction, will be forwarded by Princeton University Press to the proper persons.

CONTENTS

INTRODUCTION

LIKE the plays of the theatrical period it represents, *Recent Melodramas,* as part of the title of this volume, needs a sub-title. Recency of the plays will have to be sufficiently elastic, as part of the title, to cover a form of drama that began to make its appearance as early as the middle of the eighteenth century, reached the peak of its popularity at the turn of the present century, and may even today be seen in the repertoire of a few travelling dramatic tent shows which still perform in the more remote sections of the country.

Melodrama—drama with melody, or music—developed in France in the early years of the nineteenth century and was a reputable dramatic form until the playwrights of the Ten-Twenty-Thirty theater carried emotion, characterization, sentiment and dialogue to such lush extremes that violent revolt arose to demand theater entertainment which had some slight respect for the playgoer's intelligence and his sense of the probable. This revolt against artificiality and sentimentality has been so thorough that even today the adjective, melodramatic, is in popular usage a term of ridicule and contempt. Only in academic circles does the term remain as a definition of a valid dramatic form, and this definition is a far cry from the popular connotation of the word. It would therefore seem more accurate to identify the plays of this volume by a term other than the unqualified word, melodrama. Perhaps the best classification would be one which relates them to the type of theater wherein they found their greatest popularity—the Ten-Twenty-Thirty theater.

Subtlety was not a virtue of the Ten-Twenty-Thirty plays. It was whole hog or none. In dialogue, the soul-thrilling mock heroics and rhetorical contrast are still remembered for lines such as:

"Thank Heaven I arrived in time."

"You spurn my love, but the day will come when I can rend your heart as you are rending mine."

"I am coming back and it will be when I am least expected."

"Not without one kiss from those voluptuous lips."

Read any play of the period and you will find it plentifully filled with this heroic rhetoric which was calculated to (and did) throw the audience into a frenzy of emotion and pile up dollars at the box office.

The plots of the plays were very much alike. Audience interest was not so much in the nature of the story as in the physical heroics or mechanical sensations which might be introduced. Everyone knew what the outcome of the plot would be, but the thrill lay in watching the huge whirr of a circular saw as it approached the log to which the heroine had been tied by the villain. Not until the saw had touched the heroine's dress would the hero arrive, just in the nick of time to throw the lever and save his sweetheart from permanent bisection. Never in the history of these plays had the hero failed to arrive either a second too late—or too early. The audience revelled in this use of theatrical trickery and gave little heed to any cause and effect relationship of dramatic incident. The plays had a very simple code of morality. Villainy must always be punished and virtue always receive its just reward.

The characters of the plays were types rather than individuals. Characters had names but that mattered little. Actually they were the hero, the heroine, the villain or "heavy," the adventuress, the toby, the rube, a foreigner, etc. Characters were always one hundred per cent true to type. Never a villain with even one tiny redeeming quality nor a hero with even a suggestion of a fault. Make-up and costuming were also according to type. Blond curls and white dress for the heroine, and boots, rawhide whip and long black mustachios for the villains. Red wig and blacked-out teeth for the rube and red dresses and large jewels for the adventuress. Foreigners also were always acted according to type. Although it is doubtful if many of us ever saw foreigners behave in the way these plays represent them, it is fairly safe to say that many Americans, because of early contact with these plays, still believe all Frenchmen to be debonair, well dressed and passionate; all Englishmen to be monocled and completely lacking in a sense of humor and all Irishmen to be red-nosed, happy, and hunting a fight. Likewise the Chinaman, the Jew, the German, the Italian and others have all been typed and the impression provided by the plays of this Ten-Twenty-Thirty theater remains basic in the average American's concept of a foreigner.

There is little need for lengthy comment on the plays of this type. They are widely known and little respected. Amateurs (and professionals) produce them so that the audience may laugh at them. Critics and scholars regard them as the epitome of all that is bad in playwriting and acting. Text-books in American literature do not even mention the existence of this large field of dramatic writing. But in spite of all the indictments which can be piled up against the plays of the Ten-Twenty-Thirty theater, one rather challenging fact remains to disturb the scoffer. In spite of volumes of vitriol, these plays still remain the show pieces of a theater which came closer to reaching a universal audience than any other theater in all of history. Every village and town throughout the country had its Opera House or its Academy of Music. Each theater had four of five stock sets of scenery—the cottage interior, the palace set, the prison, the center-door-fancy, and an exterior. Travelling companies fitted their entire repertoire into these stock sets and the theater was packed nightly at admission prices of ten cents for the gallery, twenty cents for the balcony, and thirty cents for seats on the main floor. Actors did vaudeville acts in front of the curtain while between-the-act scene changes were made, and a set of dishes was given away on Saturday night to the holder of the lucky number. Throughout the country this theater flourished. Today's critics and historians speak of the American theater as having "grown up" and "matured." Perhaps so, but today's managers would give much for even the tiniest fraction of the popular support and universal enthusiasm accorded the plays and actors of the Ten-Twenty-Thirty theater.

It is unfortunate that what would have been the sixth play of this volume had to be omitted. In many respects, *The Fatal Wedding*, by Theodore Kremer, is one of the most characteristic plays of the period. Upon the author's death, rights to the play were inherited by relatives living near Cologne, Germany. The present war has made it impossible to locate these heirs and obtain the necessary permission to publish the play. However, in action, story and dialogue, *The Fatal Wedding* follows the same formula as the other plays of the volume. Its omission is regrettable primarily because of the play's importance as a leading box-office success throughout most of this period.

Theodore Kremer was a graduate, in music, of the University of Leipsig. He is the author of seventy-five successful melodramas. A. H. Woods produced approximately fifty of them and states that all were successes. *The Fatal Wedding* was the most spectacularly successful of all of Kremer's plays and it not only made a fortune for the author but it laid the foundation for the theatrical dynasties of Sam Harris and A. H. Woods.

Kremer began his career as an actor in Australia and came later to San Francisco where he began to write. His better known melodramas include such successes as *The Bowery After Dark, Wedded and Parted, Fast Life in New York, A Race for Life, Queen of the Convicts, Fallen by the Wayside, The King of the Bigamists,* and *Secret Service Sam. The Fatal Wedding* opened in Brooklyn in October 1901. Three weeks later it was presented at the Grand Opera House in Manhattan under the management of Sullivan, Harris, and Woods. For several seasons the play toured all over the country, breaking records for house receipts. In 1910 it was still one of the most successful of the stock-company offerings. Much of the play's success was due to the long series of intense situations which reached a climax in the escape of the hero across a rope over a yawning chasm.

Kremer made several attempts to write for the higher-priced houses but all of them met with failure. He retired with his fortune to a home in Cologne, Germany, where he died in 1923.

A ROYAL SLAVE

Clarence Bennett, author of twenty-eight plays which were performed during the many years he was associated with popular melodrama, is one of the most versatile personalities of the period. He began as an actor at McVickers Theatre in Chicago. There he was seen by Edwin Booth and taken on tour as a member of the Booths' company. Later, he established himself in such rôles as Hamlet, Svengali, Monte Cristo, and as a comedy Mephistopheles in his own adaptation of *Faust.* For forty-five years he was associated with a number of managers in the operation of his own companies, and during that time toured the United States, several provinces of Canada, and as far south as Mexico City.

Bennett was known not only as a highly successful actor, but also as a water-colorist and scene designer. He designed many of his own spectacular lithographs, and invented a process for painting scenery known as "diamond-dye scenery." He was among the first to paint many of his drops on scrim, thus making it possible to transport some of his most elaborate scenic efforts in trunks. He was also an early experimenter with salt-water dimmers. The Reading (Pa.) *Herald,* reviewing his production of *A Royal Slave,* comments on Mr. Bennett's skill in stage effects: "To add to the realism of the play, he has provided the finest scenic effects ever displayed on our stage, the whole forming a most exceptional entertainment. The beautiful scenery alone is well worth the price of admission."

The history of the Bennett companies is the history of a trouping family. Clarence Bennett, Mrs. Bennett, and two daughters, Edna Marshall and Lydia Marshall, were in the early companies of *A Royal Slave.* Through all of her husband's long career, Mrs. Bennett was associated in the business management of their many ventures. As part of their varied theatrical activities, the Bennetts even got out a house organ known as *The Bennett Journal.* It was circulated among the various companies simultaneously playing the Bennett successes in various parts of the country. It contained four pages of news of their repertoire and its success, and included special articles and poetry by Mr. Bennett himself.

Mr. Bennett's daughter believes *A Royal Slave* to have been written by Mr. Bennett in the '80's, but not immediately included in the Bennett repertoire. It was Mrs. Bennett who first realized its box-office possibilities. In the play's first year Mrs. Bennett booked a short tour and then "wildcatted" the rest of the season, doing such phenomenal business that the play was permanently installed in the repertoire as the backbone of the business.

By 1900 the play was protected by copyright, but the exact date of the first try-out performance is not known, nor is the program available. The first available review comes from the St. John, New Brunswick, *Daily Telegraph,* of Tuesday, April 12, 1898:

"The splendid production of Clarence Bennett's great romantic play, *A Royal Slave,* proved the greatest triumph ever scored by any repertoire company that has played in St. John. The play is remarkably picturesque in costume, scenery and situation. It offers the finest opportunities for artistic work from the brightest comedy to the most intense acting, and the entire company proved themselves equal to its most trying requirement. Mr. Bennett, the actor-manager, appears in the title rôle, and proved himself master of his art in its most noble phases, the romantic and tragic.

"The scenery was the finest ever seen here in any repertoire production. A fine orchestra and a splendid line of specialties form a most pleasing innovation in relieving the monotony between acts. Miss Maude Malton in her wonderful fire, electric, and stereopticon dances; Miss Malton in her beautiful ballads, and Miss Clayton in her fine illustrated songs, were among the most striking and their work was of the highest order. No company has won such hearty applause or created such enthusiasm as this one. The house was filled to the doors and the standing room in the balcony was at a premium."

A Royal Slave played continuously in the seasons between 1898 and 1915. Theatrical notes of the times are constantly reporting that some actor had just left to join the eastern, western or southern, *Royal Slave* companies. In 1902 they were heading for Wallace, Idaho; in 1903, for Rhinelander, Wis.; in 1904, for some one of the companies in Georgia, Alabama or Tennessee; in 1905, for Glens Falls, N.Y.; in 1906, for Ashland, Neb.—and so on for the surprising number of years during which it proved to be the *pièce de résistance* in the melodrama houses.

During its long life, the play had many casts. Clarence Bennett was the well known Aguila, and Walter Hubbell was one of the last to play the part. Bernice Belnap was one of the first Countesses, and Lulu McConnell one of the first Isadoras. James Kirkwood and Willard Mack were members of *Royal Slave* companies, and with the Gordon-Bennett company, Margaret Neville was, for a time, the feminine lead.

The script as here printed, comes directly from one of Mr. Bennett's prompt books, noted with longhand directions, and containing the author's watercolor designs for the sets. The scene plots are of particular interest in indicating the extent of the scenery which the Bennett companies carried.

Among the many other successes written by Clarence Bennett are: *Ivan's Oath, Cape Cod Folk, In Pennsylvania, The Shadow of a Crime, A Noble Revenge, Thy Neighbor's Wife,* and *Uncle Sam in Cuba.*

THE GREAT DIAMOND ROBBERY

When Colonel Edward M. Alfriend and A. C. Wheeler collaborated in writing *The Great Diamond Robbery,* they combined a varied experience in the theater. Colonel Alfriend had come to New York from Richmond, Va. He had served in the War between the States, commanding a company which he organized. In 1865 he returned to Richmond and the insurance business, but the theater always held a great fascination for him. In 1889 he left Richmond permanently and went to New York with the intention of becoming a dramatist. Among Mr. Alfriend's plays were: *A Foregone Conclusion,* produced by the Madison Square Company; *Across the Potomac,* a Civil War play in which he collaborated with August Pitou; *The Louisianians,* a romantic drama produced in repertoire by Robert B. Mantell; *New York;* and *The Great Diamond Robbery.*

A. C. Wheeler, born in New York, was a critic, essayist and novelist with a wide newspaper experience. While he was a member of the editorial staff of the *Milwaukee Daily Sentinel,* he first began to write under the pseudonym of "Nym Crinkle." He also served as a reporter on the *New York Times* and as dramatic critic for the *New York World, The Sun, The Star,* and for a number of years was the writer of the famous "Nym Crinkle" column in the *Dramatic Mirror.*

The Great Diamond Robbery had its first performance at The American Theatre in New York City on September 4, 1895, with the following cast:

"Dick Brummage," W. H. Thompson; "Frank Kennet," Orrin Johnson; "Senator McSorker," Odell Williams; "Dr. Livingstone," Joseph E. Whiting; "Clinton Bulford," George C. Boniface; "Mario Marino," Byron Douglas; "Grandfather Lavelot," Joseph Wilkes; "Sheeney Ike," B. R. Graham; "Count Garbiadorff," George Middleton; "Jane Clancy," C. B. Hawkins; "Mickey Brannigan," James Bevins; "Jimmy McClune," Gustave Frankel; "Philip," Prince Lloyd; "Frau Rosenbaum," Madame Janauschek; "Mrs. Bulford," Blanche Walsh; "Mary Lavelot," Katherine Grey; "Mrs. O'Geogan," Annie Yeamans; "Peggy Daly," Fanny Cohen; "Madame Mervane," Florence Robinson; "Mary Watson," Ray Rockwell.

Although the play received both praise and blame from the critics, there was no doubt as to its success with audiences. In 1905—ten years after the New York opening—the play was still listed by theatrical journals as one of the most popular plays from coast to coast.

FROM RAGS TO RICHES

From Rags to Riches, a classic of the Ten-Twenty-Thirty theater, is one of a long list of melodramas written and successfully produced by Charles A. Taylor. The play had its initial performance at the Metropolis Theatre in New York City on August 31, 1903, and was immediately launched on a long and successful career which took it all the way across the country. In this play, Laurette Taylor (known at that time as Laurette Cooney), made her first New York appearance, and the rôle of "Ned" was played by young Joseph Santley.

The play was presented in several New York theaters. In November of its first season it was playing at the New Star Theatre on Lexington Avenue with the following cast:

"Edward Montgomery," Theodore Kehrwald; "Robert Brown," J. O. Cantor; "Herbert Bostwick," Frank Norton; "Charles Montgomery," Biglow Cooper; "Bella," Laurene Santley; "Mike Dooley," Sidney Olcott; "Chinese Sam," William Cummings; "Louis," John O. Cantor; "Antonio Succo," Albert Livinston; "Handsome Jack," William Gane; "Fritz," Fred Snyder; "Mother," Lillian Marlin; "Albert Cooper," William Morris; "Gertrude," Anna V. Risher; "Flossie," Laurette Cooney; "Ned," Joseph Santley.

Other popular and successful melodramas written by Mr. Taylor include: *Belle of the Rio Grande, College Boy and Widow, The Child Wife, The Cradle Robber, Daughter of the Diamond King, The Derby Mascott, The Fortune Hunter, The Girl Engineer, The Girl Waif, Held for Ransom, The King of the Opium Ring, The Queen of the Highway, Rich for a Day,* and *The Scarlet Throne.*

NO MOTHER TO GUIDE HER

Lillian Mortimer, author of *No Mother to Guide Her,* was one of the best-known leading women of the country in the popular- priced theater. She was not only an author and actress but she also produced the plays in which she starred. Although she was acting in her own plays as early as 1895, her greatest success did not come until 1905 when she first produced *No Mother to Guide Her.* During the first week of August 1905 this play drew high praise from the Detroit press. On December 4, 1905, the play opened at the Star Theatre in New York City with the following cast:

"Ralph Carlton," John Lane Connor; "John Livingstone," John T. Nicholson; "Silas Waterbury," Irvin R. Walton; "Jake Jordan," Frank B. Russell; "Farmer Day," Allen Elmore; "Tommy Fisher," Ray Carpenter; "Walter Perkins," H. A. Conels; "Frank Caldwell," Rau W. Gordon; "Parson Thomas," Charles C. Connor; "Officer Keough," Eddie Sargeant; "Policeman Toad," Jake Liebermann; "Captain Hennessey," Kirt Easfeldt; "Rose Day," Alice Morlock; "Lindy Jane Smithers," May Manning; "Mother Tagger," Eva Benton; "Bess Sinclair," Grace De Foy; "The Baby," by herself; "Bunco," Lillian Mortimer.

The play was highly successful in New York and in succeeding seasons duplicated this success all over the country. For a time Miss Mortimer left the melodrama theater to become a headliner in vaudeville, but in 1911 she returned to continue her success in *No Mother to Guide Her*. The play was still being performed by her in 1913. Among Miss Mortimer's other plays were: *The Shadow of the Gallows, The Girl of the Streets, Bunco in Arizona, A Man's Broken Promise, Kate Barton's Temptation, The Heart of the Plains,* and *A Girl's Best Friend*.

BILLY THE KID

Shot well, he did,
And out of many
A tight place slid
$5,000 on his head
Catch him
Either alive or dead.

* * *

Six million people have seen Billy the Kid. Have You?

* * *

To Managers of Theatres, Opera Houses or Town Halls in Connecticut, Massachusetts, Rhode Island, Vermont, New Hampshire, Maine, New Brunswick, Nova Scotia and Prince Edward Island:

Get Ready for Big Business!
Billy the Kid is headed your way.
Has Been Witnessed by over Six Million People.
Has played every important city in every State in the U.S
Is the Champion Melodrama of the World.
Is Seven Years Old and Still Breaking Records.

SEE:

The Famous Bandit Horse, "Silver Heels."
The Battle in the Dark.
The Hairbreadth Escape of Billy the Kid.
The Kiss Auction.
The Soul Stirring Bravery of the Boy Bandit.
The Famous Broken Heart Saloon.

The above is taken from the announcement sent out by the management of *Billy the Kid* at the opening of its seventh consecutive season of touring. Five additional seasons of continuous success were still to come.

Billy the Kid, written by Walter Woods, opened its career of twelve solid seasons at the New Star Theatre in New York City on August 13, 1906. *The Dramatic News* proclaimed it "better than The Girl of the Golden West and the best melodrama I expect to see this season." The New York cast was as follows:

"Stephen Wright," Thos. J. MacMahon; "Mary Wright," Lorena Ferguson; "Billy," Joseph Santley; "Colonel Wayne Bradley," John C. Fenton; "Nellie Bradley," Marion Leonard; "Boyd Denver," Paul Barnett; "Con Hanley," Geo. M. DeVere; "Jim Storm," Frank Gordon; "Bill White," James Liet (later listed "Light"); " 'Peanut' Givanni," Robt. G. Vinola; "Bud Monroe," Thos. J. MacMahon; "Hank Burke," T. Jerome Morley; "Arizona Jake," James Early; "Molly," Jessie Lansing; "Jennie," Adele Lyndon.

Among the other plays of Walter Woods are: *Between Trains, The Chicago Boy Bandit, The Girl of Eagle Ranch, Manuella, The Reformer, The Sweetest Sin, Way of the West, Within four Walls,* and *Woman's Place.*

Garrett H. Leverton

New York City
August, 1940.

A ROYAL SLAVE

By Clarence Bennett

SCENE PLOT

ACT I.

Our leg drops in 1, 2, and 3. Our tree on 3rd leg drop. Our back drop in 4. Your wood wings to mask.

ACT II.

SCENE 1: *Same as Act I, except tree.* SCENE 2: *Our rocky pass drop in 1.* SCENE 3: *Your kitchen with jog and window set, as below. Our first act back drop.*

ACT III.

Our first act drop to back. Our third act drop in 4. Our tabs, right and left. Interior backings, right and left. Our fancy borders. Have short and long lines in 1 and 3 ready for tabs.

ACT IV.

SCENE 1: *Our cave drop must be above tormentor. Use prison wings or wood wings at tormentor.* SCENE 2: *Our fourth act drop in 5. Our horizon wings left. Use sea cloth, our set winter and ground roll. Our platform, upright against drop, our cloth to cover same.*

ACT V.

Our back drop in 5. Our drop with center opening just below this. Our cut drop in 4, between cut drop and with opening. Our platform. Our steps for platform. Our table with lines, use in Act III. Our borders. Interior backings, right and left.

PROP LIST

ACT I.

Fountain, with water connections and waste pipe complete up C. Rustic seat L.C. Tropic plants to dress stage. Cigarettes for Pedro, Jones, Countess. Knife for Aguila. Knife for Alacran. Dagger for Pedro. Bicycle for Jones. Note book and pencil for Jones. Heavy riding whip for Pedro. Purse for Carlos. Guitar L. by house tuned to play accompaniment.

ACT II.

Chimes in distance. Fencing swords and daggers for Pedro and Carlos. Locket for Pedro. Blood-stained handkerchief for Countess.

SCENE 3: Curtains, strung on rope, to draw, from stage screw C. C. 8 ft. high, to wing R. 8 ft. high. Cot bed in alcove R.C. Two chairs. Small table R. with crucifix and tumbler. Books on table. Lace scarf for Isadora. Dagger for Countess.

ACT III.

Small sofa R. of C.D. Two ordinary (light) parlor chairs R. and L. in 2. Table with handsome spread, crucifix, two handsome brass or silver candlesticks with candles, small dagger, L.2. Heavy curtains, on bar, on C.D. to close. Handsome furniture to dress stage. Swords for robbers. Knife for Alacran.

ACT IV.

SCENE 1: Chains and manacles for Juan L.1. Ditto for Aguila, C., fastened to floor, long enough for him to raise his hands as high as his breast. Whip (heavy), black bottle and combat knife for Matador. Old blankets, 1.R.1.E., one L.1.E. Riding whip for Pedro. Bunch of keys for Matador. Binding and rope for Aguila. Dagger for Pedro. Revolver for Jones.

SCENE 2: Shark ready L. Boat and oar ready and roped to draw on, L.4. Moon box lighted and ladder behind scene. Stump in island. Men to work sea cloth. Sash for Alacran. Mattress R.C. front of island. Plenty of salt and boy to throw it as directed.

ACT V.

Set same as Act III. Candles on table lighted, and matches for Padre to relight them. Dagger for Pedro. Swords for Carlos and Aguila. Trick candles for Padre. Locket for Carlos. Letter for Padre. Two soldiers, with guns ready, L.3.D. Blood-stained handkerchief for Countess.

CAST OF CHARACTERS

EL AGUILA, *an Aztec, "Child of the Sun"*

COUNT PEDRO MARTINEZ, *"El Capitan"*

HUMBOLT AGASSIS JONES, *American newspaper correspondent*

LIEUTENANT CARLOS CASTILLO, *officer in Mexican service*

PADRE DOMINGUS, *priest and physician*

JUAN ALVAREZ, *an insane captive*

BERNAL, *robber lieutenant, known as "El Alacran"*

PHILLIPPE, *robber guard, "El Matador"*

COUNTESS INEZ DE ORO

ISADORA DE ORO

BANDITS AND SOLDIERS

ANNETTA, *maid*

SYNOPSIS OF SCENES

ACT I: *Casa, or country seat of Countess de Oro, overlooking Valley of Mexico.*

ACT II, SCENE I: *Wood in neighborhood of Casa de Oro.*
  SCENE 2: *Interior of Padre Domingus' house.*

ACT III: *Countess' house or hacienda near Puebla, near east coast of Mexico.*

ACT IV, SCENE I: *Interior of cave of "El Capitan," near Puebla.*
  SCENE 2: *The islet of "El Toro," near Puebla.*

ACT V: *Same as* ACT III. *Night.*

NOTE: *The Padre can double Bernal; Carlos double Phillippe.*

ACT I.

Drop in 5. View of valley and distant city of Mexico at sunset. Popocatepetl in background. Scene to change with gauzes to moonlight. Mexican house with verandah set L.2. and 3. Low walls, gate C. Cross stage at back. Practical fountain with circular seat curb, C. Water plants in fountain, plants and flowers to dress stage. Tropical wings and borders. Countess R.C. on fountain seat. Pedro standing C.

INEZ. I hear, count, that the dreaded Capitan has surprised another silver train in the Sierra Madre, and robbed it of nearly half a million.

PED. Indeed? He is a brave fellow at all events. It seems strange that no one can capture him, or discover the secret of his identity.

INEZ. It does indeed, señor. He has carried on his depredations since I was a child, and yet no clue has been discovered that could lead to his arrest.

PED. He must be very wealthy by this time.

INEZ. It would seem so, señor. Do you know there is a slight romance in our family connected with him?

PED. Indeed, señora? I beg you will favor me with it. That is, of course, if the story is not a family secret.

INEZ. A secret? By no means! At least not from you, as you will shortly be one of the family. But I should not like the story to reach the ears of El Capitan, as it might attract his attention rather unpleasantly to us, and awaken in him a desire to investigate the mystery for himself.

PED. [*Smiling*] Have no fear, señora. I am good at keeping secrets.

INEZ. You must know, then—to begin my story, I once had a sister. I have never spoken of her to you. She fell in love with a young man named Juan Alvarez of Puebla, between whose family and ours there had existed for years a deadly feud. He was the last of his race, and on him my father centered all his enmity. When he learned of the attachment between Alvarez and my sister Mercedes, he of course opposed the union most bitterly. But in spite of his opposition, Mercedes eloped with and married her lover.

PED. What became of them?

INEZ. My father was a man of iron. He disowned Mercedes. But despite his curses, they lived happily together for about three years, when a child, a daughter, was born to them.

PED. Your story is interesting, señora. Pray go on!

INEZ. Señor Alvarez had a vast treasure in gold and jewels hidden. No one but himself knew where. Alarmed by the frequent depredations of El Capitan, he had determined to secrete it in a more secure place. And on the very day he purposed changing its hiding place, he was waylaid and murdered by El Captain.

PED. How do you know this?

INEZ. Our old peon, Aguila, who was very fond of my sister, was with Señor Alvarez at the time, and in defending him, was severely wounded and left on the ground for dead. Recovering, however, he brought back the dreadful news. My sister, nearly crazed by the death of her husband, not knowing where his treasure was hidden, exhausted her remaining resources in a fruitless search for him. And finally, driven to despair, she lost her reason and disappeared.

PED. But was the treasure never recovered?

INEZ. No, señor. Meanwhile I had married at my father's command, Señor Antonio de Oro, an old but wealthy banker of the capital. My father died, Isadora was born as the fruit of this loveless marriage. Then Señor Antonio died and I was free again! Free!

PED. But did you never try to find the treasure?

INEZ. Yes, señor. At my sister's death, Señor Alvarez' hacienda and estates at Puebla, remaining unsold, reverted to our family. I have searched there for it again and again, but always in vain. I could gain no clue to its hiding place.

PED. Do you not suppose, señora, that your old peon, Aguila, may know. You say he was with Señor Alvarez when he was murdered. Might he not have made this Indian the repository of the secret of the hidden treasure?

INEZ. No, señor. He is true to our family, and thoroughly honest. He was so fond of my sister he would certainly have revealed it to her.

PED. This old peon seems to hold a strange position in your family. He has been the nurse and confidant of three generations. He seems devoted to your race.

INEZ. He was the playfellow and friend of my father in his boyhood, my sister's guarding spirit and mine, and now Isadora's constant companion and protector. He is as devoted to her as a faithful dog. I never had any love for him, but still I keep him for his profound judgment and wisdom. His counsels have been of great value at times.

PED. His race rarely turns gray, but though he is rugged as an oak, his hair is white.

INEZ. The fever from his wound and the exposure made his long hair fall out. And when it grew again, it was snowy white.

PED. He is a strange being—humble, courteous, faithful to your family, a peon, a slave. He still has the dignity and bearing of a king.

INEZ. Because he is a king. He is the lineal descendant of the Montezumas who once ruled Mexico. His kingly grace and bearing he owes to the royal blood in his veins.

PED. [*Looks off L.U.E.*] Señora, there is Señorita Isadora and that Señor Castillo. They seem very much absorbed in each other's society.

INEZ. [*Showing displeasure*] Yes, I see.

PED. You do not seem pleased at his constant attentions to your daughter.

INEZ. Not altogether. [*Crosses R.*]

PED. Nor am I. As you know, señora, I love the señorita, your daughter, and this fellow's interference is very annoying to me. Who is he anyway?

INEZ. [*Half severely*] He is my guest, señor. But there, curb your jealousy. I promise you that I will see that you are not annoyed further. She is your affianced wife. You have my promise. That is enough. I have your interests at heart, señor. Leave her to me! But come with me. I do not wish to meet them now. Come. [*Going R.2.*]

PED. Your wishes are commands to me, señora. [*Exeunt Inez and Pedro R.2. Enter Isadora and Carlos through gate from L.U.E.*]

ISA. [*Looking at bouquet in hand*] Señor Castillo, you have as good taste as a lady in the arrangement of flowers. I shall treasure this as a token of your skill.

CARL. Ah, señorita—I have been dallying here among the roses, forgetting that I was only a soldier. But the order came this afternoon that calls me from this scene of happiness to duty. I must leave tomorrow!

ISA. [*Looking up gravely*] Oh, señor! You surely are not going away so soon.

CARL. I must. You cannot dream how bright these days have seemed to me. Bright with the glory of your presence, the sunshine of your beautiful eyes, the music of your voice. They are a sweet spell that will haunt my heart while I live.

ISA. Señor, brave men should not be flatterers.

CARL. The words that spring to our lips when we kneel before the Holy Mother, are not flattery, but devotion. Isadora, you are the saint shrined in my heart! You say I flatter, I answer "I love you."

ISA. [*Shyly*] Oh, Señor Carlos!

CARL. Tell me, Isadora—may I hope?

ISA. [*Toying with bouquet*] It is cruel, señor, to deceive those who trust us!

CARL. Can't you believe me?

ISA. [*Gives him her hand*] Yes, Señor Carlos. For our good padre says—"Out of the fullness of the heart the mouth speaketh"—and if your eyes are mirrors of your heart, I am sure it is full of truth and goodness!

CARL. [*Joyously*] It is filled with both, for it is full of you! I was but a plain honest soldier till I met you. And then the world seemed changed. The sunshine seemed brighter—the flowers sweeter, the songs of the birds more joyous that such a bright being as you was in the world.

ISA. [*Coquettishly*] How pleasant sounds the gurgle of the fountain!

CARL. Yes! It is singing to you. And that lends it music. [*Pause*] Little señorita, can you love me?

ISA. Oh, if I but dared to believe you!

CARL. Why do you doubt me? I swear to you that you have grown into my heart till, while that heart shall beat, it will enshrine your image! There is no present joy, no future hope that does not mirror your sweet face. And in my soul I would treasure and guard your love always as a holy thing!

ISA. [*Coyly*] Do you mean what you say?

CARL. Mean it! I have laid my heart at your feet. You may read its truth in my eyes!

ISA. Hearts are false and eyes too sometimes.

CARL. Why do you doubt me, Isadora?

ISA. [*Seriously*] I do not doubt you, Carlos. I love you! If you thirst for my love, the draught is yours. Take me! Our hearts shall throb in unison, our lives entwine till death, my Carlos!

CARL. [*Clasping her*] Darling! If I were dying, your kiss upon my lips would, like the wizard's fabled elixir, awake my drowsy heart to love and life again! Are you happy now?

ISA. Yes, Carlos—always, with you!

CARL. And can you trust your future, your life, your happiness to me?

ISA. If not, to whom can I ever trust them? You are my future, my life, my joy!

CARL. Bless your sweet lips for those words. [*Kisses her*]

ISA. But, Carlos, are not love and happiness like the sweet cerus bloom—a thing of beauty born at eve to fade and die ere morn? A thing too sweet to last?

CARL. Nay, trust me, dearest! Shrined in our souls, it will bloom on forever. In hearts of truth love is immortal!

ISA. Dear Carlos! How sweet it sounds to call you by that name!

CARL. Sweet indeed, breathed by your lips. [*Kisses her*] I must do as an honorable man should. I must tell your mother of our love and ask her for her little girl. May I go to her now?

Isa. Yes, Carlos.

Carl. I cannot rest till I can call you mine! Good-bye! Little sweetheart! When I come back, I hope to bring you good news. Good-bye! [*Exit R.U.E.*]

Isa. He loves me! Oh, I am so happy! Dear, dear Carlos! Sweet flowers [*Toying with them*], you were his gift! [*Kisses them*] My brave, strong, handsome lover! I am so proud of him, I love him so. [*Sings:*]

> "Will you love me always, darling,
> Fondly, tenderly as now?
> When my eyes have lost their brightness,
> When the silver's on my brow?
> Will your kiss be just as tender,
> Just as fond your strong arms fold,
> And your voice as kind and gentle?
> Will you love me when I'm old?"

[*She looks off L.U.E.*] Here comes dear old Aguila! I must tell him. [*Hides up L., amid flowers. Aguila enters C. from L.U., sets large pulque jar by fountain, and seats himself, wiping perspiration away*]

Ag. The day is as hot as a fiend's breath! None but the sun's children dare stand before him today! I wonder where my little señorita is? My little nightingale should come when the stars peep through the twilight's purple curtains. [*Isadora steals up behind him and takes his head in her hands, kisses him on the hair*]

Isa. Who is it?

Ag. An angel!

Isa. [*Laughing*] Oh, no, Papa Aguila! It's only me.

Ag. Well, I was right!

Isa. Oh, no, you weren't! You didn't know me!

Ag. Not know you, my beautiful! Does the bee know the flower whose heart is full of sweetness? Whose kiss but yours ever blesses my old white brow? And it touches it with a glory like the sunlight on the snowy head of yonder mountain. A crown more royal than the one my fathers wore. There, at its feet!

Isa. [*Kneeling L. of him*] You are a king to me, Aguila.

Ag. [*Sadly*] No, only a peon. A poor old slave! Your old Aguila!

Isa. No! You are a Montezuma! A royal child of the sun! And, more than all, my dear old papa! [*Pats his cheek playfully*]

Ag. [*Moved*] My darling child! [*Looking in her eyes*] What makes my little señorita's notes so glad and tender today? Is there some singing joy making its nest amid the white blossoms of her young heart?

Isa. [*Demurely, taking his hand between hers*] Papa Aguila, I have never had a secret from you, and I must tell you this. The dearest, sweetest secret of all! For I know that no one loves me as you do—no one shares my joys and sorrows like you. There is a joy at my heart tonight!

Ag. I know what it is. I have read the hope in your bright eyes long ago, before you dared to own it to yourself. The Señor Castillo is young, brave and tender, and my little mistress is fair, sweet and gentle—and so your hearts turned toward each other like the courses of the brooks that blend their pure tides in one channel. You love and you are loved, and in that thought as in an urn, blossom the flowers of joy!

Isa. [*With bashful joy, laying her cheek against his hand*] How good you are! How wise. You know my heart before I do myself!

Ag. Ah, my child! May you never learn the bitter lessons of sorrow that crush the hope out of young hearts! Would I might shield you from it all! All!

Isa. Sorrow seems so far away tonight! But should it ever come, you will help me, will you not, you will always love me, Papa Aguila?

Ag. [*Clasping her*] Ah, would I not, my child. As the palm loves the singing brook purling in its shadow, and bends lovingly and tenderly over its pure, deep heart, so do I love my little señorita. So would I shelter her from the fierce heat of the countess' anger, from the mad hurricane of misfortune, though it should rend my withered branches and lay my old trunk in ruin beside her.

Isa. Dear old Aguila!

Ag. [*Rising and going L. with her*] Fear not, little one! Should trouble come, leave all to old Aguila. He will win back to you the joy that shall live when he is dust! Come, my bright eyes, come! [*Exuent in house*]

Jones. [*Appears at back, C. from L.*] Well, by Jove! This is the neatest I have seen in this country. A perfect earthly paradise! Paradise and the peri. Where's the peri, I wonder? I'll reconnoiter! [*Writes in notebook*] "Hacienda embowered in feathery palms, amid whose waving plumes fitful gleams of tropic sunlight steal, like bright fairies, laying their tresses in the murmuring fountains, chasing the roseate shadows in and out among the bloom-laden bowers, kissing the perfume, breathing lips of flowers as rarely beautiful and purely bright as a saint's dream of Heaven." There! That will read well in the *Herald.* [*Enter Annetta from house, stands watching Jones*]

Ann. Buenos dias, señor!

Jones. Ah! The peri, by Jove! Your servant, señorita! I hope I don't intrude. I was coming down the pass, and seeing this beautiful spot, could not help hiding from the heat in such a charming place for a moment.

ANN. [*Curtseying*] Oh, señor, I am sure you will be most welcome. The countess' house is always open to visitors. I am sure she will be pleased to entertain the nice American gentleman.

JONES. [*Fixing his collar and tie*] Ahem! And you, my pretty little flower of Mexico! Would it please you to have me stay?

ANN. I am sure the señor would be a much more charming guest than that cross old Count Pedro Martinez.

JONES. What a lovely picture of tropic female loveliness!

ANN. A picture? Why, señor, are you an artist?

JONES. Well, no, not exactly.

ANN. I'm glad of that, for I don't like artists!

JONES. [*Quickly*] Oh, well, I am no artist! I never could draw anything, not even two pair. In fact the only thing I can draw is my salary—and mosquitoes!

ANN. You see, señor, there was an artist from San Francisco who boarded with mother, just back of the cathedral, in the city yonder; and he went away without paying his board. Mother is very poor, and could not afford to lose the money. Señor, is San Francisco in America?

JONES. What charming ignorance of geography! [*Aloud*] No, my dear, it is in China. The wretch was a Chinaman in disguise!

ANN. [*Coyly*] I am glad he was not an American! But there was a señor from New York who made a great deal of money selling shares in some silver mine, and when he left Mexico suddenly, the people here began trying to find out what they had bought, and they are still trying when they don't stop to rest and swear.

JONES. Oh, he was an Indian.

ANN. Oh, no, señor! We have Indians here. He was not dark like them. I am sure he must have been a white man.

JONES. No, you see he was from the Manhattan Reservation. They look like white men till you know them; but they are Indian savages all the same. I hope you have never had any newspaper correspondents down here.

ANN. I think not, señor. What is it like?

JONES. Well, it's a sort of gentleman angel, if you can imagine such a thing.

ANN. I cannot.

JONES. Well, there are such things, but they are rare. He goes about seeking whom he may interview, trying to be pleasant and see all that he can and get acquainted with everybody and get them to talk to him—

ANN. Oh, I see! You are a correspondent!

JONES. [*Starting towards her*] You are an angel!

ANN. [*Running into house, laughing*] Adios, señor!

JONES. She's a charmer! The prettiest girl I ever saw! I must not lose sight of her. Hello! Here comes someone! These Mexicans are like their cactuses, they blossom with welcome and wait their chance to stick you. [*Enter Carlos R.1.E.*] Señor, I beg your pardon for this intrusion, but I stumbled in here quite unexpectedly, upon this little Eden. You see, I am an American writing up Mexican society, scandal, science, stocks, soldiery, spondoolix, et cetera. My name is Humbolt Agassis Jones, at your service.

CARL. [*Recognizing him*] What! My old friend Jones?

JONES. Castillo? Shake! I'm delighted to see you.

CARL. And I to see you, señor. We have not met since that night a month ago, when your bravery saved me from El Capitan and his band.

JONES. Friend Carlos, I guess we saved each other. You fought like a lion. I guess I am more indebted to you than you are to me.

CARL. Indeed, no! Señor Jones.

JONES. [*Laughing*] Wasn't it lively fun though? If you hadn't been such a crack shot, El Capitan and his cutthroats would have fallen heirs to our petty belongings—watches, wallets, wash-bills, toothbrushes and all. To say nothing of that little indispensable to travellers called life.

CARL. It was a narrow escape, señor. And we owe it to your reckless brav-'ery. You Americans never know when you are beaten. Well, I'm heartily glad to see you. [*Shakes hands again*]

JONES. What are you doing here? You sly rogue! Daphnis and Chloe, I'll warrant! Some fair señorita? Come! Confess!

CARL. Well, I will be frank with you. That is the reason of my prolonged stay here. But "The course of true love—" you know the adage.

JONES. What's the matter, old fellow? Is the fair divinity deaf to her worshiper, or is the Duenna lynx-eyed, or, worse than all, is her mama obdurate?

CARL. Neither. On the contrary, I am certain I am not an unwelcome guest, for the Countess Inez, my hostess, treats me with the most marked kindness. But when I try to have a word alone with the fair señorita, Isadora, I am always thwarted, I don't know how.

JONES. Castillo, we are sworn friends. Let me help you. Introduce me here, and rely on my aid.

CARL. Thanks, señor! I'll do it. It seems I must be doubly indebted to you. Both for life and happiness. You are indeed a friend.

JONES. There, there! You owe me nothing! It will serve my purpose as well. It will give me an insight into Mexican high life and society.

CARL. [*Looking off R.*] Ah, here comes our hostess. And with her, that old Count Pedro. He is always in my way!

JONES. Who is he?

CARL. I fear he is a suitor for the hand of Isadora.

JONES. So! He's the stumbling block is he? Well, I'll roll him out of your way. I'll keep him so busy he'll have no time to interfere. [*Enter countess and Pedro R.1.E.*]

CARL. Señora, pardon the liberty I take! A friend of mine was passing when we met quite accidentally. I presumed on your hospitality by detaining him. Allow me to present him to you.

INEZ. Your friends are mine, señor.

CARL. Thanks, señora! Permit me to introduce my dear friend, Señor Jones, from the United States. Señor Jones, the Countess Inez de Oro.

INEZ. You are most welcome, señor. I can only thank Señor Castillo for bringing us such a pleasant guest.

JONES. [*Kissing her hand*] Thanks, señora. So royal a welcome could only come from such queenly lips.

INEZ. [*Smiling*] I did not know you Americans were such adroit flatterers. Our gallants had best look to their laurels in the fine art of compliment. But pardon me! My guest and friend Count Pedro Martinez, Señor Jones.

JONES. [*Offers hand*] I'm glad to meet you, count.

PED. [*A dead shake*] Your servant, señor. [*Folds arms. Jones does sizing up business*]

CARL. Señor Jones and I have been sworn friends since a month ago, when being fellow travellers, we one night encountered El Capitan and his band in the Passo del Rey. I owe my life to his bravery that night.

JONES. Señora, don't believe him! He is as modest as he is brave. He fought like a tiger, and is the best shot I ever saw. But for him I should have been in paradise—or—perdition—tonight and a month's rent due.

PED. Señors, you were fortunate—few men have met El Capitan and lived to boast of it.

INEZ. Which proves how brave they both were.

PED. Still, señora, their escape was little short of a miracle.

JONES. [*Aside*] Where have I seen him before?

CARL. [*Aside to countess*] Señora, may I have the honor of a word with you, alone, when convenient?

INEZ. [*Up L.*] Certainly. Count, will you kindly play the host for me for a little while, and show Señor Jones around the grounds? I wish to speak to Señor Castillo a moment, and then we'll join you.

PED. [*Down R.C.*] Your wishes are pleasures to me, señora.

INEZ. [*To Jones who goes up L.*] Señor, make yourself perfectly at home here. I am only too happy to have the pleasure of numbering you among my guests.

JONES. I shall need no coaxing, señora. An angel's invitation to a paradise is sure to be accepted. [*They talk together, Jones points off to vista at back*]

BERNAL. [*Peers from trees, R.2.*] Hist, señor! I am here. [*Aguila enters L.U., sees Bernal, stops*]

PED. Caution! Watch your chance. He, Castillo, is in my way. A quick blow and be off. You can steal my horse.

BERN. My own is near by.

PED. Good! [*Exit Bernal, R.W. Exit Aguila R.U.E. Annetta enters from house*]

JONES. [*Aside*] The angel again, by Saint Thomas Jefferson!

INEZ. Annetta, tell Parquita to prepare the west room for a guest and tell Manuel to be ready to start down to the city.

ANN. Yes, señora. May I go with him?

INEZ. Yes.

JONES. [*Crossing R. behind Inez, aside to Annetta*] I am going to stay here!

ANN. I am glad, señor.

JONES. Are you, little sweetheart? [*Inez looks around, Annetta slips into house, Jones goes up C. expatiating in pantomime on the beauties of the scene*]

INEZ [*To Pedro*] Pardon my breach of etiquette, señor. I thought you had joined us.

PED. It is nothing, señora. [*To Jones*] Come, señor—I will be your guide. [*Jones and Pedro bow to Inez and exit R.3.E. Tremolo, pianissimo, passionate, till countess off*]

JONES. [*Aside, as he goes*] It isn't the first time he has been "guyed."

INEZ. [*Coming down with Carlos*] Now, Señor Carlos, we are alone. What is it?

CARL. Señora, you have been so kind, so good, but I have the greatest of all favors to ask of you.

INEZ. Señor Carlos, what would I not do for you?

CARL. You give me courage, señora. I love your daughter. Will you give her to me for my wife?

INEZ. [*Sits on fountain seat C.*] Sit down by me, Carlos. I want to talk to you. You are a strong, brave, noble man. You do not want this child. She is not your equal in any way. She is not mate for such a man as you. This is a mere passing fancy!

CARL. A passing fancy, señora? I love her, I adore her! Won't you give her to me?

INEZ. [*Breaking forth passionately*] Oh, Carlos! I cannot! I cannot!

CARL. [*Surprised*] Cannot? Why, señora, why?

INEZ. Listen, señor, and then condemn me if you will. My father was a man of iron. His will was law. He forced me, a motherless girl of fourteen into a hated marriage with Señor de Oro, a man older than himself. His only merit was his hoarded gold. I was sold to him, body and spirit. I cannot call that hated union a marriage! I loathed him!

CARL. Poor señora! What misery, what despair!

INEZ. Do you pity me, Carlos? Nay, listen. Isadora was born as the child of that loveless marriage. I almost hated the child for her father's sake. Then he, my master, my owner—I will not call him husband!—died, and I was free at last. My heart, chilled in its budding hope, lay frozen in my breast till I met you. Turn away your face, Carlos! Do you not see all? I cannot give you to her because I love you!

CARL. [*Amazed*] You—love—me!

INEZ. Yes! Don't speak, Carlos! I love you! Your touch thrills me and makes my heart leap, my blood run riot in my veins! I never knew I had a heart till it wakened at the music of your voice! Now it is a tide of passionate love that sets toward you as the river toward the sea! She is but a child, cold and weak as her father before her.

CARL. I love her, señora! I will be a good son to you and love you as a mother.

INEZ. [*Wildly*] Mother! I am not an old woman, Carlos! As a son? Never! As my own, my lover, my husband, my life? Yes, always! With a love that defies death itself! You are the only being I have loved since my childhood. I cannot lose you thus! Oh, Carlos, forgive me. I cannot crush my love, my hope! Your words stung me till they wrung this cry of despair from my lips and tore the hidden secret from my heart! Oh, Carlos, I love you so!

CARL. Oh, I am so sorry for this, countess! Sorry for your sake, for all our sakes!

INEZ. Beware! Love passionate as mine makes us angels or fiends. If returned, its warmth and light are poured out like the sunshine on the flowers. If pent and curbed, its fierce heat blasts what it would have cheered and blessed.

CARL. Pardon me, señora! I cannot control my heart! Will you not let me be your friend, your son, giving you that pure love a son may give a mother?

INEZ. [*Starting up*] No! If you cannot be mine, I will not place before me the torturing sight of your affection for another, the caresses that might have been mine but for her. [*Pedro appears R. at back, listening*]

CARL. Think of your child's happiness.

INEZ. [*Laughs bitterly*] I have wasted my life in sacrificing my heart to the happiness of others; you have said it, "I cannot control my heart!" Listen! To watch her love for you, your tenderness to her, would drive me mad, and I should kill you both! [*Pedro exits R.3. Countess falls on knees, arms around him*] Oh, hear me, Carlos! At your feet, forgetting all my pride, I plead for your love! Strong natures such as yours crave more than the weak return of cold hearts like hers. Think of the wealth of my love for you, and contrast it with the poverty of hers! Renounce her, Carlos, and take my heart, my soul, my life if you will!

CARL. [*Freeing himself*] Woman! Are you mad?

INEZ. [*Starts up, laughing wildly*] Perhaps I am. I hope so! To breaking hearts madness is a sweet oblivion, a blest lethe of forgetfulness. [*Falls onto bench*]

CARL. Are you a mother? Can you stand in the way of your child's happiness, and let your selfishness cast its shadow over her young life? Would you doom her to suffer the misery of seeing her blighted hopes realized by the cruel mother who could have saved, and has betrayed her? Woman! The very tigress is more tender of its young!

INEZ. You spurn my love! The day may come when I can rend your heart as you are rending mine! Will I spare you then, will I show mercy? Aye! The same mercy you show me now! I have laid all on the altar of my love! You scorn the offering. Tremble lest the angry flame leap up consuming the idol at whose feet it burned! Mark me! I would kill her with my own hands before you should have her! You have your answer! Farewell, señor—Ha! Ha! Ha! [*Exits in house, laughing bitterly. Pedro comes down L. slowly, from R.3.E.*]

CARL. [*Sinks in despair on fountain*] Name of Heaven! This is terrible! Is it love or madness? Does all hope end here? [*Starts up*] No! By the angels! I will win her yet! I [*Turns R. facing Pedro*] Your pardon, señor! I did not see you. [*Crosses Pedro to R.*]

PED. [*Detaining him*] Stay a moment, señor. I am here with the countess' consent, as a suitor for her daughter's hand, and I want no interference.

CARL. [*Defiantly*] Should she ever become your wife, you would then have some right to dictate who her friends may be, certainly not now.

PED. [*Hotly*] My rights and my actions are my own, and not subject to the approval of a fortune-hunting adventurer.

CARL. [*Quickly*] Señor—[*Restrains himself*] My blood is as pure as yours, a noble! If my purse is lighter, so is my greed.

PED. [*In rage*] Greed, fellow!

CARL. It has never been necessary for my family to hide the sources of its wealth!

PED. [*Attempts to speak*] Ah—

CARL. [*Interrupts him*] Nor have I grown old in low cunning, craft and wickedness!

PED. [*Starts to strike him with glove*] Fool! Your life shall pay for this!

CARL. [*Grasps wrist*] You forget that you are playing the gentleman! We are guests here, and have no right to settle our differences before the doors of our hostess.

PED. Enough, señor! You shan't have that excuse! Words are useless between us! If your heart is as brave as your tongue, meet me tomorrow morning at sunrise, at yonder bridge. Our meeting without witnesses, and our cause to the tribunal of brave men. [*Touches sword*] These!

CARL. [*Bows*] I will be there, señor. Till then farewell! [*Exit C. and L.*]

PED. [*Countess enters from house*] Dog—I'll cut his heart out! [*Sees countess*] Ah, señora.

INEZ. You seem annoyed, count, what is it?

PED. I am annoyed, señora. I cannot brook that Castillo's attentions to Isadora. Give her to me at once!

INEZ. I will, señor. You shall be wedded tomorrow if you will.

PED. [*Kissing her hand*] Señora, you are too good! Tomorrow let it be then! And now, good-night!

INEZ. Good-night, count. Tomorrow, at noon. Good-bye till then! [*Exit Pedro, C. and R.*] Ha, ha! Carlos Castillo! The game is mine. [*Exit R.1.E. Enter Carlos C. from L.*]

CARL. My darling! I may never see her again! But if I live she shall be mine, I swear it! My dear one, my beautiful, good-bye, good-bye! [*Sees guitar by hammock on porch*] Ah, Isadora's guitar! It shall be my messenger, and bear her my adios. [*Sings. Music tremolo, hurry, pianissimo*]

> Dark night o'er the sad earth fell,
> Sad to bid the day "Farewell"!
> Sad and dark my spirit true,
> As it bids farewell to you—
> Soft the night wind's gentle sigh,
> In the rose-heart dew-tears lie.
> Thus my heart, with sigh and tear,
> Bids farewell to thee most dear!

Though the happy day is done,
There will come another sun—
Though we part in grief and pain,
Darling I'll come back again!
Love, I leave my heart with you!
Keep your heart to Carlos true!
Sad the word as tolling knell!
Oh, my life! Farewell! Farewell! [*Lays down guitar and turns to go. Up C.*]

ISA. [*Cautiously at door*] Hist! Carlos!

CARL. [*Turns quickly*] Isadora! [*Clasps her. Bernal creeps out R.2. with knife. Draws back to stab Carlos. Aguila springs on after him, wrenches knife from him and knocks him down. Chord fortissimo*]

AG. Coward!

BERN. [*Skulking off R.*] You red devil! We shall meet again!

AG. [*Picking up knife*] Never but once, and then I'll leave you for a buzzard's feast.

ISA. [*Going to him*] Are you hurt?

AG. No, estrella de mia alma!

CARL. Aguila, you have saved my life! I shall not forget this, my friend. [*Offers purse; Aguila refuses*]

AG. All for her, señor! Be kind to her and make her happy, and old Aguila will be repaid a thousandfold! [*Puts her in Carlos' arms. Going up C.*]

CARL. I will! I swear it! [*Calls*] Aguila!

AG. [*Turns*] Señor?

CARL. You are my friend. Meet me tomorrow morning, half an hour after sunrise, at yonder bridge. I may need your aid to care for a wounded man.

AG. I will be there, señor. Say nothing of that murderous dog! Leave him to me. I will guard you as though you were my own son, for you are her happiness! Good-night!

ISA. [*Rushing to his arms*] Dear old Papa Aguila! Bless you! Bless you!

AG. Flor di cielo! My darling child! [*Kisses her and exits C. and L.*]

CARL. [*Hurriedly*] My life, my hope! I must leave you. Your mother will not yield. But fear not! I will win you yet! Good-bye, my dear one!

ISA. [*Clinging to him*] Oh, Carlos! My heart will break! Must you leave me?

CARL. Yes, dearest, for your sake. But the countess must not see us together here! Aguila shall tell you our plans. If I am seen here, you will suffer for my rashness. Be brave, little woman! [*Kisses her*] I'll soon come back. [*Chord segue as before*]

AG. [*Rising at back*] Hist! Señor Carlos! Away! [*Exit Carlos C. and L.*]

INEZ. [*Coming on R.2.E., seizing Isadora's wrist*] You wretch! I saw your clandestine meeting with your lover! Girl, mark me! You shall renounce him! Tomorrow, at noon, you wed Count Pedro Martinez!

ISA. [*Starting up*] Never!

INEZ. [*Enraged*] I swear it, girl! Tomorrow you shall be his bride or death's. Choose then! Your answer! [*Chord, hurry, pianissimo, suit action*]

AG. [*Springs up, Isadora in arms*] No! [*Pedro appears at back with riding-whip. Comes down back*]

INEZ. Dare you defy me?

AG. Yes! I have been the slave of your family for sixty years! I have obeyed your slightest wish, not through fear, but love and duty to your race. That love makes me defy you now.

PED. [*R.C. Threatens with whip*] Dog! [*Aguila raises hand commandingly*]

AG. Hold! I am a peon, a slave—the Spaniard's faithful dog, as you will, but not a cur to—One cut of that whip, and I am a sleuth-hound at your throat—the blood of kings is in my veins and cannot brook a blow!

PED. [*Strikes at him with whip*] Dog! Take that!

AG. [*Wresting whip from him, throws Pedro C. on his face*] And with it, your life! [*Draws machete*]

ISA. [*Kneeling R. of Aguila*] Stay, Aguila, spare him for my sake!

AG. I can wait! [*Inez, R. opposite 2. Pedro, Aguila, C. Isadora, kneeling R.C.*]

PICTURE

ACT II.

SCENE 1 : *Eight bars lively at rise. Handsome tropic landscape, 2. Bridge to run on R.2. with connected groundpieces, to draw off. Scene fixed for boxings to revolve up from tormentors for Scene 2. Early dawn. Distant chimes ringing at rise. Valley of Mexico.*

JONES. [*Discovered sitting on bridge, writes*] "Beautiful view, snow-capped mountains, faint cathedral chimes, purple leagues, tropical sunrise, distant city, lovely valley, seen through lace-like llanos and plumy palms, fern embowered limpid brooks." Limped brooks? No! It runs crooked but it don't limp! "Staggering brooks" is better. [*Corrects*] There, that will do for the sketch. I'll put in the coloring later. [*Sings*] Hello, who's that? [*Looks back of him*] Carlos, as I live. Buenos dias, caballero!

CARL. [*Smiling, enter R.2.*] Buenos dias, Señor Humbolt. You are out early.

JONES. Yes, and you too. You see I am up to catch the tropic sunrise and dish up a little journalistic mess for that gossip gormand, the American Public. But what gets you up at this hour?

CARL. [*Evasively*] I could not sleep. Besides, I had an appointment at daylight.

JONES. Isn't the view fine from this point? I could linger here for hours admiring it.

CARL. My friend, will you do me a favor?

JONES. Certainly, Carlos. What is it?

CARL. [*Sun gradually up*] Go and find Aguila, the old Indian—

JONES. I say, Carlos, why are you so anxious to get rid of me? Oh, I see! The appointment at sunrise. I beg pardon! Oh, you sly fox! A love tryst, and this the trysting place! And I am in the way! "Two's company, three's a crowd!" Ha, Ha, Ha, Ha!

CARL. [*Gravely. Takes Jones' hand*] My friend, it is a tryst of death! I have an appointment to fight Count Pedro Martinez here, at sunrise.

JONES. I'll be your best man. No, that is, I mean, your second.

CARL. The duel was to be without seconds. That was the agreement, and I must hold to it. But I thank you. There! Leave me now and return with Aguila in half an hour. One or the other of us will need your good offices. Should I fall, tell Isadora.

JONES. [*Grasping his hand*] I will do as you wish, Carlos. But I don't trust that Señor Count. I dread foul play from him.

CARL. I have no fear. He is at least a gentleman.

JONES. [*Aside*] I doubt it! [*Aloud. Shaking Carlos' hand warmly*] Goodbye old fellow, and good luck! If Mr. Count harms you, he will owe me the next dance! It will be "Pistols for Two! Balance all, Second Couple Lead Out!" I'll fill him as full of windows as a Long Branch cottage! [*Exit R.2., over bridge*]

CARL. This is an unpleasant affair, and the sooner it is over, the better. What detains Martinez? [*Looks off R.*] Here he comes now. [*Enter Pedro, R.1.E.*] Good morning, señor!

PED. Good morning! You are prompt. [*Music through fight till Carlos falls*]

CARL. [*Preparing*] Yes. [*They drop jackets and serapes and sombreros. Serape round L. arm. Pedro drops locket. They fight. Count crowds in and hits Carlos on head with knife and stabs him. Carlos falls. Pedro rises, laughs cruelly, throws off serape. Chord fortissimo. Inez enters R.2. as Pedro kneels to finish Carlos. Inez throws him R.*]

INEZ. Hold! Murderer! You have killed him! [*Kneels, takes Carlos' head on knee, staunching blood with her handkerchief*]

PED. [*Smiling*] Yes, señora, according to the code! Dead, but all fairly.

INEZ. Fiend! You murdered him!

PED. He was your lover.

INEZ. It is false!

PED. Señora, I heard your burning words of love to him last night, by the fountain. I heard him spurn your heart! I have avenged you!

INEZ. [*Furious*] Are you my bloodhound to track to death all that offend me? Assassin! Did I bid you drive your cruel steel through that heart around which my own heart-strings had twined?

PED. No, señora. But as I am to be your son, I killed the man who insulted your love and crossed mine!

INEZ. What! You my son, and your hands red with his blood? Never! Tomorrow's dawn sees her in the convent of Santa Madre. Begone, monster! Never let me look upon your face again!

PED. [*Bowing*] As you will, señora. Farewell! You will repent your anger, and give her to me yet!

INEZ. [*Fiercely*] Never! Go!

PED. [*Smiling*] We shall see! [*Exits R.1.E.*]

INEZ. [*Passionately*] Oh, Carlos! Forgive me! Speak to me! Did I bring you to this? Look up, Carlos! I forget your words of scorn, forget all save that I loved you! [*Kisses him*] Oh, that my kisses might breathe their passionate life into your lips! Were my heart cold in death, your clasp would make it leap to life again, though my soul stood at the gates of paradise! Your kiss would lure my spirit back from Heaven to you! Oh, are you dead? [*Feels heart*] No, no! He lives! His heart beats faintly yet! Perhaps I may save him! [*Enter Jones over bridge*] Oh, Carlos! You shall not die! You shall not!

JONES. What! Carlos wounded? Ah, señora! Let me lead you away. This is no place for you. This is no sight for woman's eyes.

INEZ. But to leave him thus!

JONES. [*Kneels, feels heart*] Leave him to me. You can dispatch for a doctor, and send me aid to bear him where he can have careful nursing. Thank Heaven, he lives!

INEZ. Ah, señor, you are too kind! Save him for Heaven's sake!

JONES. Fear nothing, lady! He is my friend. I shall do all in my power for him. [*She staggers*] But you are faint! Let me help you across the bridge. [*Exit with her over bridge. Aguila and Padre enter L.1.E.*]

AG. There, padre, I have told you all. You are her friend! The Church, your sacred office, your wisdom can protect her, poor child! I can do nothing! I am only a slave!

JONES. [*Running on R.2.E.*] Aguila! Padre! Quick, Carlos has been wounded! See! [*All to body. Aguila lifts him tenderly and, after, puts him on Padre's knee for examination*]

PADRE. Wounded? Nomen coeli! Let me look! [*Takes him on knee. Aguila rises at back*] The Saints be praised! He lives! [*Pause for business*] I do not think the wound is deep. And this handkerchief has stopped the flow of blood. I can save him.

AG. [*Seeing locket. R.C.*] Ah, what is this? [*Picks it up*] Saints in Heaven! My dear lady—my Mercedes' picture!

PADRE. [*Surprised*] Mercedes!

AG. Yes! How came it here? Master Juan wore this locket the day he was captured by El Capitan! I was with him, and was left in the pass for dead.

PADRE. Then the man who lost it must have been El Capitan!

JONES. Yes, that is certain! We have got him then!

PADRE. [*Surprised*] What do you mean? It cannot have been him, for he was a mere boy at the time.

JONES. No! I mean his antagonist. He must have lost it.

PADRE. Who was he?

JONES. Count Pedro Martinez. Carlos told me, not half an hour ago, that he had an appointment to fight the count, here, at sunrise.

AG. [*Aside*] Ah, the assassin last night! I see it all! El Capitan's hireling!

PADRE. Come! Bring him to my house at once! Not a word of this to a living soul, I charge you. Come! Follow me! [*They bear Carlos off L.1.E.*]

SCENE 2.

JONES. [*Entering R.1.E. looks R. and L.*] Nobody in sight along the pass. Aguila will take some short cut, I suppose. Indian like, he knows every by-path in the country. Hello! What is that, through the trees, yonder? The flutter of a petticoat! Oh, Annetta! Sweet Annetta! Would to goodness I could get her! I would not envy kings their thrones, if she'd be Mrs. Humbolt Jones! Short meter, please!

ANN. [*Entering L.1.E.*] Oh, señor! I am so glad I have found you!

JONES. So am I, my sweet Annetta! But you look frightened. What's the matter?

ANN. I *am* frightened, señor! But it's for you.

JONES. For me? Why, what have I done?

ANN. I have an awful secret to tell you!

JONES. A woman and a secret! All right, Annetta. I'll help you keep it.

ANN. Oh, señor! this is no jest. You are the friend of Señor Castillo; and you and he fought with El Capitan's band, in the Passo del Rey and escaped from them, did you not?

JONES. [*Surprised*] Yes. But how in thunder did you find that out?

ANN. Listen, señor! Last night I went down to the city, to visit my mother, who is poor; and to whom I take my wages as often as I can go to her. Well, she was sick; and I went for a doctor for her. As I was coming home, I saw two men near the back of the cathedral. They were rough-looking men, and I was afraid; so I crept into one of the dark corners and waited for them to pass. They were talking earnestly and did not see me. I heard one of them tell the other that El Capitan wanted him to skulk around the Hacienda de Oro and kill Señor Castillo; but that the Indian had balked him; but that he would finish his work, and would not forget to put that red watch-dog to sleep, and that American too! For, said he, he finished six of the best men in the band, in the Passo del Rey; and that one of them was his brother.

JONES. Oh! He will, will he? Well, if he "monkeys" with me, he'll join his brother in the Happy Hunting Grounds quicker than a "jay" will bite a three card monte!

ANN. I was so frightened, señor! It seemed that I could not get back here quick enough to tell you.

JONES. So, you little dear, you didn't want me to be killed, eh?

ANN. Oh, no, señor!

JONES. Well, my Guardian Angel, it was very kind of you to take so much pains on my account; and I am very grateful to you. I shall be on my guard, you may be sure. But I am not afraid of them.

ANN. Oh, señor! You do not know that terrible El Capitan.

JONES. Oh, yes I do! I had a short call from him and his whole family in the Passo del Rey. It was a very lively visit, too!

ANN. They glide like snakes and bite you from the thicket, when you least expect it!

JONES. Yes, but sometimes the snake gets "snaked" out of his nest! Why don't they catch the scoundrel?

ANN. Oh, I forgot to tell you the rest. The man who threatened to kill you, told the other one the shortest way for him to go home with his goods to the cave, was by the Passo del Ferdinand, to the mouth of the Toreador's Cañon; and then to follow up the stream for a mile, where, by the large fallen pine tree across the stream, he would see the path that led to the cave.

JONES. [*Dancing for joy*] We've got him, Annetta! [*Seizing her and waltzing her around*] We've got him! Tol-de-rol-de-rol, -de-rol! Tol-de-roodle-de-ray!

ANN. Got whom, señor?

JONES. El Capitan and his whole nest full of snakes! Listen, my darling Annetta. Don't say a word of this to anyone! The Government of Mexico offers a reward of ten thousand dollars for the capture of El Capitan. Now, you say your mother is poor. You have discovered his hiding-place, and that money is yours!

ANN. Mine! Why, I cannot capture him, señor! I am only a weak woman.

JONES. See here, Annetta! Don't you breathe a word of this to a soul! You have trapped him, and I'll capture him for you. You get the money and I'll get lots of fun and a "crackerjack" of a newspaper article! Your mother will be comfortable for the rest of her life, and you can be a lady of fashion.

ANN. I don't care about myself, if mother could have a nice home in her old age and not be poor.

JONES. You are a good little daughter, and would make an angel of a wife; and that is just what I need in my business.

ANN. But, señor, you had better not try it.

JONES. What? Getting married?

ANN. No. Capturing El Capitan. You might get killed.

JONES. Then you don't want me to get killed, eh?

ANN. Why, certainly not! I—I—

JONES. [*Eagerly*] Well, "You—you" —you love me a little bit, then?

ANN. Well, I'd like you much better alive, señor.

JONES. Yes! I wouldn't be an interesting corpse! See here, Annetta! Let's get down to business! I'll catch that blankety blank robber and get the reward for you. I don't want a penny of it; but want to put your mother on "Easy Street." I've never seen her; but I like the old lady for your sake. Now I am not a bad sort; but average up pretty well on a general invoice. I love you harder than a Mexican mosquito can bite; and I want you to marry me! There! What do you say?

ANN. [*Laughing*] Much obliged!

JONES. You're welcome.

ANN. But, señor! I hardly know you!

JONES. Not know me? Why, we're partners in business! Annetta, Jones and Co. Robber Catchers, Cave Finders, Etc., Etc. Look here! If you don't consent, I'll go and get killed by El Capitan and every one of his band that I come across! I am determined to get married or murdered.

ANN. Well, don't get killed, señor; and we'll try to get better acquainted. I must have time to make up my mind, you know.

JONES. Remember! I can't hope to live unless I live to hope!

ANN. You'd better live to hope, then, señor!

JONES. [*Trying to kiss her*] My angel!

ANN. [*Eluding him*] Wait till we're better acquainted! I haven't given you my promise yet, remember! [*Exits L.1., laughing*]

JONES. No; but you will! You shall! Like General Scott, I have set my heart on the conquest of Mexico! Well, I must be off for the padre's! We'll catch that cuss as sure as Lord made little apples! [*Exit L.1.*]

SCENE 3: *Interior of priest's house. Door with curtains R. flat, window in flat, C. Set door L.U.E. backed exterior. Couch in C. at back. Large robe or mat L.C. at back. Door L. flat backed interior. Chairs R. and L. opposite 2. Carlos insensible, on couch, Jones and padre over him. Aguila on watch at window.*

PADRE. Watch close, Aguila. Warn us of anyone's approach. I think he is regaining consciousness. The wound is not deep, and he is only weak from loss of blood. He has received a hard blow on his head that has done the most of this.

CARL. [*Opening his eyes*] Water! [*Jones gives it*] Where am I?

JONES. Among friends, Carlos. How do you feel?

CARL. Very weak. Am I wounded?

PADRE. Not very badly. I will have you on your feet again in a few days if you will obey me.

CARL. To whom am I indebted for this kindness?

JONES. To the good padre and faithful old Aguila.

CARL. [*Taking Jones' hand*] And you, my more than friend!

PADRE. Yes, señor.

JONES. Padre, you should know your patient. This is Colonel Carlos Castillo.

PADRE. [*Surprised*] Son of Antonio and Maria de Castillo?

CARL. [*Surprised*] Yes, padre! How did you know that?

PADRE. Thank Heaven that I can serve you! I have not seen you since you were a child. Carlos, you are my sister's son!

CARL. [*Trying to rise*] What! My uncle, Padre Domingus?

PADRE. [*Taking his hand*] Yes. There! You must lie quiet now, my boy. The Holy Word says "Thou shalt not kill." My son, you have nearly lost your life by disobeying Heaven's command. I must heal you body and soul.

CARL. Uncle, there are some insults no man can bear. I am a soldier, and it is better to die like a man than live like a coward!

PADRE. [*Soothing him*] There, there, my son! I'll not be uncharitable to you! Young blood is hot, and who knows? Had I been a soldier instead of a priest of Heaven, I might have done as you did! Who was your antagonist?

CARL. Count Pedro Martinez.

PADRE. Did you see him drop anything where you fought?

CARL. Yes. I remember, when he threw off his serape, I saw something glitter and fall. It was about the size of a coin, and was gold.

JONES. We have the rat in the trap!

PADRE. [*Showing locket*] Might it not have been this?

CARL. I think likely. Did you find it there?

PADRE. Yes. Listen, my son! You may do the state a better service than risking your life in a duel. Fourteen years ago Juan Alvarez was waylaid and probably murdered by El Capitan. On that day he wore this locket. It contains the picture of his wife, Mercedes. It has never been seen till today. The man that lost it was probably the one who took it from the body of Alvarez.

CARL. [*Excited*] El Capitan?

PADRE. El Capitan!

CARL. [*Trying to rise*] I will go at once to the guards—

JONES. [*Restraining him*] No, Carlos! Remember your wound—

CARL. 'Tis nothing! A soldier's trade is to give and take hard knocks like a man. I will seize his servants. They shall confess.

PADRE. No! You must let your wound heal first.

CARL. [*Wildly*] And in the meantime he may win her? What! Spare my body and lose my soul's hope? What is the pain of this scratch to a broken heart?

JONES. Hear me, Carlos! Leave him to me. Aguila will guard the little señorita.

AG. Yes, with my life!

JONES. For her sake, you must remain here under the good padre's care. I'll track that wolf, and if he shows his teeth at the American eagle, there won't be enough of him left to write an epitaph over! Good-bye. I'll see you later! [*Exit door L.U.E.*]

AG. [*At window*] The little señorita is hastening up the walk. [*Tremolo pianissimo till Isadora on*]

PADRE. Quick! Help me in here with Carlos! [*They lift him off in cot D.R.F.*] My son, not a word till I bid you! The sudden shock might kill her or drive her mad. If you love her, keep silence.

CARL. I will, padre, I will! [*Padre closes curtains. Knock at D.L.3.*]

PADRE. [*Seated R.*] Enter! [*Isadora runs in, dropping shawl. Falls on her knees by padre*]

Isa. Oh, padre! Carlos, my Carlos! My love, my life, is dead.

Padre. [*Stroking her head*] There, there, calm yourself, my child. We are all mortal. Let us hope for the best.

Isa. Hope! What hope is there for me now? Speak of hope to the condemned wretch, to the castaway, struggling with the waves, for they have still a thread to cling to. But not to the woman whom death has robbed of all that life held dear to her! The word is but a cruel mockery! These are not childish tears that a caress can soothe. Mine is a loving woman's woe!

Ag. [*Wiping away his tears*] Poor child! It seems so cruel not to tell her! [*Turns to window*]

Padre. My child, remember you are a Christian! Have faith in Heaven! Through faith the dead have been called back to life! Remember the story of Lazarus. "Though dead, he yet lives."

Isa. [*Looking up*] Oh, good Padre Domingus! I see the joy in your eyes! He is not dead! You fear to tell me suddenly! See! I am strong! Tell me! If you have any mercy, tell me! Is there any hope?

Padre. Yes, my child!

Isa. Alive? Thank Heaven! Bless you for your kind words of comfort! [*Sobs on padre's breast*]

Padre. There, calm yourself, my daughter! He is alive, but it must be a close secret for a time. Can I trust you?

Isa. Trust me? For Carlos' sake? O father, yes! But why must it be a secret?

Padre. You shall know all in good time.

Isa. But where is he? May I not see him?

Ag. [*At window*] Oh, padre, the countess! [*Music, hurry, pianissimo, till countess on*]

Padre. Quick, my child! Not a word, not a breath or you are lost! Your lover is in there! In! In! [*Isadora flings open curtains*]

Isa. [*Falling on knees by couch*] Carlos!

Carl. [*Clasping her*] My darling! [*Padre closes curtains. Knock L.3.E. Aguila throws himself in L.U. corner, under rug*]

Padre. [*Killing time*] Coming! Coming! [*Opens door*] Ah, my daughter! You are welcome. Come in!

Inez. [*Enters and comes C.*] Padre Domingus, you are the skilled physician both of the body and the stricken spirit. You devote your life to healing the ills of all that come to you in sickness or affliction. I have come to claim your good offices for my poor, heartbroken child!

Padre. Your child? What do you mean, señora?

INEZ.　Padre, my daughter's lover has been killed in a duel. The blow has broken her heart. I come to you to crave an asylum for her within the convent's holy cloisters. There she may end her sad days in thoughts of Heaven, and learn consolation from the sweet and solemn service of the Church!

PADRE.　I understand you, countess, better than you think. The convent is a refuge for the world-weary spirit, not a prison in which malice or treachery locks its victims. You cannot use the Church of God to do the work of Hell!

INEZ. [*Astonished*]　Padre! What do you mean?

PADRE.　You look on your child, not with a mother's, but a rival's eye, and would make the Church the toil of your wicked plans. Thou monster!

INEZ.　False priest! You have refused her the convent's refuge, then she shall wed Count Pedro Martinez!

PADRE.　If you try to force her into such an unholy marriage, I know the secret of your cruelty to your dead sister, and will blast you with it.

INEZ. [*Startled*]　What? Do your worst! I have wealth and power, and I will crush you!

PADRE.　Though you were an empress, what were your puny power to me? I am the servant of the King of Kings! What is the little might of man matched against a holy faith, throned in the faithful hearts of millions?

INEZ.　She is my child, and must obey me!

PADRE.　We shall see! If you refuse your consent to her marriage with Carlos, I will crush you! [*Music, hurry, pianissimo, till curtain*]

INEZ. [*Catching at his words*]　If I refuse? Ah, he lives, then! [*Sees shawl*] See! She, too, has been here! [*Tears open curtains*] So! I have found you? [*Drags her L.C.*]

ISA. [*Kneeling at her feet*]　Mercy, mother, mercy! Do not tear me from him! My heart will break!

INEZ. [*Seizing her wrist*]　I care not! Come!

CARL. [*Struggles up*]　You human tigress! You shall not! Would you kill her? You have said it! You—ah! [*Sinks exhausted by bed. Padre springs to catch him*]

PADRE.　Woman! Would you have his blood on your hands?

INEZ.　I'll bend her to my will though she goes mad! [*Throws Isadora to her L., as Aguila, throwing off rug, springs and catches Isadora with his L. arm*]

AG.　Not while I live! [*Countess with a cry of rage, draws stiletto from her hair, stabs at him. He catches her wrist in R. hand. She drops dagger*]

PICTURE

ACT III.

House near the coast, at Puebla. Handsome Mexican interior. Large window with wooden shutters to open in, in C. Backed by garden in 4. Large panel pictures R. and L. of C. window. R. picture to open. Black or stone backing to panel. Set door R.3.E. Scene boxed. Dressing table L.U.E. NOTE: *This can be set with three-door fancy, or with plain chamber by having drapery over C. window. Enter countess R.3.E. At rise, eight bars of stormy music.*

INEZ. I have her safe at last! It was a good thought of mine, to bring her here to Puebla. They will not follow us here! She shall not elude me this time! Locked in this room, she cannot escape! I will send for Count Pedro at once. He shall marry her immediately. Though she kills herself at the altar, I care not! I hate her for her father's sake! What is Antonio de Oro's brat to me? I was but the slave bought with his gold! She is the child of hate, not of love! I owe her nothing. Would I had strangled her in her cradle, then she would never have risen between me and my love! Oh, Carlos, Carlos! My darling! You shall be mine. I would sell my soul for you! As for that red traitor, Aguila, he shall die! Defiance to me! His mistress! Manuel has promised to silence him forever! Poor Manuel! Poor faithful fool! He would go to his death at my bidding! He shall stab him while he sleeps. No dog of a peon shall defy me and live! [*Laughs wildly. Grasps her head*] Oh, my brain! My brain! Am I going mad? No! No! I will not! It is only this sleepless fever of desperation. With her once out of my way and Aguila dead, I can rest! [*Jones passes window R. to L.*] Who is that? [*Runs to window*] The American señor! How could he have followed us here? I must be calm! [*Calls R.1.*] Annetta!

ANN. [*Entering R.1.*] Yes, señora countess!

INEZ. There is a gentleman coming: Señor Jones. Admit him and make my excuse. I will see him presently.

ANN. Very well, señora countess. [*Exit Inez R.1.E. Jones knocks, L.U.E.*]

ANN. [*Opening door*] Good morning, Señor Jones! Come in!

JONES. [*Entering*] What? My sweet Annetta? And alone too? I'm in luck!

ANN. The countess told me to say she would be in, presently.

JONES. Then, to business! Will you marry me?

ANN. Why, you have not captured El Capitan yet?

JONES. Was that the condition? I am going today. I was only waiting for your answer. I wanted to know whether I was to get married or massacred.

ANN. Oh, you mustn't get killed! It isn't a bit nice!

JONES. To die is bitter, but it is better than to love Annetta and then not get her!

ANN. Why, señor! I am only a poor girl, a servant! I am no wife for a gentleman like you.

JONES. Annetta, the accident of position cuts no ice with Jones! Poverty is no crime; and a servant may be more of a lady than the mistress she serves! Annetta, a poor girl who is a true, pure woman and a good daughter, is a queen among women if she is crowned with a servant's cap! I want a wife who is a wife. Put your head here, please, and say: "Yes!"

ANN. [*Putting head on his breast*] Well, then, yes!

JONES. America has taken Mexico!

ANN. No! Mexico has taken America!

JONES. Well, America and Mexico have signed an eternal treaty of love and union. Let's sign the treaty, thus! [*Kisses her*] Signed, sealed and delivered! Now El Capitan is a dead man!

ANN. Is he dead?

JONES. Well, no, not yet. He's just hanging round till I get there, but he will be!

ANN. Hist! The countess! [*Enter Inez R.1. Annetta bows and exits L.1.*]

INEZ. Ah, Señor Jones! I am glad to see you. Come in.

JONES. [*Entering*] Pardon my intrusion, countess. Do not think I wish to interfere in your affairs. I have come as the friend of Carlos—

INEZ. [*Graciously*] And you are welcome! It is no intrusion, señor. I am very glad that you have come, for I can say to you what I could not say to him. You think me cruel, heartless. I am not. When you know all, you will see I am just and right.

JONES. It is not my place to question the actions of a lady under her own roof, señora.

INEZ. Will you hear me, señor?

JONES. Certainly, señora.

INEZ. Do you think I could be cruel to my own child, señor?

JONES. [*Evasively*] Such things have been before now.

INEZ. I am a friend of Carlos. To justify myself and cure him of his foolish infatuation, I must unveil the skeleton in our family. Know, then, that Isadora is not my child!

JONES. [*Surprised*] Not your child?

INEZ. No. She is the child of Señor Antonio de Oro, my husband, by a slave! Carlos is of noble blood, one of the oldest Spanish families. I love him as though he were my own son. Now what sort of hostess would I be, señor, to let him wed this child of shame?

JONES. [*Incredulously*] If this be true, señora, how came you to rear her as your own child?

INEZ. My husband was so much my senior, that my love for him was more the love of a daughter. Hence I was free from those jealousies that would have tortured a wife. He loved the bright child, and as we had lost our own daughter in infancy, to please him I reared Isadora as my own child.

JONES. Pardon me, countess! But it seems hardly credible.

INEZ. It is true nevertheless. No matter what that scheming padre may say to the contrary. He knows nothing of the truth. In fact, I have hidden all evidence of the secret so carefully that I now have no proof to confirm my statements. But the fact remains. I feel that I have only done my duty by Carlos, although he may feel unkindly toward me.

JONES. Does Señorita Isadora know of her origin?

INEZ. No, señor. No one would ever have known of it, if I had not been driven to reveal it. I will be frank with you, señor, for I feel that I can trust you. I love Carlos, and I could not bear to see him won away from me by a creature whose very existence is an insult to Heaven, and whose origin must bring the blush to every honest cheek.

JONES. [*Shrewdly*] It seems strange, señora, you did not think of this when you made her your child, gave her your name and the place of your own offspring in your house.

INEZ. Señor, could I refuse the last request of that old man as he lay there dying? He had always been kind to me, although he knew I could not love him. He had given me position, title, almost boundless wealth. Could I do less than share the name and fortune I owed to his bounty with the child he loved? My gratitude to him was stronger than my scruples. You cannot dream how hard it is for me, even now, to betray his secret! Had her love fallen on anyone in the world but Carlos, the secret should have remained buried forever.

JONES. [*Aside*] What a lawyer she would have made! [*Aloud*] I will tell Carlos what you have said, señora.

INEZ. [*Giving her hand*] Señor, you are so good! Tell him all, and then let him judge me calmly and honestly.

JONES. [*Rising*] Well, señora, I must be going. [*Aside*] Perhaps the padre can unravel this snarl of lies. [*Aloud*] Good-day!

INEZ. [*Shaking hand*] Señor, I thank you for this call, as it has given me a chance to save Carlos and vindicate myself. Good-bye! [*Exit Jones. She laughs triumphantly*] There! I have made Carlos' pride my ally. He will not wed a child of shame! Ah, Padre Domingus! I told you I would conquer yet! Woman's wit against man's power! It is a desperate game, but I have won! Aguila's lips once sealed, no one can disprove my story. [*Goes to door R.3.E.*] You may come out now. [*Music, tremolo, pianissimo, till Isadora on*]

Isa. [*Entering*] Mother, if you have one kindly feeling, if your heart is not stone, do not torture me any more! Do not threaten me with this hated marriage with Count Pedro! Or, if you are merciless still, why, kill me! I am ready to die!

Inez. Perhaps I may if you do not obey me. You marry Count Pedro at once!

Isa. [*Falling on knees*] Oh, mother! Have pity! Mercy!

Inez. [*Throwing her off*] Child, it is time this farce was ended! Listen! You are not my child! You are the child of my husband by a slave! You are a thing of shame!

Isa. [*Defiantly*] It is a lie!

Inez. [*Sneeringly*] Indeed! How do you know? I have reared you as my child, but you are not. You are a stain upon the family whose name you bear! Carlos knows this now, and he would cut off his right hand before he would disgrace his noble name by giving that hand or name to a thing like you!

Isa. You have lied. But I will use your own weapons against you. I shall tell Count Pedro Martinez this story, and he will refuse the child of your husband's slave!

Inez. [*Fiercely*] Do it if you dare! I will declare you insane. I will send you to a private madhouse. Do not think to trifle with me! You cannot escape from this room. Aguila cannot help you. I will put him beyond reach of you! You have no alternative, you must yield!

Isa. Never! I can die!

Inez. Fool! You are a feather in my hands! There is no foe this side of death to match a woman who wars for love and hate at once! Kill yourself if you will! You only serve my purpose. [*Going R.3.E.*] Beat your wings against your cage if you will, you cannot escape. [*Exit door R.3.E., laughing. Music, tremolo, till Aguila enters*]

Isa. [*Throwing off restraint*] The child of a slave! A thing of infamy! A living shame! And he believes it! He loathes, despises me! My last hope gone, a helpless captive, branded with infamy, Carlos lost to me forever. My only choice that hated marriage or a madhouse! No! There is always one hope left to despair. Death! [*Prays R.C.*] Santa Madre! Forgive me, if I do wrong! I, who have no mother! Better death than dishonor, and a marriage unsanctified by love is nothing less! Think how I am goaded to despair! Thou, who knowest all suffering, forgive my sin and take me to thyself! [*Sobbing. Goes to toilet-table up L. on which is cushion with bodkin for hair*] Oh, for some means! [*Sees bodkin*] The desperate wretch is never without a weapon against himself! This bodkin! One quick thrust will reach my heart—[*Aguila springs from panel, seizes her wrist. Chord, fortissimo, as Aguila enters*]

Ag. Child! What would you do?

Isa. [*Falls in his arms*] Aguila!

Ag. Yes! Why don't you trust me? I have sworn to guard you as my soul!

Isa. Oh, but Papa Aguila! She has told me all! Has told Carlos, and he hates and despises me now!

Ag. All! All what?

Isa. That I am not her child!

Ag. [*Astonished*] What! That you are not her child? How did she know that! I thought I alone knew the secret.

Isa. That I am a thing of shame! The child of her husband's slave!

Ag. [*Fiercely*] It is a lie!

Isa. [*Eagerly*] Oh! Is it, Aguila? Is it a lie?

Ag. Yes, my child! She herself does not know you are not her own child, but I do!

Isa. Tell me, Papa Aguila! What do your words mean? Who am I then?

Ag. Not now, my child! In time, you shall know all. 'Tis enough to know now that you are her equal. Your blood as pure as hers! Fear not Carlos' faith! He loves you too well to doubt, or give you up for a lie from lips that he knows are false as Hell!

Isa. Go to him, Aguila! He will believe you. Tell him I am not the thing she would make me! And if she tries to force me to marry Count Pedro, I will kill myself rather than be untrue to my love!

Ag. Listen, child! You need not die. You see that secret door? No one but me knows of its existence. It was built by your—by Señor Juan Alvarez, the former owner, as a hiding place for his vast treasures. I discovered it three years ago. There is a secret passage leading to the room below. There is a spring of water there, lamps and oil enough to last for weeks, and food and bed for you, my little one!

Isa. Oh, good Aguila! You have saved me!

Ag. I foresaw the coming storm, and knowing you might need a refuge, I hastened here before the countess, and stocked it with all things needful for your comfort. Now hear me, child! Only use it as a last resort. Not a word to anyone of it or what it holds. Trust old Aguila, he will not fail you! Now promise me one thing, little señorita—that you will not attempt to destroy yourself again!

Isa. But should she succeed in forcing me into this union with Count Pedro—

AG. [*Interrupting her*] Have you not a safe retreat? Even should they seize you, aye, though the priest had said the words that made you his wife, I will save you at the eleventh hour. Believe and trust me, mea alma! Has Aguila's word ever failed you yet?

ISA. But suppose she should, as she has threatened, imprison you. How could you save me then?

AG. Our good padre thought of that, and gave me this phial. 'Tis an acid that can eat away all bolts and chains. She may cage my little dove, but not the eagle!

ISA. She has some dreadful plan against you, Aguila.

AG. I know it. I was skulking amid the flowers in the garden, when I heard her bid that yellow wolf, Manuel, to stab me while I slept.

ISA. [*Appalled*] Oh, horrible!

AG. [*Fiercely*] Let her beware how she opens the gates of the hurricane, lest the tempest crush her! Fear not, Mariposa! That slimy snake will never crawl into the eagle's nest! I'll give his carcass to the kites before tomorrow! But do as I bid you, and we are safe. But as you love Carlos and trust me, never raise your hand against yourself again! Promise me, promise!

ISA. [*Kissing him*] I promise, Aguila.—I will do as you bid me to the last! I will trust you always! [*Hurry, pianissimo, to suit action till curtain*]

AG. [*Clasping her to his heart*] Bless you, my darling child! [*Looks through window*] Ah! What is that? The assassin who tried to kill Carlos? El Capitan's servant! [*Closing shutters*] The secret panel! The lion's mouth the spring! In! In!

ISA. [*Terrified*] Who can shelter us now?

AG. [*Back against shutters*] The wings of the eagle! [*Battering against shutters*] In, I say, in! [*Isadora enters panel and closes it after her. Shutters are struck, Aguila staggers; shutters burst in, Aguila falls down stage. El Capitan and robbers enter, masked. At window. Aguila staggers to his feet and strikes El Capitan in breast, felling him. Bernal and robber seize him from behind and force him to his knee*]

BERN. [*Raises machete*] Strike him!

EL CAP. [*Stopping him*] Hold, you fool! He knows the secret of the hidden treasure! He shall tell us where it is or I will flay the red dog alive! Where is the girl? Speak!

AG. [*Laughs defiantly*] Go! Seek her! Within the convent's walls! Safe from your grasp, you robber!

EL CAP. Away with him to the cave!

AG. [*Throws off robbers*] Do your worst! Ha! Ha! I defy you!

PICTURE

ACT IV.

SCENE 1: *Eight bars pathetic. Cave scene in 2. Can be braced to run off back of 1. so that R. and L. may be left clear for sea-cloth. Tropic island set back of scene before curtain goes up. Phillippe dozing on bench R.2.E. Set door R.2.E. Wing boxed L.2.E.*

JUAN. [*Chained L.2., talking to himself*] They'll not find it there! Ha, ha, ha! Oh, how my head pains me! He struck me here. I can't remember since then. No, no! I forget where I hid it! Did they kill Aguila? I saw him cut El Capitan here! Ha! Ha! It was no child's blow! Yes, yes! Where is my child, my baby Isabella? Mercedes! Wife! Where is our little sunshine?

PHIL. Shut up, ye old fool! I want to sleep!

JUAN. I won't!

PHIL. [*Starts up. Crosses L.*] What! Ye won't? Take that! [*Kicks him*] And that! [*Same business*]

JUAN. You may kill me if you want to. I will not tell. I cannot! I have forgotten!

PHIL. Silence, ye chattering old monkey! [*Crossing R.*] He's thinking of his buried treasure. There's where the Capitan's temper cost him something. When the fool wouldn't tell where it was hid, the Capitan hit him on the head, and he went crazy. Now he can't tell! El Capitan might have starved the truth out of him. But now his only hope is that he may get his wits some day and tell where it is. Damn the money anyway! Give me aguardiente and I am happy. [*Drinks*] Ah, that's the stuff! Drink fit for a saint! [*Knock—he listens*] What's that? El Capitan and the rest back so soon? [*Voices without*] Who's there?

BERN. [*Without. Music, hurry, till all on*] The wolf's litter!

PHIL. [*Unbolting door*] Back so early? [*Enter robbers with Aguila bound and blindfolded. They take off the hoodwink. Throw him C. at back*]

EL CAP. Yes, but without the girl. [*Aguila laughs*] But we have you, you dog of an Indian! He shall be of some services to us. He can tell us what that crazed fool has forgotten. And by Satan he shall, or I'll have him skinned alive at sunrise!

AG. You can tear the flesh from my old bones, but you cannot tear the secret from my heart!

EL CAP. We shall see! Listen, Aguila! I will spare your young mistress and let you and that crazy old idiot go free, if you tell the truth. Refuse, and I will torture the secret out of you or kill you!

JUAN. Aguila? Who said Aguila? You are not Aguila! No! He killed you in the pass. You are Aguila's ghost. How came you here among devils? This is not your place.

AG. What! Señor Juan, my old master, alive? Thank Heaven!

EL CAP. Yes, and you can save him and yourself by telling where the treasure is hid. Refuse, and he shall be tortured with you!

AG. [*Aside*] I dare not tell him, not even to save Master Juan, for it would betray her hiding place!

EL CAP. Answer me, you old fool!

AG. I don't know!

EL CAP. [*Music, hurry, till Aguila chained*] You lie, you dog! Men! Chain him to the wall! [*They chain him, ring bolt C. at back. Phillippe locks chain, keys in belt*]

JUAN. I'll tell you! It is hidden behind the fourth stone. [*Pauses*]

AG. [*Aside*] Saints of Heaven! If he remembers, she is lost!

JUAN. The fourth stone—the fourth toward the sea. It is in the sea! I know! No, I have forgotten all! All! I cannot tell!

AG. [*Aside*] Thank Heaven!

BERN. [*Threatening Aguila*] You stole my knife in the garden. You struck me. I always pay my debts. [*Strikes him in face*] Take that! [*Chord!*]

AG. Coward! If my hands were free you would no more dare do that than you would dare knock at the gates of Hell!

BERN. [*Laughs*] You said, when we met, you'd make a buzzard's feast of me! Do it! I'll make a handsome saddle of your hide, tomorrow! [*Seizing Aguila by the throat*] Ha! Ha! I'd like to throttle you!

AG. Would you? Why don't you do it, then? You need not be afraid, I'm chained.

EL CAP. Never mind him, "Alacran," he can wait till morning. Come here, I have work for you. Go back to the casa of Señora de Oro, watch for the señorita. I believe that old knave lies. She must be there! If you see her, seize her and bring her to me at the island. I will be there by evening.

BERN. [*Points to Aguila*] What about him?

EL CAP. He will keep till we get back.

JUAN. Aguila, call Mercedes and bring little Isabella. It is time to go.

PHIL. [*Springs at him with whip*] Shut up, you old parrot! [*Cuts him twice. Chords at whip cuts*]

AG. [*Tugging at chains*] If I were but free of these cursed irons, I'd make a stairway of your bloody corpses!

PHIL. Oh! You want your share, eh? Take it, then! [*Cuts him. Chords at whip cuts*]

JUAN. [*To himself, gloatingly*] Oh, if he would only fall asleep within reach of my chain! He'll do it sometime—then—Ha, ha, ha!

PHIL. What! Ye want more? [*Cuts him again. Drops keys on blanket. Juan sees them and covers them with corner of blanket. Gets them later*]

EL CAP. Here, matador! You make more noise than he does! Be quiet!

PHIL. [*Crossing R.*] All right, Señor Capitan.

EL CAP. [*To Bernal*] If you capture her, take her to the island, as I told you. There are two black rocks on the north side, and a narrow, deep channel between them. That is the safest and most hidden landing place. [*They drink*]

AG. [*Quickly, aside*] Black rocks, narrow channel? He means El Toro! Oh, if I were only free!

EL CAP. Once there, tie her and come off with the boat for me, you hear?

BERN. Yes, Señor Capitan. But I may need aid to seize her.

EL CAP. Take Vasquez, Miguel and Sancho with you then. Mind! No harm to the girl, or El Alacran and the rest of you shall answer to me!

BERN. [*Crosses R.1.*] Have no fear of us, Señor Capitan, you know I am always faithful to you.

EL CAP. [*To Aguila*] With the girl in my power, I think I can bend your stubborn will.

AG. [*With assumed calmness*] You will not find her, señor. She is in the convent of Santa Madre, safe from harm.

EL CAP. [*Laughs incredulously*] Perhaps. But we shall see. If we do not find her at the casa, we will storm the convent.

JUAN. Give me back the locket! It contains the picture of Mercedes, my wife.

EL CAP. [*Striking him*] Silence, you fool!

JUAN. [*Points to his head*] There is where you struck me before. It aches yet, and that was a long time ago.

EL CAP. [*Seizing him by the throat*] Be quiet, I tell you! [*Throws him down*]

AG. Have mercy! He is an old man, and mad!

EL CAP. Mercy? Ha, ha! You talk like a fool! [*Turns R.*] See here, lads! Go to the lower pass. There is a rich prize coming today. An old rich señor and his servants. Pluck the pigeons, and, if they are well behaved, let them off with whole skins. He is a fat sheep, and we may have a chance to shear him again when his new fleece has grown. So don't kill him this time, mind!

ROBBER. All right, Señor Capitan.

EL CAP. Vasquez—you, Miguel and Sancho go with "El Alacran." The rest to the Pass! Vicente, Chico and Gonzales to the lower bridge; Pancho with the others wait at the gorge above, and follow the game to the bridge, to attack them in the rear. I must go first to my hacienda, then to meet you, Bernal, at the island.

BERN. [*To two robbers*] Come, boys, let's be off! [*They exit door R.2.E.*]

PHIL. And me, Señor Capitan, shall I go with the others?

EL CAP. No, Matador, you stay here to watch your pets and guard the cave. Don't get your head so full of aguardiente that you lose your brains.

PHIL. Trust me, Señor Capitan, I am not such an ass as to put my neck in a halter.

EL CAP. Be careful that you don't. There are soldiers in the neighborhood, and your love of liquor will be the death of us all someday, I fear.

PHIL. I'll not touch another drop today, Señor Capitan.

EL CAP. Come, boys, be off now, and good luck to you! Make a quick and clean job of it, and don't let the grass grow under your feet when it is done. Be careful you are not watched, and if you are, remember—"dead men tell no tales!"

ROBBER. All right, Señor Capitan. [*They exit door R.2.E.*]

EL CAP. [*Mockingly to Aguila*] Adios, friends! I hope soon to bring a guest who will unseal your royal lips.

AG. Heaven grant you may not!

EL CAP. Watch close, Matador.

PHIL. Adios, Señor Capitan.

EL CAP. And remember, no more liquor.

PHIL. Not another drop, Señor Capitan. [*Exit El Capitan, door R.2.*]

AG. [*Remembers phial*]· Ah, the good padre's gift! The phial! [*Phillippe, as he bolts door and sees all safe, sings. During song, Aguila gets phial from hair and puts acid on ringbolt. Turns quickly as Juan calls Phillippe's attention*]

PHIL. A woman to love and a bottle of brandy,
    A good game to play and a good song to sing,
    When fat purses travel, a machette handy,
    And I wouldn't change with an abbot or king!

JUAN. They say swans sing before they die!

PHIL. Here! I want to sleep. If you make a riot and wake me, I'll fan you with this! [*Shakes whip*] I'll have another drink first, and damn the Capitan! [*Drinks. Throws himself on blanket R.2.E.*] I'll tame the cattle! I'll—I'll— [*Sleeps. Aguila bursts chains. They fall from wall with noise. Phillippe wakens. When chain breaks, hurry music till Phillippe falls*]

PHIL. Eh? Hello! What's this? [*Seeing Aguila*] What! Broke yer tether, eh? [*Draws knife*]

AG. [*Raises chains over head*] Back, I say! Or my path lies across your grave!

PHIL. [*Springing at him*] Ye will have it, eh? [*They fight. Phillippe draws knife. During fight Juan works wildly on his chains with keys*]

JUAN. [*Wild and exultant*] Kill him, Aguila! Kill him! Ha, ha, ha! Down with him! [*Aguila gets Phillippe's wrist in his teeth. With a howl of rage he drops knife. Juan bursting from his chains, picks it up and stabs him in the back*] Ha, ha! I knew I'd pay him back! [*Gets whip, cuts corpse with it*] Take that! And that! Ha, ha, ha! He drops his keys and I hid them there, in the blanket! [*Cuts corpse. Music, hurry, till Jones on*]

AG. Master Juan, where are the keys? [*Knocking at door. Aguila runs to door, raising chains as weapon*] Who's there?

JONES. [*Without*] Open in the name of the law!

AG. Señor Jones?

JONES. Yes, with my American bulldog and the Mexican army! Open this rat's nest or we will open it for you! [*Aguila draws bolts. Enter Jones followed by soldiers*] Aguila?

AG. Yes, señor.

JONES. A dead man and a maniac. Who is this?

AG. Señor Jones, that is my old master, Señor Juan Alvarez. [*Soldiers unlock Aguila's chains. L.C.*]

JUAN. [*Courteously. R.C.*] Your servant, gentlemen! Excuse me! I am killing a snake. [*Juan throws dead body off*]

AG. [*Rapidly*] Señor, the password is "The wolf's litter." They will be back by night. Take Señor Juan with you.

JUAN. [*Interrupting*] No, no! I am free! Free! [*Springs back with knife. Tremolo, pianissimo, suit action till curtain*]

AG. [*Trying to conciliate him*] Master Juan, give me the knife!

JUAN. No, no! I will not!

AG. Yes, señor. I am old Aguila, your faithful Aguila.

JUAN. So you are! [*Slowly gives knife*] Did they kill you? He struck me here. See the dent?

AG. They will take you to your friend, good Padre Domingus, and to little Isabella.

JUAN. Yes, I'll go to Padre Domingus. [*Points to Jones*] Is he the señor, your friend?

AG. Yes, master. [*Puts Juan's hand in Jones'*] Take him to the good padre, he will cure his head. [*Soldiers take up body ready for change. Tremolo*]

JONES. But you, Aguila, where are you going?

Ag. Send guards to Casa de Oro, and to El Toro after me. I go to save the little señorita, or die defending her! [*Exit followed by Jones and guards. Scene moves down to 1st grooves, followed down by sea-cloth, then runs off back of 1st grooves*]

SCENE 2: *Tropic island drop in 5. Padded platform across stage in 5. Shore- piece in 4. Cut wood and set tree on platform. Flats obliqued off in 3. to show sides of island and sea beyond. Grooves in 2. empty. Concentric turntable de- vice for shark fight. Sea-cloth, scrim. Sand-bar foreground to hold edge of sea-cloth in 1. Bernal appears L.4. in boat with Isadora bound. Lands L.C. at back*]

BERN. [*Lifting her*] Come, señorita. Here we are. You must wait here for the Capitan.

ISA. Oh, señor! Have you no mercy? What would you do? By the memory of your mother whom you must have loved, I beg you to let me go!

BERN. [*Doggedly*] Can't do it I tell you! I must obey orders.

ISA. Oh, spare me, señor! You are a brave, strong man. You cannot fight with women!

BERN. Come! No more of your whimpering! I shan't harm ye, and if ye don't put on airs with the Capitan, ye'll live like a queen.

ISA. [*Appalled*] What awful fate is hidden in your words? Oh, señor! In mercy, kill me then! Kill me! I will kiss your hands, red with my blood, and die blessing you! [*Sinks half fainting*]

BERN. Shut up, I tell ye! I must see all safe around here, and then go back for the Capitan. [*Going R.4.E.*] She's a devilish pretty one. I'd like her for myself if it wasn't for stealing her from the Capitan. [*Exit R.U.E.*]

ISA. [*Bound to tree*] I am lost, lost! Is there no hope? Santa Maria! Hear and save me! Poor old Papa Aguila! Would they had killed me as they have you! How gladly would I lie dead now in your kind, strong arms where I slept so often when a child! Come to me, Aguila! Come to me! [*Aguila appears swimming L.2.E. Chord segue, hurry till curtain*]

Ag. I am coming!

ISA. [*Cries joyfully*] Aguila!

Ag. Still! Or we are lost! [*Shark appears C.*]

ISA. See! Aguila! The shark! The shark!

Ag. Hush, I say, or you will ruin us! Fear not for me!

ISA. [*Praying*] Santa Madre Maria, save him, my old Papa Aguila! Oh, Aguila, thank Heaven! Oh, I dare not look! Ah! There he comes! [*Aguila stabs shark, who turns over and sinks. He lands*]

Ag. My child! My darling child! [*Cutting her bonds*] Thank Heaven I am here to save you!

Isa. Are you hurt? Tell me?

Bern. [*Out R.U.E.*] What riot is this? Has the little fool gone mad? [*Enters, sees them*] What! Free?

Ag. Yes! [*Springs on him before he can draw machete. Fight with knives. Aguila down. Bites Bernal's wrist, he drops knife. Aguila stabs him, turns and stabs him again. Bernal front. Throws him out in water. During fight, shark's fins show above water. When Bernal strikes water, the fin disappears. Isadora faints in Aguila's arms*]

Ag. The shark steals the buzzard's feast!

PICTURE

ACT V.

Same as Act III. Eight bars triumphant. Night backing in 4. Countess seated R. by table. Pedro C.

Ped. [*Offering hand*] So, countess, our feud is ended! We are friends once more, eh? You pardon me?

Inez. Fully, señor, and more. I ask your pardon. I am very grateful to you for using your influence to have her returned to me.

Ped. Not at all, señora! I had just received your treaty of peace, this letter, when the news of her abduction was brought to me. Of course I was almost driven wild. I ordered my horse and was off at a madman's pace to find the alcalde. Half way to town, whom should I meet but the alcalde himself, with the rescuing party. Among them that infernal Indian and that prying American. Of course she remonstrated against being returned to your house.

Inez. [*Sneeringly*] I do not doubt it! She probably threw herself on the protection of that red traitor, Aguila, and that quixotic Jones.

Ped. Yes, señora, and they espoused her cause and tried to hold her, but I told the alcalde that, as you were her mother, to deliver her into the custody of anyone else would be unlawful and equivalent to abduction. He took my view of the matter, and sent her back to you.

Inez. You have worsted our enemies. Now, if we use our time, the day is ours. I learned that Señor Castillo was not dead, and my anger against you softened. I wrote you that letter, asking your pardon for my hasty words, and requesting an interview. I wished to tell you that if you so desired, we will proceed with this marriage at once.

Ped. Señora, it is my dearest wish.

INEZ. This marriage once accomplished, we are masters of the situation and our enemies are completely outgeneralled.

PED. Yes, señora. Once in my house, as my wife, they will take their lives in their hands if they attempt to meddle with my household.

INEZ. I will bring in your bride. You will doubtless find her cold and distant at first, but firmness and kindness will soon teach her how useless it is to sigh for a lost lover, and she will soon see that her only chance of happiness is in courting the favor and esteem of her husband.

PED. Trust me, señora! I shall manage her when she is once my wife!

INEZ. [*Going R.U.E.*] Pardon me a moment, señor, and I will bring her here. [*Exit D.R.*]

PED. [*Alone*] So, I shall accomplish my purpose at last, and all legally! She shall be mine, body and soul! No human will has ever yet opposed me that I have not crushed! I will not now be balked by a puny girl! As for her lover, I can have him removed; we shall see who wins!

INEZ. [*Entering with Isadora. D.R.U.*] Señor, here is your promised wife. [*To Isadora*] Child, prepare yourself, at once, to be married to Count Pedro.

ISA. [*C. Aside*] Will Aguila keep his word? [*Aloud*] Señor, I do not love you—

INEZ. [*R. Aside. Clutching her wrist*] Beware! You know me!

PED. [*Smiling*] You will learn to in time, señorita.

ANN. [*Entering L.3.*] If you please, señora countess, there is a holy father out here who fears to go down the Passo at night, and asks permission to wait here till morning.

INEZ. A holy father? [*Aside*] Most opportune! [*Aloud*] Bid him come in.

ANN. [*At door L.3.*] Enter, father!

PRIEST. [*Entering*] Benedicite, my children! Señora countess, pardon my intrusion, but I am belated on my way to Puebla. My mule is lame, and the night is on me. These passes are infested by El Capitan and his band. I am forced to ask your hospitality till daylight, when I can continue my journey in safety.

INEZ. You are most welcome, holy father! This is Count Pedro Martinez of Puebla. [*Pedro bows*]

PRIEST. Benedicite, my son!

INEZ. Father, we need your good offices to celebrate the union of this gentleman and lady at once.

ANN. [*Aside*] I wish I had set the dogs on him!

ISA. [*R. starts up defiantly*] I will not marry him! You may kill me if you will, I care not!

PRIEST. [*Crossing R.*] Calm yourself, my child! [*To Inez*] Is she your daughter, señora?

INEZ. [*L.C., with Pedro*] Yes, father. Though a most wilful and disobedient one. She is infatuated with a young and worthless adventurer. I have selected a worthy, wealthy and honorable husband for her. One who can give her position, title and luxury. And you see how the ungrateful child opposes my love and care!

PRIEST. My child, you owe obedience to your mother! You should let her wisdom guide your impetuous youth.

ISA. [*Appealingly*] But, father, I do not love him! Would you have me make a mockery of Heaven's blessings, by letting you bestow it on a loveless marriage?

PRIEST. Have faith, my daughter, that Heaven will send you love. By faith the dead have been called back to life. Remember the story of Lazarus; though dead, he yet lives.

ISA. [*Surprised. Aside to him*] Those words! Who are you?

PRIEST. [*Warning her*] Sh! [*Smuggles letter to her. R.*]

INEZ. I thank you, father, for your holy counsel to my wayward child. We will leave you with her, while I give orders for your entertainment. And I trust she may profit by your good advice. Come, count. [*Exeunt Pedro and Inez D.R.U.E.*]

ANN. [*Half hidden in curtains*] I don't believe he's a holy father at all, or he would not try to marry poor Señorita Isadora to an old monkey that she hates!

ISA. Who are you?

PRIEST. Fear not, my child. I know your story. I am the friend of Padre Domingus, your friend. Passing his parish the day your mother brought you here, he commissioned me to prevent her placing you in a convent here, and to be your friend in need, as he would be. But read your letter!

ISA. [*Opens letter and reads*] "Trust the Holy Father. He is our friend. Let them go on with the wedding. You are surrounded by friends. We will be there at the proper time. Carlos." [*Kisses letter*] Dear, brave Carlos! [*Annetta comes down from curtains*]

PADRE. [*To Annetta*] You are her friend, are you not?

ANN. Friend! I would die for her, father!

PADRE. You are a good girl! The American señor—Ah! you blush! You love him! Now I know I can trust you. A woman may always be trusted where she loves.

ANN. Yes, padre! What are Señor Jones' wishes?

PADRE. He sends word that you should have the dogs tied on the other side of the house, away from that window. Let no one see you do it. You understand?

ANN. Yes, father. [*Exits door L.3.*]

PRIEST. There, poor child! Prepare for your wedding, and, at the final moment, there shall be a change of bridegrooms!

ISA. [*Clasping his hands*] Heaven bless you, father! [*Countess and Pedro enter D.R.U.E.*]

PRIEST. [*Signals their presence to Isadora*] There! Calm yourself, my child; go and dress for your marriage, and leave the result to Heaven.

ISA. [*Seemingly yielding*] I will do as you bid me, father! Heaven grant it may be for the best! [*Exit R.3.E.*]

INEZ. I am much indebted to you for the wonderful influence you have gained over her, father.

PED. It seems wonderful that you could so completely have subdued her opposition!

PRIEST. Kind words will lead a child where death could not drive her. I have a nephew who can be ruled by no other means. He is kind-hearted, but such a wag. I believe he would play his pranks on the saints! Here are some candles he gave me as I started. [*Unrolling package*] I tremble to use anything from his hands without first testing it, and I mistrust these innocent looking candles. [*Annetta seen peeping on at door L.3.*]

PED. Those candles? Mistrust them? And why?

PRIEST. [*Drily*] His candles do not always burn evenly! For fear that these are not staid, sober and well behaved, I will, with your permission, light one outside of the window. As its capers, if it be frolicsome, will do no harm there.

INEZ. [*Laughing*] The young rogue! To play tricks on his uncle, thus.

PRIEST. [*Preparing at window*] It is a young rascal, but I love him for it, after all; I was a boy myself, once. Heaven forgive my wild pranks! [*Lights rocket candle*] Ah! I thought so! The young monkey! Ha! Ha! Ha! [*Inez and Pedro laughing heartily. Distant pistol shot and whistle. Aside triumphantly*] They see it! [*Closes window. Isadora enters D.R.U.E. dressed as a bride. Music tremolo till Aguila on*]

ISA. Well, father, I am ready.

PRIEST. [*By table L.2., candles on it*] Ah, my child! You are a good and obedient daughter. [*Annetta crosses to R. of window*] Give your hand to this gentleman. [*She obeys. Countess R.C. Pedro C.R. Isadora C.L. Priest by table L. Whistle outside. Priest with back to others, puts out candles. Lights down. Glass crash. Guards, Carlos, Aguila on*] How stupid of me! [*Lighting candle.*

Lights up. Aguila L.C., Isadora in his arms L. His sword at Pedro's breast. Jones getting in window. Chord, fortissimo]

PEDRO. [*Amazed*] What does this mean?

JONES. It means that we are about to reverse the rule, and give away the bridegroom!

INEZ. Señors, leave my house! I am mistress here, and this intrusion is most insolent! More! It is a violation of the laws for which you shall answer.

JONES. Señora, we are here on business of the state, and can't accept your pressing invitation to take a walk. We can't tear ourselves away so unceremoniously.

INEZ. Such insolence!

JONES. Don't put your fingers in this mess of porridge, or you may burn them! [*Goes to Annetta*]

PED. Trickster! This is your work! Who are you?

PADRE. [*Throws off disguise*] Padre Domingus, who has assumed this disguise to save this poor persecuted child from the clutches of a robber!

PED. A robber! What do you mean?

CARL. It means, Pedro Martinez, you are our prisoner.

PED. Upon what evidence?

CARL. Mine, and these gentlemen's. I accuse you of being El Capitan, the noted robber chief. This locket, stolen from the body of your victim, Juan Alvarez, you lost where you fought with me, by the river. I accuse you of robbing him, attempting his life, and of all the countless crimes that have made you the scourge of the Republic for so many years.

PED. [*Laughs defiantly*] Is this your proof? Ha! Ha! I'll show you how worthless it is. I bought that locket, years ago, from a Jew in the city of Mexico. It bore so strange a resemblance to the little señorita, whom I loved even as a child. You see, señors, your evidence is trash!

CARL. [*Triumphantly*] Stay! Not so fast! Here is a witness whose evidence you cannot so easily gainsay! [*Leads Juan on L.U.E.*]

PED. [*Quickly*] What testimony do you expect to gain from him? He is mad!

JONES. [*Quickly*] How do you know?

PED. [*Confused*] Well, I could see by his eyes that he was not sane.

PADRE. He is as sane as you! You struck him on the head, and dented his skull. The blow made him insane. I have relieved the pressure on his brain, and his reason has returned. So you see, señors, he had no way of knowing but his knowledge of his previous condition. [*Pedro attempts to rush out. Stopped by guards*]

CARL. Your attempt to fly is almost enough to condemn you! [*To Juan*] Is this man El Capitan?

JUAN. Yes, señor.

PED. 'Tis false! This man is mad, I tell you! Even though he fancied he saw a resemblance, that proves nothing. Your evidence is worthless!

AG. But mine shall crush you!

PED. [*Sneeringly*]   Indeed? Since when has the evidence of a dog of a slave been sufficient to crush a man of wealth, rank and noble blood?

AG. Noble! In years gone by, in this fair land, my fathers ruled. Their gentle sway lay like a happy maid, that, smiling, slept upon a bed of roses, her fair hands clasped by either sea! The stranger came, a man like you; a robber and a murderer, who wore the cross of God above a heart where coiled things of Hell! You are the whelp of that robber! I am the child of a King!

PED. Well, wretch! What can you tell?

AG. Fourteen years ago, señors, I gave El Capitan a slash with my machete, across the left shoulder. Let us see if the noble Count Pedro bears the mark of Cain! [*Springs on him. Pedro draws knife. Aguila tears it from him and forces him to kneel. Tears open shirt and exposes scar*] Behold! [*Throws Pedro up C. into arms of guards*] Bind him, señors, and away with him.

PED. [*Struggling with guards, as they take him L.U.E.*] Curse ye all! You've trapped the lion, see that you hold him! If I break my meshes, beware!

JONES. We've clipped your claws! Your band are all killed or captured to the last man. We've got the whole business. Don Pedro, Sancho, High Low Jack and the game! [*Throwing him to soldiers*] Gentlemen of the Guard, guard the gentleman. [*Exit soldiers with Pedro*]

INEZ. Señors, now that you have disgraced my house with this scene, I trust you will relieve us of your presence! [*To Isadora*] Come here, my child!

AG. She is not your child!

ALL. Not her child?

AG. No! Your child died in its cradle the day you turned your sister Mercedes starving from your door. I told her of its death, and she begged me to save her baby's life by putting it in the dead one's place. You have reared your sister's daughter!

INEZ. [*Furious*] This is a lie! A wicked lie!

PADRE. No. It is Heaven's truth! Your sister told me the story as she was dying. How you loved Juan and hated her that she had won his heart. And of the deception practised on you. But I never knew that Aguila was her assistant. [*To Isadora*] My child, you are not Isadora de Oro, but Isabella Alvarez, and this gentleman is your father!

JUAN. [*Clasps her*] My child!

Isa. Father, Carlos, my dear old Aguila—I have you all, all! [*Tremolo, pathetic, pianissimo, till curtain*]

Inez. [*With wild laugh*] Yes, all! All! Ha, ha, ha! And I have lost all! Carlos, you were all to me, as he once was! And I have lost you! I sinned to gain you, Ha, ha, ha! Fool that I was! Fool! Fool! [*Buries face in her hands*]

Carl. [*L.C.*] Merciful Heavens, she is mad!

Inez. [*C. Starting up*] Mad! Am I mad? Oh, tell me, Carlos! You hate me now, but you will forgive me when I'm dead. Yes, and kiss me just once! Just once. I loved you so! Just once that I may know that you forgive me. Good-night, Carlos! Ha, ha, ha! [*Snatches bodkin from her hair. Stabs herself. All spring forward to prevent her. She waves them back*] Stand back, señors! [*Hands on breast*] See the roses—beautiful red roses! They are your gifts, Carlos! See how the petals fall off! No, it is blood! My blood! [*Staggers. Aguila supports her*] Aguila, don't let Carlos forget to kiss me when I'm dead. [*Gasps*] Carlos! Carl—[*Dies in Aguila's arms*]

Ag. Poor Inez! Heaven forgive and pity thee! [*Padre, Inez and Aguila C. Juan and Isabella L.*]

PICTURE

CURTAIN

THE GREAT DIAMOND ROBBERY

By Colonel Edward M. Alfriend and A. C. Wheeler

CHARACTERS

Dick Brummage

Frank Kennet

Mr. Clinton Bulford

Grandfather Lavelot

Mario Marino

Dr. Livingstone

Senator McSorker

The Count Garbiadoff

Sheeney Ike

Jimmy McCune

Philip

Jack Clancy

Mickey Brannigan

Policeman

Mrs. Mary Bulford

Mary Lavelot

Mother Rosenbaum (Frau)

Mrs. O'Geogan

Peggy Daly

Mme. Mervaine

Incidentals: Heelers, Clubman, Salvation Army Lass, Messenger Boy, Bar-keepers, Waiters, Street Gamin, Blind Musician, Guests.

ACT I.

SCENE: *Small cosy breakfast or supper room in Mr. Bulford's house on Lexington Avenue in New York set in 2. It is tastefully furnished with grate fire burning, and an easy chair and table in front of it. Room lit by gas or lamps, but not glaringly. There is a sofa R. with buffet in corner C. It is furnished with glass, silver, decanters, etc. There is an entrance R.2.E., another L. in back flat. Bitter storm outside—howling of wind heard with banging of shutter. See fire lighted and red medium for rise.* TIME: *Nine o'clock at night, late winter or early spring.* DISCOVERED: *Mrs. Bulford at half open door L. in flat. She is listening intently at door and is nervous. At the expiration of half a minute, she goes to a little table and strikes bell. Crosses R.C. and to R., then listens. Enter Philip L.*

MRS. B. Philip, that shutter in the parlor is banging.

PHIL. [*L.C.*] Yes'm. [*Is about to go*]

MRS. B. Where is my brother, Marino.

PHIL. In his room, ma'am. I smelt his cigar in the hall.

MRS. B. Tell him to come here.

PHIL. Yes'm. [*Is about to go*]

MRS. B. What have you in your hand?

PHIL. It's a letter, ma'am. It came by messenger a few minutes ago. It's for Mr. Bulford. I couldn't give it to him because he's got parties in the reception room. [*Puts letter on table*]

MRS. B. Did you see the people in the reception room?

PHIL. Yes'm. I let 'em in.

MRS. B. What did they look like?

PHIL. Like foreigners! [*Mrs. Bulford starts*]

MRS. B. Did they bring anything?

PHIL. Yes'm. One of them had a hand bag.

MRS. B. Go and fasten that shutter and tell my brother to come here.

PHIL. Yes'm. [*Exit leaving door ajar. Mrs. Bulford stands a minute in perplexed attitude looking at letter, then places it on table and going to buffet, takes a drink of water and composes her face in the glass. Enter Marino, L., with book in hand*]

MAR. Hello, dear!

MRS. B. Are you going to the club tonight? [*Crosses to L.*]

MAR. [*Yawning*]   Heaven forbid! It is almost as dull there as it is here. I was reading Daudet and smoking.

MRS. B. [*Shutting the door*]   Did you see the men who are with Mr. Bulford in the reception room?

MAR.   See them? No, I didn't know there were men there. [*Crosses to sofa*]

MRS. B. [*Relieved*]   I was going to ask you to go out in the storm and execute a commission for me. You will object, of course?

MAR. [*Sitting on sofa R.*]   Santa Maria, my charming sister, why do you insist on making me uncomfortable?

MRS. B. [*Petulantly*]   You would be comfortable on the edge of Hades. As for me I wish we were in Rio tonight. Think of it! They are celebrating the feast of St. Catherine with flowers. [*Lights cigarette at buffet C., then crosses to fire L.*]

MAR.   Aye—and the streets are filled with black eyed señoritas, who have tropical faces all the year around. I detest this northern climate. But you, who have spent a winter in St. Petersburg, ought to be comfortable in New York.

MRS. B. [*Facing him*]   I should be more comfortable in New York if I had never been to St. Petersburg. I made the mistake of my life there.

MAR.   I only know of one.

MRS. B.   What's that?

MAR.   You got married. [*Rises, crosses to C. up to buffet*] Most adorable of sisters, you did not send for me to tell me this.

MRS. B. [*Sits by fire*]   Why not? I have been telling it to you for months. You think because I wear a calm face I am comfortable. My heart is like a volcano covered with snow, but wearing a core of fire! I can play at respectability, but the play must not be too long or too tedious.

MAR.   Well, if I were going to play the respectable thing, I'd get rid of that senator you keep hanging about. It makes me feel sorry for your generous old husband.

MRS. B.   Senator McSorker is the most powerful and influential politician in New York.

MAR. [*R. of table, L.*]   And one of the most disreputable, I fancy.

MRS. B.   Nobody is disreputable in New York, unless they are unsuccessful.

MAR.   Oh, but he dresses so damnably and smokes such rank cigars.

MRS. B. [*Seated at fire L.*]   Bah—you are a child. I shall never make a man of you. In Europe we have to fight brains, finesse and diplomacy to get on. [*Rises, crosses to L.C.*] Here the canaille are the supreme rulers and we ought to be princes among them. Instead of going to St. Petersburg and marrying a respectable old gentleman because he was attached to the American Legation there, and who keeps you in cigarettes and pays your club bills to please me, we should have come direct to New York; for here every politician is a gold mine and every clever woman can defy the law. [*Crosses C. at back of sofa*]

MAR. By Heavens, if you were single, I believe you would marry that senator.

MRS. B. No. But I should like to have the chance for six months to make him think I would. [*Leans over back of sofa*]

MAR. Well, you have been scheming for six months. I hope you will not do anything to disturb our respectability and comfort. For my part, I rather like this sort of thing. [*Wind. Enter Mr. Bulford door L., evening paper sticking out of his pocket—jewel-case under his arm; looks at the pair on the sofa, shivers and places jewel-case on the table*]

MR. B. Boo-oo. I am chilled through. That reception room is like a vault. [*Wind*] Listen to that wind! Now, this is cosy. [*Warms his hands at grate fire L.*]

MRS. B. Your visitors must have had business of great importance to bring them out on such a night.

MR. B. Importance? Yes, I should say it was. It's the most extraordinary thing I ever heard of.

MAR. [*Seated on sofa; eagerly*] Why, what is it pray?

MR. B. [*Back to fire*] Do you remember the robbery of the Garbiadoff diamonds in Europe? It took place just before we left there, a year and a half ago. It was all in the papers, but I did not pay much attention to it, although I knew Garbiadoff well. We are friends in fact.

MAR. I remember it very well. They were stolen in Cracow by—

MR. B. [*Stands back to fire L.*] By the cleverest thief in Europe. They were said to be worth fifty thousand pounds. [*Mrs. Bulford C., standing*]

MAR. Fifty thousand pounds?

MR. B. The thief, who is known as Don Plon, has operated in both hemispheres. He was in this country once, I understand, but incurred the deadly enmity of a powerful criminal who is a woman, for he betrayed her son to the authorities, and she swore to be revenged. He accomplished this robbery in Cracow by introducing a handsome woman in the count's house, and while the count was carrying on an amour, the diamonds disappeared with the woman. After chasing the jewels through Europe, the Russian police got upon their track in this city and succeeded in negotiating with some of the conspirators and getting the jewels back, but so afraid were those agents of Don Plon or this woman that they came to me tonight with the property and wanted me to go to the bank with them and have the jewels deposited. There they are in that case.

MAR. [*Going to table*]   Why, this beats Daudet! Fifty thousand pounds! [*Sits at head of table L.*]

MR. B.   I told them I wouldn't go out tonight for all the jewels in the Russian Empire, but they assured me that it was in their interest that they should get them out of their hands into the safe keeping of a responsible party. [*Mrs. Bulford crosses and leans on back of sofa R.*]

MAR. [*Seated at head of table L., looking at the case*]   But do you really mean to say they are worth fifty thousand pounds!

MR. B. [*Sitting L. of table by fire*]   Yes—that is the estimate put upon them by England. There is said to be a ruby in that case worth five thousand pounds. It was known along the upper Ganges as the "heart of fire."

MAR. [*Rises*]   You are assuming a great risk by accepting the property in this way.

MR. B.   The men appeared to think they were lessening the risk by getting the property into my hands.

MRS. B.   And none know they are here, but those men?

MAR. [*Turning to Mrs. Bulford*]   Don't you wish to see them, Maria?

MRS. B. [*On sofa R.*]   No. It has given me quite a sensation. I can fancy the mysterious Don Plon hanging about our house tonight when we are asleep, and, if they should disappear—

MR. B. [*Seated L. of table, interrupting*]   Oh, nonsense! Don't say anything to the servants and I'll be responsible for them until morning. I've the count's order and I will see the jewels deposited carefully.

MAR. [*Seated at head of table, taking up case*]   Can't we see them?

MR. B. [*Seated by fire*]   No. It is sealed. You see, there is some difficulty in identifying the diamonds, owing to the absence of the count. Nobody but Don Plon or that woman of his could identify them and it would be a very easy matter to change them. [*Marino returns to the lounge thoughtfully, stands at back of it. Mr. Bulford turns around in his chair again. Enter servant L., hands card to Mr. Bulford, then stands by door L., L. of it*]

MR. B. [*Looking at card*]   Kennet—Kennet—Frank Kennet? What does he want to see me for? It's no use.

MRS. B.   Who is Frank Kennet?

MR. B.   It's a young man I put in the bank six months ago. He's got into some kind of trouble with his accounts. I feel sorry for him but it's no use running after me here.

MRS. B. [*Music for Kennet's entrance until well on*]   Oh, you had better see him. Perhaps he wishes to confess.

MAR.   I'll be in the way, please excuse me, I'll go back to Daudet. [*Exit, L.*]

MR. B. Well, I am not going into that cold reception room again. Tell him to come here. [*Servant bows and exits*]

MRS. B. [*Rises*] Perhaps I had better retire. [*Crosses a little to C.*]

MR. B. [*Rises*] Nonsense—sit still. Confound it—why can't young men go straight.

MRS. B. [*R.C.*] What is the trouble?

MR. B. There's something crooked. I've got to lay it before the directors. A case of bad habits and worse companions, I suppose. [*Enter servant L., stands R. of door L., showing in Frank Kennet who wears a great coat with collar turned up and carries a soft hat in his hand. Servant exits L. Kennet stops at entrance, disturbed that Mr. Bulford is not alone*]

FRANK. [*Up C.*] I expected to see you alone, sir. [*Mr. Bulford doubles his newspaper and places it carefully over jewel-case on table*]

MR. B. If you come into my family this way, sir, you must expect to see some of the members of it. [*Points to Mrs. Bulford*] Whatever you have to say—you can say it here [*Mrs. Bulford goes to window, looks through*] but make it short. [*Sits L. of table*]

FRANK. [*Goes slowly down to Mr. Bulford*] I came to appeal to you, sir, not to make public the charges against me until they are investigated. I am innocent.

MR. B. [*Seated L. of table*] Hum-ph! I hope so, but the business of the bank must be carried on regularly. I must report the matter to the directors tomorrow.

FRANK. [*L.C.*] Tomorrow? A day or two cannot injure the bank, but it may give me time to vindicate myself. There are others who will suffer from haste.

MR. B. Ah, there are others—of course—your associates.

FRANK. [*L.C.*] No sir—I have no associates.

MR. B. Come—come—this is idle talk. What do you mean?

FRANK. [*L.C.*] I am engaged to be married. I thought that perhaps that fact would incline you to listen to me kindly.

MR. B. Oh, there's a woman at the bottom of it, is there? I thought as much.

FRANK. Pardon me, sir, you are going too far. Some women cannot stand even the rumor of dishonesty and Mary Lavelot is that kind of a woman.

MR. B. [*Impatiently*] Well, this is all very fine, but as a bank officer, I've got to stick to the accounts. I am responsible to the stockholders.

FRANK. [*R. of table L. above it*] I did not come here as a culprit, sir. I only ask you to satisfy yourself of the injustice of these charges before making them public. Once that bank sets in to prosecute me, I have no means to fight it and no friends. I am not thinking of myself as much as others. [*Mrs. Bulford is listening from window, R.*]

Mr. B.   If you are innocent, you need not fear an official examination—in fact, there is no other way whether you are innocent or not.

Frank.   [*At head of table L.*]   But sir, what if some of the directors, in order to save the real culprit, should desire to make me appear guilty?

Mr. B.   [*Rising*]   What's that? What's that? You have a warm temper young man. It is sheer folly to accuse me of unkindness. I have done a great deal for you.

Frank.   It is that which hurts me, for you are undoing it all now.

Mrs. B.   What's the matter? Is he faint? Let me offer him a glass of wine? [*She turns to buffet C., back to audience and pours glass of wine*] We can afford to be generous as well as just on such a night.

Mr. B.   Nobody ever accused me of being either ungenerous or unjust.

Frank.   But you intend to take this action tomorrow?

Mr. B.   Young man, I shall do my duty tomorrow, if I live, as I have always done. [*Mrs. Bulford hands Frank the glass of wine, R. of him*] But you needn't go away with any hard feelings to me. Maria, you can give me a glass of sherry. [*Mrs. Bulford comes to table with glass of wine in a cut sherry glass, gives wine to Mr. Bulford, looks at them a moment and goes to window R.*] Drink that young man—it will warm you. [*Frank and Bulford drink*] Let us hope matters will not be as bad as they look. [*Frank drinks the wine, places glass on table, stares at Mr. Bulford a moment, goes to door L. where he stands irresolute*] Good night! [*Goes and sits L. by fire. Frank attempts to speak, breaks down and exits. Mr. Bulford sighs, takes newspaper from table L. and resettles himself in his chair. Fifteen seconds elapse. Mrs. Bulford tries to appear unconcerned. Business ad lib*]

Mrs. B.   [*Coming from window R., crosses to table L.*]   Oh, there is a letter for you—did you get it?

Mr. B.   No. Where is it?

Mrs. B.   [*R. of table at head of it*]   Philip placed it here on the table. Here it is. [*Gives envelope. Mr. Bulford tears it open and takes out enclosed foreign letter*]

Mr. B.   Why, this is a foreign letter sent to the care of the Russian Consul here, and by him delivered to me. It must have come by messenger. [*Opens letter and looks at signature*] It is from Count Garbiadoff himself.

Mrs. B.   [*R. of table—eagerly*]   Garbiadoff! [*Goes back a step or two*]

Mr. B.   [*Seated next to fire*]   Yes. There is his signature—Garbiadoff. It doesn't look like the signature on the order. What did I do with that order? [*Feels in his pockets*]

Mrs. B. [*Eagerly*] Never mind about the signature. Read the letter.

Mr. B. [*Looking at the two names*] Yes, the letter must be genuine. There is the count's coat of arms in the corner. I remember it very well—and there's the Imperial postmark on the envelope. Do you see Maria, do you see?

Mrs. B. [*R. of table, agitatedly*] Certainly it must be genuine. Why do you not read it?

Mr. B. [*Seated L. of table, L.*] But if the letter is genuine, the order cannot be. It must be a forgery! Why should any one forge an order to get the jewels into my hands? There is something wrong here.

Mrs. B. Let me read the letter for you.

Mr. B. [*Holding letter open and reading*] No! No! I will read it myself! "Dear Sir:

"Recalling our pleasant acquaintance while you were in St. Petersburg, I venture to address you. If in this communication I give you pain you must not blame me—necessity compels me to write as I do. You will remember that for a few weeks prior to your departure from Russia I was absent from home. I returned to find that you had married, resigned your position as Attache of the American Legation and departed for America. Curious to find whom my good friend had honored with his name, I made inquiries at the Embassy and elsewhere, but beyond the fact that you had married somewhat suddenly, a woman supposed to be French, I could learn nothing. In point of fact your old companions seemed somewhat reticent and so disinclined to impart any information upon the matter that I dropped it entirely. More than a year has passed, and today it has been brought back to me by an occurrence at once remarkable and painful. You know all about the theft of my diamonds, how I was tricked out of them by the wiles of a woman, at the time the mistress of that supreme scoundrel calling himself Don Plon. Happily for the world this villain never lived to enjoy his plunder, for he died in Paris eight months ago. I have employed the best detectives to find my property, and while I have been unable to recover it, so closely have I been on its track that a sale of the diamonds by the thieves in any of the markets of Europe has been made impossible. Today, however, a woman formerly a servant of Don Plon's mistress, was arrested by the Russian police on some petty charge, and sent for me in prison, saying if I would procure her release, she would give me information that might aid in the search for my lost property. The information she gave me was startling—even tragic. It was that the diamonds had been recently sent to America and that the wretch who had tricked me, Don Plon's partner in the theft, was"—My God!—"Marie Marino, the same woman who had married my American friend Bulford." [*Bulford starting up in great agitation—stop music*] Is this the truth? Speak, or I shall kill you where you stand. You do not answer. You cannot. Ah, I see it all now. The men who brought those diamonds here tonight were not the police but your tools! The order was a forgery and you are—you are—Plon's woman! [*Mrs. Bulford stares at him for a moment or two, goes to buffet, puts poison in glass then pours in wine, with back to audience, turns, brings glass to Bulford, behind him on his R., pours it down his throat*]

Mrs. B.   Take this, my dear it will revive you. [*He drinks*] Oh! [*Steps a step back with look of triumph then looks frightened*]

Mr. B.   Oh! My God, my God, the shame of it! The shame of it! It will kill me! It will kill me! Oh—Oh!—[*Falls, struggles in chair, dies. Mrs. Bulford stands a moment horrified, then goes around to front of chair, presses his head back with her hand. It falls on his breast. She goes to his R. at back takes the letter out of his hand, puts it in her bosom. Taps bell on table. Enter Marino L.*]

Mar.   What's the matter?

Mrs. B.   Quick, a doctor! He is dying! He says the young man who was here poisoned him, but I think it is apoplexy. [*Imperatively stamping her foot*] Why do you stand? Go! Go! [*Music till curtain is well down. Wind and rain outside. Exit Marino hurriedly L. Mrs. Bulford watches him off, clasps her head in her hands for a moment as if bewildered and listens. Then staggers and facing audience goes to table and gets sherry glass—quickly seizes it with left hand and with the right grasps jewel-case through the paper— staring wildly into space. Quick curtain*]

ACT II.

Scene: *Old Lavelot's house and shop in Houston Street. Three days later. An old-fashioned apartment littered with old clothes and personal effects on pegs and tables. Stove rear, window L. and curtains showing street. Children's shouts. Doors L. in back flat, R.1. and R.3.* Time: *Morning.* Discovered: *Old Lavelot sitting at stove doubled up, with poker in his hand. Dr. Livingstone and Mrs. O'Geogan down front C.*

Dr. L.   I'll give you a powder to put in his tea at night to keep him quiet.

Mrs. O'G.   Tay, is it? If I put tay in the medicine he wouldn't take it. He'd taste the water in a drink if it was a foggy mornin'. Sure tay is for the strong-minded sex, like meself, doctor.

Dr. L. [*R. at head of table*]   I'm sorry to find the old man such a wreck. It was lucky I happened to be in the neighborhood.

OLD L. [*At stove*] Oh, you come here too much, damme! Fire him out—fire him out! [*Strikes the stove viciously with the poker. They disregard him entirely*]

MRS. O'G. Don't mind him, don't mind him. It's very good of you, doctor. To think of the loikes of him, and you havin' so many rich people to attind.

DR. L. Don't mention it. I knew the old man when he was a political influence in his ward.

MRS. O'G. I mind it well. That was in the Fourteenth, and he ought to be goin' to Albany this blessed minute. I hear, doctor, that the women do be takin' the politics in their own hands, thank God!

DR. L. You always had your share of political influence in the Fourteenth I believe.

MRS. O'G. But nary a job did I ever get. If I'd had the scrubbin' of the City Hall and the Court House as long as Mrs. Dooley, I'd be a ridin' in me coach meself, this blessed minute. [*Goes to door L.*]

OLD L. [*Seated R. of stove*] Lay for'ed—lay for'ed. [*Strikes the stove with the poker*] How long is this thing going to last?

DR. L. [*Crosses to C.*] You had better give him two powders Mrs. O'-Geogan.

MRS. O'G. I'll give him half a dozen and choke him at wanst. It's yourself cud be doin' an honest widdy a good turn by spakin' to the senator.

DR. L. [*R.C.*] Oh, you have more influence with him than I have.

MRS. O'G. Influence, is it? May St. Peter fly away with him! He has a heart as big as his fist, but his tongue ought to melt in his mouth with his own blarney. Aha, is that you, Mrs. Dooley—you'll be comin' up to see me in my new house on the Avenoo, says he, and drink a glass of champagne with the boys, at election toime. The devil an invite do I get to the house on the Avenoo and me workin' like a nager with the gang on election day. I'm thinkin' I'll put on me trousseau at the next blow-out, and march into the house on the Avenoo. [*Imitating him with hands on her hips*] A-ha—is that you, sinator? You'll be givin' Biddy O'Geogan a mug of champagne I don't know, or divil another whack will you git of election day.

DR. L. Where is Pop Lavelot's granddaughter, Mary. I saw the girl once —in fact, I assisted at her début.

MRS. O'G. She never had it. A healthier baby I never saw.

DR. L. [*Smiling*] I mean, her first appearance. [*Music till Mary is well on*] She promised to become a very handsome girl.

Mrs. O'G.   She is a good girl and kept her promise. Didn't ye see her, doctor, she must have stepped out. I'll call her. [*Goes to door R.3. and calls*] Miss Mary—whist—here's the doctor.

Mary. [*Outside*]   I'm coming in a moment.

Mrs. O'G. [*Coming down*]   It's no place for the loikes of her with her schoolin' and tinder sinsibilities. But the old pelican there has got a pot of money, and she's the only one who can manage him. [*Going up to door R.3. Enter Mary R.3. Coming C.*] This is Doctor Livingstone, miss. He knew your mother.

Dr. L. [*Advancing to Mary*]   It's no use my telling you we have met before. You wouldn't remember it. [*To Mrs. O'Geogan*] She has kept her promise indeed! A little pale, however—and—[*Regarding her closely*] I don't like the look of worry on your face.

Mrs. O'G.   Bedad she's breakin' her heart, doctor!

Mary.   I need exercise, doctor.

Mrs. O'G. [*Aside*]   Exercise—listen to that. Does a cat need fur?

Dr. L.   Well, you will have to let me come over and look after you a little. It will never do, your eyes are red.

Mary.   It is nothing, doctor. I took a little cold in them. [*Crosses L.*]

Dr. L. [*Going toward door L.*]   Mrs. O'Geogan, don't forget two powders at night and one in the morning. Miss Lavelot, let me advise you to take care of your health. Good-bye. [*Exits L.*]

Mrs. O'G.   Good-bye! He's the foinest doctor in New York. I'll speak to Senator McSorker about him. He ought to be on the health board—his medicines are so tasty.

Mary.   You are very careless with your tongue and I am surprised at you.

Mrs. O'G.   When you have killed me with your trouble, I'll not be able to speak of it.

Mary.   I don't want it spoken of to anybody.

Mrs. O'G.   You're killin' yourself entoirely and there isn't a man on earth that's worth it.

Mary. [*Going to window*]   Oh, why does not Frank send me some word. I seem to be wandering about in a ghastly dream.

Mrs. O'G.   It's that young man Frank Kennet, that's wanderin' about with the police at his heels. [*Mary opens window and looks out; laughter; children's voices heard*] Listen to that, and our hearts are as heavy as a hod of bricks.

Mary.   There is a girl dancing for them. She is a brazen thing. [*Speaks to some one outside*] Yes, this is Pop Lavelot's. You'd better come inside, I can't hear what you say. [*Opens door L. Enter Dick Brummage and Peggy Daly.*

Door is left open. Brummage is roughly dressed as a longshoreman—pea jacket and cap, muffler, etc. Peggy wears a short coarse skirt, cheap waist tucked into it, coarse jacket, yarn stockings and heavy shoes. She is eating an apple with juicy exuberance]

BRUM. [*Laughing. To Mary*] I promised the girl to buy her a frock if she'd shake a horn pipe and blow me if she didn't kick it out on the flags like a boatswain's mate. She's got a foot like a ripple and a leg like the spar on the commodore's yacht. Shake them out a shuffle, old gal.

MRS. O'G. Oxcuse me. This is a respectable man's house!

BRUM. Well, she's respectable round the ankles. Wait till you see her.

MARY. [*L. at back of sofa*] Do you wish to buy something?

BRUM. Yes. I got to buy the girl some togs.

MARY. [*L.*] You had better go to a store. We've nothing but odds and ends.

PEG. Say, old man, will you buy me a sweater?

MRS. O'G. You had better hold your whist and get out of here. [*Mrs. O'-Geogan and Peggy scowl at each other*]

PEG. [*To Brummage*] Wait till I eat me apple and I'll take a rise out of the old woman. [*To Mrs. O'Geogan*] Say, old lady I'm the champion contortion-east.

MRS. O'G. [*R.C.*] You are, are you? Well you'd better take a tumble to yourself. I'm the Columbian terror from the Fourteenth when me rules and regulations is interfered with. [*Gets broom*]

BRUM. [*C.*] If you don't dance she'll lather you.

PEG. Lather me? Wait till I show you how I can dance? [*Wild dance ad lib; Arapahoe spasm*]

BRUM. Now, old woman—fetch her frock out.

MRS. O'G. You don't need no decent woman's frock. You'd better go over on Broadway and buy yourself a set of tights. [*Peggy goes up L.C.*]

MARY. [*Coming down from window*] Oh, get her what she wants, Mrs. O'Geogan and let her go. There's a lot of stuff in that back room. [*Crosses to R.*]

MRS. O'G. It doesn't become me to be waitin' on the loikes of her.

MARY. [*Going to door R.3.*] Very well. I will wait upon her myself. [*To Brummage*] Wait a moment, sir.

BRUM. All right. Take your time. [*Crossing to R. Peggy dancing up stage C. Mrs. O'Geogan follows Mary to the door*]

MRS. O'G. Oi wouldn't ruin me reputation by stayin' alone with them. [*Exit Mrs. O'Geogan and Mary R.3. Brummage immediately shuts door L. and returns to Peggy, who is dancing very quickly*]

BRUM. [*L.*] Now then, Peggy Daly, what are you doing in Houston Street when your beat is in Canal Street? Come, straight out with it. I'm looking at you. The old woman sent you up here—what for?

PEG. [*Frightened*] Who be you?

BRUM. You ought to know me pretty well. I'm Dick Brummage.

PEG. Dick Brummage. [*Takes a step or two towards R.*]

BRUM. I got you out of the Oak Street station, but I'll put you back there pretty quick if you don't give it to me straight—you were sent up here by Rosenbaum to watch this house.

PEG. [*R.C.*] I hope to die, if I've done anything. A gal can come to Houston Street, can't she?

BRUM. Yes, and she can go to Blackwell's Island when I've got a through ticket. The old woman sent you here to see who was hangin' about this house.

PEG. [*Beginning to cry. R.C.*] She'd broke my back if I hadn't come.

BRUM. That's all right. Keep your mouth still and I'll stand your friend yet. The old woman never bought you a frock since you've been with her. [*Peggy crosses to table R. Enter Mrs. O'Geogan and Mary R.3. Mrs. O'Geogan carries a bundle which she puts on table R. Group to table examining clothes. As Brummage speaks to Mary, she goes to window, leaving Mrs. O'Geogan and Peggy facing audience at table. While the conversation is going on between Mary and Brummage, Peggy picks up a lorgnette from table and hides it in the folds of her dress, going up R.C.*]

BRUM. [*To Mary*] I want to get some duds meself.

MARY. I don't think you'll find what you want here, sir.

BRUM. Oh, that room is full of odds and ends. I'll get the old lady to let me pick out what I want.

OLD L. Oh, take him down the cellar and give him some oats. [*Peggy looks sharply around*]

BRUM. Well, gal, you got your frock?

MRS. O'G. [*R. of table R.*] Yes; sir, there's the frock. It will cost you a dollar.

MARY. [*At window; to Mrs. O'Geogan*] The gentleman wishes to buy some things himself. You'd better show him what you've got.

MRS. O'G. [*Resignedly*] Oh, very well. Step this way, sir.

BRUM. Good-bye, Peggy. You can start a dancing school now.

PEG. [*By door L.*] So long—so long—I'm goin' to the Eyetalian Opera. [*Exit Peggy L. Mary comes down and sits L. of table R.*]

MRS. O'G. [*At door*] This way, sir.

BRUM. [*To Mary*] I'll see you again, lass, before I go. I might have something to say to you. [*As Mrs. O'Geogan and Brummage exit R.3. Mary drops her head in her hands*]

OLD L. Get over—get over. Stand round. What's the matter with you? Whoa! [*Strikes the stove with a poker as if it were a horse then rises and exits grumblingly and slowly R.3. Enter suddenly Frank Kennet street door L.; he turns, locks the door and comes C. quickly*]

FRANK. Mary! [*Going to her*]

MARY. [*Seated L. of table R. Looking up*] Frank! [*Covers her face with her hands*]

FRANK. [*L. of her*] Look me in the eyes. I'm hunted! Tell me if I am a murderer?

MARY. [*Staring at him*] Where have you been these three days?

FRANK. Trying to get to see you to see if you believed in me, for that was the only thing worth living for. [*Puts hat on table R.*]

MARY. You were hiding.

FRANK. Do you believe that?

MARY. [*Rises*] They were looking for you everywhere—why did you not face this terrible charge of murder and robbery if you are innocent?

FRANK. [*Turning away aside*] My God! Even she suspects me. [*Goes up to window*]

MARY. You do not answer me. [*Crossing to L.C.*]

FRANK. [*Comes down R.C.*] I will tell you. When I left Mr. Bulford's house on that fatal night, I started to come to you. My senses became bewildered. I was numb with cold. I must have fallen down somewhere. When I recovered my senses, I was on the deck of a South American ship, and was being carried out of the country. I waited till dark set in, cut loose one of the boats and escaped from the vessel. A strong ebb was running—no effort was made to pick me up. Almost dead with cold I succeeded in reaching the Jersey shore in the grey of the morning. When I saw the papers and saw the crime with which I was charged [*Mary sits on sofa L.*] one desire influenced me. It was to see you first and then give myself up and demand a trial. I have made my way to you to tell you I am innocent and to hear you say you believe me. The rest is fate. [*Crosses to table, takes up hat and steps up a little. Reenter Brummage dressed as Old Lavelot. Seats himself R. of stove*]

MARY. [*Rising*] What are you going to do now?

FRANK. I am going to the nearest station.

MARY. [*L. back of sofa*] Can you prove your innocence?

FRANK. [*R.*] Is that worth proving which no one will believe in?

Mary. [*L. back of sofa. Approaching him*] Frank, this is a terrible mystery. The blow has numbed me—my heart tells me that you are innocent, but the dreadful facts stare me in the face. If you are innocent, we must prove it. [*Crosses to C.*]

Frank. [*R. at head of table*] Mary, I can fight adversity, and poverty and keep my spirit, but I cannot fight fate. [*Throws his hat on table, R.*] What cursed luck was it that sent me to that house that night and put me in these toils? [*Comes down R.*] I'll tell you what it was. [*Back to C.*] I was thinking of your happiness.

Mary. You can never make me unhappy if you are innocent.

Frank. [*R.C. Turns Mary to his R.*] I am innocent and you are the only friend in the world that I thought would believe me. [*Crosses a step to L.C.*]

Mary. [*R.C.*] Oh, no! You must have a friend who can advise you and help you.

Frank. [*L.C.*] I thought so before I came here.

Mary. [*R.C.*] Well, in Heaven's name think so yet.

Frank. [*L.C.*] There is not a person on earth who will not believe me guilty after reading the newspapers. [*Goes, looks out of window*]

Mary. [*R.C.*] I don't want to believe the newspapers. I want to believe you.

Frank. Mary!

Mary. [*Looking into each other's eyes*] Let me look at you—yes—you are the same Frank to me—no matter what happens. There is no murder in your eyes. [*Embrace, C.*]

Frank. [*L.*] No, my darling, I could not put these arms around you again if they had committed a crime. All that I want you to do is to believe in me.

Mary. Oh, I must do more. I only wish that I knew how. [*Marino gives a loud knock at street door, L. They are both startled*] Go in there. [*Pointing to door R.1.*] You must not be taken yet, I have so much to say to you. Go! Go! [*Knock again. Exit Frank R.1. Mary goes to street door and, unlocking it, admits Marino*]

Mar. Are you Miss Lavelot?

Mary. Yes. What do you wish? [*Crosses L. to behind sofa*]

Mar. I am in search of Frank Kennet.

Mary. [*Aside*] He has followed him here. [*Direct*] What is it you wish to know?

Mar. [*Coming down L.C.*] I will be frank with you. I have learned that you are engaged to be married to Frank Kennet.

Mary. Well, sir—

MAR. He is suspected of murder and the theft of valuable jewels.

MARY. But he is innocent of both.

MAR. You think so?

MARY. I am convinced of it.

MAR. [*Quickly*] Ah, then you have seen him since the murder and he has convinced you.

MARY. [*Aside*] He does not know he is here. [*Direct*] He has not convinced me.

MAR. I assume that you know where he is.

MARY. But you must not assume that I would betray him if I did.

MAR. I came here to open negotiations with him through you for the recovery of the diamonds, and to discover the murderer.

MARY. I, too, am anxious to discover the murderer.

MAR. [*Eagerly*] Has the murderer wronged you? [*During the speech they are standing one each side of the table, facing each other*]

MARY. Yes, he has.

MAR. Then we ought to be able to act together.

MARY. [*R. of table R.*] To what end?

MAR. To the discovery of the murderer. If Frank Kennet is that murderer, you would like to know it, wouldn't you?

MARY. I am anxious, as I have told you, to discover the murderer.

MAR. Then we can be of some assistance to each other. Now put me in communication with him. It is much the best way. He will be caught in time and then it may be too late for us to recover the property. Think it over and I will come back and see you again. It is not my intention to annoy you. [*Goes to door, L. Politely*] I beg your pardon for this intrusion. [*Bows and exits L. Door left unlocked*]

BRUM. [*Getting up from stove, looks out of door L. Coming down C.*] Well, you got rid of him very nicely, my girl.

MARY. [*Astonished*] You? Who are you?

BRUM. An officer from Headquarters, and I am waiting to see Kennet.

MARY. [*Overcome*] Oh, Heaven! Then it's no use. I have betrayed him!

BRUM. Well, don't go to pieces. Frank Kennet is suspected of two crimes, you know that?

MARY. [*At head of table R. back to end of it*] Yes, I know it, but he never committed them.

BRUM. [*C. up a little*] He went to the Bulford's house full of revenge. He was left alone with the old gentleman. They had an angry conversation. They drank wine together, and Mrs. Bulford says that when she returned to the room, Mr. Bulford was dead and the diamonds had disappeared. Have you read the papers?

MARY. Oh, yes—everything is against him—but—he is innocent—I know it.

BRUM. It is one thing to know and another thing to prove.

MARY. Everything. [*Covers her face with her hands*]

BRUM. No, not everything. Sit down here, you are trembling. [*Mary sits on L. of sofa*] Now listen to me. The coroner said Mr. Bulford was poisoned. But the inquest could not tell with what. It might have been in the wine he drank and the belief is that Kennet slipped it in the sherry glass when Mrs. Bulford went out. He drank it out of a cut sherry glass. That is in evidence. Are you listening to me carefully?

MARY. Oh, yes.

BRUM. [*R. of sofa L.*]   Mrs. Bulford in her examination said that the two glasses were on the table when she returned to the room. But the police were in the house before twelve o'clock that night looking for the diamonds. Something had disappeared.

MARY. Yes, yes, the jewel-case.

BRUM. The cut sherry glass.

MARY. Let me think. Yes. Go on.

BRUM. Somebody had made away with it, and it could not have been Kennet. Don't you see that? [*Mary jumps up*] Don't excite yourself. Why was that glass made away with, and who made away with it?

MARY. I understand. What do you intend to do?

BRUM. I am going to save Frank Kennet if I can.

MARY. Who are you?

BRUM. I am Detective Brummage of the Central Office, the one friend that the newspapers haven't convinced. When I was a poor man and a friendless boy, Frank Kennet's father befriended me and helped me. What are you crying for? [*Goes up, opens door L., looks out*]

MARY. I suppose it is because he's got such a good friend.

BRUM. [*Comes down C.*]   I suspect there is some kind of deviltry at work in that house of the Bulfords. Do you know who that man was that just left here? It was Mrs. Bulford's brother. [*Mary rises, goes L. around sofa at back of it*] But he will not suspect that Kennet is in town when he discovers the mistake he has made.

MARY. [*Behind sofa L.*]   Oh, tell me what do you want me to do?

BRUM. It isn't much. [*Takes newspaper from pocket, points to paragraph*] Read that. [*Goes up, opens door L.*]

MARY. [*Taking paper and reading*] "Wanted—a neat maid to attend a lady—must not be over twenty-three; with good penmanship and a knowledge of hair dressing; apply in own handwriting to No. 400 Lexington Avenue." [*Speaking*] What does it mean?

BRUM. It means that Mrs. Bulford has discharged all her old servants and is hiring new ones. Can't you apply for that place?

MARY. I? In that house? [*Crosses to R., sits L. of table*]

BRUM. There are some things in that house I want to find out. Once inside of it you can help me.

MARY. [*Seated L. of table*] But you forget that Mrs. Bulford's brother who has seen me here will see me there and betray me.

BRUM. No. I don't forget. You must take the risk of meeting him in order to help me.

MARY. [*Gets up and approaches Brummage*] I will take all risks and encounter all perils.

BRUM. [*Going to her—placing his hand on her shoulder and speaking tenderly*] You must be guided by me. We must not let it be known that Kennet has returned. The conspirators think he is out of the country and that makes them careless. I will take care of him and be responsible for him. [*Door L. opens softly and Marino looks in and listens*] You must trust me. I don't want to be known. [*Marino beckons to someone outside*] If you betray me we may lose everything.

MAR. [*Aside*] The very man! Frank Kennet!

MARY. I will believe in you and trust you. [*Marino closes door and disappears L.*]

BRUM. Good! Keep your counsel. Frank shall not give himself up to anyone but me, until this is settled. Now I'll go and get these things off, or your grandfather will think his double is walking about. [*Goes to door R.3.*] Brave girl! Keep your spirits up. [*Exits R.3.*]

OLD L. [*Outside R.3.*] Mary! Mary! [*Enter Old Lavelot from door, growling; he reseats himself at stove and takes poker*]

MARY. Yes, grandpa, dear, I'm coming. I'm coming.

OLD L. I want my bran, damn it! Been chewing on my manger ever since sunrise.

MARY. Grandpa, dear, I'll get you something to eat right away. [*Enter from L. door Marino and officer. Marino advances and points to Lavelot*]

MAR. There's your man. Ah, Kennet!

MARY. Kennet!

MAR. [*With quiet triumph*] This is better than we expected. You're a pretty sly bird but your game is up.

OLD L. [*By stove*] Throw 'em down the hay-loft stairs—I'm getting tired of this.

OFF. It's no go. Will you come quietly or shall I put you out? Don't be a fool any longer.

MAR. [*Down to table; to Mary*] It is not too late. Ask him where the diamonds are. [*Crosses to C. Mary indicates by her manner that she understands the mistake and to save Frank is willing to keep it up*]

MARY. Frank—[*Breaks down; officer seizes Lavelot; business of absurd struggle in which officer succeeds in getting him out of L. door followed by Marino. The moment they are gone Mary runs to door and locks it; calls in suppressed voice*] Frank—[*Frank enters R.1.*] We have only a few moments. They have taken the old man by mistake and will be back as soon as they discover it. [*Enter Brummage R.3.*]

BRUM. I'll be responsible for you. If they lock you up now, you can't help me. I've the superintendent with me, but the people we are going to fight have only the commissioners and politicians.

FRANK. And I, God help me, have nobody. [*Brummage is between Mary and Frank*]

BRUM. Nonsense! You've got two of the best friends that any man ever had on this earth and they are going to help you.

MARY. Yes, we are going to help you.

FRANK. *You?*

BRUM. Yes, she! [*Puts their hands together*] We've got a big fight, but if you'll be steered by Dick Brummage, we will run the real culprit to earth. [*Quick curtain*]

ACT III.

SCENE: *Two days later. Dining room in Mrs. Bulford's house. Two entrances —one at portieres in rear wall L. with screen in two folds, the other a hall door well up R.3. Buffet back C. Table with cloth up C. with chair R. and L. of it. Large mirror L.* TIME: *Early morning.* DISCOVERED: *Mary at buffet with back to audience looking at glasses. She wears a white apron and is plainly but tastefully dressed as a maid.*

MRS. B. [*Outside L.*] Susanne!

MARY. [*At buffet, startled*] Yes, madam.

MRS. B. [*Outside L.*] There is a man coming with flowers—let him in and see who they are from. I am not dressed yet.

MARY. Yes, madam. [*Mary goes to hall door R.3. Enter Dick Brummage disguised as an Irishman and carrying two bouquets—one large and the other small*]

BRUM. [*Coming to table and looking around*] Where's your mistress?

MARY. You can put the flowers on the table.

BRUM. How the divil then do Oi know I'm givin' them to the right person?

MARY. Mrs. Bulford is dressing. It's all right.

BRUM. Drissin', is she? Begorra it's yourself that needs no drissin'.

MARY. You may leave the room.

BRUM. Av course I'll lave the room. D'ye think I'd be takin' it wid me? Let me speak a word in your ear, my darlint. [*They go around the table; Mary goes to hall door and opens it*]

MARY. Leave the flowers and leave the room.

BRUM. There, me darlint. [*Puts flowers on the table, approaches her, changes voice*] Lass, don't you know me? [*Goes to door L.*]

MARY. [*Astonished*] You?

BRUM. Sh-sh-sh, not too loud. Where is she?

MARY. She is dressing.

BRUM. There's something going on here tonight. Keep your wits about you. Have you discovered anything?

MARY. Nothing.

BRUM. Well, you will tonight. Keep your eye on that portiere—if you see it move signal me at once and I'll stop. I've brought these flowers so as to keep you in sight. I am going to pretend that I have brought the wrong bouquets, so as to come back again with the right ones. Do you understand?

MARY. Yes; you frighten me.

BRUM. Keep your courage up, my little woman. If anything should happen to you tonight in this place and you want to communicate with me— write a line and put it in this small bouquet. I will leave it here and when I come back, I'll get it. Is it perfectly plain to you?

MARY. What can happen to me?

BRUM. Well, not much—if you keep me informed. You haven't found out who made away with that glass?

MARY. No, I have found out nothing, yet.

BRUM. Well, keep your ears open tonight. A girl's instinct is better than a man's reason when she's got a man to save.

MARY. Yes—poor Frank. Has he given himself up yet?

BRUM. Yes—to me. I am responsible for him. [*Mary suddenly looks right at him and starts. Crosses L. Portieres move; Brummage's voice and manner change*] Phat the divil, then, do I care for the trouble. I'd carry the blissed flowers forty toimes to git a look at a pretty gurrl loike yourself, so I would. [*Enter Mrs. Bulford through portiers*]

Mrs. B. [*C. up stage*]   What's the matter?

Brum. [*At table*]   The divil of anything's the matter save meself who's brought the wrong flowers. Axin' your pardon, I'll have the right ones here before a billy goat cud eat them.

Mrs. B.   Very well, you may leave the room.

Brum. [*Taking up large bouquet and leaving small one*]   I'll lave that to sweeten your room anyhow. [*Going at door*] But with two such beauties, it's too sweet already for an Oirishman. [*Exit through hall door R.3.*]

Mrs. B. [*Looking at flowers at head of table C.*]   Who sent the flowers?

Mary.   The man was so rude I could not find out and as you heard, he brought the wrong bouquets.

Mrs. B.   Never mind. Attend the door—I expect Dr. Livingstone. [*Turns down R.*]

Mary. [*Starting*]   Dr. Livingstone?

Mrs. B. [*Turning quickly*]   What's the matter—do you know him?

Mary.   No—o. But, are you ill?

Mrs. B.   No. He calls on business. [*Door bell rings*] There he is now. Show him in here. [*Takes bouquet from table, smells it and places it on side table L. Mary opens hall door R.3; timidly screening herself with it, and Dr. Livingstone enters, walks straight in without perceiving her. He comes down hat and cane in hand; Mary exits door L.*] I am glad you obeyed my summons, doctor. [*Doctor puts hat and cane on table. Mrs. Bulford at sofa L.*]

Dr. L. [*Taking off gloves*]   Yes, you have summoned me for what?

Mrs. B.   Will you be seated? [*Indicating chair*]

Dr. L. [*Still standing*]   Proceed, madam—why have you summoned me?

Mrs. B. [*Crosses to sofa end of it L.*]   I have a woman's curiosity and I wish to ask you some questions.

Dr. L. [*Gravely*]   I trust, madam, that you will not occupy my time in gratifying your curiosity.

Mrs. B. [*Sits on sofa*]   I pray that you will be seated, doctor. [*Indicating chair. Doctor sits easy chair close to Mrs. Bulford*] On the night that Mr. Bulford died, you told me that he died of apoplexy and that you would give me a certificate, but you changed your mind and notified the coroner.

Dr. L.   You are correct, madam. Proceed!

Mrs. B.   What I wish to know is, why you changed your mind after leaving my house. [*Dr. Livingstone gets up and walks toward door R.3. and does not immediately reply. Mrs. Bulford goes to the portiere L., looks*

through, and returns to sofa] We are entirely alone so you may be confidential. Why did you change your mind after leaving my house? [*Mary appears
at L. door listening; Dr. Livingstone sits on sofa L.*]

DR. L. [*Speaking deliberately*]   Madam, I changed my mind because I
saw you.

MRS. B. [*On sofa L.*]   Not after you left the house, doctor.

DR. L.   Yes.

MRS. B.   I did not leave the house that night.

DR. L. [*Looking at her and speaking slowly*]   No, but you came to an
upper window. [*Mrs. Bulford starts but recovers herself*] You lifted the sash
and threw something out. [*Mrs. Bulford clutches arm of sofa involuntarily
but smiles and looks the doctor in the eyes*]

MRS. B.   What a curious hallucination. You must have seen my ghost.

DR. L.   Madam, that which you threw out of the window could not well
be an hallucination, for I picked it up. It was a cut sherry glass with a mono-
gram on it. It fell upon a heap of rubbish and was unbroken. [*The two look
at each other for a moment. Mary, in her eagerness to hear, has pushed herself in at door*]

MRS. B.   This is really interesting. What did you find in the phantom
glass, doctor?

DR. L.   A little of the wine adhered to the bottom of the glass.

MRS. B.   And you sent it to the chemist?

DR. L.   That was not necessary—I tested it myself.

MRS. B.   And of course—in all such romances—you found—

DR. L.   Poison.

MRS. B. [*Still seated on sofa*]   But, doctor, of course you didn't know what
kind of poison it was?

DR. L.   Fortunately, I am one of the few who are familiar with it. It was
the deadly Para poison made only in South America. It was that fact that
defied the coroner. [*Mary closes the curtains and disappears*]

MRS. B.   Capital! And what did you say when you made this charming
discovery?

DR. L.   I said to myself—a woman will undo the craft of months with the
impulse of a moment. [*Rises*] Instead of washing the glass you threw it out
of the window. It is by such miscalculations that crime is detected.

MRS. B. [*Rises*]   No, it is by such fairy stories that detection is misdirected.

DR. L.   I scarcely understand you.

MRS. B. [*Taking a few steps to C. with assumed lightness of manner*]   I
mean—that a disinterested person hearing your story would say the doctor
was a confederate of ghosts and that phantoms threw the glass out to him,

especially when he acknowledges he is one of the few persons familiar with the poison. [*Goes and stands by sofa*] Besides, he went away the next day so as not to be present at the inquest. Then too he was, in all probability, on intimate terms with the phantom and may have made her visits extra professionally—just as you are visiting me tonight. [*Crosses to C.*] Doctor.

Dr. L. [*Bitterly*]   Madam, you are not only a clever, but an unscrupulous woman.

Mrs. B.   But not so clever as you are, doctor, at inventing stories. Let me ask you—have you told this to anyone? [*Dr. Livingstone walks up and down R.*] Try and compose yourself, doctor. Let me beg of you to be seated? [*Sits L. of table C.*]

Dr. L.   I was called away early in the morning after Mr. Bulford's death by a professional appointment at Montreal, and have only returned this morning. I have had no opportunity to give it much thought.

Mrs. B.   Well, now, doctor, don't you think that in view of your own peace of mind and your future success in New York (I understand you have an eye on the position of health officer of the Port, which is a political gift— I believe), don't you think, doctor, that for your own interests it would be well to abandon these ghost stories and thus save some estimable people from a great deal of annoyance? You are so eminent in your specialty of compounding medicines that it seems a pity to assume the risk of a romancer at your age.

Dr. L. [*Seated R. of table C. After pause—looking at her*]   You are right, madam, I have compounded medicines for many years, but I never compounded a felony.

Mrs. B.   Now you are angry, doctor; I beg your pardon.

Dr. L.   If you had studied faces as long as I have, madam, you would know that what you call anger is only a man's pity.

Mrs. B.   Not pity for me, doctor, I hope.

Dr. L.   No, madam—pity for an innocent man somewhere who is accused of a crime he never committed.

Mrs. B.   But who, if the papers are correct, ran away from the crime?

Dr. L. [*Turning*]   But I am informed that he had a friend who has not run away.

Mrs. B.   Are you referring to yourself, doctor?

Dr. L.   No, I am referring to a woman. So far as I am concerned I have been trained to the rigid performances of two duties—one to my patient. [*Pause*] The other to the public.

Mrs. B. [*Rising*]   Then, doctor, I hope that you will always permit me to be your patient. [*Mrs. Bulford goes L. Doctor R.C., watching her*] Doctor, would you mind telling me who is the woman in your fairy story so interested in this matter? [*Doctor is surprised, but does not answer. Mrs. Bulford calls through portiere*] Susanne! I have a morbid desire to meet her. [*The doctor has turned toward audience and does not see her*] You and this woman both know of the phantom glass I suppose?

DR. L. [*Annoyed*] Madam, I have already told you that I just returned to town and have as yet communicated with no one. She therefore could not know it—unless—unless she had been listening to our conversation. Madam, as I can be of no further service to you, I think it would be well for you to change your physician. [*Bows. Mary enters L. Doctor goes to table to take his hat and cane and comes face to face with Mary across table. Doctor starts as he recognizes her. Mary appealingly puts her finger to her lips and signals him not to betray her; all of which Mrs. Bulford sees in the mirror L. and turns quickly in blank dismay to watch them. Doctor hesitates a moment, looks from one to the other, takes his hat and cane and comes down C. With dignity*] Madam, I wish you good evening. [*Mrs. Bulford is speechless and only glares at him. Doctor exits hall door R.3. Mary glides quickly out at R.3. Mrs. Bulford comes down to table in great agitation*]

MRS. B. [*Leaning over table C.*] What does it all mean? Let me think— let me think? They know each other—what were his words? What were his very words? Unless she has heard our conversation. There are two of them who know. I have been spied upon in my own house. Where are my wits— where are my wits. What I do now must be done quickly. Who is this woman? [*Enter Mary R.3.*]

MARY. Madam, the senator.

MRS. B. Ah! [*Mary holds door R.3. Enter Senator McSorker dressed in Prince Albert coat; wears a large diamond; typical well-to-do New York politician*]

SEN. [*Heartily*] Ah—ha—there you are, lovelier than wax. Madam, yours obediently. You look like a four-year-old.

MRS. B. A four-year-old. Do I look childish, senator?

SEN. No, no, no—I mean a horse.

MRS. B. Look like a horse—Heavens, senator.

SEN. I beg your pardon—of course not—of course not. You know what I mean—an angel.

MRS. B. [*Still L. on sofa*] I see, when you say a horse—you mean an angel.

SEN. [*Front of sofa*] What's the matter? You look as though you'd been nominated and withdrawn.

MRS. B. We all have our troubles.

SEN. [*Seating himself in chair*] I'll buy your troubles at your price and carry them around for a pocket piece. What's your price?

MRS. B. [*Coquetting with her foot*] Yes, I dare say a man with your influence could soon end my troubles—if you were sufficiently interested in me.

SEN. [*Seated R. of sofa L., looking at her foot*] Say, that's good. I like that —interested in you—do you want me to get down on my knees like they do in the play? Lock the doors—I'll do it.

MRS. B. No, no—if there is any appealing to be done, I must do it.

SEN. Ha—ha—that's good. Now I particularly like that. You appeal to me? Say—that's rich. What'll you have?

MRS. B. You're a generous man, but I want too much.

SEN. *Name it! Name it!*—put up your scale. If I haven't got it, I'll borrow it.

MRS. B. Ah, what would I have given to have met a man like you earlier in my career—how different my life would have been.

SEN. [*Slapping his knee*] Better late than never. Call off your wants.

MRS. B. You're like all men when you're in a generous mood and would play the lover.

SEN. By Heavens, I would do anything else but play the lover.

MRS. B. I am afraid I want something more than a lover.

SEN. Anything you like—how would slave do?

MRS. B. What I want is a protector.

SEN. All right—I'll protect you from other lovers and I'll begin now. [*Sits down on sofa beside her and puts his arm about her*]

MRS. B. I want protection from powerful enemies. The man that wins my favor must shield me from scandal if he has to stop the law and defy the machinery of justice. Are you able to do that?

SEN. [*Attempting to rise*] Ain't you drawin'—a—it a little strong?

MRS. B. [*Attempting to rise*] I see—your power and your devotion are not boundless!

SEN. [*Pulling her back*] Don't go off that way—I'm yours. Do you want me to start something—or stop something?

MRS. B. I want something stopped. That dreadful affair of Mr. Bulford's.

SEN. But you didn't have anything to do with it.

MRS. B. [*Snatching his hands*] I don't want anything to do with it—that's the point. I have enemies who hope to drag me into court.

SEN. Look here—I'm gone to pieces on you—see? I don't know what you want me to do, but I'll do it if you don't play me.

Mrs. B. I want you to stand between me and my personal enemies when the time comes, no matter who they may be, you will crush them with all the influence and power that your position gives you. Now do you know?

Sen. [*Fondling her*] It's a go. I'll show you how we handle these things in New York. [*Seizes her hand*]

Mrs. B. You are hurting my hand, senator—I have a sharp ring on it.

Sen. [*Looking at ring*] Gee—willikens—where did you get that blazer? You must have been in politics yourself. I've carried the district attorney's office in one pocket and the Central Office in the other, but I never had a stone like that on my finger. [*Mrs. Bulford pulls her hand away quickly*]

Mrs. B. Senator, I'm going away in the morning to a quiet place in the country.

Sen. [*Rising*] Going away! Oh, come now, you can't do that. Damn it—I beg your pardon. I've made all arrangements. [*Sits on sofa again*]

Mrs. B. Arrangements for me?

Sen. Now see here, I told you tomorrow is election day and if things go right, I'm going to give the boys a blow-out at my house on Madison Avenue and I want you to be there.

Mrs. B. Oh, but senator, I should dislike to appear in public at this time.

Sen. 'Tain't in public—it's my private house. I'm going to give a banner to the Fourteenth and I wanted you to give it away. I made all calculations.

Mrs. B. Who will be there?

Sen. Only my friends, the politicians, and they're your friends. See? And you have to stand in with them. You needn't come till late. I'll take you away as soon as it's over.

Mrs. B. You don't have to announce me by name?

Sen. No—we'll call you the glittering Goddess of Liberty—anything you like. I'll waltz you through and take care of you. That's the way to see whether I can protect you or not.

Mrs. B. [*Rising*] I suppose I must earn my protection by obeying you. [*Enter Marino hurriedly from L.*]

Mar. How-de do, senator. [*To Mrs. Bulford*] Was Dr. Livingstone here half an hour ago?

Mrs. B. Yes, yes. What's the matter? [*L.C. senator L.; goes round sofa up L. to C.*]

Mar. He is killed! A fire truck run into his carriage on the Avenue and threw him out on his head. I happened to pass at the time and the ambulance attendant, who had the doctor's book, said that his last call was here. [*Mrs. Bulford clasps her hands and shivers*]

Mrs. B. Dead!

MAR.   What's the matter?

MRS. B.   [*Laughing hysterically*]   Nothing—it is so sudden. Give me a glass of water—dead—then there is but one.

SEN.   [*To Marino, coming down C.*]   Young man, go and sit down. [*Takes Mrs. Bulford over to sofa*]

MRS. B.   Gentlemen, I shall have to ask you to leave me. You have undone me for the moment. [*Sits on sofa L.*]

SEN.   Don't forget tomorrow night, dear. Get yourself in your best—good-bye. [*Goes to door R.3.*] Young man, you're too damn sudden! [*Exit R.3.*]

MRS. B.   Come here and sit down.

MAR.   [*Sits on sofa*]   What is agitating you so? You don't usually take on in this way.

MRS. B.   Did you send the message to the old woman, that I gave you?

MAR.   Yes, I did.

MRS. B.   I must have some money and I have a few jewels that she will pay me a better price for than any one else. Is she coming?

MAR.   Yes, but I don't want to see her.

MRS. B.   No, I will spare you this humiliating business, but I must have some money. You know more about this woman than I do.

MAR.   I know too much about her to have her name linked with yours.

MRS. B.   Did you understand that she is the woman who hates Don Plon?

MAR.   Yes, he is said to have betrayed her son who was executed. What are you asking me this for, now?

MRS. B.   [*Sotto voce*]   And she has threatened to be revenged?

MAR.   Yes. What has got into your head?

MRS. B.   That is all. I wanted to be sure I had not dreamed it.

MAR.   [*Rises*]   You look as if you had a fever and a bad dream. If I were you I'd go and lie down before she comes. [*Bell heard*] There she is now. I'm going to skip. [*Music. Enter Mary R.3.*]

MARY.   Madam, a lady in black—she would not give her name.

MRS. B.   Let her in. [*To Marino*] You must be at the senator's house to-morrow night, I may need you.

MAR.   [*Going*]   Yes, but I don't like the crowd—I'm not a politician. [*Exit Marino L. door. Enter Mother Rosenbaum R.3; she advances to C.*]

ROS. [*Down to C.*]   Ah, madam, you will not come to see me in my little store, so I must come to you, when you have something to sell.

MRS. B.   [*Fastening back the portiere*]   Sit down, madam. I did think of selling my few family jewels, but I have changed my mind as I am going to remain in the city. [*Both seated on sofa*]

Ros. You have not many diamonds? Ah, madam, you are too modest. I think you have the finest jewels in America.

Mrs. B. [*Sits in chair next sofa*] What makes you think so? I am not a rich woman.

Ros. Ah, it is not the rich woman who has the most diamonds.

Mrs. B. I have a few jewels that were presents—

Ros. [*Interrupting*] They were presents to you—heh?

Mrs. B. I said—presents, but I have concluded to keep them.

Ros. Are they diamonds?

Mrs. B. Yes, but of no great value.

Ros. Have you not a ruby?

Mrs. B. [*Face to her in chair by sofa*] Now if we are to do any business, let me beg of you to be at least respectful.

Ros. Respectful, madam? I very much respect the woman who has a ruby and a large ruby—what you call—u-m. Mein Gott, woman, I could not, at my time of life, ask where people get things.

Mrs. B. You are affected with the same suspicion that besets other people, and that is that I have the Garbiadoff jewels. You and your friend Plon are both of one mind. I sent for you to get you to help me against his plot.

Ros. The dog! You say Plon is my friend and he and I are of the one mind? Oh, madam, do not say that again, or you will make me your enemy for life. Plon—the hound! It was he who made my poor and only boy suffer. The dog! I wish I had my fingers on his throat.

Mrs. B. The miscreant has a woman whom he employs to obtain his plunder.

Ros. Yes, yes—I know, I know.

Mrs. B. [*Seated R. of her*] She is here in my house. She obtained service as a maid. I caught her tonight telegraphing to a visitor. She has been eavesdropping here for a week.

Ros. [*Eagerly*] Where is she now?

Mrs. B. She is at the other end of that passage and she cannot approach without my seeing her. [*Rises and crosses to end of sofa L.*]

Ros. [*Going up and down. Hesitates, then eagerly*] How do you know that she is Plon's woman? [*Down by sofa R. of it*]

Mrs. B. [*Hesitating*] Because I discovered a letter from him in her room.

Ros. [*Viciously*] Ah—the sweet little creature—give her to me.

Mrs. B. How can you take her?

Ros. I will not take her—she will go herself—just as gently—you shall see. What is she here for? Is she not looking for the diamonds?

Mrs. B. Yes, yes—well?

Ros. Will she not know that I come to buy the diamonds—anybody can tell by my poor dress that I buy diamonds—I do not wear them. You shall tell her to go in my carriage and bring the diamonds here from my place. She will think they are the Garbiadoff's and to get them in her hands, she will be so eager she will go. [*Viciously*] But she will come away not again.

Mrs. B. But I cannot consent to any step that will imperil my character.

Ros. Gott in Himmel. If I did not respect your character, I would not be seen in your house. I have a character myself.

Mrs. B. But my friends—Senator McSorker.

Ros. If you did not have Senator McSorker for your friend then would I not do it? Of course you will marry the senator.

Mrs. B. Marry the senator?

Ros. Aye. Aye. You will marry the senator. You will go to his party to-morrow night. You will put on all your jewels and your fine dresses and when he sees you come down the staircase, he will think you came down from Heaven, like the angel you are. Now if you do not fix the senator to-morrow night, not even Rosenbaum can save you. Now let me see the jewels —the diamonds.

Mrs. B. Let you see the jewels? What for?

Ros. What for? Mein Gott! Woman, do you think I make a bargain with a cat in a bag?

Mrs. B. You are a queer creature. You are erratic.

Ros. Am I? Well, I see, I see, Rosenbaum cannot do any straight business with madam—so I'd better go. [*Starts to rise*]

Mrs. B. Stop! Sit down.

Ros. Well, I sit! Well?

Mrs. B. I cannot lay hands on the jewels at the present moment—

Ros. Yes, you can.

Mrs. B. How?

Ros. Because they are here.

Mrs. B. Here? Where?

Ros. On your person. Get them out. To save you I must see the jewels. [*Mrs. Bulford goes to portieres, pulls curtains together, then goes to chair L. of table, takes up cloth with back to audience at C. table in front of it, and pretends to take jewels out of her bosom—then goes down L. of Rosenbaum, who is on sofa. Mrs. Bulford sits, unwraps cloth. While Mrs. Bulford is at table*] I always thought she killed old Bulford, and now I know it. [*Mrs. Bulford goes down to Rosenbaum. Examining jewels*] Now shut them up. [*Mrs. Bulford rises, goes to C. table. Business*] And now let me see Plon's woman. You shall send her in my coach to my house on an errand.

MRS. B. *Very well!* [*Goes to portiere and calls*] Susanne! Susanne! [*To sofa*] Be careful, or she will suspect. [*Enter Mary L.*]

MARY. [*Down C.*] Yes, madam.

MRS. B. Susanne, pay attention. I have some jewels which this lady took to her house to sell for me, but as I have changed my mind, I want to get them back again. Can you get in this lady's coach—go to her house and bring me the jewels?

MARY. Yes, madam. [*Aside*] Heavens—the jewels! [*Direct*] Do you wish me to go now? [*Mrs. Bulford at back of sofa*]

Ros. [*Seated on sofa L.*] Right away, my dear. What a beautiful child you are. You must be careful and come right back—heh—while I wait here for you.

MARY. Yes, madam.

Ros. Come here, my child. [*Mary crosses to head of sofa, Mrs. Bulford crosses to C.*]

Ros. [*Taking her hand*] What a beautiful hand! [*To Mrs. Bulford*] Madam, it is not right to send a child on such an errand—I will go myself.

MARY. [*Nervously*] I can do it, madam.

MRS. B. There is no danger that I can see. Give her a note—she will get the package and come straight back. I would not have her take any risks. [*To Mary*] Go bring paper and pencil, Susanne. [*Exit Mary at L.*]

Ros. [*Clutching Mrs. Bulford by the arm*] I will save you, but how will you save me?

MRS. B. Save you—what do you mean?

Ros. Mein Gott! Woman, do you think I save people for the amusement?

MRS. B. [*In chair next to sofa*] What do you want?

Ros. [*With her face close to Mrs. Bulford and with hissing intensity*] I want the "Heart of Fire."

MRS. B. [*Rises and suddenly with dignity*] Why?

Ros. If we cannot understand each other, then what for do I come here? Do you think I have no heart? I have, my dear, I cannot take a young lady from such a nice home—it is too cruel. [*Sits again on sofa*]

MRS. B. I must have my jewels to wear tomorrow night at the senator's. The day after I will talk to you. Can you trust me?

Ros. I do not have to trust you when I have the young woman. [*Enter Mary at portieres with paper; place it on side table front L.; crosses to C. table and takes bouquet from table and goes to buffet with it where she is seen by audience putting a folded paper into the bunch of flowers, which she places on table while Rosenbaum is writing on side table. Mrs. Bulford is watching Rosenbaum*]

MARY. [*At C. table, aside*] If anything happens to me he said he would get this.

Ros.   Come here, my dear. [*Gives note to Mary who comes down*]

MRS. B. [*Behind Rosenbaum without turning around*] Do be careful of yourself, my child.

Ros. [*Rising and crossing to Mary*] I will tell my coachman to be very careful of her and bring her right back. [*Exit R.3. Rosenbaum and Mary. Mrs. Bulford watches them off nervously and the moment they disappear, she jumps up and walks stage to C. Enter Marino from L.—the two face each other*]

MRS. B.   You! Why have you come back?

MAR.   Did Susanne go out? [*Goes toward portiere*]

MRS. B. [*Quickly*] Yes, why?

MAR.   I wish to speak to her.

MRS. B. [*Controlling herself*] Try and behave yourself in my room— what do you want of Susanne?

MAR. [*Going up a little*] Do you know who she is?

MRS. B.   What do you mean?

MAR.   I have been thinking of her a great deal. She may know something of the murderer of Mr. Bulford.

MRS. B. [*Sotto voce*] Yes, she may.

MAR. [*Catching Mrs. Bulford by the arm impressively*] Maria, are you sure that when you returned to the room that night the jewels were gone?

MRS. B.   What are you talking about? Have you lost your wits?

MAR.   Where is the girl? [*Enter Rosenbaum at R.3.*]

MRS. B. [*Hesitating and looking at Rosenbaum*] She is gone.

MAR. [*Astonished*] Gone where?

MRS. B. [*Impressively*] I do not know. [*Walks rapidly*]

MAR. [*Excitedly*] But I will know. [*Rosenbaum and Mrs. Bulford to front L. together*] I am going to find the murderer of Mr. Bulford. [*Marino takes bouquet from table and mechanically sniffs it as he walks. Enter Dick Brummage from R.3. with flowers*]

BRUM.   Oi've brought ye the right flowers. [*Looks at bouquet in Marino's hand disconcertedly*] And Oi'd thank you to give me that one.

MAR. [*Walking, carelessly*] Oh, I'll keep this one—I like it. Leave the room.

BRUM. [*With comical distress*] Shure you wouldn't have a man lose his place, by lavin' the flowers wid ye that belonged to some one else.

Mrs. B.   Oh, give him the flowers and let him go. [*Marino throws bouquet to Brummage, who seizes it eagerly and goes to door behind screen, faces audience, looking into bouquet for paper. Marino continues walking*]

Ros. [*To Mrs. Bulford*]   You will bring me the "Heart of Fire" on Thursday.

Mrs. B. [*To Rosenbaum*]   You are sure that when she left this house, she could communicate with no one?

Ros.   Ah, when she go away from here, no one shall ever know one word from her. [*Brummage pulls Mary's note from bouquet deliberately, putting it in his pocket*]

ACT IV.

Scene: *Hoffman House Café. The set represents the room as if seen from Twenty-fourth Street. Square bar in C. with fixtures; barkeeper dealing liquors. Groups ad lib. Large frame of Bouguereau's Nymphs seen in profile L.C. lit from above. Statuary, plants, etc., and six tables arranged at equal distances in front and up R.* Time: *Eight o'clock in the evening. Brummage seated at table L. Enter countryman L.C., comes down slowly and stops in front of picture. His attention is fixed. He is amazed—looks intently, looks furtively away and looks back at the picture in the same way. Enter Mrs. O'Geogan looking at picture and then to Marino who is at the bar.*

Mrs. O'G.   Is Senator McSorker here? I came here to find him.

Mar.   No, I have not seen him.

Mrs. O'G. [*Looking at picture aghast, pointing to it*]   What's them?

Mar.   What do you mean, the picture?

Mrs. O'G.   Yes.

Mar.   The picture is called the Nymphs and the Satyr.

Mrs. O'G.   Please say that agin to me, I didn't catch it.

Mar.   The Nymphs and the Satyr.

Mrs. O'G.   That's a funny name for them women. Why they ain't got no clothes on. Why don't they put some dresses on them?

Mar.   They are painted natural.

Mrs. O'G.   Yes, they's mighty natural. There is no mistake about that. It ought not to be allowed. It is sinful. [*Pauses*] But they are daisies you bet.

Mar.   Why do you look at them, if it be sinful? [*Crosses down below*]

Mrs. O'G.   I can't help it, they fetches me so. Them gals is peaches, ain't they? Why, I can't just take my eyes off them. Natur is natur, and I'm just as natural. Air you still hungering for the flesh pots of Egypt? If you see the senator tell him his old friend Mrs. O.'G. is looking for him. Good-bye. [*She*

and Marino exit L.2. Enter Count Garbiadoff R.; he comes down front.
Dick Brummage, who has been seated at table L. since rise, sees count and
approaches him]

BRUM. Well, Count Garbiadoff, you are, I observe, taking in all the sights
of the city.

COUNT. [*Surprised*]   Who are you?

BRUM. [*Opening coat and showing badge*]   Detective Brummage. We met
at the Central Office today.

COUNT. Oh, yes. I remember now. Haf you tell me something?

BRUM. Yes. Sit down. [*They sit L.*]

COUNT. What is it, speak. I am anxious to hear.

BRUM. Could you identify your diamonds if you saw them?

COUNT. Every stone.

BRUM. Even if on the person of the woman we suspect and at night?

COUNT. Yes, under any circumstances.

BRUM. The politician under whose protection this woman is, gives a party
at his home, No. 1360 Madison Avenue. You must be there.

COUNT. What for?

BRUM. The woman will be there, and I think will wear your diamonds.

COUNT. Wear my diamonds? The audacity—it is not possible!

BRUM. I think she will wear them. A woman's vanity is always greater
than her caution. She does not believe that anybody can identify them, and
as she does not know the Count Garbiadoff is here. Be careful, remember
you are sent there only to see them.

COUNT. Oui. I came all the way from Cracow to see them and to see her.
[*Aside*] I will tear them from her—the pitiless wretch.

BRUM. Let me warn you not to be rash. If you can identify your jewels
on her it will be all we can do tonight. If you are not prudent you may ruin
us both, and destroy all chances of recovering the property.

COUNT. Mon dieu! Do you tell me I shall take only ze look and go back
to Cracow with vat you call ze tail between ze legs? Pah! You shall call the
gendarmes.

BRUM. Everything will be gained for the courts if you can identify the
woman and the jewels. That is enough. Everything else would be madness.
You do not understand this politician's power.

COUNT. Canaille, I do not understand.

BRUM. Calm yourself and meet me at the senator's tonight. Any cabman
will carry you there.

COUNT. The entrée? How will I get that?

BRUM. Walk boldly in. The company will be so mixed that the senator will not know his guests and you will not be recognized. Now we had better say good-bye for the present, as I have other work to do.

COUNT. Au revoir. [*Exit door off R. at back. Brummage waves his hand and sits L. reading paper. Enter senator L.2., followed by Marino, Clancy, Brannigan and others. He is greeted cordially by several as he comes on to front of bar*]

SEN. Well, well, boys, as I was telling you, I have always depended on the Fourteenth. She deserves the banner and tonight she gets it—see? The handsomest woman in New York, my friend Mrs. Bulford, will make the presentation. Gentlemen, Mr. Marino, her brother. He is going in politics. [*To bartender*] Set 'em up, councillor. [*The two heelers shake Marino's hand, boisterously*]

CLAN. There's nothing the matter wid the Fourteenth. She gits the banner, dat's all right; and I get me brudder out of Sing Sing, eh, senator?

SEN. You bet. Have some cigars. [*Business with cigars. First heeler takes a handful from the box and puts them in his coat pocket, conversation in dumb show*]

BRAN. Ah, what d'ye know about the Fourteenth? You was brought up in de Sixth.

CLAN. De men in de Sixth learned the trade of votin' before de Fourteenth was made.

BRAN. Ah, de Fourteenth don't depend on no votin' when dey can do de countin'. What's de Fourteenth care for voters when dey got de inspectors?

COUNT. I am very anxious to learn the political methods of New York, but I don't know at present what I am to do to help on the glorious cause.

BRAN. Well, you kin do the drinkin' can't yer, like the rest of us?

CLAN. Ah—what does the Sixth know about drinkin'? [*Sheeney Ike appears L. coming down R., stops at corner of bar L. and tries to catch the senator's eye. Brummage moves so as to see Sheeney Ike over his paper*]

SEN. [*Laughing*] You'll have to take my friend down in the Sixth and show him the ropes. [*Sees Sheeney Ike*] Excuse me a minute, gentlemen. [*Goes to corner of bar, conversation of heelers continues in dumb show*] Are you looking for me?

IKE. Yes, Mother Rosenbaum sent me up from Canal Street.

SEN. What's the matter with her now?

IKE. She says there's a special from the Central Office a workin' the Bulford lay.

SEN. Well, it's none of his business. I'm takin' care of that. Tell the old woman to brace up. What's she got to do with it anyhow?

IKE. She says they're a tryin' to fix it on the widder—Mrs. Bulford.

SEN. Oh, they are, are they? Well, it don't go, because I'm lookin' out for the widder, and he can't work no lay there for I'll call him down. I've got a party at my house tonight—going to have Mrs. Bulford present the banner to the Fourteenth. You tell the old woman to rest easy in her mind—I will see her tomorrow—they can't work no lay without me. You bet. [*Marino going. Senator and Ike's dialogue continues in dumb show. While this conversation has been going on, the two heelers have got into violent altercation in dumb show which Marino absurdly tries to prevent, and both rush to senator for a decision, coming to the corner of bar L. and opposite table where Brummage sits*]

BRAN. [*With great excitement*] Well, I'm bettin' me pile on it. [*Pulls an enormous roll of bills from his hip pocket and slaps the roll down violently on table. First heeler pulls a still larger roll from pocket and imitates defiantly*]

CLAN. Say, your money was born deaf and dumb. Here's the money what talks. [*Brummage gets up, disgustedly holding paper. Business continues between heelers in dumb show, Marino showing absurd anxiety and astonishment, senator leaning against bar and laughing at them. Senator and Ike move away from heelers*]

SEN. [*To Ike*] Who's the officer that's meddlin' in this matter?

IKE. She says it's Brummage.

SEN. Well I'll break him tomorrow, see? Have a drink, have some wine? [*Heelers coming promptly to bar again. At this moment great shouting is heard in the office and a crowd of Princeton and Yale boys shouting college cries and waving flags, singing songs, come crowding into room. Everybody yells, scenes of confusion, students cluster around the bar or sit at tables and pound bells ordering drinks. Senator and his friends form a group at bottom of bar, drinking and looking amusedly at boys. Frank is seen coming on at back mingling with the crowd. The moment he is well on, Brummage spies him and rushing across to him, takes him well R. and in a low voice but excitedly, says*]

BRUM. My God, what are you doing here? I told you not to leave the house.

FRANK. I know, I know. But I couldn't stand the suspense any longer. So I came here hoping to see you, and hear something of Mary and my own fate.

BRUM. Well, I have something to say to you, and not much time to say it in.

FRANK. Where is Mary?

BRUM. Don't look around—we may be watched. Mary's kidnapped.

FRANK. My God, then what are you doing here? [*Ike's attention is attracted by Frank's manner*]

BRUM. Do you want to tell everybody in the place what we are talking about?

FRANK. [*Dropping back in his chair*] Kidnapped on my account and I am helpless!

BRUM. I respect your feelings, but just now they are damned risky, for we've got work to do.

FRANK. Why don't you tell me—where have they taken her? Who are the miscreants?

BRUM. Well, don't shout—I'm trying to find out. I've got a letter from the girl. If you'll keep quiet I'll show it to you. [*Produces note that he took from bouquet. Subdued laughter in bar, rear. Brummage and Frank listen a moment. Brummage then hands Mary's note to Frank*]

FRANK. [*Reading with difficulty*] "I am going to Madam Rosenbaum's to fetch the diamonds to Mrs. Bulford—don't know where. I am suspicious and nervous. I depend on you if anything happens to me." [*Direct*] What Madam Rosenbaum, where has she gone?

BRUM. There's only one old woman in New York that's likely to be mixed up in this, and she's a desperate character protected by the politicians and rolling in ill-gotten wealth. She has never hesitated at murder when it served her ends, for she goes to that senator there for protection. There stands the senator and there's the old hag's man talking to him.

FRANK. [*With gesture of impatience*] My God! What iniquity!

BRUM. Well, don't telegraph it. It must occur to you that in any case they wouldn't send the girl to fetch the diamonds and if they made her believe it, it was to trap her.

FRANK. Go on—you've got the knife into me—turn it around. Is there no living show for innocence in this city?

BRUM. Well, there is if you've got patience, and if you've got your facts right. But there's something else on that paper I couldn't make out. [*Frank looks at paper*]

FRANK. Yes, there's something else, but it's rubbed. [*Holds paper to light*] Oh, yes. It says "I know all about the glass." What does that mean?

BRUM. [*Starting*] Does it say that? [*Snatches paper and looks at it*]

FRANK. What does it mean?

BRUM. It means that she knows something and they've tried to make away with her.

FRANK. For God's sake, tell me what you're going to do.

BRUM.   I'm going to get the information tonight. Tomorrow it will be too late. They are celebrating that politician's power now. Tomorrow he will stand between us and justice.

FRANK.   We are wasting time—it may be too late now.

BRUM.   Try and be cool and listen to me. The only way to save her is to get that information. [*Ike leaves senator and comes slowly and guardedly toward picture back of table where Brummage and Frank are sitting. Senator goes up R. to other groups*]

FRANK.   Very well, man, let's be quick about it.

BRUM.   The old woman has two places—one in Rivington Street—that's her store. The other in Canal Street near the river. That's her den. We've got to get in those two places tonight. If we only see Mary for a moment and get that information. [*Brummage and Frank have their heads down intent on the subject and Ike goes past them trying to listen just as Brummage has uttered the last speech*]

FRANK.   Yes, yes.

BRUM.   I am going to one place and I want you to go to the other. You can do just what I tell you. I'll write the number of the place in Canal Street on this card. [*Writes on card*] And on this side of it—[*Turns card over*] I'll give you a line to the patrolman on the beat. He will know it and will keep his eye on you. [*Hands card*] I will go to the other place. If the girl isn't there, I will be in Canal Street almost as soon as you are. We may not save the girl, but we may get the information that will save you. [*Ike is approaching the table and trying to listen*]

FRANK.   I will not be saved at such a sacrifice.

BRUM.   Never mind the rescue. See the girl—[*Brummage stops suddenly and eyes Ike fixedly. The latter seemingly does not turn his head—cowed by Brummage's gaze slinks off hurriedly at back*]

FRANK.   Well—well—why do you stop? You wanted me to go to Canal Street to this old woman—

BRUM.   But I don't want you to tell it to that ruffian who has just passed us. [*Marino, who has been intently watching all this, goes to senator and points to Brummage and Frank. Senator starts and looks in their direction*]

BRUM.   Wait a moment. Is that sheeney still there?

FRANK.   No. He has gone, but the senator is watching us closely. Does he suspect?

BRUM.   Yes, very likely. We have got to act quickly. The girl, if you can get to her, will tell you all, and if you can get away with the information, we will hang the right person.

MAR. [*Motioning his head in direction of Brummage*] Senator, there's your friend the detective, I am sure.

SEN. [*Astonished*] Brummage?

MAR. Yes, and the young fellow with him is startlingly like that young fellow Kennet I saw that fatal night at Mr. Bulford's.

SEN. You don't mean it! He would never dare—

MAR. 'Tis he. I would swear it.

SEN. [*Amazed*] I'll make a bluff and have him taken and spoil Brummage's game whatever it is. [*Senator beckons to Clancy and Brannigan. They join him. Senator talks to them in dumb show. They shake their heads knowingly and affirmatively. Frank and Brummage rise—they start towards door L.2.*]

SEN. Hold on! Both of you! Don't be in a hurry. I want you, see?

BRUM. Are you talking to me, sir?

SEN. Well, I am talking straight at you. See. I am on to you!

BRUM. Sir?

SEN. Oh, "sir" don't go, I won't have any frills. You are meddlin' in something that's my business. [*Tapping his breast*] And I'm going to call you down right here.

BRUM. You are drunk, sir, and I have no time to waste with you. [*Senator gets squarely in front of him*]

SEN. You're a liar. What are you doing? Where are you going?

BRUM. I am going out of that door.

SEN. Not yet, you ain't. You are going to stay here where my eye is on you.

BRUM. I am going. [*Slowly*]

SEN. And I am going to stop you.

BRUM. Oh, no. Remember you can't stop me tonight. You may tomorrow. [*Music till curtain*]

SEN. I'll stop both of you now. That man there with you is a murderer. [*Frank shudders*] And I am going to have him taken in. [*Motioning head toward Brannigan and Clancy. Brummage looks over his shoulder cynically at them*]

BRUM. Touch him if you dare. He is in my charge, by order of the superintendent, and while there, no man can arrest him. I represent the law, and don't you dare to put your hands on him.

SEN. Not a step shall he move until I get an officer. Patsy, Shorty seize him. [*Patsy and Shorty start to seize Frank; Brummage puts himself between them and Frank, one hand behind him on his pistol, the other on Frank, making picture*]

BRUM.   Stop! I'll make daylight shine through the man who puts a finger on him.

SEN. [*As if to draw pistol*]   You dog, I'll make an end of you here, and now, and I'll take in that murderer.

BRUM.   *Draw!* I dare you. I am prepared for that. I am doing my duty and I shall protect this man unless you kill me. [*Places himself between senator and his men, shielding Frank completely. Senator and his men make picture standing at bay*]

SEN.   Damn you—if I didn't have a party on my hands tonight, I'd have the buttons pulled off of you—you infernal hound.

BRUM. [*With intensity and deliberation*]   Your party will be over by midnight; I'll report to you at twelve o'clock. [*Goes to door L.2.*] You'll have your friends around you. That hour will be yours—till then the hours are mine. [*Arm about Frank, pistol in hand, forcing way through crowd L.C. They give way in fright*]

CURTAIN

ACT V.

SCENE: *Canal Street. Exterior of Mother Rosenbaum's house, front scene. Old fashioned house, brick with green blinds. Alley in drop with practicable door. One practical window. Music for rise until curtain is well up.* TIME: *Nine o'clock at night.* AT RISE: *Old man playing harmonica. Peggy Daly dancing to his music. Four boys looking on; they have shinny sticks; clapping hands and keeping time with their feet. Enter Jimmy McCune with girl on his arm. She is leading a dog. He wears a silk hat and the girl carries a satchel.*

PEG. [*L.*]   Where are you goin', Jimmy McCune, with your consort? How's yer sore eyes?

McC.   Don't you gull me, Peggy Daly. Here, take me dorg into the alley. I am going down to Lumpy Kidney's.

PEG.   Dere ain't no free lunch at Lumpy's today. [*Exit L.1. with dog. While they are talking, one of the boys snatches the satchel; Jimmy makes a dash at him, his hat falls off. Immediately the boys begin playing shinny noisily with it, two on a side. Peggy reappears from the alley and finally rescues the hat and gives it to Jimmy*]

McC.   I'll make the old woman pay for that. Tell her I'm down to Lumpy Kidney's. [*Exit L.1. with companion. As he goes off there is a sound of rushing wheels and a gong. Boys all strike listening attitude and boy No. 1 shouts*]

BOY No. 1.   Hi, fellers, there's a fire!

Boys. Fire! Fire! [*Exit hurriedly L.I., followed by Peggy. At the same time Sheeney Ike comes on R.I., goes to entrance of brick house. The blinds of practicable window open cautiously and Mother Rosenbaum's head appears with shawl thrown around it. Noise stops here*]

Ike. Is that you?

Ros. Yes, what's the matter?

Ike. [*Looking guardedly around*]   There's something up. I just came from the Hoffman House.

Ros. Is the senator all right?

Ike. He's all right. Where's the gal?

Ros. I've got her here—she's all safe.

Ike. They are coming for her.

Ros. Who's coming?

Ike. A young fellah's coming down here fer to get word from her. I got onto it straight in the Hoffman House by listenin'. He's to spot the cop on his beat who's a goin' to look out for him.

Ros. Who's the nice young gentleman who's a comin' to visit the old woman?

Ike. [*R. of window*]   I think it was Brummage was puttin' him up. But I steered the senator onto Brummage, and he'll take care of him. What we've got to look after, is the other one.

Ros. And the other one is coming to the pleceman on this beat?

Ike. That's the way I heard it.

Ros. And if he don't see the pleceman and comes in—

Ike. Then they'll never know he come.

Ros. Quick—where's Peggy?

Ike. There she comes—she's been down to Lumpy Kidney's. [*Pointing to L.I. Enter Peggy L.I.*]

Ros. Come here to me and mind what I tell you. [*Peggy to window*] Where's Jimmy McCune?

Peg. He's down to Lumpy's now. [*Takes a dancing step and hums*]

Ros. Stop that! Go back there and tell him to put on the cop's dress and lay for the young man what's a comin' here. Be quick about it. He's to steer this young man in here and not let the regular cop see him. Do you understand? Here's the shield—the coat's in the saloon. [*Hands out shield*] Tell him to keep out of the patrolman's sight. Go on now and if you make a mistake I'll skin you! [*Exit Peggy L.I. dancing. To Ike*] Go up to Cahill's saloon and tell the boys to keep the regular patrolman there till this is over. Here's the money. [*Gives money*] Buy whiskey, will you—no wine. Go on and come back here—I want you. We will give my young friend a chance to see [*Music till she closes window*] the old woman at her best. [*Ike takes money and hurriedly exits R.1. Rosenbaum looks up and down and then closes the shutters. Enter Peggy L.1., crosses to R. and exits through door. Enter Frank Kennet, R.1., looks about him*]

FRANK.   This must be the place. I wonder if Mary is in that dismal hole— and I am the cause of her misfortune. My God! She may be dead before this. [*Walks L. and looks about*] I wonder where I'll find the patrolman. [*Looks off L.*] Thank Heaven, here he comes. [*Music tremolo till change of scene. Enter McCune, L.1., disguised as policeman. He walks guardedly along drop. Frank advances*] Are you the officer on this beat? [*McCune assents inarticulately*] There's a card for you. [*Gives card*] I want to find Mother Rosenbaum's.

McC. [*Pointing to the house*]   You are right on top of it, see!

FRANK.   Do you understand this card? You are to keep your eye on the place if I get inside.

McC.   All right, I won't let go o' you, see!

FRANK.   If I do not come out in twenty minutes—

McC.   I'll fetch you. See? This is the way. Here, and I'll introduce you meself. See. [*Exit McCune followed by Frank through door. Dark change*]

SCENE 2: *Mother Rosenbaum's den. A large stone room in a cellar with one exit up a practicable swinging steps, C. of rear wall, with practicable door at top cut across in C., about eight feet up. On L. of room is a door to closet or dark room. Room is lit by iron grating. Small pine table extreme L. front, on which is a butcher's knife. Two wooden chairs at table. At extreme R. is a trap in 2. closed.* DISCOVERED: *Mother Rosenbaum seated at table L. Sheeney Ike and Peggy Daly half way down steps. Lights down.*

PEG. [*On steps*]   He's got the man—they're comin' in.

Ros. [*Seated at table, screaming*]   Go back to the front window and keep your eye out. [*Girl stands irresolute a moment. Mother Rosenbaum throws knife at her viciously and crosses a little to C. Peggy runs up steps and exits. Sheeney Ike picks up knife*]

IKE. [*R.C. crosses to Mother Rosenbaum*]   You'd better let me keep it. You'll have it into somebody while this fit's on.

Ros. [*Screaming*]   I'll have it into you if you don't mind your business. Give it to me. [*She clutches the knife and goes to table L. Ike shrugs his shoulders and relinquishes it*] Open that door. [*Pointing to door, L.*] I put some ointment on me beauty's head, and I want to see her. [*Comes to C. Ike unlocks door and opens it, pulls Mary out roughly. She is poorly dressed, has her head bound up and is terrified*]

MARY. [*Crosses to C., shrinking*] Do not kill me.

ROS. [*Striking knife on table*] Kill you, eh? Yes, I kill you easy enough. But first tell me who made you play the spy—who is he, eh? [*Seated at table L.*]

MARY. [*C.*] Let me go. I do not wish to play the spy. I am a helpless girl. [*Looks about piteously*]

ROS. [*Seated at table L., contemptuously*] Yes, you are a helpless girl. You have some friends, eh? Mebbe they come here and help you. [*Laughs bitterly*] Who put you up to this? You tell me who it is or maybe I cut it out of you this time. [*Viciously. Business with knife*]

MARY. You are mistaken. I do not know you. You brought me here yourself.

ROS. You lie! You were looking for the diamonds. You play the maid, eh? You shall play the maid for me. [*Rises and crosses to Mary advancing upon her*] You shall dress my hair. [*Clutching fingers*] No, I will dress your beautiful hair. You have a friend who comes to see you. I will show you what I will do to your friend. [*Mary shrinks terrified, Ike coming down and throwing Mary to R.*]

IKE. Oh, don't tear the girl to pieces. We've got enough to attend to without this.

ROS. [*R.C., swinging Ike, L.*] Don't you interfere—maybe I tear you to pieces.

IKE. [*Stepping back*] Oh, well I ain't murdering girls. You'll have the whole Central Office swarming over us.

ROS. [*Defiantly*] What does Rosenbaum care for the Central Office, you sneaking coward? If it was not for Rosenbaum you would be hanged long ago. It is Rosenbaum who has defended and released you when they had the rope on your neck, because you did what I told you. When you change your mind—pif! away you go. [*Goes up and turns*] You think Rosenbaum has no heart. Yes, you are right because it was torn out of my bosom when they killed my beautiful boy. I have lived with no heart waiting for Plon and his woman. I have laughed at the police and have bought the judges with my stolen money. And now when at last there comes to me Plon's woman, you think I will get my heart back again. Ha—ha—! you shall tear to pieces what I like. You shall do what Rosenbaum tells you or go like Red Leary and Scotty Jack. When you do not what I want you shall hang. [*Goes up, music*]

IKE. [*Astonished*] Plon's woman! Here? Why didn't you say so before. [*Crosses and seizes Mary. Crosses with her to door L. Half door at head of stairs opens and Jimmy McCune in policeman's uniform puts his head in and looks down. All start*]

Ros. Put her back there. [*Pointing to L. Ike seizes Mary and crosses with her*]

MARY. [*Piteously*] Oh, no—no—anywhere but in there. [*Appealingly to McCune*] Are you an officer? [*Ike roughly thrusts her in the dark closet and closes it*]

Ros. [*To McCune*] What are you grinning there for, McCune?

McC. [*At head of stairs*] De bloke's comin' in—here's de card he gave me. [*Throws down card. Ike picks it up and gives it to Mother Rosenbaum*]

McC. [*Looking back*] Look out for the steps. [*Frank appears at door, looks down and then slowly descends the steps. McCune leans on the half door. Ike up L.*]

FRANK. [*Down R.C.*] Are you the woman they call Mother Rosenbaum?

Ros. [*Screaming*] Shut the door McCune and stay here.

McC. All right. [*McCune starts to shut the door, and gets behind it. Brummage, disguised as a policeman, substitutes for McCune. (NOTE: Brummage and McCune must be made up alike, and be of same size and height so as to successfully accomplish substitution) Brummage shuts the door and comes down steps as if drunk, goes to the extreme upper R. where he sits down sideways to the audience on a box. He is disregarded by Ike and Mother Rosenbaum who are occupied with Frank*]

Ros. [*L.C.*] Madam Rosenbaum, if you please.

FRANK. [*R.C.*] You or some of your friends have a girl that I wish to communicate with. I come to you because—

Ros. You come to me, eh? Mebbe I brought you and you don't get away so easy.

FRANK. It is useless to threaten me for I communicated with the police before I came in.

Ros. [*Spitefully*] Yes, you tried to. Well, I stopped you. There's the card you gave to my man. The piece don't know you're here [*Flips the card up to him, then up to Brummage. Frank picks it up with some astonishment*]

FRANK. [*Aside*] What does this mean? I am trapped. [*Goes down R.*]

Ros. [*Up by Brummage, L. of him. To Brummage*] Jimmy, he thought you was a reg'lar. I'll have to be payin' you reg'lar salary pretty soon. [*Down C.—Brummage simulates drunkenness*]

FRANK. [*Alarmed*] Madam, I come here with but one purpose—it was to see the girl. I only want to speak to her.

Ros. [*Striking knife on table. Sits*] Well, I'm going to let you see her. Ikey, bring her out. [*Ike goes to closet door, unlocks it, and brings Mary out. She puts her hands to her eyes as if the light dazzled her. Sees Frank*]

MARY. Frank Kennet! You here?

Ros. and Ike. Frank Kennet! [*Mother Rosenbaum starts to her feet*]

Frank. [*Advancing to Mary*] Mary, my poor girl. What have these miscreants done to you? [*Music*]

Ike. [*Interposing*] Keep back!

Ros. Frank—ha—ha. Quick, Ikey, the steps. [*Rises and goes down R.C. presses button, throws steps up, cuts off retreat by means of a spring in the wall; at the same time Mary and Frank come together and the girl clings to him terrified*] So—o—o, you are Frank. You've been hiding from everybody since you killed the old man. Nobody knows you are in New York and nobody will miss you—and you set out to ruin the old woman. Let me look at you. For thirty years they have been trying to ruin Rosenbaum. They killed my boy. They put spies in my house. They set the police on me, they dragged me into courts. Because I am Rosenbaum. [*Goes to table and down L.*]

Frank. You dastardly wretches—you are making a big mistake.

Ros. Ha—ha—ha! Rosenbaum makes no mistakes.

Frank. Dick Brummage knows where I am. [*Music stops*]

Ros. The copper will tell him he didn't see you. If I were to let you run, you'd be tryin' to prove you didn't kill Mr. Bulford and we couldn't have that. [*Advances upon Mary slowly R.*] And I ain't going to let you run loose. [*Seizes Mary suddenly by the arms, pulls her away from Frank violently and thrusts her into chair L. As Frank attempts to interfere Ike catches hold of him behind by arms back; struggle; Frank throws him off and the three glare at each other. To Mary*] Now, you set there and see what we do with men who try to ruin the old woman. If you move an inch I'll put this into you. [*Picks up knife. Mary drops her head into her hands piteously and shudders*]

Frank. Hellhounds! If you think you can murder me without a fight for it, you've made the mistake of your lives. [*Takes his coat off and throws it behind him. Music*]

Mary. [*Half rising*] No, no, they will kill you.

Ros. [*Thrusting her back in chair*] Set down or I'll settle you first. [*Ike goes to trap R. and lifts it up (be particular about carpenters attending to steps—they fall when button is pushed). Brummage appears to be in drunken sleep*]

Frank. Mary—tell me—have you anything to say to me—what about the glass?

Mary. [*L.*] Mrs. Bulford threw it out of the window the night of the murder and Dr. Livingstone has it.

Ros. [*By Mary, L.*] Ha, that settles you—when you're both dead, the madam will be free. Ikey, open the trap. Jimmy, you drunken dog, get up. [*To Mary*] Now you sit still. [*Men struggle up and down the stage and

Frank gets the better of Ike. Ike calls on Mother Rosenbaum; women watch the fight intently. Mother Rosenbaum goes R. Mary also rises and goes L. and thence to steps. The action of the two women must be so timed that Mary arrives at the spring in the wall at the same time Mother Rosenbaum reaches steps a second after they fall. Mary touches the spring and they have come down with a bang. All three of the group turn sharply around and Mother Rosenbaum makes two impulsive steps toward Mary and stops undecidedly. Mary runs up the steps but the door at the top is locked and she pounds on it with her fists. The two men glare at each other] Can [*On foot of steps C., to Ike*] you get away with him?

IKE. [*Struggling with Frank*]   Can I? Give me the knife. You take care of the girl. [*Mother Rosenbaum tosses the knife to Ike. It falls on the floor. Ike instantly goes toward Brummage to pick it up*]

ROS.   Quick, finish him—you are man to man and even. [*Ike stoops to pick up the knife when Brummage leans forward, presenting pistol; stands up R.C. above Ike*]

BRUM.   But what are you going to do with the old man? [*Change music till curtain. Tableau*] How are you going to get away with Dick Brummage?

TABLEAU. CURTAIN. RING.

2ND CURTAIN: *Mary comes down the steps, stops at bottom. Frank jumps to her, they embrace.*

FRANK.   Mary!

ACT VI.

SCENE: *Senator McSorker's house on Madison Avenue. Music off R.2.E. for rise. Interior showing handsome corridor and grand staircase C. coming well down stage, with lamps at bottom on either side flanked by heavy tropical plants. Arcaded entrances to salon L.2.; smoking room and hall R.2. Guests in evening dress standing at salon entrance looking at guests and conversing. At rise soft chamber music heard. Burst of laughter from group.* TIME: *Eleven o'clock at night.*

CLANCY. [*L.*]   Yes, if it ain't Lumpy Kidney I hope to die.

BRANNIGAN.   Well, I never expected to see him in a dress coat. He wears it like an epileptic fit. Say, boys, there won't be any eating until twelve o'clock. Let's go over to the chophouse and get a welsh rarebit. [*All come down C.*]

CLAN.   Oh, you'll miss the show. He's going to trot out her royal highness.

BRAN.   That's what we're here for. We've got to throw our posies at her. It's a go-as-you-please. Grand entrance. Procession of maids. Burst of music

—lights up—shower of bouquets. Three cheers for the flag and the senator on top.

CLAN. Well, I like it. No invites. No airs—no introductions.

BRAN. Say, if you don't keep your mug shut, I'll shove this into it. You act as if you were on Eighth Avenue instead of Madison. De Sixth ain't celebratin' tonight. [*Music stops*]

CLAN. When I get me brudder out of Sing Sing and he's a sheriff, I'm agoin' to move on de Fifth meself.

BRAN. Yes, I hear the whole Sixth is goin' to move up. [*Both go to salon entrance L.2. Bursts of laughter from guests*]

CLAN. She's a rich widow, I hear, from South America.

BRAN. Well, what's the matter with havin' her over to the Chowder Club? Come, let's go in. [*Move toward salon entrance and group themselves. Enter Mrs. O'Geogan from R.2. She is fantastically dressed and has a feather fan*]

MRS. O'G. I wonder if the senator calls that a party. It's more like a soree. [*The male guests laugh and exit R.2.*]

BRAN. No, madam, it's a levée.

MRS. O'G. I thought a levee was something that kept the flood out. Where's the cook room? [*Going R.C. Enter second heeler*] It's yourself that's cuttin' a fine shine this evening, Mr. Brannigan, with your shwaller tail.

BRAN. Oh, I ain't cuttin' no shine. We wuz to hang around the edges for a call. But it's all guzzle and munch and no jumpin'.

MRS. O'G. I have a stick in my mind a soakin' for the senator.

BRAN. I heered you was on the school board Mrs. O'Geogan.

MRS. O'G. You did? The same to you Mr. Brannigan. I heard you was workin' a reform ticket on the Fourteenth. You'll be goin' to Albany wid your shwaller tail, I don't know. [*Enter first heeler from R.2. with his coat on his arm*]

BRAN. [*To second heeler*] Say, dere is one of the dry dock tarriers in the crowd. We don't want no dry dock tarriers among us gents, do we?

CLAN. Oh, put your coat on; why can't you act like a gent in a gent's crowd and stop for de word before you do any mussin'.

BRAN. [*Putting his coat on*] I ken tump him, if it wasn't fer de coat. What's the good of our bein' here. [*Two heelers cross toward R. When they reach R.2. they encounter Count Garbiadoff and Madame Mervaine who are entering R.2. Heelers exit R.2., Count and Madame Mervaine cross L.*]

MME. M. Thanks, count, it is so close in there that, but for your kind attention, I should have fainted.

COUNT. I am only too delighted to be of service to you, madam. You say Mr. Brummage asked you to guide me through this strange assemblage.

MME. M.   Yes—but take care how you mention that name here. [*Indicates that Mrs. O'Geogan might overhear them; then quickly to Mrs. O'Geogan*] The senator has all his friends here tonight?

MRS. O'G.   Yis, ma'am. Shure it would be a little more lively if some of his inimies were on deck.

MME. M.   Are you one of his friends?

MRS. O'G.   Of course I am—one of his best friends. I knew him when he tended bar in Tim O'Shaughnessy's and had to mix drinks in a buttoned up coat while I washed his shirt. He's got to be a great dude, has the senator.

MME. M.   Will the lady who is to make the presentation come down those stairs? [*Pointing to stairs C.*]

MRS. O'G.   Well, I'm thinkin' she wouldn't come down the fire escape, with her diamonds and starched skirts. I wonder if that door has a kitchen behind it. Sure it's starvin', I am. [*Exits R.2. Count and Madame Mervaine laugh heartily at Mrs. O'Geogan's remark and at her exit*]

COUNT.   Is zis ze sort of canaille which your mansions are filled with at evening parties?

MME. M.   Oh, count, when you are the guest of an American politician you must wonder in silence and endure silently. Fretting about your environment is quite out of order. Let's take another stroll and see if we can find Mr. Brummage.

COUNT.   Yes, I must find him. [*Aside*] And I must see zat woman. [*They exit L.2. Enter two heelers from R.2. and two college boys*]

2ND H.   Break away, here comes de drum corp. [*Enter senator L.2. He is fussy, anxious and exuberant, followed by several male and female guests*]

SEN.   Ah, ha, gents, enjoying yourselves, I hope. Don't forget to go to the saylong before the horns go off. I've arranged everything on schedule time and that's the signal that the lady's coming downstairs. I don't want you to miss it. Have you got your flowers? [*Looks around at them. The two heelers and two college boys raise their bouquets as if to throw them*] Stop! All right. Don't throw them until she gets at the bottom of the stairs. [*Looks at his watch*] Half past eleven. Great success, eh?

2ND GUEST.   Perfectly paralyzing. Beats the Wild West, senator.

1ST GUEST.   Regular coop—de-e-tat. [*Senator moves fussily toward smoking room R.2. looks in and calls*]

SEN.   Gentlemen—everybody in the saylong. The ceremony is about to begin. [*Looks at his watch again. To guests in front of stage*] Now then, gents—all in the saylong. [*Male guests move to entrance L.2. Senator crosses to L. and meets Marino, who comes from salon L.2.*] Is the lady all ready?

[*Looks at his watch*] I expect them horns to go off every minute. How does she look.

MAR. Like a goddess—she always does, senator.

SEN. [*Slapping Marino on back*] Damme! I'll make her the Goddess of Liberty. I'll have her walk in roses knee deep. It's going to be the proudest moment of her life, my boy. Just go up and see she is ready, will you? [*Marino goes up stairs and exits. Senator exits into salon L.2. followed by guests. Coutche-coutche polka. Enter Mrs. O'Geogan R.2. She is noticeably under the influence of wine. She carries a large fan and has an elaborate head-dress with two feathers*]

MRS. O'G. Oh, my! Oh, my! I've been havin' the greatest toime out there. Shure I don't know what's the matter with me. I wuz hungry just now, and —now—I'm loaded with everything good to eat and drink—ah! that pink stuff in a great glass christian bowl, with strawberries and pineapple all thrown in gratis. And they give it to you for nothin'. They kape fillin' your glass whenever it's empty, and just don't give you toime to get thirsty. [*Enter senator L.2., approaches her, and goes with great rush. Business, while senator is talking to Mrs. O'Geogan, of her leaning forward and bowing her head in acknowledgment of what he says, and the headdress feathers tickling his nose and face—he trying to escape*] It sounds like the Midway of Plaisance, I heard at the World's Fair. [*Business. Crosses to L and sits on sofa. Business*] Oh! my, oh, my. Oh, this is like the cable car, without the bumps.

SEN. [*To guests*] Mrs. O'Geogan one of my constituents—what the devil brought her here?

MRS. O'G. Mister Conductor! Mister Conductor, please let me off at Forty-Second Street. [*Business. Senator coughs, comes down C. Mrs. O'Geogan turns on sofa; sees him, rises, crosses to C., bowing*] I'm here, senator, I'm here.

SEN. Yes, I see you are.

MRS. O'G. How do you like me get up?

SEN. Gorgeous! Gorgeous! I'm glad to see you on this glorious occasion. [*Crosses L.C. turns and faces her*] The Fourth of July ain't anywhere; music —fireworks—illuminations, beautiful women. And you, Mrs. O'Geogan, are queen of beauty and the jewel among women. The Kohinoor ain't in it with you.

MRS. O'G. [*R.C.*] Oh, thank you. I don't know Mrs. Kohinoor. But, senator, I'm wid you every toime.

SEN. [*Shaking hands*] I know you are, Mrs. O'Geogan. [*Aside*] How the devil am I to get rid of her. [*Goes up L.C.*]

Mrs. O'G.   Oh, I'll always be wid ye, senator, you are the one man of my affeshuns. Come here, sinitor. [*Senator comes down to her, L.C.*] Mrs. O'-Dooley tould me that you are a great flirt.

Sen.   Damn Mrs. O'Dooley. [*Goes up L.C.*]

Mrs. O'G.   [*Sings*] "You're the only man in all the world for me," etc. [*Goes up R.C.; business; comes down*] Come here, senator. [*Senator comes down L.C.*] I can sing better than that if I like.

Sen.   Well, I hope so.

Mrs. O'G.   But, senator, I've always loved you. Senator, pardon my blushes.

Sen. [*L.C.*]   Where did she get it? [*Turns away; steps up a little; turns facing her*] Mrs. O'Geogan have you had something to eat?

Mrs. O'G.   Eat, is it? Shure, I've been down in the kitchen to see Mary the cook. Shure, Mary's an old friend of mine, and she had an elegant christian bowl full of punch, with strawberries, all floating on the top of it, and I helped myself—ah, shure I didn't have time to get thirsty. Senator—I'm loaded.

Sen.   Eh?

Mrs. O'G.   Wid the supper—wid the supper. Ah! Senator, you keep iligant liquors.

Sen.   How d'ye know?

Mrs. O'G.   Sure I imbibed—

Sen.   What? [*Goes up L.*]

Mrs. O'G.   I man, I inhaled—inhaled the aroma, and I intend to marry you—

Sen. [*Aside*]   The devil you do.

Mrs. O'G.   With your consent. You are—[*Business of patting him on the face*] my love's young dream. [*Business*] You are so beautiful, so fresh, so innocent. [*Putting her finger on his chin*] You're a daisy.

Sen.   Oh, am I? [*She leans her head on his breast; business*]

Mrs. O'G.   Sure, Mrs. O'Dooley told me. [*Putting her face close to his. He pushes it gently away. She puts her face to his again*] Senator, Mrs. O'Dooley tould me—[*Coutche-coutche polka*]

Sen.   Damn Mrs. O'Dooley. [*Goes up, listens to music which plays off L.2.*] That's the way to get rid of her. Mrs. O'Geogan, I know you love music and dancing—

Mrs. O'G.   Love music? The idea. Do you remember when we used to go speeling in Walla Walla Hall? Did you ever know an Irish lady that wasn't fond of music and dancing? Senator, will you dance a step wid me?

Sen.   What? [*Looks off L.2. turns to her*] Not on your life.

MRS. O'G. Oh, come here, that or nothin'. [*She takes him by left hand; they dance a few steps toward R., turn facing L.2., dance and exit L.2., laughing. Enter Count Garbiadoff and Madame Mervaine R.2.*]

MME. M. Mr. Brummage has not come.

COUNT. Bah—the police Americans are what you call ze grande hoom-poog.

MME. M. They are cautious, count. He probably did not want to witness this woman's triumph. Be careful, she is coming. If the earth does not open and swallow her before she gets to the bottom of the stairs, you will see the most magnificent victory of audacity. It was worth coming from Cracow to witness! [*Enter Marino from top of stairs, comes down past the sofa and speaks*]

MAR. The lady is coming. Will you not enter the salon? [*Exit Marino into salon L.2. Count rubs his glasses with his handkerchief, and leaving the sofa goes to stairs, standing off behind the plant. Mrs. Bulford appears at top of staircase in full evening dress, bejewelled and attended by maids of honor. She holds her head high and wears a triumphant look. Guests enter. The female guests are bending eagerly forward to see her, count is peering at her through his glass behind balustrade. When Mrs. Bulford has reached the middle of the stairway, Mary Lavelot suddenly steps out from behind the plants on L. of steps and stands like a statue under the lamps. At the same moment the trumpets are heard playing a fanfare. She is attired in the same dress she wore in Rosenbaum's den and her head is bound up in the same cloth. She is pale and distressed. Mrs. Bulford comes slowly and smilingly down steps, chatting and laughing to maids. When she reaches the bottom she is suddenly confronted by Mary. Fanfare stops. Mrs. Bulford starts, recovers herself and speaks, the maids forming a tableau of astonishment*]

MRS. B. Who are you?

MARY. Susanne!

MRS. B. [*Agitatedly*] What are you doing here?

MARY. Meeting you face to face for the last time.

MRS. B. [*Imperiously*] Stand aside. I cannot waste words with my servants now.

MARY. I have come out of a living grave to confront you in your triumph and to tell you that the God of Justice reigns even in New York. I cannot stand aside even if I would. [*Mrs. Bulford exhibits great distress*]

MRS. B. [*Almost at foot of stairs*] Who is this lunatic? Why is this outrage permitted? Where is the senator? Where are the police? [*Turns and looks R. Enter Brummage, R.2.*]

BRUM. Madam, the police are here and waiting. [*Mrs. Bulford turns her head and sees Garbiadoff standing a few paces down stage L.*]

MRS. B. Garbiadoff! [*Falls on steps, recovers, starts to go up steps and falls backward, falling in the arms of Garbiadoff, who is L. and Brummage who is R. Recovers again, goes up steps, struggling with Brummage who is holding her by the left wrist*] Don't touch me! Let me go! [*She is now on platform on top of steps*] My God! This is the end! [*Taking small vial from her bosom—puts it to her mouth—falls and dies. Brummage kneels by her a moment to see if she is dead. Takes the vial from her. (Brummage should carry a duplicate vial—she may lose hers.) Holds it in his right hand. Enter Marino quickly from L.2.; he looks about in wonder*]

MAR. What is the matter?

MME. M. The lady has fainted.

MAR. Fainted? Impossible! [*Rushes upstairs, looks at Mrs. Bulford in astonishment. Enter senator, L.2., followed by guests and Mrs. O'Geogan, L.2.*]

SEN. Well, what's the hitch? Where's the lady? Will somebody stop the music? [*Turning and looking off L.2.E., then turns to stairs again*] Where is she? [*Enter several other male and female guests R.2.*]

MAR. [*On top of stairs C.*] Dead!

OMNES. [*Solemnly*] Dead!

MAR. [*Kneeling by his sister*] Dead!—my God—dead!

BRUM. [*Holding up vial*] The Para poison! [*Senator takes a step or two towards stairs in rage*]

SEN. You damnable dog! [*Slight pause*] Here, Patsy, Shorty, where are you? [*Enter L.2., first and second heelers. They come left and right of senator. All the guests looking extremely anxious at stairs. Madame Mervaine at sofa looking at stairs, Garbiadoff a little above her, all looking to C. in suspense*]

BRUM. [*Who has come down a step or two holding up his hand authoritatively*] Stand back! The lady belongs to the law—her diamonds to the Count Garbiadoff! [*Pointing to the count*] Senator, it is twelve o'clock! [*Mary in Frank's arms L., a little above the senator*]

PICTURE

CURTAIN

FROM RAGS TO RICHES

By Charles A. Taylor

CHARACTERS

NED NIMBLE, *a newsboy who works his way from gutter to palace*
ALBERT COOPER, *his father under a brand of shame*
OLD MONTGOMERY, *a wealthy retired merchant*
PRINCE CHARLIE, *a gambler, his nephew*
CHINESE SAM, *a dog doctor*
MIKE DOOLEY, *a policeman*
BROWN, *the merchant's valet*
MOTHER MURPHY, *one of the real ol' sort*
FLOSSIE, *Ned's sister, who loves excitement*
GERTRUDE CLARK, *a trained nurse*
FLORA BRADLEY, *a fruit daughter of Eve*
WAITER
MESSENGER, CAB DRIVERS, DETECTIVES, POLICE, WAITERS, NEWSPAPER MEN,
   SOCIETY GIRLS, POLITICIANS, CIVILIANS
TIME, *The Present*
PLACE, *New York*

SYNOPSIS OF SCENES

ACT I.

Mother Murphy's news stand and coffee counter on the Bowery—midnight. Ned in poverty and rags. His playground the gutter. Meeting of the pauper and the prince. Price of a sister's honor.

ACT II.

Library of the merchant's home. Plot to kill Montgomery. The abduction of Flossie.

ACT III.

SCENE 1. *Broadway after dark. On the trail of the kidnappers.*
SCENE 2. *Room in the Waldorf-Astoria. Ned as a messenger boy.*
SCENE 3. *Roof of Waldorf-Astoria.*
SCENE 4: *A cellar in Chinatown. At the eleventh hour.*

ACT IV.

A palace on the Hudson. Ned as a royal host. Blood will tell. That which pays best in the end. "On the road to the White House."

ACT I.

On the Bowery—midnight. Drop in 3. shows buildings with street in fore-
ground. Center arch doorway cut in drop; half-high swinging doors attached
to this doorway. Over and under swinging doors is seen the backing which
is drinking bar and sideboard with liquor bottles and glasses. Sign over door-
way, "Concert Hall"; to the right of this doorway is painted a pawnshop; to
the left a lodging house. Set piece representing El track across stage directly
in front of drop. Profile electric train: windows illuminated to work back and
forth on this set piece. Set house representing tenement left. Doorway opening
upstage backed by practical stairway; hanging lamp over stairway; on tran-
som over door "19." Lunch counter over which is dilapidated awning up- and
downstage in front of return piece L. On return piece is painted backing for
lunch counter—coffee urn, cups, plates, pies, cakes, and so forth. In front of
counter two wooden stools. End of counter downstage barrel on top of barrel;
wide board upon which are papers, magazines, and so forth. Sign on front of
awning, "Mother's Coffee House." From end of counter upstage to return
piece L. is small backing with open window. Flat with flipper wing R.—build-
ing "Chinese quarters." Door opening off stage in 2., sign over door, "Chinese
Sam, Dog Doctor." Set lamppost, on which are police, fire-alarm, and mail
boxes, in front of this door.

Curtain rises to drinking chorus and thumping of piano offstage in con-
cert hall. Discovers Flossie, girl of sixteen—plain petticoat off ankles—old
shirtwaist—kitchen apron—rose in her hair—behind counter—wiping coffee
cups with old linen towel; and Mike—policeman—middle-age—smooth-
shaven—neat uniform—Irish character study.

MIKE. [*Enters L.3. as song ends—sticks head in window*] Ah, Flossie,
me darlin', how goes it with you this evening?

FLOS. It's not evening, Mike, it's morning. The clock struck one.

MIKE. I haven't struck one tonight, and haven't made an arrest. I never
saw the Bowery so quiet before. [*Crosses to C. Pushes open door and looks*
in Concert Hall. Men and women seen drinking—shouts off—clinking of
glasses]

FLOS. Stick around and you will find it noisy enough. Have a cup of
coffee, Mike?

MIKE. [*Comes down*] No, me darlin', much obliged. I'm looking for a drop of something stronger. Why don't you close up?

FLOS. I'm waiting for the old woman.

MIKE. And where is she?

FLOS. Looking for Ned.

MIKE. Who gave you the pretty posie that you have in your top-knot?

FLOS. Me feller.

MIKE. Truth and you have a hundred.

FLOS. But this one is the real thing, Mike. He rides in a cab and bought all of my papers—he dresses swell—has a big diamond ring. He told me I was pretty and would be a fine lady some day.

MIKE. Did he tell you anything else?

FLOS. No, but he said he would when he came back—

MIKE. So he is coming back, is he?

FLOS. [*Nodding*]

MIKE. Well, I don't blame him.

FLOS. He wanted to take me to ride but I had no one to leave with the stand.

MIKE. What's the matter? Won't it stand up alone? Going to take you to ride, is he? If he does I'll give him one in a patrol wagon! Mother Murphy should stay home and keep an eye on you.

FLOS. Don't tell her about the rich fellow, will you, Mike?

MIKE. I don't know about that. These chaps with fine clothes and pretty speeches don't visit this locality looking for wives. You're only a slip of a girl, Floss. You're well liked up and down the line and I for one would hate to see you go wrong. [*Crosses R.1.*]

FLOS. Oh, Mike [*C.*]

MIKE. What is it?

FLOS. You ain't mad, are you?

MIKE. No, but you have worried me. The old woman is a friend of mine— she's had a hard struggle to raise you and Ned. Remember you're not her children. Yu'd been in the gutter if it hadn't been for her.

FLOS. We work hard for what little we get.

MIKE. Yes, but it's a mother's care and good training. That's a whole lot, in a rough neighborhood like this. [*Exit R.1.*]

ALBERT. [*In rough clothes and under influence of liquor, pushed out of center door by man in shirt-sleeves and white apron. Reeling down C.*] That's right—when my money's gone—throw me into the street—much obliged. You're a gentleman—I don't think. [*Feels pockets*] I had it when I went in

—oh, well, it's gone like everything else—I ever had. [*Reels to counter, balances himself by stool*]

Flos. What's the matter, Pop?

Alb. Don't call me Pop. I'm nobody's papa. I'm a fool—

Flos. Oh, no you're not. It's only wise men who know when they have been foolish. Here's a hot cup of coffee. It will brace you up.

Alb. [*Getting on stool with difficulty*] I need it, girl. I can't pay for it.

Flos. That's all right—pay some other time.

Alb. They wouldn't stand for that in there.

Flos. We don't run that kind of a place. We don't burn as many lights as they do. We can afford to be generous—here's a sandwich. Mother made it for my supper—but you can have it.

Alb. Thank ye, girl. You make me ashamed of myself—I ain't had nothing but whiskey for two days.

Flos. Whiskey won't keep you alive.

Alb. No, but it helps me to forget.

Flos. Forget what?

Alb. The past, my dear, the past—helps me forget a little girl that would be just about your age if she's alive.

Flos. Was she your girl?

Alb. Yes.

Flos. Then why should you wish to forget her?

Alb. Because she may grow to be like her mother.

Flos. I don't understand you.

Alb. Her mother was bad. She ran away from me, left her two babies—ruined my life—made me a drunkard, an outcast; worse, made me a criminal. The prison brand is on me. My children lost to me forever.

Flos. Why don't you go home?

Alb. I have no home. When I got out of jail, my house was gone, my children were gone, all, everything.

Charlie. [*In long, stylish ulster, travelling cap, cane and gloves, enters L.3. Crosses rapidly to R.2.*] Chinese Sam, dog doctor. That must be the old devil I want. [*Pulls envelope out of pocket*] Yes, this is the number all right.

Flos. [*Steps downstage behind counter at Charlie's entrance, places hand upon her heart*] That's him—[*Turns and hangs head, walks*]

Char. [*Turning L.*] Hello there, neighbor—who has seen me? I'll square myself. [*Crosses L.*] Hello, Butterfly, you're up late. Time little girls were in bed.

Flos. You said you was coming back.

Char. Well, I'm here, am I not? [*Looking over shoulder at Albert*]

ALB. [*Engaged with his sandwich and coffee*]

FLOS. Yes, sir. [*Sinking down on doorstep*]

CHAR. I see you still have my rose. [*Bending over and scenting rose in Flossie's hair*]

FLOS. Yes, sir.

CHAR. Why don't you wear it over your heart? Then I shall place it upon your breast. Come, have you a pin? [*Removing rose from Flossie's hair*]

FLOS. Please don't. I must go now; mother will be back.

CHAR. Oh, hang mother.

FLOS. I don't think you could.

CHAR. Fat, is she? Well, I'm going soon as I adjust the rose. Are you going to give me a pin or—maybe you don't want this rose. Oh, very well, I'll keep it. [*Starts to place it in his button-hole*]

FLOS. Yes, yes, here's the pin. [*Pricks Charlie*]

CHAR. Ouch, you did that on purpose, you little mischief. Will you hold still! [*Adjusting rose on Flossie's shirtwaist*]

FLOS. I didn't mean to prick you—honest I didn't. [*Looks up into Charlie's face*] Mr.—Mr.—What's your name?

CHAR. Call me Prince—that's what the boys call me.

FLOS. And are you a real sure enough prince?

CHAR. Well, hardly. There now, you must pay me for that rose there. I must be going—[*Catching her by both hands and drawing her to him*]

FLOS. Pay you for it?

CHAR. Yes, give me a kiss, quick—no one's looking. Just one?

ALB. Hold on there. [*Slips from stool, staggers forward*] Let that girl alone.

CHAR. [*Turning and releasing Flossie*] You drunken fool, what right have you to interfere? [*Flossie enters door L., exits upstairs*]

ALB. No rights. No rights at all, old chap. But I interfered, didn't I? She's gone; now run home, sonny, and if you don't—well, I'm just drunk enough to put up a hell of a good scrap. [*Squares off*]

CHAR. [*Starts forward with arm drawn back to strike. Albert suddenly pauses, bends down and looks into his face, staggers back. Aside*] Albert Cooper—and he doesn't know me.

ALB. Come on, I'm not bluffing. My head's swimming so I can't see to punch straight—but I'll fight.

CHAR. Bah, I'm not fighting drunken men. [*Crosses R.*] If you don't go about your business I'll call an officer and have you locked up.

ALB. [*Staggering to counter*] Wish you would. I have no place to sleep tonight.

CHAR. He's too drunk to recognize me. I'm in luck. Curse the fellow, I thought he was in jail and out of my way. It won't do for us to come together just now. There is too much at stake. [*Exits into Concert Hall. Mike enters from R.1., crosses behind counter, watches Charlie. Goes up and pushes door open, looks after Charlie. Flossie enters from door L., crosses behind counter, watches Mike*]

BROWN. [*Plain business suit, enters L.3.*] Hello, Mike—did you catch him?

MIKE. Hello, Brown, what are you doing here?

BROWN. I'm after that fellow you're watching—[*They cross down R.*]

MIKE. Since you retired from the Force, I thought you'd given up watching crooks. Who is he?

BROWN. Don't you know him?

MIKE. Well, slightly. He poses as a gambler around here. He's known as Prince Charlie.

BROWN. He's the nephew of the man I'm working for.

MIKE. Old Montgomery, the millionaire?

BROWN. Yes, and his uncle wants to learn what he does out so late nights. You see there's a few hundred thousands coming his way when the old man dies.

MIKE. I see. And the young chap's getting his hand in so he'll learn how to spend them.

BROWN. He'll have none to spend if the old man learns what I know.

MIKE. I thought you was the old man's valet. So you've turned detective again.

BROWN. For a woman's sake, Mike. One that this man ruined and cast off—took from her husband and children, left them to die in the public hospital.

MIKE. Your heart was right when you was on the Force. Tell me more of this affair—you'll find I'm with you. Come, we'll keep an eye on the Prince. [*Crosses up with Brown through open door. They exit R.3. talking in by-play*]

ALB. Don't blame you for being angry, little girl. But somehow I felt that chap didn't mean right by you.

FLOS. They all get fresh if you give them half a chance. Men are all alike. [*Sighs*] But he seemed different than the rest. He said this rose reminded him of me. [*Crosses downstage end of counter*]

ALB. Let me see it. [*Flossie removes a rose from her dress, kisses it and hands it to Albert*]

ALB. [*Inspecting flower*] Pure white and a bud. Came from Bushman's and cost a dollar, I'll wager. Hum, buds like this one don't blossom in the hands of men like he is, my dear. They wither and decay. Killed by frosts of infidelity. [*His head falls on his breast and the flower falls from his hand*]

FLOS. [*Springing forward and picking up rose*]   Oh, sir, you have crushed my rose.

ALB.   Pardon me, little girl, I was thinking of my wife. You'll forgive me, won't you? [*Places his hand on Flossie's head, wiping eyes with sleeve*]

FLOS. [*Burying her face in the flower*]   Yes, I'll forgive you because there are tears in your eyes. I know a big man like you don't cry unless he's had a lot of trouble. See, I'm going to give you this rose. I will pin it right here on your coat. Then when you look at it you will remember someone cares for you, and you won't drink any more, will you? There, when you find your own little girl [*Pins rose on Albert's coat*] you can give her the rose.

ALB.   Thanks, child. You have put new life in me. Some day I'll come back here and hunt you up. Show you what a few kind words and a generous act will do for a man who is down on his luck. [*Crosses to R.*] From this night on I give you my promise I will keep clear of places like that. [*Points to Concert Hall and exits R.1. Laughter, shouts, and clinking of glasses in Concert Hall*]

MOTHER MURPHY. [*Stout good-natured Irish woman with shawl over her head, carrying a baseball bat, enters R.3.*] Flossie—I say, Floss—where the devil are you? Oh, there you are. What are them dirty dishes doing on the counter? Why don't you close up shop and go to bed? The Raines Law Committee will have us pinched for selling mint juleps after twelve o'clock at midnight. Is that brother of yours home yet? If I lay hands on him, I'll break this baseball bat across the soles of his two feet. What are you snivelling about? Has there been any of that Chatham Square gang around here making googlum eyes at yees?

FLOS.   No, ma'am, I'm not crying.

MOTH.   Then why are you wiping your nose on that dish towel?

MIKE. [*Enters R.3.*]   Ah, Mother, so you've got home at last. Did you find Ned?

MOTH.   Find him—you might as well look for a hole in the bottom of the East River.

MIKE.   He'll come home all right. He's probably up around the Broadway Café, trying to get a few more pennies with his extras. Ned's a hustler.

MOTH.   Yes, he'll work himself to death. I have to tie him in bed or he'd be on the street all the time. He's that way ever since I got him. Have some coffee, Mike. [*Crosses behind counter, draws coffee*]

MIKE.   Thanks—don't care if I do. Did you ever try to look up the parents of these children? [*Flossie crosses down and sits on doorstep L.*]

MOTH. What time have I to look them up? It's a bustle to live. An old merchant who I used to scrub for down on Broome Street brought them to me when they was babies and told me he'd pay for their keep. Then he moved and I moved. It was a game of checkers between us, but they got into my king row and 'twas all off. I'm thinking it's the lad's move now. They do be saying, Mike, it's a wise child that can find his own father.

MIKE. Ned will find his if he's on earth. [*Chinaman Sam, in blue blouse, smoking Chinese pipe, enters R.2. Stands in doorway smoking*]

MIKE. What kind of joint does that fellow run? [*Pointing to Chink*]

MOTH. Who, the Chineser? That's me neighbor with the slanting eye. They do be saying he's a doctor but begorra I think he's a rat catcher. He must have swallowed one and the tail is growing out behind his head.

MIKE. His sign says he's a dog doctor. Do you ever see any dogs around here?

MOTH. Yes, two-legged dogs. Lots of 'em. And some of 'em wears petticoats. Hist, Mike, I think it's what you call a joint. Get an order from headquarters to raid it, Mike, and I'll give you free coffee for a month.

MIKE. Will you sign a complaint, Mother? [*Crosses R.1.*]

MOTH. Faith, Mike, and you know I can't sign my name. But I'll put my cross on that Chink the night of the wake. [*Mike exits R.1. El train from L. to R. Shouts from Concert Hall*]

CHAR. [*Enters from Concert Hall. Looks down and L. Crosses to R.2. Chinamun bows low, pushes open door. Charlie hesitates, sees Mother, crosses rapidly to counter L., throws leg over stool*] Give me a cup of black coffee. [*Flossie looks up from step as Mother's back is turned drawing coffee—shakes finger at Charlie. Places a finger on her lips*]

MOTH. There you are, sir—something else?

CHAR. No, thanks. When do you close up?

MOTH. This blessed minute, if me boy comes home.

CHAR. Then you have a boy to support?

MOTH. Yes, and a girl too. [*Pointing to Flossie*] She's more trouble than the boy.

CHAR. Why don't you find her a good husband?

MOTH. A husband? Faith, man, she's only a child. Stand up, Flossie, and show the gentleman how tall you be. [*Flossie arises, hangs her head*]

CHAR. [*Steps around end of counter*] Why she is quite a young lady. I'd give a good deal to have a girl like that.

MOTH. Have you no children of your own?

CHAR. Well, no. You see I have plenty of money and a beautiful house—but no children.

MOTH. What will you give for mine? You can have the boy and the girl if you give them a good home. You see I'm only a poor woman and this is no place for them.

CHAR. Well, really, I can't say. I've never seen the boy, you know. But the girl's appearance pleases me very much. My wife and I may drive down tomorrow and take her to our house for the afternoon. Then we will talk the matter over. [*Flossie turns and starts as Charlie says "My wife" but he winks and she again bows her head*]

MOTH. How about that, Floss? Would you like to go with the gentleman tomorrow?

FLOS. Yes, ma'am.

MOTH. But how do I know who you are, sir? Where is it you live?

CHAR. My home is on West End Avenue. My name is—there is my card.

MOTH. Thank you, sir. I guess you mean well by my girl. I will talk the matter over with her brother. He is younger than she is, but he's a good boy and the man of the house. He may go with her.

CHAR. Oh, the boy may come some other time. There is only room for three in the cab.

FLOS. Two's company and three is a crowd.

CHAR. There is the pay for your coffee. I must be going. I will call for the girl at ten tomorrow. [*Lays bill on counter*]

MOTH. Sir, this is twenty dollars, I have no change for that.

CHAR. You seem to be a hard-working woman and as I have plenty of money you are welcome to the change. And, by the way, I wish to give the child a gift to remember me by—[*Removing ring from his little finger, stepping forward and taking Flossie's hand*] This ring should just about fit her slender fingers. It is too small for mine. [*Slips ring on Flossie's fourth finger*]

FLOS. Look, mother, it's a diamond. A real sure-enough diamond! Isn't it beautiful? [*Kissing it, crosses R.*] It's an engagement ring. He placed it on my fourth finger. Oh, I'm so happy I could cry. [*Wiping eyes with apron, rubbing ring and kissing it R.*]

MOTH. Do hear how that child goes on. Don't mind what she says, sir, you'll be spoiling her. [*Crosses C.*] Engagement ring, you goose, the gentleman has a wife of his own. He's old enough to be your father.

CHAR. Yes, certainly. [*Winking at Flossie, crosses R.C.*]

FLOS. Oh, yes. I forgot—I'm to be his little girl.

NED. [*Enters R.3. Ragged cap and coat, bundles of extras under his arm. Comes down to center, looks from one to the other*] What's up, mother? What makes you all look so happy? Someone bought all your papers?

MOTH. That's him, sir. That's my boy. See, I bought him a nice baseball bat today, and he never came home to get it. [*Holding up bat and winking at Flossie*]

CHAR. How do you do, my lad? What's your name? [*Shakes hands with Ned*]

NED. My name is Ned, sir. The newsboys call me Ned Nimble because I move around and sell more papers than they do. Give us your hand again, sir—

CHAR. Certainly, what's the matter? [*Offers hand to Ned*]

NED. I didn't like the grip you gave me last time.

CHAR. The grip? Oh, I see—you're a Mason.

NED. No, I'm only a newsboy, but when a man shakes with me I don't want to feel that half-hearted squeeze as if he was shaking dice. Give me a good, hard grip, then I know you're right. My hands will stand it. They have seen plenty of honest work. [*They shake again*] That's right. Now I'll hear what you've got to say.

MOTH. Don't mind him, sir. He has the airs of a man.

CHAR. [*Aside*] Yes, and the impudence of the Devil. [*Aloud*] I suppose Ned will be a politician some day and run for office. Then he'll change his mind about handshakes.

NED. If I ever do get to the White House it will be hands of the working man that shakes mine.

FLOS. See, Ned, what the gentleman gave me. [*Removing ring and handing it to Ned*]

NED. What is it? A rhinestone? I wonder how much you could get on it. [*Blowing it and examining stone as an expert*]

MOTH. Yes, Ned, and he gave me twenty dollars.

CHAR. That's right, Ned, I mustn't forget you—[*Pulling roll of bills out of pocket*]

NED. Hold on, partner. Put that back. I've got to earn mine—[*Crosses L.*] What did you give the gentleman in return for twenty dollars, mother? Have you sold the stand?

MOTH. No, Ned—I gave him a cup of coffee.

NED. A cup of coffee. And you, Flo, what did you give him for this ring? That stone is a full-carat diamond.

FLOS. Why, you see, I—I—mother, you tell him.

CHAR. That's all right, Ned. It's only a trifle. It don't amount to much.

NED. It amounts to a good deal to us, sir; we are very poor.

CHAR. I know, and I am willing to help you. I've taken quite a fancy to your sister—and I—

MOTH. He's going to take her to his house tomorrow, Ned, a fine, swell mansion of West Avenue.

NED. Take Flo to his house?

CHAR. Yes, just for dinner and an informal call, that's all, Ned.

NED. Are you married?

CHAR. Don't I look it?

NED. That's not answering my question.

CHAR. Certainly. I have a very beautiful wife. [*Winking as he crosses to Flossie*]

NED. Then you should go home to her, instead of hanging around here making presents of diamonds to my sister.

MOTH. Ned, how dare you speak like that?

CHAR. The boy is insulting.

MOTH. Ned! Go up to bed, sir, or I'll take this bat to you.

NED. I'll not go to bed, mother, 'till this man leaves. Give me that money he gave you. Give it to me, I say—[*Snatching bill from mother*] There is your money and your ring, sir. I'm sorry if you think me rude but we can't accept them.

CHAR. No, no, Ned. Don't get mad. You don't understand. I've made arrangements to adopt your sister and you also.

NED. Adopt us?

MOTH. Yes, Ned, that's right.

FLOS. Yes, yes, Ned. We are to be rich.

NED. Rich—at what price? How can this man adopt us? Before God we are your children till we find our own parents. Mother, this man is not what he claims he is.

CHAR. You street arab! I've had enough of your insolence. How dare you speak to me like that!

NED. Because it's the truth. I've seen you in the gambling houses of the lower Bowery; at the race track, with fast women. Mother and I battle the world day and night to support our home in poverty. But if we are compelled to purchase riches at the cost of my sister's honor, we'll remain in rags all the rest of our lives—Go—[*Hurls money and ring at Charlie, who stoops and picks them up, crosses L.3., turns and doffs his hat. Flossie starts toward Charlie. Ned catches her hand and swings her left into Mother's arms, stands between them with arm uplifted. Enter Mike and Brown R.3. People from Concert Hall and Chinese crowd out of doorway C.*]

ACT II.

Library of the merchant's home. Next day. Arch doorway R.C.—conservatory backing. Arch doorway L.C.—plain hall backing. Hat rack with mirror against hall backing. Heavy portiere arch doorway L.C. Door opening off R.2., plain chamber backing. Door opening off L.2., plain chamber backing. Fireplace and mantel L.3. Armchair before fireplace; ottoman, cushion and so forth. Plain leather couch, R. corner. Chair, foot of couch. Plain flat-top office table, partway C. Chairs behind and R. of table. Plain small table, down L., containing water pitcher. Glasses, medicine bottles, and so forth. Books, writing material, on table Center. Chair, R. and L. of arch doorway L.C. Back wall painted to represent bookcases. Pedestals, stationery, bric-a-brac, plant, potted palms, maps and so forth. Sunlight in conservatory. Blue, hallway. Red glow in fireplace. Lights full up at rise.

BROWN. [*Enters L.C. at rise. Hangs hat on rack, comes down to table, picks up packages of mail, runs it over*] Here's the morning mail unopened —proves the old man's not up. I'm in luck. I learned enough about his rogue of a nephew last night to write a novel. What will he say when he learns that the woman who poses here in luxury as Charles Montgomery's wife is only an adventuress. Here is a letter for her now—"Mrs. Montgomery"—the brazen huzzy! It bears the trademark of Powell and Mason, the wholesale drug firm. Now what does she want with drugs? Can she be responsible for the old man's sinking spells—I've learned enough to warrant further investigation. I'll look this over. [*Puts letter in pocket*]

GERTRUDE. [*Enters L.2. Handsome, middle-aged woman as nurse. Dressed in black, white cap and cuffs, small lace apron. She has smoked glass goggles that disguise her face. Over one arm a blanket, bottle and spoon in other. Lays bottle and spoon on small table—throws rug over armchair*] Good morning, Brown.

BROWN. Good morning, Miss Clark. How's the old man?

GERT. He passed a bad night, Brown. He asked for you several times.

BROWN. He gave me permission to go.

GERT. Yes, I know. But he wants either you or I with him all the time. He grows weaker every day. He is suspicious of everyone else.

BROWN. I don't blame him. Did it ever occur to you, Miss Clark, that someone might wish to hasten the old man's end?

GERT. You mean his nephew?

BROWN. Yes, and that woman who poses as his wife. [*Pointing to door R.2.*]

GERT. No, no. I can't believe Charlie is as bad as that. [*Sinking into chair C., removing glasses, wiping eyes*]

BROWN. Not after the wrong he done you? Why a man who would ruin a woman's life as he did yours would be guilty of most any crime.

GERT. Silence, Brown. They must not know. I need this humble position I fill. Need it badly. Did they know who I was I would be out into the street.

BROWN. You have more right here than she has, and I don't believe Mr. Montgomery would turn you out. You have been too kind and good to him, Gertrude. Pardon me, I mean Miss Clark.

GERT. Call me Gertrude if you wish, Brown. One name is as good as another to me. They are both false—false as I am. [*Crosses R.*]

BROWN. Why don't you go to Mr. Montgomery and tell him all?

GERT. No, no, Brown. I am afraid.

BROWN. I've learned things about his nephew that he shall know, and I mean to stick by you, little woman, through everything.

GERT. Thank you, Brown—you've been a friend. God bless you for it.

BROWN. I would be more—no matter what your past has been. I love you.

GERT. No, no. Not that, Brown. Let us remain as we are. Remember I am a wife and a mother.

BROWN. Yes, but your husband is a convict in prison, and your children lost to you forever.

GERT. Don't say that, Brown. Every hour of my life I pray for their return.

BROWN. Suppose I could place them once more in your arms. What then, Gertie?

GERT. What are you saying, Arthur? Are you jesting with me? Speak, man! You know something, you have found them—my little girl and my baby boy? [*Sinking upon her knees sobbing*]

BROWN. Hush, Gertie—don't take on like that. We'll be heard. I don't wish to raise your hopes, but [*Raising her to her feet*] I'm on a clue that promises great results. Have courage, little woman. Fate had some object in placing you in the home of the man who ruined your life.

GERT. I expect every day that Charles Montgomery will recognize and kill me—I'm careful that he never sees me without my glasses.

BROWN. All the more reason to tell his uncle the truth and have him punished.

MONTGOMERY. [*Off L.2.*] Brown, oh, Brown. Is that you?

BROWN. There's the old man now.

MONT. [*Off L.2.*] Brown—

BROWN. Yes, sir—I'm coming. [*Crosses to door L.2.*] Give me that mail quick. [*Gertrude gathers mail from table, runs with it to Brown. Business.*

Brown keeps dropping papers and letters as Gertrude picks them up. Exits L.2.]

FLORA. [*Enters R.2. in handsome morning gown*] Good morning, Gertrude. Is my uncle better this morning?

GERT. [*Bending over small table L. and adjusting her glasses*] No, ma'am, he seems much weaker.

FLOR. Has his valet returned?

GERT. Yes, ma'am, he's with him now.

FLOR. Did you see a letter for me on the table? [*Looking on table*]

GERT. No, ma'am.

FLOR. Strange, I expected one. [*Walking to conservatory R.C.*] Get my uncle's wheeling chair ready, Gertrude. You will need to change the pillows. [*Crosses to table C.*]

GERT. [*Picking up bottle and crossing C.*] I must give Mr. Montgomery his medicine when his bath is over.

FLOR. I will attend to that. You may go. Do as I tell you. [*Gertrude sets bottle on table, exits R.C. Flora picks up bottle, shakes it, removes stopper, applies her nostrils*] This is not strong enough. It's too slow, all together too slow. If I only dared use something more powerful. With this I shall never be found out. [*Charlie enters L.C. Removes hat and coat. Tosses them to butler who hangs them on rack and retires. Flora crosses L., sits on arm of chair before fire*] Prince Charlie comes home to his little wife when he has no place else to go.

CHAR. You are right, Flo, always right. Where's the old man?

FLOR. Not up yet, my dear boy—indisposed as it were. It is about time he had his drops. [*Crosses to table C. and picks up bottle*]

CHAR. [*Clutching bottle and taking it from Flora*] You avarice-, money-crazed cat, you have no more heart than a stone.

FLOR. I might say the same of you, my dear Prince, but I wouldn't be so unladylike—did you get what I sent you for?

CHAR. No.

FLOR. Why didn't you?

CHAR. Because I will not be a party to your hellish plot.

FLOR. You are a coward, Prince. You are willing I should stay here and take the risk. When it's all over you will lay back in luxury and try and convince your conscience you are innocent.

CHAR. Where's the nurse—her eyes seem always on me.

FLOR. We are alone, my dear—have no fear.

CHAR. Flo, if the old man knew you were not my wife he'd cut me off without a penny.

FLOR. That's just why—the sooner it's over the better. This won't do. [*Handling bottle*] That Chinese doctor I sent you to can give me what I want. Did you see him?

CHAR. No, I didn't get a chance.

FLOR. It's only an opium pellet, Charlie. It will leave no trace to betray us. Your uncle is dying now with aneurism of the heart. It is only a question of a few weeks or months at most. In that time he may learn the truth and cast us into the street. I can't go back to the old life in the dance halls, and what would you do without money?

CHAR. I know that, Flo, but it would be murder. My God, woman, what are you asking me to do? We may be found out, go to the electric chair. No, no, you're a fiend from hell! Go 'way from me. I don't know why I ever brought you here. [*Gertrude with wheeling chair enters R.C. Stands in conservatory near doorway*]

FLOR. To pawn me off on your uncle as the wife of Albert Cooper, the man you wronged and sent to prison for a crime committed by yourself.

CHAR. Stop, Flo, for God's sake. Someone will hear. Do you want to ruin every chance we have to live a better life? [*Gertrude reels back as if fainting. Clutches handle of wheeling chair, supports herself, turns her back*] What's that? [*Turns suddenly, sees Gertrude adjusting pillows in chair as if she has not heard*]

FLOR. That prying, pale-faced nurse. She's always about when not wanted; Gertrude—Gertrude, are you deaf? You may go.

GERT. Yes, ma'am. [*Bows low and exits R.C.*]

FLOR. Don't look so scared. She didn't hear you. Are you going to get that for me? Or must I go to Chinatown?

CHAR. Go to hell for all I care.

FLOR. If I do you'll open the door for me. See here, "my dear husband in name only," there is no love lost between you and I. It's a cold business proposition of dollars and cents. Your uncle injects enough morphine into his veins every day to kill ten ordinary men. So much for habit; his system is filled with it. Opium is the same drug in another form. My friend the Dog Doctor compounds it to put crippled Chinamen out of the world without pain. Now what is twenty-four hours more or less in a man's life? You could hardly call an act of humanity by such a cruel name as was whispered here a moment ago.

CHAR. Enough! If I do this for you, will you do something for me?

FLOR. I think I am doing a great deal for you.

CHAR. There is a young girl I want, down in the Bowery. She is hardly of age yet and we must be careful.

FLOR. Oh, you hard-hearted man! So I am to take second place? And where are you to pitch her wigwam?

CHAR. I leave that to you, Flo. Is it a go?

FLOR. Yes, there is my hand. No use fighting, Charlie. We've too much at stake. If we pull a double oar we will reach the shores of wealth.

CHAR. Yes, or land in jail. Get dressed and we'll go for a ride. I don't feel like meeting the old man just now. [*Exits L.C. with hat*]

FLOR. [*Follows to L.C., looks after him, laughs and shrugs shoulders*] Poor weak miserable fool, how I abhor him. [*Crosses down C.*] And yet he placed me where I am. Was it not for him I would be in the lowest dives of this city today. Why have I no gratitude; why have I no heart? [*Picking up bottle*] Ask the men who have made me what I am. [*Brown and Montgomery enter L.2., Montgomery a refined old gent, white hair, dressing-gown, walks with cane and leans on Brown*]

MONT. Careful, Brown, careful. My old heart is thumping like a trip-hammer. Where is my nurse? Where is Gertrude? [*Brown leads Montgomery to chair before fire, assists him to seat*]

FLOR. I'm to be your nurse this morning, uncle. Miss Clark stepped out for a few moments.

MONT. I don't want you, I want Gertrude. It's time for my hypodermic and drops. [*Rolling back sleeve of his right arm*] See the scars on my arm, Brown, hardly a place can I find to insert the needle.

BROWN. Don't excite yourself, sir. I will administer the morphine. [*Crosses up to small table*]

MONT. Send that woman away. She annoys me.

FLOR. Now, uncle, don't be cross with me this morning. [*Pats old man's head, puts arm around neck*] I'm so sorry, so very, very, sorry for you. Won't you let me be your little nurse? See what a nice nosegay I picked for you this morning. [*Takes flowers from bosom and pins on old man's gown*]

MONT. Flowers, bah! [*Pulls off flowers, throws them on floor*] Save them for my coffin. I want my drops; bring my drops.

FLOR. [*Picks up nosegay; crosses to table, returns with bottle and spoon, pours out drops, offers to Montgomery*] Here they are, uncle.

MONT. I've changed my mind. Bring me whiskey. If I'm to die I might as well have my old hide filled with rum. Morphine, Brown, the morphine! What are you doing, man? You are slower than Balaam's ass. [*Lays back in chair, throws his naked arm across his breast and clutches at his heart*]

BROWN. [*Who has filled syringe from vial at small table; crosses up and after trying flesh several places on old man's arm, injects high up*] Steady, now—easy—you will soon be yourself. [*Flora has staggered back to table center with bottle and spoon and watches the above like a hawk*]

Mont. [*Gives sigh of relief*] God bless you, Brown. That's a great relief. Heaven don't seem so far away as it did a moment ago. Flora, go get your marriage certificate. You promised to show it to me time and time again. Now I want to see it.

Flor. Yes, uncle, I'll go and search for it. I told you I mislaid it.

Mont. Well, don't come back till you've found it.

Flor. [*Aside*] Old fool—he'll soon forget. [*Exits R.2., slams door*]

Mont. My, that woman has a temper, Brown. She's a bad one. Did I believe what you told me I'd turn her out.

Brown. It's the truth. I'm going to furnish you with proofs today.

Mont. You say that my nurse, Miss Clark, is the wife Charlie took from Albert Cooper fourteen years ago?

Brown. Yes. I believe I have found the children. I have arranged to have them brought here today. You can question them yourself.

Mont. The unprincipled rogue. He has disgraced the name he bears. I have put up with him long enough. Send Miss Clark to me.

Brown. Don't tell her of the children till we are sure they are hers. [*Crosses to R.C.*]

Mont. Oh, Brown.

Brown. Yes, sir.

Mont. Have you sent for the plumber to look over the sanitary conditions of my bathroom? It annoys me.

Brown. Yes, sir. He should be here now. [*Exits R.C.*]

Char. [*Enters L.C.*] Are you feeling well this morning?

Mont. Well enough to talk business with you. Your bank account is overdrawn.

Char. I know it. You keep me down to cases.

Mont. I'll keep you down to day labor if you're not careful, young man. Where were you last night?

Char. At the club.

Mont. You're a liar.

Char. Uncle, you forget yourself.

Mont. Silence, sir. I want you to find Albert Cooper.

Char. [*Aside*] My God, does he know? [*Aloud*] Albert Cooper is dead, uncle. I've told you that repeatedly. How could I have married his wife were he alive? He was shot down while escaping from prison, years ago. He died in the hospital and was buried in potters' field.

BROWN. [*Enters R.C.*] The plumber has sent his apprentice. He's a new man, shall I let him come in?

MONT. Yes, send him in. [*Albert, dressed in overalls, with plumber's tools, enters R.C. at signal from Brown*]

BROWN. Right this way, my man. [*Crosses to L.2., opens door. Charlie staggers down C., clutches edge of table, turning his back to Albert. Albert bows, crosses behind Charlie, exit L.2. and throws down tools off L.*]

BROWN. Miss Clark is waiting to see you, sir.

MONT. Let her come in. [*Brown exits R.C.*] Charlie, you may go; I will talk with you some other time. If Cooper is dead his children must be found and justice done them before I die. [*Charlie crosses rapidly to L.2., opens door a little, looks off*]

MONT. What are you doing there now?

CHAR. Watching your plumber. He looks like a sneak thief. Better get him out of here as soon as possible. [*Gertrude enters R.C., goes down C., bows head*]

MONT. Never mind him. Leave me, I have something to say to Miss Clark. [*Charlie turns, bows low to Gertrude and exits L.C.*]

GERT. You sent for me, sir?

MONT. Yes, come over here beside me where I can see your face. [*Gertrude sits on ottoman at Montgomery's feet. Removes her glasses and keeps them off throughout the scene*]

MONT. I'm good-natured now. The morphine is in my veins. I'm not going to scold you.

GERT. You never scold me, sir.

MONT. No, because you're kind to me; you know your business. Gertrude, you've been faithful to me; a loyal, patient nurse. I shall provide for you in my will.

GERT. I expected no reward, Mr. Montgomery.

MONT. I know that. I have learned that this woman he calls his wife is an adventuress. It was you, Albert Cooper's wife, whom I believed I was aiding all these years. I tried to avoid disgrace, and at the same time aid the family my nephew ruined. He told me Cooper was dead, that he had married his widow. I forgave him for that and searched for the children.

GERT. Yes, yes, my children, where are they? Oh, sir, I have suffered more than human heart can bear. When I got out of the hospital where he left me to die, my babies were gone, my health was gone. I had lost my hair; I was so changed no one knew me. Then they took me back as a nurse. That is how you came to get me, sir.

MONT. It must have been the Almighty who sent you, Gertrude, and if suffering can atone for sin, there may be light yet for both of us. I am stricken with death, have but a few days to live, but before I die I want to see the little family so cruelly separated by my nephew once more united.

BROWN. [*Enters R.C.*] The parties I spoke of are here, sir. Will I wheel you in the garden to see them, or shall I have them come in?

MONT. Gertrude, you go and see the maid keeps her eye on that fellow in the bathroom. I will send for you when I'm done with these people.

GERT. Oh, my heart seems to be bursting with joy, Mr. Montgomery; your kind words give me new life—new hopes. [*Places arm about old man's neck and kisses him. They are both in tears. She hastens to exit L.2., wiping her eyes with handkerchief. She screams offstage, reels back, clutching at her bosom and looking off L.*]

MONT. What's the matter, Gertrude?

GERT. That man, sir!

MONT. Didn't you know he was there?

GERT. [*Slowly shakes her head. Hammering upon metal heard off L., Gertrude pushes door slowly open again. Her lips move in a frightened whisper*] No, no, it can't be, it can't be!

MONT. What are you frightened about, Gertrude?

GERT. [*Crosses rapidly to Montgomery*] Oh, Mr. Montgomery, that man in your apartments! There is something about him reminds me of Albert.

MONT. Nothing but your nerves, my girl. He's only a poor, harmless plumber. Run on now and see that he doesn't charge me for anything he's not doing. [*Gertrude adjusts her glasses and exits L.2. Ned and Flossie enter R.C. in store clothes, badly worn but tidy. They enter hand in hand, and approach Montgomery, timidly looking all about. Mother Murphy follows them on R.C., wears green bonnet, plaid shawl, and stands C. Brown and Mike, in uniform, follow Mother on R.C. and stand in doorway*]

NED. This certainly is a swell joint, and that's no idle dream.

FLOS. Ned, look at the gold handle on the coal shovel.

NED. See the big pair of curling-irons beside 'em! [*Pointing to tongs and brass-handled shovel on the hearth*]

MOTH. I must be in one of those dreams people get after eating mince pie.

MONT. Are these the children, Brown?

BROWN. Yes, sir, and this is the good woman who has cared for them.

MOTH. Top of the mornin' to you, sir.

MONT. Is this Mrs. Murphy?

MOTH. It is. Mother Murphy, as I'm known on the Bowery, sir.

MONT. Don't you remember me?

MOTH. Seems to me I do, sir.

MONT. I used to be in business on Broome Street.

MOTH. Are you the old gentleman I used to scrub for?

MONT. I am, Mother. Are these the babies I left with you in 1890?

MOTH. The very same, sir, and the devil of a time I've had scratching for their living.

MONT. I sent you money to provide for them every month by my nephew, until you moved and he could find you no more.

MOTH. Devil a bit did I ever see of your nephew or any money, sir.

BROWN. The woman speaks the truth. This officer will vouch for her honesty.

MIKE. That I will, sir, and pardon me, but you might as well know all the truth while we are at it. One of the worst gamblers of the Tenderloin poses as your nephew and obtains money by using your name.

NED. Yes, and he insulted my sister last night.

MOTH. Don't mind him, sir, it was no insult. The young gentleman was kind to us.

MONT. Enough! Brown, you have convinced me. Take them away. I must have time to think. Oh, the shame, the disgrace of it all!

NED. We're not here to disgrace anybody. If you are ashamed of us we will go. I didn't want to come. It kept me from work.

MONT. Then you work, young man?

NED. Yes, sir.

MONT. What do you do?

NED. Sell papers.

MONT. Would you work just as hard if this mansion was yours?

NED. Yes, sir. I'd have to if I wished to keep it.

MONT. Leave the boy with me, Brown, he interests me. [*Brown motions to Mother, and exits R.C. with Mike*]

MOTH. Come, Floss. [*Crosses up R.C.*]

FLOS. Can't I stay, too? Oh, it's all so grand!

MONT. Let the girl remain if she wishes. I will see you before you leave, Mrs. Murphy, and give you a check for what I owe you.

MOTH. God bless you, sir! What will I do with all that money? [*Exits R.C.*]

MONT. Come to me, children, I'll not harm you. I'm only a poor, sick old man, with a broken heart, waiting patiently for the reaper.

FLOS. [*Sitting on ottoman before Montgomery*] What's a reaper?

NED. Don't ask foolish questions, Floss. He's the fellow that reaches out and takes in all the chips.

Mont. That's right. The fellow that rakes us all in some day. Do you remember your parents, children?

Ned. No, sir, we weren't old enough.

Flos. I do, I'm older than him. I remember mama, she was always crying.

Mont. Would you like to see her again?

Flos. Yes, sir, very much.

Ned. Would I like to see her? Say, I'd eat her up. [*Pounding heard on metal off L.*] What's going on in there? Is someone tapping the till? [*Peeping at keyhole, L.2.*]

Flos. You must not peek, Ned, that's rude. I want to look at some of those books awful bad, but I wouldn't ask. [*Pointing to center table*]

Mont. You may look at them, my dear, while Ned and I go and investigate the noise in my apartments. [*Flossie crosses to center table, examining books*]

Ned. Is that your room in there?

Mont. Yes. Do you think you are able to assist me to enter? [*Trying to rise*]

Ned. Do I? Just try me. Lean on my shoulder hard as you want to. I'm strong. [*Assisting Montgomery to rise*]

Mont. [*Leaning on Ned and walking L.2. by aid of cane*] You would be a handy boy to keep around here. Wouldn't you rather work for me than sell papers?

Ned. How much do you pay?

Mont. What salary do you want?

Ned. All I can get.

Mont. We will talk it over. Easy now, don't let me fall. [*Ned pushes open L.2., exits with Montgomery*]

Char. [*Enters L.C. dressed in velvet jacket, riding boots. Crosses down R. Is about to open R.2. when he sees Flossie leaning with both elbows on table engrossed in book. Aside*] She here?

Flos. [*Looking up and smiling*] Hello, Prince.

Char. Hello, what are you doing here?

Flos. Reading a book.

Char. Did you drop from the sky?

Flos. Do I look like an angel?

Char. Yes, and a very beautiful one. What brought you here?

Flos. My feet. I don't have carriages like the one you promised to take me in.

Char. Did you come here to get the carriage ride I promised you?

Flos. Certainly, and that ring my brother made me give back.

CHAR. Are you joshing me? How old are you, anyway?

FLOS. That's pretty hard to say, seeing I don't know who my mother is or when I was born; but I feel—oh, let me see, quite a young lady—about eighteen, I guess.

CHAR. You don't look sixteen, but you are sweet enough to kiss. Then you're not mad with me after what happened last night?

FLOS. No, why should I be? You treated me all right.

CHAR. Then here's the ring. [*Places ring on Flossie's finger and goes to embrace her*]

FLOR. [*In stylish riding-gown, hat and veil, enters R.2.*] What is that girl doing here?

CHAR. You'll have to ask her. I haven't found out yet.

FLOS. My, but ain't you swell. [*Circling about Flora*]

FLOR. Who are you?

FLOS. Flossie Murphy.

FLOR. Who brought you here?

FLOS. The old woman.

FLOR. Where is she now?

FLOS. Out in the garden. [*Crosses up to R.C.*]

CHAR. This is the girl I told you about, Flo. I gave her mother my address last night but I didn't think she'd bring her girl here. The old lady needs the money and I want the girl.

FLOR. Shame, she is only a child!

CHAR. No matter; so much the better. Now's the chance to get her. You take her down to the side entrance. [*Pointing R.2.*] I'll have the carriage sent round to you. I'm going horseback and will meet you in the park.

FLOR. Suppose she won't go?

CHAR. Yes, she will. Quick now or we will be discovered. [*Pushing open R.2.*] Come here, Butterfly, do you want to take that ride?

FLOS. Sure I do, if you ask the old woman.

CHAR. You go down to the carriage with this lady. I'll go and tell your mother.

FLOR. [*Crosses R.2.*] Come, my dear, we'll not be gone long. [*Stretches her hand forward to Flossie*]

FLOS. [*Advances slowly R. and gives her hand to Flora*] My, what beautiful diamonds. See, I have one on my hand also. It's not very big, but it's my engagement ring. [*Kisses ring and looks over her shoulder at Charlie and exits*]

FLORA. Charles Montgomery, hell has no fires hot enough for you. [*Smiling*]

CHAR. How about yourself?

FLOR. Oh [*Shrugs shoulders*], I'm resigned to my fate. I don't think about such things. It's unpleasant. [*Exits R.2., closes door. Riding master appears L.C.*]

CHAR. Send James around to the side entrance with the coupé. Hold my horse ready in the front drive. [*Master salutes and exits L.C. Montgomery and Ned enter L.2., Montgomery leaning on Ned*]

CHAR. Uncle, I am waiting for a check.

MONT. You'll have to keep on waiting. [*Sits L. of table by Ned's aid. Ned stands L.C.*]

CHAR. [*Leans on table*] Don't get it? Do you want the bank to pull me up and disgrace you?

MONT. Disgrace me, you low-lived dog. You've done nothing else during your whole life. Ned, is this the man who insulted your sister?

NED. Yes, sir.

CHAR. The boy lies. I never saw him before.

MONT. Silence, sir. Where's your sister, Ned? I want her evidence, also.

NED. She must have gone out. I'll get her. [*Exits R.C. on run*]

MONT. Charlie, I want you to take this woman of yours and get out.

CHAR. How dare you speak of my wife like that? Uncle, if you were a younger man I'd—[*Raising arm as if to strike Montgomery*]

MONT. [*Rising and clutching table*] You'd what? My God, has it come to this? Raise your arm to me, after all I've done—I'll cut you off, sir! You and your adventuress you call your wife. This excitement is killing me. My heart, Charlie—it's humming away like the tongue of a monster bell. Call my nurse, Gertrude, I'm dying—help—[*Falls insensible upon rug in front of table, center*]

ALB. [*With kit of tools and short section of lead pipe in his hand enters L.2., runs forward and tries to catch Montgomery as he falls. Kneels and, laying his pipe and tools down, raises Montgomery's head*] What are you standing there for, man? Run for help. [*Charlie R.C. bending over Montgomery. Ned, Brown, Mike, Mother, enter R.C. in order named—Gertrude, wearing glasses, enters L.2.*]

NED. See, the old man has been murdered.

CHAR. Yes, cruelly murdered, struck on the head by that man, who is an escaped convict. See, his weapon lays beside him.

GERT. [*Crosses C. in front of Montgomery's body*] You lie, Charles Montgomery. It is true this man is an escaped convict, but he would not be guilty of murder.

CHAR. How do you know?

GERT. [*Removing glasses*] Because he is my husband.

ALB. [*Catching Gertrude in his arms*] Flora, my wife.

GERT. [*Freeing herself*] Yes, Albert, your wife once and for all time, had it not been for that man. [*Pointing to Charlie. Kneeling*] Mr. Montgomery was not murdered. There is no sign of a blow upon his head. He was suffering from an aneurism, the most dangerous disease of the heart. Undue excitement caused it to burst. [*Arising*] This man died of a broken heart.

CHAR. Yes, and left me his sole heir to millions. I defy you all. I am master of this house now. There is no room here for escaped convicts and beggars. So get out. [*Lawyer, white hair and Prince Albert, with legal document, enters L.2., crosses to L. of table*]

NED. [*Climbing on table and bending down so he can pat Charlie on shoulder*] Hold on, Prince Charlie. I might have been a beggar once, but I ain't no more. The old man changed his mind just a few minutes before he died, sent for his lawyer, cut you off and left his money to me. Read that and then you get out. [*Takes legal paper from lawyer, hands it to Charlie. Charlie opens it, staggers back, looks up to lawyer, who nods*]

CURTAIN

		Mother	Ned	Brown	
Mike		Montgomery	Lawyer	Gertrude	Albert
	Charlie				

PICTURE FOR 2ND CURTAIN

Mother		Brown		Charlie and Riding Master
	Mike		Lawyer	

POSITIONS FOR 3RD CURTAIN

Ned   Gertrude   Albert

PICTURE

Albert, Gertrude, and Ned in group L.C. downstage. Albert has arm about Gertrude. Gertrude has hand on Ned's head. Ned is showing will to his father, Albert. Mike and lawyer stand facing upstage talking to Mother and Brown near conservatory R.C. Charles and Riding Master in heated conversation in hallway seen through L.C. door, Charlie pulling on his gloves. Montgomery's body lies in front of table C., head L., feet R.; Butler with folded arms and bowed head at feet. Little maid with white apron and cap, kneeling, crying at his head L.

Arrange for curtain call after second curtain. Positively do not let character who plays Montgomery take this call. Let the boy come last with father and mother. Do not let Flora or Flossie take this call. This is important to further interest in play.

ACT III.

SCENE 1: *One month later. Broadway after dark in front of Shanley's. Drop in 3.—painted to represent entrance to restaurant. Arch door R.C. with interior backing. Window L.C. with interior backing. Set piece representing rear of cab R.2. There can be profiles with backings so as to show drivers on the box in livery. Curtain discovers Mike, in uniform of Broadway police, hustling supers as newsboys and venders, beggars and so forth R. and L.— supers as ladies and gents enter and exit from R.C.*

BROWN. [*In business suit enters from R.*]   Hello! Mike, been transferred?

MIKE.   Yes, promoted to the Broadway Squad. Have you found Miss Flossie?

BROWN.   Not yet. Flora Bradley doesn't deny she took the girl to ride, but says she let her out in the park and she ran away.

MIKE.   A likely story. What does the coachman say?

BROWN.   Anything for money and they have lots of it.

MIKE.   Too bad the boy Ned can't get his own.

BROWN.   Yes. Prince Charlie's attorneys claim the old man was tricked into signing his property away. The codicil reads "To Cooper's boy to provide for the mother and help find the father."

MIKE.   Yes, and the mother signed as witness. What more do they want?

BROWN.   She signed as Gertrude Clark, the nurse. Now she can't prove she is Cooper's wife or that Ned is her boy. They won't take a convict's testimony in the case. If the girl could be found, she was old enough to remember her mother. Her identification would establish the boy's right to the property.

MIKE.   All the more reason for them keeping her hid. [*Calling R.*] Here, move on. Don't bump that lady, or I'll bump your head.

MOTH. [*Enter R.1., talking off R.*]   You have a foot on you like a rhinoceros. You popped my corn for me. Oh, me, oh, my. [*Hopping on one foot*] What's that? Here, officer, arrest that Welsh rabbit, he called me a cuckoo. [*Bumps into Brown*] Excuse me, sir.

MIKE.   Don't mind them, Mother.

MOTH.   Don't mind them, who—those loafers or me corns? Oh, it's you, is it?

BROWN.   What are you doing on Broadway, Mrs. Murphy?

MOTH.   Looking for me poor gal.

BROWN.   Where's Ned?

MOTH. Doing the selfsame thing and trying to support himself. My business has gone to the devil with all my trouble. The lawyers offered to advance Ned money, but he's so proud he refused it. I hear you're doing what you can, sir, and I'm much obliged to you. Hist, Mike, can I borrow your ear for a minute? [*Crosses L.*]

MIKE. You can if you don't whistle in it.

MOTH. Walk down the street. I need protection. Excuse us, Brown, he'll be back in a wink.

BROWN. Going to get a drink?

MOTH. No. no. I said in a wink—one of those things you get on Broadway after dark. [*Winks at Brown, exits after Mike, L.1. Gertrude, in plain street dress, with small parcel of dry goods, enters R.1.*]

BROWN. Hello, little woman, I was just speaking of you. I see the governor has pardoned your husband.

GERT. Yes, Brown, he was never guilty. I found out too late that Charles Montgomery forged the checks that sent Albert to jail and turned me against the father of my children.

BROWN. And I shall help you. [*Clasping her hand*]

GERT. I understand, Brown. I only hope my daughter is in the hands of an honest man like you.

BROWN. Would you know her if you met?

GERT. I suppose not, though my mother heart should tell me.

BROWN. Where is your husband?

GERT. Looking for employment. We all want work. I'm sewing, but it takes us from the search for Flossie.

BROWN. Let me help you. [*Reaching for money*] I have money saved and you are welcome.

GERT. No, Arthur, you have done enough.

BROWN. You look tired. Won't you come in and have supper?

GERT. In Shanley's? Oh, no. I'm not dressed well enough. Besides I have this work to deliver. Ned promised to meet me here. He will be around with his extras before long. I shall walk up and down and watch the people till he comes.

BROWN. If I find him, you shall both go to supper with me. [*Exit L.1.*]

GERT. All lights, music and bright faces. I wonder if there are any hearts in there as heavy as mine. What a beautiful girl in that cab. She's going to alight. [*Looks R.*]

FLOS. [*In stylish gown, with jewels and so forth, enters R.1., passes Gertrude*] Why couldn't that stupid driver let me out in front of the joint, instead of waltzing me round the corner into a dark street. Guess he don't know who I am. Shanley's, this is the place. I won't know how to act in that swell bakery. I feel so funny in all these new togs. I want to stay on the street and show off. Charlie don't want anyone to see me. He put me in the cab and told me to keep out of sight. I don't blame him, I must look out of sight. I guess he's afraid he'll lose me. He says if the old woman gets me, she'll put me back to washing dishes. [*To Gertrude*] Who you looking at? Didn't you ever see a lady before? [*Gertrude bows head, crosses L.C.*] My, but these common people are rude. I suppose she knows I'm going to be a bride. When Charlie bought me these clothes he told me they was my wedding *trousers*. He's getting awful fresh. I don't know whether I will marry him or not. [*Exits R.C. Waiter seen seating her at window L.C. Flossie ties napkin round neck—drinks out of water bottle—jokes with waiter, whispering to him from behind. Waiter throws his head back and is seen shaking himself with laughter*]

GERT. Poor, wild, young thing. I wonder who she is. My, but she is beautiful. Her face seems to fascinate me. I will walk back this way on my return and see if she is still there. [*Starts L. but stops, watching Flossie as if fascinated. Charlie and Flora enter R.1. in evening dress without seeing Gertrude*]

FLOR. Fool, you are taking a desperate chance.

CHAR. She wouldn't stay cooped up any longer. She's so changed her mother wouldn't know her.

FLOR. I should hope not. [*Gertrude bows head and slowly exits L.1. Charlie and Flora turn and watch her*]

CHAR. Who's that?

FLOR. Some hungry beggar. Why don't you take the girl and get out to Europe before they catch you up in the game?

CHAR. She says I must marry her first.

FLOR. And will you?

CHAR. You know me. I shall make her think so. You must go on playing the sister gag. [*Exits R.C. Flora laughs and exits R.C. Drops chatelaine bag containing purse*]

ALB. [*Plain, rough, but neat clothes, enters R.1.*] I can't find employment. No one wants me. My mind is always on my lost child. Had I known her that night on the Bowery, when she gave me this rose, I might have saved all this suffering. [*Taking rose from inside vest and kissing it and replacing it; sees bag*] Hello, has my luck changed? [*Picks up bag*] A pocketbook, and filled with bills. Thank God, my prayer has been answered. This will relieve my wife and boy from want. Help us to find our Flossie. No, I can't keep this. It wouldn't be right. I'm under suspicion now. I must be careful.

FLOR. [*Enters R.C., with waiter, followed by Charlie*] There it is in that man's hands. He must have snatched it from me as I got out of my carriage.

ALB. I just picked it up, ma'am. [*Offering bag*]

FLOR. [*Snatching bag from Albert*] You were counting the money and placing it in your pocket. There is some missing.

ALB. A thief don't stop on Broadway to count stolen money. [*Mike enters L.I. Crowd gathers from R. and L.*]

CHAR. You seem familiar with their methods. Officer, this man has robbed my wife. I want him arrested.

MIKE. Cooper, what does this mean?

ALB. They are mistaken. I found the bag and returned it.

CHAR. Lock him up, officer. I know him to be a common thief.

MIKE. And I know him to be honest.

CHAR. If you refuse to arrest this man I shall prefer charges against you.

MIKE. Your word don't count for much at headquarters. You are not above suspicion yourself. Take that hand-painted fairy and go inside. [*Crosses up steps*]

CHAR. You are all witnesses that this officer has insulted me, and he refused to do his duty. That man is a thief.

ALB. Let me at him, Mike. [*Rushes at Charlie*]

MIKE. [*Catches Albert and pushes him back*] Hold on, Cooper.

ALB. I'll get you yet, Charles Montgomery. God help you when I do.

MIKE. Go on, go on, don't be a fool. [*Backs Cooper off R.I. Charlie and Flora seen standing inside beside Flossie. Charlie sits facing out, head close to Flossie's face, talking earnestly*]

GERT. [*Enter L.I.*] Yes, she's there still. [*Looking in window*] She has company. No wonder that man's talking to her. Where have I seen him before? I wish he would raise his head—my God, it is Charles Montgomery, and he has ensnared and will ruin her as he did me—as he has so many others. [*Staggers back, puts her hand to face*] If I could only warn her. Get her away from him some way.

MOTH. [*Enters L.I.*] What's this crying in the street, Mrs. Cooper? Have you gone daffy? Just as we are getting you straightened up of all your trouble.

GERT. Look, Mother Murphy, do you see that man?

MOTH. See that man? Faith, I'm not blind. I see two of them. One is making love, the other spilling soup down his back. [*Pointing to waiter who is just serving Charlie and Flossie*]

GERT. No, no, not the waiter. I mean the gentleman.

MOTH. Faith, there is no gentleman there, my dear. A man that would talk to a gal like that while she's trying to eat her victuals is no gentleman.

GERT. Don't you see who it is?

MOTH. Sure enough, it's Prince Charlie—and say, what the devil has come over my eyes?

GERT. What's the matter, Mrs. Murphy?

MOTH. The girl I'm lookin' at. Make the snakes crawl back in Ireland, but it's her.

GERT. It's who?

MOTH. That brazen huzzy in the silk petticoat. Look at her with the airs of a lady and the jewels of a Dutch heiress. Eatin' her soup with a fork. Look at her, woman. Don't you know who that is? [*Gertrude shakes her head*] That's Flossie Murphy Cooper. That's your own daughter, my dear. [*Gertrude gives a stifled scream and clutches Mother for support*] Be still now. Don't be a fool because your child is—brace up—brace up and be a man. [*Messenger boy in uniform of W.U.T.Co., about same size as Ned, enters R.1., exits R.C. Is seen again at table L.C. with Flossie and Charlie. Charlie seals and hands boy a message*]

GERT. My child, my little Flossie in the power of that man! Quick, Mrs. Murphy, we must do something to save her.

MOTH. Easy, now. Easy. We'll do that same thing but we will be diplomatic. That man is a smooth-tongued slippery cuss. You wait here and keep your eyes on him while I get a cop.

GERT. What is he giving that messenger boy?

MOTH. I suppose it's a date with another gal. He has a hundred but the divil will have him when I get back.

FLOR. [*Following messenger on R.C.*] Hurry now, catch that car and change at 34th Street. [*Messenger starts L.*]

GERT. Stop, boy, give me that message. [*Grabs message*]

FLOR. What do you mean, woman. Let that boy alone. [*Messenger dodges Gertrude and exits L.1.*]

MOTH. Here, give me that. Come back here, you little divil. I'll catch you. I'll turn you up and spank your—[*Exits L.1.*]

GERT. You adventuress, I have found you at last.

FLOR. So it's you, is it?

GERT. Yes, the nurse who foiled your plans to poison the dearest old man who ever lived. The mother of that little girl who you stole and are leading to ruin. Give her to me at once.

FLOR. Be still, woman, don't make a scene. You shall have her. See, you are attracting a crowd. [*To waiter*] Quick, Lewis, call Mr. Montgomery.

Tell him to bring the girl. [*Waiter exits. Charlie and Flossie seen to rise hurriedly and enter R.C.*]

FLOR. Quick into that carriage and get away—I will stay and have her locked up.

FLOS. Who is it? What does she want?

CHAR. Never mind. Come.

GERT. Flossie, Flossie, my child. Don't you know me? [*Stepping forth and reaching toward her*]

CHAR. Come. [*Pulls Flossie R.*]

FLOR. [*Stepping between Flossie and Gertrude*] Hands off. I will have you arrested.

FLOS. Stop. You hurt me. Let me see what she wants.

CHAR. Come on, I say. [*Jerks Flossie off R.i. by the arm*]

GERT. Oh, please, someone stop them. They are stealing my child. [*Ned with extras enters R.i.*] Ned, my boy—help—[*Starts toward Ned, staggers, fainting. Ned throws down papers. Catches Gertrude, lays her C., kneels behind her. Crowd gathers about in sympathy*]

FLOR. She's a rank imposter, deserving of no sympathy. Someone call the patrol.

NED. Stop. She is no imposter. She has fainted from worry and grief. This woman is my mother, and I am here to protect her. You are the one who should be arrested. [*Pointing to Flora*]

FLOR. Who will take your word. You're only a boy of the streets—a ragged beggar.

NED. Child of the streets, yes, but no beggar.

MOTH. [*Enters dragging messenger boy by ear*] Come on, sonny, or I'll twist your ear off. [*Sees Ned*] What's the matter? Have I come too late?

FLOR. Release that boy. I sent him on an errand. What are you doing with my message?

MOTH. Holding it for the police. Where the divil are they? When there is a fight they all run the other way.

NED. Here's the cop—it's Mike. We're all right now. [*Calling*] Mike, Mike.

MIKE. [*Enters R.i.*] Hello, Ned. What do you want?

NED. I want you to arrest that woman. [*Pointing to Flora*]

MIKE. What's the trouble?

NED. I don't know, but I am going to find out.

MOTH. That woman knows where your sister is, Ned. Flossie was in that restaurant a minute ago with Prince Charlie. They sent this boy away with a message. Here it is. I can't read, but I can run like hell, can't I, boy? [*Hands Ned the message*]

NED. [*Tearing open the envelope and reading, aside*] "Frank, meet me at the Waldorf-Astoria, Room 604. I want you to perform a mock marriage. Come quick." [*Crumbles message in his hand*] Not as quick as I will go. Here, boy, I want to trade jobs with you. Lend me your coat and cap. I will deliver this message. [*Pulls off his coat and hat. Throws them on top of his bundle of papers, jerks coat and cap off of messenger boy and puts them on*]

MIKE. What are you going to do?

NED. Turn detective. Look after my mother, Mike, and don't let that woman get away. Here, boy, you can sell those extras for me. When I get back I'll have money enough to set you up in business. [*Hands messenger boy his papers, hat and coat and exits R.1. on the run. Mother, who has been kneeling by Gertrude during this scene, raises her to her feet, just as Ned exits. Gertrude calls "Ned, Ned," stretching forth arms. Brown enters L.1. Throws his arm about Gertrude and she starts to exit L.1. between Mother and Brown. Mike has started to drag Flora off R.1. She puts up a fight and Brown handcuffs her. Crowd laughs and taunts her—"oot, oot, oot," slap Lewis the waiter with their hats and drive him in restaurant*]

LEW. [*Pulls apron, tries to make a stand*] You loafers, hoodlums. [*Shakes fist, throws flower pots and exits. Sticks head out of window, shakes fist. Lights out. Dark change*]

SCENE 2: *Same night. Room in the Waldorf-Astoria. Drop in 2. with windows R.C. backed by house-tops. Railing and ladder of fire escape seen through L.C. Arch door draped by heavy curtains R.2., supposed to lead into bedchamber. Red bunch off this entrance. Door opening off L.2. White off this entrance. Table C. containing novels, fruit, candy, flowers and so forth. Over table drop-light or standard lamp. Fancy chairs, R. and L. of table. Couch and writing desk R. Couch well downstage R. Desk R. Chair before desk, pencils, paper, pens, and so forth in desk. Fancy sofa pillow on couch. Newspaper, cuspidors, rugs, wastebasket. Full mirror downstage L. Statue of Moorish slave and flower set so as to reflect by mirror. Electric button for call bell in practical circular molding to break away, on return piece L.*

FLOS. [*Discovered before mirror in evening dress, jewels on her hands and at her throat. She is dressing her hair with flowers*] I wonder who my mother was. As I remember her, she was very pretty. I wish she was with me tonight. Charlie has gone for the minister. He's going to tie the knot right in this room. Now it's come down to saying yes, I'm scared maybe I ain't doing right. [*Crosses to couch*] I'd gone home and got Mother Murphy and Ned if they'd let me, but I'll make it all right when the job's done. I'll have money enough so they won't have to work no more. This is a bully book. It's by Laura Jean Libby. It tells about a poor girl just like me, who married and became a duchess. I don't believe I'd marry a Dutchman. [*Charlie enters L.2., closes door and listens. Flossie sitting up with book in lap*] Behold the bridegroom comes. What are you listening for, Prince? Are you scared your mother-in-law's coming upstairs?

CHAR. No, you see I have no business in the room. They are very strict at this hotel. I didn't dare to register you as my wife.

FLOS. Well, I should say not. Where's the preacher? The crimp is all coming out of my hair. [*Crosses to mirror*]

CHAR. [*Lighting cigaret*] See here, Flossie, if my friend doesn't come pretty soon we can't get married till we get over the pond.

FLOS. No, sir, you don't float me across no pond on promises.

CHAR. Now come, Flossie. Don't be obstinate. It will be only a matter of a few days.

FLOS. Yes, I know, but there's lots can happen in a few days. Suppose I get seasick, or the ship goes down?

CHAR. Then we will die in each other's arms and sink together.

FLOS. If we do the fishes will find my marriage certificate buttoned under my shirtwaist. I ain't putting myself up as any saint, Prince. I may not be as polite and soft-spoken as some girls. I use words that ain't writ down in the Bible, but I say my prayers when I don't forget about it, and when I do I ask God to keep me right for the man I'm going to call husband.

CHAR. Yes, you're a diamond in the rough, and, hang it all, I like you, Floss. I'll be truthful with you if nothing more.

FLOS. Haven't you always been?

CHAR. Not exactly. You see the fact of the matter is I can't marry anyone. [*Crosses L.*]

FLOS. Then what have you been foolin' around for all this time?

CHAR. Because I am madly in love with you.

FLOS. This book says, "Beware of him who speaks of love and not of marriage vows."

CHAR. Then you believe that book?

FLOS. Yes. It is a very good book.

CHAR. Hang what the good book says. Come over here and sit beside me. [*Seats himself on couch*]

FLOS. Promise me you'll not get fresh. That you won't start no lolly-gaggin'.

CHAR. I promise.

FLOS. Cross your heart.

CHAR. Cross my heart. [*Makes sign of cross on right side*]

FLOS. Get out. Your heart ain't on that side.

CHAR. No, but it will be when you sit down here. [*Making room on his left*]

FLOS. [*Sits down timidly and adjusts skirts; raises her eyes*] Why don't you tell me I look nice?

CHAR. You certainly are a swell looker for a kid.

FLOS. Get out. I ain't no kid. I'm most seventeen.

CHAR. Old enough to smoke. Have a cigaret?

FLOS. The old woman would beat hell out of me if she saw me smoke one of these. [*Taking cigaret*]

CHAR. But she won't see you. [*Putting his arm about her; his hand on her bare arm*]

FLOS. Take that cigaret-holder off my shoulder.

CHAR. A cigaret-holder?

FLOS. Yes, your hand. It's all stained from the smoke. [*Pushing Charlie's hand and moving down*]

CHAR. That's nicotine.

FLOS. What's nicotine?

CHAR. Nicotine comes from the cigaret. It's poison.

FLOS. Then why do you offer them to me? [*Looking at cigaret in her hand*]

CHAR. Oh, they won't hurt you.

FLOS. They won't do me no good. Let me see you make it come out of your nose.

CHAR. What?

FLOS. The smoke.

CHAR. Oh. [*Blows smoke through nose. Flossie laughs*] What are you laughing at?

FLOS. When you do that you look just like the Devil.

CHAR. [*Springing to his feet, crosses C.*] So I am, the Devil in the form of a man. God placed such bewitching creatures as you on this earth to make men what I am. Come, you have tempted me long enough. You must be mine. [*Starts forward and as Flossie springs up, clasps her in his arms*]

FLOS. Quit now. You hurt me. Let me go. What are you looking like that for, Charlie? You frighten me. [*Begins to sob and cry*]

CHAR. [*Releasing her*] Oh, if you are going to cry, I'll let you alone.

FLOS. [*Snuffling and smiling through her tears*]   Then I'll keep on crying all the time. [*Sits on couch*] My, but you're roughhouse when you get started. Worse than the Chatham Square gang what took me to Coney Island.

CHAR. See here, Floss, why can't you look at this matter in the right light? I want you to go to Europe with me. I'll give you everything money can buy. Diamonds, fine clothes, horses, carriages, servants—nothing but a good time. Christmas every day in the year.

FLOS. You must want to work Santa Claus overtime.

CHAR. I'll be your Santa Claus, and I'll not kick at my job. Come, what do you say? Haven't I given you beautiful presents already? Have you no gratitude? What more do you want?

FLOS. A plain band of gold on that finger.

CHAR. You shall have it. Anything else?

FLOS. Yes, a man with a long face, who will tell you how to put it on.

CHAR. Rot. You'll have to cut out the man with the long face.

FLOS. Then you will have to fill up the pond before you'll get me to cross it.

CHAR. See here, do you think I'm going to be foiled by a strip of a girl like you? Are you aware I have you in my power? That I can do with you as I please?

FLOS. Maybe you can if you are good to me, but if you speak like that and get me mad, I'll tear something. [*Rips lace on sleeve*]

CHAR. Don't destroy that dress. It cost me a hundred dollars.

FLOS. [*Ripping lace on other sleeve*]   I don't care if it cost a thousand. If you get me riled, I'll tear it off. [*Throws herself on couch in convulsion of sobs*]

CHAR. See here, my fine lady, if you are going to fight me like that, I'll place you back on the Bowery in rags.

FLOS. [*Springing up*]   Send me back. There's where I belong. Give me my old garments and let me go back. Then such men as you may pass me by. My soul will feel more secure with my body clothed in rags. [*Crosses C.*] There's the flowers you gave me, your rings, your diamond necklace, your dirty old picture—all you gave me. I'll give you everything, everything but what you want. [*Tearing jewels, locket, and so forth, and throwing them at Charlie; then picking up skirts and jumping couch, exits behind curtain R.2. Charlie starts after her. Ned pounds on door off L.*]

CHAR. [*Pauses and looks over shoulder in frightened manner*]   Who's there?

FLOS. [*Off R.*]   The Devil come to claim his own. Take that, and that, and that. [*Throwing shoes, corset, stockings, petticoats, undergarments, one at a time, through curtain at Charlie, who dodges these missiles C. Ned keeps up a vigorous hammering at the door. Flossie off R.*] If you come in here, Charles Montgomery, I'll kill you. [*Throwing her high-heeled shoe and striking Charlie*]

CHAR.   Oh, I'm not coming in, don't worry. [*Rubbing his arm*] Be still, Floss, there is someone at the door. [*Crosses and listens at door with back to window*] Who's there, I say. [*Aside*] Whoever it was, they have gone. [*Stands listening. Ned, as messenger boy, appears on fire escape, breaks window and springs into the room*]

CHAR. [*Staggers back and crosses down R.*]   What is the meaning of this?

NED.   I came to deliver a message, sir. [*Holding out book*]

CHAR.   Is that any excuse for breaking in like a burglar?

NED.   Yes, when the door is barred. My message is important.

CHAR.   Well, sir, what is it?

NED.   The Cooper family have elected me a committee of one to settle accounts with you and bring home my sister.

CHAR.   Come, boy, get out of here or I will throw you out of the window.

NED. [*Pulling revolver and pointing at Charlie*]   I don't think you will.

CHAR.   Put that down. What are you going to do?

NED.   Ask my sister a few little questions. If you have harmed her I'm going to kill you. [*Takes doorkey from door L.2., puts it in pocket*]

FLOS. [*Entering R. from behind curtains in her old dress and crosses, kneeling by Ned*]   No, Ned, don't do that. See, I am ready to go home with you.

CHAR.   Take that pistol away from him, girl. You can't tell what he may do. The boy's gone mad.

NED.   Mad, you bet I am. Why didn't you come and take it away?

CHAR.   If I could only get over and touch that bell.

NED.   I'll let you touch it. The answer might not be just as you expect.

CHAR.   On second thought, I guess I'll let it alone.

NED.   Yes, I think you'd better.

FLOS.   Ned, put up that pistol and take me home.

NED.   Not if you've disgraced it.

FLOS.   No, no, Ned. He tempted me. But see here are my old beads. The cross is still over my heart. You know my promise to Mother. No, no, Ned. I gave him back his clothes and jewels. I would not pay the price he asked.

NED. [*Putting up pistol in back pocket, raising Flossie to her feet and kissing her*]   I believe you, my sister. See here in his own handwriting is a plan to ruin you. [*Hands Flossie message*]

FLOS. [*Reading*]   A mock marriage. So you never meant fair by me from the first. [*Charlie springs forward and overpowers Ned. Takes pistol from him*]

NED.   Quick, Flossie, touch the bell. [*Charlie strikes Ned on head with the pistol. Ned places hand to head and falls across couch unconscious*]

CHAR. [*Dashes to Flossie and pulls her from bell*]   Come away from there.

FLOS.   Too late, I have rung the bell.

CHAR.   See, I've quieted your brother. If you give an alarm, I'll treat you the same way.

FLOS.   Oh, Ned, Ned. [*Throwing her arm about Ned*] Speak to me, Ned. Coward, to strike a boy like that. [*Picks up flower urn and dumps out flowers and breaks it over Charlie's head. Charlie catches Flossie by throat and chokes her*]

FLOS.   Help. Let me go. You are choking me. [*Charlie drops Flossie L. Bellboy pounds at door. Charlie picks up petticoat, binds it about Flossie's head, drags her off behind curtains R.2. Returns, takes key from Ned's pocket, opens door part way*]

BELL.   Did you ring?

CHAR.   Yes. You will find a well dressed Chinaman in the smoking-room waiting to see Charles Montgomery. Send him up.

BELL.   Yes, sir. [*Charlie closes door and locks it. Ned rolls off couch and tries to rise. Charlie springs forward, turns Ned on his face and ties his hands behind him with strings. He takes strings from corset that lay on the floor*]

NED.   You'll get all that's coming to you when I get away. Where's my sister?

CHAR.   She's thinking over the folly of her ways.

NED.   Do you ever think?

CHAR.   No, I'm too busy to think.

NED.   You'll have plenty of time to think in the place where I'm going to put you.

CHAR.   Where's that? Over in Blackwell's?

NED.   No, in the cell my father left vacant in Sing Sing. [*Bellboy knocking at door*]

CHAR.   Now if you holler when that door opens, I'll use this on you. [*Shows pistol*]

NED.   Oh, you'll find me game. I'll not squeal. I ain't found out all I want to yet. [*Charlie drags Ned up and throws him beneath window, pulls portieres about him and opens the door*]

BELL. [*Off L.*]   Here's your Chinaman.

CHAR. Come in, Sam. [*Sam enters L.2. with long, blue canvas bag over shoulder. Charlie shuts door and locks it. Sam unshoulders his pack*] Sam, I can't do anything with that girl. We will have to take her away in that bag. Do you think you can carry her out without creating suspicion?

SAM. I am strong. If she is still, it will all go well.

CHAR. Oh, she'll be still all right. What have you in there?

SAM. Nothing but odds and ends. [*Showing lanterns, parasol, Chinese lace*]

CHAR. Good, you will find her in there. Hide the contents of your bag under the bed.

SAM. That's my business, always to hide something.

CHAR. It pays you well.

SAM. Maybe. I don't know. We will tell better in the end. [*Exits R.2., behind curtain. Bellboy knocks at door L.2. Charlie opens door L.2.*]

BELL. [*Off L.*] Here's your cord and wrapping paper, sir. [*Hands folded heavy paper and ball of cord to Charlie*]

CHAR. You're a good boy. Tell them at the desk not to have the maid bother us in the morning. We may sleep late.

BELL. [*Off L.*] Yes, sir.

CHAR. [*Shuts door*] Now, young man. I'll fix you so you can't walk in your sleep. You might fall out of a window. [*Pulls Ned to his feet, sets him in chair, and commences to bind him to chair, down C.*]

NED. Why don't you have the Chink put me in the bag?

CHAR. I'm afraid you'd kick.

NED. You bet I would. If I had a pair of spurs I'd ride his neck.

SAM. [*Enters R.2.*] What, one more fellow? I didn't bargain for two.

CHAR. Oh, this fellow don't count.

NED. Don't I? I can count Chinese all right. Yip son, yip soik, yip sa, that means I wouldn't give three cents for a pigtail.

SAM. Boy foolem all time. He no care.

CHAR. Have you a pill that will make him sleep?

NED. Yes, roll me a couple so I can dream I'm wealthy.

SAM. [*Producing two pills, taking one out between thumb and forefinger*] You take this you think you're Morgan.

NED. If I was, I'd scuttle every ship that carried Chinamen.

CHAR. Force it in his mouth while I hold his head. [*Sam tries to put pill in Ned's mouth. Ned bites his finger, spits out pill*]

SAM. Oh. [*Jumps about shaking his hand*] Muc j-er hy—pink-I-tye—muley-coy—wene—I—jar—we—fow—gemar.

CHAR. Did he bite you?

SAM. Yes, he bites like a mad dog.

CHAR. Did he swallow it?

NED. I swallowed something. I don't know whether it was the pill or the end of the Chink's finger. Whatever it was, I'm going to throw it up. Oh, Lord, ain't I sick. [*Coughing and gagging*]

CHAR. I'll just put this bell on the bum as an extra precaution. Give me that big knife of yours. [*Sam pulls big knife from up his sleeve. Charlie takes it, pushes blade behind button of bell, hits back of blade with butt of revolver and cuts off button and wire*] Is the girl ready? [*Handing knife to Sam*]

SAM. She all right.

CHAR. Bring her along then. The boy's all right. [*Sam exits R.2. Charlie unlocks door, puts key on outside, turns out electric lights. White light streams in from hall on Ned who hangs head as if asleep. Charlie ties handkerchief over his mouth, gives his head a couple of pushes*] That pill fixed him. All right, come on, Sam. [*Sam raises curtain R.2.; dull red gleam streams out. Sam lowers curtain, goes back. Lights seen to go out. Sam bowed with bag on his back filled with dummy to represent Flossie's length. Staggers out and exits L.2. in the ray of white light that streams in from L. Charlie shuts and-locks door on outside. Lights very low, stage quite dark. Noise of cars and city bustle in the distance. Clock striking twelve*]

NED. [*Tumbles chair over and tumbles about floor. Gets handkerchief off his mouth by rubbing it on leg of table*] Help, help! If I could only get free. [*Pounding his forehead against desk*] If I could break this chair and find something to cut my hands loose. [*Working downstage and crushing legs of chair by pounding them on legs of table*] Help, help. [*Suddenly the light is turned on and Flossie is seen center with her hand on the student's lamp bending over table, looking down at Ned who lies panting on floor.*]

FLOS. Ned, Ned, my brother. Don't you know me? [*Kneeling by Ned*]

NED. Yes, Flossie. Where did you come from?

FLOS. That room. [*Pointing to R.2.*]

NED. I thought you was in the bag.

FLOS. I got out while they was giving you the pill. Where's your knife?

NED. In this pocket. Hurry, cut me free.

FLOS. [*Gets knife from pocket, starts to cut the cords that bind him*] Hold still now, or you'll hurt yourself.

NED. How did you fool them, Floss?

FLOS. I wrapped a heavy statue of Venus in the bed-clothes, put it in the bag and hid under the bed.

NED. [*Springing to his feet and trying door*] Brave girl, you've saved us both. The door's locked from the outside.

FLOS. Ring the bell.

NED. There's no bell to ring. Stay here. I'll give the alarm. [*Springs out of window*]

FLOS. Ned, Ned, don't leave me alone.

NED. I'll only be gone a minute. [*Goes down ladder. Charlie unlocking door outside L.2.*]

FLOS. What's that? [*Stops and listens*] Someone is unlocking the door, they are coming back. [*Key heard rattling in lock. Flossie starts to exit R.2.; Charlie enters, followed by Sam*]

CHAR. [*Throws door open, grabs Flossie*] Smart, ain't you. I've got you this time. [*Flossie screams; Charlie places hand over her mouth, throws her on couch*] Quick, Sam, the chloroform. That's the quickest. [*Sam throws down bag, produces bottle from folds of his frock and administers chloroform*] The boy has escaped. He has given the alarm. We are in a trap.

SAM. No, we go up, not down. Lock the door.

CHAR. [*Locks door*] What do you mean?

SAM. The roof. We are safe there; it is dark.

CHAR. I see! You mean the fire escape?

SAM. Yes.

CHAR. But the girl?

SAM. You go quick. I carry her. [*Ned and bellboy pounding on door L.2. Charlie exits, fire escape and up ladder. Sam picks up Flossie, throws her across his shoulder. Steps upon chair, from there through the window onto the fire escape and is seen ascending the ladder. Bellboy throws door open, working at pass-key. Ned enters followed by Brown and Mike. Crosses, throws open curtains R.2.*]

BROWN. Too late.

MIKE. Yes, the birds have flown.

NED. They have fooled me this time, but I'll find her if I have to search every den in Chinatown. Mike, you go down the elevator. Brown, go down the stairs. Boy, you go down the fire escape. I'm going on the roof. [*While he is speaking he has picked up the bag and opened it. Just as he finishes, he dumps out figure of Venus, from which bed-quilts fall, leaving the figure lying on the floor in the nude. Ned springs out the window and up the fire escape. Mike throws quilt over Venus and runs down stairs*]

SCENE 3: *Drop in 1.—Roof of the Waldorf-Astoria.*

CHAR. [*Enter R.1.—looks back*] Come on, Sam. They are after us. Someone's coming up the ladder behind you. [*Crosses L.*]

SAM. [*Enter R.1. with Flossie on his shoulders; looks back*] Damn, boy, he come up.

CHAR. We are worse off than we were before. A mile in the air. No way to get down. That boy has alarmed the whole house. We are on top of a hornet's nest.

SAM. We lay the girl down there. Hide behind chimney, catch boy, throw him off.

CHAR. What will we do then?

SAM. Go down same way as we come up. [*Exits L.1. with Flossie*]

CHAR. Good. Hurry, here he comes. [*Hides behind tormentor R.*]

NED. [*Enters R.1.*] I feel as if I was on Washington Monument. If that Chink went down with my sister he'll be caught. If he's up here, I'll find him. [*Charlie enters R. and creeps toward Ned on tiptoes*]

NED. [*Turns, pulls knife*] Hold on there. Your Chinese friend dropped this on the fire escape. He must have known I'd need it. [*Brandishes Sam's big knife. Charlie reaches for pistol*]

NED. Take your hand out of your pocket or I'll cut it off. [*Jumps forward and slashes at Charlie*] Throw 'em up.

CHAR. [*Throws up hands*] You're losing time. The Chinaman is the man you want.

NED. Not so bad as I want you. Show me where he is or I'll cut your buttons off. [*Slashes buttons off of Charlie's coat. Sam enters L.1.—creeps up behind Ned, pinions his arms behind him*]

CHAR. [*Takes knife from Ned*] Good boy, Sam. Now we will throw him down an air shaft. [*Catches Ned by feet, swings around with his back L. Flossie enters L.1. Creeps up behind Charlie*]

NED. Let me go. Help, help. [*Kicks vigorously*]

FLOS. [*Puts hand into Charlie's back pocket and gets his pistol, points it at Sam*] Drop him.

CHAR. [*Looks over his shoulder*] That's what we are going to do—over the edge of the roof.

FLOS. Drop him or I'll shoot. [*Charlie and Sam drop Ned to a sitting position*]

NED. Oh, what did you tell them to drop me for, Floss? They jarred all my teeth loose.

CHAR. [*Pointing L.*] There they come up through that sky light. Quick, Sam, we must fight. [*Flossie looks over her shoulder L.*]

CHAR. [*Grabs pistol from her, swings her into Sam's arms R.*] Take her down the ladder, Sam. I'll hold them off with this. Get my carriage. Don't wait for me. [*Sam exits R.1., dragging Flossie. Charlie crosses to R.1., keeps Ned off with pistol*]

NED. [*Crosses L. beckoning off*] Hurry, fellows! Here they are, quick or they'll get away. [*Charlie turns and exits R.1. Ned follows Charlie off R.1. on the run. Charlie shouts offstage R. Ned enters R.1., staggers C. clutching his arm*]

MIKE. [*Enters L.1.*] What's the matter, Ned? Are you shot?

NED. Yes, he winged me, but I still have a good pair of legs. Come on. [*Exits R.1. on the run. Mother Murphy enters L.1. with Venus in her arms upside down. Runs C. puffing and blowing*]

BROWN. [*Enters L.1. with pistol in his hand*] What did you bring that up here for?

MOTH. Faith, I don't know. Some one yelled "Fire" and I thought I'd save something.

BROWN. You have her upside down, Mother.

MOTH. So I have. All the blood will rush to her head. [*Turns Venus over and wraps her in her shawl. Brown exits R.1. on the run*]

BELL. [*Enters L.1., bare-headed, followed by police officer, with night-stick*] That's her, officer. She stole that out of Number 604.

MOTH. You're a liar. I live at Number 13 Billy-Goat Alley.

OFF. What have you in your arms?

MOTH. Me youngest child, sir.

OFF. How old is she? [*Sizing up the length of the bundle*]

MOTH. I don't know. I can't remember.

OFF. You can't remember?

MOTH. She is just getting her teeth, sir.

OFF. [*Taps Venus with night-stick*] My, but she must be a hard nut for her age.

MOTH. She has stiffening of the joints, sir.

OFF. Well, come on. I'll take you both to the lockup. [*Catches Mother and starts to pull her R. Brown shoots several shots in rapid succession in R.1. entrance*]

OFF. Owo—wo—wo. [*Dodging*] I guess we'll go this way. [*Exits L.1. on the run*]

MOTH. Come back here and help me down. [*Exits L.1. Dark change*]

SCENE 4: *Cellar in Chinatown. Drop in 3. painted like brick basement. Backed by eight-foot platform. Same as used in Act I. Hole 4'x4' cut in drop R.C., backed by prop. Bricks to break away. This hole is eight feet from floor opening onto platform. Door L.C. opening onto platform. Stairs coming down to stage. Return pieces R. and L. painted as wall of brick cellar. Holes representing dog kennels. Dogs chained to these kennels. Bulldog chained to bottom of stairs. Pile of straw up C. Barrel beside stairs, upside down with lighted candle on it. Scene quite dark. Curtain discovers Chinaman in blue trousers held up by belt; white undershirt and bare arms. He is whipping and driving dogs back into kennels with black snake whip.*

SAM. [*Enters from door at top of stairs, descends and picks up candle, holds it aloft and shades eyes with hand*] Prince Charlie, Prince Charlie! All right come down.

CHAR. [*Carrying Flossie in his arms, descends stairway; pauses part way down*] What an ugly brute. Will he bite?

SAM. All right, come on. I no tell him hurt you. He bite by and by. [*Charlie descends and stands Flossie on her feet L.C.*]

FLOS. [*Crying softly, crouches behind Charlie to get away from bulldog*] Don't let him bite me. Please don't. Keep him away.

CHAR. Oh, he's not the only dog here. Look about you. There are other dogs.

FLOS. [*Looking timidly about her as Sam holds candle aloft so she can penetrate the dark corners. She shudders and clings tightly to Charlie's arm*] Yes, I see them and you are the worst looking dog of them all. You, I mean. [*Pointing to Sam. Sam grins and shows teeth*]

CHAR. That's right. Show your teeth.

FLOS. So this is the end of my honeymoon. I would have never believed it. I expect every minute to wake up and find the past few hours a horrid dream.

CHAR. You can wake up if you only say the word. You said you preferred rags to my offer.

FLOS. And so I do. I hate you, Charles Montgomery.

CHAR. Then why do you cling to me?

FLOS. Because I am afraid of the other dogs.

CHAR. Still full of spunk. By my word, I hate to leave you here.

FLOS. You couldn't be so cruel? You wouldn't be as bad as that, would you, Charlie? [*Hands on his shoulder*]

CHAR. Do you know where you are? These dogs are mad. Their bite means a horrible death.

FLOS. I'm much safer with them than I am with you. Go.

CHAR. Come on, Sam. Bring the light. I guess a little of this will cause her to change her mind. [*Starts up stairs*]

FLOS. Please don't take the light. I'm afraid of the dark.

CHAR. Oh, it's not the dark that will hurt you. Are you going to tie her, Sam?

SAM. No. He no let her come up. [*Pointing to bulldog; mounts stairs. Chinaman whips dog back, follows Sam*]

FLOS. [*Clutches him by belt and pulls him back*] Don't go. Stay here. You have a whip, you can keep them away. [*Chinaman raises butt of whip to strike Flossie*]

CHAR. [*Pulls pistol and points at Chinaman*] Hold on, you yellow dog. Strike that girl and I'll blow your brains out. Put down that whip and come up here. [*Chinaman lowers whip, runs up stairs*]

SAM. [*Begins a string of cuss-words at other Chink*] Mucker hy—pink ky tie pepwo w-wow yip.

CHIN. Yip wow—wow yip—pink ky tie—no brow ky tie—mucker hy loo.

SAM. Mucker hy—loo—damn fool. [*Crosses Charlie on steps, followed by other Chinaman. Sam stands on the platform at top of steps and as other Chink passes, Sam kicks him, then stands at top of steps and holds candle for Charlie*]

FLOS. Why didn't you let him strike me. I'm better dead than left here. I shall die of fright.

CHAR. I don't want you to die. I didn't bring you here for that. I want to give you a chance to reflect and be a good girl.

FLOS. Be a bad girl, you mean. Do you think I could give myself to you after what you have done. No, I mean to kill myself.

CHAR. Oh, you wouldn't do that.

FLOS. Don't be too sure. [*Bows head on knees in prayer*]

CHAR. Good night. I said "Good night," Flossie. What are you doing? [*Flossie turns around and holds up the cross from the beads she is saying*]

CHAR. What's that, I can't see?

FLOS. The cross mother gave me the night she ran away.

CHAR. Bah. Cling to it. Lots of good it will do you. [*Turns, runs up stairs and slams door shut. Ray of white light shines under door and into Flossie's face as she remains kneeling and whispering her prayers. Soft music of sacred hymn. Ned heard tapping bricks of rear wall with iron bar on top of platform. Bricks fall to floor one at a time, but Flossie does not turn to see what causes the sound. Soon Ned is seen through the hole, sitting astride the sewer pipe and knocking out bricks. Mike holds a lantern down through a man-hole just above him. Rope hangs from man-hole to platform. Ned takes the lantern from Mike and ties it to the end of rope and lowers it over wall into cellar*]

NED. Flossie, Flossie!

FLOS. [*Turning*] Ned, Ned, my brother. [*Falls fainting on the straw*]

NED. She's down there, Mike. When I tell you fellers to pull, hoist her up. [*Sam, followed by Chinaman, opens door and starts down stairs. Ned pelts them with bricks and holds them at bay until Mike pulls Flossie to safety. Chinaman whirling around center with bulldog fastened by his teeth to the seat of his trousers. Other Chinks around him pelting dog with bricks but hitting the Chink. They are kept busy dodging bricks which Ned throws from above*]

ACT IV.

A palace on the Hudson—one month later. Scene shows old Montgomery summer home. Big stone mansion, well off L. Broad stairway leading to verandah, open doorway off L.2., backed by curtain. Backdrop landscape showing the river. Stone wall covered with ivy, across in 3. Center gateway with large posts. Wood wings R. and L., foliage borders. Rustic table and chairs down L. Garden bench down R. Curtain discovers:

FLOR. [*In summer gown; on the table are flowers which she is sorting*] One whole month since I heard from Charles Montgomery. He has left me in sole possession of this beautiful estate. His infatuation for that doll-faced girl was a lucky thing for me. He will never dare come back to this country with a term in prison staring him in the face.

LEW. [*Lewis, same as character in Act III. Enters L.3.*] Your lunch, madam. Where shall I serve it?

FLOR. Out here, Lewis. The weather is too nice to go indoors. I expect my attorney. You may serve for two.

LEW. I've been wishing to speak to you in private, madam.

FLOR. What is it, Lewis?

LEW. I'm obliged for your bringing me here from the city and paying me big wages, but I must give my notice, madam.

FLOR. Tired of the country life, already?

LEW. Not that. The police watch this place. They make me nervous. I got what you call the Holy Dread. [*Shrugging shoulders*]

FLOR. They are looking for Prince Charlie. You've read the papers. You know what for. They'll not molest you nor I.

LEW. I am not so sure. I am not satisfied.

FLOR. Very well, sir, you may go.

Lew. Thank you.

Flor. When your month is up.

Lew. What? When my month is up. Never. By then I will be in jail six months. [*Shaking head, exits L.2.*]

Flor. Fool, he is easily scared like all the rest. Money will do anything. The police will never molest me. I was careful to cover my moves in the game. Now I am rich, powerful. In the position I have worked so hard to gain. [*Exits R.2. Sam, disguised as common laboring Chinaman in plain blouse, black slouch hat, and small package done up in red bandana handkerchief, enters C., crosses, looks in door without seeing Flora*]

Flor. [*Reenters*]   Here, fellow, what do you want? Get out or I'll set the dogs on you.

Sam. [*Turning and showing teeth in smile*]   I no feared of dogs.

Flor. Sam, I didn't know you. How dare you come here?

Sam. Prince Charlie, he told me, he afraid.

Flor. Then he's in hiding here; didn't go to Europe?

Sam. Europe too far.

Flor. What does he want?

Sam. Money.

Flor. He won't get it.

Sam. I no know.

Flor. I do know.

Sam. I think you got green eyes.

Flor. I like your impudence.

Sam. You hate little girl with big mouth.

Flor. What! Me jealous of that little beggar?

Sam. She no beg, she fight. Her bludder, the littey feller, he fight like hell. He bloken up my business. No good.

Flor. [*Laughing*]   Yes, I read in the paper your business had all gone to the dogs.

Sam. Yes, dogs all gone. By and by police catchey me, catchey you, catchey Prince Charlie. Catch whole damn business.

Flor. Sit down, Sam. I won't let them catch you.

Sam. Me sit beside you? What I catch?

Flor. Catch me, if you do what I ask you. I'll not hurt you. Sit down.

Sam. [*Sits cautiously on end of bench*]   This like old times on Pell Street.

Flor. I want you to give me some of that stuff that puts people to sleep.

Sam. What for? Old man dead. You got plenty money.

Lew. [*Enters L.2.*]   I believe I'm standing on my head. I'm either crazy or I'm back in the Latin quarter in Paris and don't know it. [*Exits L.2. Mother*

Murphy, with an expressman bearing a small tin trunk tied up with rope on his shoulders enters C. Expressman lets trunk down with a thud. It breaks open and old shoes, petticoats, canned goods and so forth fall out. Flora springs up with a scream]

MOTH. Good morning.

FLOR. What are you doing here, woman?

MOTH. I've come to spend my summer vacation, but if you keep boarders with pigtails I'll look up another boarding house. Here, pick up those things. I'll sue you for damages. *[Expressman gets on knees and fires clothes back into trunk, pushing down with foot]*

FLOR. Here, man, take that rubbish out of my grounds; and you, woman, get out before I have you thrown out!

MOTH. Easy now, don't get excited. I was invited here by the gentleman who owns these grounds and I'll not get out.

FLOR. The gentleman who owns this estate is not in this country.

MOTH. Oh, yes, he is. I saw him this very morning.

FLOR. I don't believe you. I shall have you put out. Lewis, oh, Lewis, come here quick! *[Exits L.2. Sam takes bundle and starts for gate C.]*

MOTH. Here, Chineser, where you going?

SAM. I go buy bar of soap for my laundry.

MOTH. You'll have bars in the laundry where you're going and they won't be bars of soap either. Get hold of that trunk and help this man take it in the house or I'll run this umbrella through you. *[Poking Sam with umbrella]*

SAM. What for, you fool? I not got time. I'm busy. *[Starts up]*

MOTH. *[Catches Sam around neck with crook of her umbrella]* Come back here. I'll keep you busy. *[Sam grabs handle of trunk. Mother whacks Sam over back with umbrella and Sam and expressman exit L.2. with trunk, on the run]*

MOTH. I'll show them who's boss around here. This place belongs to me boy, and if he's not here yet I'll take possession in his name. They won't bamboozle Mother Murphy. *[Crash and bump off L.]* There goes me trunk. They let it fall downstairs. *[Picks up skirts and starts to exit up stairs]*

EX. *[Enters L.2. wiping forehead with red handkerchief]* Fifty cents, please.

MOTH. Fifty cents for what?

EX. The trunk.

MOTH. It didn't cost but forty. Look at it, look what's left of it. *[Pointing off L.]* Get out of this or I'll have you arrested for assault and battery. *[Throws expressman off of steps, chases him out of gate C., striking him over head with umbrella]* Fifty cents. I'll give him fifty cents with the bumbershoot. [*Exits L.2. Lewis enters L.2. as if thrown out. Falls down steps. Picks himself up and shakes fist off L.*]

MOTH. [*Off L.*] Out, you pigtailed heathen, out I say. [*Sam stumbles out L.2. with head stuck through an oil painting, broken frame over his shoulders. Mother throws flower pot through door at him*]

FLOR. [*Enters L.2., screaming, with fingers in her ears. Crosses R. to Lewis and Sam, who are behind bench*] See, she has ruined my beautiful oil painting of the battle of Santuary. [*Removes wreck of painting from Sam's neck*]

LEW. I think it is the battle of "Who'll run," ma'am.

FLOR. Why don't you protect me, Lewis? Why don't you put her out?

LEW. Didn't you see me put her out?

SAM. Come outside, Irish. [*Brandishing big knife. Mother throws a lamp at Sam through door. Sam jumps aside, Lewis catches lamp*]

FLOR. Run, Lewis, run and get the police. The woman's crazy.

LEW. We are going to be dispossessed. [*Looking at lamp and picking up wreck of frame, flower pot, and so forth*]

CHAR. [*Enters C. in excited manner. Wears long linen duster, driving gloves, cap, with carriage whip*] Flora, Sam, quick. I'm followed. I must hide.

SAM. Let us all hide.

LEW. In the house? [*Pointing*] Not me!

CHAR. What's the trouble here?

FLOR. That Irish woman. She's gone mad, taken possession of the house.

CHAR. I am still master here, though I am a refugee. They have me cornered and I must hide. This is the last place they will search. Follow me. We will take care of the Irish. [*Exits L.2. followed by Flora. Lewis falls upstairs, dropping bundle of wreckage, Sam has his knife out and is cautious and looking for a fight. He exits L.1.*]

MOTH. [*Enters, creeping about corner of house L.1. She has sleeves rolled up and an axe*] Now, where the divil did they go? [*Carriage containing Ned, Flossie, and Gertrude, all in stylish clothes, drives up to gate C.*]

NED. [*Jumps out, assists Gertrude to alight*] Come on, mother. [*Flossie jumps out by herself. Gertrude enters gate with arm about Flossie, who is R., and Ned, who is L. Carriage draws off R.*]

MOTH. May your shadows never grow less, but that's a sight for my poor old eyes. The mother and her children united at last.

NED. Don't cry. You shall be our mother still.

FLOS. Yes, our grandmother.

MOTH. What's that? A grandmother? I'll have you to understand I'm only four and twenty.

NED. Mother, we are rich. The lawyers tell me I've won my suit.

MOTH. Why didn't you win a swallow-tailed one while you were at it? You look like a Baxter dude; and Flossie, your heels are so high you'll break your neck.

NED. You don't understand, Mother. We have come to take the law on these people. This home is to be ours when the papers are served.

MOTH. Well, I've quit selling papers, but I've got possession here and that is nine points of the law.

GERT. My children would not wait. They were so eager to see this estate they have fought so hard to gain.

FLOS. Yes, I'm going to have Prince sent up for ten years. It would have been cheaper for him to marry me.

NED. You're a silly goose, Floss. Now you've got the money without the man.

FLOS. What is money to me without the man? [*Crosses L., looks off*]

GERT. [*Shaking head*] I believe she loves him still.

MOTH. She's a fool. A girl of her age will fall in love with anything that wears breeches.

NED. [*Sitting at table, pounding bell*] Let us have some refreshments. Is there no one at home? Sit down, Mother. Sit down, Floss.

MOTH. Hist, Ned, there's a hornet's nest around here somewhere. You don't want to stir it up.

NED. What are you doing with that axe?

MOTH. There is a monkey here with a tail as long as me arm. I'm going to amputate it.

LEW. [*Enter L.2.*] What did you ring for? This is no public garden.

NED. I rang because I was hungry. Bring out all you've got and be quick about it.

LEW. You're a loafer. I'm not here to serve you.

NED. Then I'll hire somebody that will. I'm proprietor of this joint. [*Crosses*] There's your first week's wages, including tips. Now get to work. [*Pulls out big roll of bills, hands Lewis several*]

LEW. Five, ten, fifteen, twenty-two, twenty-seven [*Throwing up both hands and thrusting money in pocket*], I haven't time to count it. Oh, Lewie, Lewie, you must be smoking! You are a gentleman, monsieur. I serve you for the rest of my life. Ladies, what is your pleasure?

FLOS. Bring me a cocktail with a cherry and some low-necked clams.

GERT. Floss, I'm surprised at you.

LEW. She shall have them, madam, if I dig them myself. One minute I will serve you with wine. [*Exits L.2.*]

NED. Hear that, ma, we're going to have wine. I tell you, girls, money is the thing that talks. [*Pulling a big handful of bills and commencing to shuffle them like cards*]

MOTH. If it could beat that waiter talking I wouldn't want that roll under me pillow. Me, oh my, that must be a million dollars. Think of all that talking to I need.

NED. Here, Mother, buy yourself a house and lot. [*Hands Mother several bills*]

MOTH. You're getting extravagant. You'll be broker in the morning and back to selling papers. How much is this? I can't read.

NED. Sixteen hundred dollars.

MOTH. [*Drops axe and places hand to her head, staggers over and falls on bench*] Do you want me to die of heart disease? [*Turns back to Ned, pulls up dress and stuffs money in her stocking. She has on old stockings, one red and white; the other light blue. Lewis enters in rush, L.2. Places tray with bottle of wine and glasses on table. Ned, throwing feet up on table and tilting chair back and peeling off bill from roll, which he hands Lewis. Lewis stumbles up stairs in his haste to exit, L.2.*] What's the matter with that fellow? He must have the blind staggers.

NED. He has the disease they all get when they see the long green.

MOTH. I'm going to look for that Chineser. [*Ascends steps L.*]

GERT. My children! You have just been restored to me. I don't wish to deny you any pleasure, but the wine cup will be your ruin. Promise me you will drink no more.

FLOS. I promise, mama. I thought it was the swell thing to do.

LEW. [*Enters L.2. with bottle of wine*] Pardon, monsieur, if I have kept you waiting. This is one hundred years old.

NED. No wonder you was a long time getting it. Take it into the house and drink it yourself.

LEW. We—we, Gates—[*Exit L.2.*]

NED. I'm a Gate this time, next time I'll be a door. I guess I'll introduce myself. [*Starts up steps*]

GERT. Where are you going, Ned?

NED. To look for trouble. You stay here.

GERT. Better wait till your attorney arrives.

NED. Tell them I've taken possession. [*Exits L.2.*]

CHAR. [*Enters L.1., doffs cap*] Ladies, this is a pleasure, I assure you.

GERT. Charles Montgomery, what are you doing here? [*Raising her arm and throwing it about Flossie*]

CHAR. If you will permit me to be so bold, I might ask you that same question.

GERT. We are here to claim our own. The courts have granted the estate to my son.

CHAR. Indeed, and what is to become of me?

GERT. That is for the courts to decide. If you are caught, you will likely go to the penitentiary, where such men as you belong.

CHAR. See here, woman, I'm desperate. I know I've wronged you, but you've had revenge enough. I'm ruined. You have all the money and property which is rightfully mine, I am at your mercy. These grounds are surrounded by officers of the law. Your damned husband and boy have run me into a trap. My only chance to escape is that you will aid me. Come, what do you say?

GERT. No! After the disgrace, the sorrows you have brought into my life, I have no feeling for you but contempt. I shall be glad to see you punished.

CHAR. Then you refuse?

GERT. Yes.

CHAR. And will tell them you have seen me here?

GERT. Yes.

FLOS. I won't, Charlie. I'll cut my tongue out first. Please, mama, let him go.

GERT. I'm not stopping him. Look into my face. Do you love this man, Flossie? [*Flossie bows head, begins to cry*] Look, Charles Montgomery; see what your lying tongue has done for this poor child! Robbed her of an affection that should have been bestowed upon someone more worthy. A love so pure and strong it would shield you now. For her sake, go, and our lips shall remain sealed.

CHAR. I love the girl and would make her my wife. Give her to me and I will try and atone for the past.

GERT. Too late. I would rather see her dead. You are a criminal. You have nothing but disgrace to offer her.

CHAR. You're right, I'm a lost soul. There's not a ray of light or hope before me.

FLOS. [*Advancing and giving him her hand*] I shall pray for you every night, Charlie, just as long as I live.

CHAR. Good-by. I shall never be taken alive, but if I escape, your kind words and the knowledge of the love I once cast aside will help me to be a better man. Good-by. [*Bends and kisses Flossie's hand, crosses up to gate. Flossie puts handkerchief to eyes, crosses down L. to Gertrude who puts arm about her*]

ALB. [*Enters C. in neat business suit*] Hold on. I have something to say to you before you go.

CHAR. Albert Cooper, what the hell do you want?

ALB. Satisfaction for the long days and nights I lay in a cell and grieved for a wife and children you stole from me, and then left to die of starvation and hunger.

CHAR. Can't you forgive me? Your wife and daughter have done so.

GERT. It is false. I did not forgive you; neither has my daughter. We were only sorry to see you fall so low.

ALB. There are some wrongs you can't ask a man to forgive. Come, Charles Montgomery, you must give me satisfaction. [*Throws off coat. Flora enters L.2. Stands at top of steps*]

CHAR. If it is any satisfaction to see me die, look with all your eyes. [*Pulls pistol, attempts to shoot himself in heart*]

ALB. [*Springs forward and wrestles with him*] Kill yourself? Not if I know it! [*Pistol is discharged between them*]

FLOR. [*Places hand to her breast*] Charlie, Charlie, you've shot me! [*Falls to porch and rolls down the steps. Albert and Charlie separate, Albert L. with pistol, Charlie R. Lewis enters to top of steps*]

CHAR. Cooper, that is your work. You have killed that woman.

ALB. [*Kneels by Flora, places hand on heart*] Her heart beats. She's not dead. Quick, someone, get a doctor. We will take her in the house. [*Mike and Brown enter C. Mike crosses L. to Albert. Charlie starts up C.*]

BROWN. Stop. Where are you going?

CHAR. To get a doctor. That woman has been shot.

BROWN. Who shot her?

CHAR. That man with the pistol.

FLOR. [*Raising herself and clinging to steps*] Help, I want water. Charlie, I'm dying. Why did you shoot me?

BROWN. She says you shot her.

CHAR. She don't know what she is saying. It was an accident.

BROWN. Oh, then this man didn't shoot her?

CHAR. No, we struggled for the weapon. I meant that bullet for myself. [*Gertrude kneels by Flora. Lewis enters L.2. with glass of water; hands to Gertrude, who places it to Flora's lips. The water turns red as she drinks*]

FLOS. Oh, why doesn't someone run for a doctor?

GERT. It would do no good. The woman is dying.

CHAR. I wish it was me instead of you, partner. We've played a losing game.

FLOR. I got what I deserved. I made you what you are, Charlie. It was all my cursed love for gold. Lots of good it will do you beggars. [*Staggering to her feet*] Take me inside the house, Lewis, away from these. Don't look at me with pity. I don't want it. If you gain possession here, it will be over my dead body. I hate and defy you all. [*Lewis, supporting Flora, leads her off L.2.*]

CHAR. Let me go to her. [*Starts L.*]

MIKE. No, you must come with me. I have a warrant for your arrest. [*Produces handcuffs*]

FLOS. [*Crosses C.*] Let him see her, Mike, just a few minutes, for my sake.

CHAR. I'll not run away or do myself any harm. I promise you that.

FLOS. Please, Mike. [*On her knees*]

MIKE. All right, go ahead.

LEW. [*Enters L.2.*] Quick, sir, the madam wants you. She is dying. [*Charlie exits L.2. followed by Lewis and Mike. Flossie bows head crying*]

ALB. [*Throwing arms about her*] Don't cry, daughter. He's not worth it.

FLOS. Father, have you that rose I gave you the first night we met?

ALB. Yes. It's been over my heart every hour since then. [*Hands Flossie rose from inside pocket*]

FLOS. It shall remain on mine till the judgment-day.

MOTH. [*Enters L.1. leading Sam with a rope about his neck, his hands tied behind his back, and Ned hanging back on his cue*] Come along here, you son of Pekin.

NED. Here he is. This is the man you want. Go 'long, Sam. Get a bag, Floss, and we'll throw him in the river. [*Brown takes rope from Mother and pulls Sam over R. Handcuffs him*]

NED. Hello, father, what's the news?

ALB. I've the deeds for your property, my son. [*Handing legal papers*] We have received justice at last. My little family is united. We will begin a new life from today. [*Messenger boy enters gate followed by newsboys and characters from the Bowery*]

NED. Father, this is the gang from Chatham Square. I've invited them up to dinner.

THE END

NO MOTHER TO GUIDE HER

By Lillian Mortimer

SCENE PLOT

ACT I

Landscape drop in full stage. A set house on the left side of stage. Porch with raised platform if convenient. A fence with gate center, up stage in front of drop. There is a garden bench or chair down R. If desired there is a tree center. Other furniture to dress stage as a farmer's home.

ACT II

Should be a dense woods, with a gypsy camp in foreground. There should be a tree over left. Or left center. A tripod with fire effect under kettle is right. There may be the back of an old wagon showing, if available and desired. Stumps or kegs to represent same about the stage. And a small tent up stage.

ACT III

Livingstone's room, as described in Act.

ACT IV

A wood, or rocky pass, or almost anything of this type will suffice. Or same set or same exterior used in former act will do. Except there is a cabin on stage left.

PROPERTY PLOT

ACT I

Small kitchen table, and cover. Two chairs. Two books. Double-barrelled shotgun. Newspapers. Rocking chair. Sofa. Market basket. Suitcase. Bundle of sticks.

ACT II

Four grass mats if available. Three stumps, or kegs. Bass drum for thunder.

ACT III

Telephone. Fancy chairs and rocker. Dresser, if available. Carpet and rugs. Center table and cover. Fire log, andirons and tongs. Small clock. Glass for crash off stage. Soap box. Step ladder. Hassock. Rope.

ACT IV

Table. Stumps, etc. Drum—bass. Kitchen chair.

CAST OF CHARACTERS

JOHN LIVINGSTONE, *a bank robber*

RALPH CARLTON, *in love with Rose*

SILAS WATERBURY, *the town constable*

JAKE JORDAN, *an escaped convict*

FARMER DAY, *Rose's father*

ROSE DAY, *secretly married to Ralph*

LINDY JANE SMITHERS, *in love with Silas*

BESS SINCLAIR, *a shop girl*

MOTHER TAGGER, *a tool of Livingstone*

BUNCO, *comedy soubrette*

HARRY PATENT

TOMMY FISCHER

WALTER PERKINS } *the sweet-singing gypsies (off stage)*

FRANK CALDWELL

PARSON THOMAS

OFFICER KEOUGH

POLICEMAN TODD } *officers*

CAPTAIN HENNESSY

TIME: PRESENT.

PLACE: NEW YORK STATE.

SYNOPSIS OF SCENES

ACT I: HOME OF ROSE DAY. THE MURDER.

ACT II: THE GYPSY CAMP. TORNADO.

ACT III: IN THE BIG CITY. THE BANK ROBBERY.

ACT IV: OLD HUT IN THE HILLS. THE WAGES OF SIN.

ACT I.

AT RISE: *Lively music. Lights, sunshine. Strong yellow lights. Farmer Day discovered seated on rocker on porch L. reading paper. Lindy standing at gate shading her eyes. Has sunbonnet on.*

DAY. See anything of Rose, Lindy?

LINDY. No, and it's nigh about time she was comin' home. Three weeks is a long enough visit fer any gal. There comes that city feller. I don't like him. I think he's set on makin' love to Rose.

DAY. Well Lindy, he seems like a pretty good feller.

LINDY. Good? Shucks I wouldn't trust him as fur as I can see with my eyes shut. If I was a gal I'd ruther have that other feller. He's lookin' mighty calf-like at our Rose too. Oh but I'll be glad when both of 'em is gone. I don't like keepin' summer boarders nohow. [*Livingstone enters gate up C.*]

LIV. Ah, Miss Lindy, how well you are looking. [*Lindy business. Crosses R.C. and sits*] Reading the evening paper, Mr. Day? What's the news? [*Livingstone standing R.; business with shotgun*]

DAY. Hain't read none yet. Got a job?

LIV. No, but Farmer Bailey wants someone to oversee his farm next month. I can have that if I want it.

DAY. That's a good job—better take it.

LIV. I think I shall. I've got some money put away but I don't want to use it till I get married, to buy a little home.

LINDY. [*Sitting under tree, C.*] And how much do you happen to have, young feller?

LIV. Oh, about ten thousand.

LINDY. Make it yerself?

LIV. No, my grandmother left it to me.

LINDY. More fool she.

LIV. Well I'm not a fellow to beat around the bush Mr. Day. I'm in love with your daughter.

LINDY. There now, what did I tell you?

LIV. I'd like to marry her—buy a little home and settle down.

LINDY. Well, ef Rose was my gal—

DAY. Hush, Lindy. Wall—I'm in no hurry fer my gal to marry, Mr. Livingstone, but whoever wins her heart kin have her—I'll not stand in her way.

And when I'm gone there'll be a tidy sum for her too, so she won't be beholdin' to her husband.

LIV. Oh, you have some money in the bank here? [*Crosses down below steps L.*]

DAY. No siree. I don't trust no banks with my money. I·keep it right here in the house.

LINDY. Yes, and a bigger fool I never see. Some morning you'll wake up with yer throat cut from ear to ear.

DAY. I'm not afraid, Lindy. [*Silas enters, glasses on and newspaper open*]

SILAS. Gosh—see the paper?

LINDY. What's up?

SILAS. Stebbin's bank broke into and robbed at three o'clock this morning.

DAY. You don't say? [*Looks at his paper*]

SILAS. Yes siree. Found the watchman tied hand and foot.

DAY. Get much?

SILAS. Five hundred dollars.

LINDY. Land sakes. [*Looking over Si's shoulder at paper*]

SILAS. Town constables are lookin' up the records of all strangers in town. [*Looks at Livingstone*]

LIV. [*Laughs*] Lucky I can give a clear account of myself—I was in bed by ten o'clock last night.

DAY. That's what ye were, Mr. Livingstone, but yer pardner wasn't in last night, was he? [*Rises*]

LIV. [*Crosses R.*] No, he hasn't come back from the city yet. I expect him tonight. [*Silas busy C. following Livingstone*]

DAY. I guess I was right about the banks, eh Lindy? [*Exits in house*]

LINDY. Oh, I don't know. [*Crosses to house*]

SILAS. Oh—that reminds me—

LINDY. Comin' inside, Si?

SILAS. Don't mind ef I do. Got something to say to you, confidential. He, he.

LINDY. Oh you get aout. [*Exits in house*]

SILAS. Wait for me Lindy. [*Trips on stairs*] Dern them steps. [*Exits after Lindy*]

LIV. [*Crosses to house*] Well, I suppose the safest thing for me to do would be to light out. That was the neatest job I've done in some time, and if I wasn't so in love with that girl Rose—[*Mother T. enters gate from C.L., looks round, sees Livingstone*]

MOTH. T. St. John. [*Weird music*]

Liv. Mother! What are you doing here? Anything wrong with the money?

Moth. T. That's safe enough but I'm afraid we had better move on. They'll be sure to suspect us.

Liv. Well they can't prove a thing. I want you to hang around for a day or two—I may have work for you. But don't come here again unless I give you the signal. You shouldn't leave the camp.

Moth. T. But I must have a leetle whiskey, my boy—a leetle drop of whiskey. I can't send anybody—[*Close to him*]

Liv. Whiskey? Why you're stupid with whiskey now. [*Crosses to R.*]

Moth. T. Cruel boy—I haven't had a drop today. [*Follows him R.*]

Liv. Bah!

Moth. T. It's the beautiful truth, I swear.

Liv. Shut up. Here. [*Gives her flask*] Now be careful. Don't get drunk and blab.

Moth. T. Trust me, darling. Whiskey makes Mother Tagger's brain work. Without it, it would stop. [*Drinks, puts bottle in apron pocket*]

Liv. Well, be careful.

Moth. T. I have some news for you. Fine news—he, he, he.

Liv. Well, stop your cackling and tell me.

Moth. T. The child is dead.

Liv. [*Crosses L.—then back to her*] Sh-hh—How did you manage it?

Moth. T. With those hands. Choked the life out of it. Ah—it's so easy to wring their little white necks. I love to hear them sputter and choke—He, he, he.

Liv. [*Crosses L.*] You make my blood run cold. Where is the body?

Moth. T. Buried in the wood darling. Buried where the beautiful violets grow. Ha, ha, ha. [*Music stops*]

Liv. Well, the kid's done for and if the girl causes me any more trouble she'll go the same way.

Moth. T. Where is she now?

Liv. I left her in New York—the fool.

Moth. T. Ah—young blood—young blood—he, he, he. [*Drinks*]

Liv. [*Crosses to R.*] Beats the deuce how the women love me. I can't help it.

Moth. T. And now there's another one, eh? The girl with the pretty face. [*Points to house L. Lights change to red sunset*]

Liv. Yes, but she doesn't seem to be in love with me. I can't understand it. But if she'll have me I'll settle down and be honest. If she won't—well there'll be another job for you, mother. She'll love me. They always do.

Moth. T. Oh, you wicked boy. He, he, he.

Liv. You'd better go now.

Moth. T. Oh you wicked boy—he-he, he. [*Exits gate C. to L.*]

Liv. [*Pause, crosses to gate*] Useful old devil. Well I'll go and jolly the old man, and find out where he keeps his money, then if the girl marries me, all well and good. If not I'll take her by force. Once in the Gypsy camp in Mother Tagger's clutches, she'll do as I say. [*Exits into house*]

Rose. [*Runs on from R. with Ralph; runs up steps on porch laughing*] Oh, how good it seems to be home again. Now don't look so blue, Ralph dear —it will all come out right, I know.

Ralph. [*C.*] I'm afraid it was a wild thing to do, dear. I ought to have asked your father's consent.

Rose. Oh but it's so much nicer to have a secret all to ourselves. Won't they all be surprised when I tell them we've been married for three long weeks. [*Laughs*]

Ralph. You are so happy dear. May you never have cause to regret it.

Rose. Regret it? Why should I Ralph?

Ralph. Well I've been rather wild, I'm afraid.

Rose. Oh, Ralph—

Ralph. Yes, dear.

Rose. Come here and sit down and tell me truly—[*Pushes Ralph to tree seat, sits L. of him*] Mind now—not even a little white fib. Did you—did you —ever love any other girl?

Ralph. Well, sweetheart, I'll tell you truly if you'll also speak truly. Did you ever love any other man?

Rose. Why Ralph—I—[*Crosses quickly to steps*]

Ralph. [*Laughs cheerfully*] Never mind dear, you needn't. I know you love me best of all. You are my wife and I am going to make you happy. But I have been wild. [*Crosses to Rose*]

Rose. But you have sown your wild oats now dear.

Ralph. Yes, yes, but if you should hear that I have done something. [*Takes hand*]

Rose. Oh hush—you couldn't do anything so bad—if you had—

Ralph. Well—?

Rose. You are my husband and I shall stand by you as a wife should.

Ralph. God bless you, dear. [*Kisses her hand*] I'll try to be worthy of your love, and if in the future you should hear stories of me, remember how dearly I love you. My mother died when I was a boy. [*Crosses to R.*] Had she lived —But there—I have you to love me now. Let me tell your father tonight.

Rose. No, no—I shall tell him myself. I'm going in now. Oh, what a sensation I shall create. Come in presently. [*Livingstone enters from house*] Oh good evening, Mr. Livingstone. [*Ralph sits C.*]

Liv. Good evening, Miss Rose. Your visit has done you good. You look charming. [*Takes her hand*]

Rose. Thank you. [*Exits into house*]

Liv. Hello, Ralph. [*Crosses to him*] I just got in. Lucky you were not at home last night. The bank was robbed and all strangers are under suspicion.

Ralph. [*Rises in alarm*] You don't mean—

Liv. Yes I do. Made a good job of it too. [*Crosses to L.*] Say what are you hanging around Rose for. You let her alone. I've made up my mind to marry her.

Ralph. What?

Liv. You heard what I said, and if you bust in, I'll make it damned hot for you. Understand? [*Close to Ralph*]

Ralph. Don't try to intimidate me, Livingstone. I know you are capable of anything but you can't frighten me.

Liv. Have you forgotten the Camden case?

Ralph. I was innocent of that crime.

Liv. Yes, but the evidence was all against you and we had to jump out. Now I've stood by you and if you don't stand pat, I'll send you to Sing Sing. Nothing could save you. [*Laughs and takes out cigar*] Have a cigar? [*Ralph ignores him*] Oh, take a cigar, and let's take a walk and talk this matter over. I don't mean you any harm. [*Takes Ralph's arm; they go to gate*] But don't interfere in my game, that's all. [*They exit C. to L.*]

Bunco. [*Enters C. from R. Looks around*] Well, dis place looks kinder respectable. Guess I'll have to hang out here tonight. Bess can't go no furder. Well here goes to tackle de landlady. Gee me feet is so heavy dey feels like hams. [*Knocks at door*]

Lindy. [*Calls loudly from within*] Who's there?

Bunco. [*Jumps back to C.*] Gee—me heart's bumpin' a hole in me ribs. [*Lindy opens door*] Howdy.

Lindy. Heavens on earth, child.

Bunco. Is it? First I'd heard of it.

Lindy. Where did you come from?

Bunco. Aw say, lady—don't look at me like dat. I haven't got me Sunday clothes on cause I was afraid de walkin' might spoil em. Me automobile broke down and me and Bess had ter tramp from New York.

Lindy. New York? Child alive, ye ain't walked from New York?

Bunco. Dat's right.

LINDY. Where's yer father and mother?

BUNCO. Dead.

LINDY. Both of 'em?

BUNCO. Yep—poor things.

LINDY. How did they die?

BUNCO. Cut their throats eating peas with a knife.

LINDY. Good Lord. An' ain't ye afraid to be tramping the country all alone?

BUNCO. Nope—I always carries dis. [*Shows revolver*]

LINDY. [*Screams*] Oh—Good Lord—[*Pushes it away*]

BUNCO. Don't be afraid, lady—it ain't loaded.

LINDY. [*Sits on steps*] Well I never—What are you wearin' them there clothes this hot weather fur?

BUNCO. Dese?

LINDY. Yes.

BUNCO. Well ye see, lady, dese is de only chilly weather clothes I got. I have to wear 'em—[*Shows bundle*] cause me trunk is full. Oh say now, lady, I don't care for myself, but poor Bess is so hungry, and sick and tired. If you could take her in tonight and give her something to eat, I'd work for it. I don't know much about farmin' but you bet your life I could learn.

LINDY. And who is Bess?

BUNCO. A poor girl what's seen lots of trouble. We worked in de factory togedder—then a smooth-tongued feller comes along, and won poor Miss Bess—den—den left her wid her little baby.

LINDY. A baby? I can't take her in. [*Rises and goes up steps*]

BUNCO. Oh, don't say dat, lady. Don't be too hard on poor Bess. You see she's an orphan and ain't got no mother to guide her. She was just planning dying, so I thought if I could get her to the country, de beautiful trees, de green grass and flowers would do her good. [*Pleading*] Bess loves de flowers, she does.

LINDY. Where is she now?

BUNCO. Out there. [*Points R.*] Settin' under a tree, waitin' till I come back. Say, take her in, won't you an' I'll work like de devil to pay you back.

LINDY. You go fetch her right in.

BUNCO. Say, you'se de real article—you'se are. I'll work fer you as dough you was my husband. [*Exits gate C. to R.*]

LINDY. Well I never. That's a strange child.

SILAS. [*Enters from house*] I say, Lindy—

LINDY. Was you a speakin' to me, Silas Waterbury?

SILAS. [*L.*] Yes, I was a sayin'—

LINDY. Well say it again, and remember to call me Miss Smithers.

SILAS. Now what's the use of bein' mad, Lindy.

LINDY. *Miss Smithers!* [*Turns*]

SILAS. Lindy, ain't ye ever goin' to change it to Mrs.?

LINDY. Mebby I be—mebby I been't. When I see a man as *is* a man.

SILAS. Gol dern it, Lindy—what am I?

LINDY. The biggest fool I ever saw.

SILAS. Oh you get out. [*Sits on steps*] Lindy I'm as tired as Tom Turner is busy.

LINDY. What? Lazy Tom Turner.

SILAS. He ain't lazy no more.

LINDY. No?

SILAS. Nope. He's the busiest man in town.

LINDY. Dew tell?

SILAS. [*Crosses to her*] Yep—he's got the seven year itch and a Waterbury watch, and when he ain't scratchin' he's windin' his Waterbury.

LINDY. [*Crosses up stage*] You git out.

SILAS. And that reminds me, when I was up to New York State last fall— [*Crosses up to gate*] Jake Tod said to me, sez he—Jumpin' Crocodiles—look at that.

LINDY. Shut yer head—[*Turns to Bess and Bunco who have entered*] Come here, you pore young 'un.

BUNCO. [*Crosses to C.*] Dere now, Bess—don't get skeered. Old Spinach won't hurt ye.

SILAS. That gal's makin' fun of my whiskers.

LINDY. Ye pore critter—how white ye look. There now—don't be afeared —and fer the land's sake don't cry. Si Waterbury—what are ye standin' there for like a bump on a log. Go tell Miss Rose to come here. Step lively.

SILAS. I'm a steppin'. [*Trips upstairs*] Dern them stairs.

LINDY. That's right—break yer neck. [*Bunco leads Bess C. to bench*]

SILAS. Not yet, by Ginger. [*Exits into house*]

LINDY. Now you see here a minute. [*Kneels beside Bess*]

BESS. Oh you are very kind. I have not been well. I—I—

LINDY. Heaven's on earth—don't flop. [*Rises*]

BUNCO. Hully gee, Bess—brace up. You see, lady, she ain't had nothin' to eat since yesterday. [*On knees beside Bess, R.*]

LINDY. Lord love us—nothing to eat since yesterday. You come right inside. [*Rose enters from house*]

ROSE. What is it, Lindy?

LINDY. Land sakes, this poor critter ain't had nothin' to eat since yesterday.

ROSE. Oh, you poor child. [*Crosses to Bess*]

BESS. I'll be better soon.

ROSE. Come right in. [*Helps her up steps*] You poor child. [*Exits with Bess into house*]

LINDY. [*L. of Bess*] Yes come right in. We'll get you something to eat. [*Exits with others into house*]

BUNCO. [*Crosses to house*] We're goin' to get somethin' to eat. I can feel it in my bones. Gee—dis must be a dream. [*Exits into house after others*]

JAKE. [*Enters gate C. from R.*] Dis must be de place all right. Looks as dough de Gov'ner struck it rich. He had a finger in de bank robbery you can bet, and de pretty girl dat lives in here is his game or I'm a gentleman. [*Sits C.*] Wonder where he left de poor shopgirl he took a fancy to when he was in New York. Well dat's none of my business—I'm broke and he's got to give me some coin. [*Starts for house*] Here comes de young lady. [*Exits quickly gate C. to R.*]

ROSE. [*Enters, speaking to Aunt Lindy in house*] All right, Aunt Lindy. [*Enters with basket*]

LINDY. [*Calls from inside*] Rose—Rose—

ROSE. Yes.

LINDY. Get two pounds—don't forget.

ROSE. Yes—two pounds of granulated sugar—is that all?

LINDY. Yes. [*Rose goes to gate singing*]

LIV. [*Enters gate L.*] How happy you are, Miss Rose.

ROSE. Of course.

LIV. Can you spare me a moment? I have something to say to you.

ROSE. No, no—not now. I must run to the store. Aunt Lindy has taken a couple in; poor things are half starved. I am going to the grocery store to get some things.

LIV. Let me have a few words with you tonight?

ROSE. No—no—not tonight. [*Exits laughing, gate C. to R.*]

LIV. She is not indifferent to me. I'll win her yet. She shall be my wife before the month is over. [*Up C. outside gate looking after Rose. Enter Bunco with pan of potatoes and knife*]

BUNCO. Hully gee—look at de swell guy. Do you belong to dis house?

LIV. [*Crossing down fiercely*] What's that to you?

BUNCO. [*Backing away*] 'Cause if you do I'm goin' to move. I don't like de cut of yer lip, see?

LIV. Get out, you tramp. Don't talk to me or I'll—

BUNCO. [*Points knife at him*] Look out—don't run up against dis—you might get a puncture.

LIV. [*Laughs*] Say, you're not half bad. I like you.

BUNCO. Well—like me furder off. [*Points knife again*]

LIV. Well, you are a character.

BUNCO. You're annoder.

LIV. I'll see you later. [*Crosses up C. to gate*]

BUNCO. Yes—you will.

LIV. Au revoir, fair lady.

BUNCO. Over the river—you big bluff. [*Livingstone exits gate C. to R., laughing. Bunco crosses to R., sits thinking*] Gee, I wonder who he is? I hope he don't own dis house. [*Bess enters from house*] Oh, Bess, come here and sit under de tree and see me peel potatoes. We're goin' to have dem for supper. Don't yer stomach feel just grand? I never was so full in my life.

BESS. [*Crosses and sits L.*] It's just heavenly, Bunco. I'd be so happy if my heart didn't hurt so.

BUNCO. Oh, now, Bess—don't say that.

BESS. Oh, Bunco, I want my baby—[*Cries*] My little baby.

BUNCO. Now don't worry and de first baby I see layin' around loose, I'll swipe fer you. I will—honest.

BESS. But that wouldn't be my baby, Bunco.

BUNCO. Gee—that's right. Well, all kids look alike to me.

ROSE. [*Enters gate C. from R.*] Here you are. Do you feel better? So Aunt Lindy has put you to work has she, Bunco?

BUNCO. Yes'm. She's going to keep Bess here till she's strong and well again.

ROSE. I'm so glad. [*Crosses to L.*] There—I've forgotten the sugar.

BUNCO. Oh, gee. [*Laughs*] Let me go and get it for you. [*Pan on seat R.*]

ROSE. I left it on the counter of the little store on the corner.

BUNCO. [*Crosses up C.*] De little store over dere on de corner? [*Points R.*]

ROSE. Yes—straight ahead, Bunco.

BUNCO. All right, miss, I'll be right back. [*Exits gate C. to R.*]

ROSE. Would you like a book to read, Bessie?

BESS. No, thank you, miss.

ROSE. Perhaps you would like to come in and lie down.

BESS. I'll stay here if you don't mind, miss.

ROSE. Why, certainly I don't. There now, you mustn't worry. No doubt the future has much happiness in store for you.

BESS. God grant it. But it looks very dark, miss.

Rose. You must be brave. I'll be back in a little while to keep you company. [*Crosses to house*]

Bess. Thank you, miss. [*Rose exits house*]

Bunco. [*Enters gate C. from R., singing. Carries sugar and a bunch of flowers*] Say, Bess, you ought to see de guy what keeps de store down on de corner. [*Laughs*] He's a peach. Say, you can buy anything in dat store from a paper of pins to a beefsteak. Ain't dese sweet? Dey are fer you. [*Gives Bess flowers*]

Bess. Oh, thank you, Bunco.

Bunco. I found dem growing right by de roadside. Oh, say, Bess, yer eyes is all wet. You've been crying again. Oh, gee. [*Crosses down, gets pan*] Just wait till I get dese in de house—den I'll come out and tell you a funny story. [*Laughs*] Oh, brace up. [*Exits house*]

Bess. Dear little flowers, I love you—I love you.

Liv. [*Enters gate C. from L., sees Bess*] By Jove—there she is. Now's my chance. [*Crosses to tree*]

Bess. [*Startled, recognizing him*] John!

Liv. Bess!

Bess. [*Into his arms*] Oh, John, I've found you at last!

Liv. [*Annoyed*] Now how did you get here?

Bess. I have been so ill, John. Our baby has been stolen, but you'll find it for me, won't you, John? And now we'll be married, won't we? You promised, you know, and I knew when you didn't come you were ill and in trouble.

Liv. [*Nervous*] Yes—

Bess. They discharged me from the shop. The girls wouldn't speak to me—all but Bunco. She brought me here.

Liv. Sh-h—don't talk so loud. Listen, you must come with me at once.

Bess. Where?

Liv. To be married. [*Bunco enters, listens*]

Bess. Oh, you are glad to see me, aren't you, John?

Liv. Yes, yes, of course. [*Tenderly*] Come, dear—come with me. [*Crosses up C.*]

Bunco. Where are you going, Bessie?

Liv. [*In a rage*] Stand out of the way.

Bunco. Well, I guess not. Bess, don't go with that guy. He means you harm.

Liv. Come, Bessie.

Bunco. She shan't. [*Stops Bess, takes gun out of boot*] Come and take her. Come in the house, Bessie.

Bess. [*Pleadingly, to Bunco*] Oh, Bunco.

Bunco. Go in, kind lady. [*Bess exits R. Bunco crosses to him*] Say, I know you now. Listen, don't you come foolin' around Bess again or I'll put a bullet through your sky-piece. [*Crosses up steps*] Dat's straight. [*Exits house*]

Liv. [*Extreme R., starts for her as she exits*] Well, I'm in a devil of a hole if that girl blabs. I must go and see old Mother Tagger at once. [*Starts for gate*]

Rose. [*Enters, apron on, fanning herself*] Supper will soon be ready.

Liv. [*Taking her hand*] Rose, will you be my wife?

Rose. Oh, Mr. Livingstone, I'm so sorry you said this.

Liv. Why?

Rose. Because I am already a wife.

Liv. What?

Rose. I like you so much and want you for a friend, but I have been married for three weeks.

Liv. To whom?

Rose. To Ralph Carlton.

Liv. [*In a rage*] Ralph Carlton! God! [*Staggers*]

Rose. [*Cross R.*] I am so sorry.

Liv. [*Shakes hands*] I wish you every happiness.

Rose. Let us always be friends.

Liv. Thank you, Rose.

Rose. [*As she crosses to house*] You'll be in to supper?

Liv. [*Sadly*] Not tonight.

Rose. I am sorry. [*Exits into house*]

Liv. [*Crosses to house in a rage*] So Ralph Carlton, you have come between me and the woman I love. Well, you'll have a short honeymoon, my lady! Ha, ha—you'd look well in widow's weeds. [*Turn at gate. Ralph enters C. from L.; slowly down R. Savagely*] Congratulations!

Ralph. What do you mean?

Liv. [*Angrily*] Oh, you know what I mean. Your wife has told me all. Married for three weeks, eh? Nice way to treat an old pal. Why didn't you tell me before? You knew I loved Rose.

Ralph. [*C.*] She didn't love you. [*Livingstone crosses L.*] Now, Livingstone, I'll admit I've been weak, but I swear from tonight on I intend to be a man, and make Rose proud of me.

Liv. [*Crosses to Ralph*] And I swear that you shall go to Sing Sing.

Ralph. For God's sake, Livingstone, you wouldn't do such a fiendish thing. What about Rose—it will only break her heart. [*Sinks into seat C.*]

Liv. Listen. The money I got from the bank last night I sent away. I'm going to jump out to 'Frisco and I'll need money. Now the old man has got money in the house. Tonight I want you to stand guard while I get it, then I'll go. We may as well part friends. Will you do it?

Ralph. No!

Liv. What? Then it's war?

Ralph. [*Rises*] Yes—if it must be.

Liv. [*Crossing L.*] Do you dare defy me?

Ralph. We may as well understand each other now. I am innocent. Why should I fear you? But I believe I know the true murderer. [*Jake enters gate C. from L.*]

Liv. What do you mean?

Ralph. I mean that I think you killed the old banker.

Liv. [*Draws knife, starts for Ralph*] So—you suspect *me*?

Jake. [*Comes between them*] Hold on, pardner.

Liv. [*Amazed*] Jake Jordan.

Jake. Glad to see me, eh? [*Business with Livingstone; knife. Then with revolver*] Hold on—dat's no way to treat an old pal. Give me dat knife.

Liv. What?

Jake. Give me dat knife. [*Does so*] Dat's a nice boy. [*Ralph exits gate C. to R.*]

Liv. [*Crosses to L.*] What do you want?

Jake. Just a little expense money, gov'nor.

Liv. I haven't any.

Jake. What? And de bank robbed last night, too?

Liv. Sh-h-h—how much do you want?

Jake. Dat's business. A twenty-dollar bill will do, gov'nor.

Liv. How long do you intend to bleed me?

Jake. Jest as long as I need de money. But if ye get tired, ye can make a test wid a rope around yer neck, fer I'll squeal as soon as the money stops.

Liv. [*Starts for him*] What?

Jake. Hold on! Give me de dough.

Liv. Here—[*Gives him money*]

Jake. Don't try to throw me over, gov'nor. I've got ye—and I'm goin' to keep ye. Good-night. [*Exits gate, L.*]

Liv. Damn him—if I could only get a hold on him, I'd—[*Ralph enters gate. Has a complete change of manner toward him*] Oh, Ralph—let's be friends. I was too hasty. Help me tonight—it will be the last time—then I'll go away. It's the easiest way to get rid of me.

Ralph. Let me think.

Liv. All right—meet me in the orchard at ten. [*Exits gate, C. to L.*]

Ralph. [*Sits under tree*] What shall I do? I'd give ten years of my life to dig up the wild oats I've sown.

Rose. [*Enters*] Is that you, Ralph?

Ralph. [*Trying to appear happy*] Yes, yes.

Rose. [*Crosses to him*] What is it? What's the matter?

Ralph. Nothing, dear, nothing.

Rose. I thought I heard you heave such a dreadful sigh. Supper is ready—come in. [*Hesitates*] You might ask me to kiss you before we go in.

Ralph. [*Kisses her*] Rose—God bless you.

Rose. I'm so happy, Ralph.

Ralph. May you always be happy, dear. [*Exits with arm about her*]

Liv. [*Enters gate, C. from L., followed by Mother Tagger*] Hang around for a half an hour or so. The girl from New York is here. Take her to your camp—dope her with whiskey—and keep her hid till we are ready to leave. [*Mother Tagger nods*]

Moth. T. Yes, yes.

Liv. Can we depend upon Jordan?

Moth. T. Yes, yes.

Liv. Good. Go now.

Moth. T. He, he, he—oh, you wicked, wicked boy. [*Exits C. to L.*]

Bess. [*Enters from house*] Oh, my heart aches so. I couldn't breathe in there. [*Crosses and sits at tree*]

Liv. My luck is with me. [*Crosses to her*] Sweetheart. [*Very tenderly*]

Bess. [*Rises in fear*] John!

Liv. Come with me, dear—we'll be married at once.

Bess. [*Retreating*] No, no—I won't.

Liv. You won't?

Bess. No, I can't trust you, John.

Liv. [*Quickly*] You won't come, eh? [*Catches her*] Then I must force you. Come. [*Bunco enters from house*]

Bess. [*Screams*] No!

Liv. [*Hand over her mouth*] Shut up! You'll trouble me no more. [*Forces her up stage as Mother Tagger enters C. Jake enters following Mother Tagger*]

Bunco. [*C. Takes gun from boot*] Let her go. [*Mother Tagger hits Bunco on head—she is unconscious*]

Liv. Good. Come, come! Hurry! You brought the horse and wagon, Jake. Help us put her in. [*Exit Bess, Livingstone, Mother Tagger and Jake C. to L.*]

BUNCO. [*On floor, coming to*] Ouch! I was knocked out, eh? [*Gets gun*] Now look out fer me, Mr. Bluff, 'cos dis time I'm goin' to shoot. [*Exits gate, C. to L. Silas and Lindy enter*]

SILAS. It's goin' to be a right smert night tonight, Lindy. That reminds me. One beautiful moonlight night in the summer old Doc Brown fell down a well and was instantly killed.

LINDY. Land sakes! What was the coroner's verdict?

SILAS. He said he should have attended the sick and let the well alone.

LINDY. [*Looking around*] Si Waterbury, I wonder where them gals is gone. [*Crosses to gate, C.*]

SILAS. [*At gate*] I'm afraid you've got a white elephant on yer hands, Lindy Jane. And that reminds me—

LINDY. Shet yer head. Somethin' always reminds ye of somethin' else. [*Crosses down C.*]

SILAS. [*Follows her*] Everything always reminds me of you, Lindy. Say, Lindy, when are ye goin' to say yes? This sweeteartin' fer ten years is gettin' monotonous.

LINDY. Oh, it is? Then quit it. [*Goes to gate, C.*]

SILAS. I can't. It's a habit now.

LINDY. Well, dern yer buttons. [*Crosses to him*]

SILAS. [*Sweetly*] See the stars up there?

LINDY. What stars?

SILAS. That reminds me—[*Kisses her*]

LINDY. Si Waterbury—ef you do that agin, I'll scream.

SILAS. I never heerd ye scream, Lindy. [*Kisses her again*]

LINDY. Oo—ooo, Si Waterbury. [*Crosses down L.*]

SILAS. Did ye see stars, Lindy? [*Laughs*] Good-night, Lindy. [*Exits gate, C. to R.*]

LINDY. [*Angry*] Well, I never see sich a man. [*Giggles*] But he do kiss the sweetest. [*Crosses to gate, sits C., sighs softly*]

DAY. [*Enters from house*] That you, Lindy?

LINDY. [*Fans herself with apron*] Yes, it is, sir.

DAY. It seems to me yer gettin' too old to be larkin' round this time o' night. [*Crosses and sits R.*]

LINDY. Oh, shet yer head. [*Exits into house*]

LIV. [*Enters gate*] Lovely night. I'm tired—I guess I'll go to bed. Good-night. [*Exits into house*]

DAY. Nice young man. [*Rises and cross up*]

LINDY. [*Enters and crosses to gate*] I can't understand where them two gals be.

DAY. Guess they've gone, Lindy. You took them in—gave them something to eat, and now they're on the tramp agin.

LINDY. Land sakes, I never would have believed that. Well, I'm goin' to bed. Good-night. [*Exits in house. Rose and Ralph enter from house*]

ROSE. Let's go out on the porch. Oh, is that you, father?

DAY. Yes.

ROSE. Isn't it a lovely night?

RALPH. I'm going for a little stroll. I've got a headache.

DAY. You won't be long?

RALPH. [*At gate*] Oh, no. [*Exits C. to R.*]

ROSE. Father, I have something to tell you.

DAY. Not tonight, daughter—I'm too tired. I know it's a love affair. He has spoken to me.

ROSE. He? Who?

DAY. Mr. Livingstone.

ROSE. Oh!

DAY. Good-night, daughter.

ROSE. But, father—

DAY. See that the doors are locked. Lots of robberies lately.

ROSE. I'm not afraid with my little revolver under my pillow.

DAY. [*Laughs*] You'd be afraid to use it.

ROSE. Would I? Don't you believe it.

DAY. Well, good-night, daughter.

ROSE. Good-night, daddy. [*Kisses him. Day exits to house*] I wonder where Ralph went. [*Runs up to gate*] Oh, there he is—I'm going for a little stroll with him. [*Exits gate, C. to R.*]

LIV. [*Sneaks on from behind house*] I must meet Ralph. He'll do as I say tonight. [*Looking off*] Hello—there he is and Rose is with him. [*Hides behind tree, C. Ralph and Rose enter gate*]

ROSE. Yes, both girls have disappeared. I suppose we'll never see them again. I wouldn't have believed they could have been so ungrateful. Well, I'll go in now. Good-night, dear husband.

RALPH. Good-night, dear wife. [*Kisses her*]

ROSE. Good-night. [*Exits, house*]

RALPH. Poor little woman—I'm afraid I've wrecked your happiness. Whichever way I turn, ruin seems to stare me in the face. But prison or no prison, I've sworn to lead a new life and I'll keep my word. Now to find Livingstone. [*Turns up, exits gate C. to L.*]

LIV. [*Comes from behind tree*] Yes, and tomorrow shall see you in custody, if my plan succeeds. His dear wife! I could kill him myself, with pleasure. [*Exits gate, C. to L.*]

BUNCO. [*Enters C. from L.*] Gee, I'm tired. [*Crosses to R.*] I followed the horse and buggy until we came to the gypsy camp where they took poor Bess. I can't do nothing tonight, but tomorrow I'll tell Miss Rose everything. I wonder if dey'll take my word against his. [*At gate*] Gee, whiz! Here he comes back. Me out of sight! [*Hides behind tree. Ralph and Livingstone enter gate, L.*]

RALPH. I tell you I won't, Livingstone.

LIV. Don't be a fool. It's easy enough and no danger. Just wait in the hall and watch. If you hear a noise—give me the signal. [*Crosses L.*]

RALPH. But think what it means to me. My God, Livingstone, is there nothing I can do instead of this?

LIV. Nothing. Come on—cover your face up. [*Takes out revolver*]

RALPH. You are not going to use that?

LIV. If I have to. Come! [*Exits into house*]

RALPH. [*Aloud*] Yes, John Livingstone, I will stand by the door and watch, but I'll give the alarm and put you behind the bars where you would send me. [*Exits into house*]

BUNCO. Christopher Columbus! Burglars! I thought dere was somethin' crooked about dat guy. De oder one didn't want to do it. Hully gee—what'll I do? Guess I'll have to take my trusty and go after dem. Dey're comin' back. [*Hides again*]

LINDY. [*Off stage, screams*] Help, help! Rose, Rose! [*Ralph fires three shots inside. Rose rushes on*]

ROSE. What was that? Burglars? My revolver.

BUNCO. Miss Rose—dey're comin' out. [*Ralph enters from house, runs to gate, Rose shoots*]

RALPH. [*Staggers—falls*] Oh, my God!

BUNCO. She's killed him.

SILAS. [*Enters gate*] What's the matter?

LINDY. [*Enters from house*] Rose's father has been murdered.

SILAS. Burglars?

LINDY. Yes.

LIV. [*Enters from house in bathrobe*] Did you get him?

ROSE. [*Enters from house*] Have I killed him?

LINDY. Look! Look!

ROSE. [*Staggers*] Oh, my God!

LIV. He's killed your father.

Rose. No! No!

Liv. It's true as Heaven.

Bunco. [*Coming from behind tree*] You lie like hell!

ACT II.

At Rise: *Gypsy camp. Mother Tagger sits by the fire. Bess is in a stupor L. by tree. Jake looking at Bess.*

Jake. Say, dat gal looks mighty bad. What's de gov'nor going ter do wid her, eh?

Moth. T. That's his business, dearie.

Jake. I'm all right when it's face to face with a man, but when it comes to frighten women, hah, I'll leave dat to de white-livered dogs dat sticks a man in de back. [*Crosses down right*]

Moth. T. Don't speak like dat, dearie, he might hear you.

Jake. Who?

Moth. T. Your master.

Jake. Livingstone?

Moth. T. Yes, yes.

Jake. [*Laughs and crosses to L.*] My master? Why if I wanted to squeal the electric chair would have his black heart forever.

Moth. T. But think of yourself, dearie.

Jake. Oh, I'm not afraid of de prison bars, and dat's de worst dey could do with me. Say, why don't you put that gal in there so she can lie on the mattress?

Moth. T. No, I like to hear her groan, and see her white face turned up to de stars, he, he, he.

Jake. Well, if dere's a hell, there's a hot place waiting for you. [*Crosses to C.*]

Moth. T. He, he, he, burn higher, and higher. How I love to see you dance and play, throwing your fiery arms around each other. He, he, he. [*Looking above*] It's going to storm, eh? Well, let the wind blow. [*Sings*]

"Blow, blow, winds

While the pot bubbles, oh.

We're wrapped in warmth

And care not for trouble, oh. [*Thunder heard in the distance. Drinks whiskey and puts bottle away on floor*]

Liv. [*Enters C. and slaps Mother Tagger on back*] What the devil are you doing there?

MOTH. T. [*Rises and screams*] How you do frighten a body, creeping around like a snake. [*Crosses to fire*]

LIV. Guilty conscience, eh? [*Laughs*] Always croaking and drinking. You make my blood run cold. [*He shivers and warms his hands by the fire. Sits*]

MOTH. T. Then warm up, darling. Drink, he, he, he. [*Points to bottle*]

LIV. Shut up that cackle. [*Drinks from bottle*]

MOTH. T. What news, eh?

LIV. Rose is going to marry me tonight. [*Rises and crosses to C.*]

MOTH. T. What?

LIV. Yes. I've persuaded her it would be so romantic to be married by moonlight in the gypsy camp.

MOTH. T. He, he, he, and the boy, her husband—has she forgotten him?

LIV. No, she believes him dead, as I told her.

MOTH. T. Yes, yes.

LIV. And for three months while she had the fever, I was devotion itself. She believes me to be her best friend, and to save her good name, she has consented to be my wife. [*Laughs*] And she will marry me to give the *child* a name. [*Bess begins to come to*]

MOTH. T. How you must love her.

LIV. Love her? Yes, I am determined to call her mine. Perhaps it will be for a week, a month, but I shall make her my wife.

BESS. [*Rises to her knees weakly*] You shan't do it, y' shan't do it, I'll tell her all.

MOTH. T. [*Starts back*] What?

LIV. What the devil! I thought you had her out of the way.

BESS. I am your wife in the sight of Heaven, you shan't ruin her life too.

LIV. Shut up, or I'll choke you. [*Has crossed to her and chokes her*]

MOTH. T. Be careful, my darling, and don't squeeze too hard. It's a thin little throat, he, he, he. [*Goes up behind Livingstone*]

LIV. You keep your mouth shut if you're wise, or I may be tempted to put you out of the way altogether. Give me the drugged whiskey. I told you to keep her under the influence, why haven't you done so?

BESS. [*On knees*] Oh please, please, don't make me take that dreadful stuff. I'll be quiet. Oh, let me go away from here. I won't trouble you any more. But don't torture me like this. [*Mother Tagger takes drugged whiskey from stocking leg*]

LIV. No, I can't trust your blabbing tongue. You must stay with Mother Tagger until we leave the village.

BESS. But she is so cruel to me. Why can't I die.

Liv. It's a devilish pity you can't. I'd help you if I dared. [*Throws her on stage and takes bottle*] Here, drink this.

Bess. No, no, I'll be quiet, I'll be quiet.

Liv. Drink it, I say. [*Bess holds it to her mouth*] There, that will keep her quiet until the wedding is over. [*Bess spits it out as he turns away*]

Moth. T. He, he, he.

Liv. Let's put her in the tent mother, here take care of this. [*Gives her the bottle. They put Bess in tent. Mother Tagger puts bottle back in her stocking—as Livingstone looks at his watch*] Now I'm going, I'll be back soon. Keep the girl in the tent and don't you dare get drunk. [*Exits R.*]

Moth. T. Don't get drunk, eh? [*Screams*] Leave you to have all the fun, while Mother Tagger does all the work, no, no, no, my pet, my pretty pet. [*Takes out bottle, drinks*] Oh, oh, it's the drugged whiskey, oh, Lord! I'm poisoned, I've drunk the drugged whiskey, what will I do? It may kill me. Oh, oh, I must go to the apothecary shop. Oh, I'm poisoned, I'm poisoned. [*Does funny business and exits R.*]

Bunco. [*Enters R. Looks around*] Dere's no one here, I'll just call Mr. Ralph and let him rubberneck. [*Calls off*] Mr. Ralph, oho, oho—[*Ralph enters R.*] Oh, I say now Mr. Ralph, don't ye go looking fer trouble, yer too weak.

Ralph. Don't be afraid, little girl, I'm stronger then you think.

Bunco. But dere's three to one. I'll do all I kin to help ye, but what's a girl in a bunch like dis?

Ralph. Well, you've got a heart that's too big for your little body. [*Sits L.*]

Bunco. Oh, my heart's all right, all right. And I've worked in de factory and I kin hold my own where dere is people dat's honest. But when you're bumped about de outside world ans have shuffeled fer yourself, you soon learns to tell a good man from a bad one. Say, you're all right. [*Puts out her hand*]

Ralph. Thank you, Bunco. [*They shake hands*]

Bunco. But say, don't stay here now Mr. Ralph, there's danger.

Ralph. You mean well, little girl, but you don't understand. When a man through his own folly has tangled the threads of his own life, there's nothing left for him to do but to untangle them again. I must see this man Livingstone, tonight. [*Crosses up stage*]

Bunco. He's de guy, the spider that will tangle you in his web again. Mr. Ralph, I tell you he is de devil.

Ralph. [*Crosses to Bunco*] But I have you by my side, and you are my little guardian angel.

Bunco. Yes, but I've lost my wings.

RALPH. [*Sits by fire*] Oh, Bunco, you're the only friend I have in the world. When everything looked dark you stood bravely by me. [*Rises*] Oh, little woman, your start in life was not too brilliant, but you have it in your power to grow up to be a noble woman. And Bunco never do anything that you'll regret all your life.

BUNCO. Well, I'll regret it if I stay here in this gypsy camp. I'll show you a short cut to the next town through the fields. If you stay here, they will pinch you sure. [*Crosses to tent R.*]

RALPH. [*Hands up to fire*] No—I'll wait. Come now, tell me about Rose.

BUNCO. Say, I never saw a man so stuck—

RALPH. I'm going to walk by the old farm house, perhaps I'll catch a glimpse of Rose. [*Exits L.*]

BUNCO. Gee—he's de grandest man I ever seed. I wonder where Bess is. She *must* be here somewhere.

BESS. [*Comes out of tent*] Bunco!

BUNCO. Bess, Bess. [*They embrace. Bess staggers*] What's the matter, honey, is ye faint? What have dey done to ye?

BESS. Oh, Bunco, I feel so ill, I believe I am going to faint.

BUNCO. Hully Gee, don't faint. Dere, we'll go far away from here where no one will find us. [*Bess starts to sink to floor. Bunco tries to help her up*]

BESS. [*Cries*] Oh, I can't, Bunco, I can't walk. I'm so weak, my head swims.

BUNCO. Dere, dere, dearie. Try again, Bessie, try again, dat's de way. [*Helps her*]

BESS. I can't, Bunco. [*Falls*] You go, Bunco, don't let him get you. Go, leave me here to die.

BUNCO. Well, I guess not. Try again. Put your arms around my neck. So, dat's right! Don't be afraid honey, I'll take care of ye.

BESS. [*Trying hard*] Oh, we'll get away, won't we?

BUNCO. You bet. [*They start up R.*]

MOTH. T. [*Enters R.*] Ho, ho, what's dis? So, so, and where do you think you are going, eh?

BUNCO. Oh, you get out.

BESS. [*Bess drops to her knees*] Oh, Bunco!

BUNCO. Don't be afraid, Bess. [*Takes gun from her boot Livingstone enters R., sneaks down behind Bunco*] Don't you be afraid, Bess. I got my old trusty and if dey lay a hand on ye, de devil will have two new angels to shovel coal for him.

LIV. [*Grabs Bunco*] Mother Tagger, take the girl. [*Mother Tagger drags Bess to tent R.*]

Bunco. [*Struggling with Livingstone*]   You let her go!

Liv.   Ha, ha, ha, you little devil, I'm glad to get my hands on you.

Bunco.   Oh, you great big coward, if I was a man I'd beat ye tell ye had to walk on crutches for the rest of your life.

Liv.   Oh, you would eh? Give me the chloroform bottle, mother. [*Mother Tagger exits*]

Bunco.   No, no, I won't be chloroformed. [*Tries to get away*]

Liv.   You *would* come into the lion's den, eh?

Bunco.   Lion? You're only a measly yellow pup.

Moth. T. [*Enters with handkerchief*]   Here, dearie. [*Gives him handkerchief*]

Liv. [*Struggles with Bunco, gives her chloroform*]   I guess you'll keep quiet now. Mother, get me one of those sacks, hurry up. I'll just tie her into it, and after dark, put her in an empty boxcar and ship her where she'll never come back.

Moth. T.   He, he, he. [*Gets sack. Drags Bunco to L. Silas and Lindy heard off R.*]

Lindy.   I tell you nothing on earth could make me do such a fool thing. [*They enter from R. and come down R.*]

Liv. [*Bows*]   How do you do? I'm just arranging for the marriage.

Lindy. [*Sees Bunco*]   Good land!

Liv.   Yes, they are a very bad lot. They're very wild. I fear this one is quite intoxicated.

Lindy.   Oh, the wicked child. [*Crosses to L.*]

Silas. [*Crosses to L.*]   Don't look intoxicated to me.

Lindy.   What do you know about 'toxication?

Silas.   Well—er—not much.

Moth. T. [*Looking at Bunco*]   Oh dear, these gals will break my poor heart. When their father died he left me to take keer of them, but they're a bad lot. Take after their father who was an awful one for them 'toxication liquors.

Silas.   Smells as if the old gal likes 'em pretty tolerable. [*Crosses in front of Livingstone*]

Liv.   I'll put her inside for you.

Moth. T.   Thank you, my good kind gentleman. [*Quickly puts Bunco in tent and goes up stage*] Can I do anything for you, dearie? [*She speaks to Silas*]

Silas.   Yes, I wanter have my fortune told.

Moth. T.   Well, I'll do my best. I must get in communication with the spirits. [*Sits L. Drunk*]

SILAS. If she communes much more with the spirits, I'm afraid she won't be able to commune at all.

MOTH. T. Give me your hand. He, he, he.

SILAS. Hi, hi, hi. [*Crosses to her*]

MOTH. T. [*Looking at his hand*] I kin see yer a great favorite with the ladies.

SILAS. Hear that, Lindy? [*Proudly*]

MOTH. T. You have many sweethearts.

SILAS. You said it.

MOTH. T. The gals all love you.

LINDY. Well, I never!

MOTH. T. But there is one you'll marry.

SILAS. Humph, I guess not.

MOTH. T. [*Looking closely at his hand*] She loves you and you love her.

SILAS. Bet your gollushes I do.

LINDY. Humph!

MOTH. T. I kin see her now. [*Looks up into the air*]

SILAS. She's on to you Lindy.

LINDY. Guess I ain't up in the air.

SILAS. Yes, sir, most of the time.

MOTH. T. It's a little woman with black hair.

SILAS. Black hair?

MOTH. T. Yes, black hair.

SILAS. That lets you out, Lindy. I wonder if it's Sally Tomkins?

MOTH. T. Yes, yes, that's her. Sally Tomkins, she loves ye, darling.

SILAS. I'll be darned. Guess that's about all I wanted to know. [*Turns to Lindy*] Going to have your fortune told, Lindy?

LINDY. Well, I reckon not. I don't believe in such foolish truck.

SILAS. [*Reaching into his pocket*] How much, mother?

MOTH. T. One dollar, darling.

SILAS. Here ye air. That's cheap enough to find out that Sally Tomkins loves me, eh Lindy? [*Crosses up to R.*]

LINDY. Si Waterbury.

SILAS. Ma'am?

LINDY. You've been flirting with Sally Tomkins.

SILAS. Get out. Well now, Lindy, I've been a courtin' you fer the last twenty years, and I can't wait twenty more for I git a wife.

LINDY. Then ask Sally Tomkins to marry you.

SILAS. [*At door R.*] I will by thunder.

LINDY. [*Following Silas*] Silas Waterbury—

SILAS. By the great tadpoles, she'll jump at me, you don't want me. [*Turns to go*]

LINDY. Yes, I do.

SILAS. What?

LINDY. [*Falls into his arms*] Oh Si—[*Enter Livingstone*]

SILAS. She's mine. By Hickory she's mine. I say Mr. Livingstone, ye kin fix up a double wedding tonight. [*With his arm around Lindy they exit R.*]

LIV. [*Laughs*] Quick, mother, get the bag, hurry up, there is no time to lose. [*Mother Tagger gets bag as Livingstone drags Bunco out*] There, now, over her head, give me a cord. [*They put her in bag and tie it shut*] There, now, my wise little shopgirl, I guess when you wake up, you'll wonder what it is all about, and what all happened. [*Mother Tagger exits into tent, drags Bunco to side of tent*]

RALPH. [*Enters L.*] John Livingstone.

LIV. Ralph Carlton, well, well, where did you drop from. [*Advances to tent, R.*]

RALPH. You know well enough, you scoundrel. From the hospital. I knew that as soon as I was well enough I'd be carried away to jail, so I took advantage of my first walk into the grounds, to get away and see you once more, my good kind friend. [*Advances toward him*]

LIV. Now don't be sarcastic, Ralph. I am your friend and will do all I can to help you. [*Crosses to Ralph*]

RALPH. How very noble! And my wife, you'll help her too won't you? I hear her father did not die.

LIV. Now see here, Ralph, I can't help if our plans turned out so devilish bad.

RALPH. Good you mean, for you. I'm going to see Rose and tell her all. [*Starts*]

LIV. She wouldn't believe you. You're very foolish old fellow to expose yourself. Better get out of the country.

RALPH. And leave Rose to you? No, I'll tell her; she will believe me. I'll tell her it was you who tried to kill her father.

LIV. Hush, you fool. Better get out of the country while you have a chance. [*Jake enters L. and remains up C. Then advances on Ralph*]

RALPH. I'll stay and face my accusers. And if I go to jail you shall go with me.

LIV. Seize him, Jake. [*Jake grabs Ralph, they struggle. Mother Tagger enters, as Ralph's revolver explodes. Livingstone hits Ralph with a billy, Ralph falls, and Jake drops on knee behind him. Livingstone draws knife and offers it to Jake*] Good, the fool! Here, Jake, kill him.

JAKE. Why don't you do it yourself, governor? [*Rises*]

LIV. [*Picking up Ralph's revolver*] I will, and while I am about it I'll just settle my account with you, Jake Jordan.

JAKE. What do you mean, Livingstone?

LIV. I mean my opportunity to get rid of you with no danger to me. You have hounded me long enough, Jake Jordan.

JAKE. Would you kill a man without giving him a chance?

LIV. Yes.

JAKE. You do. [*Crosses to him. Jake makes rush for Livingstone, who shoots Jake and he falls. Then drops the revolver near Ralph, then picks up Jake's knife. Mother Tagger looks down at him*]

MOTH. T. Is he dead?

LIV. Well, if he ain't he soon will be.

MOTH. T. You wicked, wicked boy. He's moving.

LIV. Shut up. [*Livingstone lifts Ralph to his feet*] There, there old pard, brace up, this is a bad business.

RALPH. [*Rousing himself*] What is it, what is the matter?

LIV. [*R.*] He's dead.

RALPH. Dead; who's dead? [*Sees Jake*]

LIV. [*Crosses to L.*] It's too bad, but luck seems against you. Of course it wasn't in cold blood, but in the tussle.

RALPH. I shot him?

LIV. Yes.

RALPH. I don't believe it.

LIV. I tell you you killed him. Look at your revolver.

RALPH. [*Crosses to Jake, picks up revolver*] Well, I'll go. The odds are against me just now. They may send me to prison, John Livingstone, but some day I'll meet you again, and God shall judge between us. [*Exits L. Jake has been coming to during this speech*]

LIV. [*Looking after him, then turns and crosses up to Mother Tagger*] He's gone and he will never come back. Come quick, we'll put this fellow in the wagon, he can stay there until after the wedding, and then I'll drive him to the river and throw him in. If the body is found it will be easy to fasten the crime on Carlton. Look, Mother Hag.

JAKE. [*Has risen*] You dog. [*Rushes at Livingstone who knocks him down, drags him to door of tent R.*] Now I'll put the police on Carlton's track. Don't you leave here until I return. [*Exits R.*]

MOTH. T. Don't leave here? Why darling I must have something to steady my nerves. [*Looks in tent, and following him*] She's all right. A murder and a wedding in one night. [*Kicks Bunco who is still in bag*] Everything looks safe. Now I'll get just one little drop. [*Exits L.*]

BUNCO. [*Rolling down C. and trying to get out of bag*]   Help, help!

BESS. [*Enters from tent*]   She's gone.

BUNCO.   Help, help!

BESS.   Oh Lord, what's that?

BUNCO.   Bess, Bess. [*Bess runs up stage calling her, then crosses to upper L.*] Here in the sack, Bess.

BESS. [*Going to her*]   Is it you, Bunco?

BUNCO.   I guess so—what's left of me. Hully Gee—let's get out quick.

BESS.   Oh, Bunco, my hands tremble so I can't untie it. There. [*Opens bag. Bunco jumps out*]

BUNCO.   Gee, I'd like to live in that sack.

BESS.   Did they put you in there?

BUNCO.   Gee, I feel pale. My head's just swimming.

BESS. [*Starting up*]   Come, Bunco, let's go. If they find us they'll kill us.

BUNCO.   No, Bess, I can't leave now—I've got business here. [*Goes up and sees Jake*] Try to get a little air, pardner. Quick—some water Bess, quick. Is dat better? [*Getting Jake out and trying to revive him*]

BESS. [*Getting bottle of water*]   Here, Bunco. [*Hands her bottle of whiskey*]

BUNCO. [*Starts to give Jake a drink, stops*]   No, that may be drugged stuff.

BESS.   No it ain't, Bunco.

BUNCO.   Are you sure?

BESS.   Yes, Bunco.

BUNCO.   Here pardner, drink this. [*Jake takes drink*] Are you much hurt?

JAKE.   The bullet just grazed my head. [*Partly rising*] You're a brick, kid. I'm all right now. [*Sits up. Mother Tagger laughs off L.*]

BESS. [*Frightened. Runs in tent as she speaks*]   She's coming back. [*Sound of horses' hoofs approaching*]

BUNCO.   Duck, pardner—quick. [*Bunco and Jake exit R. quickly*]

MOTHER T. [*Enter laughing from L.*]   Ha-a, I feel better now. Ah—they are coming. [*Looks into tent*] Ha, the girl's asleep yet. [*Goes down R. Livingstone enters R. followed by Rose. They go down R. Si enters with Lindy, followed by Parson. Si and Lindy go down L. Parson down C. Lindy speaks as she enters; she goes down L.*]

LINDY.   Oh, Si, I feel so nervous.

SILAS.   What for?

LINDY.   I never was married before.

SILAS. Well, you'll get used to it.

LIV. [*Has been talking to Rose, aside*] There cheer up, Rose. You look as if you were going to a funeral.

ROSE. I can't help it John, I have a horrible feeling of fear. If I could turn back now. A vision of Ralph arises before me as a warning. I have seen him in my fancy several times today. Oh, John, are you quite sure he is dead?

LIV. *You* saw the certificate. He died while you were quite ill. I buried him myself, poor boy.

ROSE. You are very kind, John. I'll try and be a good wife to you so you'll never forget your great love for me.

LIV. My one wish is for your happiness, Rose. Come, dear—you will soon be my wife. Come smile—I want to remember this as the happiest day of my life. Come, Parson. [*Parson goes C.*]

LINDY. Oh, Si, I've changed my mind.

SILAS. All right, I'll get Sally Tomkins. [*Starts; she catches his coat-tails*]

LINDY. [*As Parson prepares for the ceremony*] Oh, Si, I shall faint—I know I shall. [*Growing dark*]

PAR. [*Parson is C. Rose and Livingstone R. Silas and Lindy L.*] Are you ready? [*All bow, Lindy and Rose in dread*] If there be anyone here who sees a reason why these people should not be joined in the holy bonds of matrimony, let him speak now [*Loud thunder*] or forever hold his peace, and be silent.

BESS. [*Enters at tent*] I *do!*

ALL. Bess!

BESS. [*Coming down*] I should be in her place. He has promised.

ROSE. Bess—why are you here.

LIV. She is the old woman's grandchild and is insane. [*Mother Tagger comes down and grabs her*]

BESS. No, no—Miss Rose—don't marry him.

MOTH. T. Come, my poor crazy child. Come, dearie, come. [*Pushes her into tent. Parson goes up and talks to Mother Tagger. Silas and Lindy talk aside L.*]

LIV. Come, dear.

ROSE. Oh, John—I can't—I can't.

LIV. Sweetheart, will you allow the ravings of a poor demented creature to affect you?

ROSE. Oh, I'm afraid, John.

LIV. Come dear, come. You're nervous. You'll soon be my dear little wife. Go on, Parson.

PAR. [*Coming down C.*] Do you, Rose Day, and Lindy Jane Smithers, take these men, John Livingstone and Silas Waterbury to be your lawfully wedded husbands, to love honor and *obey* until death do you part?

ROSE and LINDY. [*At the same time—meekly*] We do.

LINDY. Oh, Silas!

SILAS. You're mine, Lindy—you're mine—at last. [*Starts to embrace her. There is a big roar of thunder and they jump*]

PAR. Then I pronounce you man and wife, and whom God has joined together, let no man put asunder. [*Rose swoons and faints*]

LIV. She's fainted.

LINDY. [*Crossing to her*] Rose—my poor Rose.

SILAS. The kerridge is waiting. [*Lifting her up*]

LIV. Yes, you take her home. I will follow you. Go at once before the storm overtakes you. I'll settle with this good woman.

SILAS. We'll wait for you.

LIV. No, no—go at once. [*Pushing them off R. As they all exit, the fury of the storm increases, with wind, thunder and lightning*] Now, mother—quick—[*Looks for Bess*] By Heaven—she's gone!

MOTH. T. Gone?

LIV. [*Looking for Jake*] Is he still here? [*Jake appears at door of wagon*]

JAKE. [*As he appears*] Yes, and ready to settle with you.

LIV. We'll see. [*Pulls knife. They fight. Livingstone gets the better of the knife fight—stabs Jake and throws him off. Livingstone starts for Jake again with knife, to give him another thrust, and as he does so, Bunco enters from R., shoots him; he staggers. During all this action there is a terrible storm raging*]

ACT III.

The scene is a room in which the Livingstones are living. It is supposed to be a room where there is a bed but a cot may be substituted if a bed is not available. There are doors R. and L.U., and there is a window in center at back. There is a dresser up stage against the wall. Fireplace down L. in front of which is a chair. The bed is down R. There is a house screen up L. There is a large closet against the wall up R. or, if desired, a door leading into a supposed closet up there. A table R., and a couple of plain chairs. One to be placed R.C. At rise, Rose sitting in front of fireplace.

LIV. [*At dresser tying his tie, preparing to go*] I may be in at ten.

ROSE. Can't you stay in tonight, John?

LIV. [*Irritated*] No—No! I say. I have business to attend to.

Rose. What business?

Liv. [*Still busy with tie*]   Oh, I can't explain it to you.

Rose. And why not? The baby is not well and I may have to send for a doctor. I don't like to be left alone.

Liv. Oh, I can't help it. It's not my kid.

Rose. [*Rising*]   John! [*Crosses to bed, puts baby down*]

Liv. [*Laughs*]   What's the matter?

Rose. [*With spirit*]   Oh, I won't bear it any longer—I won't—I won't. Business! What business keeps you out night after night and until all hours in the morning. We have been married a year and in all that time you have scarcely spent a night at home. What business is it that must be done tonight, while all day you never leave the house?

Liv. See here, Rose, don't pry into my affairs or you'll be sorry. [*Going to her*] What I want you to know I'll tell you—and if you don't like it—well you know what you can do. [*Exits abruptly R.U.*]

Rose. Oh, what a fool I've been—what a fool. I didn't love him when I married him and now I hate him. But it serves me right—I am a coward. Afraid to face the world with my baby. [*Picks up baby from bed*] Because your father was a criminal I dared not claim him. Well he has given you a name so we must be content, I suppose. [*Lays baby down again*]

Bunco. [*Calls off stage R.*]   Hey—Rose! Who-hoo—Rose—can I come in?

Rose. [*Comes down to L.C.*]   Yes—Come on in.

Bunco. [*Enter R.U.*]   I saw old Pain-in-the-Face go out so I thought I'd slip in. Is the kid asleep? [*Goes to baby*]

Rose. Yes. Be careful and don't wake him.

Bunco. I wonder if dis kid's goin' to look like its father.

Rose. I hope so.

Liv. [*From outside off R.*]   All right—wait a few moments.

Bunco. [*Running up and looking off*]   Gee—it's old Pain-in-the-Face—I'll duck. [*Runs behind screen up L. Livingstone enters door R.U., goes quickly to dresser, takes out jewelry*]

Rose. [*Comes toward him*]   What are you doing?

Liv. I'm in trouble. I want money.

Rose. Don't take those. They belonged to my mother. Here—take this. It's all I have—but leave those. [*Offers purse or moneybag*]

Liv. [*Takes money*]   I'll need it.

Rose. No! I've changed my mind. You shan't have it. [*Resisting him*]

Liv. Let go, you fool—[*Jerks money from her*] Now give me those rings —[*In desperate tone*] Quick—hurry! [*Rose, frightened, gives rings*] Now give me the other.

Rose.   My wedding ring?

Liv.   Yes. Hurry up, I tell you. I'm in trouble.

Rose.   Well—take it, but give me back the others. [*Takes ring, looks at it*]

Liv.   Ralph's ring, eh?

Rose.   Yes. Now give me back the others.

Liv.   I guess not. I need them all. [*Puts them in his pocket*]

Bunco.   [*Has slipped from behind screen and down back of him. Takes jewelry and money from his pocket*]   And so do I. [*Bunco exits L.*]

Rose.   Oh, John—John.

Liv.   Let go. [*Throws her off*] Shall I tell you why my business takes me out at night? It's because I'm a thief—a housebreaker. Now will you hold your tongue? I'm in hard luck tonight, but tomorrow we may have plenty. So cheer up, Rose—Cheer up! [*Laughs and exits door R.U. Bunco enters L.*]

Rose.   Good Heavens, Bunco, did you hear what he said?

Bunco.   You bet I did and it's true—every word of it.

Rose.   Bunco, do you know what you are saying?

Bunco.   Yes I do. He's a devil, he's a thief, a bankrobber and worser.

Rose.   A *worser?*

Bunco.   Yes—a *worser*—a murderer.

Rose.   *Bunco!*

Bunco.   Why I believe it was he who tried to kill your father.

Rose.   My God!

Bunco.   Den he ruined poor Bessie's life, and tried to kill dat poor feller Jake in dat gypsy camp, and den made poor Ralph think he done it.

Rose. [*Crossing to L.*]   Stop—Please, Bunco. For God's sake do you know what you are talking about?

Bunco.   Yes, I'm talkin' about old Pain-in-the-Face.

Rose.   You say you saw Ralph at the gypsy camp?

Bunco.   Well, I didn't exactly see him, 'cause I couldn't see. But I heard his voice and I know it was him.

Rose.   Can it be that Ralph—my Ralph—is alive and innocent. Oh, I begin to see it all now. [*Sink in chair L.*]

Bunco. [*Holding out money she took from Livingstone's pocket*]   Here —you may need dis. And if I was you I'd put on Mr. Ralph's ring again. [*Rose takes ring*] Say, Miss Rose, did you marry him?

Rose.   Yes—yes—and if he is alive I shall go mad.

Bunco. [*Picks baby up, upside down—funny business*]   De baby's wakin'.

Rose. [*Screams*]   Oh, Bunco! [*Lindy and Silas knock on R.U. door*]

Lindy. [*Outside*]   Air ye home, Rose?

Rose. [*Holding the baby*]   Open the door, Bunco.

BUNCO. [*Opening door*] Howdy! [*Dances C. to music. Lindy and Silas enter L.*]

LINDY. Where on airth did you come from?

BUNCO. Oh, I've got a good job taking keer of two kids in the flat next door.

LINDY. Well, I never. We've been to the opery, Rose. [*Crosses C.*]

SILAS. Drammer, Lindy.

LINDY. Opery! It was at the Opery House.

ROSE. Did you enjoy it?

SILAS. Yep. We had two good seats.

LINDY. [*Crossing to him confidentially*] Preserved seats.

SILAS. Yep. They were good ones anyway and you oughter see Lindy blubber.

LINDY. Hersh yer head. I guess you blubbered too when the poor gal was druv out by her hard-hearted paw. Yes—and the villain—say ye oughter see him Rose—he was a bad 'un. I'll foller her to the end of the airth, by Gum.

SILAS. [*Funny business with Lindy*] An' when the villain crep' up behind her with a big bowie knife—before he could jab him the hero pulled out his gun and *bang*—[*Shot heard outside*]

LINDY. Good Lord—what's that? [*Crosses to Silas, R.*]

BUNCO. [*At window*] Hully Chee—two coppers runnin' across the yard—and oh—oo a man is climbing up the balcony.

LINDY. Oh, Lord save me.

SILAS. Me too, oh, Lord. [*Both business of ad lib under the bed*]

BUNCO. Hully Gee! I'm pinched. [*Goes to closet R. Ralph enters through window in prison clothes*]

ROSE. Merciful Heavens!

RALPH. Lady—for God's sake, hide me.

ROSE. Ralph!

RALPH. Rose! [*Embrace*] My Darling!

BUNCO. [*Enters, sees Ralph*] Hully Gee! [*Exits in closet*]

ROSE. You are in danger.

RALPH. Yes, the police are after me.

ROSE. What shall I do?

BUNCO. [*Enters*] Get under the bed. [*Shot outside*]

ROSE. Quick—quick— [*Shot*] Here. [*Turns down cover. Ralph gets into bed*]

BUNCO. Now sleep like the devil. [*Rose C. turns down lights. Knock at R.U. door. Gets baby. Officers knock*] Hully Chee—dere's de cops. [*Crosses to chair, L.*] We ain't in. [*Funny business*]

Rose. Open the door, Bunco.

Bunco. [*Opens door*] Sh—hh—You'll wake the baby.

Off. We must come in. [*They enter*]

Bunco. My master is awful sick.

Off. [*L.C.*] Stand aside.

Rose. What is it sir? Why were those shots fired?

Off. We must search the house, lady. We are after an escaped convict. He was seen to climb the balcony. I can't say whether he came here or the flat above. But we must search.

Bunco. A convict. Oh, Gee! [*Crosses L.*]

Rose. Mercy, he isn't here, sir. You may search but please be as quiet as possible. My husband is very ill and has just fallen asleep.

Off. [*Quietly*] Sorry to trouble you, lady—[*Searches closet and under bed*] Hello—come out here—[*Pulls Silas out shaking; funny business*]

Bunco. Oh, Gee—isn't that funny!

Lindy. Oh, please, Mr. Policeman, don't take us to jail.

Silas. Shut up, Lindy—nothin' to be afraid of. We don't know nothin'.

Off. I can see that. What were you doing under that bed?

Silas. I was under there to bring Lindy out.

Rose. The shots frightened them, officer—sh-h-, dear. [*To Ralph*] It's nothing.

Off. Come. [*To policeman*] We must go through the other rooms. [*Exit L.*]

Lindy. My teeth is jest a chatterin'.

Silas. This ain't no place for a constable. I'm goin' home. [*Exits R.U.*]

Lindy. Silas Waterbury, wait for me. [*Exits U.*]

Rose. God protect you, dear. Have courage. Sit here, Bunco—quick. [*Bunco sits beside Ralph, Rose walks floor with baby*] There, there, dearie— sh—sh-h.

Bunco. Gee, ain't this excitin'? [*Crosses right to bed*]

Off. [*They enter*] Sorry we had to trouble you, missus. He's not there. We must go upstairs. Good-night. [*Crosses to C.*]

Rose. Good-night, officer. I hope you find him. It makes me nervous to think of a criminal at large.

Off. Oh, we'll get him. [*They exit R.U.*]

Bunco. Yes—you will. [*Puts key in door*]

Rose. Quick, quick, Ralph, put on this suit of clothes in the closet. [*Ralph goes to closet, puts on suit, hat, etc.*] Bunco, watch. Oh, God help me to get him away.

BUNCO. Hully Gee, Miss Rose—don't flop—[*Runs to window*] Don't be afraid, Miss Rose—God will help him, *you bet.*

ROSE. Don't leave the window, Bunco. Watch—watch. [*Bunco does fancy business, back to window*]

RALPH. [*Enters*] Rose—why are you here? And the *child*—

ROSE. Our child, Ralph.

RALPH. My God!

ROSE. He told me you were dead. I married him.

RALPH. Livingstone?

ROSE. Yes.

RALPH. Oh, God! Where is he?

ROSE. No, no—for my sake, Ralph, you must get away. I have proof against him. This girl heard it all—that night at the gypsy camp. But first you must get away.

BUNCO. Old Pain-in-the-Face is coming back.

ROSE. Too late.

RALPH. I'll meet him.

ROSE. No, it would be madness. See, the child is ill. You are the doctor—do you understand?

RALPH. Yes.

BUNCO. [*Gets chair for him*] Sit here, Mr. Ralph, de baby is sick and you are de doctor. Hully Chee—now he's a doctor. [*Livingstone sings drunken song off R.*] Hully Chee—if I'm discovered I shall be found. [*Bunco makes funny exit into closet*]

LIV. [*Enters R.U.*] How's the girl, eh? Miss her hubby? [*To Ralph*] Who the devil are you?

ROSE. Oh, John—the doctor. The baby is ill.

LIV. Too bad, hic—[*Laughs*] Let it die, doc—it's better off. [*Crosses L.*]

ROSE. John! [*Livingstone laughs*] This way, doctor. You will call again in the morning?

LIV. [*Faces Ralph*] What ails the kid, doc? [*Faces him*] By Heaven, I know you. [*Snatches off Ralph's hat*] Ralph Carlton!

RALPH. Yes, John Livingstone—I said we'd meet again. [*He rushes at Livingstone. Rose screams. During the struggle Livingstone hits Ralph on the head with butt of revolver, catches him as he struggles, throws him in closet*]

ROSE. You've killed him.

LIV. Shut up, you fool. [*Throws her C.*] I'll fix your Ralph Carlton—I'll call the police. [*Goes to phone. As he locked closet door Rose has gotten scissors and cut phone wire*] What have you done? Oh, I see—you want to save him, eh? [*Struggles with her*]

ROSE. Yes.

LIV. Drop those scissors.

ROSE. I won't.

LIV. [*Shakes them to the floor, strikes Rose; she falls C.*]   Try to save him! I'll fix you, eh. [*Gets rope at window*]

ROSE. [*Rises, runs to closet*] Ralph—Ralph—[*Livingstone catches her, drags her to bed*] Oh, you devil—you murderer.

LIV. I am, eh? [*Chokes her with handkerchief, throws her on floor, cuts rope line and ties her to bed*] There—I guess you'll be quiet now. There's another telephone downstairs, I'll use *it*. I'll lock the door and keep the key in my pocket until I come back. [*Exits R.U.*]

BUNCO. [*Crawls over transom, unlocks closet door*] I'll be with you in a minute, Mr. Ralph.

RALPH. [*Enters*] My darling, are you hurt? Bunco, get some water, quick!

BUNCO. I'll turn up the lights. [*Does so, cuts rope*] Some water. Yes, sir. Hully Gee, dis door is locked. [*Tries closet key*]

ROSE. I'm all right now, dear. Get away through the window before he gets back.

RALPH. Not without you. Will you come with me?

ROSE. Yes.

BUNCO. Come on—de door's open. I'll get de kid. [*Goes L. of bed for child. Ralph and Rose start for door. Livingstone opens it*]

LIV. The devil!

BUNCO. [*On bed, with revolver in hand*] Throw up your hands. Hurry up! That's right. Now, Mr. Ralph, give him a knock on the coco.

RALPH. Take off your coat.

BUNCO. Take off your coat.

LIV. Ah-h! [*Not taking coat off*]

BUNCO. [*Crosses to him, poking revolver in his stomach*] There! Take off your coat or I'll puncture you. [*Livingstone crosses L. and takes off coat*] Dat's right.

RALPH. Now put on these.

LIV. Huh?

BUNCO. [*Has gotten convict's clothes from closet*] Put 'em on! [*Covers him with gun*] Hurry up! [*Livingstone does so. Bunco jumps up and down on bed*] He won't put them on. Oh, no!

RALPH. Now the coat—[*Livingstone starts for Ralph*]

BUNCO. Oh, Gee, ain't we got fun—[*Pokes Livingstone in back with pistol*] Hurry up. [*Livingstone starts toward bed*]

RALPH. [*Ties him*] I guess the police will be as glad to get you as to get me, John Livingstone. [*Gags him, speaks to Rose*] Now we are going. I have a long account to settle with you. The end is not yet.

ROSE. Bring the baby, Bunco.

BUNCO. Yes, ma'am. [*Jumps off bed. Livingstone starts to move bed and all*] Whoa, Bill. [*Takes baby. Funny business across room with gun. Rose and Ralph exit R.U.*] How do you feel now, old Pain-in-the-Face? [*Kicks him*] I'll see you when the robins bloom in the spring, tra la. [*Exits after others*]

LIV. [*Struggles, works gag out of mouth*] Help—help—

MOTH. T. [*Enters at window*] Is that you, darling?

LIV. Mother Tagger—what luck! Come here and cut these ropes.

MOTH. T. How did you get into this, darling? I've been hanging around to tell you that Jake Jordan is free.

LIV. Jake Jordan free? The devil he is.

MOTH. T. True as Heaven, darling. [*Crash, scream outside*] What's that?

LIV. I'm off. [*Officers at door, R.U. Livingstone crosses and gets revolver from dresser drawer. One policeman jumps through window, other R. Jake enters R.U.*]

OFF. [*At window*] Here's our man. [*Livingstone shoots at officer at window. Jumps out. Others follow him. Officer falls to floor wounded, then rises and crosses to window. Jake shoots out of window*]

MOTH. T. [*On knees, starts praying*] Oh, oh, it's all over now! It's all over now.

ACT IV.

Over run from up L. Lindy enters L., skirt caught up, very tired. Sunrise, red and blue lights. Silas follows Lindy on; has shoes in hand and an open umbrella over his head.

LINDY. For land's sake, will you hurry? I never seed such a man in my life. Here's a tent—we can ask the way. And the next time I let you take the lead and follow you, you can lam me good. And as fer show theaters I'll never go again, 'less I'm sure we can ketch the last car home. My feet is so swelled and tired, I could jest lay down and die. Do you spect we're any nearer than when we started?

SILAS. Durned ef I know. We've walked about five thousand miles now I reckon.

LINDY. What?

SILAS. Five hundred miles.

LINDY. How fur?

SILAS. Five miles, I said. [*Wilting at her each time*]

LINDY. What on earth are you doing with your shoes in your hands?

SILAS. Ain't goin' to wear 'em out, by cracky. Paid a dollar and twenty cents fer them shoes.

LINDY. Why don't you take off your socks too? Paid ten cents fer 'em, ye everlastin' idiot. Well, air you goin' to the tent and ask where we air?

SILAS. Reckon I might. [*Goes to tent, looks in*] Jumpin' catfish! [*Jumps back, frightened*] The Devil must live here.

LINDY. The Devil must live here? What air you talkin' about?

SILAS. There was somethin' sittin' over the fire noddin' her head and laughin' and in the corner on some straw was a poor, wild-lookin' critter moanin' and groanin'.

LINDY. Let's go, Silas—we'll be murdered yet.

SILAS. If you had stayed and spent the night with Rose as ye was goin' to—

LINDY. What? And her with a convict hidin' in the bed? I guess not. Come on. Oh, Lord—my feet! [*Limps*]

SILAS. Gosh all hemlock—

LINDY. What's the matter?

SILAS. Stepped on a splinter. [*Picks splinter out of foot*]

LINDY. Then put on your shoes.

SILAS. Not for fifty splinters, by tar. [*Exits R. with Lindy*]

BUNCO. [*Enters up L. and runs down. Looks around*] Wonder what time it is. Must be six o'clock. I feel like breakfast. Oh, dere's a tent. Maybe we can all get a cup of coffee. [*Calls off stage*] Hoo-oo, hoo! Come on, yes, all right. [*Crosses back as Ralph and Rose enter up L.*] Give me de baby. Dere, dere—you poor child, is you cold?

RALPH. [*Down run*] Be careful, dear—be careful.

BUNCO. Shall I go to the tent and ask for some breakfast?

ROSE. No, no—don't do that, Bunco. I'm so afraid, dear, that we might meet someone who would know us and betray us to the police.

RALPH. Sit here, dear. Now listen. We can't wander around as we have done all night. I'll give myself up, dear.

ROSE. No, no, Ralph.

RALPH. It's the only thing to do now. I am innocent. Bunco there can prove that.

BUNCO. You just bet I can. [*Crosses up stage, back to audience*]

RALPH. Don't look so downhearted, Rose. Our sun will shine again. Already my heart feels light.

ROSE. Oh, Ralph, you inspire me with confidence. I couldn't bear to lose you again, dear.

RALPH. We must be brave and try to face with cheerful hearts whatever the future has in store for us. I feel sure that in the end all will come out right.

ROSE. But what shall we do with John Livingstone?

BUNCO. Put him in a cage and throw sugar at him. [*Crosses to tent*] Hully Gee. Sneak!

ROSE. What's the matter!

BUNCO. We're up against it. De old gypsy hag is in dat tent.

ROSE. Oh, what shall we do?

BUNCO. Come on dis way.

RALPH. Don't be so frightened, dear. Be brave.

ROSE. For your sake, I'll try.

RALPH. My brave little woman. [*All exit up L.*]

MOTH. T. [*At door of tent*] No sign of him yet, and I heard bloodhounds a-bayin'. I'm afeared they'll get him, the poor darlin', and if he should squeal, then my poor neck would be stretched. Oh, this is a sad, sad world. [*Drinks out of bottle. Bess appears at door*] Here, you come out—do you hear? [*Bess comes out*] Go to the spring and get the bucket filled. Hurry up, you lazy hussy. Hurry, I say. [*Pushes her*]

BESS. Oh, I can't—[*Falls*] I can't go so far and carry that heavy bucket. I'm so weak and sick and I've had nothing to eat today.

MOTH. T. Well, I've been away on business. He, he, he. [*Coughs and crosses to R.*] D'ye hear? Haven't had time to go to town for groceries. One day's starving won't hurt you. Ye ought to be used to it by now.

BESS. Yes, if one can get used to starving. I've been hungry often enough. Oh, why don't you let me die at once and not kill me by inches?

MOTH. T. It's safer by inches, darling. Then there's no danger. Oh, I'd have strangled you long ago if I'd dared. Get up! [*Kicks her*] Get the water before I beat you again.

BESS. I won't. [*Rises and faces her*] You may beat me till I die. I won't. I won't be your slave any longer.

MOTH. T. What? He, he, he. We'll see, my fine lady—[*Drinks*] We'll see. [*Crosses into tent*]

BESS. [*Falls on knees, sobbing*] Oh, dear God, let me die, let me die. Perhaps somewhere in Heaven I may have a *mother to guide me*. I'm so terribly alone here—so terribly alone.

MOTH. T. [*Enters with whip*] So you'll stand out against me, eh? Get up —do you hear? [*Crosses to L.*]

BESS. I wont'—I won't!

MOTH. T. [*Strikes her with whip*] Then take that, you lazy whelp. I'll teach you to mind. [*Raises whip again*]

JAKE. [*Enters L.U., catches whip*] You she devil! If ye wasn't so old, I'd cut ye in pieces and leave yer bones fer the crows to pick.

MOTH. T. Jake Jordan!

JAKE. Yes. Thought I was in jail, eh? Well I've served my time. Ye've forgotten that, eh? Git up, sis. [*Helps Bess up*] Ye'll get no more beatin's.

BESS. God bless you, sir. [*Sits R.C. on stone*]

MOTH. T. [*Screams*] What do you mean?

JAKE. Jest this. I've made a full confession. If the cops land Livingstone tonight, he'll take his last rest at the end of a rope.

MOTH. T. Would you squeal on a pal?

JAKE. Pal? Has he been square with me? Tried to murder me in cold blood and you helped him—you dried-up old mummy. But I'll leave the Devil to settle wid ye.

MOTH. T. Oh, don't talk that way, darlin', ye make my bones rattle. [*Crosses L., drinks. Dog barks*]

JAKE. De hounds. Dey is on de trail again.

MOTH. T. Oh, Lord. Oh, Lord—[*Starts to go*]

JAKE. Stay where you are—de cops'll need you. Get into dat tent.

MOTH. T. Oh, oh, darlin'—my sweet boy.

JAKE. Don't darlin' me—you old crow. Get in there. [*Pushes her into tent*]

BESS. Oh, sir, will they catch John Livingstone?

JAKE. Yes—unless he is sharper than those bloodhounds that are after him.

BESS. What's that? Oh, it's Bunco—it's Bunco! [*Bunco singing old song off stage, "When the Robins Nest Again"*]

BUNCO. [*Enters L.*] Hully Gee—does me lamps deceive me? Bess! [*Embraces her*] And me old college chum—shake, Jake. [*They shake hands*]

JAKE. You bet. Well, kid—you're all right.

BUNCO. Well, say, where did you two drop from? I feel as if I'd found my family. Oh, Gee. Say, I helped you once, old pal—now you must help me. I know I kin trust you. De dearest friend I have in de world is in trouble. Will you stand by me?

JAKE. Till death, kid.

BUNCO. [*Shakes hands with Jake*] De same. Well he's just escaped from de pen and found his wife. Hully Gee—she's got two husbands now.

JAKE. She married Livingstone, didn't she?

BUNCO. Yes. Livingstone's de guy dat sent him to de pen. Dey are in de woods hidin'. De cops have turned de bloodhounds loose.

JAKE. I know somethin' about his case.

BUNCO. You do?

JAKE. Yes. Bring them here.

BUNCO. You bet. [*Exits down R. Sunlight till curtain. Bess sways and faints*]

JAKE. Dat kid's all right. Sit down, sis. Dere—don't tremble so. You're safe. De cops will run Livingstone down, den de sun will shine brighter fer you. I've had a few ups and downs myself, but now I'm goin' to be honest. We're all lookin' fer happiness in dis life and it's wisest to be getting it by being straight, than by being crooked. [*Goes to stump, R.*]

BESS. Oh, it is, is it?

JAKE. Dere now—you've got a friend in me, sis, and don't you forget it.

BUNCO. [*Outside*] Come on, Mr. Ralph—here's de guy.

JAKE. Hello—dey're comin'. [*Ralph, Rose and baby enter L. Bunco runs to Bess*]

RALPH. Mr. Jordan! [*Holds out hand*]

JAKE. Jake, pardner.

RALPH. You'll help me out of this?

JAKE. You bet—and I kin do it too. I know you're innocent.

ROSE. [*Crosses to L.*] Bessie—if you had only known!

BESS. Oh, Miss Rose, will you let me see your baby?

ROSE. Don't wake him, Bessie.

BESS. Oh, baby—baby—[*Sobs*]

ROSE. There, there, you shall come home with me and have him as long as you like.

MOTH. T. Oh, oh, let me out. Good, kind gentlemen—let me out.

JAKE. Here comes a cop. [*Rose, Bess and Bunco cross up stage C.*]

MOTH. T. Oh, Lord. [*Officers enter with dog up R.*]

OFF. Hello, Jake—is that you?

JAKE. Yes, gov'ner—see any sign of him?

OFF. Dogs seem to have lost the trail. Who's that?

JAKE. A friend of mine, gov'ner. I say, ye might question de old hag in dere. She's de old hag who has done Livingstone's dirty work for years. I've got her in there. Question her.

RALPH. [*Crosses to C.*] One moment, Officer. I'm Ralph Carlton, escaped from Sing Sing. I want to give myself up until you have evidence of my innocence, and that will be soon.

OFF. Yes, we have the confession of Jake Jordan here, which looks well for you. However, I'll have to put the bracelets on you just as a matter of form. I believe you are an innocent man. [*To police*] See if the dogs can find the scent again. I have business here. Start for the caves, men. [*Other officers have their dogs*] Hallowell and Cane, have their dogs on the trail to the west. [*Police exit L.U. over run with dogs*] Now I'll see the old woman. [*Opens door to tent*] Come out, madam.

BUNCO. [*Down stage*] Oh, Gee— now mudder is goin' to get it.

MOTH. T. [*Enters from hut*] Oh, oh, oh, I'm an innocent woman, darlin'. Oh, oh, oh!

OFF. Innocent, are you? Well, Livingstone says not.

MOTH. T. What—have they got him? [*L.C.*]

OFF. Yes, and he will be condemned for murder.

MOTH. T. Oh, the wicked, wicked boy.

OFF. And it looks as if you'd die with him, my woman.

MOTH. T. Me? Oh, good Lord. Darlin'—what for?

OFF. Well, Livingstone has confessed that you were implicated in the Cosden robbery and the murder as well.

MOTH. T. He lies—he lies! The dog. He did it himself.

OFF. Also the attempted murder of the young lady's father.

MOTH. T. Oh, the hound. I was at the camp at the time. He did it himself.

OFF. Then how did you know he did it?

MOTH. T. He told me himself.

OFF. [*Making notes*] Ah, very good. I think I shall have to borrow your bracelets, Mr. Carlton. [*Does so. Mother Tagger starts to run*]

BUNCO. Hold on, mudder—[*Catches her*] We need you.

OFF. [*Puts bracelets on Mother Tagger*] Allow me.

MOTH. T. Oh, oh, darlin'!

BUNCO. How do you feel? Kinder natural, mudder?

MOTH. T. Wait till I get out.

BUNCO. Oh, I'll wait.

OFF. Oh, I'll take care of you. [*Exit L.U. Hounds bay*]

JAKE. The hounds are on the scent again. Sounds as if they were over by the falls. [*Goes up and exits, L.2.*]

ROSE. [*Crosses to Ralph*] Oh, Ralph, I'm so afraid.

RALPH. Go into the tent, dear. I'll be right back. [*Goes up and exits, L.*]

BUNCO. Where are you goin', Mr. Ralph? Hully Gee, I wish I was on the police force. [*Livingstone fires revolver off R.2. Rose exits into tent*]

BUNCO. [*Off stage*] Oh, look—*look*—he's coming.

Liv. [*Enters R.2.*] Stand out of my way. [*Throws Bunco R. Shots are heard outside. Livingstone covered with blood, revolver in hand. Ladies scream, dogs bark. Bess is R. Crosses to L. Rose R.*]

Silas. As the constable of this county I order you to surrender.

Liv. I'll see you in hell first. [*Snaps revolver at him. He is out of shells*] Damnation! [*Up on run*]

Silas. Surrender, or I'll fire.

Liv. Fire, and be damned. [*Runs to L.2. Jake comes out on run, meets him, knife in hand*] Jake Jordan!

Jake. Yes.

Liv. I have no knife.

Jake. [*Throws knife away*] Neither have I. The best man wins. [*Fight. Livingstone hits Jake on head, starts to exit L.U. Meets Ralph*]

Ralph. John Livingstone, I said we'd meet again. Fate has made me the instrument of justice. [*Backs Livingstone down run*] For years you have made me suffer. Now you shall pay for it to the last penny.

Liv. Have mercy!

Ralph. What mercy did you show me?

Bess. Ralph—for my sake. [*Grabs his arms. Ralph turns a second to Rose. Livingstone starts for him with knife. All scream. Jake shoots. Silas catches Livingstone*]

Jake. Livingstone, old pal, you've planned your last crime. [*Officers enter*]

Silas. We've got your man. He's dying. Take him away.

Liv. Jake Jordan, I'll meet you in Hell.

Jake. No, guv'ner—I ain't goin' that way. [*Officers exit with Livingstone. Bess crosses to entrance. Bunco puts arm around her*]

Ralph. Rose!

Rose. Ralph!

Silas. *Lindy*, come into *camp*!

CURTAIN

BILLY THE KID

By Walter Woods

DESCRIPTION OF CHARACTERS

WRIGHT, *a man of sixty. White hair, long white moustache.*

MARY, *a woman of thirty-five.*

BILL, *fifteen at opening of play.*

BRADLEY, *a military looking man of sixty-five. Moustache and chin whiskers.*

NELLIE, *about Bill's age.*

DENVER, *a well preserved man of forty; looks younger.*

CON, *Denver's age and looks older.*

MOSE, *a clean-shaven old man.*

PEANUT, *black moustache and beard, low forehead, long hair.*

BUD, *a tough-looking character, stubby moustache.*

COSTUMES

BILL: *Act I: Ballet shirt, knee pants, soft hat. End of act, long coat, mask.*
  Act II: Black velvet coat, wide-necked shirt, light riding breeches, top boots, light sombrero.
  Act III: Leather breeches, blue shirt, red handkerchief about neck, cartridge belt with revolvers.
  Act IV: Same as Act II, with addition of long gray rain coat.

DENVER: *Act I: Traveling suit.*
  Act II: Black suit, outing shirt, slouch hat.
  Act III: Same, soiled and torn.
  Act IV: Same, more soiled and torn.

COLONEL: *G.A.R. uniform.*

MOSE: *Same.*

CON: *Act I: Overalls and jumper.*
  Act II: Cowboy outfit.
  Act III: "   "
  Act IV: "   "

WRIGHT: *Act I: Plantation suit of light crash.*

PEANUT: *Mexican suit. Last act, cloak.*

MONROE: *Cowboy.*

MOLLY: *Flashy dress.*

JENNIE: *Act I: Flashy dress.*
  Act III: Plain maid's dress.
  Act IV: Same, with wrap.

NELLIE: *Act I: Light summer dress.*
  Act II: Western riding habit, short skirt, shirt waist, sombrero.
  Act III: Neat house dress.
  Act IV: Walking suit with wrap.

(Three sets of scenery are necessary. Last act is the same as Act I, with the addition of a transparent return to house)

CHARACTERS

IN ACT ONE

STEPHEN WRIGHT, *a ranch owner.*   *(Old man)*
MARY, *his wife.*   *(Juvenile)*
WILL, *Mary's son.*   *(Lead)*
COLONEL WAYNE BRADLEY, *a retired army officer.*   *(Character)*
BOYD DENVERS, *an Eastern gentleman.*   *(Heavy)*
CON HANLEY, *a hand.*   *(Comedy)*
MOSES MOORE, *an ex-orderly.*   *(Character comedy)*
MAID   *(Utility)*
NELLIE

IN ACT TWO

BILLY, THE KID, *a Western desperado.*   *(Lead)*
CON HANLEY, *his lieutenant.*   *(Comedy)*
BOYD DENVER, *owner of the Broken Heart Saloon.*   *(Heavy)*
"PEANUT" GIVANNI, *manager of Broken Heart Saloon.*   *(Character heavy)*
BUD MONROE, *a bad man.*   *(Character)*
HANK, *bartender.*   *(Utility)*
COLONEL WAYNE BRADLEY, *still retired.*
MOSES MOORE, *still an "ex."*
MOLLY ⎫
JENNIE ⎬ *women of the Broken Heart.*
NELLIE BRADLEY   *(Lead)*
MINERS, DEPUTY SHERIFFS, ETC.

      NOTE: Cast can be doubled to seven men, three women.

SYNOPSIS

ACT I.   EXTERIOR OF WRIGHT'S COTTAGE
            "THE OATH OF VENGEANCE"

ACT II.   THE BROKEN HEART SALOON (THREE YEARS LATER)
            "YOU SHALL FOLLOW ME"

ACT III. COLONEL BRADLEY'S DINING ROOM (ONE WEEK LATER)
            "POLLY HAS ARMS OF HER OWN"

ACT IV. SAME AS ACT I
            "VENGEANCE IS MINE"

ACT I.

SCENE: *Landscape in 5. Picket fence at back. Large Southern home with porch L. Canary in cage hanging from porch. Well curbing, foot and a half high, up L. Table and chair R.* DISCOVERED: *Con seated on well curb, smoking. Enter Maid from house, with bottles and glasses. Puts them on table. Enter Wright R.U.E. followed by Denver.*

WRI. Con! [*Con jumps up and gets busy*]

CON. Yis, sor.

WRI. Have the niggers bring up a few loads of gravel and fill that old well. [*Goes to table, sits L; Denver sits R.*]

CON. Well, well. All's well that ends well.

WRI. What's that, suh?

CON. I said, very well, sor. That would end the well, sor. [*Exit L.*]

WRI. [*Pouring drinks*] Somebody will fall in there yet. It's a nuisance. It's thirty feet deep and dry as a bone. We get all our water from the artesian well, yonder.

DEN. Thirty feet deep? A dangerous hole.

WRI. Yes, suh. Why a person could fall in there and no one would ever know what became of him.

DEN. [*Half to himself*] Excellent.

WRI. What's that, suh?

DEN. The—ah—whiskey is excellent.

WRI. You're a gentleman, suh. Any man who is a judge of whiskey is a friend of mine. [*They shake hands*]

DEN. I'd often heard of your Southern hospitality, and rather doubted its existence myself; but during my short stay here you have converted me for life.

WRI. Tut, tut, tut, suh! You have only received the treatment that any gentleman may expect. Have another drink. And remember, until you are ready to leave this—rather dismal landscape, you are my honored guest.

DEN. It's a beautiful spot—beautiful. And you have a charming wife and a wonderful son. No wonder you are contented.

WRI. Contented? Contented is not the word, suh. Happy, suh, downright happy!

DEN. [*Slight sneer*] Indeed?

WRI.   Yes, suh. Why hang it, I'd like to see the man who could *help* but be happy with Mary for a wife. A lady, suh—one of your sort from up North. How she ever came to care for an old codger like me, is more than I can guess.

DEN.   You underrate yourself.

WRI.   Not a bit of it. My youth is far behind. I'm rough in my ways, and I never took a prize in a beauty show. [*Denver laughs*] Although I am well fixed financially—

DEN.   [*Still laughing*]   Well, there, there! That last remark doubtless—

WRI.   Hold on, my friend. I was going to say that although I am well fixed financially, Mary would never wed for money, and if any man was to hint at such a thing, I believe I would kill him. [*Denver suddenly ceases laughing; he looks at Wright*]

DEN.   [*Intense*]   I believe you would.

WRI. [*Light*]   You and she must become great friends, suh. Perhaps—perhaps she sometimes feels sort of lonesome, way out here in the West, and you two can talk over New York until this ranch will seem like a suburb of the great city.

DEN.   I am sure Mrs. Wright and myself will become great friends but I hardly think we will discuss the East. During our short interview this morning, I could see that her whole interest lies with her home, husband and boy.

WRI. [*Huskily*]   That's kind of you to say that, suh. Yes, suh—[*Fills glass to hide his emotion, spills liquor*] Yes, suh.

CON. [*Enters L.U.E.*]   For the love of Hiven, don't spill it.

WRI.   What the devil is the matter with you, Con?

CON.   If I hadn't arrived just when I did, you would have poured it all on the ground.

WRI.   Thanks for getting here in time. [*He talks to Denver*]

CON. [*Aside*]   Thanks is it? That's a mighty dry reward for saving a man's whiskey. [*Aloud*] I've told 'em, sor.

WRI.   Eh? Told who? Told what?

CON.   Well, well, well, how forgetful ye are. I've told the niggers.

WRI.   Oh, yes. About filling the well.

CON.   That well and me, sor, are alike in one respect; and then again we differ with the advantage all on the side of the well.

WRI.   How is that, Con?

CON.   Well—we're both as dry as a bone. [*Wright and Denver laugh*]

DEN.   Very good, Con.

CON.   But the well is going to be filled up.

Wri. [*Rises, crosses to Con, C., laughing*] So are you, Con. Help yourself, but go light on it. [*Goes up L. Con crosses to table, takes bottle and glass, all the time watching Wright. Seeing his back turned, is about to drink from bottle when he turns and sees Denver watching him*]

Con. Turn yer head, can't ye? What do ye want to be watching a man drink for? [*Growling*] Old Tom the peeper! My, my, but it's a beautiful pair of eyes ye have in your head. I love to look at 'em. [*Pours glass full and drinks*] Well, how did ye like the way I did it?

Den. You seem to have taken a dislike to me, Con.

Con. I have not. I wouldn't take the trouble.

Den. [*Low*] One word to Wright of your insolence to me today and he would kick you off the place.

Con. One word to him about the little talk I overheard ye having wid his wife this morning and ye would never leave the place alive.

Den. [*Rises, uneasy*] What did you hear?

Con. That's none of your dom business. Turn yer head, will ye? I want another drink. [*Denver turns, agitated. Con drinks from bottle*]

Den. Have another, Con?

Con. What's the use? The more I drink the less I talk.

Den. [*Hurriedly*] Before you tell Wright anything I wish to see you alone.

Con. No, I'm not going to tell him. That seems to relieve ye, don't it? No, I wouldn't spoil his happiness for the world. But I'll keep me eye on you, my laddy buck, while ye stay here—which had better not be long.

Den. Meet me here, in an hour—alone.

Con. All right. In the meantime, me and the well will proceed to get full together. [*Goes up stage*]

Den. [*Aside*] And you, my friend, will be at the bottom of it.

Wri. [*As Con joins him*] Will the niggers start on the well at once? [*Con shakes his head*] No, suh? Why not, suh?

Con. Billy is using 'em for cattle, sor. He's learning to be a roper, sor.

Wri. I'll rope him. Tell him I want him. Tell him—*tell him*.

Con. T'ell with him.

Wri. What?

Con. I said I'd tell him, sor—[*Exit L.U.E. Wright laughs*]

Den. The servant seems on excellent terms with the master.

Wri. [*Comes down*] Servants? Haven't a one on the place; they are all my friends. Master? There is but one Master—above. [*Crosses to table*]

Den. [*Up L.*] And one servant who never fails us—below. [*Looks in well*] A dangerous hole, dark and deep. [*Con enters L.U.E. behind Denver and overhears his last remark. Wright is busy mixing a julep and does not hear the following*]

CON. Nice place to pitch a man, eh?

DEN. [*Starts*] Damn you! [*Shows anger; Con stares at him insolently*]

CON. Look at the purty eyes on him!

DEN. [*Recovers himself and laughs*] You possess the true Irish wit, Con. I see you are trying to have fun at my expense by making me angry, but I refuse to be a victim. You and I shall be friends. [*He holds out hand*]

CON. [*Takes hand*] Whenever I meet you, I shall always be glad to hold your hand like this.

DEN. Thank you, Con.

CON. So ye can't stick a knife in me. [*Denver, in anger, attempts to snatch hand away; Con holds it*]

DEN. Let go of my hand, you Irish cur, you are hurting me. Let go I say!

CON. I'll let go when I get through wid it. You gave it to me. I didn't ask for it. [*Pinches his hand at every chance. Denver shows signs of pain*] There. [*Throws hand*] I'm through with that hand—forever.

DEN. I'll make you smart for this!

CON. What's the use? I'm smart already. You said I had the true Irish wit. [*Laughs and crosses down to Wright*]

WRI. [*Enters R.3.*] Hello, Con. Did you tell Billy? Is he coming?

CON. Yes, sor. No, sor.

WRI. Yes, suh—no, suh! What do you mean?

CON. Yes, sor, I told him. No, sor, he ain't coming.

WRI. Why not?

CON. He's practising wid his revolver. He wants to be a crack shot.

WRI. I'll crack him when I see him, confound him.

CON. Yes, confound him, but Con couldn't bring him wid a yoke of oxen. [*Exit L.U.E.*]

DEN. [*Crosses to table*] That boy of yours, Billy, seems full of mischief.

WRI. Full of life, love and kindness, sir. A better boy never lived. A little wild perhaps but that will wear off in time. Brave and reckless as any cow-puncher on the ranch; a hard rider, a good roper and a sure shot. But he ain't mine, more's the pity. You see, Mary was a widow when I married her. Had a little boy baby. But he's grown up just like mine and will never know the difference.

DEN. [*Surprised*] She had a child when she married you?

WRI. Yes, poor thing. She had married a cur, a sneak who deserted her. Then he died, which I reckon was the only decent thing he ever did in his whole life.

DEN. [*Aside*]   She had a child.

WRI.   Mary is only half my age, suh. But our love is as young as a honey-moon. There's only one mar to my happiness. I'm sorry the scoundrel who caused her such unhappiness is dead. I should like the pleasure of killing him. [*Crosses to house*]

DEN. [*Aside*]   A dangerous fool. I must be careful.

MAID. [*Enters on porch*]   Supper's ready, sir. [*Exits*]

WRI.   Supper! That's welcome news to a couple of hungry men, come in, suh. Come right in. [*"Marching Through Georgia." Exit house*]

DEN. [*Following*]   She had a child. [*Exit house*]

COL. BRADLEY. [*Outside*]   Column right, march! [*Enter R.U.E. in single file, Colonel, Mose and Nellie. They march down C.*] Halt. [*They do so*] On left into line. March! [*They line up. Nellie L., Mose C., Colonel R.*] Now we'll call the roll.

MOSE.   No, sir.

COL.   Never, sir. Damme, sir.

MOSE.   Never, sir.

COL.   When I have to swear, I can do it myself, can't I?

MOSE.   I—should—say—you—could.

COL.   Where's that girl? [*Calls*] Nellie—I mean, Sergeant, come here.

WRI. [*Enters from house*]   Hello, Colonel. Glad to see you. [*They shake hands*] You are just in time. Drop the tactics and we'll go in and have a julep before supper. Mose, you are a deacon so I mustn't tempt you. Just make yourself comfortable.

MOSE.   Thank you, sir. [*He drops military air and goes up, filling his pipe*]

COL.   That's it. The army is demoralized by the accursed drink.

WRI.   Why, I thought you would like a little something after your long ride. [*Calls in house*] Sam, never mind the juleps.

COL.   Hold on there, never countermand an order. Besides, I didn't say *I* didn't want one. I said it demoralized the army. I am an officer. [*Exit both, laughing, arm in arm*]

MOSE.   Wish this army had a little demoralizing. Deacon, eh! Only on Sundays. [*Sees bottle on table*] Attention! Forward march! [*Goes to table, salutes and picks up bottle*]

CON. [*Enters*]   Heave to! [*He throws shovel of sand in well*]

MOSE.   Heave two? I haven't had one yet.

CON.   What are ye doing wid that whiskey?

MOSE.   Whiskey? What—me a deacon? This ain't whiskey.

CON.   The saints protect me. I've lost me taste. What is it?

MOSE.   It's a—a—nerve tonic.

CON. Well, me nerves are all on edge. Give me a taste.

MOSE. [*Filling glasses*] Mind this is only medicine.

CON. I know it. Make mine a big one. [*Mose takes glasses. Hands one to Con*] Well, here's looking at you. [*Con C. Mose R. of C. Enter Bill, R.U.E. He comes down between them*]

MOSE. Happy days. [*Both drink. Bill slaps them on back and both spit out liquor*]

CON. Heave two.

MOSE. One's enough for me.

BILL. At it again, eh? Mose, I'm ashamed of you, a deacon.

MOSE. Only on Sundays, Billy.

BILL. Con, I thought you signed the pledge.

CON. I did not. I only swore off. There's nothing to prevent a man swearing *on* again, is there?

BILL. [*Laughing*] You are a pair of frauds.

CON. Supper's waiting for ye, Billy.

BILL. Well, I'll wait till you go, to keep you out of temptation. Besides, I want to tell you how well I'm getting on with my shooting. I hit the bull's eye ten times hand running.

CON. Ye did?

BILL. And I roped seven niggers out of eight.

CON. Billy boy!

MOSES. Better study your schooling. All them things won't do you no good.

BILL. Won't eh? Oh, yes, it will 'cause I'm going to be a pirate.

MOSE and CON. A what?

BILL. A pirate on the high seas. I'm going to hold up trains and stages.

MOSE. What? On the high seas?

BILL. No-o. I'm mixed. The book I've been reading last was about a knight of the road, not a pirate.

MOSE. Leave them books alone, son. They'll fill your head with trash.

BILL. No trash about this. I'm going to be one of 'em and Con is going to be my lieutenant. Ain't you, Con?

CON. [*Winking at Mose*] Sure thing, Billy.

BILL. No fooling now.

CON. Divil a bit.

BILL. Put her there. [*Holds out hand*]

CON. [*Wiping his hand on his pants*] Wait a bit, Billy; I shook wid a blackguard a while ago. [*He shakes his hand*]

MOSE. Now, Con, don't go putting that boy up to any foolishness.

BILL. This ain't foolishness, Mose. We're going to hold up only the rich people and carry them off to our cave for ransom.

CON. What is a ransom, Billy?

BILL. I don't know.

CON. Well, how in blazes are ye going to hold 'em for it if you don't know what it is?

BILL. Oh, it means—death; hold 'em until they die, see?

CON. Well I think that will be a heap of trouble. Why not take a gun and ransom 'em as soon as we capture 'em?

MOSE. Con, stop teasing the boy.

BILL. Then we'll capture Nellie and I'll marry her.

CON. Oh, ho! Nellie is it? Sure yer stuck on her.

BILL. Never you mind, Con. She's going to be my wife some day.

MOSE. Great guns. What notions—Pirates, ransoms and matrimony.

COL. [*Inside*] Forward march!

BILL. Here she comes now.

MOSE. And here comes the Colonel. [*Stands at attention. The Colonel enters from house, followed by Nellie*]

COL. Halt! Where's the rest of the army?

NELL. Billy! [*Rushes to him*]

BILL. Nellie! [*They shake hands and retire up stage*]

COL. Attention! About face—Halt, do you hear? [*Bill and Nellie pay no attention. Con rushes down beside Mose, and presents arms with a spade*]

CON. Prisent.

COL. What are you doing here?

CON. I am a sub-sti-tchute.

COL. Get out, both of you. [*Con goes L. Mose does not move*] Well! What are you waiting for?

MOSE. The proper command, sir.

COL. Left face, forward march! [*Mose exits in house, followed by Con imitating his manner. Colonel crosses to table*] Now then, you young rapscallions. [*Sits*] I say, you—[*Bill and Nellie walk toward house, talking*] I'll have you on the—a—hip, sir. On the hip—hip—

CON. [*Enters at door*] Hurray! [*Exits. Colonel fumes; turns to bottle*]

BILL. When I'm a man, Nellie—

NELL. When you are a man. [*They kiss. Nellie exits in house*]

COL. [*Turns*] Eh? What's that?

BILL. What's what?

COL. That noise. Sounded like—[*Smacks lips like a kiss*]

BILL. O-oh—that? Why that was the little bird. Birdy chirped. [*Smacks lips at the bird*] Didn't you hear birdy chirp?

COL. Yes, but hang it, I never heard her chirp like that before.

BILL. [*Still making noise at bird*] Birdy wants her chickweed.

COL. I think birdy *got* her chickweed.

BILL. Say, Colonel, I want to whisper something to you.

COL. [*Rises, goes C.*] Well, what is it?

BILL. [*Whispering*] I love Nellie.

COL. Eh?

BILL. [*Louder*] I love Nellie.

COL. What's that?

BILL. [*Yells*] I love your niece, Nellie.

COL. Ouch! Well, you needn't take my head off. I'm not deaf. Say, Bill, I want to whisper something in your ear.

BILL. Go ahead.

COL. [*Whispers*] So do I.

BILL. Soda what?

COL. [*Louder*] So do I.

BILL. What kind of soda?

COL. SO—DO—I.

BILL. Ow! All right, Colonel, but I've won her and we're going to be married when I'm a man.

COL. [*Mocking Bill*] When you are a man, Billy. [*Smacks lips. Both exit, laughing, L.1.E. Enter Denver from house, followed by Mary Wright*]

MARY. You wish to speak to me alone? Speak quickly, I can grant you but a moment.

DEN. Indeed? [*C. Looks at her*] What a change. How—happy you must be.

MARY. Why—why did you come here. To torture me?

DEN. Bosh! I torture? I am going to take you away from this life of monotony to one of pleasure.

MARY. I am happy with my husband.

DEN. Your husband? You flatter me. You were never divorced to my knowledge. I still bear that title.

MARY. [*Putting hand to head*] Oh, I had forgotten. I fear I shall go mad —I thought you dead. This morning when you came like a black cloud from the wretched past, my heart stopped beating. I would gladly have died. After a little, rather than cause my—the man whose name I bear—the sorrow that your real identity would bring him, I decided to remain silent. But do not torture me more with your presence. My patience has a limit, and rather than endure your sneers and insinuations, I will tell Mr. Wright all.

DEN. [*Frightened*]   You would tell him? Have you forgotten the love you once bore me?

MARY. [*Sits on steps*]   Yes. As completely as you did when you so cruelly deserted me. Oh, my struggles for an honorable living were bitter but I bore them, until an honest love crept into my barren life and showed me true happiness. [*Wearily*] And now—it is all over.

DEN.   Nonsense. I don't want you to leave him—that is, not yet.

MARY.   And do you suppose I would pass another day under his roof knowing that I am not his wife?

DEN.   Why not? He has certain deeds that I must get. You can help me in this. Then we will clear out forever.

MARY.   Shame! When will your evil heart grasp the fact that I am not your tool?

DEN.   Sh-h! [*Wright appears at door*] As you say, your husband is a prince among men. I do not wonder you are proud of him. [*Wright, thinking he has been unobserved, quietly exits, house*]

MARY.   What treachery!

DEN. [*Smiling*]   Diplomacy, my dear.

MARY.   One word from me to the man you are so basely deceiving, and he would kill you.

DEN.   Yes. I am aware of his bloodthirsty tendencies, therefore I have no thought of allowing you to tell him. Suppose I took to supplying him with past history. For instance, you spoke of your virtuous struggles from the time I left you until you married Wright, but I learned today that when you came to him you had a child.

MARY.   Why that child is—

DEN.   There, there. I don't care for explanations; they are tiresome. Enough that I know you—and you know me. At present I am in something of a hole—shady transaction back East. I had to leave suddenly. Wright has the very deeds I was supposed to have forged. By hook or crook I must have them. I came here, never dreaming of finding my charming consort of sixteen years ago. Fortune favors me. You will be of great assistance.

MARY. [*Rises*]   Enough. I will at once inform my husband. [*Starts*]

DEN.   He is not your husband. You are a bigamist. One word from me will land you in jail.

MARY.   Do you think I care for that? I will tell the truth, take the consequences—and let you do the same.

DEN. But the boy—he has a home, a *name*. What would he think of you if he knew.

MARY. My boy!

DEN. Be reasonable—for his sake.

MARY. I will keep your secret today. Tonight I will take my boy and leave this place forever.

DEN. You'll help me get the papers and go with me, eh?

MARY. You contemptible cur—*No,* I would rather die.

DEN. Curse your tongue. Take care or I'll—[*Raises hand to strike*]

MARY. Oh, no, you won't. You are too cowardly to strike me. You know there are those who would call you to a swift account for assaulting me. You will vent your spite on the woman you have so cruelly wronged, in a more cowardly fashion and at a time when there will be no one to aid her.

DEN. You're right, I will. [*Mary exits*] Oh, I'll get even. I'll touch her heart. She's soft on her boy. Mothers always are. [*Laughs*] I'll lead that boy to a life of dissipation—crime, if I can manage it. Oh, I'll touch her to the quick. I'll shrivel her heart up like the blackened embers of a discarded camp fire. How I hate her brat. I could kill him by inches. I'd like to tear his heart out! I'd like to—[*His hand is raised above his head. Enter Bill L.1.E. Denver changes manner*]—to take you by the hand, my dear boy. I've heard so much of you. [*They shake hands*]

BILL. From Con?

DEN. Why—ah—yes, from Con.

BILL. Well, don't believe anything he tells you. He's the biggest liar in the state.

DEN. [*Laughs*] I don't believe he exaggerated in your case.

BILL. Well, if he didn't, it was an accident but he means it for the best. He's my pal.

DEN. Considerable difference in your ages, for pals, don't you think?

BILL. Oh, that don't make any difference. You see I never had any boys to associate with. I have been brought up with men. [*Crosses to table*]

DEN. Con said you were as much of a man as any of them. What do you intend to become—a scout?

BILL. A pirate.

DEN. [*Laughs*] A pirate?

BILL. That's what Con and I play we are going to be. [*Laughs*] It's only in fun, sir.

DEN. But you are too big and brave a lad to play at adventure, why not have a real one? Let's have a drink?

BILL. No, sir, I never—

DEN. What! You don't mean to say that a man like you never—? Oh I see, don't want the old folks to know, eh? Well, you can trust me. Here, take a drink.

BILL. [*Flattered, takes bottle*] Guess I can stand a pull. [*Drinks*]

DEN. The people around here don't appreciate you, not even your father. I hear you are a fine shot.

BILL. Oh, I can shoot some, sir.

DEN. I'll wager you can. What sort of a gun do you use?

BILL. This one. [*Shows Colt*]

DEN. [*Takes it*] Oh, a Colt. An old out-of-date pattern, too. [*Tosses it on table*] Let me show you something modern. [*Takes pistol from pocket*] See; a double-acting, self-cocking, shell-extracting revolver. [*Hands it to Bill*]

BILL. Gee! What a beauty!

DEN. It shall be yours if you are the lad of spirit I take you to be. [*Takes pistol, puts it in pocket*] Now let's play a little joke on your father, just to show him the stuff you are made of.

BILL. [*Drinks. Shows a recklessness from the effects*] I'm your man— what is it?

DEN. You know he keeps his private papers in the—ah—

BILL. Little safe in his bedroom.

DEN. That's it. Of course you don't know the combination—

BILL. Oh, but I do though.

DEN. All the better. Now here's the plan. Your father has boasted there is not a man in the state who would dare hold him up for anything. And as for cracksmen, he defies the cream of them to get anything from his safe. Now, if you will get all his papers—don't touch the money, that would be stealing—but just the papers, and bring them to me, I will tell your father there is one man in the state that was a match for him and show him the papers to support my statement. He, of course, will be thunderstruck, and when he asks who this wonderful fellow is, I will introduce, Billy, the Prince of the Road. [*Laughs*] What do you think of it?

BILL. [*Laughs*] That would be a fine joke, wouldn't it? I believe I'll try it.

DEN. Of course you'll try it. You couldn't let such an opportunity slip.

BILL. When shall we do it?

DEN. Tonight. They will all leave the house in a few moments to see the Colonel start for home. That is our opportunity. Get a piece of black cloth and make yourself a mask. Saddle your horse and tie him yonder. After the folks leave the house, you slip in the back way. Now go.

BILL. [*Starts*] Won't Con be surprised? My, but that stuff makes you dizzy, don't it?—and Mose laughed at me. I'll make them all proud of me yet. [*Exits L.U.E.*]

DEN. Fool! When I get the papers, I'll set the officers on his track. Two birds with one stone—the papers, and the mother's heart broken over a worthless boy.

CON. [*Enters from house*] Well, what divilment are ye hatching out now?

DEN. Con, you are hard on me. Let us forget the difference between us for the time. Here is ten dollars. [*Gives money*] Go to the station and see if there is any mail for me.

CON. Tin dollars fer going to the station? Yer paying mighty high fer a small service. [*Throws down money*] I won't go.

DEN. [*Angry*] Why not?

CON. I think you want to get rid of me, eh, me laddy buck?

DEN. You are a suspicious fool.

CON. Yes, that's the reason I'm going to keep me eyes on you. And ten thousand dollars wouldn't make me take them off.

DEN. [*Up stage*] Keep them on as much as you like, my meddling friend, but it won't save Billy or the Wright family.

COL. [*Inside*] Forward march! [*Enter from house Mose, Nellie and Colonel. Mose crosses and exits R.U.E. Nellie goes up L.*] Goodnight, Mr. Wright, we're off for home. You and the Mrs. be sure to come over next Sunday, good-night.

WRI. [*At door*] Wait a moment, Colonel. We'll see you off. Wife's in her room getting her hat or something.

COL. Don't bother, Wright. We know the way, good-night. [*Crosses and exits R.U.E.*]

WRI. Wait a minute, Colonel. [*Exit house, calling*] Mary, Mary!

NEL. Where can he be?

DEN. Looking for someone, Miss Bradley?

NEL. Yes, I was looking for Billy.

DEN. You are too pretty a girl to waste your time on a country lout.

NEL. Sir! I do not understand you.

DEN. A city man would be more to your liking, eh? [*Chucks her under the chin. She is astonished*]

NEL. Mr. Denver—!

DEN. There, there, don't be frightened. Give me a kiss before you go.

NEL. [*Slaps his face*] You cur! [*Crosses to R.U.E.*]

DEN. [*Hurriedly*] A thousand pardons. It was only a joke, I assure you.

NEL. We will see if the "country lout" looks at it in that light. [*Exits*]

DEN. The sting of that blow will cost you dearly, my lady. Damn their Southern pride, but I'll shrivel them all up before I'm through with them. [*Exits R.U.E. Enter Mary from the house, followed by Wright*]

WRI. Mary! For God's sake listen to me. You do not—you cannot mean that you are going to leave me forever.

MARY. Don't question me, I must.

WRI. Oh, I do not need an explanation. [*Bitterly*] Youth weds with old age. It could not last. I might have known it.

MARY. Stephen, it is not that. God knows I love you better than all the world. But I must leave you.

WRI. But why—why if you love me?

MARY. I cannot explain. It would kill me—it would kill us both.

WRI. You do not mean—disgrace?

MARY. Yes. [*Wright sinks on porch, overcome*] My heart is breaking. I must go. [*Staggers to C.*]

DEN. [*Enter R.U.E. not seeing Wright*] Yes, and you go alone.

MARY. I am going with my boy.

DEN. You can't. He's going to jail.

MARY. What do you mean?

DEN. That I acted on your suggestion, refrained from blows and struck at your heart. By this time your son is a criminal and answerable to the law.

MARY. [*Half screams*] What have you done?

DEN. Revenged myself on your son.

MARY. And yours as well. Fool, could not your cold heart have prompted the truth? He was your own child. You have sent your own flesh and blood to destruction.

DEN. You lie.

MARY. I speak the truth.

WRI. [*Who has overheard. Rising*] What does this mean? [*Denver frightened*]

MARY. It means that there stands the man who blighted my past as·well as my present happiness. It means that he is Boyd Bradley, my husband, and the father of my boy.

WRI. Wait a bit, wait a bit. I can't seem to get these things straight somehow.

DEN. [*Drawing revolver*] Then get it through your head quickly. She is my wife and she is going with me.

WRI. [*Low and intense*] So—this is the man who caused my Mary's unhappiness—the man we thought dead. And now he returns to wreck afresh the life of the woman who trusted him. [*Slowly approaches Denver*]

DEN. Be careful. Keep your distance. I am armed.

WRI. And do you think I care for that? All the weapons this side of Hell couldn't keep my fingers from your throat. [*Wright grapples with Denver. They struggle. Mary screams, goes down R. Revolver explodes, killing Mary. They struggle toward the well. Denver gets his pistol hand free and shoots Wright. He falls half in well, head first. Denver stands frightened, looking around*]

DEN. It was self-defense—he tried to murder me—he threatened to kill me—Mary heard him. [*Sees Mary*] Mary! Fainted! [*Goes to her*] Dead! God! I did not mean it. I did not mean it. [*Overcome, sinks on knees. Suddenly starts up*] They'll lynch me. [*Crying*] I am innocent. It was an accident and self-defense. They'll not believe it—they'll not believe it. [*In frenzy*] I must get rid of the bodies somehow. The old well—thirty feet deep and dark as a pocket. [*Throws Wright in*] My revolver, this must not be found. [*Drops it in well*] They will fill the well and all traces will be lost. His property will go to my wife—she is dead. But the boy—he stands between me and a fortune. Pshaw! He is an outlaw! I will put him where he will never trouble me again.

BILL. [*Enters from house, black mask on*]   Here are the papers—why, what is the matter? [*Drops papers*] Mother! [*Runs to her*] Mother, Mother, speak to me! [*Looks up in agony, husky voice*] Mr. Denver—look at me—look me in the face. What has done this?

DEN. I—I—don't—know.

BILL. You are not speaking the truth. Where is my father?

DEN. Your mother was going to leave him—they had a quarrel and—

BILL. [*Half screams*]   Answer me. Did my father do this?

DEN. Your father! Your father? [*Realizing that he is the boy's father*] Your—father—yes!

BILL. [*Strong, but not loud*]   I do not believe it.

DEN. As God is my judge, I speak the truth.

BILL. My father shall be found. From his lips I will learn the truth.

DEN. But you have no time for this. Do you realize that you are an outlaw? You have robbed your father's safe. Who will believe you did not kill your mother in an attempt to escape?

BILL. You scoundrel!

DEN. I know you are innocent, but will the law believe it, too? Make good your escape and leave me to find your father. I will take good charge of these. [*Stoops for papers Bill has dropped*]

BILL. [*Takes pistol from table*]   Drop those papers. [*Denver does so*] My mind is dazed by this calamity. But one thing I know, the guilty shall be made to suffer. It shall be the one object of my life. [*Kneels before Mary*]

Mother, if you can hear me from above, record my oath of vengeance. And you—[*To Denver*] You who have plotted my destruction shall live to hear the outlaw you have created. Go, and leave me with my dead. [*Falls over body of Mary*] Mother! Mother! [*Denver slinks off L.U.E.*]

ACT II.

TIME: *Three years later.* SCENE: *Interior of the Broken Heart Saloon and dance hall. Low-roofed, rough interior. Bar R. Two tables and several chairs L. Entrance to dance hall in L. jog. Exterior door C. Small door behind bar. Door to dance hall is covered by long curtain. Oil lamp on bar; three more in bracket on the walls. All lighted. Reward notice pasted on R. of door.* DIS-COVERED: *Hank behind bar, cleaning glasses. Peanut leaning against bar. Bud at table with three rough-looking cowboys, playing cards. An old piano is heard in the dance hall, together with the shuffling of feet.*

BUD.   Did I tell y'u about butting into Red Mike yest'day?

PEA.   Some-a de boys tella me something about.

BUD.   Mike used to be a bb-ba-ad man. But he got made a dep'ty sheriff and that spiled him. Got proud. Me an' him used ter sorter sidle sideways o' one another, both hearin' a bit that t'other was handy with his gun. But when he got made dep'ty his pride swallered his caution.

PEA.   What was de trouble all about?

BUD.   Just nuthin' at all. I went into Pete's place as meek as a kitten. Some-body says as how Red Mike had give it out that no one was to do any shoot-ing in town but him. I allowed he couldn't make his bluff good. He hap-pened to be there, so he pulled and I dropped him.

PEA.   What-a de people do?

BUD.   Offered me his job. [*All laugh*] Mike lost his nerve. It's all up wid a bad man when he once loses his nerve. Then a kid can make him take water.

PEA.   And you never lost your nerve?

BUD.   Not much. I ain't afraid of man, devil or the world to come, but 'spose my time will come with the rest. Until it does, I'm going to be a terror to these ba-a-ad men.

PEA.   Why you no-a go after dis-a one? [*Points to reward circular*] Den dere be a five thousand dollars for you.

BUD. [*Turning*]   Who's that? [*Peanut goes up. Con enters C., goes to bar*]

PEA. [*Reading*] Five t'ousand dollars reward for de capture, dead or alive, of one, William Wright, better known as Billy, the Kid. Age eighteen, height five feet t'ree inches, weight one hundred and twenty pounds—

BUD. Why, a baby.

PEA. —light hair, blue eyes, even features.

BUD. A baby *gal*.

PEA. Is the leader of the worst band of desperadoes the Territory has ever had to deal with.

BUD. Fairy tales.

PEA. De above reward will be paid for his capture, or for positive proof of his death. [*Con has been interested; Peanut turns to Bud*] Dere, what-a you tink of dat?

BUD. Nuthing.

PEA. Why you no getta him?

BUD. [*Rise*] Why, Peanut, I wouldn't waste no good powder on that youngster. If I had taken that job as dep'ty, I'd just land de kid an' give de coin ter charity. 'Cause it would be just like findin' it.

PEA. Dey say he vera badaman. Dey say he kill in fair fight, as many men as he has years on his shoulders.

BUD. De kid is a bluff, I tell you.

PEA. Man tole me yesterday de government he send from Washington a Secret Service man to capture Billy. Man go to Billy, say, "I a-want to joina-a your band." Bill he say, "Where you come from?" Man says, "Me work at Hick's ranch." Bill tell him to hole out his hands; man does. Dey are soft and white, not like a cowpuncher's. So Billy shoot him dead.

BUD. Peanut, if ever that kid comes in here while I'm here, I'll make a monkey out of him! *I'll* show you how bad he is.

CON. Sure, it's not fer me to be telling ye yer business; only this—when you come to mix it wid him, don't be sorry fer him on account of his youth!

PEA. Do you know-a him?

CON. Know him? I trotted him on me knee when he were a baby. I've watched him grow up into a fine, strapping boy, wid his head full o' nonsense about pirates and ransoms and things. Then I see him receive a shock that turned him into a man, fearless, reckless and brave.

BUD. And did he do all them things they tell about?

CON. Most o' them stories be lies.

BUD. That's what I thought. De kid is a bluff.

CON. Does that look like it? [*Points to circular*]

BUD. Well, just let me see him, that's all I ask. Just show him to me.

CON. Don't worry. You'll see him—some time; and it's meself that's think-ing ye will take a fancy to the lad—[*Sotto voce*] if ye live. [*Bud goes to table*]

MOLLY. [*Enters from dance hall*] Who wants to dance? Well—don't all speak at once.

CON. Sure if we did, you'd have a picnic instead of a partner.

MOLLY. Well, speak for yourself, Irish.

CON. It's a bright girl ye are, to discover me ancestry. Well, I'll admit it, I am Irish—but I don't dance.

MOLLY. You can buy a drink, can't you?

CON. I have the power and I have the price but not the inclination.

MOLLY. You're a cheap skate.

CON. And while I'm about it, I may as well tell ye that I prefer to choose me own associates—present company not excepted.

BUD. D'ye mean that for an insult to me?

CON. No, sor, I don't. When I want to insult you I'll make it so plain ye won't have to ask who I mean. [*Turns to bar*]

BUD. [*Reaching for pistol*] That's an insult.

PEA. Hold on, Bud, dat only Irish wit.

BUD. Well, he don't want to get fresh around here. [*Con fills glass*]

DEN. [*Enters door in flat, hurriedly*] Hello, boys. [*Goes to bar, down stage*]

ALL. Hello boss, etc.

DEN. Whiskey. [*Hunk sets bottle and glass before him, then goes to table to watch the game. Con is about to drink when Denver turns and sees him. Denver, in fright, stares at Con*]

CON. For the love of Heaven, turn your head. I never see a man so fond of watching me drink as you are.

DEN. You—here?

CON. Great guns! Can't you see I am? Sure, ye have eyes enough.

DEN. Where—is—the boy?

CON. None of yer dom business. Glad ye found out? [*Denver turns to bar and gulps down drink*] Now ye are getting sensible. Keep yer face at same angle 'til I get mine. [*Drinks*]

MOLLY. [*Comes down*] Hello, boss. Why what's the matter, you're white as a sheet?

DEN. Don't bother me. [*Crosses to C.*]

MOLLY. [*Laughing*] Hey, boys, the boss has seen a ghost.

DEN. [*Aside*] Yes, the ghost of my past misdeeds. The ghost of coming retribution. [*To table*] Peanut, do you know that man at the bar?

PEA. Yes, dat Con Hanley. He came here two—three times before.

Bud. If he makes a move at me—yes. [*Bud is seated behind table. Peanut at the R. Denver stands beside him. Jennie enters from dance hall, goes C. sullen and downcast*]

Molly. Gee, here's Miss Innocence. What are you doing in the barroom, going to come to the drink after all?

Pea. What you want here? Get back in the dance hall. [*Pause*] Well, do you hear!

Jen. Yes.

Pea. Why don't you obey den? Are you-a going?

Jen. No.

Pea. What! Why not?

Jen. Because I am sick of it—life, most of all.

Pea. [*Rise*] I'll take dat-a out of you.

Den. Hold on a minute, Peanut. [*To Jennie*] Now then, what's the matter with you? [*Pause, sneeringly*] Haven't you had all the place affords—and—money?

Jen. [*Passionately*] Money! Was it money that lured me to this dive? No, it was you. Did I pledge my honor for money? No, for you. Did you keep your promise to make me your wife? No. You liar and deceiver!

Den. You infernal cat. [*Slaps her in face, she reels. Con catches her*]

.Con. [*In anger*] Strike a woman? [*Threatening*]

Den. Bud, drop him. [*Bud pulls pistol*]

Con. [*Holds out hand to Bud*] No need of that; I'm unarmed. Besides ye are six to one. I'll swallow me tongue and keep me own council. But, Mr. Denver, some day you and me will meet on an equal footing, then I'll kick the livin' daylights out of you. Come, me girl, brace up and forget it. Come into the hall wid me. [*Both cross*]

Jen. [*Crying*] If I could only die. [*Both exit to hall*]

Molly. For Heaven's sake, somebody let the girl die.

Den. [*Angry*] Why the devil didn't you drop him?

Bud. Why the poor fellow wasn't even armed.

Den. [*Crosses to bar*] What difference did that make? You are getting chicken-hearted.

Bud. Chicken-hearted? I'm in fer a scrap at all times—even or odd, but I gives every man a chance for his white alley. [*Rises*] Now if you think I'm chicken-hearted, I'll give you a chance to prove it.

Pea. [*Rises*] Hold on, Bud. [*Men rise*]

Den. [*Frightened*] I did not mean it, Bud. Truly I did not. I was angry at that Irish lunk-head and forgot myself. Come and have a drink. We won't quarrel.

PEA. He alla right, Bud. Put up-a de gun.

DEN. Come on, boys. Come, Moll—everybody take one on me. [*All go to bar. Denver down stage—Molly next, then Bud, Peanut and others at back*]

BUD. We'll let it go this time, Denver, but don't get flossy with me again.

MOLLY. Gee! I thought something was doing that time and it all petered out in talk.

DEN. Set out the good bottle. [*Hank sets out bottle and glasses. General conversation ad lib while they fill glasses*]

MOLLY [*To Denver*] Here's to the girl you would like to see most of all tonight.

DEN. I'll drink to that with a vengeance. [*All drink. Bud, Peanut and Denver go back to table*]

MOLLY. Gee whiz! You must love her.

DEN. I *hate* her.

MOLLY. Then what do you want to see her for?

DEN. To get even. I spoke to her one day, three years ago; she struck me in the face. Less than a year ago I met her while she was riding her pony. I apologized for my rudeness on the former occasion and she cut me with her riding whip. I carried the mark for many a day; and the longer it remained the stronger grew my hatred.

MOLLY. Gee, she must be a dandy. Wish we had a few spunky ones like that around here.

DEN. Well, this place would soon take the spunk out of them.

CON. [*Enters from hall, singing "Some day ye may be President or a gineral in th' army." Goes to bar, pushes Denver to one side*] Don't block up the bar when ye see a customer coming! [*Denver goes C. very angry, doubles fist as though about to strike Con. Con winks broadly at him and laughs*]

HANK. What'll ye have?

CON. A glass of water.

HANK. Water? What for?

CON. To drink. Did ye think I wanted to go in swimming? [*Hank gives him a glass of water. Con takes it and starts L.*]

DEN. I remember your insolence of three years ago—

CON. Well, forget it. [*Exits to hall*]

MOLLY. I believe that's the ghost you saw awhile ago, boss.

DEN. Have another drink?

MOLLY. To the same girl? [*Crosses to the bar*]

DEN. Yes. [*They fill glasses. Enter Mose, C., followed by Nell*]

MOSE. Halt. [*Salutes*] Who's in command here?

PEA. I run-a dis place.

Mose. Well, sir, we need assistance. The darkness overtaking us while in the hills, we lost our way. If you have a guide that can conduct us to Bradley's Place, he will be well paid. [*Denver turns at the mention of Bradley's and sees Nellie*]

Den. [*Aside*] God! It is she!

Pea. De night's very bad and de way is long and difficult. But maybe I find you a guide.

Den. By no means. These are friends of mine and I could not let them run the risk of getting lost. They shall remain here tonight.

Mose. Impossible. [*To Peanut*] Will you get us the guide?

Den. Never mind the guide, Peanut. They shall remain here tonight. I am sure it will be agreeable to *dear*—Nellie. [*Denver sneeringly takes off hat*]

Nel. At our last meeting I gave you a striking proof of my regard for you. Do not compel me to repeat that disgraceful scene.

Molly. Gee! Here's the girl that licked the boss.

Den. The scene, if repeated, will not be so onesided this time.

Pea. She very fin-a girl. Me like to have her here.

Nel. What a horrible place this is. Come, Mose, let us leave here at once. [*They turn*]

Den. Boys, guard the door. [*Two men spring to C. door*] Do not, I beg of you, leave us so suddenly. [*All laugh*] The dance, the wine, all the pleasure the establishment affords, are at your disposal.

Mose. You scoundrel. Open that door at once or I'll—[*Comes down, raises cane to strike Denver. Bud knocks him down*]

Nel. You scoundrel. To strike an old man! [*Kneels beside Mose*]

Bud. If he hadn't been an old man, I'd have put a bullet in him.

Nel. [*Rise*] You contemptible cur. A paid assassin for that coward. [*Points to Denver. Enter Jennie from hall*]

Bud. Wha-a-t? [*Raises fist to strike her. Jennie runs between them*]

Jen. Strike me, Bud, I'm more used to it than she.

Bud. Git out of the way. [*Throws Jennie violently against table; raises fist again*]

Den. [*Steps between them*] Hold on, Bud.

Bud. What the devil have *you* got to do with it?

Den. She's mine. Oh, she shall be humiliated. But let *me* do it.

Jen. [*Struggles to her feet*] You shall not do it, Boyd Denver. I've seen enough suffering here—I've suffered enough myself and I won't *let* you add another victim to your list.

Den. Indeed? And what can you do?

JEN. I will inform Con Hanley, he is in the dance hall. [*Starts; Peanut grabs her, places hand over her mouth, drags her across stage*]

DEN. Put her in the dark room, Peanut, until she gets some sense. Bud, watch the door, rope the Irishman if he attempts to enter. Hank, drag the old man behind the bar. [*They suit action to his words. Jennie is thrown in door behind bar. Bud goes L. Hank drags Mose behind bar. Men at door seize Nellie and drag her down stage and put her in chair*]

NEL. You shall pay for this outrage, with your miserable lives, every one.

PEA. If she-a going to squeal. [*He threatens her*]

DEN. [*Holds up hand*] Don't worry, Peanut. Now for the festivities first. A drink, to put the lady in good humor. Hank, bring me a cup of brandy. The lady may not like it; she may even refuse to drink with us. In that case, we will force it down her throat. [*Hank brings Denver tin cup*] Will you drink with us *willingly*, my dear? [*He is holding cup in right hand. Nellie, still held by the men, suddenly kicks cup, throwing the contents in Denver's face*]

NEL. That is my answer. [*All laugh*]

MOLLY. Gee! Can't she kick, though?

DEN. [*Very angry*] Laugh! That's right. The joke is on me this time, but the second portion of the entertainment cannot fail. Now, which of you gentlemen would like the first kiss from these fair lips?

ALL. Me—I would—*etc.*

DEN. One moment. As we seem unanimous on the subject, let us auction off the privilege. We will bid for the *first* kiss. Moll, you be auctioneer.

MOLLY. Here's a lark. [*Mounts chair*] Now then, gents, here's a prize. A kiss from pretty lips, unsullied by contact with coarse moustaches, such as yours. How much am I bid—

PEA. I bid ten cents. [*All laugh; Nellie hangs head in shame*]

MOLLY. Bid's too low; can't accept it. Come, come, gentlemen, bid up, bid up.

BUD. A dollar.

HANK. Two dollars.

MOLLY. Two dollars, two, do I hear any more. Who will make it three—anybody? Two, two—

DEN. Five dollars.

MOLLY. Now we are coming on. Five, five, who will make it ten? Going cheap, gentlemen. Five—five—do I hear any more? Five once—five twice—

JEN. [*Bursting through door R.*] I bid ten dollars.

DEN. You meddling brat. Get back in that room. [*He starts for her*]

JEN. [*Behind bar, picks up bottle*] Don't come near me, Boyd, or I'll brain you.

DEN. [*Turns to others*] My bid stands. She's not in this anyway.

MOLLY. Why not? She's got the money and her bid goes, eh, boys?

BOYS. Yes—certainly—*etc.*

MOLLY. The bid stands, according to the jury. Ten dollars, I'm bid. Ten dollars I'm bid—ten—ten—

DEN. Twenty-five. [*Jennie is about to bid when Peanut claps hand over her mouth and forces her under bar*]

MOLLY. Twenty-five—a good bid—any more? [*All shake heads*] Where's Jennie? Twenty-five—once—twice—three times and sold. The first kiss to Boyd Denver. [*Gets down*]

DEN. Here's your money. [*Gives Molly roll of bills*] Now for the reward! [*Bill enters door C.; all watching Denver, do not see him. Denver approaches Nellie with a laugh, as he stoops to kiss her, he glances up and sees Bill. Starts, recoils and begins to walk backward*]

MOLLY. Well, why don't you go ahead? You've paid enough for the privilege.

BILL. What's going on here? [*All turn. Men release Nellie who staggers up stage and sinks on chair R. Mose drags himself from behind bar and goes to her. Hank has released Jennie and both stand behind her looking at Bill*] Answer, some of you, what is the meaning of this?

PEA. A little sport. Just a little auction.

BILL. Well, stop it.

BUD. *What?*

BILL. Stop it.

BUD. Who says stop it?

BILL. I do.

BUD. And who are you?

BILL. Billy, the Kid. [*All these speeches are very quiet on Bill's part*]

BUD. Oh, you are, eh? Well, I've been looking for you.

BILL. That so?

BUD. Yes, it's so. You've heard about me, all right. I do nothin' but eat up ba-a-ad men—and bad kids, too. See that gun? Each of those notches stands for a bad man what ain't no more. That new one is for Red Mike planted yest'day. And there's room on there for a dandy, stuck up chap about your size. *I'm* Bud Monroe.

BILL. Never heard of you before. How are you? [*Takes Bud's hand. Bud astonished*]

BUD. How *am* I? How *am* I? Why, I'm in the pink of condition, I am. Ready to have it out with anybody.

BILL. [*Wiping his hand with his handkerchief*] Why don't you wash your hands? They are filthy.

BUD. *What!* Do you mean that fer an insult? [*Hand on gun*] If you do—

BILL. For Heaven's sake, don't talk so loud. I am not a thousand miles away. Lend me your hat a minute. [*Takes Bud's hat from his head*] The roads are very dusty. [*Dusts boots with hat*]

BUD. [*Astounded*] Here—you—[*Plucks at Bill's sleeve*]

BILL. Take your hand away. I told you they were filthy. Take—them away. [*Looks steadily at Bud. He removes hands, still astonished. Bill finishes dusting his boots; when through throws hat on floor*]

BUD. Draw—quick—[*Reaches for pistol. Bill's hand goes like lightning to Bud's side. Grabs his hand containing pistol as Bud draws it*]

BILL. What are you reaching so often for? [*Takes pistol from Bud*] Oh, a Colt. An old out-of-date pattern too. Ask Mr. Denver—he is a judge of firearms.

BUD. Gimme my gun. [*Plucks at Bill's sleeve*]

BILL. [*Whacks his fingers with pistol*] I told you to keep your hands off me. [*Goes to bar, tosses pistol on bar*] Here, bartender, give us a drink on the great Bud Monroe's shooting iron. [*During this scene everybody has remained motionless as though expecting something to happen. Now the strain is relaxed, all take in long breaths of surprise and saunter to the bar, except Bud who remains motionless and Denver who crosses to Bud*]

MOLLY. Gee! Ain't he the winner, though? [*General conversation as glasses are filled. Denver talks to Bud in dumb show, draws knife and offers it to Bud. The latter shakes his head. Denver in anger sneaks up behind Bill who is at bar with his back turned. When he is within striking distance, Denver raises knife. Bill wheels suddenly and faces him. Denver tries to conceal knife and gently drops his arm. Bill catches hand as it descends*]

BILL. Why, hello, Denver. Come up to shake hands, eh? [*Shaking*] I had no chance to do it before. What's that? A knife? Bad place to carry it, Denver, you might cut someone. [*Takes knife from him and tosses it across room*]

DEN. I—thought—you—might have trouble with Bud, so I slipped it up my sleeve to have it handy, in case I could be of service to you.

BILL. Very kind of you, I am sure. Come, get in line, there's a drink coming to you. [*Denver lines up to bar. Bill on the end, down stage. Bud has worked himself into a fury, crosses to Bill and slaps him on back*]

BUD. Look-a here, me young sport—

BILL. [*Wheels suddenly*] Well—what is it? [*Sharp*]

Bud. [*Wilts*] Why—why—don't I get no drink?

Bill. To be sure. Edge along, boys, and give the mighty Bud Monroe room. [*All drink and talk ad lib. Jennie leans over bar and whispers to Bill*]

Jen. For God's sake, get her away from here if you can. [*Bill nods*]

Con. [*Enters from hall*] Well, if there ain't Billy. The top of the evening to ye, Billy.

Billy. Con, you are just in time. I want you to safely conduct Miss Bradley and Mose to their home.

Con. I'll do it wid pleasure.

Pea. [*Has crossed back to Bill; is on his L.*] Hold on. I have something to say to that.

Bill. [*Beside him*] Well? [*Hank sneaks up close to Bill's right*]

Pea. Dat-a a lady no-a leave here tonight.

Bill. She will leave this place in one minute.

Pea. I no permit it. [*Angry*]

Bill. How can you prevent it?

Pea. [*Draws knife*] I'll show you. *Strike*—Hank. [*Both spring at Bill at the same time. He knocks Hank down, grabs Peanut by hair with left hand, forces him over table and, with right, takes knife away, holding it at his— Peanut's—throat.* note: *This action must be like lightning*]

Bill. I could kill you before you could raise an eyelash.

Pea. Mercy—mercy!

Bill. I am not in the habit of having my will disputed, don't *you* try it again. [*Throws Peanut to floor; tosses his knife after him*] Now, Con, we are ready. [*Con goes to C. door, Mose follows. Nellie starts, then turns*]

Nel. God bless you, Billy; you have saved me.

Bill. Thank Heaven I arrived—in time.

Nel. You will come with us?

Bill. No. I remain here.

Nel. But these men, they will kill you.

Bill. It is because I prefer death, I suppose, that my miserable life is spared.

Nel. Oh, Billy, is there no turning back?

Bill. None. Good-night. [*Takes her hand, kisses it. She exits C. followed by Mose and Con*] Could my life be rolled backward but three short years! [*Leans against door*] Could the weight of blood and crime be lifted from my guilty soul, what happiness might await me there. Oh, I must not think of her—not here—not *here*. [*With an effort he rouses himself*] Come, my girl. [*To Jennie*] We will dance; why it seems ages since I have had a dance. You shall be wined and dined to your heart's content tonight. Come! [*Takes Jen-*

nie's arm and they exit to hall. For a second after their exit no one moves. Bud and Denver are still at bar. Hank behind it, bathing his eye, Peanut is grovel-ling on the floor where he has fallen. Three men are at back R. talking]

DEN. [*Rousing himself and going to reward circular*] Well, are you all hypnotized? Or is money so plentiful that $5,000 grows on every bush? [*Taps circular. Peanut rises*]

BUD. I don't need the money. That fellow is a ba-a-ad man.

DEN. Are you all *afraid?*

PEA. [*Feels neck*] Well-a are you?

DEN. Of course not. But I have all the money I require. [*Peanut laughs*] Here, there are six of you. I'll give you two hundred dollars apiece if you will wipe him out. The reward you may divide to suit yourselves.

BUD. Now if I had only taken that dep'ty job—

DEN. [*Hurriedly*] He is now in the dance hall. There's a little door at the other end behind the piano. Go out this door. [*Indicates door C.*] Slip around and in the other. Get down behind the piano; when he passes, nail him. Don't be afraid of hurting Jen, she's outlived her usefulness, anyway. You can't fail. Surely there is one shot among you.

BUD. *One* shot? Give me my gun, Hank. [*Takes it*] What do ye say, boys?

ALL. We'll do it—yes—*etc.*

PEA. You come-a too, Boyd?

DEN. No-o, I'll watch the bar.

BUD. Ha-ha—chicken-heart. Come on, boys. [*They exit C.*]

DEN. [*Goes to door, looks after them*] They cannot fail. At last I shall be rid of him. How I fear him—how I fear him. My own son—son? Bah! I wish he had been throttled in infancy. [*Comes down*] There is the Wright place going to ruin—he cannot claim it, being an outlaw. I dare not claim it while he lives. What's that? The back door closing. They must be in position by this time. I must see the sport. From this doorway I shall see the end of Billy, the Kid. [*Goes L. to curtain, pulls it aside. Bill is standing in doorway. Denver starts back in terror. Bill enters*]

BILL. I thought I would find you alone. Kind of you to send the others away. Be seated. [*Denver drops in chair R. of table. He seems stunned. Bill sits L.*] I sought you out tonight, because you were a witness, three years ago of my oath to find my father.

DEN. [*In whisper*] Yes.

BILL. Well—I have found him.

DEN. [*Aside*] Caught. He knows me.

BILL. I had another object in wishing a private interview with you. To restore you a lost and valuable article. [*Throws pistol on table, Denver sees*] *it, shakes with terror and clutches the table*] A double-acting, shell-extracting, self-cocking revolver. We found it at the bottom of the old well. It is not in very good condition now, being rusted and choked with sand. Three loaded shells remain in the chambers, two have been fired. When you have a moment to spare, see how this bullet compares with the ones still remaining in your revolver. [*Throws bullet on table. Denver picks it up*] It was taken from my mother's breast. [*Denver drops it. Bill lights cigarette. Denver grabs pistol, points it at Bill and tries to pull trigger. It will not work. He drops it in despair. Bill does not move or show the least concern when Denver picks up pistol. Continues to light cigarette*]

DEN. [*As he drops pistol*] The devil aids you.

BILL. I told you it was out of order; a little oil will fix that, then you can try again.

DEN. [*In husky voice*] What—what do you want me to do?

BILL. Follow me until I am ready for the hour! Heaven has appointed me your executioner but the hour has not arrived. From now until your death you shall never leave my side.

DEN. Give me a chance—only a chance to prove my innocence.

BILL. You shall have sufficient opportunity. We will stand beside my mother's grave and you will tell me the truth. [*Rises*] We had best start before the others return. Bring that pretty revolver; I will need it. Come. [*Goes up to C. door. Denver takes revolver, struggles to his feet*]

DEN. No—no—I cannot—will not go.

BILL. *Will* not? You shall go with me though the whole world tried to stop you. [*Draws two pistols. Bud, followed by others, enters from hall. They scatter across stage during the following dialogue. Bud extreme R., Peanut next, three men C., Denver L., Hank R. of Denver*]

BUD. He ain't there.

PEA. Where he-a go?

DEN. [*Throwing table on end and getting behind it*] There! There! At the door! Shoot! [*General fusillade of shots. Lights are shot out, leaving the stage in total darkness save the flashes from the pistols. Some twenty shots fired in all and from small caliber pistols so that the noise will not be startling. Suddenly firing ceases; silence and darkness for a second*]

DEN. [*In a shaky voice*] Billy—Billy—are you there? [*Pause*] He is dead! Bud!

BUD. Hello—is that you, Denver?

DEN. Yes, strike a light—light up everything for Billy, the Kid, is dead. [*While speaking he arises from behind table. Bud has risen from behind table*

after lighting candle. As lights go up Peanut is discovered lying C., Hank L. Three men lying at the feet of Billy, who is standing C. a pistol in each hand]

BILL. Come, Denver—you—go—with—me. [*Denver sneaks out of door C., Bill follows. Bud still standing behind bar holding candle as curtain falls*]

ACT III.

TIME: *One week later.* SCENE: *Colonel Bradley's dining room. Large window. Breakaway opening to floor C. Old flag draped L. of window. Closet door L.2., small table beside it. Exterior door L.U. Door R.3. Long table R.C. set for seven people. Tablecloth long enough to touch floor on sides, but short, so audience can see under in front. Small table L. of C. window. Chairs, etc. Canary in cage, up L.* DISCOVERED: *Nellie and Jennie putting table in order.*

JEN. [*Finishing story*] And then the lights were shot out. All was in darkness and the stillness of death prevailed. Suddenly somebody lighted a candle and there stood Billy, without so much as a scratch on him. Oh! It was wonderful.

NEL. Wonderful indeed!

JEN. That was my opportunity to escape. I couldn't stay there, miss, so I slipped away. Yours was the first kind, honest face I had seen in my two months' imprisonment in that awful den, and I wanted to come and tell you I had made up my mind to start all over again. I never expected you to offer me the place of maid, miss.

NEL. Let us say no more about it. Stick to your resolution to do right, and this funny old world, that trampled you under foot yesterday, will receive you with open arms today.

JEN. Do you think there is any hope for me? But, there, I don't need to ask that question. Your actions have shown that you do. [*With a desire to change conversation*] Was it not kind of your uncle to hold this little reception in honor of Billy's gallantry in saving you?

NEL. Not half what he deserves, Jennie. Oh, it was so noble of him!

JEN. You love him, miss?

NEL. Nonsense, Jennie, I only—

JEN. We, who have had our affections worn smooth by hard contact with the sharp edges of the world, have quick eyes for the flash of love, the ready blush, the catching of the breath at the sound of a name—things that we have forever lost.

Nel. You are mistaken, Jennie; at least in thinking that I care for him. It —it is impossible. He is an outlaw. Why, he and I could not be further apart if one of us were dead.

Jen. Perhaps he might reform.

Nel. It would make no difference. In this cold, hard world, when once one has fallen, all the angels in Heaven could not place him right again in the eyes of his fellow men.

Jen. [*Crying*] There is no hope, then, for me.

Nel. Forgive me, Jennie. It was thoughtless and cruel of me. [*Arms about her*] There, there, don't cry. We will make you the exception that proves the rule. [*They embrace*]

Mose. [*Enter R.3.*] Attention! How dare you waste your time hugging one another? It's a waste of sweetness. You never saw two men hugging, did you? If you must hug somebody, hug me.

Nel. You old sinner! I have hugged you nearly to death on several occasions and you offered absolutely no resistance. In fact, I really believe you enjoyed it.

Mose. Of course I did. A good soldier likes arms about him, don't he?

Nel. Well, as you are so fond of feminine arms, I wonder you never married.

Mose. I did. That's why I became a soldier.

Nel. Oh, tell me about her. Black hair?

Mose. Red.

Nel. Blue eyes?

Mose. Yellow.

Nel. Nonsense. Why, that would be—

Mose. A cat. Honest, that's what she was.

Nel. [*Laughs*] Then your matrimonial venture did not turn out well?

Mose. Oh, yes, it did. Turned *me* out.

Nel. Honest, Mose?

Mose. True as I'm standing here, and all because the dearest, sweetest little widow—

Nel. Bother. Served you right! What became of your wife, Mose?

Mose. Dead. [*Feels in pocket*] Confound it! I always weep when I get to that point and I can't find my handkerchief.

Nel. [*Laughs*] You are an old fraud but the best old fraud that ever lived, so I'll give you a hug. [*Does so*]

Mose. Bully.

Nel. —for the sake of your wife.

Mose. [*Disgusted*] Don't. [*Nellie laughs; goes to table*]

COL. [*Enters R.3.*]   Oh, there you are, eh? [*Mose stands at attention*] Gossiping like a schoolgirl, I'll bet.

MOSE.   Superintending the spreading of the feast, sir.

COL. [*Surveying things*]   Looks pretty well, eh?

MOSE.   I am very well satisfied, sir.

COL.   Oh *you* are, eh? Well, I'm glad it pleases you.

MOSE. [*Peevishly*]   A body can't say a word but you must get sarcastic.

COL. [*Blustering*]   What—what—sir—

NEL.   There, there. We'll have no quarrel today. Haven't time for it. Postpone it until tomorrow.

MOSE.   Now, Nellie, I'll leave it to you if I said anything—

NEL.   But you are doing a lot of it now.

COL.   Of course he is. If he couldn't keep that mouth of his going—

NEL.   Uncle! Will you change the subject.

COL. [*Growling*]   U-m-m!

MOSE. [*Growling*]   U-m-m-m! [*They scowl at one another*]

NEL.   Who have you invited, uncle?

COL.   All of Billy's friends that want to come. Don't know how many he will bring but I guess seven plates will be enough. Nellie, Billy and myself are three. Then there will be four plates for friends. In case the places are not filled, Jennie, you and Mose shall be of the party.

JEN.   Thank you, sir. [*Exits with dish, R.3.*]

MOSE.   Well, I'll be one of the party anyway. Do you suppose I am going to give up my place to a lot of robbers?

COL.   Attention! Billy is the son of my old friend, Steve Wright. Today he shall be treated as such. He and his friends are to be my guests and I don't need you or anybody else to tell me what is due a Southern gentleman's guest. Today I shall forget the lawless boy and remember only the wild harum-scarum youngster I used to love. Tomorrow, Billy the Kid may go his way. I never want to see him again.

NEL.   Oh, uncle!

COL.   My child, our roads lie apart. Today we will overlook that fact. [*Sighs; Nellie wipes her eyes*] Mose!

MOSE.   Present.

COL.   Set the wine near the head of the table. [*Mose does so*] And, Mose—

MOSE.   Countersign is correct, sir.

COL.   Remove that bird. Birdie won't need any chickweed today.

MOSE.   Yes, sir. [*Takes cage and exits*]

NEL.   What a tease you are.

COL. Well, I know Billy is overly fond of dicky birds and I want to put temptation out of his way.

NEL. Well, if you think an old excuse like that—

COL. There's one other thing, miss. Don't try to work off any extra champagne cork-popping. I've got the bottles counted. [*Mose enters with plate of cabbage salad*] And I know every pop. [*Nellie laughs*]

MOSE. It's a wise cork that knows its own pop.

COL. [*Laughs*] Very good, Mose. [*Nellie laughs and exits R.3.*]

MOSE. [*Tasting salad*] And it's a wise cow that knows its own fodder.

COL. [*Sharply*] Fingers out of the dish, Mose. You are not a cow.

MOSE. [*Indignant*] No, sir, I'm not. Do you know what I am?

COL. A—a—jackass?

MOSE. Yes, sir, I am. I mean, no, sir, I'm not. But I ought to be after associating half my life with a mule.

COL. What! Call me a mule?

MOSE. No, sir, I don't—you are a-a-a confounded old crank.

COL. Insubordination! You shall be courtmartialled.

MOSE. No, I won't. We are not on the battlefield now. I know my rights—I am a free-born citizen and have a vote.

COL. [*Snorts*] Vote! What good does that do you? You never voted.

MOSE. I never got my price.

COL. Nice citizen you. Talking about a price.

MOSE. I know my business. I've got a say in the management of this household and I'm going to have my rights.

COL. [*Furious*] Attention!

MOSE. We're not on the field now.

COL. No, confound you. If we were, I'd have you hamstrung.

MOSE. Sit down there and listen to me. [*Colonel sits, astonished*] To begin with, Nellie don't like the tactics, therefore, she must be relieved from all duty henceforth.

COL. You don't say so?

MOSE. Then—Nellie loves Billy, and you pretty near broke her heart when you told her she must never see him after today. That order must be revoked.

COL. Must, eh?

MOSE. Don't you call me musty. You're as old as I am.

COL. [*Rises*] Damn, this has gone far enough. I am commander of this post, and I won't have any rebellion. No opposing forces shall mar my peace. You get out of here as fast as you can go.

MOSE. [*A little frightened*] Get out!

Col. Bag and baggage. I won't put up with your interference another minute.

Mose. [*Blustering*] Hm! Hm! You can't discharge me. I'm your orderly.

Col. We're not on the battlefield now. You can go.

Mose. [*Voice trembles*] Go? Go where?

Col. To the devil for all I care. I've stood enough from you to try a saint. [*Sits*]

Mose. I ain't got no home but this, sir.

Col. Well, get another.

Mose. [*Whimpering*] I'm too old to start all over again.

Col. You're a free-born citizen—got a vote, you know.

Mose. Colonel, you ain't going to turn me out, are you?

Col. Yes, I am, confound you, and don't you go snivelling around Nellie to be taken back. I won't have it.

Mose. [*Firing*] You never heard me snivelling at Antietam, did you?

Col. We're not on the battlefield now.

Mose. No. If we were, I'd tell you to take your horse and go to thunder. Oh, I'll go. [*Goes up*] It won't take me long to pack. I ain't not nothing but my bugle.

Col. Well, take it along. I'll be glad to get rid of it. You've nearly driven me crazy with your tooting, the last fifteen years.

Mose. I was going to give it to you, Colonel—but I'll not—trouble you any more. [*Wipes eyes on flag*] Why here's the old flag. I'd like to take that, Colonel.

Col. Well, take it along.

Mose. 'Member how at Antietam, the color-bearer was shot down and you grabbed up this same old flag?

Col. Certainly. No soldier would let the colors trail in the dust.

Mose. How the boys cheered you as you led 'em along. Why, it just put new life in 'em.

Col. Ah, they were a fine lot.

Mose. And then you were shot in the arm. I picked you and the flag up together and carried you back—out of the firing.

Col. That you did, Mose. A brave deed—bullets zipping all around us—men falling everywhere.

Mose. And then when the surgeon went to probe for the bullet—ha, ha—you said: "Drat your picture, stop it. It's the other arm—that's my vaccination"—[*Laughs*]

Col. [*Laughing heartily*] I remember, Mose, I remember. One on the doctor, eh?

MOSE. More like one on you. You got the worst of it.

COL. So I did. Ha, ha—glorious times, Mose.

MOSE. All over now, Colonel. We're both old, and I'm turned—out. [*Wipes eyes*]

COL. [*Rises, goes to him*] Mose, dear old friend, forgive me. [*Holds out hand*] This tent is yours as long as you will share it with me. [*Mose shakes, still wiping eyes*]

NEL. [*Enters R.3.*] Well! Are you two quarrelling again? I declare, that selfsame quarrel and reconciliation has occurred at least once a year, as far back as I can remember.

COL. We need it, my dear, to strengthen old ties. And to serve as a reminder that we are still comrades. [*Pats Mose on back*] But I think Mose is an old friend. He gets these quarrels up on purpose, knowing discipline will be relaxed for a week or two, so he can run the place to suit himself.

MOSE. Don't you believe it, Miss Nellie.

NEL. Of course I don't. Uncle is equally to blame. Well, everything is ready now. I hope they are on time. [*Horse effect outside*] There! Run and see who it is, Mose.

MOSE. [*Saluting*] Once more the army is himself. [*Exit L.U.E. Sounds of several horses stopping. "Whoa," "Back Up," etc., outside*]

COL. Seems to be quite a lot of 'em.

NEL. [*Disappointed*] I was in hopes he would come alone.

COL. He knows his business best. Maybe it is not safe for him to travel alone.

MOSE. [*Enters announcing*] Friends of Mr. Billy, the Kid. [*Enter Bud followed by three plainsmen. All have revolvers in belt at back. Blue shirts, broad hats, boots, etc. As Bud enters, Nellie starts back in alarm and watches them suspiciously*]

COL. Welcome, gentlemen, to this little feast given in honor of your noble comrade. [*Shakes with Bud*]

BUD. Thanks, Colonel, it's mighty kind of you all right—all right, but he's deserving of it. He's one of the gamest men in this section. And b-a-a-a-d? Well I guess. Me an' him used to be kinder on the outs, but he licked me an' a few more in a fair fight. So I struck me colors and joined his forces—an' I'm his'n for life. [*Nellie seems to accept his explanation*] This is Hank Burk, this is Bill Burnside and this is Bald Pete. Gentlemen, Colonel Bradley, one of the heroes of our last late war.

COL. And gentlemen—my niece, Miss Bradley. [*They bow awkwardly*] Now, sit down and have something while we are waiting for Billy. Mose, go out and keep watch for him.

Mose. [*Aside, looking at Bud*] If that ain't the man that knocked me down a week ago, I'm a marine. [*Doubles up fists, looks at them and exits L.U.E.*]

Col. Nellie, see how the dinner is coming on. [*She exits R.3. Men in the meantime have seated themselves. Counting from downstage end of table Bud sits second chair R. Man third chair R. Man second chair L. The other third L. This leaves vacant, first chairs R. and L. and chair at head of table. Colonel sets two bottles of wine on table. General conversation while bottles are being opened*] Now, gentlemen, help yourselves and I'll give you a toast. Wait—I must get a julep for mine. Anybody else like one?

Bud. This'll do us, Colonel.

Col. Just excuse me for a second. [*Exits R.3. Bud jumps up and runs to window, opening it*]

Bud. Come in, Peanut. [*Peanut enters by window, head tied up where he has been wounded*] Quick, under the table. [*Peanut dives under the table, downstage, so audience can see him. He has two large revolvers in back of his belt*] If they see you they may get suspicious.

Pea. Yes. De girl she a know a me quick. Don't you tink Billy will tumble when he sees you?

Bud. Not a bit. I can square him all right—all right. Say, Peanut, how did you tumble to this banquet racket?

Pea. De fool boy dat a de Colonel send with de invitation to Billy come to my place. I read a de note and den sent it on to Bill.

Bud. Think he'll come all right?

Pea. Sure. He a sweet on the girl.

Bud. Wait a minute. [*Rises, goes up, gets bottle, places it on table by closet*] When the wine is about all gone, I'll call Billy's attention to this bottle. And ask him to get it. When he turns his back, that's the signal to jump on him. [*Resumes seat*] You understand?

Men. Yes—we understand, *etc.*

Bud. Mind, we got the law on our side. I'm dep'ty now, so don't let the old Colonel bluff you.

Pea. What! You tink de Colonel could bluff—

Bud. Shut up, he's here. [*Kicks him*]

Pea. O-o-o, dat my shin.

Bud. Sh-h-h.

Col. [*Enters*] Ah ha! Here is the real article. A genuine Southern mint julep. [*He holds up glass*] All filled up, gentlemen?

Pea. All but a me. [*Bud kicks him*] Ouch!

Col. Eh? What's that?

BUD. I just bumped my foot, Colonel.

PEA. Well, don't bump it on a me.

COL. Now for the toast. Here's to comrade Bill Wright. [*All drink*] And death to his enemies. [*Colonel drinks. Bud chokes and spits out liquor*]

PEA. Good-a joke. [*Laughs. Bud kicks him*] Sacré-damn.

BUD. 'Scuse me for swearing, Colonel; it went down the wrong way.

COL. Never mind, fill up and have another.

BUD. Cut out the toast this time, Colonel. [*Glasses filled; horse effects outside*]

NEL. [*Enter R.3.*] They're coming, uncle. [*"Whoa," etc., outside*]

COL. Just hold the next round for a minute, gentlemen, and we'll have it together. [*Goes up*]

BUD. [*Low*] Keep up your nerve, boys, he don't know any of you.

PEA. Pass me a drink, to keep a up *my* a nerve.

BUD. [*Kicks him*] Shut up.

PEA. Wow! [*Loud*]

NEL. [*Turning*] Why, what was that?

BUD. My dog, miss, under the table. [*Low, to Peanut*] Growl, you Indian, growl. [*Peanut growls*] He's very cross, miss.

PEA. Cross? He's—a *mad*. You kicka me again and I'll—bite.

MOSE. [*Enter L.U.E., announcing*] Mr. Con Hanley, First Lieutenant to Captain Billy. [*Enter Con. Colonel shakes and motions him to seat. Con pauses at sight of the men*]

CON. My—my. But it's choice society the Colonel do be keeping. [*Sits first chair R.*]

MOSE. Mr. Boyd Denver. A—a—gentleman. [*Men all start and look up*]

COL. [*Astounded*] What!

NEL. That man—here? [*Enter Denver cowed and sneaking, slinks to table without raising hand or noticing anybody. Sinks in chair at head of table, head drops in hands*]

MOSE. Captain William Wright—Billy, the Kid. [*Enter Bill, stops at sight of men at table. Hand goes swiftly to pistol; glances sharply at Colonel*]

BILL. Quite a gathering, I see. [*Extends hand to Colonel*] Colonel.

COL. Sir, I did not think you would insult my little banquet, given in your honor, by inviting that man here. [*Pointing to Denver*] Still, I shall not refuse you my hand. [*Shakes*]

BILL. Colonel, some day I will explain. Now, I cannot. [*Crosses to Nellie*] Nellie—[*Holds out hand*]

NEL. [*Ignoring it*] Billy, how could you? [*Tosses her head, turns and goes to door R.3. Breaks down, cries and exits. Bill sighs and turns away, looks*] *sharply at men again fingering pistol. Men are uneasy. Bill with sudden determination removes belt and pistol, handing them to Colonel*]

BILL. Colonel, here are my only weapons. While your guest, I shall forget my hostility towards society.

COL. [*Takes belt*] May you enjoy yourself, Billy. But I cannot—nor can I allow any of my household—to sit at the table with your *friend*. Come, Mose. [*Exit Colonel and Mose R.3.*]

BILL. [*Comes to first chair L.*] Now, gentlemen, what's the game?

BUD. Honest, Bill, there ain't none. The Colonel invited us to come. Asked me if I felt sore at you. I said "No, he licked me in a fair fight, and I takes me hat off to him." I'm square, Bill, and there's me hand on it. [*Holds out hand. Bill hesitates a moment, then takes hand*]

BILL. If you are not square, Bud Monroe, the hand you are holding now will help you into eternity. [*Bud attempts to withdraw hand*] Don't take it away, Bud. I like to feel the pressure of an honest hand, even if it does tremble like a girl's and is cold and clammy. Bah! [*Throws hand away*] What poor liars some of us are!

BUD. [*To cover his confusion*] Come on, boys. Fill up, fill up and we'll drink to Bill's health. [*All fill glasses but Denver*]

PEA. [*Glancing from under table*] He no gotta de pistol now. Why dey no jump on him? [*Sees Con*] Oh! De Con man have dem.

BUD. Now boys—[*All raise glasses*] Here's to the worthy Captain Bill. A b-a-a-d man. [*All raise glasses to lips*] And to the gentlemanly proprietor of the Broken Heart, Mr. Denver. [*All drink but Bill and Con. Denver raises head, looks hopefully at Bud*]

BILL. [*Aside*] Drink to—him? No. [*Aloud*] I—ah—think there is a fly in my glass. [*Tosses contents under table; hits Peanut in face*]

CON. Billy, I believe there is an elephant in mine. [*Dashes contents under table, hits Peanut. He sputters and turns around so his rear view is toward audience; his two pistols stick out in plain view*]

BUD. Well, try some more. [*Fills Bill and Con's glass, then attends to other end of table*]

BILL. [*Looking at glass*] This looks rather dark. [*Goes to toss it under table, sees Peanut, motions Con. Both reach down and each slips a pistol from Peanut's belt. Action is very quick*] Rather dark looking, eh, Con?

CON. Looks kind o' black to me. [*Bill slips pistol in his boot*]

BUD. Well, try some from this bottle. [*Goes to pour*] Why, it's empty. There's another bottle right behind you, Bill, will you get it? [*Nellie enters R.3.*]

BILL. Certainly. [*Bill rises, goes toward bottle on table L. Con has been eyeing the rear view of Peanut and contemplating his boot. As Bill's back is turned, all men rise slowly*]

BUD. Now, boys.

NEL. Look out, Bill. [*Bill without looking around, dashes in closet and closes door. Two men L. reach it almost at the same time. Con, without seeing the action of the others, has delivered an awful kick to Peanut, just as Bud speaks. Bud and man R. grab Con and bind him. Peanut is kicked from under table L. rushes to closet door, turns key which was in the lock and puts it in his pocket. Denver is standing and watches the scene in a dazed fashion*]

PEA. Gooda! We-a gota him!

CON. [*Who is bound*] Yes, and I gota one, too.

PEA. Sacré! [*Rubbing himself*] I have-a not forgotten.

CON. No? I think meself the sting of that kick will linger for some time on yer—memory.

PEA. Sacré! I geta even.

BUD. Where does that door lead to?

PEA. Nowhere. It is a blind closet. [*Shows key*] He-a is our prisoner.

DEN. [*Huskily*] Thank God, I am free. Give me some wine, I am choking. Oh, you shall be well paid for this. Shake. [*Shakes hands all around; drinks*]

NEL. [*At back*] I must warn uncle. [*Starts R.*]

PEA. Here, girl. [*She stops*] What a in data closet?

NEL. [*Comes down L. and speaks as Bill will hear*] Nothing—nothing but some dresses of my maid Polly. She will be here in a moment to serve you.

PEA. No-a weapons in-a dere?

NEL. None whatever. I will send my maid, Polly. [*Starts*]

PEA. Stop! You staya here. Let Polly come if she-a want to but I no-a have de house aroused by you.

BUD. I'll just lock these doors to keep anyone from butting in. [*Locks door R.3. and L.U.E. Goes back to table. The others have resumed places about table, all are drinking and laughing. Nellie stands L.C. watching them*]

PEA. Here-a girl. Give-a me dat bottle of wine. [*Points to bottle on table L.*]

NEL. Yes, sir. [*Gets bottle, comes to Peanut, pours him out drink with right hand, with left she steals key out of his pocket*]

PEA. Data a gooda girl. You learn to obey easily.

NEL. Yes, sir. [*She returns bottle to table, quickly slipping key in lock, unlocking door and taking key out again*]

PEA. Here, here! Bring back data bottle, I no-a tella you to take him away.

NEL. Yes, sir. [*She brings bottle, pours drink for Peanut and slips key back in his pocket, placing bottle on table.* NOTE: *Key business must be made very apparent to audience*]

CON. [*Who has been watching Nellie*] Nellie, fer the love of Heavin' give me a drink, before I choke wid laughter.

BUD. What you got to laugh about, cull? [*Nellie goes up to window*]

CON. It's too fine a joke to penetrate that thick skull of yours. But one thing I'd like to ask ye; what right have ye to bind me up this way?

BUD. I'm dep'ty sheriff, I am. [*Shows badge*]

CON. Oh, ho, ye are?

PEA. [*Mocking*] Ho, ho, yes he is.

CON. Go on, ye pizen-faced pup. I didn't ask you.

PEA. [*In rage*] I-a killa him.

BUD. Hold on, Peanut.

PEA. He-a kicka me.

CON. That seems to hurt your feelings, dago.

PEA. It-ah hurta my pride.

CON. Well, never carry your pride in your pistol pocket.

DEN. [*Getting drunk*] Kill him—kill them both. Oh, God! I could shout for joy at my deliverance. To be free again—free! Listen, men, for seven days I have been dragged in mortal terror, from place to place, by that fiend in yonder—tortured by the threat of approaching death, that increased my terror the longer it was delayed. I was given nothing but whiskey to drink in all that time—whiskey until I was driven mad. When I begged for water, he said: "you filled me with whiskey and then tempted me to my first crime. Your path to the grave shall be a river of it." [*Takes glass*] Come, fill up— fill up. This will be a glorious day. [*All crowd around table and fill up. Bill slips from closet disguised as maid. Goes to door L.U.E. tries to open it, finds it locked*]

NEL. Oh, here is Polly. [*All turn*]

PEA. How she-a get-a in?

NEL. Through the window.

BUD. I'll just lock that, too. [*Goes to window, locks it*]

NEL. Polly, will you serve the gentlemen?

BILL. Wiz pleasure. [*Goes to table; serves drinks. Mose appears outside window. Nellie up quick*]

NEL. [*Aside to Mose*] Mose, can you hear? [*Mose nods*] Quick! Stampede all the horses but Billy's, bring his to this window. You understand? [*Mose *nods*] When it is done, give me some signal—sound your bugle. [*Mose nods and disappears*]

BUD.   Here, you girl, don't try to get out that window.

NEL.   I am not trying to. [*Bill has been busy filling glasses. All have seated themselves. Peanut first chair L. Bud R. Billy is beside Peanut*]

PEA.   Oh, dat-a Polly—a very pretty girl. [*Pats Bill's cheek*]

BILL.   Zank you, m'sieur, you are ver'—ver' 'andsome.

BUD.   Ho—ho. She's stuck on the dago.

BILL.   You 'ave such *beautiful whiscaires.* May I not 'ave a souvenier. [*Pulls hair out of his beard*]

PEA.   Ouch! Sacré! What you-a do? Dat-a hurt like blazes. [*All laugh*]

BILL.   I am ze sorry. [*Puts arm around him*]

PEA. [*Flattered*]   Dat-a all right.

BILL.   More wine, zentlemen? [*Goes to Bud. Takes pistol from his belt*] O-o-o! What a terr'ble big pistol. 'Ow do he work?

BUD.   Well, pretty, I'll show yer. Pull the trigger an' somebody's dead, see?

BILL.   Pull ze trigaire, an' somebody dead, oui? [*Points it at Peanut*] Bang.

PEA.   Hold-a on. Don'-a you practise on me. [*Bill laughs*]

BUD.   Pull the catch and out come the cartridges, see?

BILL. [*Empties cartridges*]   Magnificent! Let me put zem back, eh?

BUD.   Go ahead.

BILL.   Zere is one—two—three—four—five, all in. [*Lets audience see he does not replace cartridges. Places revolver back in Bud's belt*] Zere! Now I have fixed you—plenty. [*Tosses shells away*]

NEL. [*At window*]   Oh, why don't Mose blow the signal?

DEN.   Here, girl, give me some wine—wine.

BILL.   Ze zentleman want wine? 'E shall 'ave it. Plenty—plenty, rivers of it. [*Goes behind Denver's chair*]

DEN. [*Glancing up uneasily*]   What did you say about rivers?

BILL.   Ze river of wine, in which to drown your sorrow.

NEL. [*Down, aside to Bill*]   When you hear a bugle call, be prepared to escape. [*Bill nods*]

DEN.   Good girl! Glorious wine. Oh this is a happy day.

BILL.   Be 'appy today, m'sieur, for tomorrow you *may* be dead.

DEN.   What do you mean?

BILL.   Zat is an old quotation from my country. Zat is all. [*Goes to man, L.*] Have wine? [*Steals his pistol, pulls up skirt and puts it in boot*]

NEL. [*At window*]   No signal yet.

PEA.   Come here, Polly.

BILL.   O-o-o—I am forgetting my dear 'andsome man. [*Goes to him*] Such a *beautiful* beard. Can you not spare me one little— [*Pulls hair out of his beard*]

PEA.   Oh! Hella! Diable! What you—a do? [*All laugh. All getting rather mellow*]

BILL.   I 'ave ze two hair, soon I have 'nough for ze watch chain.

PEA.   Not-a out of my—a whiskers. [*Nurses his face. Bill has gone to man R. steals his revolver and comes C. finds both boots full, at a loss what to do with it for a moment, then pulls dress up and puts it in pocket. Work this for comedy*]

NEL.   Oh, why doesn't Mose sound the signal?

PEA.   Here, Polly girl. How you-a like to come-a to my place? Wine, dancing, fine clothes, plenty de mon. Eh?

BILL.   I love to go—if you give me just one mo—[*Pulls out whisker*]

PEA.   Stop-a dat or I cut-a de neck. [*All laugh*]

DEN.   Let's have him out, boys, and kill him.

PEA.   I have-a de key. [*Rises, shows key, goes to door*]

NEL.   Will Mose never come?

PEA. [*Pauses at door*]   All get-a ready boys. Shoot as soon as he comes out if he no have his-a hands up. [*All rise. Bud has playfully chased Billy around table to C.*] Polly, go up-a by de window, so you not-a get hurt. [*Bill starts up*]

BUD.   Wait a minute, Polly, I want to put my arms around you.

PEA. [*Impatiently*]   We got-a no time.

BILL. [*Retreating*]   Polly don't want your arms.

BUD.   Polly has *got* to have some arms. [*Sharp bugle call. All turn. Nellie gives cry of joy. Bill grabs chair and dashes it through window. Mose appears behind broken window, bugle in one hand, leading horse with other. Bill reaches down, pulls up skirt and draws two pistols from boots*]

BILL.   Gentlemen, Polly has all the arms she needs. [*All reach for pistols, find them gone. Except Bud who snaps his unloaded one. Peanut throws open closet door. Finds the closet empty*]

PICTURE

2ND PICTURE: *Colonel and Nellie R., Mose L., pointing pistols at men. Jennie down R., releasing Con. Bill astride horse, pulling Denver towards him by means of a lasso that is about Denver's body. Denver struggles but is slowly drawn up to window. Bud, Peanut and men down stage.*

ACT IV.

SCENE: *Same as Act I., except the whole act is moved nearer C. Return to house L.1. transparent when light is behind it, showing interior of room. Fireplace, at back; sofa and chairs. Windows on porch and windows in room boarded up. Porch, fence, etc., show signs of neglect and decay. Broken tree branches and leaves scattered about the yard. Pile of sand beside well, as though it had been dug out. Rope from porch to unseen flagstaff, supposed to be on top of house. Two long pieces of rope C. Con enters at rise, R.U.E. He is dirty and worn looking.*

CON.   Sure, the place is just as we left it two weeks ago. [*Goes to porch; sits*] It's a foolish thing of Billy to come back here. They're sure to get him. An' think me own life ain't none too safe. They're hot on our trail. 'Tis a hard fight we had—and lost. The old gang do be broken up for good. What wasn't killed was captured—'cepting Billy and me. I wanted him to jump for the bad lands, but no—he must come here, back to his old home and—his mother's grave. Why, it's ten to one shot they'll watch this place. I made him stay in the little grove of trees back there a ways, 'til I had a look around. If it's all O.K. I run a little flag up to the top of the house. That's the signal for him to come. [*Rises*] Well, I guess it's all safe enough. [*Looks L.*] Hello! Who the devil do be this a coming. I don't know. [*Hides behind corner of house L.*] I'll make a quiet investigation. [*Peanut enters L.U.E.; glances around cautiously*]

PEA.   He no-a here yet. But he-a come. He come because his mother buried out there. Dat-a good-a joke. We capture de kid through his-a dead mother. [*Laughs*] De boys wait back of de hill. When I-a sight him, I run-a dis flag up to de top of de house, den we-a have him. [*Crosses to R.*]

CON.   Dago, if ye make another break like that, I'll blow the ends off yer whiskers.

PEA.   Yes, you-a very funny man. But maybe you won't be so funny bye and bye.

CON.   Well, mebby you will be and that will even things up a bit, fer ye look like a funeral just at present. [*They cross the stage eyeing each other suspiciously*]

PEA.   [*Aside*]   Billy must-a be near, I give-a de signal. [*Begins to unfasten rope on porch; takes out small Mexican flag*]

CON.   What are ye going to do, dago?

PEA.   Dis-a one Mexican holiday. I will-a celebrate by running up dis-a flag.

Con. [*Drawing pistol*] Do ye want a little fireworks, to help out the celebration?

Pea. [*Turns, throws up hands*] No-a shoot, Con, no-a shoot.

Con. Then drop that flag. [*Peanut drops it*] Now, we will celebrate in the decent way. [*Hands him small American flag*] Run *this* up to the top of the house. [*Peanut looks at it in disgust and hesitates*] Go ahead, or I'll start the fireworks.

Pea. Sacré! [*Picks up American flag and hoists it*] Sacré!

Con. Don't ye call me that again! Now elevate yer hands while I remove the arsenal. [*Peanut holds up his hands. Con takes the pistol*] Now, dago, I'm going to promote ye. You shall be my valet.

Pea. What-a dey?

Con. Why, me man, you must clean me boots.

Pea. I'll see you-a in Hell first.

Con. All right, ye can start now. [*Raises pistol*]

Pea. [*In fright*] Hold on. I shina de boots!

Con. And ye must keep me wardrobe nicely brushed and pressed.

Pea. All-a right. I press-a de ward.

Con. And trot around after me wherever I go.

Pea. Trot? You take-a me for a leetle dog?

Con. [*Raises pistol*] Good-bye, dago.

Pea. Hold on. I—I trot.

Con. [*Throws him key*] Here, open the front dure.

Pea. [*Taking key and going to door*] Dusta de clothes, blacka de boots, waga de tail, trot. Sacré! [*Opens door*]

Con. Now, me bucko, we will go around to the stable, and you shall have the honor of stabling me horse. Come—trot. [*Exit L.U.E.*]

Pea. Bud, he maka me bark like a dog, and now dis-a man, he mak-a me trot. Sacré! [*Trots off stage after Con. Enter R.1.E. Colonel, Nellie, Mose and Jennie, very unmilitary; Mose is carrying old flag and bugle. Colonel is carrying satchel. Nellie has bird cage and Jennie a large medicine case*]

Col. The army is demoralized.

Nel. Uncle, we can't stay here.

Col. Well, we can rest a minute, can't we? We've got to water our horses; besides, we want a look at Wright's old place before we leave the neighborhood forever. [*Wipes his eyes*]

Nel. [*Sees him*] Not forever, uncle. This will blow over.

Col. Blow over? How can it? To think of that measley—low—contemptible blackguard getting out warrants for our arrest, for "aiding, abetting and propensitating the escape of an outlaw."

Mose. And here *we* are, trying to aid and abet our own escape.

Jen. Oh, Colonel, it is a shame! [*She cries on his shoulder; Nellie cries on other*]

Col. Shame! Shame! It's a—Hold on, Mose, don't you *dare* to swear in the presence of ladies.

Mose. Why, I wasn't going to.

Col. Yes, you were. You were just watching for the chance. There, there, girls, don't cry! We'll pull through somehow, even with that profane Mose along.

Mose. *Me* profane? Huh? You're the champion cusser in this state—and proud of it, too.

Col. What, me? This to my face? You—old—sinner, look at these poor girls, crying their eyes out. All your fault. Why didn't you let 'em take Billy and be done with it?

Nel. [*Drawing away*] Oh, uncle!

Col. I mean it. [*Jennie draws away*] Then we wouldn't be in this fix. [*To Mose*] You brought his horse for him—and brought all this trouble to us, so I may as well tell you now, to get out.

Mose. I am out, Colonel, and so are you.

Col. That's so—both out—no home. Mose, old friend, put it there. We'll stick together through thick and thin. [*They shake*]

Nel. What a wreck the old place looks!

Col. Just as we left it three years ago, when Wright and his wife were killed. The lawyers locked up the place until they could find the heirs. Billy being outlawed, he didn't count. So far none have shown up.

Nel. [*Has crossed to porch*] Why, the door is open.

Col. Somebody must be here—sheriff, maybe.

Mose. Let's hide, quick.

Jen. What will *become of us?*

Col. Stand your ground like a soldier. If we must go to jail, let us go like gentlemen.

Mose. Women and all?

Col. Silence. [*Calls*] Hello there, anybody at home?

Con. [*Outside*] Hello—let go me arm.

Pea. [*Outside*] Hello—Sacré! You kick-a me!

Con. I know it. [*Outside*]

Mose. Had we better retreat in good order?

Col. A good plan, Mose. [*Colonel, Mose and Jennie turn R. and begin tiptoeing off*]

Nel. [*On porch*] Halt! [*They do*] Stand your ground.

Col. But my dear, a retreat in the face of overwhelming odds is always honorable.

Nel. Overwhelming odds? Fiddlesticks! There are but two men and I recognize the voice of one. It's Con Hanley. [*Con enters L.U.E., followed by Peanut*]

Con. Well, if it ain't the Colonel—and family. How are ye?

Col. Mighty glad to see *you*, Con. [*Shakes*]

Mose. Mighty glad you're not the sheriff.

Con. And there's Jennie. [*Raises hat*]

Pea. Jennie! [*Points at her*] She run away. She-a my girl. [*Jennie frightened*]

Con. [*Slapping Peanut's hand*] Put down your pointer, dago. What do ye want wid a girl anyhow? Ye've been married three times.

Pea. Well, dey all-a dead.

Con. Dead yer grandmother. Where do they be buried?

Pea. Dey no-a be buried. I have-a dem cremated.

Con. My! My! You've had wives to burn, haven't ye? And now ye want another. Bad cess to ye. I ought to give ye another kick.

Pea. No—no, no-a kick.

Col. Let him alone, Con. The poor devil is frightened to death already.

Con. Just as ye say, Colonel, but what are ye all doing here?

Mose. We're all outlaws now.

Col. You see, Con, warrants have been sworn out for our arrest because we helped Billy and you escape.

Con. The divil ye say? Well, one good turn deserves another. So Billy and me will help *you* all to escape. Just as soon as Billy takes a last look at the old place, we will all jump for the East.

Pea. [*Aside*] I knew Billy would come-a here.

Col. Don't believe I care to go that far, Con. Just over the border somewhere until this cursed thing blows over. Where would be a good place to stop?

Con. Right here.

All. Here? [*As Nellie speaks, Con turns and sees her for the first time*]

Con. [*Starts toward her, hand outstretched*] Hello, Nellie. [*Looks at Peanut*] Come on, valet, foller me up.

Pea. Bow wow! [*Trots over to Con who is shaking hands with Nellie*]

Con. Yes, sir, stay right here. Ye are over the border—just. No one ever comes this way and ye would be as safe as a bug in a rug as long as ye wanted to remain.

COL. By jove, you're right. We're over the line. I had forgotten that. Hurrah, we're safe. [*Hugs Mose, hugs Jennie, hugs Peanut. When he sees who it is throws him off in disgust*]

PEA. Dat-a worse dan being a dog.

NEL. Your hand is hot, Con, and you are shivering all over.

CON. It's them Texas mothers, miss.

NEL. Nothing of the kind. You are ill. [*Crosses down*] Uncle, Con has chills and fever, have you any medicine?

COL. Best in the world, quinine and whiskey. Brr-rr-rr, I feel a chill myself. [*Picks up satchel*]

JEN. Oh, I hope Con is not going to be ill.

CON. [*Coming down*] Divil a bit, Jennie; just the weather, that's all.

COL. Jennie, you and Mose move that table over here. [*They move table C.*] I'll soon have him all right. [*Puts satchel on table*]

MOSE. B-r-r, I feel a chill.

COL. Those chills that come just when the whiskey bottle is opened, don't go, Mose. [*Opens satchel*]

MOSE. Well you just had one.

COL. Mine were genuine. Why, I'd take the quinine if there wasn't any whiskey. [*Paws around in satchel*] Jennie, you and Nellie go in and start the fire. Brrr, I've got an *awful* chill!

NEL. Hurry, Jennie, or uncle will have a fit. [*Both exit in house laughing*]

COL. Hm! Don't see anything to laugh at. Made fuss enough when Con shivered.

MOSE. I *have* got a chill, Colonel. [*Shakes as hard as he can*]

COL. [*Still fussing in medicine case*] Won't work, Mose.

PEA. Brr. I got-a de chill—awful. [*Shakes*]

CON. Hold your whisht. Don't speak until I tell ye. Sit up on yer hind legs and beg.

COL. Come, what are you doing with that fellow in tow?

CON. Found him spying around here, so I captured him and made him me valet.

COL. Oh, where—the—devil—is—Mose, did you put that bottle of whiskey in the satchel or the medicine case?

MOSE. You wouldn't let me touch it. You said you would attend to it.

COL. What! [*Sinks in chair*] Alone—no friends—no home—and no whiskey.

MOSE. Never mind, Colonel, I didn't want it.

COL. *You* didn't want it—you—

MOSE. Hold on, Colonel, you never swear, you know.

Col. Oh no, *you* didn't want it. Well I'll have to give Con the quinine straight. [*Fumbles with boxes on table*]

Mose. You must take some quinine yourself, Colonel.

Col. What for?

Mose. Why, that awful chill of yours. You said you'd take it if there wasn't any whiskey. [*Colonel glares at him*]

Col. Give me the canteen, Mose.

Mose. [*Unslinging canteen from his shoulder*] If you don't take it, Colonel, I'll think you were faking.

Col. I wish you would mind your own business. Here, Con, take this. [*Gives him powder*] Wash it down with—water. [*Hands canteen. Con takes it*] Suppose I'll have to take one just to satisfy that old doubting Thomas, there. [*Takes powder*] Ugh, but this is awful. Anybody else? [*Mose and Peanut shake heads*] I knew it. Fakes, both of you.

Con. [*Sits on steps*] My, my! But that stuff was bitter.

Col. [*Sits*] Of all the lunk-heads—no whiskey—

Jen. [*At door*] Are you better, Con?

Con. I'm a dom sight worse.

Jen. I'm so sorry. [*Exits in house. Colonel and Mose ransack satchel and medicine case again*]

Con. Sure, it's a fine girl she is.

Col. I *must* have packed that bottle, Mose.

Mose. Hurry up and find it. Me mouth tastes like a glue factory smells.

Col. That quinine tastes like the—the very devil.

Mose. Say, Colonel, which box did you get those powders out of?

Col. This one, of course. [*Points to box*]

Mose. [*Astounded*] This one? [*Colonel nods*] Good-bye, Colonel, old comrade, good-bye, Con, old friend. [*Shakes with both*]

Col. Where are you going?

Mose. *I'm* not going. You are going. These powders are marked, morphine, poison. [*Colonel and Con clutch Mose by the arm*]

Con. Do ye mane it?

Mose. Read. [*Shows box; both read and stagger back*] Good-bye, friends.

Pea. Ha, ha! Dat-a good-a joke.

Con. Laugh—ye hyena. But before I die, I'm going to wind up your worldly career.

Col. [*Hoarsely*] Mose, old friend, don't let me go to sleep. *Don't let* me go to sleep. Walk me. That's my only chance. Keep me moving. [*They link arms and go out L.U.E. Con has been toying with his pistol, Peanut appealing to him in dumb show*] For Heaven's sake, Con, don't stand there. Walk, man, walk. Your life depends on keeping awake. Keep moving.

CON.   Dago, keep me walking. Don't let me lie down. If I find meself getting sleepy, I'll put an end to ye're dialect.

PEA.   I no let-a you sleep. [*Grabs him by arm*] Come, like one leetle dog—trot. [*Rushes Con off R.1.E.*]

NEL.   [*Appears at door*] Come in, the fire is so cheerful. Why, where have they gone? [*Enter Colonel and Mose L.1.E. singing "While We Are Marching Through Georgia"; cross stage*]

NEL.   Oh, uncle, the coffee is ready. Uncle!—*Mose!*

MOSE. [*Stops*] Eh? What?

COL.   Don't stop, you idiot. Do you want me to die right here? Keep moving. [*Grabs Mose and both exit R.1.E. singing "While We Are Marching Through Georgia"*]

NEL.   O-o-o-o, it's the medicine. I knew uncle couldn't stand the whiskey. [*Cries*] To think of it—and at such a time, too!

JEN.   [*Enters*] What is the matter, dear?

NEL.   The medicine—was too much—for uncle. [*Exits in house crying*]

JEN.   Why, what can have happened?

JEN.   [*Enter Con and Peanut R.U.E. Con is singing: "He Marched Thim Up the Hill, Me Boys, and He Marched Thim Down Again"*] Oh, Con, come and get some hot coffee. Con—Con!

CON.   [*Stops*] Eh? What, me dear?

PEA.   No-a stop. I want-a me dialect. [*Drags him along*]

CON.   Farewell my dear, if I hadn't taken the stuff—

JEN.   Was it the medicine, Con?

CON.   I should say it was. Good-bye. Perhaps in another world—

PEA.   No-a sleep—keep moving. [*Drags him off L.U.E. Con sings "He Marched Thim, etc.," in distance*]

JEN.   Nellie! Nellie! Come here, quick. [*Nellie enters*] Something has happened to uncle. Con just went by, singing as though his heart would break.

NEL.   So did uncle.

JEN.   Con said it was the medicine.

NEL.   Yes—whiskey.

JEN.   O-o-oh! [*Enter Mose and Colonel, L.U.E., Colonel tired and frightened*]

COL.   Mose, if I ever get out of this, you shall be promoted to Major. [*They come down C.*] Oh, what an end for a brave soldier! Mose, I'm tired.

NEL.   You look tired, uncle. Sit down and rest.

COL. Rest? Girl do you want to be a murderess? Out of my way! Keep moving, Mose, keep moving. [*Exit L.1.E. singing "While We," etc.*]

NEL. They have gone crazy.

JEN. What can we do? [*Enter Con and Peanut L.U.E.*]

CON. Dago, if I ever walk this off you shall go free.

PEA. Good-a boy. [*They come down C.*]

JEN. Con, what *is* the matter.

CON. [*Stops*] Well ye see, me dear—

PEA. Don't-a stop. Keep moving. [*Drags him away*]

CON. [*Being dragged backwards by Peanut, talking to Jennie*] I hain't got the time ter explain now. Perhaps in another world.

PEA. Come-a on! [*Con turns, begins singing "He Marched," etc. Both exit R.1.E.*]

NEL. We must stop them.

JEN. How can we?

NEL. [*Determined*] We will lasso them.

JEN. But I can't lasso.

NEL. You can try. Here. [*Picks up piece of rope*] Make a noose in the end of that. I'll take this piece. Slip it over Con's head and I'll do the same to uncle. [*They fix ropes. Enter from R.1.E. Con and Peanut. Enter from L.1.E. Colonel and Mose. They stop near C. and glare at each other. Jennie slips behind Con and Nellie behind Colonel*]

COL. [*Glaring at Con*] There stands the cause of all this. If it hadn't been for that confounded chill—

MOSE. Don't stop. Keep moving.

CON. [*Glaring at Colonel*] There stands me murderer.

PEA. Don't-a stop—Keep-a de move.

CON. I won't stir an inch further. I'm going to die before his very face.

COL. [*Folds arms*] So am I. [*Nellie slips noose over Colonel's head; Jennie same business with Con*]

MOSE and PEA. Walk. [*Tries to pull them*]

NEL. and JEN. Stop! [*Both sides pulling*]

COL. Here! Stop it. Let go, some of you.

CON. What is this—a tug of war?

NEL. Now stand where you are and tell me what is the matter?

PEA. Tell her while-a walking.

COL. [*Desperately*] We've taken morphine for quinine. [*Groan. Nellie and Jennie scream; both run to table and examine boxes*]

MOSE. Keep a-moving.

COL. Not another step. Let me die with my face to the foe.

NEL. There must be an antidote, somewhere.

CON. Dago, I'm getting sleepy.

PEA. [*In fright*] No-a sleep. Keep-a de move.

CON. It's no use. [*Sits on ground*] Dago, pull off me boots.

PEA. [*Pulling off boots*] Oh, I lose-a de dialect.

CON. I always swore I would never die wid me boots on.

MOSE. Want your boots off, Colonel?

COL. No, sir. This is the way a soldier should die.

CON. Shot in the stummick wid morphine powder. [*Mose shows Nellie box*]

NEL. Uncle, how many morphine powders did you have?

COL. [*Groans*] Just an even dozen.

NEL. Well, they're all here. Mose made a mistake in the boxes, that's all. [*They all look foolish*]

COL. [*Reproachfully*] Mose, how could you? This was all hatched in your infamous brain. Just to get me to promote you. [*Sadly goes to house, rope trailing behind*]

MOSE. On my word of honor, I did nothing of the kind. [*Following*]

COL. *Your* word of honor? Don't—don't add falsehood to your other crimes. [*Exits in house, followed by Mose, still arguing*]

NEL. How ridiculous it all was! [*Exits in house, laughing*]

CON. Dago, pull on me boots. [*Peanut does so*] Now, although I have lost me dignity [*Rises*], likewise me chance for a dacent burial, I'll keep me word with you. You can go.

PEA. Oh, tank-a you. [*Goes up L., aside*] Now to tell-a de gang. [*Exits L.U.E.*]

JEN. Come in to the house, Con, and get a cup of coffee. It will make you feel better.

CON. Sure I feel like a bird—cleaned and picked. I'm sorry to disappoint ye about the funeral.

JEN. Oh, Con, wouldn't it have been dreadful if you had taken morphine.

CON. Well, I dunno. Nobody would care a rap—except Billy.

JEN. Con, how can you say that. I would.

CON. [*Looks at her in surprise*] Jennie, me girl, if I thought ye would be glad to see me alive, I could die happy.

JEN. [*Laughs*] But I don't want you to die. [*Serious*] Ever since the night you tried to shield me from those wretches in the Broken Heart, I have felt for you as I never felt for another being except—my mother.

CON. [*Astonished*] Jennie! [*Holds out his arms*]

JEN. [*Drawing back*] No—no, not that.

CON. I thought the feeling was all on my side—

JEN. Don't say any more. I don't want pity—the old life is past.

CON. [*Thoughtfully*] Me work here is finished. In five minutes I leave this place forever. Me life is uncertain and me prospects more so. Jennie, will ye share me lot, whatever it may be? Will ye be my wife?

JEN. Your wife?—Oh, Con, I cannot. My life has not been—

CON. Neither has mine. The good book says; "Let him without sin cast the first brick." I'm not here to judge. I love ye. I offer ye an everlasting devotion and a strong arm, that will fight me way to the front when I get to New York. Will ye come?

JEN. [*Puts hands in his*] Yes—Con.

CON. Hurrah! I'm glad the dom stuff wasn't quinine. Jen, give me a hug. [*They embrace*] Now, let's not tell the folks anything about it. I'll leave a note for them explaining matters. My horse and the dago's is in the stable. We'll be married at the first station, then for New York.

JEN. What are you going to do in New York, Con?

CON. Why, be a policeman, of course. [*They exit L.1.E. Enter Denver and Bill R.1.E.*]

BILL. Have you lost your tongue? We stood beside my mother's grave and you shook like an aspen, but refused to speak. Why do you gaze at that well? You seem frightened.

DEN. A grave—a grave—my grave. [*Sinks down*]

BILL. Very likely. You know why I brought you here.

DEN. I am innocent. Don't kill me.

BILL. You killed my parents.

DEN. You have no proof. You are trying to compel me to confess to something I did not do.

BILL. You killed them.

DEN. I saw them die. Give me a chance and I will tell you how.

BILL. You killed them.

DEN. As God is my judge.

BILL. You killed them.

DEN. Yes—[*Head sinks in hands*]

BILL. Ah! [*More of a long drawn sigh than a word*]

DEN. [*Shivers*] I am so cold.

BILL. You shall give me the details but we must be quick. As we came along I saw a number of horsemen circling about the hill yonder. In ten minutes this place will be surrounded. They are coming for me.

DEN. With your own life in the balance, why can you not be merciful? Let me escape while there is yet time.

BILL. No power on earth would make me release you. As for death, my work is nearly finished. I did not rush blindly into this trap. I knew the stakes and am prepared to pay the price. We shall die—almost—together—

DEN. [*Shudders*] I—am—so—cold.

BILL. Go into the house. Con has a fire, I suppose. I will join you in time to hear your story, go!

DEN. [*Sneaking to house*] We—shall—die—almost—together. [*Exits in house. Bill sits at table. As Denver enters house the interior is lighted up, showing Colonel, Mose and Nellie seated. Denver goes to fire without noticing anybody and sinks down before it*]

NEL. How comes that man here? [*Goes to exterior door*]

COL. Come, Mose, we will go elsewhere. [*Exits with Mose door L. Lights go out in house. Nellie enters from house*]

NEL. Billy! [*Runs to him*]

BILL. [*Rises astonished*] Nellie! What has happened? Why are you here?

NEL. We are in hiding. The law is hounding us for aiding your escape.

BILL. [*Bitterly*] Noble law! To wage war on two women and two inoffensive old men.

NEL. But I am glad it happened. We are all going East for a while. And Con said you were going too. So we shall all be united, where there is no trouble, sin or sorrow.

BILL. Where there is no trouble—sin—or sorrow. Yes, that's where I am going. But I take a different road than you.

NEL. Why can't we all go together?

BILL. I cannot go your way. I would not have you go mine.

NEL. Billy! You don't mean you are going to stick to this for life?

BILL. God forbid. I am done with—everything. Our paths lie apart.

NEL. Billy, have you forgotten the boy and girl vows we made? Our paths did not lie apart in them. Do you remember how we planned for a happy future—when you became a man? Our paths did not lie apart then. Billy, I have always loved you, for my sake will you not come with us and begin that other—better life?

BILL. Don't! Don't! You torture me. Do you fancy I never think of those things? Out of the waste and desert of my life, with its memory of the fair prospects—the husk and the swine. I seem to be looking through a window at a peaceful life—as a hungry, lonely tramp may limp to a lamp lit window, and, peering in, see father, and mother, and round faced children, and the table spread whitely with the good sure food that to these people is a calm certainty, like breathing or sleeping—not a joyous accident, or one of the great things that man was taught to pray for. The tramp turns away with a curse or a groan, according to his nature—and goes on his way, cursing or groaning—or, if the pinch is too fierce, he tries the back door. With me the pinch is great and I feel like trying any door—not to beg for the broken meats of pity—but to enter as master of all the happiness that should be mine. But it is too late.

NEL.   It is never too late to mend. Oh say you will come with us.

BILL.   Nellie, I must tell you something. When I saw you just now, I almost cursed the fates that brought you, but now I am thankful I shall at least have about me, those I love, during my—last—moments.

NEL. [*Startled*]   Billy, what do you mean?

BILL.   This is the final chapter in my career. I am about to avenge the murder of my parents, but the effort will cost me my life.

NEL.   Billy!

BILL.   The house is already surrounded. I can never leave here. It is better so; otherwise I might be tempted to seek for happiness in that other life, with you. No, no. It is better as it is. Go—go in the house. I have but a short time to prepare for—[*He leads her to house; she is crying*]

NEL.   You must escape. Go now.

BILL.   I cannot. The effort would but hasten my end. Bear up, it is better so. [*Leads her in house; both exit. Enter Peanut followed by Bud, L.U.E. They crawl around to porch*]

PEA.   I tell-a you dat was-a him.

BUD.   Well, I wanted to be sure; that long coat fooled me.

PEA.   You got-a all de men stationed so he no get away?

BUD.   Bet your life I have. If he shows his nose at door or window he's a gonner.

PEA.   Shoot-a to kill. And mine, if dat-a Con man dere, I want-a him. He shin-a de shoes, he dust-a de ward, he wag-a de tail, he t-r-o-t!

BUD.   Get over there behind that wagon. Don't expose yourself and don't fall asleep. We'll have him, if it takes a week.

PEA. [*Going up L.*]   I get-a de Con man, don't forget. [*Exits L.U.E. Bud exits R.U.E. Lights go up in house; Bill and Denver discovered*]

BILL.   You say my mother's death was an accident and my father was killed in self-defense?

DEN. [*Wearily*]   I am speaking the truth.

BILL.   And the motive for this attack on you?

DEN.   He sought my life on learning my true identity.

BILL.   Which was—?

DEN.   My name is Boyd Bradley. Your mother was my wife.

BILL.   What!

DEN. When she married Stephen Wright, she thought me dead. I had been unkind to her—even deserted her. You see, I am not sparing myself; I am telling the truth.

BILL. You monster! And do you think the truth will save you after your cruelty to my mother?

DEN. I don't care for mercy. I am past that. I wanted you to know all before we—both—go—almost—together, for I am your father.

BILL. My father—you!

DEN. Had you a chance to live, you could easily prove my statement; your birth is duly recorded in New York. I took the trouble to look it up. You were a year old when your mother married Wright.

BILL. [*Stunned*] You—my—father.

DEN. I have told you all. Now kill me if you wish.

BILL. Oh, God, how little we know of Your greatness—Your power. This —is my revenge. My father—the father I should love and cherish—I have been hounding to his death, thinking I was carrying out Your divine will. I bow to Your mighty wisdom. I am justly punished. [*Sinks on knees, overcome*]

DEN. [*Goes to him*] My son—

BILL. [*Rises*] Don't touch me. Go—go, you are free. Go and let me have a minute alone—with my Maker.

DEN. There is no hope of your escape?

BILL. If there was, I wouldn't take it. Go! [*Denver starts to door*] Father! [*He stops*] Take my coat. You are thinly clad and deadly cold. My hat also; you are without one. [*Denver puts them on*] Here, father, is my revolver, I shall not need it—again. [*Gives him pistol*] Good-bye—father. [*Holds out hand. Denver clasps it, then passes through door, leaving door open. Bill sinks on knees, Denver pauses outside, near well*]

DEN. Free, free at last. He will be dead in ten minutes and then—a fortune for me. [*Looks through door*] There he is, praying. Pray, damn you. It won't do you any good. Suppose he should escape? He has done it before. I'll take no chances. [*Raises revolver, aims at Bill through open door. Two gun shots heard from R.U.E. Denver throws up hands, screams and falls in well. At sound of shots, Bill springs to door and closes it. Enter Bud followed by two men, R.U.E. Enter Peanut followed by one man, L.U.E. All run to well*]

BUD. [*Listens for a second*] Not a sound. Hurrah! Billy the Kid is dead! [*Enter from door L. Nellie, Colonel and Mose*]

NEL. [*Half screams*] Billy dead? [*Sees him at door*] Billy!

BILL. Sh-h-h!

PEA. Let's get-a him out.

BUD. Too much trouble. Why ye can't see the bottom. Let him stay down there. I'm off for the reward. If the authorities won't believe he's dead, let 'em come and dig him up. Eh, boys?

ALL. Yes. That's it, *etc.*

BUD. Come on boys, I want that dough in a hurry. [*All go up R.*]

PEA. [*Following*] I wanted de Con man [*Others exit R.U.E.*] to shine de shoes, to dust-a de ward—[*Exits R.U.E.*] To—[*Outside*] to—t-r-o-t!

BILL. To the law I am dead. Today my life begins anew. Come Nellie— we'll wander down life's pathway together, where the sun shines always—

NEL. Billy! [*Embraces*]

CURTAIN

America's Lost Plays

In the context of 'innumerable meanings' and the illumination of the inhabitants of all the worlds in their six states, it is not surprising that their progress towards Buddhahood is seen as comprising a great variety of practices. These are listed at length in verses uttered by the bodhisattva Maitreya, who is able to see them all as a result of the illumination. They include such things as alms-giving, renunciation of the world, eremitical meditation, proclaiming the teaching to others, emitting radiance to save the denizens of hell, observing the precepts of Buddhism, persevering under persecution (a recurring theme in The Lotus Sutra), paying homage to relics and building stupas.[27] This is a very wide range of practices, some being elementary forms of devotion and others being parallel to the teaching and saving activity of the buddhas themselves.

As to the buddhas active in all the many worlds, Maitreya can observe them relating the teaching which they give to the numberless and variegated throng. Thus Maitreya says:

'And then I can see all the buddhas,
The holy masters, the lions,
Expounding the sutra
Mysterious and supreme;
Their voices are clear and pure
And send forth softly sounding tones,
Teaching the bodhisattvas
In their innumerable myriads;
Their divine voices, deep and wonderful,
Give joy to those who hear.
Each in his own world
Proclaims the true Dharma;
By various karmic reasonings
And innumerable stories
They reveal the Buddha-Dharma
And awaken the understanding of all the living.'[28]

The idea that *various* arguments about karmic connections, and innumerable illustrative stories are used to indicate the central teaching, is one which has already been observed to recur frequently in the context of skilful means, especially in Chapter II of the sutra. Here already there is also a distinction between the three ways of the *śrāvakas*, the *pratyekabuddhas* and the 'sons of the Buddha', that is, the bodhisattvas:

---

[27] T IX 3a-b, cf. KSS 12-17.
[28] T IX 2c 又覩諸佛 聖主師子 演說經典 微妙第一 其聲清淨 出柔軟音 敎諸 菩薩 無數億萬 梵音深妙 令人樂聞 各於世界 講說正法 種種因緣 以無量喩 照明佛法 開悟眾生 cf. KSS 10f.

'If there are those who have met with suffering
And are weary of age, disease and death,
For these they proclaim nirvana
To bring an end to all sufferings.
If there are those who are in a state of happiness,
Having paid homage to the buddhas
And devoted to the quest for victorious Dharma,
For these they proclaim pratyekabuddhahood.
If there are sons of the Buddha
Disciplined in their various practices
And seeking for the supreme insight,
For these they proclaim the path of purity.'[29]

It will be noted that the three types of teaching are specifically correlated with the condition of those who receive it. In the story of the former Buddha the same is found again, though it is more precisely formulated. 'For those who sought to be *śrāvakas* he taught in accordance with the Dharma of the four truths, for crossing beyond birth, old age, disease and death, to ultimate nirvana. For those who sought pratyekabuddhahood he taught in accordance with the Dharma of the twelve causes. For the bodhisattvas he taught in accordance with the six pāramitās, to bring them to supreme, perfect enlightenment, and to the attainment of comprehensive knowledge'.[30] In one sense the three are differently evaluated: *śrāvakas* are at the most elementary level and bodhisattvas are the most advanced. Yet on the other hand these 'vehicles', as they are specifically called in the last stanzas of the chapter, are all in the same position with respect to the ray of light which illuminates them, or with respect to the previous buddha Sun-Moon-Light-Tathāgata who expounded them. All three find themselves superseded in terms of the new interpretation to be delivered following on the emission of the ray of light. The closing stanzas of Chapter I need to be quoted in sequence to gather up these points. Mañjuśrī says:

'I have seen the Buddha of Light long ago
Send out a ray, an omen like this.
Therefore I know that the present Buddha
Intends to proclaim the Dharma-Flower-Sutra.
The present sign is like the previous omen;
It is the skilful means of all the buddhas.
The present Buddha sends forth a ray of light
To help reveal the meaning of true reality.
All men should now know,
Waiting with folded hands and minds prepared,

---

[29] T IX 2c-3a　若人遭苦　厭老病死　爲說涅槃　盡諸苦際　若人有福　曾供養佛　志求勝法　爲說緣覺　若有佛子　修種種行　求無上慧　爲說淨道 cf. KSS 11.

[30] T IX 3c　爲求聲聞者。說應四諦法。度生老病死究竟涅槃。爲求辟支佛者。說應十二因緣法。爲諸菩薩說應六波羅蜜。令得阿耨多羅三貌三菩提成一切種智。cf. KSS 20-1.

> The Buddha will rain down the rain of Dharma
> To satisfy those who seek the way.
> Of all those who follow the three vehicles,
> If any one has a doubt or a regret,
> The Buddha will do away with it
> So that none whatever remains.'[31]

The ray of light is the skilful means which both illuminates multiple worlds and differentiated activity, and prepares the way for the final appearance of consistent meaning. Thus although this Chapter I may seem at first sight like an irrelevant mythological scenario, its patterns reflect the same understanding of Buddhism which appears more explicitly in the main body of the sutra already discussed.

The equivalence of all buddhas

Apart from the varied inhabitants of this and other worlds Chapter I of The Lotus Sutra also brought into view a large, indefinite number of buddhas. The ray of light illuminates eighteen thousand worlds all of which have their very own buddhas 'existing at present in those lands'.[32] Moreover the ray of light now emitted by 'the' Buddha is said to be quite equivalent to that sent forth long ago by the earlier buddha whom Mañjuśrī remembers, so that there is an equivalence in time-succession as well as in space. Similar scenes are present in Chapter XI and indeed are generally current in Mahayana Buddhism. How is it that buddhas can thus be multiplied endlessly while at the same time the very idea of a Buddha who lives for eighty years, attains enlightenment and enters nirvana, is itself undermined?

The idea of a series of buddhas is of course not unique to the Mahayana, nor even in a sense distinctively Buddhist; for the literature of the Jains includes the lives of a whole series of Jinas (conquerors) based on that of the historical founder-figure Mahāvīra.[33] In the Buddhist Pali Canon it is the traditional and more or less historical story of Gautama which is projected on to the accounts of presumed precursors in long distant time, as for example in The Mahāpadāna Suttanta of The Dīgha Nikāya.[34] While it is not impossible that legendary reminiscence of earlier holy men may have provided some of the impetus for the development of such schemes, it is clearly to be

---

[31] T IX 5b 我見燈明佛　本光瑞如此　以是知今佛　欲說法華經　今相如本瑞　是諸佛方便　今佛放光明　助發實相義　諸人今當知　合掌一心待　佛當雨法雨　充足求道者　諸求三乘人　若有疑悔者　佛當爲除斷　今盡無有餘 cf. KSS 31.

[32] T IX 2b 彼土現在諸佛 cf. KSS 7.

[33] Recounted in the first part of the *Kalpa Sutra*, cf. *Sacred Books of the East, Vol. XXII*, trans. H. Jacobi. Mahāvīra himself was represented as the most recent of twenty-four who have appeared in the present cycle.

[34] Cf. *Dialogues of The Buddha (Dīgha Nikāya)* Vol. II, T. W. and Mrs. Rhys Davids, Pali Text Society, London 1910 and 1972. This has a series of seven buddhas while the *Buddhavaṃsa*, of the *Khuddaka Nikāya*, has a longer series.

understood mainly as a mythological construction which places a particular, known figure of authority in the context of endlessly renewed cycles of time. For Buddhism in general, regardless of sectarian divergences, such a picture already implies that being a Buddha is something more than simply managing to achieve enlightenment (Buddhahood) in one of one's lives. While the notion of achievement is maintained in the progression from first resolve to final Buddhahood, the regularity of the process of training through many existences until the final fruition meant that the appearance of Buddhas was seen as part of the way in which the universe is supposed to be. That this is so is clear from the fact that the stories are not a collection of the achievements of great spiritual leaders understood in their natural diversity from a historical, humanist point of view. On the contrary, the earlier buddhas are utterly devoid of distinctive individuality, and the phases of their life are introduced by the phrase 'it is the rule that . . .'[35] It represents a certain stage in the apotheosis of the man Gautama, who comes to be represented not so much as a distinctive man with a message hitherto unknown or undiscovered, but as a special being unlike ordinary humanity, who did what he did because that is what buddhas do when they appear. This way of thinking is one of the presuppositions of Mahayana writings such as The Lotus Sutra, but it is a presupposition which was shared by all schools of Buddhism at the time.

The matter is massively extended in The Mahāvastu, which is neither a Theravada work nor yet Mahayanist, and where the number of buddhas listed as being those under whom the Buddha Śākyamuni (the historical Gautama) previously acquired merit reaches no less than five hundred.[36] These buddhas simply appear as a long list of proper names, which was presumably assembled by some particularly enthusiastic monk. The Mahāvastu also proliferates buddhas in spatial terms. Not only are there various buddha-fields (*buddha-kṣetra*) in the eastern quarter of the world, in the southern, western and northern quarters of the world, and in the nadir and the zenith of the world, but 'There are besides thousands of other buddha-fields and yet other thousands, of which one cannot reach the end in enumerating'.[37] The number of buddhas is only limited by the requirement to match up with human expectations. Rarity is important in itself so that humans do not complacently rely on the appearance of a buddha whenever they happen to be reborn, a point already observed to be important in The Lotus Sutra.[38] Moreover while many worlds are without a buddha at all, there is also a strict limitation to one buddha per buddha-field. There is a reason given for this too. 'If one man of vision were not equal to the conditions of Buddhahood, then two great-hearted Tathāgatas would be expected to appear. But men reject this notion of the inadequate nature of the great seers, and hence two valiant men are not born in one and the same

---

[35] Cf. the last-mentioned text, *passim*.

[36] Jones, *op. cit.* pp. 108ff.

[37] *Ibid.* p. 98.

[38] Chapter Three above, note 78 and context. Cf. also Rhys Davids, *op. cit.* p. 263.

field'.[39] Yet again it is the effect of the mythology on people's reactions which is the criterion for its character. Nothing must be incorporated which would reduce confidence in the overriding power of the Buddha's achievement for the benefit of his followers and believers. This is not an idle cosmological speculation, but an entirely soteriological concept. Moreover there seems to be a tacit understanding that the total picture is essentially a contrived one.

It is not surprising that the composers of The Mahāvastu also expressed the view that a Buddha is essentially ultramundane (*lokottara*), and is manifested as a Buddha in human form for the sake of conformity with the world. This view is clearly formulated in the following statements taken from a well-known extended passage.

'Although they could suppress the workings of karma, the Conquerors let it become manifest and conceal their sovereign power. This is mere conformity with the world.

It is true that they eat food, but hunger never distresses them. It is in order to provide men with the opportunity to give alms that in this respect they conform to the world . . .

They put on robes, and yet a Conqueror would always be covered without them and have the same appearance as devas. This wearing of robes is mere conformity with the world . . .

Although the Sugata's corporeal existence is not due to the sexual union of parents, yet the Buddhas can point to their fathers and mothers. This is mere conformity with the world . . .

Although in the worlds both of devas and of men they condemn upholders of wrong beliefs, they yet resort to heretics. This is mere conformity with the world.

Although, for the sake of all beings, they have awakened to the unsurpassed enlightenment, they yet put on the appearance of a lack of zeal. This is mere conformity with the world.'[40]

The dating of the Mahāvastu is a complex matter as it was compiled over a long period, and it may be that in some respects it was influenced by early Mahayana writings. However it does illustrate how significant developments in ideas about the Buddha could arise organically on the basis of the earlier tradition. There is no reliance in The Mahāvastu on the Mahayana doctrine of 'emptiness' (*śūnyatā*), and there is no radical polemic vis-à-vis earlier tradition, as there is in the Mahayana writings.

But although the concept of skilful means is not associated here in The Mahāvastu with the supra-historical view of Buddhahood, as it has been seen to be in the chapter on the Tathāgata's life-span in The Lotus Sutra, never-

---

[39] Jones, *op. cit.* p. 96.

[40] *Ibid.* pp. 133f. It is this view of the Buddha as *lokottara* which gives the name Lokottara-vadins to the school of thought which The Mahāvastu represents, see the introduction by Jones and the opening of the writing itself. The whole conception has obvious analogies with the transformations of bodhisattvas discussed later below.

theless the whole pattern of world systems in time and space is so geared as
to offer an overwhelming picture of the way the world ineluctably is, coupled
with maximum stimulation for individuals to take advantage of present
opportunity. The buddhology is tailored, and to a certain extent consciously
so, to the way in which human beings tend to react.

The Mahāvastu also contains an instructive scene concerning sunshades. A
throng of celestial beings (*devas*) are described as putting up sunshades in
honour of the Buddha who in response shows himself to be sitting beneath
each and every one. Each *deva* believes himself to be particularly honoured
and is not aware of the fictitious character of his own buddha, who is after all
no different from all of the others whom he does not see. The story is not
explained in the text itself, but it strongly suggests that the appearance of
any one buddha in the world is essentially illusory and effected for the benefit
of those who see him.[41]

A quite similar story is found in The Śūraṃgama-samādhi Sutra, a
Mahayana text translated by Kumārajīva into Chinese (see also Appendices
A and G). Here the Buddha appears simultaneously on a vast number of
lion-thrones prepared for him by various *devas*, but each *deva* sees only the
buddha on the throne which he himself had prepared. Each one then proudly
proclaims that the Buddha is sitting on his own throne and not on the throne
of the others.[42] At the appropriate moment all the buddhas are revealed to
all the *devas*, and one of them asks which is real, his own buddha or all the
others which he can now see. The answer to this is that as all dharmas are
void in their fundamental character, like a magical apparition, so all these
buddhas who are not dependent on the superficially apparent co-ordination
of dharmas are equally 'real'.[43] In reality all constituent factors of the world
are fundamentally equal, and as the buddhas do not depart from the fundamental character of things so they too are fundamentally equal.[44] The
apparent multiplicity of buddhas is brought about by special power which is
simply withdrawn when no longer required, so that only one buddha is seen
again.[45]

[41] *Ibid.* pp. 218ff.

[42] Lamotte, E. *La Concentration de la Marche Héroïque (Śūraṃgamasamādhisūtra)*, Brussels
1965, pp. 126f.

[43] *Ibid.* p. 129. T XV 630c 一切諸法皆空如幻 and 是諸如來皆是眞實。云何爲實是諸如
來本自不生。是故爲實。是諸如來今後亦無。是故 爲實: 'All dharmas are void, like a
magical apparition . . . All the tathāgatas are real. Why are they real? From the beginning
and in themselves these tathāgatas are not born; that is why they are real. These tathāgatas
do not exist either now or in the future; that is why they are real. (etc.)'. Lamotte explains
that the Tibetan version refers to the 'irreality' rather than the 'reality' of the tathāgatas, but
as he says, it amounts to the same thing.

[44] T XV 631a 是故諸佛名爲平等。梵王。是諸如來不過一切諸法如故。 cf. Lamotte,
p. 130f.

[45] T XV 631a, whole context. The supernatural power is 神力, but the ability both to
penetrate the equality of all things and at the same time to manifest his *rūpakāya* (色身) is
ascribed to the *samādhi* which the sutra extols. Cf. Lamotte p. 131.

This writing also makes the equivalence of all buddhas plain in other ways. In one passage Śākyamuni rises up into the air to the height of seven palm trees, sits cross-legged and lets out a light which illuminates innumerable universes in the ten directions. The assembly then can see the innumerable buddhas of all these universes, all preaching The Śūraṃgama-samādhi Sutra to their own assemblies, without adding or subtracting anything. This means that they are precisely equivalent to each other. Then in complementary fashion all those buddhas themselves rise up into the air to the height of seven palm trees, sit cross-legged and let out a light which illuminates innumerable universes in the ten directions. All the beings of those universes are then able to see the Buddha Śākyamuni.[46] This complementary reversal of the illumination has the effect of relativising the position of Śākyamuni. The degree of prominence which he enjoys is prominence relative to this present universe, the one in which his function is performed. Otherwise he is in principle identifiable with all or any other buddhas. Śākymuni is indeed specifically identified with the Buddha Vairocana, in the Śūraṃgama-samādhi Sutra, and the two buddhas are said to have exactly the same length of life.[47] This is of special interest because the same link is also reflected in The Lotus Sutra.[48] In the former the power which makes this identification possible is the very power of the *samādhi* (concentration) which the sutra serves to extol. This power, which underlies the multiplication and identity of all the buddhas, equally real or unreal, occupies in The Śūraṃgama-samādhi Sutra the same position as the ray of light in Chapter I of The Lotus Sutra. That is, it is connected both with the consistency of a buddha's insight into the fundamental equality of all dharmas and with his skilful means or saving activity with respect to all living beings.[49]

One of the more striking, and certainly one of the more famous accounts of such relationships between buddhas is found in The Lotus Sutra itself, in Chapter XI, the chapter on the seven-jewelled stupa of the Buddha Many-Jewels (Prabhūtaratna). This chapter is really, *mutatis mutandis*, the Buddhist equivalent of a theophany, and the impression which it makes cannot be conveyed adequately at second hand. It has served as a basis for iconographical activity and is a chapter of some special interest in the study of The Lotus Sutra for general reasons.[50] In the present context it is important

---

[46] Lamotte, p. 264b. (T XV 644b).

[47] Lamotte p. 267ff.

[48] Lamotte points out (p. 167 n. 339) that the universe of Vairocana, named Pratimaṇḍitā, is referred to in Chapters 23 and 25 (Ch. XXIV and XXVII). In the first of these the bodhisattva Gadgadasvara is said to be the protector alike of those who are born in the *Sahā* world (this world) and of those born in the *Vairocanaraśmipratimaṇḍitā* world.

[49] The term skilful means is found much less often in The Śūraṃgama-samādhi Sutra, and discussion of the explicit usage is therefore left to Appendix F. Nevertheless the basic parallelism of thought is quite apparent.

[50] W. Baruch made a special point of translating it in his *Beiträge zum Saddharmapuṇḍarī-kasūtra*, Leiden 1938. Chapter XI is the first chapter of substance after the break discerned in the sutra by Fuse. It is also the last point at which the Sanskrit and Chinese chapter numeration agrees. On these and related matters see Appendix B.

because it draws together many themes already pursued and links them with the idea of skilful means, thus affording another clue as to how the mythological patterns are to be understood.

First the stupa itself appears in the sky, bedecked with jewels and receiving the homage of multitudes of heavenly beings. From within it is heard a loud voice which testifies to the authenticity of Śākyamuni's announcement of The Lotus Sutra. This gives rise to great wonderment, and Śākyamuni explains that it is the 'whole-body'[51] of a Buddha named Many-Jewels who functioned in the distant past, innumerable worlds away to the east. As a bodhisattva he had made a vow that on becoming a buddha and attaining extinction he would cause the stupa containing his 'whole-body' to appear in every world where The Lotus Sutra is proclaimed, thus bearing witness to its authenticity and its excellence.

The assembled throng then wish to see the 'whole-body' of the extinct buddha within the stupa, and they are told that for this to be possible it will be necessary for the present Buddha Śākyamuni himself to draw back all the emanated buddhas[52] now preaching in many different worlds. To do this he sends out a ray of light from the circle of white hair between his eyebrows, just as in Chapter I, and illuminates all these worlds with their buddhas. These then return, direction by direction, and space is made for them to assemble in this very world of Śākyamuni Buddha which is levelled off and bedecked with jewels for their reception. Each one takes his place on a lion-throne beneath a jewel-tree, and when all are assembled Śākyamuni himself rises up into the sky where the stupa is suspended and opens the door with his right finger. The Buddha Many-Jewels is then visible to all, seated on the lion-throne in a position of meditation. Once again he certifies The Lotus Sutra, receives homage, and invites Śākyamuni to sit beside him on the same seat. (This motif of the two buddhas sitting side by side within the opened stupa became a regular iconographical subject.) All those assembled feel rather left behind and so they too are raised up to the sky by the Buddha's supernatural powers. From this shared vantage-point they too are urged to preserve and transmit The Lotus Sutra, for it is soon to be the turn of Śākyamuni to enter nirvana.[53]

The verse account which follows is a very briefly summarised repetition of the prose, followed by extended exhortations to preserve and to transmit The Lotus Sutra. These passages reinforce the equivalence of the various buddhas involved in the tableau, for if anyone proclaims The Lotus Sutra he will be deemed to have worshipped the Buddha Many-Jewels, and the Buddha Śākyamuni, and all the emanated buddhas.[54] Such a one will also be

---

[51] 'Whole-body', 全身, e.g. T IX 32c.

[52] 'Emanated buddhas',分身諸佛, e.g. T IX 32c, or literally 'partial-body buddhas', cf. preceding note.

[53] For all the above, which is highly summarised as the details do not affect the meaning of 'skilful means', cf. KSS 235-243.

[54] T IX 34a 其有能護　此經法者　則爲供養　我及多寶...亦復供養　諸來化佛　cf. KSS 246.

deemed to have seen all of these, who are again enumerated.[55] The exhortations seem to expand the closing lines of the prose account, but just at the point of climax between the description of the tableau itself and the beginning of the consequent exhortations there is a line of great importance which runs:

'By this skilful means
I cause the Dharma long to abide.'[56]

It may be that this case of *fang-pien* is an interpretative elaboration by Kumārajīva himself,[57] but however that may be it refers here not to some miscellaneous aspect of the scene but indeed to the whole story of the appearance of the stupa, the Buddha Many-Jewels, and the emanated buddhas. The purpose of the complete operation is to establish the meaning of Buddhism, and it is quite in line with the main teaching of The Lotus Sutra to see this phantasmagoria as being a skilful means. It is indeed most similar to the mythological preamble in Chapter I of the sutra, where the term skilful means does not itself appear on every line but where it is appropriately used to designate the whole.

A general tendency to mythological elaboration has been observed which is not peculiar to Mahayana Buddhism, and not necessarily always linked explicitly with the idea of skilful means. This general matrix of thought however implies that the number of buddhas is not itself important, nor is their length of life. Nor indeed is extinction, for the power of Buddha Many-Jewels' vow persists in the differentiated world long 'after' his attainment of final nirvana. There is no aspect of Buddhist mythology or cosmology which necessarily demands to be understood in terms less subtly elaborating and deflating, or more persistently assertive, than the concept of skilful means in The Lotus Sutra suggests. Buddhas are very mobile, it would appear, and always in strictly appropriate ways, their appearance and their absence being regulated by the psychological requirements of those who are to benefit from either of these. Superficially these may appear to be rather like a series of magical tricks, and the term 'supernatural powers' is sometimes employed to describe a particular manoeuvre. The underlying conception however is that buddhahood lies at the fundamental level of the voidness and equality of all differentiated things. In these terms there is no concern about the number of buddhas, one, two or many. From the fundamental standpoint of The Lotus Sutra, that things are always nirvanic in themselves from the beginning, as stated in Chapter II,[58] it is as skilful means, fully consistent with this, that the worlds are illumined and the buddhas mobilised.

---

[55] T IX 34a 若說此經　則爲見我　多寶如來　及諸化佛 cf. KSS 246. The emanated buddhas are defined here with a different term, difficult to translate briefly and suggesting a creative conjuring for soteriological purposes.

[56] T IX 34a 以是方便　令法久住 cf. KSS 245.

[57] There is no equivalent in the extant Sanskrit, nor in Dharmarakṣa's version, though this does not indicate conclusively that Kumārajīva did not find it in the text available to him.

[58] Cf. Chapter Two, note 47 above.

Transformations of a bodhisattva

It is a remarkable fact that after the important Chapter XVI (15) of the Tathāgata's life-span the term *fang-pien* only occurs four times in the remaining twelve chapters of The Lotus Sutra as translated by Kumārajīva. This is no doubt because of changes in subject matter, which in turn reflects the fact that these chapters represent late stages in the original development of the sutra (c.f. Appendix B). It is therefore of some interest that the only one of these occurrences which can also be paralleled in Dharmarakṣa's version is to be found in Chapter XXV (24), which is about the bodhisattva Avalokiteśvara. This bodhisattva is also commonly known by the Chinese name Kuan-yin and the Japanese name Kan-non, or, among the devout, Kannon-sama. In the Chinese text itself the name appears in a longer form, namely Kuan-shih-yin, and this is pronounced Kan-ze-on in Japanese. So much for general orientation; the name itself has been the subject of detailed discussion which need not be surveyed here.[59] Such a radiant and versatile figure as Avalokiteśvara or Kuan-yin is a good example of those celestial bodhisattvas who play an important part in the devotional side of Mahayana Buddhism. It is therefore of some interest to observe how the account of this figure fits into the main lines of thought of The Lotus Sutra, dominated as these are by the concept of skilful means.

References to the bodhisattva are found in various Mahayana texts, but most later developments of this saviour figure seem to assume the characterisation of Avalokiteśvara which is already found in The Lotus Sutra.[60]

---

[59] The second part of Marie-Thérèse de Mallmann's *Introduction à l'Étude d'Avalokiteçvara* (Paris 1967, Presses Universitaires de France), is entirely dedicated to the problem of the meaning of the Sanskrit name and also surveys the relevant literature. In conclusion she offers the following comprehensive interpretation: 'le Seigneur Brillant, Étincelant, ou (par extension) le Maître de la Lumière' (p. 82). This is not intended to exclude secondary interpretations such as 'the lord who looks down from above' or 'the lord who looks down in compassion' (cf. p. 80). It is this latter aspect which is stressed by Professor Edward Conze with reference to The Heart Sutra and The Lotus Sutra in his *Buddhist Wisdom Books* (London 1958, George Allen and Unwin) where he writes on page 78: "Avalokiteśvara is called Avalokita because he 'looks down' . . . compassionately on the world . . . He is called Lord (*īśvara*) because he has sovereignty over the world and power to help suffering beings, as for instance explained in the famous twenty-fourth chapter of the *Lotus of the Good Law*.' The Chinese name Kuan-shih-yin 觀世音 was at one time supposed to be an incorrect corruption of the Sanskrit. But Europeans who stressed this were themselves mistaken in their reading of the Chinese as was pointed out by Carlo Puini in 1873 (*Avalokiteçvara Sutra, Traduction Italienne de la Version Chinoise avec Introduction et Notes*, in Atsume Gusa (Textes 6), Paris and London, pp. II-V). The Bodhisattva Kuan-shih-yin is the Bodhisattva who regards the cries of the world. As Puini pointed out, the name is explained in the text itself and moreover in a manner not inconsistent with the overall characterisation of the bodhisattva given also in the Sanskrit text, whatever the etymological niceties of the name itself. Kuan-shih-yin is the one who takes into consideration the voices or the prayers of the world, or as Burnouf also put it, 'the lord who regards with compassion the beings suffering the evils of existence' (Burnouf, *Lotus de la Bonne Loi*, p. 226).

[60] Four such texts are reviewed by Marie-Thérèse de Mallmann (*op. cit.* pp. 36-56), namely *Lokeśvara-śataka, Kāraṇḍa-vyūha-sūtra, Mañjuśrīmūla-kalpa* and *Sādhanamālā*. All are later

Indeed the chapter in question, Chapter **XXV** (24), which was certainly an addition to the main body of The Lotus Sutra and may even have first existed independently of it, has itself been a most influential text as a separate item. Even today it circulates separately, though in Kumārajīva's version, and as such is used in various Japanese denominations such as Zen-shū, Shingon-shū and Tendai-shū, under the title of *Kannongyō*. Although the term *fang-pien* itself only appears twice in the re-edited version which circulates, the way of thinking with which it is closely associated here has worked itself deep into popular Buddhism in Japan.

The characterisation of Avalokiteśvara or Kuan-shih-yin in this text has three phases, and the first of them portrays him as a miracle worker. Non-

than The Lotus Sutra, even by some centuries, and none seem to add anything of importance to the concept of skilful means. Conversely however, since The Lotus Sutra is the major early starting point for thought about Avalokiteśvara throughout Mahayana Buddhism the concept of skilful means cannot really be subtracted from any later discussion of this bodhisattva. The same applies to the iconographical developments studied in detail by Marie-Thérèse de Mallmann.

The earliest texts in which the bodhisattva appears are undoubtedly the *Sukhāvatī-vyūha-sūtra*, first translated into Chinese by Lokakṣema (147-186 A.D.), and the chapter of The Lotus Sutra now under consideration. It is impossible to say which of these two is the earlier, because even if the main part of The Lotus Sutra is earlier than the *Sukhāvatī-vyūha-sūtra*, the chapter on Avalokiteśvara, which was linked with The Lotus Sutra at an advanced stage in its compilation, could still have originated later. However the references in the *Sukhāvatī-vyūha-sūtra* are quite brief and incidental. They are mainly of interest as the probable starting point of a later more elaborate relationship between Amitābha, the central figure of this sutra, and Avalokiteśvara. The general context may be examined in Max Müller's translation in *Sacred Books of the East* Vol. XLIX, Part 2, pp. 48 and 52. The first mention is of Avalokiteśvara as an interlocutor for Amitābha, here Amitāyus, and in the second case he is a light-spreading companion to the latter, along with Mahāsthāmaprāpta. The relationship between these figures is explored in the fifth chapter of Henri de Lubac's *Amida*, Paris 1955, which also contains a detailed survey of the whole cult of Avalokiteśvara.

A few verses on Amitābha were eventually added to the chapter on Avalokiteśvara in The Lotus Sutra, though this must have been at a very late date indeed and they do not appear in Kumārajīva's version (stanzas 28-33, cf. Sakamoto and Iwamoto III p. 269). More important was the elaboration of Avalokiteśvara's role, along with the bodhisattva Mahāsthāmaprāpta, as a companion to Amitābha. The main text here is the *Kuan-wu-liang-shou-ching* 觀無量壽經 (J. Kanmuryōjukyō), first known in Chinese in the early part of the fifth century A.D. Iconography is closely related to meditation and the standard form in China and Japan where the Amitābha cult flourished is a triad with Amitābha in the centre and the two bodhisattvas to left and right.

Other texts and iconographical development show Avalokiteśvara as a figure of devotion both in his own right and in association with other representatives of the Mahayana pantheon. In some of these, especially in Tibet and Nepal, Avalokiteśvara was taken through into the tantric phase of Buddhism. Cf. Henri de Lubac, *op. cit.* esp. pp. 108-111, on the formula *Oṃ maṇi padme hūṃ* addressed to Avalokiteśvara, the feminine double, Tara, evidences of symbiosis with Indian divinities, and eventually the veneration of the Dalai Lama as an incarnation of the bodhisattva and of the Potala as his proper residence. Other literature is noted there.

Another important text current all over East Asia is The Heart Sutra, in which the bodhisattva is firmly linked both with the mantric tradition and with perfection of insight thought. See further below.

Buddhist sources may have influenced this development,[61] but however that may be, and it is certainly not proven, the account of Kuan-shih-yin as a miracle worker here is given in response to the question put to the Buddha about why the bodhisattva has this name. The answer given, by the Buddha, is that Kuan-shih-yin uses supernatural powers to deliver living beings who suffer pain and distress. Such supernatural powers are supposed to be available to buddhas and bodhisattvas generally in any case, and the stress here is on the compassion shown by this bodhisattva and the practical forms which it takes. Those in need should call upon his name for all they are worth and they will be delivered from such things as fire, flood, shipwreck in a land of demons, violent attack, robbers, and the bondage of manacles and fetters, whether one is innocent or guilty.[62] These forms of deliverance have an obvious popular appeal and became a subject for illustration from the caves of Tun Huang onwards. The formula to be used is *Na-mo Kuan-shih-yin P'u-sa* (in Japanese: *Namu Kanzeon Bosatsu*), and is therefore very similar to the formula for calling on Amitābha Buddha.[63] In this chapter of The Lotus Sutra merchants carrying jewels along a perilous road are expressly encouraged to chant the formula addressed to Kuan-shih-yin in concert, because 'the Bodhisattva is able to give courage to all the living'.[64] One can imagine how relevant such a proposal must have seemed on the caravan routes of Central Asia, and in ancient China and Japan too as the sutra spread.

Such benefits which appeal to the basic instinct of self-preservation, are intimately juxtaposed with more spiritual benefits. These include being set free from the vices of carnal passion, irascibility and infatuation. Admittedly these problems are elementary in the religious life, but they seem to be widespread and persistent. To be truly set free from them as a result of bearing in mind the Bodhisattva Kuan-shih-yin would clearly be seen as a worthwhile first step in the training of Buddhists. Immediately associated with the above there comes a passage, much pondered in later times, which says that a woman devoted to Kuan-shih-yin will give birth to a son if she desires a son and to a daughter if she desires a daughter.[65] Petitions offered with respect to matters of such personal and social importance have far-reaching effects in religion and it is not surprising that sons and daughters arriving in this way are also confidently expected to be virtuous, sufficiently virtuous no doubt to cherish the devotional tradition. In this way a common human wish is linked to an encouragement of Buddhist virtue. Finally it is argued that anyone who reveres Kuan-shih-yin for only a moment will

---

[61] De Mallmann, *op. cit.* p. 93, adduces an interesting parallel with the Avestan god Srausha in the *Zend-Avesta.*

[62] Cf. KSS 404-6.

[63] T IX 56c 南無觀世音菩薩 cf. KSS 406. The Amitābha formula is best known in its Japanese pronunciation: Namu Amida Butsu 南無阿彌陀佛. The same basic formula found innumerable uses in the Sutra of Buddha Names (T440 and T441), extensive recitations which Kumārajīva apparently never felt called upon to translate.

[64] T IX 56c 是菩薩能以無畏施於衆生 cf. KSS 406.

[65] T IX 57a, cf. KSS 406-7.

obtain innumerable blessings, equal to those obtained by a person who reveres innumerable other bodhisattvas. It belongs to the general style of the Mahayana that one can instantaneously receive an immeasurable amount of blessing in one moment which is precisely equal to the amount one would achieve by performing innumerable meritorious acts in a very long time. This is no more strange than that one can enter the Buddha-way by entering a temple with a distracted mind and calling but once on the name of the Buddha, as was observed in Chapter II of The Lotus Sutra.

The second phase of the characterisation of Kuan-shih-yin is firmly patterned on the activity of a buddha. The Bodhisattva Akṣayamati, who puts the questions in this chapter, now asks how Kuan-shih-yin wanders in this world, how he preaches the Dharma to living beings and how his power of skilful means may be described.[66] The Buddha answers with a long catalogue of the forms taken by Kuan-shih-yin: buddha, *pratyekabuddha*, *śrāvaka*, Brahma, Śakra, Īśvara, Maheśvara and many others including elders and citizens, monks and nuns, wives of elders and citizens, youths and maidens, gods, dragons and demons. All of these have in common that Kuan-shih-yin may appear as one such for the benefit of those who are to be saved by him in just that particular form. This is how he roams the world, this is how he proclaims the Dharma, and this is the power of his skilful means. The list of transformations is not defined item by item as skilful means, but it is quite clear from the introductory question that the whole list is so understood. Skilful means is simply assumed to be the principle behind all transformations of the bodhisattva. Indeed it may be said to be the principle of his preaching of the Dharma in general, for which the benefits otherwise distributed are nothing other than a preparation. The first two phases of characterisation are intermingled in the concluding passages.[67]

The transformations of Avalokiteśvara were popularised and systematised far beyond those of any other bodhisattva in Mahayana Buddhism, and the classifications have been very conveniently set out by Alicia Matsunaga.[68] Some of the forms taken by the bodhisattva seem to reflect in further ways the concept of skilful means. For example the eleven-faced Avalokiteśvara, which has eleven extra faces above the main face of the statue, is sometimes said to represent 'eleven faces of *upāya* and one true face representing Absolute Truth'.[69] Or again, the thousand arms of the 'thousand-armed Avalokiteśvara' are supposed to represent the measureless skilful means which he uses to save sentient beings.[70]

One of the most popular series consists of no less than thirty-three different forms of Kuan-yin or Kannon, each with some distinct way of demonstrating the variety of ways in which Kuan-yin aids and saves sentient beings, or

[66] T IX 57a 云何遊此娑婆世界。云何而爲衆生說法。方便之力。cf. KSS 407.

[67] Cf. KSS 409.

[68] Matsunaga, *op. cit.* pp. 120 ff.

[69] *Ibid.* p. 124.

[70] *Ibid.* p. 125.

symbolising oneness or non-duality.[71] In Matsunaga's notes on these is found the interesting if drastic story about the Kuan-yin who nearly became the wife of a certain Ma-Lang. This Kuan-yin, appearing as a beautiful girl, managed to cut down the number of her suitors by demanding that they learn first the Kuan-yin chapter of The Lotus Sutra, then The Diamond Sutra, and then finally the whole of The Lotus Sutra. Ma-Lang was the only one who could stay the complete course, but the girl died immediately before the wedding leaving behind a total of twenty men more or less versed in the scriptures.[72] It is interesting to notice the implications of the selection of scriptures referred to in the story. For one thing it shows that the Kuan-yin chapter could be treated as a more or less independent entity. Then again it shows the close association held to obtain between Lotus Sutra thought and the *prajñā-pāramitā* tradition as represented by The Diamond Sutra.

Images of the bodhisattva scattered through Tendai and Shingon temples in Japan are even now the focal point of pilgrimage routes used for centuries. A handbook for one of these describes the pilgrimage as a skilful means (*zengyō-hōben*) for entering into the faith of this Kannon who saves the suffering beings of the world.[73] A modern Japanese booklet on the different forms of the bodhisattva, published by the 'Sunday School' (*nichiyō-gakkō*) of a temple in Hokkaidō, brings out the dialectic of the matter even more explicitly than in the sutra itself. It is out of compassion for sentient beings in the six states that Kanzeon (Kannon) takes on different transformations. The six Kannon, the seven Kannon, and the thirty-three Kannon are skilful means (J. *hōben* = Ch. *fang-pien*), while the underlying body of the bodhisattva is a unity.[74] In the pilgrimage booklet quoted earlier, the underlying body or fundamental body is said to be the Buddha who fills the whole of the universe.[75] Since both of these booklets refer explicitly to the *Kannon-gyō* (that is, Chapter XXV (24) of The Lotus Sutra) and also use the term *hōben* even at this relatively popular level, it seems appropriate to understand the whole development and the present practice of the Kuan-yin or Kannon cult in terms of the dialectic of skilful means characteristic of The Lotus Sutra as a whole, even though the term itself only appears once, albeit in a key place, in the chapter in question.

The third phase of the characterisation links Avalokiteśvara with the buddhas. It is sometimes felt that Avalokiteśvara seems to supersede or supplant 'the' Buddha, but the action described in the closing passage of Kumārajīva's prose in Chapter XXV contradicts such a view. Akṣayamati

---

[71] *Ibid.* pp. 130-134.

[72] *Ibid.* pp. 133f.

[73] 西国巡禮案內記 (*Saikoku Junrei Annaiki*, published continuously from 1933 onwards, by the Office of the Society for Places of Pilgrimage in Saikoku.) *Zengyō-hōben:*善巧方便, p. 1.

[74] 絵入意譯觀音聖典 (*Eiri Ishaku Kannon Seiten*), 1958 in Hokkaidō. The basic body of the bodhisattva is defined as the *hontai* 本體, and the others as skilful means 方便, (on unnumbered introductory page).

[75] *Op. cit.* p. 1. Again 本体 (equals 本體).

speaks first to Śākyamuni and asks permission to make an offering to Avalokiteśvara. He then offers a costly pearl necklace, which Avalokiteśvara however declines to accept. Akṣayamati presses him to accept it, out of compassion.[76] Śākyamuni adds his voice and says that Avalokiteśvara should accept it, out of compassion for Akṣayamati, for the four groups of people present and for gods, dragons and many other types of beings. So Avalokiteśvara does accept it, out of compassion. He then divides it into two parts and offers one part to the Buddha Śākyamuni and one part to the stupa of the Buddha Many-Jewels (Prabhūtaratna). In this way the symbolic offering which Avalokiteśvara receives on account of his many works of salvation is carried back to the presiding Buddha of The Lotus Sutra, Śākyamuni himself, and to the Buddha who had appeared in Chapter XI to certify the authenticity of Śākyamuni's preaching of The Lotus Sutra. Therefore the works of Avalokiteśvara are to be seen as part of the total setting in motion of the process of salvation, as this is conceived in The Lotus Sutra as a whole.

The courtesies with the necklace are significant also for another reason. Avalokiteśvara knows how to behave as a bodhisattva. He is of course not interested in receiving precious gifts, but out of compassion he will receive them. Once received, the necklace is redistributed to the buddhas. This means that in principle any offering to Avalokiteśvara is an offering to the buddhas, even if that is not the initial and explicit intention of the donor. The whole passage on the transformations of Avalokiteśvara is an exposition of the power of his skilful means, and it belongs to the total dialectic of his activity that the devotion which accrues to him, symbolised by the costly pearl necklace, is redirected to the presiding Buddha. This is the routine of skilful means: an endless elaboration of devices, in this case transformations, all of which find their ultimate validation in Buddhahood.

This famous bodhisattva is in a sense the epitome of Buddhism as a popular religion, and one might be tempted to contrast such a colourful cult as this with the more introvertly intellectual or 'philosophical' type of Buddhism found in The Perfection of Insight Sutras. Nothing could be more misleading, as can easily be made clear by brief reference to The Heart Sutra in which Avalokiteśvara is also named. This text is widely used in Japanese Buddhism and it is so short that it can be regularly recited *in toto*, not only in temples but also in homes and schools (private schools only). It is also a source of quotations for gravestones, and like the cult of Avalokiteśvara or Kannon-sama itself it is widely current in all denominations. The text in general use is attributed to the translator Hsüan Tsang,[77] but it was also translated earlier by Kumārajīva, and it bears a close relationship to a passage in the

---

[76] The character for 'compassion' (as it is translated in KSS) is 愍 (*ming*) meaning to sympathise with or take pity on, and is not the term often used for the more or less technical expression *karuṇā*. See T IX 57 b-c, cf. KSS 410.

[77] T251 known as the *Hannya-haramitta-shingyō* 般若波羅蜜多心経 or as the *Hannya-shingyō* for short.

latter's translation of the Great Perfection of Insight Sutra.[78]

As far as the Sanskrit is concerned, Conze stresses the compassionate 'looking down' of the bodhisattva more than did Suzuki.[79] It may be that this is justified by the very association of the name of Avalokiteśvara with the thoughts which follow in the sutra, which are a famously succinct statement of the Mahayana doctrine of emptiness (*śūnyatā*). That is to say, the same bodhisattva who in The Lotus Sutra uses supernatural powers to deliver living beings who suffer pain and distress of all kinds, here surveys the five constituent factors of personal existence (the *skandhas*) and sees them to be empty, that is, as having no persistent ontological status in themselves.[80] As The Heart Sutra is a relatively late manifestation of *prajñā-pāramitā* thought the character of Avalokiteśvara as a deliverer must be taken to have been established in the minds of the creators and early users of the text. There is plenty of support for this connection in the *prajñā-pāramitā* literature generally, which is the matrix of The Heart Sutra in particular.

The connection is brought out more explicitly by an extra clause found in the translations both of Kumārajīva and of Hsüan Tsang,[81] which makes the opening passage run: '. . . he perceives the five skandhas to be all empty, and does away with all afflictions and calamities'.[82] This form of the text identifies the skilful salvific activity of the bodhisattva with his perception of the fundamental emptiness of the 'beings' whom he delivers. It is of course also entirely consistent with the rest of the text which identifies form and emptiness etc.

The Lotus Sutra characterises Avalokiteśvara as a deliverer who uses supernatural powers and an exponent of the *Dharma* who uses skilful means. The Heart Sutra shows him as a bodhisattva who relies on the perfection of insight and perceives the true nature of the world in its emptiness. This combination is entirely appropriate as may be seen from the famous argument of another very widely used Mahayana sutra, namely The Diamond Sutra. According to this text (Kumārajīva's version) the attitude of a bodhisattva should be as follows: 'Whatever kinds of being there may be . . . I should get them to enter nirvana without remainder and let them cross away. Yet although incalculable, innumerable and limitless beings are led across in this

---

[78] Kumārajīva's version is T250. The association with the 習應品 (Chapter II) of Kumārajīva's 摩訶般若波羅蜜経 (T223) is made by Nakamura (Hajime) and Kino (Kazuyoshi) in their jointly translated and edited *Hannya-shingyō, Kongō-hannya-kyō* (Iwanami Bunko 6285-6, Tokyo 1961), p. 16, note 3.

[79] E. Conze, *Buddhist Wisdom Books*, (George Allen and Unwin 1958) pp. 78-9. Cf. also D. T. Suzuki's discussion in *Essays in Zen Buddhism*, Third Series, (Rider & Co. 1970), pp. 222-238.

[80] The Sanskrit has *svabhāvaśūnyā*, while the Chinese just has the single character 空 (*k'ung*) Japanese *kū*), see T VIII 847c 照見五陰空 (Kumārajīva's).

[81] According to Nakamura and Kino the evidence suggests that this clause was always present in Hsüan Chuang's translation and that it was probably inserted by the translator himself, *op. cit.* p. 18-19, note 8. But it is also present in Kumārajīva's.

[82] The additional phrase is: 度一切苦厄 T VIII 847c and 848c.

way, in truth there is not one being who attains nirvana.'[83]

Neither of these two very short sutras contains an example of the term 'skilful means' which can be quoted in this context, but an entirely consonant passage may be adduced from The Great Perfection of Insight Sutra, Kumārajīva's Chinese version of which is the natural home of the shorter pieces. It runs: 'When this *bodhisattva-mahāsattva* is practising the *prajñā-pāramitā*, by his power of skilful means he sees the living beings attached in their confusion to the five constituents. In what is impermanent they see permanence, in suffering they see pleasure, in what is impure they see purity, where there is no self they see self, they are attached to that which has no existence. This bodhisattva, by reason of his power of skilful means, and immersed in that which has no existence, plucks out the living beings.'[84]

The theme of transformations in general is widely current in Mahayana texts, and is not even exclusively Mahayanist.[85] There is a remarkable parallel to the chapter on Avalokiteśvara or Kuan-shih-yin in The Lotus Sutra itself, namely in Chapter XXIV which is about the bodhisattva Gadgasasvara.[86] By way of conclusion at this point some little known verses from Chapter VIII are the most appropriate. They arise in connection with a

[83] Nakamura and Kino, *op. cit.* pp. 42-44 (English by present writer). Cf. also E. Conze's translation from the Sanskrit in *Buddhist Wisdom Books*, p. 25, and the whole general context explained there. The text is T235.

[84] T VIII 412c. 是菩薩摩訶薩行般若波羅蜜時。以方便力見眾生。以顛倒故著五陰。無常中常相。苦中樂相。不淨中淨相。無我中我相。著無所有處。是菩薩以方便力故。於無所有中拔出眾生。

[85] Cf. quotations from The Mahāvastu above, especially indicating how the Buddha dissembles his supramundane character in favour of conformity with the world. It is perhaps indicative of a general continuity in Buddhist thought that the one reference to *upāya-kauśalya* (skill in means) in The Mahāvastu is to be found in the section on 'apparitions' in the account of the tenth *bhūmi* (the *bhūmis* are stages in the development of bodhisattvas towards buddhahood, and the tenth stage is the last). In this section the various apparitions are usually produced *by* the Buddha, but he himself is presented as appearing in the form of the former king of Kalinga to a present king of Kalinga, and also as Indra. Whether the Buddha himself is appearing in the form of someone else or whether the agents are produced more or less independently by his power as in the case of five thousand monks produced at once, the main point is that the apparitions are able to offer Buddhist teaching in a manner precisely appropriate to the situation. First the Buddha produces an 'apparition', and 'then he who is skilful in his expedients explained to Upāli the words spoken by the apparition' (Jones, *op. cit.* p. 140). So runs the introductory comment, relevant to the whole section. No reader of The Lotus Sutra would be surprised, either, by the subsequent concluding stanzas, translated by Jones as follows:

'The Buddhas, who understand good and bad conduct, know all the thoughts of others. In their various existences they examine the dispositions of all beings.

'By the gentle eloquent guidance of him who has insight into worth many men are converted by the understanding Buddha.

'Those who have drawn nigh to the highest friend and are converted by his wisdom, are in no wise reborn, nor grow old, nor die.

'All the wise Buddhas, with bodies all radiant, severally discover the profound way of life, which is of infinite light.' (*Ibid.* p. 151.)

[86] The distinction between bodhisattvas and buddhas is obscured here in that Gadgadasvara appears variously as a bodhisattva or as a buddha in conformity with what is required for the

bodhisattva named Pūrṇa, who in the prose passage is already said to have
mastered the teaching of voidness taught by the buddhas, and by his skilful
means to have benefited innumerable beings.[87]

> 'Monks, listen carefully to me!
> The way this buddha-son has practised,
> Because of well-learned skilful means
> Is quite beyond conception.
> Because the bodhisattvas know
> That people take delight in lesser teachings,
> And quail before the greater insight,
> They make themselves as *śrāvakas* and *pratyekabuddhas*.
> By skilful means without number
> They convert the various sorts of living beings
> Declaring themselves to be *śrāvakas*
> Still far from the Buddha-way.
> They release innumerable beings
> Who all attain complete realisation.
> Even the unambitious and lazy ones
> Are gradually brought to become buddhas.
> They practise bodhisattva-hood as an inward secret
> While outwardly they appear as *śrāvakas*.
> Their desires are few and they despise the round of birth and death,
> For in reality they are purifying their own buddha-land.
> To the crowd they show themselves subject to the poisons of passion
> And give the appearance of holding heretical views.
> This is the way that my disciples
> Use skilful means to bring across all the living.'[88]

salvation of different men. The system, or rather the method, is exactly the same in principle
as that of The Lotus Sutra as a whole, as may be seen from the assertion that to those who
must be saved by extinction he reveals himself as extinct, a clear parallel to the thought of
Chapter XVI (15), where the Nirvana of the Buddha was argued to be a skilful means.

The story of the bodhisattva Gadgadasvara is also firmly set within the authority of the
Buddha Śākyamuni and the Buddha Prabhūtaratna. He too pays homage to both of these
Buddhas before returning to his own land, having already presented Śākyamuni with a
necklace on his arrival. At the same time the fact that he reports about his visit to his own
'world-honoured one' brings out once again the equivalence of all buddhas and the non-
absolute quality of any one. Cf. KSS *ad loc.* for the whole chapter.

[87] T IX 27c 又於諸佛所說空法。明了通達...而富樓那以斯方便。饒益無量百千衆生。
cf. KSS 202-3.

[88] T IX 28a 諸比丘諦聽　佛子所行道　善學方便故　不可得思議　知衆樂小法　而畏
於大智　是故諸菩薩　作聲聞緣覺　以無數方便　化諸衆生類　自說是聲聞　去佛道甚
遠　度脫無量衆　皆悉得成就　雖小欲懈怠　漸當令作佛　內祕菩薩行　外現是聲聞
少欲厭生死　實自淨佛土　示衆有三毒　又現邪見相　我弟子如是　方便度衆生 cf. KSS
205-6. 'Subject to passions' is literally 'having the three poisons', and KSS is followed here in
finding the expression too obscure to count as a translation. The three poisons are greed,
anger and folly (貪，瞋 and 癡), cf. Sakamoto, *op. cit.* Vol. II, p. 336. The point is not in the
enumeration summarised by the expression 'three poisons' but in the submission of bodhisattvas to the strains and responses of ordinary human life.

Needless to say, the bodhisattva Pūrṇa is declared to be a fine example of this, and his future buddhahood is predicted. Such dissemblings and ultimate intentions are also the main feature of the bodhisattva Vimalakīrti, a most entertaining figure characterised in a text independent of The Lotus Sutra and to which we now turn.

5 SKILFUL MEANS IN THE TEACHING OF VIMALAKĪRTI

The skill of a Buddhist saint

The Teaching of Vimalakīrti is a work which has been widely used among the schools and sects of Mahayana Buddhism, and Kumārajīva's Chinese version remains popular in Japan to this day.[1] One reason for this is undoubtedly the fact that the leading figure in it, Vimalakīrti, is a layman with whom other laymen in ordinary walks of life can identify themselves. As a layman however he is by no means the model of subservient piety which clergy the world over have traditionally preferred, but instead a devastating leveller. Leading monastic disciples of the Buddha dare not visit Vimalakīrti when he is ill, for fear of being worsted in debate on the meaning of the Buddha's doctrine. Only Mañjuśrī will go to see him, and when these two meet together the result is a major discourse on the Mahayana logic of equality associated with the term *śūnyatā* or 'emptiness'. Vimalakīrti is also a model of the skill required to cultivate the qualities of a buddha-to-be in the contingencies of daily life, and is famed for his ability to perform 'contradictory acts' as Lamotte has termed them.[2] The household life is supposed

---

[1] T475. Apart from the text itself, reference has been made to the following translations: Idzumi Hōkei's English translation in *The Eastern Buddhist*, serially in Vols. II-IV, 1922-1924; Jakob Fischer and Yokota Takezo, *Das Sūtra Vimalakīrti* (*Das Sūtra über die Erlösung*), Hokuseidō Press, Tokyo 1944; Étienne Lamotte , *L'Enseignement de Vimalakīrti* (*Vimalakīrtinirdeśa*), Louvain 1962 (translated from a Tibetan version, not from T475); Charles Luk, *The Vimalakīrti Nirdesa Sutra*, Berkeley California 1972; Fukaura Masabumi's Japanese translation in the *Kokuyaku Issaikyō, Kyōshūbu* VI, Tokyo 1933 (國譯一切經, 經集部六); Hashimoto Hōkei 橋本芳契, into Japanese from three parallel Chinese versions including Kumārajīva's, in *Yuimakyō no Shisōteki Kenkyū* 維摩経の思想的研究, Kyōto 1967; and finally a draft English translation in typescript by R. H. Robinson. Quotations given below are not dependent on any one of the above, for none seemed to be exclusively appropriate, but advice has been drawn from all to a greater or lesser extent. It is perhaps of interest that a brief outline of the sutra was given by D. T. Suzuki, with the words that 'it expounds the fundamental teachings not only of Zen but of Buddhism generally', in *Zen Buddhism and its Influence on Japanese Culture*. (The Ataka Buddhist Library IX), Kyoto 1938, pp. 175ff. The influence of the sutra in Japan is partly due to the fact that it is one of the three sutras on which Prince Shōtoku (seventh century statesman and patron of Buddhism) is supposed to have written commentaries. On the influence of the sutra in China see P. Demiéville's appendix 'Vimalakīrti en Chine' in Lamotte's *L'Enseignement de Vimalakīrti*.

[2] Lamotte, *op. cit.* p. 84. 'Mais sa présence ici-bas n'était qu'un artifice salvifique (*upāya*) pour convertir les êtres à la loi du Buddha et aux doctrines du Grand Véhicule. Théoriquement, il ne croyait ni aux êtres ni aux choses; pratiquement, il travaillait au bien et au bonheur de toutes les créatures. De là ses actes contradictoires, relevant à la fois de la sagesse (*prajñā*) et de la grande compassion (*mahākaruṇā*), qui le font apparaître tour à tour comme un sceptique et comme un apôtre.'

to be full of hindrances, but the portrait of this housholder who is at the same time a freely ranging bodhisattva has proved to have great attraction for the practically minded. In all this the idea of skilful means (*fang-pien*) is closely associated with the way in which his behaviour and self-understanding are characterised.

The *tour de force* of the sutra is Vimalakīrti's encounter with Mañjuśrī, and it is in that context that many occurrences of the term *fang-pien* are clustered. Indeed Chapter V contains about two fifths of the total incidence of the term. The important opening chapters which set the scene and delineate Vimalakīrti's character have their fair share, but the remaining chapters have scattered cases only. Some very incidental usage refers to the skilful means of the Buddha himself, along the lines observed already in the Lotus Sutra. In Chapter XI for example we read that 'the skilful means of the buddhas are inconceivable'[3] and 'Śākyamuni Buddha certainly has ability in this clever practice of skilful means'.[4] In Chapter XIII however, the only other case in the whole of the last six chapters, we read: 'If someone hears a sutra like this, believes and understands, receives and preserves, reads and recites it, and by the power of skilful means he explains it in detail and makes its meaning clear for the sake of all the living, then because he has preserved the Dharma this will be called the worshipful celebration of the Dharma.'[5] In this case therefore it is the follower who is called upon to exercise skilful means, and indeed, by contrast with much of The Lotus Sutra, the usage in The Teaching of Vimalakīrti is mainly concerned with skilful means as an ability commanded by bodhisattvas. It refers both to bodhisattvas in general and of course to Vimalakīrti in particular.

The main initial portrait of Vimalakīrti himself is given in the second chapter of the sutra, which is even entitled 'Skilful Means' (*fang-pien*).[6] He is described as an elder living in the city of Vaiśālī who has already made far-reaching progress in Buddhism. His many abilities have come to fruition under countless Buddhas in previous times and he has vanquished the evil tempter, Māra. We then find the concept of skilful means acting as a hinge between his own attainment and his service to others, when we read as follows: 'He had entered the gate of deep Dharma, was able in the exercise of insight, was thoroughly conversant with skilful means, had brought great vows to fruition, knew the mental tendencies of living beings, and could

---

[3] T XIV 554b 諸佛方便不可思議。

[4] T XIV 554c 釋迦牟尼佛乃能於此善行方便。

[5] T XIV 556c 若聞如是等經。信解受持讀誦。以方便力爲諸衆生分別解說顯示分明。守護法故。是名法之供養。('Celebration', i.e. in the sense of a religious offering or ritual reverence.)

[6] T XIV 539a. Lamotte translates the Tibetan as 'L'inconcevable habileté salvifique', *op. cit.* p. 126, cf. the phrase 方便不可思議, in note 3 above. Cf. also the chapter title 顯不思議 方便善巧品, T XIV 560c in the later translation by Hsüan Tsang (T474). The oldest Chinese version does not contain this idea, cf. T XIV 520c. Cf. also the tenth occurrence of *fang-pien* in the Śūraṃgamasamādhi-sūtra in Appendix F below.

distinguish the sharpness or obtuseness of all their faculties.'[7] This means
that he disposes of the kind of insight and knowledge which a Buddha has,
and like a Buddha he is in a position to be active in many ways calculated to
bring beings across from their ignorance and suffering.

There follows an extensive catalogue of the ways in which Vimalakīrti
accommodates himself to the ways of the world, in order to bring out the
meaning of Buddhist teaching in a manner suited to those who are in need of
it. But this extremely varied list of activities is prefaced and concluded by
the controlling term *fang-pien*. Thus the very fact of his living in Vaiśālī is due
to his 'skilfulness in means', applied 'because he wished to save people'.[8] At
the end of the list of his activities it is said that the town elder Vimalakīrti
'brought abundant benefit to living beings by the use of countless skilful
means like these.'[9] The importance of these two occurrences can scarcely be
exaggerated, for they mean that the content of the list occurring in between
gives body to what is meant by 'skilful means'.

The portrait really shows Vimalakīrti as being 'in the world but not of it',
if a phrase external to the tradition but unavoidably appropriate may be
allowed. The appearances are of one sort and the realities of another. The
appearance is of a layman living as a householder with wife and children,
wearing decorative ornaments, and eating and drinking. The reality is of one
who within the household life is not attached to the world, but who delights
in continence, isolation and meditation. We read, in sum, of one who, though
living in the world, cultivates the discipline normally associated with a
religious ascetic. Such a vantage point may seem subversive of organised
religion, for if this is a desirable style it might be asked what then would be
the role of the religious who leave the world and renounce the household life.
Indeed various aspects of monastic life are quite critically treated later in
the sutra.

Nor does Vimalakīrti stay within his house. He is to be seen in lawcourts,
businesses and schools, brothels, drinking houses and gambling dens. He
converses with brahmans, officials and princes, with harem girls, with the
ordinary people in general, and with the various kinds of deity. None of these
activities however disturbs his resolute establishment in the great vehicle. On
the contrary he is able in each case to give just what is needed to those who
are entangled in these various walks of life.

Immersion into some such aspect of everyday life is the device or means
(*fang-pien*). The resolution of the device, the ripening of its fruit, seems to

---

[7] T XIV 539a 入深法門善於智度。通達方便大願成就。明了衆生心之所趣。又能分
別諸根利鈍。

[8] T XIV 539a 欲度人故以善方便居毘耶離 The expression 善方便, unusual for Kum-
ārajīva, presumably reflects an original *upāyakauśalya*, cf. Lamotte *op. cit.* p. 127, but as it
stands of course it can be taken simply as 'good means', or if we keep to our standard 'skilful
means' for Kumārajīva's *fang-pien*, then 'good skilful means'. For Kumārajīva's normal usage
see the two immediately subsequent cases of the term, 以方便 T XIV 539b, and that quoted
in the next note.

[9] T XIV 539b 以如是等無量方便饒益衆生。

take place according to one or other of two principles. In some cases what is evil or unsatisfactory is steadily confronted by the unshakeable qualities of the bodhisattva, while in other cases the good which lies within samsaric existence is singled out and confirmed by his friendship and guidance. Thus the patience of the bodhisattva takes care of those who are spiteful or angry, a good result being achieved by the appropriate display of a relevant opposite. Or when the bodhisattva is with princes he takes a place of honour among them and brings out their qualities of loyalty and filial piety, thus confirming and developing a provisional good which is already present.

The first of these functions is particularly prominent at the beginning of the portrait which is based on the six perfections (*pāramitā*) as follows.

(i) charity (*dāna*), 'having incalculable riches he assisted the poverty-stricken';

(ii) proper conduct (*śīla*), 'by observing the precepts with purity he assisted those who transgress';

(iii) patience (*kṣānti*), 'by regulating his behaviour with patience he assisted the enraged and the angry';

(iv) vigour (*vīrya*), 'with much efficient perseverance he assisted those who are shiftless or lazy';

(v) contemplation (*dhyāna*), 'by single minded-contemplation he assisted those whose thoughts are in turmoil';

(vi) insight (*prajñā*), 'with his steady insight he assisted those who are without wisdom'.[10]

In this way the six perfections which a bodhisattva is supposed to cultivate are made to be, not qualities to achieve in splendid isolation, but rather qualities which take their very meaning from the vices over against which they stand. The implication of this usage is clearly that the cultivation of these qualities for one's own good is inseparable from their cultivation for the good of others. Each one of them is a skilful means relating both to an inadequacy or a vice on the one hand and to the goal of Buddhism on the other hand. In some Mahayana formulations *upāya-kauśalya-pāramitā*, or 'perfection of skill in means', was added as a seventh perfection, and there is an incidental case of this in Chapter I of The Teaching of Vimalakīrti.[11] However

---

[10] T XIV 539a 資財無量攝諸貧民。奉戒清淨攝諸毀禁。以忍調行攝諸恚怒。以大精進攝諸懈怠。一心禪寂攝諸亂意。以決定慧諸無智。

[11] T XIV 537a 布施持戒忍辱精進禪定智慧。及方便力無不具足。 The formulation illustrates how *fang-pien* is appended to the initial unpunctuated list. The Tibetan version raises the number of perfections to ten, cf. Lamotte, *op. cit.* p. 99, an indication of relative lateness. Cf. also Har Dayal, *The Bodhisattva Doctrine in Buddhist Sanskrit Literature*, Routledge and Kegan Paul 1932, p. 248, where he says that *upāya-kauśalya* was 'subsequently raised to the rank of a *pāramitā*; but one could also see this as a demotion to being a mere item in a list. Dayal's whole treatment of the concept is singularly disappointing, for he sees it as being mainly about tricks and frauds for propaganda. On the other hand he also includes a catalogue of definitions for the *saṅgraha-vastus* (kindlinesses which help to convert people), the *pratisaṃvids* (different kinds of knowledge of phenomena relating to the expression of Buddhist teaching) and *dhāraṇīs* (spells for protection), pp. 251 ff. These are all rather loosely connected with skilful means in the general sense that they are aspects of a bodhisattva's relations to others, and the references are scattered through a much wider range of texts than those considered here.

there is a sense in which such an addition is redundant if, as here, *all* the *pāramitās* (perfections) are seen as skilful means to begin with. In this passage the skill lies in displaying the appropriate facet or quality of the good way, within the evil world, in order to help those who need a specific form of assistance. Each one of these qualities is applied as an exercise in skilful means.

The other kind of case, in which an existent though provisional good is confirmed and developed by the bodhisattva, is also not without interest because it provides a rationale for positive correlations between Buddhist teaching and various kinds of social action. The bodhisattva shares in law-making and in the defence of accused persons, he legitimises filial piety, supports education, warns against the dangers of brothels and bars, strengthens the patience of householders and the readiness of the common people to earn merit.

This social involvement has been important in two ways. For one thing it indicates that the life of the world has its own, albeit provisional, value of which the sincere Buddhist layman need not be ashamed. Secondly it is not unknown, for Japanese Buddhists at least, to identify themselves not merely with the ordinary inhabitants of society with whom Vimalakīrti so subtly consorts, but indeed with the latter himself. The understanding then advanced is that they are doing business without really being attached to it, etc., on the basis of 'gaining worldly profits without taking pleasure in them'.[12] The stress on aspects of ordinary daily life in this text is quite strong and noteworthy for an early Mahayana sutra. Reference to the advanced instruction of mythical gods, who are taught insight and the truth of impermanence, is by contrast relatively incidental.[13]

Finally the dangers to conceptual orthodoxy to which the bodhisattva exposes himself should not be overlooked. For one thing Vimalakīrti understands worldly writings, while continuing to rejoice in the Buddha-dharma.[14] This implies an acceptance of secular literature and concepts while maintaining a Buddhist viewpoint, which was surely of importance in the domestication of Buddhism in China and Japan.[15] Similarly it is said of the bodhisattva that 'He accepted all heterodoxies without transgressing against the true faith,'[16] with which should be taken the statement that 'He entered the halls of disputation to lead people on with the great vehicle.'[17] These

[12] T XIV 539a 雖獲俗利不以喜悅。

[13] T XIV 539b.

[14] T XIV 539a 雖明世典常樂佛法。

[15] This point is generally recognised. Cf. especially Demiéville's piece mentioned in note 1 above. Kenneth Ch'an has summed it up well: 'Incidentally, the layman Vimalakīrti is described in such a manner that he might easily be taken as a perfect Confucian gentleman, being pure in self-discipline, obedient to all the precepts . . . Such a way of life could indeed be a model for the cultivated conservative Chinese scholar and gentleman.' *Buddhism in China, A Historical Survey*, Princeton 1964, pp. 208f.

[16] T XIV 539a 受諸異道不毀正信。

[17] T XIV 539a 入講論處導以大乘。

indications are very brief, and indeed the whole chapter is remarkably concise, but they indicate in principle a whole theory of correlation between Buddhist thought and other systems of thought. The fundamental point is that Buddhism does not reject other thought systems, but associates with them with a view to maintaining the integrity of Buddhist thought itself. Thus it is in places of doctrinal danger or ambiguity that the Dharma emerges to new clarity.

This portrait of the specific bodhisattva Vimalakīrti is backed up at various other points in the text in more general ways. The very first chapter is not about Vimalakīrti himself but relates a discourse given by the Buddha when visited at Vaiśālī by another layman named Ratnakūṭa. Apart from some wide-ranging Mahayana phantasies the main point explained is that the so-called pure land[18] of a bodhisattva is set up for the sake of living beings in accordance with their natures. In fact the living beings and the various characteristics of a bodhisattva in training are all identified in turn with the pure land. In other words, things as we ordinarily know them can also be seen as the pure land. This is applied to the six perfections and also to skilful means, thus: 'Skilful means is the bodhisattva's pure land; when the bodhisattva becomes a buddha, those living beings who through skilful means are unimpeded with respect to all dharmas will be born in that country.'[19] The pure land of a buddha (as a bodhisattva becomes when his pure land is realised) is of ambivalent status. On the one hand it can be seen with all its variety and unevenness, that is, as our ordinary world is articulated to match the defective views of the unenlightened. On the other hand, when the bodhisattva's mind is pure, the land appears bejewelled and even. The ambivalence is demonstrated miraculously to Śāriputra when the Buddha taps his toe on the ground, and shows this present world as a purified Buddha country for a few minutes before letting it return to what we know as normal. Later on, in the famous Platform Sutra of Ch'an (Zen) Buddhism, this demythologised meaning was applied to the pure land of the Buddha Amitābha (of Pure Land Buddhism). The passage in question includes the specific quotation from The Teaching of Vimalakīrti that 'In accordance with the purity of the mind the Buddha land is pure'.[20]

In Chapter I of The Teaching of Vimalakīrti the pure land of a bodhisattva is not explicitly defined as a skilful means *per se*, but in Chapter VIII the theme is taken up again in a series of verses, one of which reads:

'Although he knows that all buddha-countries
And all living beings are empty,
Yet he always prepares a pure land
For the salvific instruction of the multitudes.'[21]

---

[18] Cf. Lamotte's discussion of *buddha-kṣetra, op. cit.* pp. 395-404.

[19] T XIV 538b 方便是菩薩淨土。菩薩成佛時於一切法方便無礙衆生來生其國。

[20] T XIV 538c 隨其心淨則佛土淨 Cf. Philip B. Yampolsky, *The Platform Sutra of the Sixth Patriarch*, Columbia University Press 1967, pp. 156 ff.

[21] T XIV 550a 雖知諸佛國　及與衆生空　而常修淨土　教化於群生 The nearest to a

This verse is of particular interest here because it lies in a series of verses on various aspects of a bodhisattva's activity which are all controlled by the concept of skilful means. Indeed, the passage is effectively a re-statement of the portrait of Vimalakīrti found in Chapter II. Vimalakīrti is asked who his mother and father are, etc. and he replies allegorically in the first verse of the series:

> 'Perfection of insight is the bodhisattva's mother,
> And skilful means, we may say, is the father;
> Of all the leaders of the multitudes
> There is not one who is not born from these.'[22]

Apart from a couple of more or less doxological stanzas, the closing passage further along repeats the same partnership of insight and skilful means.

> 'In accordance with what they require
> He gets them to enter the Buddha-way;
> By his good power of skilful means
> He can provide them with all they need.
> Thus his ways are uncountable
> And his practices have no limit;

complete identification is found in Chapter XI when the earth is suddenly made to appear most magnificent and the assembled disciples to appear golden in colour. The dictum quoted earlier that 'The skilful means of the buddhas are inconceivable' is followed by the sentence, 'In order to bring across living beings, they display differences in buddha-countries in accordance with what is appropriate', T VIII 554b 爲度衆生故隨其所應現佛國異。Literally, it is the differences which are displayed, but the overall association of ideas certainly suggests that the very appearance of the buddha-country itself depends upon the skilful means of the buddha responsible for it. The same chapter gives an account of a miraculous perfume produced by Vimalakīrti by his 'power of supernatural proficiency' 神通之力 T VIII 554a. By such power he also brought the whole assembly with their 'lion-thrones' into the Buddha's presence, T VIII 553b. Clearly the exercise of such supernatural power is to be thought of in the general context of skilful means, and Chapter XI is an example of the overall association of the two. However reference to such supernatural power of the bodhisattvas is not sufficient to indicate the meaning of skilful means. Conversely however, one might say that in so far as supernatural power is used as a mode of indicating Buddhist meaning it is to be understood as skilful means just as other forms of Buddhist communication are, such as the four noble truths.

[22] T XIV 549c 智度菩薩母　方便以爲父　一切衆導師　無不由是生 Note that the male-female imagery plays only a slight role in the texts studied, although in later centuries it became somewhat more important without adding much to the basic concept of skilful means. The main points conveyed are the complementariness of insight and means, and the slight suggestion of an active role implied for 'skilful means' by its association with the male side. Cf. also Chapter Six, note 10.

His insight is infinite
And he brings to liberation a countless multitude.'[23]

The preparation of a pure land is but one of the many ways mentioned here in which a bodhisattva fulfils his function. Others listed in the other verses are too long to quote in full, but suggest a fantastic range of transformations not only into various living forms but also in the elements, and as food and drink for the hungry.

Yet other transformations are referred to also in Chapter VI, which similarly concludes 'This is named the entrance of insight and skilful means for a bodhisattva who abides in marvellous release.'[24] The main idea associated with this concept of 'marvellous release' is that the bodhisattva is able to manifest himself quite freely in any way necessary to help others. Even the tempting devils and tormenting oppressors who make life difficult for bodhisattvas in training may themselves secretly be bodhisattvas. By putting obstacles in the way of their colleagues, the argument runs, they help them to develop steadfastness. The net meaning of this rather severe description of mutual aid, the techniques of which are explicitly described as skilful means,[25] is presumably to encourage believers to interpret hardships as opportunities. In these varied and general ways therefore this writing supports the common Mahayana understanding of a bodhisattva as one who through his combination of insight and skilful means is able to save living beings.

It is in this context, already adumbrated in the discussion of Avalokiteśvara and others earlier, that the portrait of the legendary householder Vimalakīrti is to be understood. The special stress on his lay status and lay involvement, although it has often proved attractive to lay persons, is therefore not a petty anti-clericalism; for the mere fact that he dwells as a layman in Vaiśālī is a skilful means, a provisional state of affairs with a hidden meaning. Nor on the other hand should this be taken to imply an ultimately reserved position assuming the value of the homeless i.e. the monastic or 'religious', life by contrast with that of the householder. Indeed the monk Rāhula was taken to task by Vimalakīrti (Chapter III) for teaching the importance of abandoning the household life. One is not allowed to settle in the view that one or other of these alternatives represents some kind of a solution in itself. This means incidentally that an account of the 'laicisation' or 'secularisation' process which took place under the aegis of Mahayana Buddhism could easily be too facile. Both lay and monastic status have provisional meaning only, and that is why generally speaking both are maintained in Mahayana Buddhism.

[23] T XIV 550b 隨彼之所須　得入於佛道　以善方便力　皆能給足之　如是道無量　所行無有涯　智慧無邊際　度脫無數衆

[24] T XIV 547a 是名住不可思議解脫菩薩智慧方便之門。

[25] T XIV 547a 以方便力教化衆生現作魔王。...以方便力而往試之令其堅固。'By their power of skilful means, for the salvific instruction of the living, they appear as Māra-kings .... By their power of skilful means they go to test them to make them steadfast.'

Vimalakīrti's illness

The portrait of Vimalakīrti is followed by the story of his illness which begins in Chapter II and provides the main narrative framework for the rest of the sutra. The first sentence is the key: 'As such a skilful means he gave the impression of being ill in his body'.[26] This had the result that he was visited by numerous worthy lay people, kings, princes, brahmans, householders and various officials who all solicitously enquired about his welfare. When they visited him he took the opportunity he had created to preach the Dharma to them, in the form of a meditation on the body, which is a classic theme in Buddhism.

His exposition stresses the impermanence of body and its susceptibility to suffering. By his own feigned illness Vimalakīrti was himself a visual demonstration of his teaching. He uses the standard similes. The body is like foam, like a bubble, like a mirage, like a dream or an echo. Not only is it unstable, it is also unpleasant like a poisonous snake. One should take delight not in this perishing physical body but in the 'Buddha-body'.[27] 'The Buddha-body is the Dharma-body,' he goes on.[28] The Dharma-body arises out of the cultivation of all the qualities which a bodhisattva is supposed to cultivate.[29] Above all, he says, 'He who wishes to attain the Buddha-body and cut off the afflictions of all living beings should raise the thought of supreme, perfect enlightenment.'[30] The chapter concludes with the comment that Vimalakīrti had expounded the Dharma in a manner *appropriate to* those who came to enquire about his sickness.[31] Thus the positive teaching which he gave, about the Buddha-body or the Dharma-body, is framed to fit over against the negative account of the physical body arising out of his supposed illness. This short exposition is thus a representative example of the correlational method of Buddhist teaching.

The two subsequent chapters continue the plot of the narrative begun in Chapter II, only now instead of laymen going to call on Vimalakīrti we read of the perplexities into which the closest and leading disciples of the Buddha find themselves to be pitched. Chapter III begins with a fine irony as Vimalakīrti is supposed to say to himself that while he lies there in his (feigned) illness the compassionate Buddha will surely not leave him to suffer alone. Not surprisingly the Buddha reads his thoughts and plays the game by telling his disciples and bodhisattvas to go and visit the sick elder.

---

[26] T XIV 539b 其以方便現身有病。

[27] T XIV 539b 佛身. This sutra predates a clear formation of the '*trikāya*' doctrine, which contrary to the impression given by many textbooks is not typical of the early phase of Mahayana Buddhism.

[28] T XIV 539c 佛身者即法身也。

[29] These are all rehearsed itemised lists, and one of the items listed is, incidentally, skilful means. Since Vimalakīrti's illness has just been prominently described as a skilful means, one implication may be that Vimalakīrti is giving rise to the Dharma-body or Buddha-body through his feigned illness.

[30] T XIV 539c 欲得佛身斷一切衆生病者。當發阿耨多羅三藐三菩提心。

[31] T XIV 539c 爲諸問疾者如應說法。

It is a straight continuation of the skilful means set up in Chapter II. One by one the disciples demur, and to excuse themselves they each tell their story of an encounter which they had already had with Vimalakīrti and which led to their extreme discomfiture. It would lead too far afield even to summarise all of these one by one, but the principle which they have in common is that each time the disciple is shown as taking some aspect of the Buddha's teaching in a literal and pedestrian manner, which Vimalakīrti then reinterprets in terms of transiency and voidness. The cases of Kāśyapa, Subhūti and Maitreya are perhaps best known, through D. T. Suzuki's English summary of the sutra.[32] One further example may be given in a little detail here, namely the case of Ānanda, which is of special interest since it reflects the skilful means character of Vimalakīrti's own illness.

Ānanda was standing at the entrance to the house of a rich brahman, bowl in hand, when Vimalakīrti turned up and asked him what he was doing there. Ānanda explained that the Buddha was feeling slightly ill and that therefore he was trying to beg some milk for him. At this Vimalakīrti expressed great shock and told Ānanda to stop at once. The body of the Tathāgata was like diamond, he said. How could it possibly be susceptible to illness? The Buddha-body is freed from the conditioning of ordinary existence and does not suffer illness. Ānanda should be careful not to bring the Buddha into disrepute. Not surprisingly Ānanda is perplexed at this, but fortunately for him a voice is heard from the sky, or space,[33] which affirms that Vimalakīrti, who after all is just a householder, is correct in what he says. The Buddha behaves in this way because he has come out into the world in order to bring across and release living beings. Nevertheless although what Vimalakīrti says is right, says the voice from space, Ānanda may take back some milk for the Buddha, discreetly, without feeling ashamed.

The illness of the Buddha is acted out on the side of the unenlightened, but at the same time it provides the occasion for indicating the true character of a Buddha-body. Kumārijīva does not here use the term *fang-pien* of the Buddha's illness, though it would obviously be appropriate. Interestingly enough, the same story is quoted in the vast 'Treatise on the Great Perfection of Insight' ascribed to Nāgārjuna and also translated by Kumārajīva (T1509). In this case the Buddha's request to Ānanda to fetch him some milk is explicitly declared by Vimalakīrti to be a skilful means.[34]

It will be noted that the declaration that an activity of the Buddha is a *fang-pien* or skilful means does not imply that it should be suspended. Vimalakīrti checks Ānanda in order to bring him to the realisation of what is going on; but the voice which confirms the correctness of what Vimalakīrti says goes on to instruct Ānanda to carry out his errand nevertheless. Vimalakīrti's encounters with the other disciples all bear a similar message.

---

[32] *Op. cit.*, see note 1 above.

[33] T XIV 542a 即聞空中聲曰。 The 空 is natural for 'sky' but it also means void(ness), i.e. *śūnyatā*.

[34] T XXV 122b 此雖佛勅是爲方便。

He seems to strike at the root of the renunciation of the household life, of begging for alms, of meditation and of teaching, all taken in a very straightforward manner by the disciples in question but reinterpreted in a contradictory way by Vimalakīrti. Thus, to Śāriputra, 'Meditation does not mean just sitting there . . . meditation means showing neither body nor mind in the triple world; meditation means not giving up the achievement of cessation yet maintaining the forms of wordly dignity; meditation means not discarding the Dharma of the Way, while at the same time being active in the affairs of the common people,' etc.[35] In another encounter Subhūti is permitted to receive the food offered to him by Vimalakīrti, 'if you do not see the Buddha and do not hear the Dharma'[36] or 'if you enter all false views and do not arrive at the other shore'.[37] Similarly he berates Maitreya for misleading people with talk about future states. The Buddha may have predicted the future buddhahood of Maitreya, but when he attains it so too will all beings, and when he is in complete nirvana so too will all beings be in complete nirvana. The reason for this is that 'the buddhas know that all living beings in the last analysis are in a state of nirvanic peace, that is, they are marked with nirvana and do not go into cessation all over again.'[38]

In this way, one by one, many items of doctrine and practice from the central tradition of Buddhism are restated in terms of their emptiness and their original nirvanic quality. The logic of equality which flows from this and which is typical of the Mahayana leads to the contradictory equation of monkhood and laity, leaving the household life and being immersed in the world, of saviour and saved, of future possibilities and latent states. The followers of the Buddha should follow their practices and give their teachings, but always with a view to their dismantlement from within. The rationale for this is stated in some detail in the dialogue between Vimalakīrti and Mañjuśrī, the only one of the Buddha's followers who did feel ready to call on the sick householder. This discussion, which must now be examined, links up the important Mahayana concepts of 'emptiness', 'insight' and 'skilful means'.

Vimalakīrti and Mañjuśrī

Mañjuśrī is a wise yet unpretentious bodhisattva. He has a fair respect for Vimalakīrti, whom he describes as 'hard to answer',[39] etc. and 'altogether accomplished in insight and skilful means'.[40] Vimalakīrti greets him with the words: 'You come well, Mañjuśrī. With the mark of non-coming, you come,

[35] T XIV 539c 不必是坐爲宴坐也。夫宴坐者。不於三界現身意。是爲宴坐。不起滅定而現諸威儀。是爲宴坐。不捨道法而現凡夫事。
[36] T XIV 540b 若須菩提不見佛不聞法。
[37] T XIV 540c 入諸邪見不到彼岸。This whole context supports the readiness of a bodhisattva to enter an area of doctrinal dubiety, referred to earlier.
[38] T XIV 542b 諸佛知一切衆生畢竟寂滅即涅槃相不復更滅 Cf. the teaching of The Lotus Sutra that all dharmas are nirvanic from the beginning, Chapter Two above, note 47.
[39] T XIV 544a 難爲詶對。
[40] T XIV 544b 其慧方便皆已得度。

and with the mark of non-seeing you see.'[41] Mañjuśrī replies in similar vein, as if to show that he understands what Vimalakīrti is up to, but then he casually suggests leaving the matter aside and goes on to ask about the householder's illness. It is as if he is prepared to go along with Vimalakīrti's dissembling in order to generate the discussion which will lead the assembled throng to enlightenment. The plot of the narrative is complicated by the fact that just before Mañjuśrī's arrival Vimalakīrti had magically emptied his room of all the people and objects which it contained. This was symbolic in itself and gives rise to a discussion of its own.

In the meantime Mañjuśrī plays the game and asks Vimalakīrti about the cause of his illness, how long he has been ill and how long his illness will continue. The last part of the question seems to imply that Mañjuśrī already recognises the illness to be deliberate. Since the reader of the sutra already knows that the illness is feigned, it is not surprising that Vimalakīrti now relates his illness to the sickness of all living beings. His illness arises because of the ignorance and craving of the world. When living beings are no longer sick the bodhisattva will also be free from sickness. The illness, already designated a skilful means, is said to arise through great compassion.[42] The workings of 'skilful means' and the workings of 'compassion', it may therefore be noted, follow the same track, namely that 'the bodhisattva enters birth-and-death (i.e. *saṃsāra*) for the sake of living beings.'[43] If we ask what the compassion of a bodhisattva is like, the simile used in this context is that the bodhisattva's attitude is like that of a father and mother towards an only son. 'When the son becomes ill the father and mother become ill too. If the son gets better, they get better too. It is the same with a bodhisattva. He loves all living beings as if they were a son. If the living beings are ill, then the bodhisattva is ill, if the living beings get better, the bodhisattva gets better too.'[44] The sickness of Vimalakīrti, it is stressed, has of itself no characteristics or 'marks', and is not dependent upon the body, mind or elements.[45] Yet the sickness of the bodhisattva is aligned with the sickness of the living beings which does arise because of these. Thus the sickness of Vimalakīrti had two facets. On the one hand it bears the marks of the sufferings of the world but on the other hand it has no marks. As a skilful means Vimalakīrti's illness both follows the lines of the suffering of the world and bears within it the latent resolution of this suffering.

How is such a resolution possible? Or, as Mañjuśrī asked, how is a sick

---

[41] T XIV 544b 善來文殊師利。不來相而來。不見相而見。

[42] T XIV 544b 是疾何所因起。菩薩病者以大悲起。

[43] T XIV 544b 菩薩爲衆生故入生死。

[44] T XIV 544b 其子得病父母亦病。若子病愈父母亦愈。菩薩如是。於諸衆生愛之若子。衆生病則菩薩病。衆生病愈菩薩亦愈。 The motif of father and son is also used in The Lotus Sutra, both as a simile and as a direct metaphor. It should be clearly understood that it is supposed to convey an understanding of the *relationship* between a bodhisattva (or buddha) and the world of living beings, but that it has no further implications of an ontological kind such as are often thought to be entailed by a theistic position.

[45] T XIV 544c 爲何等相...我病無形不可見 etc.

bodhisattva to be 'consoled', and how is he to 'tame his mind'? The explanation continues along the lines indicated. In so far as the sickness arises through ignorance and craving and in so far as the bodhisattva is sharing in the problems of all existence it is possible to speak as if it were real. In this sense it is said that the suffering arises from distorted ideas, and from passions, and from clinging to self. But ultimately there is no self, and therefore the bodhisattva (who is taking all beings with him) should relinquish the idea of self and the idea of living beings. Not only that, but having used the idea that the body is just made up of many elements or factors combining with each other,[46] his critical attention should now be turned to these factors, which he ought not to take more seriously than one takes the idea of self. After all, 'these factors do not know each other',[47] and 'When they arise they do not say 'I arise', and when they cease they do not say 'I cease'.[48]

The movement of this argument follows the standard pattern of the Mahayana reform. Early Buddhism had vigorously undermined any notion of a permanent soul or self, partly by stressing the various constituent factors which go to make up what seem at first in ordinary life to be important individuals, namely ourselves. The analysis and classification of these factors in turn came to be a haven, it seems, in which the monkish mind began to take a substitute refuge. In order to maintain the original drive towards liberation from mental attachments it became necessary to declare that these factors, or dharmas, were empty of 'own-being', that is, that they had no more substantial ontological status than any 'soul'. Similarly causality was declared 'empty' of connections so that the Buddhist system based on an analysis of cause and effect could not itself become an obstacle to liberation.[49]

The bodhisattva therefore must free himself from 'distortion', 'self' and 'dualism'.[50] To free oneself, or to 'depart from dualism' means 'not thinking of factors as inner or outer' and 'treating things with equality'.[51] This manner of treating things, or taking things, leads to a paradoxical rehabilitation of the notion of self which has just been attacked, for if we say 'What is equality?' the answer is that 'self and nirvana are equal' because 'self and nirvana are both empty' and they are 'indeterminate in nature'.[52] They are described as empty only because of the terminology otherwise used for them, which needs to be controlled or checked by the notion of emptiness.[53] When such an

---

[46] I.e. dharmas, 法 (Ch. *fa*, J. *hō*).

[47] T XIV 545a 又此法者各不相知。

[48] T XIV 545a 起時不言我起。滅時不言我滅。

[49] Cf. Th. Stcherbatsky's *The Central Conception of Buddhism*, London 1923, and *The Conception of Buddhist Nirvāṇa*, Leningrad 1927 and The Hague 1965, and various literature cited in Chapter Six below.

[50] T XIV 545a 顛倒, 我, 二法。 'Dualism': more literally, 'dual dharmas'; it is sometimes argued that words ending in 'ism' are a new-fangled western invention, but there seems little doubt that what is meant here is the practice of thinking dualistically, for which the best brief English term is dualism.

[51] T XIV 545a 離二法...不念內外諸法...行於平等. On the latter expression note that 行 is literally 'proceeding' or 'coursing' as bodhisattvas 'course' in the world.

[52] T XIV 545a 云何平等...爲我等涅槃等 ...我及涅槃此二皆空...無決定性。

[53] T XIV 545a 但以名字故空。

equalisation is realised there is no more sickness.[54] All that could remain would be 'the sickness of emptiness', in so far as one might be entangled in the notion of emptiness itself.[55] This 'sickness of emptiness' therefore also has to be treated with the notion of 'emptiness'.[56] To use other words, the notion of cancelling has to be withdrawn simultaneously with the cancelling out of discriminations. In this way the bodhisattva must train himself to attend to the world even while he sees through it. He seeks nirvana not in some special recess, but in the fundamental equality of all factors of existence.

Withdrawing from one's attachment to emptiness is the final movement of the Mahayana dancer. It is spelled out again in the text. By the unreality of his own sickness, which, we should recall, is a skilful means, the bodhisattva recognises the unreality of the sickness of living beings.[57] But if while thinking this he should feel compassionately attached to living beings, he must discard the thought again.[58] If he does not, the compassion which he generates will be determined by clinging views which view life-and-death (Skt. *saṃsāra*) with disfavour. This is a limitation from which also he must be free in order to be able to preach to living beings in a way which will release them from their bonds. How can a bodhisattva maintain such a dynamic balance? The argument, which has been explained in summary form up to this point, continues with a passage on insight and skilful means (*fang-pien*) which needs shortly to be quoted in full.

First however there comes a reminder that even the ordinary standard components of Buddhist practice have to be taken properly; for 'To be greedily attached to meditation and concentration is the bodhisattva's bondage; but to be born as a skilful means is the bodhisattva's release.'[59] Kumāra-jīva's version here may be a conflation because we find a more elaborate parallelism in Lamotte's translation from the Tibetan version: 'To liberate oneself from existence without making use of salvific means is a Bodhisattva's bondage. Conversely, to penetrate the world of existence with the aid of salvific means is deliverance. To enjoy the taste of ecstasies, concentrations and contemplations without salvific means is a bodhisattva's bondage. Conversely, to enjoy the taste of ecstasies and contemplations with recourse to salvific means is deliverance.'[60] The meaning of this is that Buddhist practice can be either retrogressive or helpful depending on the status

---

[54] T XIV 545a 得是平等無有餘病。

[55] T XIV 545a 唯有空病。

[56] T XIV 545a 空病亦空。

[57] T XIV 545a 如我此病非眞非有。衆生病亦非眞非有。

[58] T XIV 545a 作是觀時。於諸衆生若起愛見大悲。即應捨離。

[59] T XIV 545b 貪著禪味是菩薩縛。以方便生是菩薩解。

[60] Lamotte, *op. cit.* p. 233, 'Pour le Bodhisattva, se libérer de l'existence (*bhavamukti-parigraha*) à l'exclusion des moyens salvifiques (*upāya*), c'est un lien. Au contraire, pénétrer dans le monde de l'existence (*bhavajagatpraveśa*) à l'aide des moyens salvifiques, c'est une délivrance. Pour le Bodhisattva, goûter la saveur (*rasāsvādana*) des extases (*dhyāna*), . . . des concentrations (*samādhi*) et des recueillements (*samāpatti*) en l'absence de moyens salvifiques, c'est un lien. Au contraire goûter la saveur des extases (*dhyāna*) et des concentrations (*samāpatti*) en recourant aux moyens salvifiques, c'est une délivrance.'

accorded to it and how it is used. The 'salvific means' (Lamotte's 'moyens salvifiques') referred to here are not other than the practices in question, and the phrase 'with the aid of' may be redundant, strictly speaking, because it suggests that there are some other unspecified means to go with the practices. The import is that one has to treat the practices and activities as 'skilful means', that is, one has to continue to make use of them while simultaneously not being greedily attached to them. Not to be attached to techniques of spiritual training is quite hard for would-be saints who seriously invest in them. Kumārijīva's phrase 'as a skilful means' brings out the meaning clearly, as one would expect, although he only has two half-sayings. Simply to try to get out of the world is bondage, but to immerse oneself in it as an exercise in skilful means brings deliverance.

The passage linking insight and means, which may now be brought forward, is set out in similar parallel statements.

(i) 'Again, insight without skilful means is bondage, but insight with skilful means is release.'[61]

(ii) 'Skilful means without insight is bondage, but skilful means with insight is release.'[62]

These four possibilities are then explicated in more detail as follows:

(i) 'What does it mean to say that insight without skilful means is bondage? It means that a bodhisattva disciplines himself in the teachings of emptiness, no marks and no action, decks out a buddha-land and brings on the development of living beings, but all the time has a mind full of clinging views. This is called the bondage of insight without skilful means.'[63]

The 'clinging views' referred to here are not perhaps as deplorable as they might at first sound. They are after all a form of love, clinging views such as

---

[61] T XIV 545b 又無方便慧縛。有方便慧解。 *Fang-pien* is translated throughout this section as 'skilful means', as argued for in Chapter One above, but of course one could argue simply for 'means' if a close literal accuracy were preferred to the overall usage and meaning in Kumārajīva's versions. Similarly insight is given for 慧, while others might prefer 'wisdom'.

[62] T XIV 545b 無慧方便縛。有慧方便解。

[63] T XIV 545b 何謂無方便慧縛。謂菩薩以愛見心。莊嚴佛土成就衆生。於空無相無作法中而自調伏。是名無方便慧縛。 According to Lamotte the Tibetan version runs very differently, and he does not remark on this discrepancy. It runs: 'Quand le Bodhisattva se dompte lui-mome (*ātmanaṃ niyamati*) par la pratique de la vacuité (*śūnyatā*), du sans-caractère (*ānimitta*) et de la non-prise en considération (*apraṇihita*), mais s'abstient (d'orner son corps) par les marques physiques primaires et secondaires (*lakṣaṇānuvyanjana*), d'orner son champ de Buddha (*buddha-kṣetrālaṃkāra*) et de faire mûrir les êtres (*sattvaparipācana*), c'est une sagesse non-assumée par les moyens salvifiques et c'est un lien.' Pp. 233f. There is nothing in Kumārajīva's version for the 's'abstient' and no negative of any kind, so that the whole drift is different. The Tibetan version just seems to mean that the bodhisattva trains himself but does not go on to act for the salvation of others at all. Kumārajīva's version by contrast means that a bodhisattva starts doing the things which he is supposed to do, training in emptiness *and* bringing on other beings, but gets tangled up in them because of his clinging views. In other words he fails to bring across living beings while realising that there are no living beings brought across. The pedestrian Tibetan version is probably secondary.

may be connected with compassion, indeed 'great compassion', towards living beings.[64] In spite of the nobility of intention, however, the insight which informs such compassion may fall short of full insight or true insight precisely because of the compassionate involvement, if skilful means is lacking. Skilful means is required to achieve both thinking it important to save living beings while at the same time not looking at ordinary life with disfavour. The association of 'skill' is almost more important in Kumārajīva's concept of *fang-pien* here than is the notion of 'means'.[65]

The second of the various possibilities is explained as follows :

(ii) 'What does it mean to say that insight with skilful means is release? It means that a bodhisattva disciplines himself in the teachings of emptiness, no marks, and no action, and without weariness or repugnance, and then decks out a buddha-land and brings on the development of living beings without having a mind full of clinging views. This is called release through insight with means.'[66]

In this case the bodhisattva does all that he is supposed to do but without being attached to the matter. He is skilfully able to do it without particularly minding. He is not upset by emptiness; nor does he get ensnared by his own compassionate works.

The passage continues by commenting on the difference made by the absence or presence of insight, as follows :

(iii) 'What is meant by saying that skilful means without insight is bondage? It means that a bodhisattva plants many roots of virtue but persists in greed, anger, wrong views and all sorts of passions. This is called the bondage of skilful means without insight.'[67]

(iv) 'What is meant by saying that skilful means with insight is release? It means that he withdraws from greed, anger, wrong views and all sorts of

[64] For 愛見 cf. note 58 above, 愛見大悲。Ota defines 愛見 as 'loving people in an attached way', *Bukkyō Daijiten, ad loc.*

[65] So strong is this implication that one might expect the original Sanskrit to have been *upāyakauśalya* and not just *upāya*. There is in fact no direct evidence for the Sanskrit text at this point, although there is evidence for *upāya* alone in the opening clause quoted earlier, in the 1st *Bhāvanakrāma*, see Lamotte, p. 233, note 25. The later Chinese version has the idea of skill throughout this section by using the term 巧方便, see T XIV 569a-b.

[66] T XIV 545b 何謂有方便慧解。謂不以愛見心莊嚴佛土成就衆生。於空無相無作法中。以自調伏而不疲厭。是名有方便慧解。 Again the Tibetan version is different, cf. Lamotte *ad loc.*, and indeed comparisons with the other Chinese versions do not produce any consistency, cf. T XIV 526b and 569a. Fukaura, *op. cit.* p. 350, took the negative 不 with the whole of 以愛見心莊嚴佛土成就衆生. This is grammatically not at fault, but the original is ambiguous and Hashimoto is surely right to read, from Kumārajīva, 愛見心を以てせず。 'Not (doing those things) with a mind full of clinging views', if it is to be contrasted with the previous paragraph must mean, not just failing to do what bodhisattvas do, but rather *doing* all those things without getting tangled up in them through having a mind full of clinging views. 'Skilful means' and 'release' is all about doing what is to be done without getting stuck in it.

[67] T XIV 545b 何謂無慧方便縛。謂菩薩住貪欲瞋志邪見等諸煩惱。而植衆德本。是名無慧方便縛。

passions, and plants many roots of virtue, which he turns over to supreme
perfect enlightenment. This is called release through skilful means with
insight.'[68]

Here the term skilful means seems to refer rather generally to the bodhisattva's practice. The bodhisattva begins to do what he is supposed to do, but
without insight he cannot achieve the penetration into his own attitudes and
activities which leads to release from them. In this case his skilful means does
not have its true value, and he remains floundering in the world of discriminated objectives. At this level it is quite understandable that various
kinds of emotional attachment continue to arise. Only through insight can
he dedicate his activities to enlightenment.

The precise relationship between the terms 'insight' and 'skilful means' and
the factors associated with them is not spelled out in great detail in the text.
The main stress is simply on the need for both of them to be present in the
bodhisattva's practice. Indeed the lack of either one has a similar effect,
because if there is no insight the problem is a mind full of clinging views, while
if there is no 'skilful means' the problem is entanglement in greed, anger,
wrong views and passions. 'Skilful means' itself sometimes suggests the
various forms of a bodhisattva's activity which may, or may not, turn out to
be controlled by full insight and lead into 'supreme perfect enlightenment'.[69]
Thus it is that insight, the recognition of emptiness and equality, is the key
without which skilful means just goes astray or gets stuck at an inappropriate
point. Sometimes, on the other hand, it is skilful means which represents the
last subtle twist in the bodhisattva's own understanding of himself; for, given
his recognition of true reality and given his ready acceptance of a bodhisattva's compassionate way of life, it remains necessary for him not to be
taken in by all this as a view of the world and a life-style, so to speak, in
which he might settle. Thus it is scarcely possible to say that one is more
important than the other, or somehow prior to the other, and indeed the very
search for a conclusion like this would betray an inappropriate desire for a
universal last term or basic principle such as this text does not offer. All one
can say is that the two are most intimately related.

A clearer differentiation appears in the remaining parallel sentences on the
subject, where 'insight' has the meaning of a penetrative if static analysis,
while 'means' has the meaning of well directed action.

(i) 'Yet again, seeing the body in terms of impermanence, suffering,
emptiness and non-self, this is called insight.'[70]

(ii) 'To stay in birth-and-death even though the body is sick, bringing
benefit to all and not getting disgusted or tired, this is called means.'[71]

[68] T XIV 545b 何謂有慧方便解。謂離諸貪欲瞋恚邪見等諸煩惱。而植衆德本。迴向阿
耨多羅三藐三提。 是名有慧方便解。

[69] *Anuttara samyak sambodhi*, a standard technical phrase which Kumārajīva always keeps
in transliteration.

[70] T XIV 545b 又復觀身無常若空非我。是名爲慧。

[71] T XIV 545b 雖身有疾常在生死。饒益一切而不厭倦。是名方便。

(iii) 'Yet again, when seeing the body, to see that the body is never without sickness, and that sickness is never without the body, to see that the sickness is the body and that there is no renovation and no passing away, this is called insight.'[72]

(iv) 'To recognise that the body is sick and yet not to enter eternal cessation, this is called means.'[73]

These quotations bring out clearly the characteristic direction of a bodhisattva who, though he sees through the world and is not attached to it, nevertheless is turned towards it and not away from it. This is not so heroic as it sometimes is presented. In terms of the emptiness and equality of the dharmas there could be no individual cessation while the rest of the world burns on. As Vimalakīrti told Maitreya, when one bodhisattva attains the supreme goal, so do all sentient beings. But it is easy to find oneself bound through developing insight without skilful means. It is the dynamic, free balance which requires skill.

The discourse by Vimalakīrti goes on to describe at further length the paradoxical character of the bodhisattva's course, freely moving in the world of life-and-death and in the discipline of Buddhism, while not being bound by any of it. He is conformed to the ultimate purity of all dharmas, and at the same time he is conformed to what is appropriate and manifests his body in the world. Finally the bodhisattva is called upon 'to gain the Buddha-way, to turn the wheel of Dharma, to enter nirvana, and *still* not to discard the way of a bodhisattva.'[74] Admittedly there are no italics in the original text, but it does seem rather different from the commonly met idea that a bodhisattva 'postpones' his nirvana! Vimalakīrti is indeed hard to pin down. This is because every form of religious language, when conceived in terms of skilful means, is first allusive and then disposable. This applies to 'teaching Buddhism', that is 'turning the wheel of Dharma', and it even applies to 'entering nirvana' as observed before in The Lotus Sutra. In short it applies not merely to the preliminary suggestions of the religious system, but above all to its fundamental assumptions and final terms.

[72] T XIV 545b 又復觀身身不離病病不離身。是病是身非新非故。是名爲慧。
[73] T XIV 545b 設身有疾而不永滅是名方便。
[74] T XIV 545c 雖得佛道轉于法輪入涅槃而不捨於菩薩之道。是菩薩行。In full, 'Even though gaining the Buddha-way, turning the wheel of Dharma and entering nirvana, he does not discard the bodhisattva way. This is the bodhisattva's practice.'

6 SKILFUL MEANS IN THE PERFECTION OF INSIGHT LITERATURE

Insight and skilful means

It is sometimes assumed that The Perfection of Insight sutras are either historically or doctrinally prior to The Lotus Sutra or The Teaching of Vimalakīrti, as if the latter were more popular offshoots off the main tree. Yet when all is said and done there is no clear knowledge about the dating of these early Mahayana sutras, so that precise historical relationships cannot be determined. They are all composite, and even rough attempts at dating consist mainly in pushing back presumed phases of growth into a plausible distance from the earliest Chinese versions. Above all, even though it may be possible to discern the main outlines of development within a single corpus, it really seems to be impossible to correlate with any sureness the presumed developmental phases of two or three sutras with each other. As to the contents, one party might take the more 'philosophical' parts to be the most fundamental, while another might take a system such as Chih-I's to show the supremacy of The Lotus Sutra. Yet the non-partisan observer finds difficulty in driving a wedge of any strength between the various materials to be considered. They are all neither other than nor less than thoroughly Mahayanist. There are certain differences of emphasis. It may fairly be said that The Lotus Sutra is more attentive to the role of the Buddha and the right way of understanding his appearance, his teaching and his nirvana. The Teaching of Vimalakīrti is more concerned with the polemics between the bodhisattva Vimalakīrti himself and narrower interpreters of Buddhism. The Perfection of Insight Sutras are mainly about bodhisattvas in general and their practice of the qualities which define them. Nevertheless all these writings have many features in common, including some important ones. In spite of various secondary elements all clearly contain the Mahayana teaching of voidness (Ch. *kung*, Skt. *śūnyatā*), all contain a radical critique of the received Buddhist tradition, and all take the concept of skilful means as a key to understanding the status or role of particular ideas or practices.

The literature of the 'perfection of insight' (Skt. *prajñā-pāramitā*) consists of various sutras which are more or less repetitious of each other, and which are mainly known to the English speaking world through the translations from Sanskrit made by Edward Conze.[1] As to the East Asian tradition, the Chinese versions by Kumārajīva are again of major, though not exclusive, importance. They include T223 and T227, referred to above in Chapter One, and consisting of 90 and 29 chapters respectively. The shorter of the two may be taken as a more or less standard form of the sutra, corresponding approximately to what is extant in Sanskrit as the *Aṣṭasāhasrikā Prajñā-pāramitā Sūtra*, so that for general context the reader may refer to Conze's translation of the latter.[2] Conze's text in thirty two chapters is based on mediaeval manuscripts which apparently have more in common with later Tibetan and Chinese versions than with Kumārajīva's earlier Chinese version.[3] If anything the term *upāya-kauśalya* ('skill in means') seems to have come to be used more frequently than when Kumārijīva translated what he had before him. Occurrences of the term *fang-pien* ('skilful means') have also been examined in T223 and some cases are adduced below. However T223 is a rambling and repetitive text and the usage does not importantly diverge from that of the shorter T227. In the two sutras together there is a total of about three hundred cases of the term, no mean score, and this means that there is an average of more than one case per printed page in the form in which they appear in the Taishō Tripitaka. Naturally some of the occurrences are grouped together in a particular context, and it is mainly such passages from T227 which form the basis for the discussion below.

The longer sutra is contained, by way of repetition, in a massive commentary entitled 'Treatise on the Great Perfection of Insight' (T1509, see Appendix A). This very long work is ascribed to Nāgārjuna, conceivably by a pious fiction, and it was translated by Kumārajīva between the years 403

---

[1] The main translations in question are given in the bibliography below. A completely survey of the various texts and versions is given in Conze's *The Prajñāpāramitā Literature*. *Indo-Iranian Monographs No. VI*, Mouton and Co., 'S-Gravenhage 1960. In view of the magnitude of Conze's contribution one can only diverge from his consistent terminology with hesitation and regret. Thus, 'insight' is found below where he would use 'wisdom', as also above throughout, and following Erich Frauwallner's use of 'Einsicht' in *Die Philosophie des Buddhismus*, Berlin 1956, Akademie-Verlag); 'characteristic' (相) corresponds to Conze's perhaps unnecessarily mystifying 'sign', for Skt. *nimitta* (defined in his own glossary of *The Short Prajñāpāramitā Texts*, p. 215, as '(1) Object of attention. (2) Basis of recognition of an object. (3) An occasion for being led astray by objects.', the third of these meanings being the special matter of Buddhist interpretation discussed again below); and thirdly of course while 'skill in means' is absolutely right for the Sanskrit *upāya-kauśalya* the English used below is 'skilful means' because this is thought better to express Kumārajīva's rather conflating Chinese term *fang-pien* 方便, as explained above in Chapter One.

[2] Recently published in a corrected edition: *The Perfection of Wisdom in Eight Thousand Lines and its Verse Summary*, the Four Seasons Foundation, Bolinas 1973 (ISBN 0-87704-049-4) (distributed by Book People, 2940 Seventh Street, Berkeley, California 94710). These full details are given because in the Appendix page numbers of occurrences of *upāya-kauśalya* corresponding to Kumārajīva's *fang-pien* are given to aid general orientation. It should be remembered however that the one is *not* a translation of the other.

[3] *Ibid.* pp. xi-xii. Relations between the various versions may be pursued in Lewis Lancaster's *An Analysis of the Aṣṭasāhasrikā-prajñāparamitā-sūtra from the Chinese Translations*, Diss. University of Wisconsin, 1968.

and 405.[4] This was quite a feat, as may be illustrated from the fact that even Étienne Lamotte's massive three-volume translation into French, in over 1700 pages, covers less than one third of the original.[5] As a commentary it is still drawn upon by Japanese exegetes dealing with The Perfection of Insight sutras. However since it is itself by no stretch of the imagination a popular work it has not been exhaustively examined for occurrences of the term *fang-pien*. The concept of *fang-pien* in T223 and indeed T1509 has already been discussed in a brief and useful Japanese article by F. Masuda, but the present account will be seen to diverge somewhat from his argument.[6]

If The Perfection of Insight sutras themselves had not taken *prajñā* (Ch. *po-jo*, J. *hannya*)[7] for their titles, one might almost dare to rename them 'the perfection of insight and skilful means literature', so often does one find within them that these two terms are inseparably associated. This is not just a lexicographical fortuity, but arises from the key role assigned to 'skilful means' as a necessary complement to 'insight' along the lines already observed above in The Teaching of Vimalakīrti.

Similes in Chapter XIV of the smaller sutra stress this combination as being the key characteristic of a bodhisattva who wishes not to fall to the level of mere elementary discipleship.[8] Unless he is sustained by '*prajñā-pāramitā* skilful means'[9] he will surely come to grief, like a badly fired water-jar which will not carry water, or like a neglected sea-vessel which will not safely voyage. Similarly an old man aged one hundred and twenty, who is also ill, could not walk far down the road unless he were sustained by two healthy fellows. The two turn out to be none other than perfect insight and skilful means.[10]

There are cases where the pair of qualities is brought in as a synonym for the perfection of insight alone. Thus one who perfects insight is said to surpass all the saints, from those who definitely enter the path ('stream-

---

[4] Cf. Robinson, *Early Madhyamika in India and China*, p. 76.

[5] Étienne Lamotte, (trans.) *Le Traité de la Grande Vertu de Sagesse*, 3 vols. Louvain 1944-.

[6] Details in Chapter One, note 2. Masuda begins by stressing the importance, with skilful means, of not being attached to characteristics (相), and then goes on to discuss the connection with insight, compassion and voidness.

[7] 般若 The Chinese 若 is usually transliterated *jo*, e.g. in *Hōbōgirin, Fascicule Annexe*.

[8] In Kumārajīva's version Chapter XIV actually begins with these similes, running from the middle of page 185 in the Conze translation (the middle of his Chapter 14). Reference below is always to Kumārajīva's chapters, etc.

[9] T VIII 560b 般若波羅蜜方便。

[10] T VIII 560c. This is an unusual simile, and although no gender is given (二健人) the presumption must be in this case that they are male, which suggests that at the time this text was created there was no general assumption that *prajñā and upāya* were thought of as male and female respectively. The latter idea is a late and quite secondary line of thought which does not particularly add anything apart from re-confirming the link between the two concepts. Cf. Chapter Five, note 22.

winners'[11]) to those who individually win enlightenment (*pratyekabuddhas*, referred to earlier); while at the same time 'he also surpasses bodhisattvas who practice the perfection of giving but are without *prajñā-pāramitā* and have no skilful means.'[12] The same argument is given for the remaining four perfections of a bodhisattva: proper conduct, patience, vigour and contemplation.[13] In this way skilful means shares the controlling function of insight with respect to a bodhisattva's practice. The whole passage referred to here was further elaborated in the Sanskrit text translated by Conze, with several repetitions of the key pair of 'perfect wisdom and skill in means'.[14] A little later in Kumārajīva's version skilful means is declared to be that by which a bodhisattva can avoid being reborn among 'the long-lived gods', (which may sound quite pleasant but represents continued bondage in *saṃsāra*).[15] If we ask what this skilful means is, then the answer comes that 'it arises from the perfection of insight', so that 'even though he can enter *dhyāna* he is not reborn in terms of *dhyāna*.'[16] In sum, skilful means is the crucial concomitant of insight properly understood, as a result of which the bodhisattva is able to do what he is expected to do without getting caught out by it.

Other things also depend on this pair of qualities. The bodhisattva Sadaprarudita in Chapter XXVII displays a remarkable earnestness by piercing his own arm and thigh as a preliminary to giving his present body for a sacrifice. The merit from this act will provide for him, in a future life, to be trained in perfect insight and skilful means, and following on from insight and means he anticipates attaining 'supreme perfect enlightenment, a gold-coloured body, the thirty-two marks, continuous and unlimited radiance, great compassion and great mercy, great rejoicing and great renunciation, the ten powers, the five fearlessnesses and four unobstructed knowledges, the

---

[11] 'Stream-winners' (須陀洹), the first of four classes of disciples which also include the happy terms 'once-returner' and 'never-returner', followed by *arhat*.

[12] T VIII 573a 亦勝菩薩離般若波羅蜜無方便行檀波羅蜜。

[13] T VIII 573a 亦勝離般若波羅蜜無方便行尸羅波蜜羼提波羅蜜毘梨耶波羅蜜禪波羅蜜。

[14] *Op. cit.* pp. 242-3; each perfection is spelled out separately, with its own reference to skill in means, and as the texts reconverge Conze's translation recalls once again that such a bodisattva 'surpasses also the Bodhisattvas who are not skilled in means'.

[15] T VIII 574a 須菩提。菩薩如是學者。不生長壽天。何以故。菩薩成就方便故。 'Subhūti, the bodhisattva who trains like this does not get reborn among the long-lived gods. Why? Because this bodhisattva accomplishes skilful means'.

[16] T VIII 574b, in full: 何等為方便。所謂從般若波羅蜜起。雖能入禪而不隨禪生。'What is this skilful means? It can be called that which arises from the *pāramitā* of insight; (so that) even though he can enter *dhyāna* (*ch'an*) he is not reborn in terms of *dhyāna*.' Conze's overall result for this and the immediately preceding passage varies slightly: 'For there is his skill in means, and endowed with that he does not get reborn among the long-lived Gods. But what is that skill in means of a Bodhisattva? It is just this perfection of wisdom. And he applies himself to this skill in means in such a way that, endowed with it, the Bodhisattva enters into the trances without being reborn through the influence of the trances.' *Op. cit.* p. 250. In Kumārajīva's version skilful means is to be conceived of in terms of the perfection of insight but is not absolutely identified with it, as in the above.

eighteen uniquely attained dharmas, six supernormal powers, etc. etc.'[17] This
list includes attributes of an advanced bodhisattva, and also characteristics
of a 'great man' (Skt. *mahāpuruṣa*), that is, of a buddha, namely the gold-
coloured body, the thirty-two marks and unlimited radiance. This body of
blissful, compelling radiance, later organised under the much misunderstood
'three-body' doctrine, arises out of a bodhisattva's paradoxical combination
of attainment and non-departure, based on insight and means.[18]

It is beyond argument that insight and skilful means are most intimately
related, and this is stressed by Masuda Hideo in the article referred to earlier.
He also argued however for a similarly close connection between skilful means
and 'compassion', and it must be observed that this latter link is less evident
if the matter is pursued strictly, for the term 'compassion' does not itself
appear in any of the five quotations which he then adduced.[19] There are
indeed passages *expressive* of compassion, such as 'By the power of his skilful
means he proclaims the Dharma and he releases living beings by the teaching
of the three vehicles . . . by his power of skilful means he severs the attach-

---

[17] T VIII 582b-c 是人當爲我說般若波羅蜜方便力。我隨中學當得阿耨多羅三藐三菩提。
金色之身三十二相。常光無量光。大慈大悲大喜大捨。十力四無所畏四無礙智十八不共
法。六神通... 'This man', who will do the exposition of insight and skilful means, is
another bodhisattva named Dharmodgata. For the whole story, cf. Conze, *op. cit.* pp. 277ff
at length.

[18] Probably the main cause of widespread misunderstanding comes from Chapter X of D. T.
Suzuki's book *Outlines of Mahayana Buddhism*, which is one of the most widely used sources
of general knowledge about Mahayana Buddhism. Although this was first published in 1907,
it was republished in 1963 with a commendatory essay by Alan Watts who alas missed a great
opportunity to put it into historical perspective and to guide the unwary. Chapter X, 'The
Doctrine of Trikaya', suffers from two major defects. The first defect is an inordinate desire to
make use of Christian terminology, e.g. in the sub-title '(Buddhist Theory of Trinity)', while
overlooking that the Christian doctrine of Trinity arose as an attempt to deal with ontological
problems, about God in his relation to the world, the two natures coinhering in the person of
Christ, etc. The second defect is that the whole account is based on the assumption that it was
Aśvaghoṣa who first recorded the *trikāya* doctrine on the basis of existing Mahayana tradition
as early as the first century before Christ. In fact The Awakening of Faith in the Mahayana
(*Ta-ch'eng ch'i-hsin lun*, J. *Daijōkishinron* 大乘起信論 T1666, in T XXXII) was almost
certainly erroneously ascribed to Aśvaghoṣa, and indeed cannot be dated in any way prior to
AD 550, the year of the first Chinese 'translation'. On the general position see Y. S. Hakeda's
The Awakening of Faith, New York and London 1967, pp. 3ff. The first documented statement
of the *trikāya* doctrine as usually formulated (*dharmakāya, samboghakāya, nirmāṇakāya*) is to
be found in the fifth century AD in Asanga's *Mahāyānasūtrālaṅkāra*, then also in the
Suvarṇaprabhāsottama-sūtra, see J. Nobel's 2 volume edition and translation by that title,
(Chapter III in Chinese, but not extant in Sanskrit). Of course the whole concept is based on
various anticipations which do go back further in Mahayana and indeed Buddhist thought
generally, the most obvious one being the three-fold formulation in The Laṅkāvatāra Sutra
(giving *dharmatā-buddha, vipāka-buddha*, (or *niṣyanda-buddha*) and *nirmāṇa-buddha*), discussed in detail by Suzuki in *Studies in the Lankavatara Sutra* (1930), pp. 308ff.

[19] Masuda, *op. cit.*, p. 114a. In conclusion he writes (p. 114b); 'As shown above the word
fang-pien 方便 is used in the Prajñā Sutra 般若經 in a manner which links it both with the
view of emptiness 空觀 (great insight 大智) and with great compassion 大悲, or rather the
word *fang-pien* itself is used to bear the meanings both of the view of emptiness and of great
compassion . . .'

ments of living beings and peacefully establishes them.'[20] We are left therefore with the rather general point that 'skilful means' is used with respect to
the work of saving and converting others and this is linked with the idea of
'great compassion'. The connection does not seem to be a close phraseological
one such as is found in dozens of cases for skilful means and insight.[21] Masuda
brings in the idea of compassion so that he can go on to argue that 'skilful
means' has two meanings, one representing the movement from the ordinary
world to 'true voidness' or 'true suchness',[22] and the other the movement
from suchness to living beings, for their salvation. This is indeed a convenient
way of beginning to talk about skilful means and one which is often found in
brief explanations. Fortunately Masuda goes on to say that these two are to
be conceived in a unitary way. His best illustration is from The Treatise on
the Perfection of Insight: 'Skilful means is to see that there are ultimately no
dharmas and no living beings, while saving living beings.'[23] He also adduces
a passage in this context which does bring in the idea of compassion explicitly:
'Skilful means involves knowing that all dharmas are void because of.
thoroughly completing the perfection of insight, and taking pity on living
beings because of great compassion. By the power of skilful means no deep
attachment arises with respect to these two dharmas. Even though he knows
that all dharmas are void, because of the power of skilful means he does not
abandon living beings. Even though he does not abandon living beings he
knows that all dharmas are in reality void.'[24] The terminology seems to
overlap somewhat but that is because the argument moves forward. At first
the paired dharmas are voidness and compassion, and skilful means is the key
to their correlation without attachment to either. Then the focus of attention
shifts precisely to the combining role of skilful means. Skilful means is
therefore not just a synonym for a compassionate attitude towards the living.
It refers rather to ability, or adeptness, in operating contradictory lines of
thought on the basis of a unified intention. Although dharmas are void the
bodhisattva does not abandon the living, and although he does not abandon
the living he knows that dharmas are void.

[20] *Ibid.* p. 114a (T VIII 280c) 以方便力而爲說法，以三乘法度脫衆生。…以方便力斷
衆生愛結安立衆生。The term 'compassion' (大慈大悲 i.e. 'great mercy and great compassion')
does in fact appear in a further passage which he quotes from the Treatise on the Great
Perfection of Insight, but it is not closely associated with *fang-pien*.

[21] Perhaps Masuda shows slight unease himself in the expressions he uses: 'that is, linked
with the standpoint of compassion' (*ibid.* p. 114a) and 'none other than compassion' (*ibid.*
p. 115a). His claim that the link between skilful means and both insight and compassion have
been demonstrated in terms of the etymology of the Sanskrit term *upāya* also seems to be
unwarranted in terms of what is adduced. To bring in the root *upa/i* and to speak of *upāya*
as bearing the meaning of 'to approach' or 'to arrive' may contribute to our background
understanding in a very, very general sense, but it scarcely demands the doctrinal pattern
which follows. Cf. also Chapter One above, page 12 and note 25.

[22] *Ibid.* p. 115a. 眞空 and 眞如.

[23] *Ibid.* p. 115a (T XXV 697c) 方便者畢竟無法亦無衆生而度衆生。

[24] *Ibid.* p. 115a-b (T XXV 262c) 方便者具足般若波羅蜜故知諸法空、大悲心故憐愍衆
生。於是二法以方便力不生染著。雖知諸法空方便力故亦不捨衆生。雖不捨衆生亦知諸
法實空。

This stress on the close association of insight and skilful means is of great importance over against popular conceptions of the idea as being one of mere expediency, as Masuda and other Japanese exegetes point out (cf. also Chapter Eight below). Nor would it be right to argue simplistically that the sutras now being considered have some kind of pure interest in insight or 'wisdom' for the specialised adept, while others such as The Lotus Sutra deal with the popular expedients of Mahayana Buddhism. For one thing, as has been seen earlier, The Lotus Sutra has a deeply unsettling effect on the central concepts of Buddhism, an effect brought about entirely because of the concepts of voidness and skilful means. The Perfection of Insight sutras on the other hand precisely do not allow individualistic navel-watching. The bodhisattva *must* use his skilful means to face both ways at once, and he must not get entangled in a particularist attention to insight or voidness as if it were something different from everything else. Indeed his power of skilful means is what enables him to recognise, unfalteringly, the simple equality of voidness and the existence and needs of living beings.

Skilful means as a way of taking things

These assertions do not in themselves explain in what way skilful means helps to keep a bodhisattva upright in his path. For that one must look more closely at the argument of the sutra. Above all the point is that by his power of skilful means a bodhisattva is able to avoid making the mistake of 'practising in characteristics'[25] or signs. This matter arises in the first chapter of the smaller sutra (T227) and though it may sound cryptic it is one of the subjects most frequently discussed when the term 'skilful means' is used.

The matter may be introduced by reference to the five constituents of empirical individuals, the first of which is form. 'If a bodhisattva practises in terms of form he is practising with respect to a characteristic of things. If he practises in terms of the arising of form he is practising with respect to a characteristic. If he practises in terms of the cessation of form he is practising with respect to a characteristic. If he practises in terms of the abandonment of form he is practising with respect to a characteristic. If he practises in terms of the emptiness of form he is practising with respect to a characteristic. If he thinks "I am performing this practice" then this "practising" is a characteristic.'[26] The same reasoning is then applied to the other four constituents, up to consciousness. It will be observed that reference is made to 'arising' and 'cessation', which are perhaps the two most fundamental

[25] Or as Conze says, *op. cit.* p. 86, etc., 'coursing in signs'. 行 means to 'go' or 'course', but above all, in religion, to 'practice', that is, to practice that review of the nature of existence which plays a role in Buddhist meditation. 相 translates both *lakṣana* and *nimitta*, here the latter, and may be taken to refer to the differentiated characteristics of the phenomena which we experience, by which we recognise them. Cf. note 1 above.

[26] T VIII 538a 菩薩若行色行爲行相。若生色行爲行相。若滅色行爲行相。若壞色行爲 行相。若空色行爲行相。我行是行亦是行相。The printed text has 壞 'ruination', but two Sung editions have 離 'abandonment' which makes better sense.

categories in terms of which Buddhists understand the phenomenal world, then to 'abandonment' which is the spiritual value most evidently counter-balancing the problem of 'attachment', then to 'emptiness' which is the most famous badge of perfection of insight thinking, and then to the very thought of one's practising a practice at all. Finally the matter is related to *prajñā-pāramitā* and skilful means: 'If he has the idea that one who practises like this is practising *prajñā-pāramitā*, then this practising is at the level of characteristics. One should know this bodhisattva to be one not yet well acquainted with skilful means.'[27]

The meaning of this is that the Buddhist analysis of experience into its various factors is all very well, but that the spiritual discipline of internalising this analysis, of making it one's own, can alas go quite astray. The mistake is to get stuck in a perpetual review of the various characteristics of experience, even including the difficult and necessary ones such as voidness. Self-consciously rehearsing these is simply to walk about on the surface of the matter. It might seem important to maintain most carefully ideas like the five constituents of individual experience (Skt. *skandhas*) in order to ward off the thought of a permanent soul, and then indeed to entertain the idea of the voidness of these five constituents, from form to consciousness, as announced most famously in The Heart Sutra. What is required above all however is to make use of some such account of things while not settling in it, not striving to maintain it and not rehearsing it. Even emptiness can come to be taken as a 'characteristic'. What is required is that the bodhisattva knows the emp-tiness of form while contemporaneously freeing himself from the concept which induces this knowledge. This demands the application of skilful means. That is to say, truly practising the perfection of insight demands knowing characteristics as means. Otherwise, however systematically they are pur-sued, the practising remains at the level of mere characteristics without turning them to spiritual advantage.

The same principle is expounded with respect to merit, for the correct transformation of merit into full enlightenment requires both the recognition of a pattern of merit and freedom from seeing it in terms of characteristics. It requires in fact the combination known as '*prajñā-pāramitā*—skilful means'.[28] The argument is rather spread out, but in summary it means that merit is no longer to be weighed in terms of the particular actions which originally seemed to be its justification. All meritorious actions are, so to speak, equidistant from enlightenment. When this recognition is internalised through the practice of insight and skilful means it is termed 'the great transformation', thus: 'This transformation achieved by a bodhisattva is called the great transformation; because of skilful means it outweighs the

---

[27] T VIII 538a. 若作是念。能如是行者。是行般若波羅蜜。亦是行相。當知是菩薩未善知方便。

[28] Cf. T VIII 548b, where the phrase occurs three times, *prajñā-pāramitā* being trans-literated, followed by *fang-pien* to make one more or less unified concept (般若波羅蜜方便).

merit which can be achieved by a bodhisattva's cultivation of giving (i.e. the first perfection); why? because this transformation achieved by a bodhisattva is what is ensured by *prajñā-pāramitā*.'[29]

All the works of a bodhisattva are to be seen in this same light. The disciple Subhūti points out that if a bodhisattva increases or decreases in the perfections (the six *pāramitās*) he cannot approach supreme enlightenment because he would be thinking in discriminative terms. 'Quite so', replies the Buddha, 'For that which is beyond words there is no increase or decrease. When a bodhisattva who is well versed in skilful means practises the perfection of insight and disciplines himself in the perfection of insight, he does not ask himself whether he is increasing in the perfection of giving or decreasing in it, but thinks "This perfection of giving is but a name".'[30] This applies to the other perfections as well, even including the sixth perfection itself, which has a controlling function with respect to the others. The bodhisattva does not consider whether or not he is increasing in the perfection of insight, for this would be to depend upon its *name* and hence to fall short of it. Rather, if he is skilled in means, he practises it while at the same time recognising its status as mere nomenclature.[31] Thus skilful means is the ability to maintain a correct view of the status and role of religious language.

This is not to be understood as a kind of spiritual farewell, however, for 'The bodhisattva does not learn it by thinking, "I will practice the bodhisattva way and break off all discriminations in this present life". If he breaks off all these discriminations and does not yet entirely attain the buddha way, he will relapse into elementary discipleship. Your reverence! A bodhisattva's great power of skilful means lies in knowing all these discriminated characteristics while not being attached to non-discrimination.'[32]

Continued immersion in the world is the link between the ideal bodhisattva portrayed in these sutras and the picture given in The Lotus Sutra and The Teaching of Vimalakīrti. Sometimes it might seem, as above, that it is his own spiritual welfare which is at stake, and so in a sense it is. It is essential that the bodhisattva is neither trapped nor departs. He enters *ch'an* (Skt. *dhyāna*, J. *zen*) in such a way that he does not get himself reborn in accordance with this practice.[33] That is, he has to practise *ch'an* with skilful means in order not to get reborn among the 'long-lived gods'.[34]

More centrally stated, however, the bodhisattva practises the perfection of insight and sees all the factors of existence as they really are, but without

[29] T VIII 549a 是菩薩迴向名爲大迴向。以方便故。勝於有所得菩薩布施福德。何以故。是菩薩迴向爲般若波羅蜜所護故。For the extended argument cf. Conze, *op. cit.* pp. 127ff. His excellent term 'transformation' is followed here for: 迴向 (= Skt. *pariṇāmanā*) often thought of rather pedestrianly as a more or less calculated transfer of merit to others.

[30] T VIII 567a 如是如是。須菩提。不可說義無增無減。善知方便菩薩行般若波羅蜜修般若波羅蜜時。不作是念。檀波羅蜜若增若減。作是念。是檀波羅蜜但有名字。

[31] T XVIII 567a, as preceding with 般若 for 檀.

[32] T VIII 567b 是菩薩不如是學。我行菩薩道於是身斷諸相。若斷是諸相未具足佛道。當作聲聞。世尊。是菩薩大方便力。知是諸相過而取無相。(Subhūti is speaking).

[33] T VIII 574b 雖能入禪而不隨禪生。

[34] T VIII 574a 菩薩如是學者。不生長壽天。何以故。菩薩成就方便故。

seizing upon this realisation or attainment.[35] The Buddha continues to Subhūti: 'Because this bodhisattva does not abandon the multitude of living beings, he thus conceives his great vow. Subhūti, if the bodhisattva resolves not to abandon the multitude of living beings but to deliver them, entering the gate of deliverance of the *samādhi* of voidness, and the gates of deliverance of the *samādhi* of non-discrimination and non-action, then the bodhisattva will refrain from realising true reality in mid-course. Why? Because the bodhisattva is one who is maintained by skilful means.'[36] The style may be a little repetitive, even liturgical, but this is a clear expression of the ideal bodhisattva. He enters the three 'gates of deliverance' while refusing to leave the multitude of beings behind him. The paradox lies in recognising the voidness of all things, not taking them to be marked out by characterisation or subject to the workings of karma, while at the same time resolving to bring the multitude of living beings through with him. The piece continues: 'Furthermore, Subhūti, if a bodhisattva desires to enter those deep contemplations, that is, the gate of deliverance of the *samādhi* of voidness and the gates of deliverance of the *samādhi* of non-discrimination and non-action, then the bodhisattva should first think as follows. All living beings have for long been attached to the characteristic of being living beings. They are attached to the idea that there is some existence that they get. When I attain supreme perfect enlightenment I will sever all these views by proclaiming Dharma; and thus I enter the gate of deliverance of the *samādhi* of voidness. Because this bodhisattva is so minded and has prior power of skilful means he does not realise true reality in mid-course, and he does not lose the *samādhi* of merciful compassion, rejoicing and detachment. Why? Because this bodhisattva is accomplished in the power of skilful means.'[37] This theme

---

[35] T VIII 569a 能如是學亦不取證。'He can learn like this and not seize upon realisation.'

[36] T VIII 569a 是菩薩不捨一切衆生故。發如是大願。須菩提。若菩薩生如是心。我不應捨一切衆生。應當度之即入空三昧解脫門無相無作三昧解脫門。是時菩薩不中道證實際。何以故。是菩薩爲方便所護故。Non-discrimination: i.e. not attending to things as having characteristics—literally, the *samādhi* of (things) not (having) characteristics (無相). For the whole passage, cf. Conze, *op. cit.*, p. 225: 'For the Bodhisattva has not abandoned all beings. He has made the special vows to set free all those beings. If the mind of a Bodhisattva forms the aspiration not to abandon all beings but to set them free, and if in addition he aspires for the concentration on emptiness, the Signless, the Wishless, i.e. for the three doors to deliverance, then that Bodhisattva should be known as one who is endowed with skill in means, and he will not realise the reality-limit midway, before his Buddha-dharmas have become complete. For it is this skill in means which protects him.' Conze refers to the standard gates of deliverance, the third of which ('The Wishless') is also known in Chinese as 無願, but Kumārajīva's text is different here.

[37] T VIII 569a-b 復次須菩提。菩薩若欲入如是深定。所謂空三昧解脫門。無相無作三昧解脫門。是菩薩先應作是念。衆生長夜著衆生相。著有所得。我得阿耨多羅三藐三菩提。當斷是諸見而爲說法。即入空三昧解脫門。是菩薩以是心及先方便力故。不中道證實際。亦不失慈悲喜捨三昧。何以故。是菩薩成就方便力故。It may be observed that although the expression used here is 方便力 rather than just 方便 it does not really make any difference to the basic line of thought beyond just adding the association that skilful means is a 'power'. With or without the 'power' it is skilful means which a bodhisattva has at his disposal to determine correct practice. Passages such as these reinforce the conviction

is repeated with the variation that the multitude of living beings have long been exercising themselves with the characteristic of selfhood.[38] From these passages it may be seen that it is not so much a question of a bodhisattva 'postponing' his attainment of nirvana in the sense of spending extra time in the miscellaneous service of others before proceeding further. The text articulates the matter graphically in saying that he does not realise his goal 'in mid-course', but this image must be rightly understood. Drawing the sentences a little more closely together one might say that it is even while not relinquishing the living that he recognises the voidness of things. The bodhisattva does not exactly give up his nirvana. He steels himself not to aim for it, as it were, prematurely, as if he could attain it satisfactorily all by himself. When his shot drives home it bears with it the deliverance of all. Skilful means is the right judgement which makes this possible.

Mādhyamika connections

The Perfection of Insight literature has a natural outgrowth in a series of treatises associated with the Mādhyamika school of Nāgārjuna and others.

The Treatise on The Great Perfection of Insight (T1509) has already been referred to because it is a commentary on the sutra. Three other treatises, all translated by Kumārajīva, form the textual basis for the Three Treatise School (Ch. San-lun-tsung, J. Sanron-shū). These are:

The Middle Treatise (T1564),
The Twelve Topic Treatise (T1568),
and The Hundred Treatise (T1569), (see Appendix A for details).

Of the three the most important is The Middle Treatise, for the simple reason that it contains the famous verses of Nāgārjuna. In this respect The Middle Treatise is parallel to the seventh century commentary by Candrakīrti in Sanskrit (the Prasannapadā), which contains substantially the same verses.[39] The Middle Treatise is therefore a basic source for the thought in terms of which Nāgārjuna, as a historical person, is defined.[40] It is also important for Kumārajīva, who thought of himself as carrying on the Mādhyamika tradition.

It must be admitted forthwith that there is only one occurrence of the term *fang-pien* in The Middle Treatise, and that by contrast with the sutras considered above this represents a very low average in a text which runs to thirty-nine printed pages in the printed Chinese Tripitaka. The single occurrence is not even in the verses themselves but in the commentary. It therefore offers no evidence that Nāgārjuna personally used the term. On the

that *fang-pien* for Kumārajīva includes by implication all of '(power of) (skill in) means', which can fairly be conflated to 'skilful (operation of) means' or just 'skilful means'.

[38] T VIII 569b.

[39] Cf. Robinson's discussion in *Early Madhyamika in India and China* pp. 30ff. The small variations do not affect the substance.

[40] Cf. *ibid.* pp. 39ff.

other hand the passage in question brings out very clearly the relationship between the idea of skilful means and Mādhyamika method.

The question put is: 'If the buddhas proclaim neither self nor non-self, if all mental activity goes into extinction, if the route of expression in words is closed, how do they get people to know the true nature of all dharmas?'[41] The answer runs: 'The buddhas have the power of countless skilful means, and the dharmas are indeterminate in nature; so to bring nearer all the living beings, the buddhas sometimes declare the reality of all things and sometimes their unreality, sometimes that things are both real and unreal, and sometimes that they are neither real nor unreal.'[42] Each of these four logical possibilities is considered to be wrong in itself, yet depending on the occasion each one may provide a provisionally true basis for the teaching of release.

Preceding sentences refer in a similarly ambivalent fashion to the teaching of 'self' and 'non-self'. The teaching of non-self is advanced to bring down the determinate view of self, while if a determinate view of non-self were held, the declaration of self would be made to unfix it. A bodhisattva intending to practice perfect insight fails to do so if he asserts the existence of self *and* he fails to do so if he asserts non-self.[43] Thus each of these alternative teachings has a role which is eventually to be superseded. Each is to be maintained by the bodhisattva, as it is by all buddhas, in a manner skilfully adapted to the needs of living beings, yet which betrays no trace of mental clinging. There is an interesting parallel to this in The Lankavatara Sutra, where the teaching of the *tathāgata-garbha*, the 'tathāgata-womb', is described as a skilful means devised because of the way in which the teaching of non-self is liable to be mistakenly received.[44]

It will be seen readily by those familiar with the Mādhyamika method that the role of any of the possible declarations about 'self' or about the 'reality' of things, selected by the buddhas through their power of skilful means, is quite analogous to the role of 'provisional' truth as contrasted with 'absolute' truth. This latter distinction is known within Nāgārjuna's verses themselves, and indeed his use of that distinction may explain why he did not use the term 'skilful means'. The parallelism of thought may be allowed to appear for itself by a brief quotation from the verses of Chapter XXIV in The Middle Treatise.

(8) 'The buddhas depend on two truths
When they proclaim the Dharma for living beings.
Firstly they depend upon worldly truth
And secondly upon the truth of the supreme principle.

[41] T XXX 25a 若佛不說我非我。諸心行滅。言語道斷者。云何令人知諸法實相。
[42] T XXX 25a 諸佛無量力便力。諸法無決定相。爲度衆生或說一切實。或說一切不實。或說一切實不實。或說一切非實非不實。
[43] T XXX 24c 如般若中說菩薩有我亦非行。無我亦非行。
[44] Cf. D. T. Suzuki, *The Lankavatara Sutra*, p. 69. 'No, Mahāmati, my Tathāgata-garbha is not the same as the ego taught by the philosophers; for what the Tathāgatas teach is the Tathāgata-garbha in the sense, Mahāmati, that it is emptiness, reality-limit, Nirvana, being unborn, unqualified, and devoid of will-effort; the reason why the Tathāgatas who are Arhats

(9)   If a person is not able to know
       The distinction between the two truths,
       Then he cannot know the principle of true reality
       In accordance with the profound Buddha-Dharma.

(10)   If he does not depend upon worldly truth
       He cannot attain the supreme principle.
       If he does not attain the supreme principle
       Then he does not attain nirvana.'[45]

This whole section of the verses is on the subject of the status of the four noble truths of Buddhism, and is a response to the 'Hinayana' criticism that Mahayana Buddhism undermines the 'real' importance of the Buddha, the Dharma and the Sangha.[46] Nāgārjuna's reply, apart from criticising the Hinayana position for inherent weaknesses, is to explain the Mahayana view of the nature of Buddhist method. In a sense it *does* undermine concepts such as Buddha, Dharma, Sangha, and the four noble truths, if by this is meant that these are not themselves to be thought of as absolutes, immovables, or eternally existents. Positively however these items of Buddhist doctrine all have a provisional role at the worldly level. It would be quite wrong to think that they are not required, because it is only on the basis of discriminated knowledge that 'the supreme principle' can be conveyed. The dialectic is exactly similar to that between the three 'discriminated' vehicles and the one vehicle or the undivided Dharma, which is explained in The Lotus Sutra. The only difference is that in the latter case it is explained in terms of skilful means. It therefore seems possible to claim a harmony of approach or understanding between the Mādhyamika text and the sutras considered earlier, so that it would be correct to assume an implicit acceptance of 'skilful means thought'.

Of the other two works linked with the Three Treatise School, The Twelve Topic Treatise, which is based on The Middle Treatise, is not particularly important in Japanese Buddhism, nor, according to Robinson, was it much quoted by Chinese writers.[47] It contains three incidental instances of the term

and Fully-enlightened Ones, teach the doctrine pointing to the Tathāgata-garbha is to make the ignorant cast aside their fear when they listen to the teaching of egolessness and to have them realise the state of non-discrimination and imagelessness. I also wish, Mahāmati, that the Tathāgatas preach the egolessness of things which removes all the traces of discrimination by various skilful means issuing from their transcendental wisdom, that is, sometimes by the doctrine of the Tathāgata-garbha, sometimes by that of egolessness, and like a potter, by means of various terms, expressions and synonyms.' Note also the reappearance here of the simile of the potter found in Chapter 5 of The Lotus Sutra, (Sanskrit only), c.f. Chapter Three above.

[45] T XXX 32c-33a (8)諸佛依二諦　爲衆生說法　一以世俗諦　二第一義諦　(9)若人不能知　分別於二諦　則於深佛法　不知眞實義　(10)若不依俗諦　不得第一義　不得第一義　則不得涅槃

[46] For the general context cf. Jacques May (*trans.*) *Candrakīrti: Prasanna-padā Madhyamakavṛtti, Douze chapitres traduits du sanscrit et du tibétain*, Paris, 1959, *ad loc.*

[47] *Op. cit.* p. 33. This in spite of Seng-jui's judgement that it was 'concise and to the point', *ibid*, p. 28.

fang-pien which are listed in the Appendix.

Of greater importance is The Hundred Treatise which Kumārajīva translated twice (in 402 and 404) and which he is said to have studied and recited particularly frequently.[48] The work consists of ten chapters commenting on verses by Āryadeva, the follower of Nāgārjuna. It contains several instances of the term *fang-pien*, including one within the verses themselves.

As early as the first chapter, on 'Dispensing with sin and happiness' there is an interesting point made with respect to what is 'auspicious' and what is 'inauspicious'.[49] Concern with what is auspicious and what is not is severely attacked as heretical. It is only 'foolish people without skilful means', who go about saying that one thing is auspicious and another not.[50] The reason for it is that they desire pleasure. Thus skilful means is identified here with the ability to be detached from whether things turn out gratifyingly or not.

The distinction between blessedness and evil is itself a problem which has to be dealt with. 'Evil can be got rid of by blessedness, but how can blessedness be got rid of?' says the commentary,[51] to which the perhaps rather cryptic answer is 'Marklessness is the supreme.'[52] Fortunately there is an explanation. 'Those who seek happiness will be born in the heavens, while those who seek evil will be born in the hells. That is why non-discriminative insight is the supreme.'[53] Although being born in the heavens might seem preferable to being born in the hells, neither represents the goal. The explanation continues: 'Marklessness means not calling to mind all the characteristics of things. It frees us from all grasping, so our minds are not attached to factors of the past, the future or the present.'[54] This is the standard Mahayana or Madhyamika form, or rather critique, of dharma-theory, 'factors' here being dharmas.[55] The argument continues: 'Because all dharmas have no own-being, there is nothing on which they depend, and this is called marklessness. Because of this skilful means it is possible to discard happiness.'[56] In this way the insight into marklessness, into the nature of dharmas as being without any permanent characteristic of existence upon which they depend, is itself identified as the skilful means which leads to release.

The other passage of interest comes in Chapter IX, entitled 'Against

---

[48] *Ibid*, p. 34.

[49] T XXX 168c 吉不吉。

[50] T XXX 168c 汝愚人無方便。強欲求樂。妄生憶想。言是事吉。是事不吉。

[51] T XXX 170c 依福捨惡。依何捨福。

[52] T XXX 170c 無相最上。Marklessness means not having characteristics, as earlier, but the briefer term is kept to maintain the pungency.

[53] T XXX 170c 取福人天中生。取罪三惡道生。是故無相智慧最第一。Non-discriminative is used for 無相 here when it qualifies insight. Cf. note 25 above. Since the word is used with a variety of functions it is difficult to translate with a single terminology.

[54] T XXX 170c 無相名一切相不憶念。離一切受。過去未來現在法心無所著。 Or: 'Not-having characteristics means not calling to mind all the characteristics of things . . .'

[55] Cf. the explanations given in the context of Vimalakīrti's encounter with Mañjuśrī in Chapter Five, above.

[56] T XXX 170c 一切法自性無故。則無所依。是名無相。以是方便故能捨福。

Permanence'.[57] The line of Aryadeva reads, 'That which functions can be described in terms of: bondage, those who can be bound, and skilful means.'[58] The commentary goes on: 'Bondage refers to the passions and karma, those who can be bound refers to the living beings, and skilful means refers to the holy eightfold path. If the path is maintained and bondage is expounded, the living beings obtain release. Granted nirvana, there is nothing further to these three things which would (still) function. Or again, if there are no passions it means that there is nothing to which existence is attached. If there is no basis of existence a cause is not generated.'[59] The dialogue partner then compares nirvana to non-being, but the exposition continues: 'Where these three, bondage, those who can be bound, and skilful means, are absent, that is called nirvana.'[60] Thus 'nirvana' is the name given to the redundancy of the three functioning factors which all belong together. The main point of present interest is that in so far as the eightfold path is defined as a skilful means, much of the Buddhist religion is in principle so treated, for the eightfold path can be taken more or less as a summary at least of the disciplined structure of Buddhism as a practical working religion. It is the operation of the skilful means, that is, the eightfold path, with respect to 'bondage and those who can be bound', which brings about the resolution of all three factors in nirvana. Given that, there are no other karmic factors which carry on operating. It has already been seen earlier that central Buddhist concepts and practices are to be seen as skilful means. Now we find once again that Buddhism as a working system, 'that which functions', is entirely related to its problem, and does not claim any persistence or even any non-being beyond the solution of this problem. That is what is meant by describing the eightfold path, or as by now we might presume to say, Buddhism, as a skilful means.

From the examination of these cases we may conclude that although the number of occurrences in the treatises is relatively low, the idea of 'skilful means' found in them is consistent with that of the sutras considered earlier. It is also consistent with the general mode of thinking characteristic of the treatises themselves.

This is an appropriate point at which to raise, if perhaps not to solve, a problem which has ramifications beyond the scope of the present study. This question is whether the concept of skilful means can be considered entirely as an aspect of a religious *method*, or whether it is so closely associated with the

---

[57] T XXX 17b 破常品 or perhaps 'Permanence exposed' (i.e. for what it is, namely, an illusion). Robinson inexplicably ignores the 破 in this and other cases, *op. cit.* p. 33.

[58] T XXX 180c 縛可縛方便異此無用。

[59] T XXX 180c 縛名煩惱及業。可縛名衆生。方便名八聖道。以道解縛故。衆生得解脫。若有涅槃。異此三法。則無所用。復次無煩惱。是名無所有。無所有不應爲因。

[60] T XXX 180c 若縛可縛方便三事無處。是名涅槃。This sentence in the commentary seems to be a subtle qualification of the interlocutor's close association of nirvana and non-being (無). The point would be that when the eight-fold path (the skilful means) has led to the release of those who are bound, there is nothing further which requires or is patent of discussion; one may therefore call it nirvana.

concepts of insight and emptiness that it has material implications about the way the world is.

The question may seem simple but it is complicated by the fact that the Mādhyamika School in a general way places a high value upon its own method, while at the same time it is only concerned negatively or critically about the way the world is. In a certain sense it has to be admitted that the Mādhyamikas do not advance a position about the nature of the world, for not to admit this at all would be arbitrarily to misconstrue their account of themselves. On the other hand it would seem that not everything has yet been said about their manner of not advancing a position, for it is possible both not to advance a position and not to be a Mahayanist or a Mādhyamika. Is there perhaps some way of taking seriously their non-advancement of a position while at the same time indicating how their mode of going about these matters has definite significance? Could there possibly be something about the way things are, which, if different, would have some effect on the way in which the Mādhyamikas go about them? To put it another way, granted that they are concerned above all with a certain manner of taking things, is it possible to conceive of anything about the way things are which would make it evidently more appropriate for them to take things differently? Their way of taking things is after all not everybody's way of taking things, and it does have something to do with the way in which they understand the nature of experience. As a general question this matter must be left herewith on the table. The present enquiry does not depend upon its solution.

With respect to the more specific question about skilful means it would be convenient if one could conclude that Mahayana Buddhism in general and Mādhyamika method in particular have no implications whatever about the way the world is. It would then follow that the concept of skilful means itself is not at all entangled in any such implications. However it does not seem to be settled beyond further discussion that Mahayana Buddhism and Mādhyamika method, positionless though they may be in an important sense, do in fact have no such implications. A short cut along those lines seems to be unacceptable at present.

The problem can also be approached in a different way, namely by distinguishing between the analysis and characterisation of experience in terms of dharmas, voidness, etc. as these are explicitly carried out in Buddhism, and discussion or exhortation about the nature of such analyses and concepts. If we look at the matter in this way it seems fair to maintain that 'skilful means' is about the nature and role of religious language. In other words 'skilful means' is a kind of clue about the appropriate way to put into operation the religion which one has, that is, in the case of the Mahayanists, Buddhism. Given the detailed exposition made above it seems right on balance to say that this is mainly what the idea is about. It enables one to pursue the Buddhist analyses in the right place and time, and in the right way. It stops one getting the perfection of insight wrong.

7 SKILFUL MEANS IN PRE-MAHAYANA BUDDHISM

The decision to proclaim Dhamma

If the concept of skilful means is of such central importance in early Mahayana Buddhism the question inevitably arises as to what role it played in early Buddhism or even in the teaching of the Buddha himself. As far as the latter is concerned it must be stated forthwith that there is no evidence whatever that the Buddha himself ever used the terminology of skilful means. On the other hand, it is very difficult to make any definite statement in any case about what the Buddha taught in person and what belongs to later explication and schematisation. Even if there were more information than is in fact available about the pedigree of the terms 'means' and 'skill in means' it would probably still remain a matter of judgement as to whether the idea should be associated with the person of the Buddha or not. The fact of the matter is that we cannot say that the Buddha himself used these terms, while at the same time the terms themselves say something about the nature of his teaching which it would be very difficult to dissociate from the initiator of the Buddhist tradition.

Historically speaking the precise point of emergence of skilful means terminology must lie in the impenetrable mists of textual studies in the Buddhist Hybrid Sanskrit sutras with their early Chinese versions. In what has preceded, the Chinese versions have been used as more or less coherent unities. No attempt will now be made to unravel the process by which the Sanskrit originals were originally compiled. Even if it could be shown, for example, that there were some portions of some texts in which the terminology were less important and that these portions were particularly early, it would not really change very much. The general situation would still be that the idea of skilful means, as presented above, was widely current in the early stages of the Mahayana. As far as the history of religious ideas is concerned this leaves the general question as to how this idea is to be related to pre-Mahayana Buddhism in general. Questions of early and late are complex, and though the Pali Canon of the Theravadins does not necessarily have a special claim to hoary doctrinal purity it does provide a developed and rounded alternative tradition reaching back to Buddhist origins. Above all therefore, how does the Mahayana concept of skilful means relate to the Buddhism represented by the Pali Canon of the Theravadins?

It is immediately striking that the term skill in means occurs only rarely in the Pali Canon, and then incidentally or in late texts. This means that it is not possible to develop a history of the idea on the basis of terminological details.[1]

[1] Cf. F. L. Woodward *et al. Pali Tipitakam Concordance*, 1952ff, Pali Text Society, *ad loc.*,

Typical of the general situation is that there is only one case in the whole of the *Dīgha Nikāya*. Even that one case is found in the *Sangīti Suttanta* which is scarcely of central importance within the *Dīgha Nikāya*, for it is simply a recital of lists of doctrinal concepts arranged on the principle of their numerical order, as in the *Anguttara Nikāya*. Among the 'threes' we find 'three kinds of skill: skill in progress, skill in regress, and skill in means'.[2] These terms may be presumed to be technical in the sense that all such itemised terms are more or less technical, but they remain undeveloped as concepts. A similar case is found in the *Anguttara Nikāya*. Here the same three terms are in use when in Hare's translation we read of a monk who 'is unskilled in entering, in leaving, in approach'. Any such monk who also 'has no wish to attain unattained skill in Dhamma, preserves not his skill attained, nor stirs to persevere . . . cannot attain unattained skill in Dhamma, nor increase his skill therein.'[3] The converse is then also given, so that one who is skilled can attain. Hare's 'skill . . . in approach' is *upāyakusalo* (=Skt. *upāyakauśalya*), so we perceive that while Rhys Davids stressed the integrity of the word *upāya* by freely explaining it to be 'means of success', Hare preferred to bring out the etymology of the word in his English translation.

for the references. Tilak Kariyawasam has a chapter on *upāyakauśalya* in a Ph.D. thesis entitled *The Development of Buddhology in the Early Mahayana and its Relation to the Pali Nikayas*, Lancaster Univ. 1973, in which he notes the same few references available and then summarises usage in various Mahayana writings. Kumoi Shōzen, *op. cit.* (Chapter One, note 2), has a more complex argument in which he tries to show that pre-Mahayana Buddhism thought of *upāya* as means by which people approach the goal of Buddhahood, while Mahayana Buddhism thought of it as means provided by the Buddha from the point of view of the Buddha. The number of references available scarcely supports this argument however, the *Sutta Nipāta* case (see below) could be said to contradict it, and the *Jātaka* references have to be taken as anticipations of the Mahayana usage. Moreover he admits on page 327 that both aspects of skilful means thought are present in the Mahayana usage. In short it is not possible to argue for two clear phases in the development of this idea, one in the Pali Canon and one in Mahayana texts.

[2] J. E. Carpenter (ed.) *Dīgha Nikāya* 1910, Vol. III p. 220, *Tīni kosallani, aya kosallam, apāya kosallam, upāya kosallam.* T. W. Rhys Davids translated: 'Three proficiencies, to wit, proficiency as to progress, regress and the means of success.' *Dialogues of the Buddha*, Part III, p. 213.

[3] E. Hardy (ed.) *The Anguttara-Nikāya Vol. III Pancaka-Nipata and Chakka-Nipata*, Luzac and Co. for the Pali Text Society, London 1958, pp. 431ff. 'Idha bhikkhave bhikkhu na āyakusalo hoti, na apāyakusalo hoti, na upāyakusalo hoti, anadhigatānaṃ kusalānaṃ dhammānaṃ adhigamāya na chandam janeti, adhigate kusale dhamme na sārakkhati, sātaccakiriyāya na sampādeti.

'Imehi kho bhikkhave chahi dhammehi samannāgato bhikkhu abhabbo anadhigatam vā kusalam dhammam adhigantum adhigatam vā kusalam dhammam phātikātuṃ.'
The converse follows on in parallel.

'Idha bhikkhave bhikkhu āyakusalo ca hoti, apāyakusalo ca hoti, upāyakusalo ca hoti, anadhigatānaṃ kusalānaṃ dhammānaṃ adhigamāya chandaṃ janeti, adhigate kusale dhamme sārakkhati, sātaccakiriyāya sampādeti.

'Imehi kho bhikkhave chahi dhammehi samannāgato bhikkhu bhabbo anadhigataṃ vā kusalam dhammam adhigantum adhigatam vā kusalam dhammam phātikātun ti.'
Translation by E. M. Hare, *The Book of the Gradual Sayings, Vol. III*, Luzac & Co. for the Pali Text Society, London 1961.

This was pursued also by some Japanese writers (cf. Chapter One, note 25). Admittedly the related terms *āya*, *ap-āya* and *up-āya* do indicate that the derivation from the root *i*, 'to go', or at least the play on words, was probably once in somebody's mind. Nevertheless it seems a slender basis on which to construct the meaning of this idea. It appears that the three terms are concerned with the spiritual attitude of a monk. If we take them together with the other three of the six mentioned above, 'wishing to attain' etc., the text demands at one and the same time persistence of intent and agility of spirit. This is not without interest for the subject of skilful means in general, but unfortunately both the passages in which the triplet occurs remain isolated and obscure.

The only other direct reference to skill in means of any real interest is in the *Nāvasutta* of the *Sutta Nipāta*, where the wise man who knows *Dhamma* is compared to the skilful boatman who has the ability to ferry others across a dangerous river. There are those who do not understand the meaning of Dhamma, and when they find themselves in a strongly flowing river they are swept away, unable to help themselves or others. The good teacher on the other hand is:

> 'As one who boards a sturdy boat,
> With oars and rudder well equipt,
> May many others then help across,
> Sure, skilful knower of the means.'[4]

The great interest of this occurrence is that skilful knowledge of means is here related to the bringing across of others, which is of course a constant theme in Mahayana Buddhism. In this sense it may be said to complement the famous simile of the raft, referred to below. The image of the boat and the boatman bringing people across the river is very clearly presented, but unfortunately the special term in which we are interested is just thrown in without very much elucidation or development.

The term *upāya* by itself also occurs a few times in the Pali Canon, but hardly rises to the level of a regular technical concept. It is after all just an ordinary word for 'method', 'means' or 'device' in Sanskrit, so it would be hardly surprising if the Pali equivalent (which happens to be identical) were never to appear at all in such a large corpus of writing.[5] Some of the *Jātaka*

---

[4] D. Andersen and H. Smith (eds.) *Sutta-nipāta*, Luzac & Co. for Pali Text Society, London 1913, 1965, p. 56:

> 'Yathā pi nāvaṃ daḷham āruhitvā
> piyen' arittena samaṅgibhūto
> so tāraye tattha bahū pi anne
> tātrûpayannū kusalo mutīmā.' (verse 321)

Andersen and Smith also give the variant reading *-upāya* at *-upāyannū*. Translation by E. M. Hare in *Woven Cadences of Early Buddhists*, Sacred Books of the Buddhists Vol. *XV*, 1945, Oxford University Press, London, p. 47.

[5] The 'Vedabbha-Jātaka', Jātaka No. 48, is probably such a case, though Tilak Kariya-wasam quotes it to illustrate Buddhist skill in means. The story is of a brahmin who knew a charm which brought the seven precious things raining from the skies at a certain conjunction

occurrences, which are few enough, link one or other of the terms with *paññā* (Skt. *prajñā*), and this is not without interest because, as has been seen, this is one of the links which is important in the early Mahayana texts. However there is insufficient reason to presume these cases to be significantly pre-Mahayana.[6] All in all, the term *upāya* is not explicitly connected with early or central features of the Pali Buddhist tradition, and it is not developed in any complexity.

In view of the relative paucity of usage in the Pāli writings, the emergence of the terms *upāya* and *upāyakauśalya* to a position of major importance in the early Mahayana is striking. This is not evidence in itself however for significant discontinuity between Mahayana Buddhism and early Buddhism, whatever reasons there may otherwise be for stressing the discontinuities. On the contrary, the way in which the term comes to prominence in the Mahayana reflects characteristics of early Buddhism which are themselves generally reckoned to be of central importance. For this reason it is necessary to consider not so much the admittedly limited and miscellaneous usage of the terms as such, but rather certain well-known passages in the Theravada Canon where it so happens that the terms themselves do not appear. The passages which are adduced below indicate that there is a coherent matrix in pre-Mahayana Buddhism for the emergence of the more or less technical terminology of skilful means. They show that there was a real continuity in the way in which the nature and intention of the various specific forms of Buddhist teaching were supposed to be understood.

The first passage from the Pāli Canon to be taken up in this way is the story of the Buddha's decision to teach Dhamma (Skt. *Dharma*), when he was entreated to do so by the god Brahmā. The story is given in the section

of the stars. The bodhisattva, i.e. the Buddha in a former life, was his pupil, and one day the two of them were taken prisoner by robbers who sent the bodhisattva off for a ransom, keeping the brahmin. The bodhisattva warned the brahmin not to repeat the charm or else a calamity would befall him, but as it just happened to be the right conjunction of the stars the brahmin thought he would escape more quickly by showering riches on the bandits. Unfortunately a second band of robbers fell upon the first, and as the time of the conjunction was past the brahmin could not satisfy them also with treasure. The second band slew the brahmin, killed all the first band of robbers and seized the booty. Then they fought among themselves until only two were left. One of these brought poisoned rice for the other, who slew the former and then ate the poisoned rice, thus leaving nobody. The bodhisattva returned, found the various bodies and the treasure, and reflected that a misguided use of means for selfish purposes leads to disaster. The main point of the story as reflected in the commentarial prose seems to be that *self-will* leads to disaster, so that the story is not really about skilful means. On the other hand since the story itself really illustrates that going about things the wrong way leads to disaster it could be taken as an illustration of the concept of 'skilful means' if one already had the concept in mind. For the story in full cf.. E. B. Cowell (*ed.*) *The Jātaka*, (1895ff.) 1969, Vol. I, pp. 121ff. Cf. V. Fausbøll (*ed.*) *The Jātaka*, Luzac & Co. for Pali Text Society London 1962 Vol. I pp. 252ff., beginning 'Anupāyena yo atthanti'.

[6] E.g. Jātaka No. 214: 'In a previous life too the Tathāgata had insight and skilful means', cf. Cowell, *op. cit.* Vol. II, p. 121; Fausbøll, *op. cit.* Vol. II p. 173. See also *Jātaka* No. 463 in which the Buddha is said to have 'great wisdom! wide wisdom! ready wisdom! swift wisdom! sharp wisdom! penetrating wisdom! his wisdom hits on the right plan for the right moment!' (this latter being *upāyapaññā*), Cowell, *op. cit.* Vol. IV p. 86; Fausbøll, *op. cit.* Vol. IV p. 136.

entitled *Mahāvagga* of the *Vinaya-Piṭaka*[7] and also in the *Ariyapariyes-anasutta* of the *Majjhima Nikāya*.[8] It is a narrative sequence quite fundamental to Buddhism, and as the theme is also elaborated in both Chapter II and Chapter VII of The Lotus Sutra it is very important for the present argument. It will be seen that in some ways the special teaching of The Lotus Sutra is a more dynamic articulation of principles already present in early Buddhism, a view adumbrated before in the treatment of Chapter XVI of The Lotus Sutra (Chapter Three above).

The story in the *Mahāvagga* is preceded by reference to the Buddha's enlightenment, and followed by the beginning of the teaching itself and the founding of the *sangha*. The link with the founding of the *sangha* is no doubt the reason for the inclusion of the cycle in the *Vinaya-Piṭaka* in the first place, which after all is otherwise mainly concerned with the rules of monastic discipline. The repetition of the story in the *Majjhima Nikāya* is found in the context of a longer discourse on Dhamma. Like the *Mahāvagga* it also includes an account of the proclamation of Dhamma to Upaka the naked ascetic, who was not convinced, and to the five ascetics who accepted it. The parallels in The Lotus Sutra are not verbally close, but they are elaborations which clearly presuppose the familiar tale. The main aspects of the decision to teach

---

In the story the ship's captain Suppāraka, representing the Buddha in a former life, is also described as 'wise and skilful', (cf. *Sutta Nipāta* 321, quoted above!) but the story does not really illustrate the concept of skilful means. *Jātaka* No. 478 also describes the Buddha as skilled in means, not only as the Buddha but also in previous lives. It also refers incidentally to another story as an *upāya*, namely the story of Nanda in *Jātaka* No. 182. This latter story does not itself use the technical terminology at all, but it probably comes nearest to the Mahayana sense of skilful means. In brief, it tells how the Buddha trained a disciple named Nanda, said to be his younger brother, who hankered after a beautiful lady. The method was to show him five hundred beautiful nymphs in the heavens and then to say that he could win these by living as an ascetic, which Nanda pledged to do. The Buddha tells all the other disciples, and Sāriputta puts it to Nanda that if he is living the ascetic life in order to win the nymphs he is no different from a labourer who works for hire. Nanda hears this from so many other disciples that he is finally put to shame and genuinely works to make spiritual progress. When he becomes an arhat he comes to the Buddha and offers to release him from his promise, whereupon the Buddha replies that if Nanda has achieved sainthood he, the Buddha, is thereby released from his promise. Cf. Cowell, *op. cit.* Vol. II pp. 63f. The logic of this story is analogous to that of the deal done by the devas with Mara in The Śūraṃgama-samādhi Sutra, see Appendix F below.

The dating of the *Jātakas* is however very uncertain. The verses upon which they are pegged may be very old, and the idea of a *jātaka* as such is also very old, as is evidenced by the illustrations at Bharhut and Sanchi. According to Cowell however the prose commentary containing the stories themselves, as well as the introductory and concluding comments (in which most of the above cases are found) cannot be put as pre-Buddhaghosa. This seems extreme and the text as we have it must have had a long evolution before his time. Winternitz says however that 'much of the prose assuredly belongs to the Christian era', M. Winternitz, *A History of Indian Literature*, Vol. II (1933) 1971, Russell & Russell, New York, pp. 113ff. All in all these few references certainly cannot be counted as significant pre-Mahayana materials for the study of the idea of skilful means.

[7] I. B. Horner (trans.) *Book of the Discipline Part IV*, Sacred Books of the Buddhists Vol. XIV, Luzac & Co., 1962, esp. pp. 6-10.

[8] I. B. Horner (trans.) *The Middle Length Sayings I*, Luzac & Co. 1967, pp. 210ff.

are paralleled but the meaning of the story is more clearly articulated by the concept of skilful means.

The simple outline of the story is that the Buddha, on attaining enlightenment, is at first not inclined to teach Dhamma. On the contrary he inclines towards 'little effort'. The reason is that while the Dhamma is deep and subtle the people who would hear it are too engrossed in sensual pleasure and steeped in ignorance to recognise its value. The god Brahmā Sahampati realises this and regrets what the Buddha is thinking. He appears miraculously in the world and pleads with the Buddha to teach nevertheless. There are those, he argues, who through not hearing Dhamma are decaying, but who on hearing it would grow. The Buddha listens to this entreaty and when he surveys the world with a Buddha's eye perceives the variety of levels, faculties and dispositions of men. These are compared to a pond of lotuses, some of which grow up through the water and rise undefiled above it. Thereupon he decides after all that he will teach Dhamma. Even so, it is still important to him to consider who might be able to understand the Dhamma 'quickly', and this is another evidence of the recognition that there is a problem about relative degrees of understanding among different people. There follows the teaching to the five former companions, a teaching which includes (in the *Mahāvagga*) the teaching of the middle way and the four noble truths of ill, the uprising of ill, the cessation of ill, and the eightfold path towards the cessation of ill.

The Lotus Sutra in Chapter II contains this same story with some different details, and with a greater stress on the reflectiveness of the Buddha on what he is doing. Thus he is portrayed as recollecting 'what former buddhas performed by their skilful means'.[9] With this in mind he conceives of proclaiming the way in three vehicles, and is encouraged by the buddhas of the ten directions. It is then stressed that to do this is to follow all the buddhas and to use skilful means. Men of little wisdom take delight in petty teachings and lack confidence that they can attain buddhahood. Hence skilful means are necessary. The Buddha then goes to *Vārāṇasī* and teaches his five former companions. The nirvanic character of all existence (of all *dharmas*) cannot be stated in words and so he teaches them by using skilful means. This 'turning of the wheel of the Dharma', it is said, gives the 'sound' or promise of nirvana and the 'differentiated terminology' for *arhat, dharma,* and *sangha.*[10]

The original story, which was the common property of all Buddhists, already contained the idea that there is a problem about communicating *Dhamma* to anybody. Yet in spite of the Buddha's hesitation, he did go on to articulate his teaching to the five ascetics. The Lotus Sutra is simply drawing out the implications of this tradition when it emphasises the

---

[9] T IX9c 尋念過去佛　所行方便力 Cf. KSS p. 63.

[10] T IX10a 諸法寂滅相　不可以言宣　以方便力故　爲五比丘說　是名轉法輪　便有 涅槃音　及以阿羅漢　法僧差別名 Cf. KSS p. 64 N.B. KSS adds the gloss '(the first) Rolling of the Law-Wheel', but this seems to be gratuitous. 'Differentiated terminology': 差別名。

Buddha's initial refusal to teach at all, and then argues that through skilful means it became possible and worthwhile.

As to the final intention of the teaching, 'the supreme way' or 'the undivided Dharma', this is in itself inexpressible in words, but is realised when the Buddha 'honestly discards skilful means'.[11] It has already been seen that when this takes place it is not some new form of articulated teaching which appears in place of accommodated forms, but rather the secret lies in the very discarding of the hitherto cherished concepts such as nirvana. The real meaning of the Buddha's teaching can only be recognised in so far as one appreciates that it is at first formulated in a manner appropriate to the entanglement of the hearers in passions and ignorance. The formulations which make possible the escape from passions and ignorance are themselves only necessary in so far as they lead to the disentanglement. As the Theravada text similarly says, the *Dhamma* itself is 'tranquil' and 'beyond dialectic'.[12] This relationship between the articulated form and inexpressible goal finds many echoes in other famous Theravada passages, for example in the simile of the raft and in the discussion of the undetermined questions (on which see again below). Indeed in a broad sense at least it is not even peculiar to Buddhism. What is special to Buddhism is its built-in position in the legendary narrative about the very founding of Buddhism as a religion. And what is special to the Mahayana form of the story is the introduction of the term skilful means (or 'skill in means') when it is a question of communicating the inexpressible. This term emphasises at once the difficulty and yet the possibility of the communication of Dharma. It is also a check or reminder to ensure that the form of the communication does not fail to be converted into the full realisation of its intention.

The same story of the Buddha's decision to proclaim his message is found again in Chapter VII, as was mentioned above in Chapter Three in connection with the story of the magic city. Here the hesitation of the Buddha is dramatised at great length.[13] The Dharma finally proclaimed is the traditionally central teaching of the four truths and the twelve links.[14] There follows in due course the characteristic break-through of The Lotus Sutra with the assertion that the term 'nirvana' is of limited value. It is firmly linked to the deplorable state of living beings, thus: 'The Tathāgata's skilful means enters deeply into the character of living beings and he knows that they wilfully delight in trifles and are deeply attached to the five passions; for their sakes he proclaims nirvana, and if they hear it they will receive it in faith.'[15] At the same time this should not be construed as an easy polemical slapping down of a 'hinayana' teaching. The status of any form of the Buddha's teaching is ambiguous. On the one hand we read: 'In the world

---

[11] T IX10a 無上道; 無分別法; 正直捨方便。Cf. KSS p. 65.

[12] Horner, *op. cit.* p. 211.

[13] Cf. KSS p. 170ff.

[14] Cf. KSS p. 184, and also cf. p. 194.

[15] T IX25c　如來方便深入眾生之性。知其志樂小法深著五欲。爲是等故說於涅槃。是人若聞則便信受　N.B. 知 is misprinted as 如 in T. Cf. KSS pp. 189f.

there are not two vehicles for attaining extinction; there is only the one Buddha-vehicle for attaining extinction.'[16] But on the other hand we also read: 'Only by the Buddha-vehicle will they attain extinction; there is no other vehicle remaining apart from the teachings of the *tathāgatas*' skilful means.'[17] It is quite natural and appropriate that there should be 'skilful means' teachings given by all the buddhas, for otherwise there would be no discernible teaching at all. It is not a question of this teaching competing with that. All the provisional teachings lead into the Buddha-vehicle, or to state it more precisely, they are dismantled in favour of the one Buddha-vehicle which was the sole consistent intention from the beginning.

It must be admitted that the tale of the Buddha's decision to proclaim the Dharma is more elaborated in the two versions in The Lotus Sutra than in the Theravada texts, although the latter also have mythological elements. What matters is that the fundamental relationships between the Buddha, his own inward realisation or attainment, his form of teaching and those taught remain consistent in all the versions. These relationships are glossed in The Lotus Sutra by the concept of skilful means which helps to articulate them. The concept of skilful means does not distort the original tale. Rather, the original tale is a natural home for it.

A natural complement to the stories of the Buddha's decision to proclaim the Dharma is found in some famous verses of Nāgārjuna. The verses on the two kinds of truth were already quoted in Chapter Six above because of the parallelism of this line of thought to the idea of skilful means. The point was that the Buddha's teaching has to be understood as operating at two levels, at a worldly level, and at the level of its real meaning or supreme principle. The true reality can only be known through worldly teaching, but knowing the difference between the two levels of truth is also indispensable. The stanzas continue (in The Middle Treatise):

(11) 'Failure to see emptiness correctly
       Leads the dull-witted to do themselves an injury,
       Just like someone who misapplies magic
       Or does not handle a poisonous snake properly.

(12) The world-honoured one knew this Dharma
       To be so deeply mysterious,
       That the dull-witted could not attain it,
       And therefore he was reluctant to proclaim it.'[18]

Nevertheless the verses are based on the premise that he did proclaim it, and therefore, as in the more elaborated stories, the key lies in the correct discernment of the status of the 'worldly' articulation of the Dharma. In this

---

[16] T IX25c 世間無有二乘而得滅度。唯一佛乘得滅度耳。Cf. KSS p. 189.
[17] T IX25c 唯以佛乘而得滅度。更無餘乘。除諸如來方便說法。Cf. KSS p. 189.
[18] T XXX33a (11) 不能正觀空　鈍根則自害　如不善呪術　不善捉毒蛇　(12) 世尊知是法　甚深微妙相　非鈍根所及　是故不欲說 Cf. also J. May, *Candrakīrti: Prasannapadā*, ad loc.

sense the Mādhyamika account has the same matrix in pre-Mahayana
Buddhism as that which The Lotus Sutra had earlier claimed.

This fundamental conception of the manner of the Buddha's beginning to
teach has far-reaching implications. A teaching which relates to diverse
needs in a differentiated world clearly requires a great flexibility and this
was legitimated by the way in which the Buddha's own activity is understood. The flexibility of Buddhist teaching has many aspects. For one thing
it is expressly permitted to be translated into many languages,[19] and the use
of any one language, whether it be Pali or Chinese, as a kind of special holy
language is secondary. A great variety of literary forms is accepted as
appropriate in all schools of Buddhism, and it has been seen that in The
Lotus Sutra the various genres of Buddhist teaching are all conceived in
terms of the Buddha's skilful means. Even the rules of religious practice
submit to many re-adjustments. The laxity of the Mahāsanghikas and the
Mahayanists has found its way into the histories of Buddhism, but the
analogous flexibility of Theravada discipline is often overlooked. In general
it is fair to say that the idea of a differentiated yet consistent teaching was
the basic style of pre-Mahayana Buddhism anyway, presumed to stem from
the Buddha himself. Skilful means is the Mahayana name for this style.

Buddhist correlational technique

In the discussion of The Teaching of Vimalakīrti (Chapter Five above) it
was observed that the model bodhisattva was associated, as part of his
skilful means, with the main forms of secular life. For one thing he had a
distinct social involvement, expressing solidarity with all normal forms of
life. He also understood secular literature while maintaining a Buddhist
standpoint, and even 'accepted all heterodoxies without transgressing against
the true faith'.[20] It was pointed out that this implies in principle a whole
theory of correlation between Buddhism and other thought systems which
is controlled by the idea of skilful means. The practical working out of such
correlations means that Buddhism does not reject other thought systems but
associates with them, with a view to realising the intention of the Buddhist

---

[19] A fact given prominence by Edgerton in his grammar of Buddhist Hybrid Sanskrit, see
the opening paragraphs and documentation there.

[20] T XIV539a 受諸異道不毀正信。 It was pointed out before that Vimalakīrti was an
important model in the acculturation of Buddhism in China (Chapter Five, note 15 and *ad
loc.*) but of course the idea of skilful means had an effect on this process through other channels
as well. A most interesting case is the application of the notion by Hui-yüan, roughly contemporary with Kumārajīva, to the relations between Buddhism, Confucianism and Taoism:
'It is said in a sūtra: "The Buddha is naturally endowed with a divine and wonderful method
to convert (all) beings by means of expediency (*upāya*), widely adapting himself to whatever
situation he may meet. Sometimes he will become a supernatural genie or a saintly emperor
Turner of the Wheel (*cakravartin*), sometimes a chief minister, a National Teacher or a Taoist
master." ' Quoted in E. Zürcher, *The Buddhist Conquest of China*, Leiden 1972, p. 310. Hui-
yüan's overall argument is quite complex and links up with the idea that the early Taoist
saints were really Buddhists in disguise; the whole matter should be followed up in Zürcher's
treatment.

system. The striking thing is that this mode of correlation may involve a paradoxical, provisionally positive acceptance of ideas which are quite different from and even contradictory to the central intention or meaning of Buddhism itself.

This phenomenon can be illustrated from the Theravada Canon although it is not yet there related to the concept of skilful means. To begin with it is only necessary to link up with the argument offered in Alicia Matsunaga's book *The Buddhist Philosophy of Assimilation.*[21] The whole of her first chapter brings out very well the tendency of early Buddhism to convey Buddhist teaching in terms borrowed from elsewhere and on the strength of aspirations which are in themselves not particularly Buddhist. She refers particularly to the *Tevijja Sutta*[22] of the *Dīgha Nikāya*, in which the Buddha adjudicates upon the best method to be pursued in order to attain union with the god Brahmā. This positive attitude to what is a non-Buddhist goal needs careful attention, especially as it ultimately is seen to be related after all to the goal of Buddhism.

It is two young Brahmans who ask the Buddha's opinion about the best method to attain union with Brahmā, that is to say, the best method from among those offered by Brahman teachers versed in Vedic doctrines and practice. The Buddha replies, true to form, by criticising the speculative vagaries of those who claim to offer union with Brahmā while they themselves have never seen him. Then he criticises ritual exercises and stresses instead the importance of the cultivation of certain qualities referred to as those of the *Brahma vihāra*, of the dwelling of Brahmā. These qualities are four which have since become of regular importance in Buddhism, namely: love (*mettā*), compassion (*karuṇā*), sympathy with joy (*muditā*) and serenity (*upekkhā*). To cultivate these, it is argued, 'is the way to a state of union with Brahmā'.[23]

The point of interest about this tale is that the Buddha is shown as teaching the best way to attain a state with which Buddhism is otherwise not concerned. There is more to this than meets the eye. The situation is clarified by a different story in the *Dīgha Nikaya*, namely that of the high steward (*Mahā-govinda Suttanta*) who also led his followers into union with Brahmā.[24] It turns out that the steward was none other than the Buddha in a previous birth, so that again it appears that the Buddha personally accepts responsibility for a positive evaluation of the goal of union with Brahmā. Nevertheless, the Buddha goes on to say, rebirth in the Brahmā-world is a lesser achievement than nirvana. His own religious system is different because it 'conduces wholly and solely to detachment, to passionlessness, to cessation of craving, to peace, to understanding, to insight of the higher stages of the Path, to Nirvana.'[25] It is further defined as the eightfold path.

[21] Cf. Chapter One above, note 2.

[22] Matsunaga, *op. cit.*, pp. 10ff. Cf. Rhys Davids, *Dialogues of the Buddha*, Part I.

[23] Rhys Davids, *op. cit.* pp. 301ff.

[24] Cf. Matsunaga, pp. 12f., and Rhys Davids, *Dialogues of the Buddha*, Part II.

[25] Rhys Davids, *op. cit.* p. 280.

Matsunaga explains that this correlation of the teaching about how to attain union with Brahmā, here given in a form stressing moral and spiritual cultivation, and the teaching of the eightfold path leading to nirvana, is a method of teaching designed to begin where the audience is and then to lead them on towards enlightenment. She goes so far as to link it specifically with the term *upāya*, although this does not appear in the texts, and states the dialectic clearly as follows:

'This method of teaching non-Buddhists by instructing them in an idealized practice at their own level of understanding is a peculiar Buddhist device known as *upāya* or 'skilful means'. First the minds of the audience must be conditioned to the practice of virtue and from that point it is a simple matter to lead them to accept Buddhism and the path to Enlightenment'.[26]

Although the term *upāya* is anachronistic here, strictly speaking, the way of thought which it represents surely is not.[27] The interest and value of Matsunaga's work lies precisely in the fact that she is able to discern a consistent thread in the way in which Buddhism as a religion was able to draw in and make use of so many elements of Indian, then Chinese, and then Japanese culture and religion to serve as preliminaries to its own teaching. Presumably the same would apply to Tibetan Buddhism. This 'philosophy of assimilation' as she calls it, is entirely consistent both with the procedures of Buddhism tied up with the term *upāya* and also with the style of the teaching of the Buddha as this is characterised in the pre-Mahāyāna sources.

That Buddhist thought moves in such a fashion is relevant to every context in which central aspects of Buddhism are found to be somehow correlated with other kinds of religious belief or culture. For example, the same general principle seems to apply to the relations between Theravada Buddhism and the popular belief systems of the countries in which it has prevailed. Recent studies by Spiro, Tambiah and Gombrich have made it quite clear that the central or 'orthodox' belief system is highly tolerant of many beliefs and practices which in themselves have implications inconsistent with a strict or refined grasp of Buddhist doctrine.[28] It is with such elasticity that Buddhism actually functions as a living, working religion.

The relations between Buddhism and popular beliefs go back a long way, indeed probably to the beginnings, and an account of particular interest in connection with the present discussion is T. O. Ling's *Buddhism and the Mythology of Evil*[29] in which he attempts to characterise and locate the role

---

[26] Matsunaga, *op. cit.* p. 13.

[27] Cf. Chapter One above, note 2.

[28] Melford E. Spiro, *Burmese Supernaturalism, A Study in the Explanation and Reduction of Suffering*, Englewood Cliffs 1967, and *Buddhism and Society; A Great Tradition and its Burmese Vicissitudes*, Allen & Unwin 1971; S. J. Tambiah, *Buddhism and the Spirit Cults in North-east Thailand*, Cambridge 1970; R. F. Gombrich, *Precept and Practice; Traditional Buddhism in the Rural Highlands of Ceylon*, Oxford 1971.

[29] T. O. Ling, *Buddhism and the Mythology of Evil*, London 1962. James W. Boyd's *Satan and Māra*, Leiden 1975, does not affect the present discussion. Cf. also an earlier application of Ling's book in a related context, Michael Pye and Robert Morgan (eds.) *The Cardinal*

of the personification of evil in Buddhism, Māra. Māra is not essential to Buddhist doctrine in at least one important sense, for it is quite possible to state the four noble truths, etc. without any reference to him at all. On the other hand it appears that he was invented specifically by Buddhists on the basis of various mythological antecedents. As well as the fallen gods, the *asuras*, he is closely associated with a whole variety of malignant spirits, *piśācas*, *yakkhas* and *rakkhasas* (Skt. *piśācas*, *yakṣas* and *rakṣasas*) who populated the Indian imagination in general, and whose modern successors are found in the *yakās*, the *nats* and the *phis* of Ceylon, Burma and Thailand respectively. Buddhism did not and does not discourage belief in any of these spirits, but the key is that in so far as they are gathered up in the co-ordinating symbol of Māra they are led to defeat through the Buddha's enlightenment, when he vanquished all the malignant forces which Māra could summon together. It is striking that Ling began his discussion of how the Māra symbol functions with a quotation from T. R. V. Murti, writing on the Mahayana: 'It is possible to utilize any means appropriate to the person . . . for leading him to the ultimate truth. There is no limit to the number and nature of the doctrinal devices that may be employed to realize this end'.[30] For Ling himself, 'Māra is a symbol whose roots are in popular demonology . . . Such a symbol would have a particular appropriateness for the purpose of leading towards the ultimate truth those whose native mental world was largely coloured by demonological ideas.'[31] Ling then describes the practical use of Māra-related terminology in a passage too long to quote but finely illustrative of skilful means thought, and then concludes as follows: 'The matter may be summed up by saying that the Pāli Buddhism of the Canon does not close the frontier of thought where it touches animism and popular demonology; it allows it to remain open, but controls it from the Buddhist side, and for Buddhist purposes. The means by which such control of this frontier between popular demonology and Buddhist doctrine and methods is maintained is the symbol of Māra, the Evil One.'[32]

It is fascinating to see that the term *upāya* is nowhere adduced from the materials used by Ling in this study, and yet when he brings it in from Murti's writing on the Mahayana it fits like a glove. This demonstrates again that the very character of early Buddhism and of Theravada Buddhism is entirely consistent with skilful means thought. The implication of this is that correlations between Buddhism and other thought systems should also at least be considered in terms of the skilful means dialectic. One should not restrict attention to the unsophisticated village beliefs in spirits and so on, which anthropologists find particularly interesting. The persistent attempt by intellectual Theravada Buddhists to correlate their system with rational

---

Meaning, Essays in Comparative Hermeneutics: Buddhism and Christianity, The Hague 1973, pp. 40f.

[30] Ling, *op. cit.* p. 72, quoting T. R. V. Murti's *The Central Philosophy of Buddhism*, Allen & Unwin 1955, p. 246.

[31] Ling, *op. cit.* p. 78.

[32] *Ibid.* pp. 79ff.

Western humanism, thus giving a kind of 'modernist' Buddhism, is in principle based upon the same correlational method.[33] The same applies to the correlation between Buddhism and political symbols, from the ancient symbol of the wheel-turning monarch onwards to other involvements more characteristic of the present. Whatever the value of these suggestions it is clear that there was a natural context in Buddhist correlational procedures in general, in which the Mahayana concept of skilful means was able to develop.

The persistence of Buddhist meaning

The proliferation of varied forms of teaching, practice and devotion, and the provisional acceptance of thought-forms not ultimately required by Buddhism, lead eventually to questions of selection and control. For all its accommodations and flexibility Buddhism does not altogether disappear in a general *mêlée* of miscellaneous religious and other cultural activities. Or indeed, one may admit that it perhaps sometimes has so disappeared, but yet a recognisably Buddhist tradition has maintained itself through many centuries in truly diverse cultures. If Buddhism is so tolerant of many modes of expression and accepts so many diverse starting points in non-Buddhist culture, how does it maintain a grip on its own central meaning?

If we turn immediately to the concept of skilful means, as this has been examined above, we might say in summary that an apparently inadequate vehicle is accepted because latent within it is the possibility of its being transformed or resolved into a fully Buddhist meaning. To the early Mahayanists this was understood precisely because they had terminology for it, the terminology of skilful means. Because they understood it they were able to take a particularly relaxed view of cultural diversification. There could always come a day when, for some person or other, the skilful means arrives at its true destination of Buddhist meaning. The idea entails that every item of Buddhist communication has incorporated within it the requirement that it should eventually be dismantled. Thus skilful means involves not only proliferation but also, as has been seen, a critique of accumulated tradition. No statement of the religion should persist in arrogant self-assertion, and every provisional entanglement is liable to be deflated into pure Buddhist meaning. In principle the Mahayanists applied this critique even to their own terms, although it might be argued that not all Mahayanists have since maintained this degree of consistency.

The question now remaining is whether there is also an underlying matrix

---

[33] Gombrich, *op. cit.* pp. 40ff, esp. p. 55f, perhaps drives too much of a qualitative wedge between orthodox Sinhalese Buddhism and recent modernist developments which might be 'heading towards the first genuine syncretism in Ceylonese Buddhist history', p. 25. After all, the latter correlate certain contemporary needs with central Buddhist roots, just as the traditional orthodoxy of the villages did and does. It is surely better to see Buddhism as *regularly* syncretistic, as the wider history of Buddhism demands, although of course care must be taken over the term 'syncretism'.

for this aspect of skilful means thought in early Buddhism. Once again there is no help to be found in a merely terminological enquiry, but there are some extremely well-known passages which have a bearing on the subject, including the famous similes of the arrow, the pith, the water-snake and the raft. These passages show that there was a clear note of conceptual constraint and directedness, and also that perception of true Buddhist meaning was understood to depend upon critical awareness and spiritual attainment.

It may seem curious, in seeking antecedents to Mahayana Buddhism, to speak of conceptual restraint. The point is that Buddhism takes form in accordance with the karmic status and dispositions of those who require it, while at the same time it does not advance intellectual systems extraneous to the requirements. One might adduce the obvious case of the Mādhyamikas' claim not to advance a position, but in principle the same holds good for Mahayana in sutra form, in spite of the *use* of mythology etc. This is because Buddhism taking a form *is* skilful means, and nothing else. If this underlying conceptual restraint holds good for Mahayana Buddhism it is also a distinct current in Theravada Buddhism, as is seen in the famous simile of the poisoned arrow. This is found in the *Lesser Discourse to Mālunkyā* (*Cūla-Mālunkyasutta*) in the *Majjhima Nikāya*.[34] The context is the discussion about the famous undetermined questions, to which the Buddha refused to give an answer. The problems are about four topics, namely whether the world is eternal or not, whether the world is finite or not, whether the life-principle is the same as the body or not, and whether or not the Tathāgata exists after death, or both is and is not, or neither is nor is not. Mālunkyāputta is a questioning monk who puts these problems to the Buddha, saying that he should either give answers to them or admit that he does not know the answers. The Buddha however replies that this was never part of his programme when inviting monks to follow the path, and nor did Mālunkyāputta himself stipulate that these things should be explained when deciding to follow the path.

To demand answers to such questions before following the path of the Buddha would be to behave like a man who is pierced by a poisoned arrow and who refuses to have it drawn out by the surgeon until all possible questions about where it came from have been answered in detail. Saving the man from the effects of the wound and the poison is not dependent on knowing who shot it, where he came from, what the arrow is made of, etc. etc. Similarly "the living of the Brahma-faring" is neither dependent on the view that the world is eternal nor on the view that it is not eternal. However the world may be, whether eternal or not, it is sure that there is birth, ageing, death and suffering, and it is to these facts of existence that the Buddha offers a solution. The speculative questions are irrelevant, and therefore they remain unanswered.[35]

---

[34] See I. B. Horner (trans.) *The Middle Length Sayings* Vol. II, 1957.

[35] T. R. V. Murti, *op. cit.* has argued that the undetermined questions are an important antecedent for the Mādhyamika method in general, and there is no doubt much truth in this.

The undetermined questions appear also in *The Delectable Discourse* (*Pāsādika-suttanta*) in the *Dīgha Nikāya*.[36] Here they are treated similarly and it is argued that all comments on the various possible opinions about the beginnings and the hereafters of things should be 'expunged'. Of particular interest is the reference in this context to the Tathāgata's knowledge of past existences. Such knowledge is by no means brought forward simply because it is available. On the contrary, 'If the past mean what is true, what is fact, but what does not redound to your good, concerning that the Tathāgata reveals nothing. If the past mean what is true, what is fact, and what does redound to your good, concerning that the Tathāgata knows well the time when to reveal it.'[37] It is on this principle and this principle alone that stories about the past are used in the Buddhist religion. Since the same criterion is supposed to apply to information about the present and the future, it provides a rationale for the inclusion of some of the nine or twelve types of teaching traditionally listed as taught by the Buddha, namely at least for *jātakas*, *nidānas* (former occasions) and *vyākaraṇas* (predictions of future destiny). On the other hand this rationale has a selective application. Not just any story at all will do, but only stories which gear in eventually to the final meaning of Buddhism. It will be recalled that these various types of teaching were explicitly described in The Lotus Sutra as skilful means.

To give a further example of this from the Theravada Canon, there is a passage in the *Bhayabherava-sutta* of the *Majjhima-Nikāya* about why Gautama frequented lonely places in the forest. This might seem to imply that he himself, for all his claims, was still not yet free of attachments and aversions. Indeed the first reason given, early in the *sutta*, is that he went in order to conquer fear, by testing it out and waiting for nothing to happen; hence the title: *Discourse on Fear and Dread*.[38] Yet, on being freed from the three 'cankers' (*āsavas*) of sense-pleasures, becoming and ignorance, this should really no longer be required. So two better reasons are given. The first is that he is enjoying 'an abiding in ease here and now'.[39] The second, which is particularly relevant to the present argument, is that he is 'compassionate for the folk who come after'.[40] What does this mean? Miss Horner quotes the commentary as follows: 'The young men of family, gone forth from faith, seeing that the Lord dwells in the forest, think that the Lord

There is also the theory that the questions are left undetermined because they are in themselves fundamentally misconceived, e.g. existence or non-existence are not alternatives which are appropriate when considering a Tathāgata *post mortem*. However not only is this theory not advanced in the text now being considered, it would seem to attract the criticism of the analysis which *is* advanced. In any case what is stressed here is simply that the proliferations and correlations of Buddhist teaching are not intended to float off into miscellaneous speculations without good reason.

[36] See Rhys Davids, *Dialogues of the Buddha Part III*, pp. 127ff. It will be observed that the formulations vary. The one given earlier simply followed the text under discussion.

[37] *Ibid*. p. 126.

[38] See I. B. Horner (trans.) *The Middle Length Sayings* Vol. I, 1954, pp. 26f.

[39] *Ibid*. p. 30.

[40] *Ibid*. p. 30.

would not undertake forest lodgings if there were not something to be known, something to be got rid of, something to be developed, something to be realised—so why should not they? And they think that they should dwell there. Thus do they quickly become endmakers of anguish. Thus there comes to be compassion for those who come after'.[41] It appears from this that the Buddha is understood as going into the forest as a demonstration of practice, and not any longer because it has value in itself. In principle, though of course not explicitly, this anticipates the Mahayana argument that the very nirvana of the Buddha was undertaken as a demonstration that the ending of ill is possible. In a small way this passage indicates a mode of thinking characteristic of pre-Mahayana Buddhism (whatever the date of the commentary) which made possible the Mahayana formulations themselves.

According to its own intention Buddhist teaching is pragmatically or soteriologically orientated rather than being speculative. This character of the teaching is entirely consonant with the way in which the Buddha is represented as having begun to teach at all. He did not begin to teach for fun, nor in order to solve miscellaneous questions of a speculative kind, not to offer a theory of the universe, but rather to bring release to beings entangled in ignorance and suffering. In what sense Buddhist teaching may be said to be 'empirical', as the apologists love to claim, is a question on its own. However that may be, Buddhist teaching is related to a particular problem and a particular end. Since the teaching of the Buddha is like this, and was known from the beginning to be like this, it was quite appropriate for the Mahayanists to say that its articulation in some form is to be understood as skilful means. In this way the Mahayana stresses that it is a teaching differentiated according to needs and fashioned entirely in the light of the problem and its resolution.

Even granted the constraints of this pragmatic approach to the articulation of doctrine, the Buddhist disciple is still made aware of a rather large quantity of 'Dhamma'. In his own personal development each disciple is faced with the problem of seeing what really matters. The simile of the pith is of interest here, found in the *Majjhima Nikāya*, in the *Greater Discourse on the Simile of the Pith* and the *Lesser Discourse on the Simile of the Pith* (*Mahāsāropamasutta* and *Cūḷasāropamasutta*).[42] There is a large pithy tree of which the pith itself is quite desirable. There are monks who though making some progress nevertheless run into various snags in the spiritual life and fail to take hold of the pith. Some become famous and then indolent, others achieve moral perfection and become indolent, others achieve success in concentration and become indolent, yet others avoiding these traps attain knowledge and insight but still exult in this and become indolent. These are like those who take hold of the branches and leaves, the young shoots, the bark and the softwood of the great pithy tree, but fail to take the pith. As to the pith itself, the definition is as follows: 'That, monks, which is unshakable

[41] *Ibid.* p. 30, note 4.
[42] *Ibid.* pp. 238ff.

freedom of mind, this is the goal monks, of this Brahma-faring, this the pith, this the culmination.'[43] It is a question of discerning an elusive meaning which is all too easily but wrongly identified with various subsidiary attainments.

When the principle is expounded in the lesser discourse the brahman Piṅgalakoccha responds with a string of similes which indicate that the Dhamma has to be perspicaciously and correctly understood: 'It is as if, good Gotama, one might set upright what had been upset, or might disclose what was covered, or might point out the way to one who had gone astray, or might bring an oil lamp into the darkness so that those with vision might see material shapes—even so is *dhamma* made clear in many a figure by the good Gotama.'[44] In this case the Buddha himself is seen as playing a part in aiding discernment. But it is not as if it were simply a question of setting out pure unencumbered doctrine from the beginning. The same simile is used elsewhere in the *Majjhima-Nikāya*, where we read: 'without having cut off the bark of a great, stable and pithy tree, without having cut the softwood, there can be no cutting out of the pith . . .'[45] Thus although one should not become entangled in the preliminaries they are nevertheless indispensable.

If one function of the concept if skilful means in the Mahayana is to bring out that the same teaching may be wrongly or rightly understood by those who receive it, and that the same item of doctrine may be both a barrier and a door depending on how it is used, there are even sharper anticipations of this in the Pali writings. An example is found in the *Discourse on the Parable of the Water-snake* (*Alagaddūpamasutta*) in the *Majjhima-Nikāya*.[46]

In this exposition a distinction is made between two kinds of men who master Dhamma. That which they *all* master, in a sense, is nothing less than the whole conceptual system of the Buddhist religion. It is referred to as a whole string of varieties of teaching: 'Discourses in prose, in prose and verse, the Expositions, the Verses, the Uplifting Verses, the "As it was Saids", the Birth Stories, the Wonders, the Miscellanies'.[47] This is a list of nine types of teaching which a Buddha is supposed to give, similar to that given in Chapter II of The Lotus Sutra, where all are referred to in the context of the accommodated teaching of the Buddha. The Lotus Sutra goes on to say: 'I expound this nine-fold Dharma accommodating it to all living beings with the basic intention of leading them into the Mahayana (i.e. the great vehicle), and that is why I am expounding this present sutra (i.e. The Lotus Sutra)'.[48] In the same context there is the distinction made between 'the dull who delight in

---

[43] *Ibid.* pp. 244f.

[44] *Ibid.* p. 253.

[45] *The Middle Length Sayings* Vol. II, p. 104.

[46] *Ibid.* Vol. I. pp. 167ff. Tilak Kariyawasam, *op. cit.*, also refers to this passage, but note that the Theravada text does not explicitly refer to *upāya*. It is analogous to *Jātaka* No. 48, see note 4 above, as Tilak indicated.

[47] *Ibid.* p. 171.

[48] T IX8a 我此九部法　隨順衆生說　八大乘爲本　以故說是經 Cf. KSS p. 50.

petty dharmas'[49] and the 'sons of the Buddha, whose minds are pure'.[50]
Needless to say it is the latter who will see the great vehicle in the nine
divisions and who will accomplish the Buddha-way.

In the *Discourse on the Parable of the Water Snake* the distinction between
the two kinds of men is not dissimilar. Both receive the nine-fold teaching.
Firstly there are 'foolish men' who indeed 'master' Dhamma in a sense. But
they do not test its meaning by 'intuitive wisdom'. On the contrary they
simply master the form of the teaching 'for the advantage of reproaching
others and for the advantage of gossiping'. Moreover, the text goes on, 'they
do not arrive at that goal for the sake of which they mastered *dhamma*'. The
others by contrast do test the meaning of Dhamma by 'intuitive wisdom'.
They do not master Dhamma for the sake of reproaching others or in order
to gossip about it, and they achieve the intended goal.[51]

The difference between the two kinds of men is that the ones grasp the
teachings badly or wrongly, while the others grasp the teachings well. This
is like grasping a water-snake. If it is grasped too low down, on a coil or on
the tail, it is able to turn and bite its captor bringing death or great pain. If
on the other hand the snake is first secured with a forked stick it can then be
properly seized just below the head, and then it is not dangerous. Thus the
monks are supposed to understand the *meaning* of what the Buddha teaches.[52]
The same teaching can have two quite different outcomes depending on
whether or not one presses through to its real purport. It is no accident that
Nāgārjuna used the same simile of the snake with respect to the teaching of
emptiness, as quoted earlier, and that the ambivalent status of the teaching
was linked with the hesitation of the Buddha about saying anything at all.[53]

To return to the Theravada text, there is a further well-stressed distinction
between those who are 'unskilled in the *dhamma* of the pure ones' etc. and
those who are 'skilled in the *dhamma* of the pure ones'.[54] A 'pure one' is one
who has got rid of the conceit of his own persistent existence, and who thereby
becomes 'untraceable' like a Tathāgata.[55] But if the monk has to grasp
rightly the Dhamma which he has mastered discursively, and make his own
the skill of the pure ones, this is only possible because the Dhamma from the
beginning was taught in an appropriate way. What does this mean? It means
that it had to be taught in an articulated and discursive fashion, that is, the
wheel of the Dhamma had to be set in motion; yet also that in a Dhamma
taught thus discursively to the ignorant, some kind of initiation into the
central meaning was also essential to lead them into that real knowledge
which characterises only the trackless. The Theravada text states this too:
'Thus, monks, is *dhamma* well taught by me, made manifest, opened up,

[49] T IX7c 鈍根樂小法。
[50] T IX8a 佛子心淨。
[51] Horner, *op. cit.* pp. 171f.
[52] *Ibid.* p. 172.
[53] See note 17 above, and *ad loc.*
[54] *Ibid.* pp. 174ff.
[55] *Ibid.* p. 179.

made known, stripped of its swathings. Because *dhamma* had been well taught by me thus, made manifest, opened up, made known, stripped of its swathings, those monks who are perfected ones, the cankers destroyed, who have lived the life, done what was to be done, laid down the burden, attained their own goal, the fetter of becoming utterly destroyed, and who are freed by perfect profound knowledge—the track of these cannot be discerned'.[56]

The adducement of these various passages is not intended to show that the teaching of the Mahayana sutras and of the Pali Canon is the same with respect to particular items of doctrine, or even that the Mahayana movement in general is consistent with the doctrinal norms of Theravada Buddhism. Those are questions in themselves. What does appear, and it may have a bearing on such questions, is that there is a profound consistency in the manner in which the style and intention of Buddhist teaching is understood. In particular, it has just been observed that there is a common concern with the question of discerning the real meaning of the elaborate tradition of doctrine and practice. This is viewed as a task in the development of the Buddhist disciple himself. Early Mahayana writings such as The Lotus Sutra bring it out particularly clearly by their use of the concept of skilful means. At the same time this call to the discernment of real meaning was already at home in pre-Mahayana Buddhism.

This part of the argument may be concluded by reference to the very well known parable of the raft, which has no skilful means terminology but which is probably the clearest and simplest statement of skilful means procedure in the Theravada Canon. It is given in the same context as the simile of the water-snake.[57] The story is simply that of a man who crosses a great stretch of water by means of a raft made of 'grass, sticks, branches and foliage'. When he arrives at the other bank he considers what to do with the raft which has been so useful to him. Should he carry it with him on his head, or on his shoulder, or should he just leave it on the beach or push it back into the water behind him? The Buddha explains that though the raft has been very useful for crossing the water the right thing to do now is indeed to leave it behind and walk on without it. In the same way Dhamma is 'for crossing over, not for retaining'.[58]

There is little detail in the story, and perhaps it is fair to draw attention to the miscellany of materials which go to make up the raft: 'grass, sticks, branches and foliage', clearly what is to hand and what is required. This symbolises the ready acceptance of raw materials and invention of forms noted earlier. Conceptual restraint is seen in the pragmatic use of the raft to arrive at the other bank, for Dhamma has no other referent in the story. Finally the function of the raft has to be correctly discerned before the journey proceeds beyond. It was for crossing over, not for retaining, and therefore it is left at the beach in favour of an unimpeded departure.

---

[56] *Ibid.* p. 182.
[57] *Ibid.* pp. 173f.
[58] *Ibid.* p. 173.

The sutta goes on to say that monks, 'by understanding the Parable of the Raft, should get rid of (right) mental objects, all the more of wrong ones.'[59] This point was taken up again in The Diamond Sutra with a special twist as follows: 'That is why one should not seize on dharmas and one should not seize on non-dharmas. It was with this meaning that the Tathāgata always taught you monks: "Those who know that I taught Dharma as analogous to a raft should discard dharmas indeed, but still more so non-dharmas." '[60] The Theravada text distinguished between good and bad mental objects (dhammas), while the Mahayana text has shifted the ground to dharmas as existent and dharmas as non-existent; that is, not only should one not seize on dharmas as existent but above all one should not seize on them as non-existent. In this way The Diamond Sutra is consistently applying the critical principle of seeing Dharma as a raft not only to pre-Mahayana dharma-analysis, but also to the polemical Mahayana account of dharmas as non-dharmas. In both texts however the main point is the same, namely that Buddhist analysis is not to be pedantically maintained, but used and discarded. The central premiss was already present in the Theravada text, namely that Buddhist Dhamma itself, in general and as a whole, is to be treated as a raft.

Applying this analogy to the treasured concepts of a religious system in which one has a life-long involvement is a hard thing to do, and this is why the Mahayana critique became necessary. In effect The Lotus Sutra taught, for example, that the concept of nirvana is a raft to be left behind. It was to develop and maintain this critique that the concept of skilful means was born. It is by skill that a buddha or a bodhisattva knows when to establish and when to dismantle a specific form of teaching. It is as a bodhisattva himself that the follower is required to discern that what he was given must finally be abandoned. Only as the ambiguity of skilful means is fully used can initial progress be completely resolved into attainment. In this sense forms of Buddhist teaching are not only selected for their appositeness, they are also controlled by their final intention, whatever the initial appearances may be.

It has emerged that Buddhist teaching is offered after some hesitation. It seeks forms which are appropriate to the recipients who are rooted in diverse cultural contexts. In spite of its rich variation of form, the teaching is not uselessly speculative but pragmatically related to its goal. Its meaning must be correctly grasped. Although the teaching is indispensable it is eventually disposable. It is in these ways that all knowledgeable Buddhists understood the workings of their religion. For the Mahayanists in particular, these procedures were gathered up in the idea of skilful means.

---

[59] *Ibid.* p. 174, 'wrong ones'; *adhammā*, cf. the Mahayana text below.

[60] T VIII 749b 是故不應取法。不應取非法。以是義故。如來常說汝等比丘。知我說法 如筏喻者。法尚應捨何況非法。Cf. also E. Conze's discussion in *Buddhist Wisdom Books*, Allen & Unwin 1958, pp. 34ff, where the distinction between a moralistic and a metaphysical interpretation of *dharmas* is brought out clearly. Does Conze perhaps make a little too much of the idea of a 'hidden meaning'?

8 THE TERM HŌBEN IN MODERN JAPANESE

Colloquial Japanese: uso mo hōben

The Japanese term for skilful means is *hōben*. This is the Japanese pronunciation, it may be recalled, for precisely the same two written characters which form the original Chinese word *fang-pien*. Since the Chinese Buddhist texts studied above have been widely current in Japan for many centuries it is interesting to see how this term is now used both among Japanese people in general and among those who are self-consciously Buddhist.

If the average Japanese is asked what is meant by the term *hōben* he may be at a loss as to how to answer. The reason for this varies according to the person. Some persons simply do not recognise it in relative isolation, in speech. Some of those who do recognise it and know it to be a Buddhist term are not sure what it means. Others who recognise it and have some idea of what it means are unsure how to begin to explain it to a western questioner. In general the slight uncertainty of reaction no doubt is connected to the fact that the word is not very commonly used in daily speech. Unlike the Sanskrit and Chinese originals it is not an ordinary obvious word for 'method' or 'device' (which would be *hōhō* or *shudan*, etc.). Nevertheless, the term is available in the vocabulary of most Japanese and it is found in children's dictionaries.

An entirely different impression is obtained if one asks about the expression *uso mo hōben*, that is, 'even an untruth is a means'. This expression is generally known and arouses no feeling of difficulty. If an explanation is pressed for in detail one receives an illustration of ambiguous behaviour, usually of a kind deemed to be socially necessary. One example is the case of the father of a very young child whose mother has died. He explains to the child that the mother has gone away on a very long journey so that the child, who has no previous experience of death, and does not know what it means, can gradually become accustomed to the sustained absence of the mother. In a sense such an explanation is an evasion of the truth directly stated, but it is felt to be an inevitable one because in practice the plain truth would be incomprehensible to the child. What to a non-participant observer appears to be an untruth is felt to be the effective form of communicating the real state of affairs, namely that the mother is absent in a sustained manner. Another illustration is the case when someone is secretly trying to remain on good terms with two other people who are themselves mutually inimicable. This is of course what diplomacy is often about, but the application of the expression *uso mo hōben* is, in this context, intended to suggest that an untruth may become inevitable because of the regrettable ill-feeling between the two unfriendly parties. The untruth is perpetrated by the mediator, but the reason for it is not any lack of moral uprightness on his own part but rather the relative weakness of the other two.

It will be known to those who have lived in East Asia that this is not a question of rare cases of great moral conflict. On the contrary, these illustrations reflect the whole style of living together which is not characteristic of, say, Western Europe. The avoidance of face-to-face contradictions is of axiomatic importance. It is achieved by allowing divergent contexts to demand their own various and contradictory responses. That these varied responses contradict each other does not surprise the oriental observer of his fellows. Consistency, he would presume, is to be sought in another realm, somewhere behind the scenes, not in anything so mundane or transient as what people say to each other in acceptable conversation. Of course it would be impossible to show that this style of conducting relationships is the result entirely of Buddhist concepts, though it is also difficult to think that the latter have had no influence on such matters. In the case of Japan there is a close symbiosis of social and religious styles in this respect. Certainly Buddhism as a working religion fits easily enough into the general social rules which have just been briefly described. On the other hand articulate Buddhists are not very happy about the phrase *uso mo hōben*. The two illustrations given above show that the term *hōben* in this phrase does have some relationship to the meaning of the term in Buddhism. On the one hand an untruth described as a *hōben* is perpetrated because of the needs of those towards whom it is directed. On the other hand it is considered not to reflect an inconsistency on the part of the one who initiates it. Nevertheless those who think of themselves as positively Buddhist, and who take pains to articulate the meaning of Buddhism, consistently reject the phrase *uso mo hōben* as being contrary to the Buddhist meaning of *hōben*. Even though the popular usage is not entirely dissonant with the Buddhist meaning there is some justification in the Buddhist reaction. To understand this a closer look at the expression *uso mo hōben* is necessary.

The illustrations given have so far been interpreted in a positive ethical sense at least in so far as no doubt has been cast on the fundamentally good intentions of the persons involved. Indeed it is hard to imagine that a Japanese Buddhist would particularly object to the use, on occasion, of an untruth in situations such as those described. The saying 'even an untruth is a *hōben*', however, is in itself simply a general proposition which can easily be understood as giving approval to falsehoods whenever it seems convenient. Buddhists certainly wish to dissociate themselves from it in this sense. The position can be brought out clearly by considering two possible English parallels.

The most obvious parallel is the expression 'telling a white lie'. Westerners may debate about whether there are any circumstances under which it is justifiable to tell a 'white lie' and this is not the place to start such discussion much less to encourage the telling of white lies (lest any reader misunderstand). The hidden personal assumption of the writer is probably western to the point of naturally preferring the hard line, even to the extent that hurtful truth is expressed. Nevertheless there is of course a possible case for 'telling

a white lie', and circumstances of great stress where a white lie might in fact
be beneficial to the person who hears it present the strongest situation in
which such a course can reasonably challenge the ethical desideratum of
strict adherence to truth. If the white lie is not to be excluded on principle
the question of its justifiability must turn on the relation between the
enormity of divergence from truth and the extent of the benefit to the other
party. Unfortunately a decision which does justice to the complexity of a
situation does not spring automatically from the phrase 'white lie' in itself,
which could equally well be applied much more vaguely to petty lying in the
service of self-interest. Hence westerners are usually reluctant to extend
toleration to 'white lies' without any qualification. This general vagueness,
and in particular the lack of any directed control over intentionality is
exactly what is worrying to a Buddhist about the phrase *uso mo hōben*. A
Buddhist 'skilful means' may in itself be an inaccurate description of a state
of affairs, but it is nevertheless a controlled one.

The second English phrase worth reflecting on briefly is 'honesty is the best
policy'. This is just the opposite of *uso mo hōben* in the sense that it encourages
consistency with fact whereas the Japanese phrase allows inconsistency with
fact. Nevertheless, the English phrase is really based on an utterly dubious
if not always consciously devious ethical stance. The implication is that one
should tell the truth because it will lead to one's own benefit, at least eventually. Admittedly it may sometimes be of some wider social value in the
sense that the advantages of 'going straight' might provide a basis for the
rehabilitation of criminals. Nevertheless the main implication of the idiom
is that telling the truth does not commend itself simply as a categorical
imperative but because it is supposed to lead to a desirable state of affairs
for the person concerned. In this respect it is not different in principle from
the use of untruths as devices to ease social disharmony. It might be argued
that it is preferable if the best policy also happens to coincide with statements
of brute fact, but the self-centred motivation seems to be the primary
implication. The un-Buddhist aspect of such a line of thought or action is
that it is centred upon a desired future situation for one's self, however much
it may be beneficial for others as well.

These two English parallels are of course not present in the mind of the
Japanese speaker, but they have been adduced to illustrate to the English
reader the character of the phrase *uso mo hōben*, and the way in which a
reflective Buddhist feels unease with respect to it.

It may be noted furthermore that the Japanese term *uso* itself is rather
vague. It can refer to an intentional untruth. However it is far less rude than
the term 'lie' in English, and Japanese speakers of English have to take care
not to say 'lie' when they would naturally and not necessarily impolitely say
uso in Japanese. This holds even when intentionality is imputed, but the
word is also used to refer to cases when a person is simply mistaken without
any intention to deceive. Analogously, in English, 'I am telling the truth'
can mean both 'what I say is factually correct so please take note of it' and
'I am not saying this with the object of deceiving you'. When a former prime

minister of Japan uttered the dictum *uso wo iimasen* (I do not say false-hoods) it was a rather vague and generous claim to reliability.

Because of the vagueness of the term *uso*, and because *uso mo hōben* can so easily be used to justify telling untruths for the sake of a rather general interest almost indistinguishable from self-interest, this popular usage is not able to offer a satisfactory reflection of the Buddhist meaning of *hōben*. The phrase *uso mo hōben* simply does not rise to the dialectic implied by the term *hōben* in a truly Buddhist sense. The falsehood is not controlled by its dissolution into truth. it is not revelatory of that which would validate it. It is not a refractive symbol of the real (*jitsu*).[1] It cannot be said to be 'not other than the real', as demanded for example in the formula *gon-jitsu fu-ni*, 'the provisional and the real are not two'.[2] A mere falsehood can remain all too easily on the side of self-centred unenlightenment. Thus the phrase *uso mo hōben* is both the main colloquial context for the term *hōben* and an embarrassment to articulate Buddhists who see it as bringing the idea of skilful means into disrepute and aligning it with mere arbitrary expediency. This whole state of affairs indicates to the observer that the term can easily be misunderstood in this way, but that from the Buddhist point of view it is not supposed to be. Buddhist corrections will be given more attention shortly, but first the spectrum of general usage should be completed.

Spectrum of usage in reference works

The Japanese are great lovers and users of dictionaries, great encyclo-pedists, and great believers in the contents of reference books. The very complexity of the written language ensures that children become accustomed to the physical procedure of looking up words from an early age, and much more thoroughly than, say, their English counterparts. There are in principle two types of Japanese dictionary. One type is arranged phonetically, and while it gives a brief explanation of the meaning of the word it is also used to find out which are the correct characters for writing it. Such dictionaries are sold in their millions. Countless schoolboys have their own dog-eared *kokugo jiten* ('dictionary of the national language'). Countless families have their own copy of the *Jikai* or the *Kōjien*, two of the most famous diction-aries of this type, whose pleasant names mean literally, if subliminally, 'Sea of Words' and 'Grand Garden of Words'. The other type is the *kan-wa* dictionary, that is, the Sino-Japanese dictionary, which lists Japanese words of Chinese origin according to the proper arrangement of the characters, and gives the pronunciation and meaning. These too range from simple word lists for children to the great Morohashi dictionary which, because of the intimate relationship between the writing systems of the two languages becomes in effect a dictionary of Chinese literature. Alongside these two

[1] Jitsu (実) is normally opposed to *gon* (権), the provisional.

[2] 権実不二 The relationship between *gon* and *jitsu* is really a parallel to the relationship between *hōben* and *shinjitsu*, as may be seen immediately by reference to the standard Japanese dictionaries of Buddhism. (権実＝權實)

types of dictionary are the many-volumed encyclopedias covering subjects ancient and modern which also serve as reference dictionaries.

The entries for *hōben* in Japanese dictionaries, which because of their wide use may be taken as genuinely reflective of public usage, bring out quite clearly the spectrum of meanings from the specifically Buddhist to that which Buddhists specifically reject. Indeed an example of a Buddhist writer stepping into this arena to criticise the entry in a major dictionary will be given later.

The simplest dictionaries do not indicate any Buddhist meaning at all. A *Kan-wa* dictionary for middle-school children gives:

'a temporary measure,
a method which suits the circumstances.'[3]

A similar one also based on the 'characters for general use'[4] gives:

'means,
temporary measure used for achieving an abjective.'[5]

A third designed along similar lines has the following:

'a purely temporary course of action, suiting the circumstances and intended to realise something desired,
a measure,
example: *uso mo hōben.*'[6]

A fourth popularly designed dictionary, but rather larger and containing characters beyond those taught in compulsory schooling has:

'a method suiting the circumstances,
something used once only,
example: *uso mo hōben.*'[7]

The overall view of *hōben* here is of a makeshift course of behaviour designed to suit the circumstances, 'or in other words, expediency pure and simple. In

[3] Hoikusha, *Chūgaku-kanwa-shinjiten* (保育社, 中学漢和新辞典, Tokyo 1964).
The entry runs: 一時的なてだて。つごうのよい方法。
[4] The 'characters for general use' or 'general purpose characters' (*Tōyō Kanji* 当用漢字) are a list of characters stipulated by the Japanese Ministry of Education as being those to be taught in compulsory schooling. They number 1850 in all and the different ways in which they are allowed to be read number just over three thousand. Further information on the use and the spread of these characters may be found in the present writer's *The Study of Kanji* (Hokuseidō Press, Tokyo 1971). The two characters which form the word *hōben* are officially supposed to be introduced in the second and fourth years of primary schooling, which means that the components of the term under study are easily available to every Japanese child. Moreover, as is seen from the fact that entries from the elementary dictionaries adduced in the text can be given at all, the term itself is reckoned to be a rather ordinary one.
[5] Chūkyōshuppan, *Tōyō-kanji-jiten* (中教出版, 当用漢字辞典, Tokyo 1961). The entry runs: てだて。ある目的のために利用される一時の手段。
[6] Ōbunsha, *Tōyō-kanji-jiten* (旺文社, 当用漢字辞典, Tokyo 1964). The entry runs: 望みをなしとげるために，いちじだけ使うつごうのいいやり方。てだて。例：うそも方便。
[7] Kyōiku-tosho-kenkyukai, *Tōyō-kanji-jiten* (教育図書研究会, 当用漢字辞典, Tokyo 1959). The entry runs: つごうのよい方法。そのときかぎり使うもの。例：うそも方便。

two cases the phrase 'even an untruth is a means' is explicitly adduced as an example of appropriate usage.

The above-mentioned dictionaries are really designed for those working to master their own writing system and do not in any sense claim to be Sino-Japanese reference works. They simply reflect popular usage. A very well known single-volume *kan-wa* dictionary (Kadokawa) has the following entry:

'occasion (*the dictionary illustrates this with a quotation from a Chinese dynastic history compiled in the T'ang period*), (Buddhism) measures provisionally devised by the Buddha for the guidance of living beings, measure, expedient, (colloquial) opportuneness.'[8]

It is evident that the popular usage here appears in the last two explanations. The Buddhist usage is specifically mentioned, though in a very introductory and unambitious way. No quotation is felt to be needed, perhaps because there is too wide a variety of contexts which might be known to a culturally accomplished Japanese. The first sense given, by contrast, is really not a very common one, and it is provided with a literary source proving its genuine Chinese pedigree. It is surely not without accident that this part of the entry is simply an abbreviated form of the first part of the entry in the great Morohashi *kan-wa* dictionary. It gives the literary basis in classical Chinese but in a fairly digestible form. It then moves from what to the average Japanese user of the dictionary is relatively little known, through the Buddhist usage which is imperfectly known, to the colloquial usage which needs no quotation or even explanation, but merely needs to be listed.

The standard Morohashi *kan-wa* dictionary is authoritative in a sense, though its influence on mainstream Japanese usage is difficult to assess. Two basic meanings are given. The first is defined as 'occasion' or 'opportunity', with the literary quotation illustrating this which was referred to above.[9] The second is the Buddhist sense, defined as follows:

'(Buddhism) measures provisionally administered by the Buddha for the guidance of living beings. By extension, emergency measures, expedient methods'.[10]

---

[8] Kadowaka, *Kanwa-chūjiten* (角川, 漢和中辞典, Tokyo 1965). The entry runs: 機会。(quotation omitted). (仏)仏が衆生を導くために, 仮に設けた手段。手段。まにあわせ。(俗)好都合。

[9] Morohashi, *Dai-kanwa-jiten* (諸橋轍次, 大漢知辞典) 。The following entry consists of the term *hōben-bukuro* (方便嚢) which means 'an occasional bag (for carrying things)'. It should also be noted that more extensive explanations of the term *hōben* are in fact given under the term *hōben-mon* 方便門, which is said to be synonymous with *hōben* and identifiable with Buddhism (*bukkyō* 仏教). However *hōben-mon* is already a slightly more technical term and not confluent with a word used in ordinary speech, as is *hōben*. For this reason attention is restricted to the way in which *hōben* is treated.

[10] The term translated 'occasion' or 'opportunity' is 機会 (J. *kikai*). The entry for the 'Buddhist' meaning runs as follows: 佛が衆生を導くために施すかりの手段。轉じて, 臨機の處置, 便宜の方法をいう。

It will be noted that the independent meaning for *fang-pien* of 'means' or 'convenience' referred to by Sinologists and in Sino-English dictionaries[11] is not given independently here, but is entered only as an extension of the Buddhist meaning. For the Japanese compilers at least, the Buddhist meaning seems to be treated as if it were more important than the meaning 'occasion', even though it is listed second, for the explanation just quoted is followed by two quotations from Chinese Buddhist writings. These are not however a mere illustration of usage. They both contain 'etymological' interpretations of the term *hōben* (i.e. the Chinese *fang-pien*), of the sort which have entertained Chinese and Japanese *literati* for centuries. It goes almost without saying that the really valid historical starting point for explaining the term as a Buddhist term should be its use in Chinese Buddhist texts as the translation for a Sanskrit original. Didactic Sino-Japanese tradition however allows that any term which consists of two characters in Chinese can be 'explained' in terms of its constituent characters. Such explanations are themselves mainly of interest to us as indicating how the explainers wished or wish to understand the term. Since the two explanations adduced in Morohashi are themselves not identical their parallel form and divergent trend can be most easily expressed in a simple table as follows.[12]

	fang (J.*hō*)	*pien* (J. *ben*)
Daizōhōsū[13]	method	expediency
Hokke Monku[14]	Dharma	use (application, function)

This method of explaining the meaning of *hōben* is still used with variations in modern Japanese writings (see below in another context), in accounts of Buddhism prepared for foreigners, and even in uncritical secondary accounts

[11] See quotations above in Chapter One, note 29.

[12] The associations between the characters are of some importance, being stronger in the first text than in the second:

fang-pien:	方	便
Daizōhōsū:	方法	便宜
Hokke Monku:	法	用

There is a proper sense in which character associations can be taken into account in a linguistic assessment of meaning. I.e. for modern Japanese the character *hō* 方 bears with it something of its use in words such as *hōhō* 方法 (method) *hōshin* 方針 (policy) and *hōsaku* 方第 plan; means), while the character *ben* 便 reminds one of *benri* 便理 (convenient) and *bengi* 便宜 (expedient), and even *ben-jo* 便所 (toilet, or literally 'convenient place'). Special tests would be necessary to assess the precise weight to be placed on any sub-liminal character associations. Perhaps they tend if anything to be overestimated by foreigners, sinologists and Japanese pedagogues.

[13] *Daizōhōsū*, Ch. *Ta Ts'ang Fa Shu* (大藏法數).

[14] *Hokke Monku* (法華文句), i.e. *Myōhōrengemonku*, Ch. *Miao Fa Lien Hua Wen Chü*, (妙法蓮華文句) T1718. One of the more famous writings of Chih-I (智顗), known in Japan as Tendai Daishi (天台大師).

by westerners.[15] As far as the present discussion is concerned the main point of interest here is that the Morohashi dictionary operates quite definitely in terms of Chinese scholastic tradition, without quoting from the fundamental Mahayana sutras which introduced the concept into China as a specifically Buddhist concept in the first place. The dictionary's own direct definition of the term does not contain anything more specifically and accurately Buddhist than the entry in the single-volume *kan-wa* dictionary quoted just before. Though it is of course correct as far as it goes, it would seem that it should be just as open to criticism by Buddhist scholars as the entries in smaller dictionaries.

The *kan-wa* dictionaries based on Chinese characters as such provide a spectrum of explanations running from the Chinese literary sources and scholastic Buddhist tradition to the contemporary colloquial. What about dictionaries of Japanese words arranged phonetically, that is, *kokugo* dictionaries which contain both native Japanese words and Japanised Chinese words, not to speak of compound words based on elements of Chinese origin but put together in Japan, and words of European origin such as *gasu-sutōbu* (gas-stove) or *kasutādo* (custard)? It will be sufficient to bring reference here to three such dictionaries including two of the most famous, namely the *Jikai* and the *Kōjien*, referred to already. The *Jikai*, which is slightly shorter, offers the following:

(1) '(Buddhism) skilful measures used for the salvation of living beings by buddhas and bodhisattvas; (skilful measures) (winning over by skilful means) (the bow of skilful means),

(2) An expedient measure used for achieving an objective, means, method, instrument; (arms are no more than an expedient measure).'[16]

By contrast with the cases given so far the Buddhist meaning is given first and the general meaning is given second. The phrases in brackets are phrases illustrative of use, without being quotations. For the Buddhist meaning the phrases are of course from Buddhist writings and are in fact formulations of Chinese origin. For example, the term translated just above as 'skilful measures' is *zengon-hōben* (Ch. *shan-chüan fang-pien*), the term used to translate *upāya-kauśalya* in the first Chinese version of The Lotus Sutra.[17] As far

---

[15] Inada and Funabashi, *Jōdo Shinshū*. This book, in English, argues that the *hō* of *hōben* means *hōsei* 方正 or 'correct', while the *ben* means *kōmyō* 巧明 or 'skilful', p. 100. This rather confused 'etymology' is reproduced in Joseph J. Spae's *Christian Corridors to Japan*, Tokyo 1965, p. 33, where *hōben* as such is defined as 'expedients, i.e. partial understanding' and then more satisfactorily as 'the correct, adapted way which leads to salvation'. The explanation is based on Pure Land Buddhist tradition going back to the Chinese patriarch T'an Luan, J. Donran 曇鸞.

[16] *Jikai* (辞海, Tokyo 1968). The entry is: (1) (仏) 仏菩薩が衆生救済のために用いる巧みな手段。(善巧方便)(方便引入)(方便の弓)。 (2) 目的おとげるために用いる便宜の手段。てだて。方法。道具。(武力は方便に過ざない) The bow of skilful means is a metaphor for skilful means, stressing the conscious directing activity of the Buddha who 'feathers an arrow' for his bow, c.f. Heibonsha's *Daijiten*, Tokyo 1936, Vol. 23, p. 131.

[17] 善權方便 cf. Chapter One, note 30.

as the second meaning is concerned it is notable that the compilers did not
demean themselves by entering the colloquial expression *uso mo hōben*, but
preferred something which displays at least a wider refleetion on civilisational
matters.

A similar dictionary, but one which specialises in traditional Japanese
allusions, is the *Shinchō Kokugo Jiten*. This gives the same two basic
meanings, in the same order, and following almost verbatim the formulations
of the *Jikai*. The phrases in brackets are replaced by allusions to Japanese
literature, and the article is then after all completed with the phrase *uso mo
hōben*[18].

Thirdly, the *Kōjien*, a somewhat larger but still a single-volume dictionary
in general use, has to be considered:

(1) '(Buddhism) (Sanskrit *upāya*) (a) skilful measure for the teaching and
    guidance of living beings, (b) a form of teaching set up provisionally to
    tempt people into the true teaching.
(2) An expedient measure used to attain an objective, means, deceit.'[19]

This basic entry is followed by three more compound phrases which reflect
the two fundamental meanings in miscellaneous ways.[20] It will be seen that
the same double set of meanings is given, first the Buddhist one and secondly
the general one. The Buddhist part is given with a little more elaboration
than in other cases, not least by the introduction of the Sanskrit *upāya*
rather than by any prior indication of a Chinese literary use. The quotation
above may even do less than justice to the original for the simple reason that
the order of words in Japanese usually has to be more or less reversed when
they are rendered into English, and this plays havoc with emphasis based
on word order. As a result, the two subdivisions of the Buddhist meaning
may seem to be very similar indeed. The distinction which is being emphasised is the stress on the 'living beings' in the first one ('living beings'
comes first in the Japanese), who are so ignorant as to *need* such skilful
measures; and 'the true teaching', or 'the teaching of reality' (*shinjitsu no
kyōhō*, which again comes first in the Japanese) which is really the main
point of the second one. *Shinjitsu*, for which translations rightly waver
between 'truth' and 'reality', is, so to speak, the omega-point of Mahayana
Buddhism. It is that which transcends discriminative thought, and indeed
precisely that to which *hōben* stands in a dialectical relationship.[21] Admittedly

---

[18] *Shinchō-kokugo-jiten* (新潮国語辞典, Tokyo 1965), *ad loc.*

[19] *Kōjien* (広辞苑, Tokyo 1963). The entry is: (1)(仏)(梵語 upāya)(イ)衆生を教之導く
巧みな手段。(ロ)真実の教法に誘い入れるために仮に設けた法門。(2)目的のために利
用される便宜の手段。てだて。たばかり。

[20] The term *hōben-dango* (方便団子) 'liars' dumplings' is referred to again below. *Hōben-
bukuro* (方便嚢) is the same as that given in Morohashi and reflects an incidental Chinese
usage. *Hōben-riki* (方便力) 'power of skilful means' is an expression frequently occurring in
Buddhist texts, such as The Lotus Sutra, c.f. Chapter One, note 37.

[21] The Morohashi *Dai-kan-wa-jiten* entry for *hōben-mon* referred to in note 9 above contains
a fine quotation from Chih-I's *Hokke Monku* where he speaks of 'opening the gate of skilful
means to reveal the mark of true reality' (開方便門示眞實相). Indeed the phrase *hōben to*

this relationship is not particularly clearly pointed out in this short dictionary entry, and its importance suffers further by association with the second general meaning given, which ends with the word 'deceit' (*tabakari*). Even though the phrase *uso mo hōben* does not appear, this angle is sufficiently covered by the term 'deceit', and by one of the illustrative compound phrases, namely *hōbendango*, 'liars' dumplings' eaten ceremonially to erase the lies of the preceding twelve months.[22]

In sum the *kokugo* dictionaries also reflect a spectrum of usage from the popular to the more literary and historical. They are different from the *kan-wa* dictionaries however in showing no interest in any independent Chinese origin for the word, while the meaning 'occasion' (*kikai*) does not appear at all. The Buddhist meaning, briefly explained, is always given first, reflecting no doubt the persistent influence of Buddhist writings on the Japanese language ever since the beginning of the literature. It must not be forgotten that not only did the Japanese never know a Chinese language uninfluenced by Buddhist ideas and terminology, but the early intrusion of continental culture was spearheaded by Buddhist texts such as The Lotus Sutra, which were used very frequently in public ritual as well as in temples.[23] At the same time there is a clear recognition of a more general use of the term to mean 'expedient', 'method', 'means', and even 'deceit'. This links up both with the general meaning of the term *fang-pien* in Chinese and with the popular usage in Japan which, although it does not appear in every dictionary, can be best summed up by the phrase *uso mo hōben*. Now that the general range of usage has been spelled out, at least in this summary form, more detailed attention can be paid to the way in which articulate Buddhists themselves relate to and comment upon this usage.

Response of Buddhists to general usage

Both the phrase *uso mo hōben* in particular and the whole tarnishing of the Buddhist concept of skilful means with the extended general implication of mere expediency are rejected by Buddhist writers. This statement is based on the content of numerous conversations, but can also be illustrated by varied written documents.

Take first a popular and readable book by the founding president of the Risshō Kōsei-kai, Niwano Nikkyō.[24] Niwano is the genial spiritual leader of a few million devoted followers for whom Buddhism is a matter of explicit day-to-day importance and not just a cremation service. His books are printed in large numbers and it is fair to suppose that they are widely read. In a single-volume commentary on The Lotus Sutra, which is the primary

shinjitsu 'skilful means and true reality' appears now and then as a sub-heading in modern books on Buddhism.

[22] Cf. the *Kōjien* entry on *usotsuki-iwai*, 'liars' ceremonies'.

[23] Cf. de Visser's *Ancient Buddhism in Japan*, *passim*.

[24] Niwano founded the Risshō Kōsei-kai in 1938, seceding from the Reiyūkai (霊友会)。 Cf. also Chapter One, note 3 and *ad loc.*

scriptural basis for the movement, he went to some length to counter the popular view of skilful means as a more or less dishonest device by referring to another 'etymology' of the term. 'If we look up the character *hō* of *hōben* in a dictionary we find that it means 'dead square' (*masshikaku*) and thus also 'correct' (*tadashii*). *Ben* means 'measure' (*shudan*). Therefore the term *hōben* means 'correct measure'. It is a pity that the way of understanding it has gradually become distorted as for example in the expression *uso mo hōben*. Originally it meant a teaching device which exactly fits the person and the circumstances.'[25] This etymology is of the same sort as that noted above in connection with the great Morohashi dictionary but seems to be very close to an interpretation current in Pure Land Buddhism.[15] Were the ancient interpretations perhaps devised originally with the same practical intention as Niwano's, namely to safeguard the serious Buddhist meaning? In this particular case it is directed specifically against the phrase *uso mo hōben*. It should be admitted that the term *shudan*, translated 'measure' here and earlier, is itself not entirely unassociated with the idea of 'stratagem', 'device', and the like, though the element of expediency would have to be brought out fairly specifically with a qualifying term such as *ichiji no*, 'temporary', etc. The English term 'measure' is perhaps just a little more straightforward than *shudan*, but it is kept as a translation here because the whole tenor of Niwano's explanation is to stress the correctness and lack of deviousness involved.

Naturally there does remain the question of the inconsistency apparent between the *hōben* and the objective considered in itself, all protestations notwithstanding. But against this two things may be said, which reflect things said in conversation by the above quoted writer. For one thing, it is argued people cannot be taught the truth of Buddhism except by the use of *hōben* through which the full truth is indeed displayed. This of course follows the line of thought within The Lotus Sutra itself. It is only because of the 'trace' Buddha that we can know of the 'essential' Buddha.[26] Secondly, the criterion for distinguishing between a genuine *hōben*, which is ethically acceptable, and a trick, which is not, lies in the intention of the person who establishes the measure in question. If the intention is one of love, as of a father to his children, and if it leads to the wisdom or insight of Buddhahood, then it is a genuine Buddhist skilful means. If the intention is to deceive or to cheat someone then of course it is completely different. The criterion does assume the truth of the 'truth' towards which the skilful measure leads people, and its validity depends upon that truth. At the same time the independent observer can see for himself that it is an honest claim to validity, since it rules out real cheating by definition. If it is understandable that such

---

[25] Niwano Nikkyō, *Hokkekyō no Atarashii Kaishaku* (法華経の新しい解釈, 'A New Commentary on The Lotus Sutra'), Kōsei Press, Tokyo 1966, p. 96.

[26] These terms reflect acceptance of the traditional Tendai pattern of exegesis. The 'trace' Buddha (*shakubutsu* 迹仏) is the historical, but merely provisional Buddha, while the 'essential' or 'basic' Buddha (*honbutsu* 本仏) is the Buddha whose duration of life is unlimited, that is, the 'real' Buddha. Cf. also below under the heading *Hōben in sectarian Buddhism*.

a useful concept as skilful means should have been misunderstood, as Buddhists would say, by those who see things largely from a selfish point of view, then it is also required of the observer that he take note of the protestations of articulate Buddhist leaders and recognise that *hōben* are both necessary and controllable within the Buddhist system. Indeed it is quite clear that, for Buddhists, if a skilful means does not lead consistently into the truth with which it is related, it is simply invalid.

A more academically conceived argument was developed by Kumoi Shōzen whose article 'Hōben to shinjitsu' ('skilful means and true reality') was referred to earlier.[27] He too was concerned to correct misapprehensions in Japanese usage. His starting point was the entry in the *Kōjien* dictionary referred to above and in the popular phrase *uso mo hōben*.[28] His conclusion however is to reject this usage and to stress the connection with insight or wisdom. 'Speaking generally, have we not been misinterpreting the term *hōben* in various ways? Even leaving aside the generally current colloquialism *uso mo hōben* the meaning of *hōben* has usually been presumed to be 'substitute' (*kari no mono*), 'a mere device' (*tan naru shudan*) or 'method' (*hōhō*). But is it really right to interpret *hōben* in this sense of expediency? From the Buddhism of the *Āgamas* onwards to its high tide in Mahayana Buddhism, *hōben* thought has been seized on as the content of wisdom. It may even be said to have signified the internal characteristic of Buddha-wisdom. It was certainly not the mere expedient method or device which it is commonly supposed to be . . . *Hōben*, that is to say, skilful means (*zengyō hōben*), in so far as it takes its origin in the wisdom of the Buddha cannot be conceived of apart from its connection with wisdom.'[29]

Sawada Kenshō had argued similarly a little earlier in *Bukkyō Bunka Kenkyū* (Studies in Buddhist Culture). *Hōben* is usually taken to mean a 'measure', a 'temporary measure' or a 'means', he says, but he goes on to argue that the real Buddhist meaning is deeper than that. After a brief survey of the development of the term he concludes that it has two basic meanings. It refers both to the system of manifestations which the Buddha provides for the salvation of beings, and also to the system of methods used by these beings in their attainment of nirvana or release. Thus it certainly does not have the mere meaning of device or measure. On the contrary, the term can more or less be equated with the term Mahayana.[30]

Another voice is that of Masuda Hideo who published his article on usage in The Perfection of Insight Literature at about the same time. After stressing the connection between skilful means and insight, he concluded as follows. 'The term *hōben* has come to be associated with vulgarised meanings such as *uso mo hōben* although really it affords great possibilities with respect to the investigation of Buddhism, and particularly the bodhisattva way of the Mahayana. I think it is necessary to wash away the meanings which have

[27] Cf. Chapter One, note 2, above.

[28] Kumoi, *op. cit.* p. 323.

[29] Kumoi, *op. cit.* p. 350.

[30] Sawada, *op. cit.*, cf. Chapter One, note 1, above.

nowadays become attached to the word and re-establish its original, fundamental meaning.'[31]

In such ways as the above, various Buddhist writers find it necessary to try to turn the tables against the distortion of the meaning of *hōben* in the popular mind. A similar effect is found, though not explicitly argued for, in some discussions of the term in encyclopedias where a named authoritative writer is asked to write a short article.[32] In two such encyclopedias of the nineteen thirties, which, it should be emphasised, are general encyclopedias and not specifically on Buddhism, the term is explained entirely in the Buddhist sense. One of these may be quoted in full.

'*Hōben* (*Buddhism*). Two meanings, one as compared with insight and one as compared with reality. In the first, knowledge leading to suchness is called insight, while knowledge tending towards the benefit of others is called skilful means. In accordance with this the whole of Buddhism, whether Mahayana or Hinayana, is a skilful means. In the second, that which signifies the return to the ideal is termed true reality, while that which is established as a substitute and maintained temporarily is termed skilful means. Popularly it means a measure, and in this sense the Hinayana is an expedient teaching if it is a gate leading into the Mahanaya. Similarly the three vehicles were established in order to lead into the one vehicle, so that these two are expedient teachings.'[33] It will be seen that there is only the slightest nod of the head towards the popular meaning here, and even then it is equated with the polemical use which it sometimes has within Mahayana Buddhism. The basic meaning is given in terms of its dialectical relationship with either insight (*hannya*,=Skt. *prajñā*) or true reality. In terms of the basic meaning the whole of Buddhism is to be understood in terms of skilful means.

The other article is longer and contains a summary account of the term in the 'Hannyakyō' (i.e. sutras of the *Prajñāpāramitā* class) and in The Lotus Sutra. It stresses firmly the interdependence of insight and means:

[31] Masuda, *op. cit.* (cf. Chapter One, note 2 above), p. 117.

[32] Not all encyclopedias follow this pattern. For example, Heibonsha's *Daijiten* (大辭典) (Tokyo 1936) has shorter unnamed entries, that for *hōben* being in Vol. 23, p. 130. Basically this is like the *kokugo* dictionaries already treated as it gives two meanings, the Buddhist one and the general one (measure, method, expedient, deceit). The Buddhist meaning as given here strongly stresses that *hōben* are expedient doctrinal devices. It quotes from The Teaching of Vimalakīrti along these lines, ignoring the dialectics with 'insight' in that sutra considered in Chapter Five above. It also quotes from the Heike Monogatari, where various appearances of a deity are said to be so many *hōben* (方便區區). If this entry is strongly biased towards taking *hōben* as mere expedients it is fair to add that it is followed by a whole series of compound words including *hōben*, thus giving generous space to the ramifications of the idea. At least one modern encyclopedia, by contrast, *Nihon Hyakka Daijiten* (日本百科大辭典) (Tokyo 1955), has no entry for *hōben* at all.

[33] *Kokumin Hyakka Daijiten* (國民百科大辭典) (Tokyo 1936), volume 11. The entry runs: ほうべん（佛）般若に對すると，眞實に對するとの二意前者は眞如に達する智を般若，利他に向う智を方便という。之によれば大小乘一切の佛教は方便。後者は究竟の歸旨を眞實，假を設け暫くにして發するを方便という。俗にいうてだて，之によれば小乘は大乘に入るの門なれば方便教。三乘は一乘に通ずる為に設けたものであるから之も亦方便教。

'. . . based on the correct knowledge of insight, not sinking into signless, non-discriminated voidness, but bubbling up just at the point where the denial of discriminated marks is penetrated, to plant and train all good virtues, this is skilful means. Thus skilful means is an emergence from voidness to being, it is an amplification and an application. Therefore skilful means must be accompanied by insight. Similarly voidness is realised through skilful means, and therefore a coursing in voidness which forgets skilful means is not the bodhisattva way but a relapse into Hinayana.'[34]

Passages such as these, which indeed reflect passages in the ancient sutras studied earlier, show that Buddhists conceive of the whole idea of skilful means as intimately related to that of insight, or equivalent terms for the omega-point of Buddhism. On the one hand the intention of the Buddhist system as a whole is the criterion for controlling the establishment and operation of skilful means. On the other hand, coursing in voidness without skilful means is inadequate, or, voidness is only to be realised by the route of skilful means, or, the whole of Buddhism as a working religion is skilful means. Such is the tenor of twentieth century Mahayanist views.

Hōben in sectarian Buddhism

The sectarian development of Mahayana Buddhism displays a rich inter-weaving of traditions, and subtle shifts in the relative importance of the main sutras and symbols. The writings of patriarchal figures such as Nāgār-juna and Vasubandhu, Chih-I and the Ch'an masters in China, and in Japan Kūkai, Hōnen and Shinran, Dōgen, Nichiren and so on, take on an import-ance of their own in defining the shape and the meaning of the tradition. It would be a task in itself, one both massive and intricate, to trace the fortunes of the term *hōben* within the huge literary deposits which have resulted. At this point it will suffice to note what seems to be one regular characteristic of contemporary sectarian usage in Japan.

It has been seen that in principle any formation of Buddhism may be interpreted in terms of *hōben*. The tendency of sectarian devotion however is not to understand the central symbols of the sect in question as *hōben*, but to leave this term for interpreting the symbols of other sects and various peripheral practices common to all the sects. It must be admitted that this proposition can only be tentatively advanced, partly because of the sheer mass of data for living Buddhism in modern Japan, partly because a com-plete discussion would involve correlating different levels of articulation within even one sect, and partly because leading persons in a Buddhist group

---

[34] *Daihyakka Jiten* (大百科事典) (Tokyo 1933), Vol. 23, p. 422. (般若経に於ては) 般若の正智に立ち，空の無相無分別に沈没することなく，差別相の否定に徹するところに涌き出づる，諸の善徳を植修することを方便といふ。故に方便とは空から有への出動であり，擴充または應用である。かふる方便は必ず般若に伴ふべきものであり，空は方便によって生かさるるものであるから，方便を忘れた空行は菩薩道ではなく，聲聞に堕落したものとする。*Shōmon* is rendered Hinayana in translation for the sake of clear reading.

are themselves not always certain about whether or where they wish to draw the line between what is *hōben* and what is not. Nevertheless it is evident that the previously documented response of Buddist apologists to popular usage is not always entirely backed up by the nature of sectarian usage, and the impressions to be offered below suggest that some Buddhists think of *hōben* as being mere devices for the ignorant which have little to do with the true Buddhist doctrine and practice which they themselves cultivate. The matter can be briefly illustrated with respect to Tendai/Nichirenite, Shingon, Sōtō Zen and Shinshū Buddhism.

The Tendai (Chinese: T'ien T'ai) system formed by Chih-I in China is not really under discussion as such here, because Chih-I himself seems to have understood The Lotus Sutra and Mādhyamika principles to apply to all the various means at the disposal of Buddhists.[35] As to the Tendai foundation in Japan, this was really more of a comprehensive national church than a sect (if these terms may be used[36]), and it was partly from within its broad embrace that the more distinctive sects emerged. However there are two lines of thought formulated by Chih-I and transmitted in Tendai Buddhism which had a particular effect on later Buddhism relevant to the present discussion. One was the *p'an-chiao* (Japanese *hankyō*) system of arranging sutras in a sequence of graded importance or development. The other was the division of The Lotus Sutra into sections for exegetical purposes.

The *p'an-chiao* system does not need to be described in detail as it is given in various books,[37] but we may recall that the main point of it is to make The

---

[35] Yet there is a strangely secondary use of the term *fang-pien* in his major work on meditation, the *Mo Ho Chih Kuan* (摩訶止観 J. *Makashikan*, T1911). This contains reference to five sets of five points of preparation for meditation, known collectively as preparatory skilful means (*ch'ien fang-pien* 前方便) and adding up to the 'twenty-five skilful means'. These are listed in Hurvitz, *op. cit.* and include a variety of physical and mental preparations. Cf. also the Japanese translation *Makashikan*, ed. by Sekiguchi Shindai (関口真大), Iwanami Bunko, Tokyo 1967, Vol. I, pp. 196ff and 377ff.

[36] The problem of classifying religious groups belongs partly to the sociology of religion as well as to the phenomenology of religion. The church/sect distinction going back to Ernst Troeltsch is now antiquated, but modern refinements are equally unsatisfactory as yet. The term 'church' though often loosely used in journalism touching on East Asia is quite inappropriate for Buddhist organisations except in the most vague and general sense, and is probably best eschewed altogether. 'Sect' is used here without any intention of technical precision.

[37] The best account is in Hurvitz, *op. cit.* because he also gives systems other than Chih-I's. The five stages in Chih-I's system include the first brief but unfortunately incomprehensible statement of the Buddha's teaching (*Kegon*), Hinayana teachings (*Agon*), preliminary Mahayana teachings which indicate the provisional character of the preceding (*Hōdō*), the teaching of the perfection of insight (*Hannya*) which overcomes the differentiation between the two preceding, and finally the Nirvana and Lotus Sutras (*Hokke-Nehan*) which announces the Buddha-hood of all and the immeasurability of the Buddha's life, (terms in Japanese). One of the most interesting precursors of Chih-I in this connection is Tao-sheng (道生, fl. 397-432) who wrote the oldest Chinese commentary on The Lotus Sutra which is still extant. He asserted the universality of Buddha-nature and also stood for sudden rather than gradual enlightenment. Of particular interest here is his division of the Buddha's teaching into four

Lotus Sutra the final culmination of the Buddhist teaching and to relegate other sutras to the realm of provisional truth. This is not necessarily inconsistent with the basic idea of skilful means. It all depends how one understands The Lotus Sutra itself. Properly understood the sutra has no new content at all. It simply makes clear, in terms of the teaching of skilful means, how Buddhist teaching is to be treated. Understood in this way it does not present a usurpation of any kind, or a sectarian self-assertion. Stated in terms of the *p'an-chiao* scheme, it could be said that The Lotus Sutra is only needed in the final position because of the intervening stages. These in turn were required because the initial teaching of the Buddha, the first of the five stages in Chih-I's system, was not understood. It is only because the teaching had to be unrolled in various provisional forms that The Lotus Sutra was finally required to roll them back together again. However it is far from clear that all subsequent devotees of The Lotus Sutra understand it in this way, even though they may pay homage to the memory of Chih-I. Rather they see the sutra as a simplified focus for an absolute devotion superior to other forms of devotion. This is true especially for the various Nichirenite sects and groups, because there is no doubt that the net effect of Nichiren's work was to reinforce the tendency to pay exclusive devotion to The Lotus Sutra as a sacred writing.[38]

This tendency is undergirded also by the second line of thought bequeathed by Chih-I, namely that The Lotus Sutra should be divided up into sections for exegetical purposes, and that in particular a major distinction should be made between the first fourteen chapters and the second fourteen chapters (of Kumārajīva's version). The first half of the sutra then is the realm of the 'trace' Buddha, while the second half is the realm of the 'essential' Buddha, the first dominated by the chapter on skilful means, the second by the chapter on the unlimited life of the Tathāgata.[39] It has already been shown most interestingly by Alicia Matsunaga how this concept influenced the idea of *honji-suijaku*, which eventually helped to regulate the relations between Buddhist bodhisattvas and the indigenous Shintō gods in Japan (*kami*).[40] In Nichirenite Buddhism the distinction between *shaku* ('trace') and *hon*

kinds or aspects (perhaps anticipating Chih-I's 'four principles' or 'four methods' rather than the *p'an-chiao* classification). These were 'the good and pure (善淨 *shan-ching*) wheel of dharma', 'the skilful means (方便 *fang-pien*) wheel of dharma', 'the true reality (眞實 *chen-shih*) wheel of dharma' and 'the residue-less (無餘 *wu-yü*) wheel of dharma' (c.f. Hurvitz, *op. cit.* p. 198). This might make the skilful means teaching look rather elementary, but the point is that skilful means leads into true reality and the conclusion or final resolution of the matter is 'without residue', that is, without karmic remainder.

[38] This statement could of course be qualified in various respects, especially taking account of Nichiren's own use of many Buddhist scriptures in his writings (the *Kaimokushō* is a prime example), and bearing in mind that other important sutras such as The Heart Sutra are very well known to some of his devotees.

[39] The overall arrangement is much more complex, with subdivisions going down to individual chapters. It is explained in Ōchō Keinichi's *Hokekyō Josetsu* (横超慧日：法華経序説), Kyōto 1962, p. 116; and in G. Renondeau's *La Doctrine de Nichiren* (Paris 1953) p. 242-3 (note), and of course in many other places.

[40] Matsunaga, Alicia, *The Buddhist Philosophy of Assimilation.*

('essential') had the special effect of taking the second part of the sutra out of the realm of skilful means and turning it into an absolute focus of devotion. As a result of this there sometimes seems to be a finality and a fixity about some forms of devotion to The Lotus Sutra or to the *honbutsu*, that is, the so-called eternal Buddha, which belie the internal message of the sutra itself. This trend seems to be the result of a rather inflexible acceptance of Tendai tradition. Chih-I's systems are taken as being in themselves a plan of salvation, instead of being recognised for what they are, namely exegetical devices. Concomitant with this stress on a new absolute point of devotion is the tendency to view other Buddhist sects with some suspicion, following the lead of Nichiren himself, and to emphasise The Lotus Sutra as being the only vehicle of salvation. It is ironical that Nichiren, who criticised Amidism and Shingon for setting up misleading alternatives to the central meaning of Buddhism, not only provided a new mantra and a new mandala but also created a focus of devotion which was itself so easily open to misinterpretation.[41] On the other hand it should be admitted that Nichiren and his various followers have had an undeservedly bad press among western observers.[42] Nichiren himself was a subtle mediaeval theologian, and many of his modern followers have a view of Buddhism at least as broad as that held in other Buddhist sects.

The main counterpoise to the Tendai school in the early formative period of Japanese Buddhism was Shingon Buddhism, a system of tantric elements consolidated by Kūkai (774-835) on the basis of Indian and Chinese models. Shingon has complex rituals involving the physical symbolism of gestures (*mudras*) and mandalas, especially the *Taizōkai Mandara* and *Kongōkai Mandara*, painted on *kakemono* and used as focal points for meditation.[43] All forms of Shingon ritual have as their ultimate objective the identification of the adept with the cosmic Buddha named as Dainichi Nyorai (Skt. Vairocana Tathāgata) and identified with the *dharmakāya* itself.[44] It is perhaps not surprising that the 'three mysteries' of the esoteric teaching (*mikkyō*) namely body, speech and mind, have also been termed the 'three skilful means'.[45] Kūkai himself stressed the immediacy of the identification with Dainichi Nyorai, and wrote of 'attaining enlightenment in this very

[41] See Nichiren's criticisms, especially of Hōnen, in the important *Risshō Ankoku Ron*, (French translation by G. Renondeau in T'oung P'ao). Nichiren's mandala is reproduced and explained in Renondeau's *La Doctrine de Nichiren*, pp. 180-1.

[42] E.g. strictures by Sansom in a piece appended to Sir C. Eliot's *Japanese Buddhism*, London, 1964.

[43] See especially Tajima Ryūjun, *Les Deux Grands Mandalas et la Doctrine de l'Esotérisme Shingon*, Tokyo and Paris, 1959, (Bulletin de la Maison Franco-Japonaise, Nouvelle Série, Tome VI).

[44] In a sense this is a curiosity because the whole point of the term *dharmakāya* was to refer to an ineffable principle of buddhahood by contrast with the more or less speakable and tangible *sambōghakāya* and *nirmaṇakāya*. Dainichi Nyorai by contrast acts as a revealer. However it would be fair to observe that the 'bodies' here are not so much muddled as identified, which in the last analysis is consistent with any form of the *trikāya* doctrine.

[45] Ui Hakuju, *Bukkyō Konsaisu Jiten*, article *san-hōben* (三方便) *ad loc*. Note also 'nine hōben' (九方便) referring to preparatory rituals only.

existence' (*sokushin jōbutsu*)[46]. Enlightenment and wisdom are to be found in one's own mind 'because it is originally pure and bright', stressed Kūkai, on the basis of the opening argument of the *Mahā-vairocana sūtra*, the centrally important writing of the sect.[47] When asked in the sutra about the nature of this 'wisdom', the Buddha Dainichi (Mahavairocana) himself replies: 'The enlightened mind is the cause, great compassion is the root, and skilful means is the ultimate.'[48] At the same time Kūkai had a distinct sectarian consciousness, strengthened no doubt by his personal toil in establishing the Shingon system over against an influential Tendai establishment which itself allowed of esoteric practices within its limits. One of his important writings was *The Precious Key to the Secret Treasury* in which he elaborated ten stages of spiritual development. The system is analogous to the *p'an-chiao* systems. Although the concept of skilful means is not explicitly applied, it is argued that the Buddha produces a variety of medicines out of compassion for beings in various imperfect states. The whole idea is exactly consonant with the concept of skilful means found in The Lotus Sutra. Parables in the same sutra are unavoidably recalled by the statement that men are unaware of the treasure which they possess and the rhetorical question: 'If they refuse to take the medicines that have been offered, how can they be cured?'[49] The first nine stages are medicines 'to sweep away the dust covering the surface of the mind and dispel its illusions,' but then comes the turn of the Shingon teaching or practice itself. 'Only in the Diamond Palace are men able to open the inner treasury and receive the treasures therein.'[50] The practices and ideas otherwise current in the Buddhism of the time were fitted in by Kūkai with the later stages of the scale, but the final conclusion is that 'the Shingon teaching is the ultimate Truth, transcending all other teachings.'[51] The first nine stages of development are all seen as 'stepping stones' towards the next, but Shingon Buddhism by contrast is the supreme truth revealed by the Dharmakāya Buddha. It is this emphasis no doubt which makes it difficult for Shingon Buddhists today to conceive of the central Shingon concepts and practices themselves as being skilful means.

When it comes to the relationship between Shingon Buddhism and various popular forms of religion it is a different story. Shingon has always been very closely interwoven with indigenous practices of various kinds, just as tantric Buddhism was closely entangled with shamanism in Central Asia. Historically, the relationship between buddhas and *kami* elaborated under the formula

---

[46] 即身成佛, translated thus by Y. S. Hakeda in a recent study entitled *Kūkai, Major Works*, New York and London 1972. The phrase is the title of one of Kūkai's writings.

[47] The Japanese name for the sutra is *Dainichikyō* (大日経, T848).

[48] Quoted by Hakeda, *op. cit.* p. 87.

[49] *Ibid.* pp. 157ff. The first varieties of medicine mentioned represent Confucianism, popular Taoism and Hinduism, explicitly referred to also by Nichiren as skilful means in the *Kaimokushō*, which is indeed a somewhat similar writing, (cf. Renondeau, *La Doctrine de Nichiren*, p. 67).

[50] Hakeda, *op. cit.* p. 161.

[51] *Ibid.* p. 161.

shinbutsu-shūgō, similar to the *honji-suijaku* theory referred to above, is a clear example of the ability of Mahayana Buddhism to assume and dominate popular forms of religion. Whether this phase should be understood explicitly in terms of skilful means is open to question, but as a procedure it has obvious affinities with this way of thinking.[52] In modern times Shingon is still intricately bound up with popular religion. Mount Kōya, the mountain fastness of the sect, is the beginning and end of a pilgrim circuit running mainly round the island of Shikoku, and of which most stopping places are Shingon affiliated temples. Kūkai, or Kōbō Daishi as he is respectfully termed, is himself the centre of an elaborate cult. Pilgrims visit his tomb on Mount Kōya. They may perform the exercise of one hundred circumambulations, which in practice means hurrying backwards and forwards between the front of the tomb, where reverence is paid, and a stone marker post some metres to the side. The life of Kōbō Daishi is a tale told with great marvel in many editions, simply written and lavishly illustrated. Kōbō Daishi charms (*o-mamori*) are bought to ward off illnesses and other misfortunes, and this along with the use of spells (*majinai*, Sanskrit: *dhāraṇī*) is simply the Shingon version of a common thread in Japanese religion in general. How is this flourishing yet touristic and incidental religion to be understood in the context of the mystical writings of Kūkai himself and what has it to do with 'attaining enlightenment in this very existence'? They have all been described to the writer as skilful means (*hōben*) designed to develop the faith of the people in general, who because of the pressures of time and economics cannot enter into the system at a more profound level. They are thought of as the elementary stages of a progressive spiritual development, just as are the non-Shingon forms of Buddhism.

Thus once again in the context of a distinct sectarian development there is a reluctance in everyday discussion to concede that central formulations of the Shingon tradition itself are skilful means (though an interpretation of Shingon probably *could* make out a case for this). On the other hand the concept is used to justify practices of popular religion, which at first sight might seem to be mere casual superstition and to have little if anything to do with enlightenment or wisdom.

In Sōtō Zen one meets the admission that all is *hōben* except for *zazen* itself. For many members of the Sōtō sect this may be just a matter of denominational pride in the achievements of the patriarch Dōgen. It may also be argued however that the position makes sense in so far as *zazen* itself is a point at which an articulated differentiation of means does not take place. *Zazen* considered by an independent observer might look like having the status of a means, but *zazen* carried out existentially passes beyond the elaboration of means. Such an interpretation reflects the self-dissolving nature of Buddhist skilful means when these are properly used. By all accounts, *zazen* truly practised is an effortless, perfect living of suchness, being no longer a technique or a method, nor even a symbol, but a direct and undifferentiable statement of buddhahood. On the other hand it is possible

[52] Cf. Matsunaga, *op. cit.*

for a person to practice *zazen* in good faith on the basis of denominational loyalty, but with a sad lack of perfection. There are those who train for monkhood out of family reasons, there are those who seek in *zazen* a re-creation and a relaxation which will stand them in good stead in the bustle of secular life. In a sense *zazen* is being used, and indeed this is not in itself disallowed. It seems difficult to maintain however that a *zazen* meeting which contains all the criss-crossed elements of human motivation does not operate as much on the level of skilful means as on the level of the perfection of insight. The danger of mere denominational assertion might be reduced by a greater readiness to apply the *hōben* dialectic explicitly to *zazen* itself.

In Shinshū, the Pure Land Buddhism in the line of Shinran, one meets a similar reluctance to conceive of the central workings of the faith (which is what it is) as skilful means. Some facets of the written tradition suggest that it should be so understood. Admittedly, just as Dainichi Buddha is identified in the Shingon tradition with the *dharmakāya* itself, so too in Shinshū is Amitābha or, in Japanese, Amida Buddha. Is it of any importance that a further distinction is made here between the *hosshō hosshin* (*dharma*-nature dharma-body) and the *hōben hosshin* (skilful means dharma-body), and that Amida is defined as the latter?[53] One of Shinran's own stanzas suggests that the Vow of Amida, which is the central soteriological agent of the religion, is to be thought of as a skilful means, or perhaps indeed as *the* skilful means:

> 'The Divine Power and the Original Vow!
> The Perfect, Clear, Firm, and Fulfilling Vow.
> Inconceivable is the Compassionate Means.
> Take refuge in the Truly Unfathomable One.'[54]

Yet the main drift of Shinran's teachings was perhaps rather to stress the expedient character of all that went before. Thus:

> 'In all the life-time teachings of Sakyamuni Buddha, the attainment of Enlightenment in this world is called the Path of Sages, which is also called the Path of Difficult Practice. In this path there are the Mahāyāna and Hīnayana, the Gradual and Abrupt teachings, the teachings of the One Vehicle, Two Vehicles, and Three Vehicles, the Expedient and Real teachings, the Exoteric and Esoteric teachings, and the teachings of Vertical Going-out and Vertical Transcendence. These are all ways of self-power, or provisional, expedient teachings (*hōben gonmon no dōro*) expounded (by Bodhisattvas) in the stage of benefiting and teaching others.'[55]

An even sharper distinction is made in another stanza from the *Jōdo Wasan:*

> 'In the temporary expedients (*gonke no hōben*) of the Path of Sages
> Sentient beings have remained long,

---

[53] *Jōdo Wasan* (Ryūkoku Translation Series IV) Kyōto 1965, p. 31 note. The distinction goes back to T'an-luan (J. Don-ran) and is a standard subject of discussion in Shinshū theology.

[54] *Jōdo Wasan*, p. 66.

[55] *Kyō Gyō Shin Shō* (Ryukoku Translation Series, III) Kyōto 1966, p. 179.

Only to suffer transmigration in various existences.
Take refuge in the One Vehicle of the Compassionate Vow.'[56]

It is this latter usage which reflects the most common *de facto* attitude among Shinshū believers, and hence we see that once again there is a tendency to shift from the formative usage of the idea of skilful means. Instead of skilful means being a concept with which to understand the role of each and every vehicle of Buddhist meaning, it is used to refer particularly to those symbols or systems which are dialectically rejected in favour of the new truth. When Amida's Vow *is* the 'one vehicle' (*ichijō*), as in the stanza quoted above, it tends to appear as a new, positive exclusivism. As in the other schools of thought the pressures of denominational organisation and of individual piety reinforce this tendency.

This very brief sketch of attitudes towards the idea of skilful means in the context of some varied sectarian traditions is intended mainly to reflect the tenor of conversations with their living representatives. No attempt has been made to document systematically the vagaries of the term *hōben* in the sectarian literary traditions. However there seem to be two trends of interest. Firstly, popular practices of peripheral interest to Buddhism are described as *hōben*. Secondly, there is a tendency to see what others do as *hōben*, implying that it is a *mere* skilful means, and to hypostasise one's own central symbols or practice as a final resolution or summation of Buddhist teaching or Buddhist meaning. Both of these trends to some extent reflect and reinforce the popular way of understanding *hōben* against which Buddhist writers otherwise react sharply when attending specifically to the term.

One single conclusion about contemporary usage is therefore not possible. The term *hōben* is generally known among those who are self-consciously Buddhist, but its fundamental meaning as once given in the major Mahayana sutras tends to be overshadowed by the sectarian influences. Moreover while there are explicit variations at the official doctrinal level there is also variation in the manner in which different individuals understand the same forms of religion. Two people in one organised religious context will make use of the same materials very differently. One will use them for self-definition and self-assertion. Another, or the same person at a later date, will use them without this kind of affirmation or attachment, as skilful means in a truly Mahayana manner. The observer must always reckon with a coexistence and miscellany of use and misuse, as it might seem to be from a purist point of view. Similarly one should always bear in mind the possibility of a long-term dialectic of skilful means, not only expressed doctrinally but also articulated in a particular sectarian social form. With Buddhism, one might say, it does not matter if it is not fully understood or resolved until later.

---

[56] *Jōdo Wasan*, p. 104.

9 GENERAL OBSERVATIONS

Skilful means is not quite so tidy a concept as a systematic investigator might hope. The materials studied above show that it is sometimes of central importance and sometimes rests in a merely secondary niche. However as far as the history of religious ideas is concerned the main meaning must be taken as that which it had in the early Mahayana texts. Even though this was not necessarily always understood by later Buddhists, who may have used the term in a derivative and perhaps misleading way, the fundamental idea can no longer be entirely subtracted from our understanding of any later phase of Buddhism. This view is reinforced by the argument advanced above that the idea in any case had a natural starting point in the very nature of pre-Mahayana Buddhism.

Sometimes specific teachings or entertainments, invented by the Buddha or by bodhisattvas in order to help ordinary beings on their way, are referred to as skilful means. Sometimes the idea finds concrete reference in particular practices which one performs in order to make spiritual progress. One should not think however that skilful means are therefore just elementary or peripheral aspects of Buddhism. For one thing the fact that the idea seems to come up in the two divergent ways just mentioned is deceptive. They are but two different ways of speaking about the same total range of elements in the articulation of Buddhism as a working religion. This deeper undercurrent becomes evident if one tries to itemise all the things referred to now and then as skilful means in the main texts studied. It simply transpires that all possible ways of giving expression to Buddhist Dharma are to be so understood. This applies to elementary or peripheral devotions but also to central matters such as the four noble truths and the story of the Buddha's life, including his final nirvana. It also applies to special Mahayana ideas such as that of the bodhisattva bringing across other living beings, for it is by his skilful means that he does this while not being attached to the characteristics of the process. How could a bodhisattva free others if he were bound himself by the problem of their deliverance? Thus in terms of skilful means a bodhisattva's true practice and the deliverance of others belong together. The Mahayanists saw the whole Buddhist religion as a vehicle for 'crossing over' and for 'bringing over', which are inseparable. In short, Buddhism is skilful means.

When we speak of 'the Buddhist religion' we do well to remember that it probably never was a single set of concepts and practices, however much our long historical perspective may press us to simplify it in this way. Of course there were dominant formulations and techniques which have persisted throughout, but the great strength of Buddhism as a cultural force has lain in its positionless, mediating, method. It has always thrived on control

159

through syncretism. Syncretism is not a Buddhist word for these correlation procedures, but skilful means is. It is because Buddhists understand the functioning of their religion in terms of skilful means, or if not, then instinctively along the lines which the term skilful means sums up, that they have been so easily able throughout history to acclimatise their religion in diverse societies. On the one hand they are able to show patience in accepting heterodox and even contradictory tendencies in their surroundings, and on the other hand they are both persistent and sophisticated with regard to the eventual recoupment of Buddhist meaning. This does not imply that Buddhists do not resort to polemics, as is popularly but erroneously supposed. On the contrary it means that the appraisal of Buddhist polemics is particularly complicated.

Skilful means may be described as a hermeneutical control for Buddhists, in the sense that it allows for expressions of Buddhism to be developed while indicating that they are not to be misapplied or taken wrongly. An expression of Buddhism is supposed to be aligned with the karmic condition, and thus the culture, of those for whom it is intended, while bearing hidden within it the implication that they are already nirvanic in quality from the beginning. Such an expression of Buddhism is a skilful means. In so far as it is properly understood by those for whom it is intended, if they are not conceited, do not get tangled up in it, do not practice it 'as a characteristic', etc. then its initial ambiguity should be resolved into the original or final Buddhist meaning, leaving the empty shell of the device, whatever it was, behind. Of course similar devices will be used repeatedly throughout Buddhist history, which may give an air of cultural conservatism in some cases. This is because even though an expression of Buddhism understood as skilful means bears within it the seeds of its own dismantling, others similar to it need to be continuously reconstituted for successive Buddhists. The same principle allows enough room for creative modernists. It is of course difficult for the mere historian of religion to distinguish at any one time between truly operating skilful means and the fossilised jetsam of former times. After all, the normative discernment of skilful means entails an interpretative activity within the tradition, that is to say an activity analogous to what in the western world is known as theology. It was activity of this sort in which the composers of the early Mahayana sutras were engaged, when they used the term skilful means to indicate the way in which their Buddhist tradition ought really to be understood.

While Buddhism certainly does function in this way at the socio-cultural level, and this may indeed be the most evident aspect of the matter to historians and other observers, it should not be overlooked that the resolution of the ambiguities of skilful means takes place in the experience of successive individuals. This means that while phases of tradition and patterns of acculturation naturally form the materials for much of the activity of interpreting Buddhism, it is also possible to reflect upon the matter in a less time-bound way. Whatever the truth may be about the recurrence of buddhas, ordinary individuals do recur in the sense that they follow each other countlessly along analogous patterns of development. The expressions of Buddhism include words such as *anātman* or *śūnyatā*, stories and legends, political patronage, the language of rites and yoga, temple bells and cemetery stones; but all these expressions undergo shifts of meaning in the context of individual development. At first they are not understood, but they are acceptably present in a world which seems more or less definitely existing. Later they come to be understood, but their disappearance, together with that of the transitory world, is anticipated. So it is that all religious language and symbolism comes to be de-literalised. This maturation can be understood in terms of skilful means, namely as a move from profligate differentiation towards an inward consistency. This explains why it is quite appropriate for many ritualised individual predictions of Buddhahood to be made in The Lotus Sutra, once the principle of skilful means has been expounded and understood.

The idea of skilful means may operate in various ways at a varying pace. Fundamentally it refers to the very nature of the Buddhist religion. But the speed at which this is expressed and worked out varies in accordance with socio-cultural conditions. The reflective insights of early Mahayana were only possible on the basis of lengthening historical perspective. For example, it would not have been possible to say that the nine literary forms of Buddhist teaching were skilful means until these nine forms had all been elaborated and itemised. It was later quite natural for Chinese Buddhists to give expression to the same basic idea in terms of *p'an-chiao* theories of various kinds. In modern times it may be appropriate for Buddhists to align themselves with the historical understanding of the development of Buddhist literature, which does not in the least conflict with the concept of skilful means provided by the early Mahayanists. The main point remains that, once the tradition was sufficiently extended, it was possible for individual Buddhists, at varying speeds, to come to an understanding of the historical diversity within the tradition in terms of skilful means. Exactly the same applies with respect to the geographical diversification which Buddhism accepted from the start. The individuals influenced by Buddhism in any one context of cultural syncretism come to recognise, at varying speeds, the inward meaning or intention of the expressions which Buddhism adopted. In the meantime the contexts in which these recognitions take place continue to exist as long as the same socio-cultural conditions obtain; this is for the benefit of further persons involved. The teaching is never dismantled just because one individual has understood its character as skilful means. It remains in existence for others to see through. When the socio-cultural conditions change, then new expressions of Buddhism may be expected, as for example in both China and Japan today.

To anyone who has read this far the idea of skilful means may prove suggestive in the interpretation, or perhaps the better appreciation, of a whole range of religious phenomena: religious language and ritual in general, religion in its social and psychological outworkings, even those aspects of religion which to the rationalist appear as fabrications and frauds. In particular an understanding of the way Buddhism moves among all the other socio-cultural factors in its world, sharpened by the concept of skilful means, provides a clue to the provisional and ambiguous character of all syncretisms. It is relevant to the interpretation of all religious and ideological systems which proliferate themselves through new forms of communication acceptable to their changing environment. This means, in effect, all the great religious and religio-ideological systems which the world has ever seen; though admittedly not all operate with the same patient acceptance of heterodox tendencies or the same persistent sophistication in the eventual recoupment of their underlying intention.

It is easy to observe that the proponents of every religious and ideological system are continuously engaged in identifying the true meaning of successive expressions of their tradition. Every system has its narrow-minded conservationists of literal form and its tolerant if not woolly liberals, tussling between them over the meaning which their tradition bears. The matter is always complicated by the varying pace of change in the perspective of individuals. The idea of skilful means has a potential application, if the protagonists care to transfer it, to many an ideological or theological controversy. This is because every such system really requires both relentless criticism of the received forms and expressions while maintaining and indeed bringing out the meaning. Skilful means implies that there is a time to articulate a particular form or expression and a time to relegate it or dismantle it.

There is a sense in which every religion is pitched into the world, having its time and place, meeting the circumstances and bearing a meaning which is addressed to those circumstances. Every religion which can be named is what Lessing called a 'positive' religion, positively present in the world and thereby subject to historical relativism. An approximate contemporary of Lessing, the Japanese writer Tominaga Nakamoto, saw different religions but the same principle. Indeed our common knowledge of the physical universe in modern times now raises the inescapable probability that all specific religions will eventually disappear, without trace. The transmission of religious meanings depends therefore on a kind of suspense between the appearance and departure of a specific form. The ability to handle this suspense, speaking now very generally, is analogous to the skilful means cultivated by a bodhisattva in Mahayana Buddhism. Putting it another way, it is in tune with the way of the world to understand any expressions of religion in terms of provisional articulation and eventual dismantling, the meaning being given first in alignment with the 'karma', that is, the history, the society and the psychology, and then coming to fruition while the expression itself vanishes with them.

It would lead too far actively now to attempt the interpretation of a quite different religion in terms of this Buddhist concept. Different readers would no doubt prefer to consider different cases. The main religion of the writer's own society is Christianity, and it seems that in that connection at least there are many interesting matters which arise. Indeed the analogy between skilful means and some Christian materials has already been pointed out in print by earlier writers in a peripheral way. It is notable that recent decades have seen among Christian theologians one of the most sustained attempts in history to dismantle a religious tradition from within. Perhaps never before have the original and subsequent forms of a religion been so severely and systematically reviewed by international teams of professional theologians who nevertheless seek not to discard the persistent meaning of the tradition in question. Perhaps never before have so many religious leaders shocked so many religious followers. But the crisis has been great, and still is, at least in part because there is no concept adequate to articulate the debates except in terms of various forms of orthodoxy or betrayal. There is no concept traditional to Christianity which has enabled people to speak adequately of the relations between the proliferation and disposal of the various elements which have gone into the making of Christian religion. On the other hand it is readily evident to most westerners who have the concept of skilful means brought to their notice that Christianity provides natural analogies to the Buddhist procedures understood as skilful means.[1]

It should be admitted that the idea of skilful means does introduce a certain initial stress for those brought up in the western world. The three monotheistic religions which have dominated the west, Judaism, Christianity and Islam, have all appeared to be quite uncompromising in their account of what is true and what is false. The westerner might feel moved to say that he does not want to be tricked into understanding; to which the eastern Buddhist replies (has replied) that if he were, he should not complain, but be grateful. In any case the western traditions themselves are not necessarily quite what they seem to be. For one thing there is the question of inexpressibility as a truth-value, particularly in the context of the substantial mystical tradition in the west. It is perhaps even more important, if less obvious, that the element of contrivance in all western religions has never been properly characterised or understood. This refers not only to the acting and story-telling by which religion is elaborated and carried on in general,

---

[1] The problem to which one may refer for simplicity's sake as that of speaking about the essence of Christianity is probably best solved not by referring to particular doctrinal statements but by identifying the characteristic style or method with which it meets otherwise existing structures. It took its birth in a critical, ambivalent stance towards Jewish religion of the time, and while it later accommodated itself to dominant social forms in many ways it has again and again thrown up a reformatory concern for the rightly directed use of religious belief and practice. Christianity has always had a subtle relationship to its contextual religious and ideological systems, especially if we take its more naive protagonists as parts of a more complex overall phenomenon. This can be observed in the earliest syncretisms evidenced by the New Testament materials, through the Apologists and right down to modern times. Moreover, there has always been a fascinating symbiosis of literalism and non-literalism, as for example in the resurrection stories, but also in many other matters. Moreover, even leaving on one side the elitist stratifications found in Gnosticism, Christianity has always recognised in one way or another that change and maturation are appropriate in the Christian's own understanding of his religion. It seems reasonable to suggest therefore that particular expressions of Christianity in a situation, in a life, in a society, in fact have a status quite anal-

but also specifically to the fundamental self-understanding of the three religions mentioned as being historically occasioned. Of course, the religions have often been described as false or illusory; but, without assigning levels of value at this moment, they ought to be critically appreciated as *contrivances of truth*.

In the meantime skilful means remains a way of understanding Buddhist method. Although it has been treated more or less peripherally in modern writings, there seems little doubt of its general importance in Buddhism. It offers a coherent rationale for the diverse cultural and social proliferations of Buddhism. It makes sense both of the intellectual and experiential aspects of understanding. Moreover it has surely gone beyond Buddhism in a tightly defined sense to influence the art and politics of East Asia. There are many concepts and practices which may convey the meaning of Buddhism, but no one of them can finally pin it down. Buddhism needs to be understood as a working religion. The strength of Buddhism lies in its method as skilful means.

ogous to that ascribed to the various expressions of Buddhism. That is, they are expressions quite necessarily particular to the occasion and dispensable with it. They disappear ultimately with the individual historical circumstances in which and for which they were conceived. Seen in this perspective the idea of skilful means may be relevant to central questions such as the function of language about God. It might also facilitate a 'christology' appropriate to the relativism of the modern world and, as it were, ready to give way with the world. Such an approach would no doubt be full of pitfalls and it would be a distortion to pursue them further here, but it may be helpful to note that the writer has attempted some other groundwork elsewhere. Specific attention is given to the syncretistic proliferation of religion in 'The Transplantation of Religions', *Numen* XVI, 3 (1969), 'Syncretism and Ambiguity', *Numen* XVIII, 2 (1971), and 'Assimilation and Skilful Means', *Religion* I, 2 (1971). Presuppositions of the appraisal of religions in the perspective of historical relativism are considered in 'Aufklärung and Religion in Europe and Japan', *Religious Studies* 9 (1973); and in *Ernst Troeltsch, Writings on Theology and Religion*, Duckworth 1977, co-translated and co-authored with Robert Morgan (cf. especially the section on 'Interpreting religious traditions' in the essay 'Troeltsch and the Science of Religion', which comments on Troeltsch's own major essay translated as 'What does "essence of Christianity" mean?'). Finally, there is a direct approach to the problem of transferring hermeneutical concepts from one religion to another in the essay 'Comparative Hermeneutics in Religion' in *The Cardinal Meaning, Essays in Comparative Hermeneutics: Buddhism and Christianity*, The Hague 1973, co-edited with Robert Morgan.

APPENDIX A
BRIEF NOTE ON THE MAIN TEXTS USED

T numbers and Vol. numbers refer to the *Taishō Shinshū Daizōkyō*.

T262 (in Vol. IX) 妙法蓮華經
Ch. *Miao-fa-lien-hua-ching*
J. *Myō-hō-ren-ge-kyō*
Eng. Sutra of the Lotus Flower of the Wonderful Dharma
Conventional J. *Hokekyō*
Conventional Eng. The Lotus Sutra
Cf. Sanskrit *Saddharmapuṇḍarīka-sūtra*
T262 has seven 'rolls' and 28 chapters, while the Sanskrit has 27 chapters
(cf. table in Appendix B). Cf. also T263 and 264 and discussion of relation-
ships in Appendix B.

T475 (in Vol. XIV) 維摩詰所說經
Ch. *Wei-mo-chieh-so-shuo-ching*
J. *Yui-ma-kitsu-sho-setsu-kyō*
Eng. Sutra of the Teaching of Wei-mo-chieh
Conventional J. *Yuimagyō*
Conventional Eng. The Teaching of Vimalakīrti
Cf. Sanskrit *Vimalakīrti-nirdeśa-sūtra* (only quotations extant)
T475 has three 'rolls' and 14 chapters, while the Tibetan differs (cf. Lamotte,
L'Enseignement de Vimalakīrti, p. 79).

T642 (in Vol. XV) 佛說首楞嚴三昧經
Ch. *Fo-shuo-shou-leng-yen-san-mei-ching*
J. *Bus-setsu-shu-ryō-gon-zam-mai-kyō*
Eng. Sutra of the Buddha's teaching on the Śūraṃgama-samādhi
Conventional J. *Shuryōgongyō*
Conventional Eng. The Śūraṃgama-samādhi Sutra
Cf. Sanskrit *Śūraṃgamasamādhi-sūtra* (only fragments extant)
T642 consists of two 'rolls' and is not divided into chapters. It should not
be confused with T945.

T223 (in Vol. VIII) 摩訶般若波羅蜜經
Ch. *Mo-ho-pan-jo-po-lo-mi-ching*
J. *Ma-ka-han-nya-ha-ra-mitsu-kyō*
Eng. Great Prajñā-pāramitā Sutra
Conventional J. *Daihannyakyō* (but N.B. not T220 in Vols. V-VII),
Daibongyō or *Daibonhannyakyō*

Cf. Sanskrit *Pañcaviṃśatisāhasrikā-prajñāpāramitā-sūtra*

T223 consists of no less than twenty-seven 'rolls' and contains 90 chapters. On relations between Prajñā-pāramitā texts cf. Conze's *The Prajñā-pāramitā Literature.*

T227 (in Vol. VIII) 小品般若波羅蜜經
Ch. *Hsiao-p'in-pan-jo-po-lo-mi-ching*
J. *Shō-bon-han-nya-ha-ra-mitsu-kyō*
Eng. Shorter Prajñā-pāramitā Sutra
Conventional J. *Shōbongyō*
Cf. Sanskrit *Aṣṭasāhasrikā-prajñāpāramitā-sūtra*

T227 consists of ten 'rolls' and 29 chapters, while Conze translated from a Sanskrit text in 32 chapters (*The Perfection of Wisdom in Eight Thousand Lines and its Verse Summary*). *Hōbōgirin* gives the official name of this sutra as being identical with 223, but the *Taishō Shinshū Daizōkyō Mokuroku* enters it as here, and so does Vol. VIII itself.

T235 (in Vol. VIII) 金剛般若波羅蜜經
Ch. *Chin-kang-pan-jo-po-lo-mi-ching*
J. *Kon-gō-han-nya-ha-ra-mitsu-kyō*
Eng. Diamond Prajñā-pāramitā Sutra
Conventional J. *Kongōkyō*
Conventional Eng. The Diamond Sutra
Cf. Sanskrit *Vajracchedikā-prajñāpāramitā-sūtra*

T235 consists of one 'roll' only; for the Skt. text, translation and commentaries cf. Conze and Tucci in *Serie Orientale Roma* Nos. XIII and IX respectively.

T250 (in Vol. VIII) 摩訶般若波羅蜜大明呪經
Ch. *Mo-ho-pan-jo-po-lo-mi-ta-ming-chou-ching*
J. *Ma-ka-han-nya-ha-ra-mitsu-dai-myō-ju-kyō*
Eng. Sutra of the Great Prajñā-pāramitā's Great Bright Spell
Conventional J. *Daimyōjukyō*
Conventional Eng. The Heart Sutra
Cf. Sanskrit *Prajñāpāramitā-hṛdaya-sūtra*

T250 covers less than a page. A different version (T251 by Hsüan Tsang) is more commonly used and contains the name 'Heart Sutra' in its title. But cf. also an important parallel passage in Kumārajīva's T223, TVIII 223a.

T1564 (in Vol. XXX) 中論
Ch. *Chung-lun*
J. Chū-ron
Eng. The Middle Treatise

T1564 consists of four 'rolls' and may be compared to Sanskrit *Madhya-makaśāstra* in so far as both contain Nāgārjuna's Middle Stanzas, on which they are commentaries. The authorship of the Chung-lun commentary is discussed in Robinson's *Early Mādhyamika in India and China,* who concludes that Kumārajīva himself has much responsibility for the final Chinese text (pp. 29ff.).

T1568 (in Vol. **XXX**) 十二門論
Ch. *Shih-erh-men-lun*
J. *Jū-ni-mon-ron*
Eng. The Twelve Topic Treatise
T1568 consists of one 'roll' only and was attributed to Nāgārjuna.

T1569 (in Vol. **XXX**) 百論
Ch. *Pai-lun,* or *po-lun*
J. *Hyaku-ron*
Eng. The Hundred Treatise
T1569 is a commentary in two 'rolls' on stanzas by Āryadeva, a follower of Nāgārjuna. The commentary is ascribed to Vasu, whose identification is otherwise uncertain, cf. Robinson, *op. cit.* p. 33.

N.B. Occurrences of the term *fang-pien* 方便 in the above writings are catalogued in Appendices C-F below.

APPENDIX B
HISTORICO-CRITICAL PERSPECTIVE ON THE LOTUS SUTRA

The above examination of the concept of skilful means was based on the premise that Kumārajīva's Chinese version of The Lotus Sutra may fairly be viewed as a literary unity. There is a historical appropriateness to the premise, but it is of some importance to locate that literary unity in its proper context in the history of the sutra's emergence. Moreover, as there is no adequate introduction to the Lotus Sutra presently available in English, the following very brief perspective may also be of some general use to readers.

The critical study of the text of The Lotus Sutra may be said to have begun in China, for the editors of the third Chinese version discussed in a preface the manuscripts which they consulted (see below). Modern study of the text however really began when the first Sanskrit manuscripts were collected in Nepal in the early nineteenth century, since when the discovery and comparison of various manuscripts has been slowly advanced with the co-operation of scholars in various countries. A general account of the European discovery of Buddhist Sanskrit literature may be found in G. Welbon's *The Buddhist Nirvana and its Western Interpreters*. As far as the text of The Lotus Sutra is concerned the main landmarks of progress are the Sanskrit editions published by Kern and Nanjio (1908-1912), by Wogihara and Tsuchida (1934-5) and by Nalinaksha Dutt (1953). (Details of these and other works mentioned below will be found in the bibliography.) The first of these used several Nepalese mss. and also indicated variations in a Central Asian source known as the Petrowski Manuscript. The Wogihara-Tsuchida edition was based on Kern-Nanjio but referred also to the Chinese and Tibetan versions. The Kern-Nanjio edition was most severely criticised by W. Baruch in his *Beiträge zum Saddharmapuṇḍarīka-sūtra* (1938). It is most unfortunate that his own edition ('Das Manuskript einer Neuausgabe des Saddharmapuṇḍarīkasūtra's liegt nach mehrjähriger Arbeit druckfertig vor.' p. vii) never saw the light of day. Baruch also recorded his deep suspicion of the Wogihara-Tsuchida edition, based as it was on Kern-Nanjio, although it appears that he never examined the work in detail. Wogihara-Tsuchida was reviewed in detail by F. Weller in the *Orientalistische Literaturzeitung*, 1937, Nr. 2, pp. 118-125. Nalinaksha Dutt's edition was based on the two previous editions, but took note of readings from Central Asian manuscripts collated by N. D. Mironov, cf. the latter's 'Buddhist Miscellanea II: Central Asian Recensions of the Saddharmapuṇḍarīka', JRAS 1927. Because of the dependence of the later traditions on Kern-Nanjio, Iwamoto Yutaka was still able to describe it as the '*editio princeps*' (Sakamoto and Iwamoto, *Hokekyō*

Vol. 1, 1962, p. 396), in his review of Lotus Sutra studies. It is a sorry state of affairs that there is not an up-to-date critical edition which commands general confidence and which makes use of all of the available sources. Even the Chinese versions, which have been available for long enough, have never been properly collated with the Sanskrit manuscript tradition.

As to translations from Sanskrit, it must be recognised that the pioneer translations by Burnouf into French (1852) and by Kern into English (1884, not 1909 as indicated by Iwamoto, *op. cit.* p. 396) preceded even the first critical edition of the text itself. They reflect only a section of the manuscript tradition as a whole. Kern's translation also suffers from more general terminological defects and although it first appeared in the prestigious *Sacred Books of the East* series edited by Max Müller, and was recently republished in unrevised form, it should only be used with great caution to obtain a general indication of the contents of the sutra. The best English translation for general use at present is that of Katō, Soothill & Schiffer from Chinese, see Chapter One, note 4. There are no up-to-date translations from Sanskrit in European languages, though readers of Japanese can make use of Iwamoto's critically annotated translation, *op. cit.*

The general position with regard to the relationships between the various texts and versions is as follows:

Texts (*Buddhist Hybrid Sanskrit*)	*Versions* (*Chinese and Tibetan*)
I (a) Gilgit ms., Kashmir, three-quarters of whole text, 5th-6th century A.D.	
(b)	*Cheng-fa-hua-ching* 正法華經 (J. pronunciation: *Shōhokkekyō*) T263, Chinese version by Dharmarakṣa, 286 A.D.
(c)	*T'ien-p'in-miao-fa-lien-hua-ching* 添品妙法蓮華經 (J. pronunciation: *Tenbonmyōhōrengekyō*) T264, Chinese version by Jñānagupta and Dharmagupta, 601 A.D. (revising T262, see below)
(d)	*Dam-paḥi chos pad-ma dkar-po shes-bya ba theg-pa chen-poḥi mdo*, Tibetan version by Surendrabodhi and Sna-nam Ye-śes sde
(e) Nepalese mss., various mss. dating from 11th century A.D.	
II (a)	*Miao-fa-lien-hua-ching* 妙法蓮華經 (J. pronunciation: *Myōhōrengekyō*)

                                        T262, Chinese version by
                                        Kumārajīva, 406 A.D., based on
                                        ms. from Kucha in Central Asia

(b) Central Asian mss., various
    fragments from fifth century
    onwards including lengthy
    Petrowski ms. from Kashgar

The table is based on a similar table in Iwamoto, *op. cit.* p. 412, and further bibliographical and other information, especially on the various manuscript fragments which have been discovered, can be found in his review as a whole.

Note that the Gilgit ms. is not complete, and even that of it which remains after a deplorable dispersal has not yet been assimilated in a critical edition. The Tibetan version is said to be close to the late Nepalese mss. Since the Central Asian mss. are also fragmentary, the Chinese versions are a most important source of information. It is of particular significance that Ib (T263) and IIa (T262) fall into different groups.

Baruch strove to group them the other way round, relating T263 to the Central Asian manuscripts and T262 to the Nepalese group, but there are many inconsistencies in his treatment of T262. Ic (T264) is secondary. Its position in group I arises only from the fact that it contains some additions and 'corrections' typical of that group, for the text in general follows Kumārajīva's form of translation.

Some attention must now be paid to the relationships between the three Chinese versions. The first, by Dharmarakṣa in A.D. 286, was made more or less redundant by the much more widely used translation of Kumārajīva. The differences between the two no doubt arise partly because Kumārajīva was a mediating thinker who wished to express the meaning of the sutra in clear and direct Chinese. Whether this meant that his version was more faithful or less faithful to his original Sanskrit is a complex problem. A more faithful translation could be at the same time less useful for textual information. Unfortunately, since the manuscripts which the two translators used are not themselves available little progress can be made on this matter.

Of immediate interest however is the fact that Kumārajīva seems to have made use of a manuscript which was different from that which underlies T263. The preface to the third Chinese version states this explicitly. Indeed the writer of that preface claimed to have seen two different manuscripts of The Lotus Sutra in a sutra store house. One of these was written on palm leaves and the other in a script used in Kucha, where Kumārajīva lived for thirty years. The latter manuscript, it is said, agreed very closely with Kumārajīva's Chinese version. The palm leaf manuscript, on the other hand, agreed with Dharmarakṣa's version. Although Dharmarakṣa's version appeared first it should not be thought that the manuscript used by him necessarily represented an earlier form of the textual tradition. The only real evidence which we have about this is to be drawn from a comparison of the contents and arrangement of the two versions. As will be indicated below the likelihood is rather that the manuscript underlying Kumārajīva's version represented the earlier form of textual tradition.

The producers of the third version, T264, attempted to iron out the differences of content and arrangement which the first two versions displayed. For this reason it was called the *T'ien-p'in-miao-fa-lien-hua-ching*, that is, the *Miao-fa-lien-hua-ching* with additional material. The preface mentioned earlier not only refers to manuscripts close to those which the earlier translators must have used, but also gives important evidence about variations of content and arrangement with respect to which they themselves had to adopt a policy. They also refer to others before them who added to Kumārajīva's version. The passage is so important that it must be quoted. The numbers in brackets indicate the *T'ien-p'in*/Sanskrit chapter numeration for every reference, excepting of course for the Devadatta chapter which has no separate number in those texts.

'In former times the Tun Huang *śramaṇa*, the Indian Dharmarakṣa, in the generation of Wu of the Chin dynasty, translated the *Cheng-fa-hua-ching*. In the later Ch'in, at the request of Yang Hsing, Kumārajīva made a new translation, the *Miao-fa-lien-hua-ching*. When we examined the two translations we found that they are not the same text. Dharmarakṣa followed the palm leaves, while Kumārajīva followed the Kucha text. We also investigated the sutra store and looked closely at two books, one on palm leaves which agrees exactly with the *Cheng-fa* and one in Kucha script which is just the same as the *Miao-fa*. Furthermore, there are some neglected places in Dharmarakṣa's leaves while Kumārajīva's text has no such gaps. Nevertheless what is lacking in Dharmarakṣa's is the verses of the P'u-men-p'in 普門品 (24), while what is lacking in Kumārajīva's is half of the Yo-tsao-yü-p'in 藥草喻品 (5), the beginnings of the Pūrṇa-p'in 富樓那品 (8) and Fa-shih-p'in 法師品 (10), the Devadatta-p'in and the P'u-men-p'in (24) verses. Kumārajīva transposes the Chu-lei-p'in 囑累品 (27) before the Yo-wang-p'in 藥王品 (22). Both put the *Dhāraṇī*-p'in (21) after the P'u-men-p'in (24). There are some other points of divergence which cannot be recorded in detail. As to the Devadatta-p'in and P'u-men-p'in verses, we observe that former worthies have continued to give them out, following the fashion of adding what is lacking. Furthermore, we respect received tradition and make this pattern our rule. In the first year of the Jen Shou period of the Great Sui dynasty, Bitter-spirits year, at the request of the *śramaṇa* Shang Hsing of the monastery P'u-yao-ssu, I re-examined the Indian palm leaf text together with the Dharma masters Jñānagupta and Dharmagupta at the monastery Ta-hsing-shan-ssu. The beginnings of the Pūrṇa-p'in (8) and the Fa-shih-p'in (10) were also lacking in the text we examined. We have re-added the other half to the Yo-tsao-yü-p'in (5), inserted the Devadatta-p'in into the T'a-p'in (11) made the *Dhāraṇī*-p'in (21) follow the Shen-li-p'in 神力品 (20), and restored the Chu-lei-p'in (27) as the conclusion at the end.' (T IX 134b-c).

Kern quoted Nanjio's translation, but although he realised that Kumārajīva may have used an older manuscript (*Saddharma-puṇḍarīka*, p. xxi) he did not draw out the full significance of this preface. Baruch also failed to do so because of his prejudice against the possible value of Kumārajīva's version (*op. cit.* pp. 32-35). Even Iwamoto, who like Kern, also quoted the preface, came out with a preference for T263's closer literal similarity with *later* Sanskrit manuscripts and irrelevantly criticised the use of Kumāra-jīva's version by present day 'fanatics' (*op. cit.* p. 409). It will be observed that the preface refers to no less than *five* previous stages in the textual transmission of which three are no longer available to us. These are: the 'palm leaf' manuscript, Dharmarakṣa's translation, the Kucha manuscript, Kumārajīva's original translation (which we will hasten to call Kumārajīva I before anybody comes up with *Ur*-Kumārajīva), and Kumārajīva's trans-lation with the verses added to Chapters XII and XXV by the 'former worthies' (which we may call Kumārajīva II). Baruch treats this latter information as if it suggests that plenty of other changes were made to Kumārajīva's original version (*op. cit.* p. 35) but there is no evidence for this at all, and indeed it seems unlikely that such changes would have gone unremarked. The information contained in the preface, plus what is known of the texts which survived, enables us to compile the following table. It indicates the presence or absence of six portions of text.

	Kucha text	Kumā-rajīva I	Palm-leaf ms	T263, Dharma-rakṣa	Kumā-rajīva II (= T262)	T264, T'ien p'in	Extant Sanskrit
Latter half of ch. 5	—	—	in	in	—	in	in
Passage near beginning of ch. 8	—	—	—	in	—	—	—
Passage at beginning of ch. 10	—	—	—	in	—	—	—
Verses of Devadatta chapter (11, or XII in T262)	—	—	in	in	in	in	in
Verses 1-26 ch. 24, (ch. XXV in T262)	—	—	—	—	in	in	in

Verses 27-33
of ch. 24,
(ch. XXV in
T262)   —   —   —   —   —   —   in

The most important fact demonstrated by this table is that none of the passages in question appeared in Kumārajīva I or the Kucha text, while all are found in the later Sanskrit manuscripts except for the two extra passages peculiar to T263. The question is whether people were leaving things out or putting things in. It is often supposed that Kumārajīva simply left things out, and that the full-blown Sanskrit manuscripts, to which Dharmarakṣa's earlier Chinese version more nearly approximates, are the measure of the original text. This view arises for two reasons. One is that Dharmarakṣa's version is known to be older and hence naively thought to represent 'the' original Sanskrit more accurately than Kumārajīva's version. However there is no *a priori* justification for this assumption. The other reason is the unfor-tunate term 闕 which was used in the preface quoted above to describe the absence of certain passages. Literally speaking the translators may appear as the agents in 'omitting' passages, but the real implication of the term may be more restrained, namely that the passages are 'lacking'. Admittedly the very fact that the *T'ien-p'in* version made up some of the lacking passages might imply that they considered them to have been omitted; but on the other hand they did not make up all 'lacking' passages.

There are in fact strong reasons to presume that the passages were not omitted, but added. None of the passages in question is represented by a disruption when it is not present. Nor is there any specific reason to suppose that any specific passage was omitted by anybody, whether by accident or on purpose. On the other hand the whole psychology of sutra transmission is precisely to hand down, with reasonable circumspection, everything which posterity may need. Hesitant additions gradually come to be established, acceptance coming by fits and starts. Thus the *T'ien-p'in* editors wanted to put in all that should be put in, having looked over what was available. They approved of the 'former worthies' who added verses to Kumārajīva I, and they followed suit. They also touched up the text in other ways, for example by adding to the chapter on Avalokiteśvara a short exchange between two bodhisattvas of 62 Chinese characters, (not indicated in the table above). The verses on Amitābha (verses 27-33 chapter 24), found only in the Sanskrit texts, are another example of exactly the same process taking place else-where, representing an addition which just happened not to gain currency in China at the right time.

If this general supposition is correct it is quite clear that Kumārajīva I, and the Kucha manuscript, represented an older textual tradition than that carried forward by the 'palm leaf' manuscript and T263. The only thing which Dharmarakṣa's version 'lacks' are the Avalokiteśvara verses (chapter 24, verses 1-26), but we also *know* that these were coming in at a later date, being contributed for example to Kumārajīva II (our present T262). Kumārajīva I however lacked no less than four items contained in T263. It does not matter in the least that T263 pre-dates Kumārajīva I by just over a century. The point is that compilation was further advanced in the manuscript used by Dharmarakṣa than in the manuscript used by Kumārajīva. Kumārajīva must have known of Dharmarakṣa's existing version, which he chose not to copy. He may have had access to manuscripts such as Dharmarakṣa used; that we do not know. Could it be that he actually preferred the text from Kucha?

T263 has *some* relationship to the Nepalese manuscript tradition, though not a perfect one, but it seems to have been treated by the Chinese not only as a dead translation but also as a doubtful textual tradition. The *T'ien-p'in* editors incorporated materials from elsewhere, but only used T263 where it was corroborated by the 'palm leaf' manuscript. Thus they did not take up the passages in chapters 8 and 10, and since these now turn out not to be in the Nepalese manuscripts either they deserve to be congratulated.

The numeration and arrangement of chapters also provides evidence which strongly supports the view indicated above. Before commenting on details however there follows, for general reference, a synoptic view of the chapter headings and numbers of Kumārajīva's version (T262) and the extant Sanskrit text. The contents of each chapter correspond to that in the column opposite except where otherwise indicated, except for minor variations.

Kumārajīva's Chinese version		*Extant Sanskrit*	
I	Introduction	1	The occasion
II	Skilful means	2	Skill in means
III	An allegory	3	An allegory
IV	Faith-discernment	4	Disposition
V	Parable of the herbs	5	Herbs (*plus extra material*)
VI	Prediction	6	Prediction
VII	Parable of the magic city	7	Parts played in a previous life
VIII	Prediction about the five hundred disciples	8	Prediction about the five hundred monks
IX	Destiny of those training and trained	9	Prediction
X	Expositor of the Dharma	10	Expositor of the Dharma
XI	Beholding the precious stupa	11	Appearance of a stupa
XII	Devadatta	—	(*includes* XII *opposite*)
XIII	Exhortation to hold firm	12	Fortitude
XIV	Carefree life	13	Carefree life
XV	Springing up out of the earth	14	Appearance of bodhisattvas from the gaps of the earth
XVI	Duration of life of the Tathāgata	15	Duration of life of the Tathāgata
XVII	Discernment of merit	16	Allocation of merit

XVIII	The merits of joyful acceptance	17	Exposition of the happiness of heartfelt conversion
XIX	The merits of an expositor	18	Benefits received by an expositor of the Dharma
XX	The bodhisattva Never-despise	19	Sadāparibhūta
XXI	The divine power of the Tathāgata	20	Demonstration of the super-human powers of the Tathāgata
XXII	The commission (*equals* 27)	21	Spells (*equals* XXVI)
XXIII	The original story of the bodhisattva Medicine-king	22	The part of Bhaiṣajyarāja in a previous life
XXIV	The bodhisattva Wonder-sound	23	Gadgadasvara
XXV	The universal gate of the bodhisattva Regarder-of-the-cries-of-the-world	24	Samantamukha (*plus extra verses, verses* 27-33)
XXVI	Dhāraṇī (*i.e. spells,* equals 21)	25	The part of King Subhavyūha in a previous life (*equals* XXVII)
XXVII	The original story of King Resplendent (*equals* 25)	26	Samantabhadra's encouragement (*equals* XXVIII)
XXVIII	Encouragement of the bodhisattva Universal-virtue (*equals* 26)	27	The commission (*equals* XXII)

The chapter headings of T264 follow those of T262, except that Chapter XII of T262 does not appear as a chapter in T264, and the titles of chapters XV and XVI in T262 are shortened in T264 where they appear as XIV and XV. Chapter VIII is referred to in the preface quoted earlier as the Pūrṇa Chapter, Pūrṇa being the name of the bodhisattva most referred to, but T264 follows T262 in the printed text today. The chapter headings of T263 naturally display more variations when compared with those of T262, but the details need not detain us.

It will be noticed that from Chapter XI/11 onwards the numeration of chapters does not coincide as between T262 and the Sanskrit text, and care should be taken not to confuse them. This is partly because the chapter on Devadatta was for some time treated as an independent chapter, as it still appears in T262, whereas in the present form of the Sanskrit it has been incorporated into Chapter 11. Both T263 and T264 already made this conflation, and therefore they too have a total of twenty-seven chapters only. Baruch's treatment of this matter, *op. cit.*, is hopelessly impaled on the later Chinese rationalisation that Kumārajīva or unspecified redactors separated an original Chapter 11 into two parts. The matter cannot now be pursued in detail, but the most widely held view is that the Devadatta chapter was a relatively late addition to the sutra, and that this is illustrated by its separateness in T262. Indeed it has been doubted whether Kumārajīva's original work, Kumārajīva I, contained the chapter at all. Sasaki Kōken has concluded that it was probably inserted some time in the late fifth century or in the sixth century A.D. (in Mochizuki Kankō (ed.) *Kindai Nihon no Hokke Bukkyō*, Kyoto 1968, pp. 564-570). However that may be, the peculiarity of Kumārajīva's version in this respect is a further indication that it is based on a manuscript in an older state than that used for T263.

The arrangement of the last seven chapters needs special consideration. Kern's diagram to illustrate this (in the introduction to his translation), and others made by Japanese authors, are far from clear. In the following table the numeration of the Chinese versions is given in Roman numerals and the numeration of the extant Sanskrit is given in Arabic numberals. In addition the numbers of the quivalent Sanskrit chapters are given in brackets for each Chinese version, so that the easy way to compare the arrangement is to look at the Arabic numerals only. It will be seen that T264 is exactly equivalent to the Sanskrit, while the other two versions indicate displacements which are indicated by asterisks.

T262		*T263*		*T264*		*Sanskrit*
XXII	(27)*	XXI	(22)	XXI	(21)	21
XXIII	(22)	XXII	(23)	XXII	(22)	22
XXIV	(23)	XXIII	(24)	XXIII	(23)	23
XXV	(24)	XXIV	(21)*	XXIV	(24)	24
XXVI	(21)*	XXV	(25)	XXV	(25)	25
XXVII	(25)	XXVI	(26)	XXVI	(26)	26
XXVIII	(26)	XXVII	(27)	XXVII	(27)	27

Firstly, chapter 27 seems, in the textual tradition followed by Kumārajīva, to have preceded chapters 21-26. It is usually concluded from this (e.g. Kern, *op. cit.* p. xxi) that it formed the conclusion of the sutra at some time when it consisted of twenty-one chapters only. This hypothesis is supported also by the character of the contents of chapter 27 which is clearly a chapter of conclusion, and also by the contents of chapter 20 which are natural enough for a penultimate chapter. It is likely therefore that chapters 21-26 circulated at first as a kind of appendix to the main body of the sutra until finally the concluding chapter was moved along in order to appear at the *de facto* end. If this is so it is a third indication that, even though T263 is older as a translation than T262 Kumārajīva used a manuscript which had a more ancient arrangement.

The second displacement is that of chapter 21. If the order of precedence for antiquity of arrangement is: T262, T263, T264 and extant Sanskrit, then it is tempting to conclude by analogy with the above that chapter 21 was moved back to its present position in T264 (and Sanskrit) at some point later than the compilation of the manuscripts used for the previous Chinese versions. The motive for this may have been to range the chapter as nearly as possible with earlier chapters having a similar import. It may be objected that chapter 21 is rather a unique chapter in that it deals with the giving and listing of spells or talismanic formulae. However the point of the spells is that they protect those who keep The Lotus Sutra in their memory or in a book, and it may be argued therefore that the chapter is not so much interested in the spells themselves, but rather in the people who keep and transmit The Lotus Sutra. In this respect it displays a significant community of interest with chapters 10, 12, 13, 16, 17, 18 and 19, all of which deal with the life-style, the problems and the solaces of expositors of The Lotus Sutra. Again, it might be supposed that if someone were re-arranging chapters in this way a position between chapters 19 and 20 would have been more appropriate. However, chapter 20, as was noted above, was one of the concluding chapters of the earlier body of the sutra, and therefore it would have been natural to hesitate to push chapter 21 back before that while yet wishing to move it back as far as possible among those chapters known to have been appended. All the other remaining chapters are concerned with various great bodhi-sattvas, etc., and so it would be quite appropriate for the chapter on spells to be made to precede them. There seems to be no particular reason why the displacement should have been made the other way round, i.e., from the present position in the Sanskrit to the position between chapters 24 and 25 which is represented in the two earliest Chinese versions. If the two displace-ments are thus or similarly to be accounted for, it may further be concluded that the order of the last six chapters of T262 is most likely to be the order in which they were originally appended to the earlier and shorter sutra.

All in all, there are three distinct reasons for presuming that the text which Kumārajīva used represents the most ancient stage of the textual tradition about which we have knowledge. Firstly, it contained significantly less materials than the other stages that we know about; secondly, the chapter on Devadatta was still numbered separately; and thirdly, the arrangement of the last seven chapters is the most archaic stage known to us in the process of their incorporation into the whole. Dharmarakṣa's version by contrast is of positive importance for the very different reason that it represents a *later* stage of textual tradition at an *earlier* date, which has implications for the overall dating of the sutra (see below).

The variations of content and arrangement have already led to a discussion of some aspects of the compilation of the sutra. Further clarification of this process depends on an examination of more detailed characteristics of the text. This was first attempted by Fuse Kōgaku who published his results in a work entitled *Hokekyō Seiritsu Shi* (i.e. 'History of the Formation of The Lotus Sutra') in 1934. His general conclusions have been accepted by Japanese scholars down to the present day, and he summarised them himself in 1966 in an article for the general public entitled 'Hokekyō Seiritsu no Rekishi' (see bibliography). Fuse used both the Chinese versions and the Sanskrit of Kern and Nanjio. It is conceivable that a complete collation of more recently discovered fragments would provide a text which might yield slightly different conclusions. However, Iwamoto *op. cit.* pp. 417 ff., sur-veying the linguistic evidence recently, could only find hints that the sutra first stemmed from the Maghada district, or at least from eastern India, and offered no suggestions for a new linguistic approach to the problem of the compilation of the sutra. Note also that Rawlinson has made a detailed study (*op. cit.*), mainly on the basis of the Sanskrit text, and independent of Japanese research. The discussion below is based on Fuse's approach.

Fuse gave three reasons for distinguishing a major fissure in the sutra between chapter 9 and chapter 10, as follows:

(i) In chapter 10 the word *pustaka* appears for the first time to refer to 'the sutra' alongside the words *sūtra* and *dharmaparyāya* which had been used in the preceding chapters. This is significant because while the two latter words can refer to 'teaching' whether written or not, the term *pustaka* definitely implies a written sutra. (Kern translated it as 'book', *op. cit.* p. 214, etc.)

(ii) Chapter 10 also sees the introduction of three new forms of devotion to the sutra which imply its existence in written form. These are 'chanting' in the sense of reciting from a text, 'copying' and 'honouring', i.e., with flowers and so on. Forms of devotion to the sutra mentioned in the earlier chapters such as memorisation, recitation (from memory) and explanation, did not imply that it existed as a text. Indeed the assumption was that the sutra was heard from the mouth of the Buddha himself.

(iii) Finally there is a new emphasis in chapter 10 on the *caitya*, a shrine within which is deposited a copy of the sutra, as opposed to the *stupa*, which is a repository for the relics of a Buddha. Indeed, in spite of the very significant magical stupa which appears in chapter 11, there is in chapter 10 a specific recommendation to the effect that a *caitya* is as valuable as a *stupa* and should be so honoured.

These three facts are not merely incidental differences of vocabulary, but they betray rather a new and different point of view from which it is possible to look back and speak of the sutra as a physical entity, indeed as an already existing book. On the basis of this evidence and many other considerations about the contents of the various chapters Fuse concluded that the main part of the sutra was compiled in two main stages, namely (in the Sanskrit numeration):

I: chapters 1-9, and chapter 17 (which he thought displayed an approach similar to the early chapters).

II: chapters 10-20 and 27 (excluding the Devadatta section and excluding chapter 17 referred to above).

He also compared the prose and verse portions of the chapters in question. Whereas Burnouf had argued for the priority of the prose, Fuse agreed with Kern's later judgement that the verse was written first, at least as far as the first part of the sutra was concerned. In the second part he found no sufficient reason to reckon either as predating the other. (Chapters 21-26 contain no significant verse of early date. The stanzas of chapter 24 have been referred to already, and apart from these there are some nine stanzas scattered among chapters 21, 22 and 25, all of them being brief sentences of address).

Altogether then, Fuse saw the growth of the sutra as having had four main stages. They are, with the approximate dates which he assigned to them, as follows:

I:	chapters 1-9 and 17, verse;	1st century B.C.
II:	chapters 1-9 and 17, prose;	1st century A.D.
III:	chapters 10-20 and 27 (except the Devadatta chapter and 17);	circa 100 A.D.
IV:	chapters 21-26;	circa 150 A.D.

To these may be added a fifth stage which would include the Devadatta section and other small additions. Nearly all of these must have been in existence before 286 A.D., the date of Dharmarakṣa's translation.

If Fuse's analysis of the main stages of growth is right, we have to take the original nugget of The Lotus Sutra as having consisted of the verses of chapters 1-9, or as some part thereof. (Fuse's association of chapter 17 with these earlier chapters is, I think, of incidental interest rather than of fundamental importance.) It is within these portions that the original growing point of the sutra is to be discerned. It may be that one more step forward can be taken by means of a simple form-critical approach. Chapters 1-9 include four main types of material, namely: (i) an introduction, namely the occasion (*nidāna*) of a preaching to be given by the Buddha; (ii) the preaching itself, given directly; (iii) stories (*aupamya*) which illustrate the meaning of the preaching in an indirect, allegorical way; (iv) announcements or predictions (*vyākaraṇa*) concerning the future destiny of those hearing the preaching. Although there are one or two anomalies in the arrangement as it now stands, there seems little doubt that the thread running through chapters 1-9 was spun in terms of these four main types of material and that the various chapters contribute in their various ways to a coherent literary whole. There is only one chapter of which it could reasonably be argued that it once stood alone as an independent unit, and that is chapter 7. Moreover, this chapter, alone of the chapters in question, contains within itself all four of the main types of material which are found in chapters 1-9 as a whole. It is a story set in the distant past, entitled *Pūrvayoga* (i.e. 'Parts played in a previous life'), and it is in effect a miniature Lotus Sutra. Is it too far-fetched to suggest that the ideas characteristic of The Lotus Sutra as a whole were first intimated in that fairly short writing, in a manner which did not in itself provide too stark a doctrinal challenge, and that these ideas then fired the imagination of a reader or readers skilled enough to expand them into the more grandiose scheme of chapters 1-9? The alternative, namely that someone conceived the extensive contents of chapters 1-9 as a unity, without working on the basis of an existing scriptural stimulus, seems to be unattractive in terms of the psychology of sutra writing. However this is only a hypothesis which may serve to stimulate further investigations on these or similar lines. It may be that linguistic evidence will rule out this particular suggestion, but it is high time that form-critical methods were applied to Buddhist documents.

The above considerations all have some implications for the dating of the sutra. It should be remembered that we are speaking throughout of presumed Sanskrit manuscripts on which the Chinese versions are based. The Chinese seem to have been more concerned to follow what they took to be authoritative sources than to make fresh compilations themselves. The changes made by the editors of T264 were made in order to improve Kumārajīva's version in accordance with authoritative sources. The changes in arrangement considered above must then have been completed in the Sanskrit manuscript tradition long enough before the production of T264 for them to have had time to become authoritative. Indeed, one of the adjustments, namely the shifting of chapter 27, must have taken place, analogously, some time before T263 was produced in A.D. 286. Before that date the additional chapters had to have been added and have come to be considered worthy of being treated as an integral part of the text. Bearing in mind that T263 is not the oldest stage in textual tradition, even of the full-length text, of which we have knowledge, this can scarcely have happened later than the early years of the third century A.D. Furthermore, since the additional chapters are not particularly closely associated with each other, it is not intrinsically likely that they were all composed and added at once. On the contrary, it is likely that they were added piecemeal. This demands if anything the postulation of a longer period of time and it seems not at all unreasonable to suppose that it began during the second century A.D. rather than the third. The three earlier stages of the growth of the sutra outlined by Fuse, however they need to be adjusted in detail, must be presumed to have been composed during the preceding century or so. To this may be added the general principle of contemporaneity with similar writings. L. de la Vallée Poussin pointed out that the sutras relating to Amitābha were translated into Chinese in 148 and 170 A.D. and display a buddhology as developed as that of The Lotus Sutra ('Lotus of the True Law', Hastings' *Encyclopedia of Religion and Ethics* VIII). It is also widely thought that the Perfection of Insight literature was begun around the turn of the millennium. Thus Fuse's dating must be about right.

It remains unclear to what extent The Lotus Sutra became the centre of a particular cult in India. It has already been indicated that in the third phase of its development, represented by chapters 10-20 (with the exceptions noted) devotion to the sutra was believed to bring merit, while its devotees clearly thought they had to reckon with various trials and hardships. Watanabe Shōkō has called attention particularly to this group of people, who produced and promoted the sutra, and his emphasis is praiseworthy since it is all too easy to treat the sutra merely as a unit in a scriptural tradition, forgetting the real people to whom it was important. (*Nihon no Bukkyō*, pp. 183f.)

One of the points made by Watanabe is that the story of the millionaire and his poor son, who rose from utter degradation to enter finally into the inheritance of his father's possessions, would be inconceivable in terms of the Indian caste system. Moreover, although the caste system was not observed within the Buddhist sangha itself, it was not denied by them with regard to society in general. For this reason the story may be thought to have arisen in some kind of separate community lying apart from the influence of Brahmanism (*ibid.* p. 184). Against this it may be pointed out that there are wider problems about the development of Buddhism in relation to Brahmanism strictly conceived; while at the same time there is no doubt that in other respects The Lotus Sutra makes free use of widely current Indian terminology. The inventiveness of the storyteller should also not be overlooked. After all, to take a close parallel, in what real society could the details of the story of the burning house be set?

Watanabe also suggested that since the representation of Devadatta as the teacher of the Buddha in former times is quite contrary to the normal Buddhist account of him as a straightforward enemy of the Buddha, there may have been a time in the development of The Lotus Sutra when the community among whom it was important was to some degree separated from the main line of the Buddhist tradition (*ibid.* p. 184). Against this it might be argued that the story about Devadatta is intended to make a point which is fully consonant with the teaching of The Lotus Sutra as a whole, in that it asserts the future Buddhahood of one in whose case it would be precisely not expected. Along with the story of the daughter of the Nāga-king, the story of Devadatta adds a polemical pointedness to the doctrine that all beings will become Buddhas. Thus there is no reason why the Devadatta chapter should indicate the existence of an isolated group any more than that the existence of the sutra as a whole should do so.

In sum neither of these suggestions seems to be particularly compelling or indeed particularly informative. Watanabe seems to be too anxious to paint The Lotus Sutra as being the concern of an outcast community which in turn harshly rejected the doctrines of others. He notes, somewhat exaggeratedly, the polemics against 'Hīnayāna' Buddhism (*ibid.* p. 184), but fails to complement this by recognising for example that Śāriputra, representative of the earlier wisdom, is the first of whom future Buddhahood is predicted in terms of the new teaching. He fails also to do justice to the subtlety of the relationship between the three vehicles and the one Buddha vehicle. Is it possible that Watanabe is influenced in this approach by his image of a contemporary movement based on The Lotus Sutra, namely the Sōka Gakkai, of which he appears to disapprove? It is perhaps significant that widely differing types of piety can be inspired by the sutra today, and this in itself should make us hesitate to draw too quickly the portrait of the group among whom The Lotus Sutra was at first important almost two thousand years ago. Rather than having been the sole standard of an exclusivist sect, it seems far more likely that The Lotus Sutra was carried along as one Mahayana text among many. Several important Mahayana texts give the impression that they alone offer the real meaning of Buddhism, and those written in sutra form regularly fail to make mention of their fellows; but the general overlapping of ideas leaves little room for doubt that they sprang up and were cherished in the context of a widespread Buddhist tradition and not in narrow conventicles, each being passed with greater or less interest from community to community.

A commentarial tradition specially devoted to The Lotus Sutra does not seem to have developed in India. The only Indian writing especially devoted to it of which there is any trace is a commentary ascribed to Vasubandhu (fourth century A.D.). Two Chinese translations have survived, but according to Ōchō there is no attempt in this work to relate the contents of The Lotus Sutra to the Yogācāra doctrines for which Vasubandhu is famed (*Hokke Shisō*, p. 293). This is not necessarily surprising in view of the general character of the extensive systematising literary activity for which the Yogācārins are equally remembered. With regard to this, E. Conze said, 'A great deal of what they wrote consisted in just 'working up' traditional fields of knowledge, such as the Abhidharma or the Prajñāpāramitā . . .' *Buddhist Thought in India*, p. 250. The commentary in question also seems not to have had the influence on later Buddhism which Vasubandhu's works on the *Daśabhūmika Sūtra* and the *Sukhāvatīvyūha Sūtra* had on the Hua-yen (J. Kegon) and Pure Land schools respectively. Indeed Ōchō wonders whether the commentary was really by Vasubandhu at all (*op. cit.* p. 213). It may be added that according to Watanabe the Tibetan canon of Buddhist scripture contains various treatises and commentaries from the Gupta dynasty, but nothing of Indian origin on The Lotus Sutra (*Nihon no Bukkyō*, p. 185).

In spite of the relative lack of early commentary, there is no doubt that The Lotus Sutra quickly came to be considered a Mahayana sutra of major importance along with others. Its influence can be seen in the frequent use of themes drawn from it in the Buddhist iconography of central Asia and north-western China (cf. J. L. Davidson, *The Lotus Sutra in Chinese Art*) and in the respect which the Chinese accorded it during the introduction of Buddhism to that country. It was not until the time of Chih-I (538-597) that a more specialised doctrinal basis for the later sects associated with The Lotus Sutra was clearly laid. Some see his approach to the relations between the various sutras and the analysis of their contents as a departure from the way in which The Lotus Sutra had been understood up till then, while others see it as a justifiable elaboration in terms of Mahayana Buddhism. But that is a question which goes beyond the present discussion.

APPENDIX C
OCCURRENCES OF *FANG-PIEN* IN THE LOTUS SUTRA

The following is a list of all the occurrences of the term *fang-pien* 方便 in Kumārajīva's version of The Lotus Sutra (T262), giving page numbers in T Vol. IX, and following his chapter numeration. Alongside are shown the appropriate equivalents in T263 and also the page numbers of the English translation by Kern, Soothill and Schiffer (KSS) for general context.

No.	Page ref.	Chapter	T263 equiv.	KSS
1	5b	I	67c	31
2	5b	II	67c	32
3	5c	II	68a	32
4	5c	II	—	32
5	6a	II	68c	32
6	6b	II	68c	38
7	6b	II	68c	38
8	7a	II	—	43
9	7b	II	69c	45
10	7b	II	69c	45
11	7b	II	—	46
12	7b	II	—	46
13	7b	II	—	47
14	7c	II	70a	48
15	7c	II	70a	49
16	8a	II	70b	50
17	8a	II	70b	51
18	8b	II	—	54
19	8b	II	70c	54
20	8c	II	71a	55
21	8c	II	—	55
22	9a	II	71c	59
23	9b	II	—	59
24	9b	II	72a	60
25	9b	II	72a	60
26	9b	II	—	61
27	9b	II	—	61
28	9c	II	72b	63
29	9c	II	72b	63
30	9c	II	72b	63
31	10a	II	—	64
32	10a	II	72c	65
33	10a	II	—	65
34	10b	II	73a	67
35	10b	II	—	67
36	10c	III	—	70
37	11a	III	74c	74

No.	Page ref.	Chapter	T263 equiv.	KSS
38	11a	III	74c	74
39	11a	III	—	74
40	11b	III	—	75
41	12a	III	—	81
42	12b	III	75b	82
43	12c	III	75b	84
44	13a	III	—	85
45	13a	III	75c	86
46	13a	III	75c	86
47	13b	III	75c	87
48	13b	III	76a	87
49	13b	III	76a	87
50	13b	III	—	88
51	13c	III	76b	90
52	14b	III	77b	97
53	15a	III	78a	101
54	15a	III	—	103
55	15a	III	78b	104
56	15a	III	—	104
57	17a	IV	—	120
58	17a	IV	80b	120
59	17a	IV	—	121
60	17b	IV	81a	123
61	17c	IV	81a	124
62	18a	IV	—	128
63	18a	IV	—	129
64	18c	IV	82c	134
65	18c	IV	82c	134
66	19a	V	—	139
67	20b	V	84c	149
68	20b	V	85a	151
None in Chapter VI				
69	25c	VII	92b	189
70	25c	VII	—	189
71	26a	VII	—	190
72	26a	VII	92c	190
73	26a	VII	—	191
74	26a	VII	92c	191
75	26c	VII	93c	196
76	27a	VII	94a	197
77	27a	VII	—	198
78	27a	VII	94b	198
79	27b	VII	94b	198
80	27b	VIII	94b	201
81	27b	VIII	94c	201
82	27c	VIII	95c	203
83	28a	VIII	96a	205
84	28a	VIII	96a	205
85	28a	VIII	96a	206
86	28b	VIII	96b	207
87	29a	VIII	97b	212
88	30a	IX	98b	218
89	31c	X	—	229
90	34a	XI	—	245

No.	Page ref.	Chapter	T263 equiv.	KSS
None in Chapter XII				
91	36c	XIII	—	268
92	38a	XIV	—	277
93	38c	XIV	109b	281
94	39a	XIV	109c	285
95	39b	XIV	110a	286
None in Chapter XV				
96	42c	XVI	113c	309
97	42c	XVI	—	309
98	42c	XVI	—	310
99	42c	XVI	—	311
100	42c	XVI	114a	311
101	43a	XVI	114b	313
102	43b	XVI	114b	314
103	43b	XVI	114c	314
104	43b	XVI	114c	315
105	43c	XVI	115a	317
None in Chapter XVII				
106	47b	XVIII	—	339
None in Chapters XIX—XXIV				
107	57a	XXV	129b	407
108	58a	XXV	—	413
				(see below)
None in Chapter XXVI				
109	59c	XXVII	—	423
110	61b	XXVIII	—	434

Case no. 108 is located in the verses of Chapter XXV, which probably did not form part of The Lotus Sutra as Kumārajīva himself originally translated it (cf. Appendix B). For case no. 51 there is a misprint in the T263 parallel on 76b.

Of the parallels in T263, some use close equivalents rather than the term *fang-pien* itself. Even so there are forty-one cases (or forty excluding case no. 108) which have no specific parallel in T263. On the other hand there are twenty cases in T263 which are not found in T262, as follows: Ch. II, 70a; Ch. III, 79a; Ch. IV, 81a, 81b; Ch. V, 84a, 84c, 85b, 86b; Ch. VII, 90b; Ch. VIII, 95b, 96a, 97b; Ch. X, 100b; Ch. XI, 102c-103a; Ch. XIV, 112a, 112c, 112c; Ch. XV, 114b; Ch. XVII, 118a; Ch. XXI, 127a; (N.B. following T263's chapter numeration in this case). All in all it is fair to conclude that the term was more important for Kumārajīva, because he used it more often and more consistently.

The spread of occurrences by chapter in Kumārajīva's version is as follows:

I	1
II	34
III	21
IV	9

V	3
VI	0
VII	11
VIII	8
IX	1
X	1
XI	1
XII	0
XIII	1
XIV	4
XV	0
XVI	10
XVII	0
XVIII	1
XIX-XXIV	0
XXV	1 (or 2)
XXVI	0
XXVII	1
XXVIII	1

This distribution indicates that the main usage of the term is concentrated in the chapters which Fuse took to represent the first phase of the growth of the sutra (cf. Appendix B). Thus there is a statistical base to the reader's general impression that it is a leading theme of the opening series of chapters in particular. The only chapter outside the first group which has a significant number of occurrences in Chapter XVI (= Skt. 15). Not surprisingly it is also the main chapter in the later part of the sutra to pick up again the other leading themes of the sutra, the critique of the concept of nirvana, the nature of the Buddha's teaching, etc. The account of Avolakiteśvara in Chapter XXV has only one occurrence in the original prose part, as was admitted in Chapter Four above; however it is an important single occurrence, as explained earlier, and the whole conception of Chapter XXV closely mirrors that of the bodhisattva Pūrṇa in Chapter VIII, where there are several relevant occurrences. The general pattern of occurrences is not contradicted by Dharmarakṣa's usage. The only noteworthy flurry of extra occurrences outside the first phase of the sutra is in his chapter 14, and in those cases there is no extra support in the extant Sanskrit texts to presume an *upāya* or *upāyakauśalya* which Kumārajīva might perchance have disregarded (cf. Wogihara and Tsuchida, *op. cit.* pp. 262ff.) Thus all in all, apart from indicating the textual basis of the earlier discussion, the list of occurrences shows that whether one conceives of the sutra doctrinally, giving the traditional prominence to Chapters II and XVI, or whether one conceives of it historically along the lines of Fuse's theory or some refinement of it, the concept of skilful means plays an irreducibly leading role.

APPENDIX D
OCCURRENCES OF *FANG-PIEN* IN THE TEACHING OF VIMALAKĪRTI

Lamotte has provided a detailed concordance of all extant historic versions (*op. cit.* pp. 21ff.); and the reader may easily find the general context for cases of the term 'skilful means' in any of the various modern translations mentioned in Chapter Five, note 1. The following is therefore simply a list of all the occurrences of the term *fang-pien* 方便 in Kumārajīva's version (T475), giving the page reference in T XIV and the location by chapter.

No.	Page ref.	Chapter
1	537a	I
2	538b	I
3	538b	I
4	538b	I
5	538c	I
6	539a	II
7	539a	II
8	539a	II
9	539b	II
10	539b	II
11	539c	II
None in Chapter III		
12	542c	IV
13	543c	IV
14	544b	V
15	545b	V
16	545b	V
17	545b	V
18	545b	V
19	545b	V
20	545b	V
21	545b	V
22	545b	V
23	545b	V
24	545b	V
25	545b	V
26	545b	V
27	545b	V
28	545b	V
29	545b	V
30	547a	VI
31	547a	VI
32	547a	VI
33	547b	VII
34	549a	VIII
35	549c	VIII

No.	Page ref.	Chapter
36	550a	VIII
37	550b	VIII
None in Chapter IX		
None in Chapter X		
38	554b	XI
39	554b	XI
40	554c	XI
None in Chapter XII		
41	556c	XIII
None in Chapter XIV		

The locution *fang-pien-li* 方便力 occurs in six of the above cases, namely nos. 1, 13, 30, 31, 37 and 41. It could perhaps be maintained that this phrase is preferred when it is a question of a bodhisattva directing his salvific activity towards living beings, but there are so many cases in Kumārajīva's usage when this is referred to with *fang-pien* alone that there does not seem to be an importantly distinct function for *fang-pien-li*.

APPENDIX E
OCCURRENCES OF *FANG-PIEN* IN THE PERFECTION OF INSIGHT SUTRAS ETC

The following is a list of all the occurrences of the term *fang-pien* 方便 in Kumārajīva's version of the Shorter Prajñā-pāramitā Sutra, T227, giving page numbers in T Vol. VIII, chapter locations, and cross-references to Conze's English translation from Sanskrit (abbreviated as C), *The Perfection of Wisdom in Eight Thousand Lines and its Verse Summary*. The latter may be used for indications of general context, but it should be remembered that the texts translated by Kumārajīva and by Conze were by no means identical. A cross-reference does not necessarily imply an *upāya* or an *upāya-kauśalya* for Conze's text, though of course there usually will be one. The chapter numeration is also different. An x in column four (Insight) indicates that Kumārajīva closely associates *fang-pien* with the perfection of insight, as e.g. in the linked phrase 般若波羅蜜方便. An x in column five (Power) indicates that the case in question is 方便力, or 方便之力, 'power of skilful means', rather than just 方便 'skilful means'.

No.	Page ref.	Chapter	Insight	Power	C
1	538a	I	x		86
None in Chapter II					
None in Chapter III					
2	543c	IV	x	x	109
None in Chapter V					
None in Chapter VI					
3	548b	VII	x		129
4	548b	VII	x		129
5	548b	VII	x		129
6	549a	VII			132
7	549a	VII			132
8	549b	VII			132
9	549b	VII			132
None in Chapter VIII					
None in Chapter IX					
None in Chapter X					
10	556c	XI			167
11	556c	XI			167
12	556c	XI			167
13	556c	XI			167
14	557b	XI			169
15	557b	XI			169
16	557b	XII			170-1
17	557b	XII			170-1
None in Chapter XIII					
18	560b	XIV	x		185
19	560b	XIV	x		186

189

No.	Page ref.	Chapter	Insight	Power	C
20	560b	XIV			186
21	560c	XIV	x		186
22	560c	XIV	x		186
23	560c	XIV	x		186
24	560c	XIV	x		187
25	560c	XIV	x		187
26	563a	XV	x		195
27	563a	XV	x		195
28	563a	XV	x		196
29	563a	XV	x		196
None in Chapter XVI					
30	566a	XVII	x		209
31	566c	XVII			211
32	567a	XVII	x		212
33	567a	XVII	x		212
34	567a	XVII	x		212
35	567b	XVII		x	215
36	567c	XVII	x		217
37	569a	XVIII	x		224
38	569a	XVIII			225
39	569b	XVIII		x	225
40	569b	XVIII		x	225
41	569b	XVIII		x	226
42	569b	XVIII		x	226
43	569b	XVIII		x	226
44	569b	XVIII		x	226
45	570b	XIX			230
46	570c	XIX			232
47	570c	XIX			232
48	571a	XIX	x		234
49	573a	XX	x		242
50	573a	XX	x		243
51	573a	XX	x		243
52	574a	XXI			250
53	574b	XXI	x		250
None in Chapter XXII					
None in Chapter XXIII					
None in Chapter XXIV					
54	579a	XXV	x	x	272
55	579a	XXV	x	x	272
56	579a	XXV	x	x	273
57	579a	XXV	x	x	273
None in Chapter XXVI					
58	580b	XXVII		x	278
59	580b	XXVII		x	278
60	582a	XXVII	x	x	283
61	582a	XXVII	x		283
62	582a	XXVII	x		284
63	582b	XXVII	x		285
64	582b	27	x	x	285
65	582c	27	x		286
66	583c	27	x	x	290
67	584a	27			290
68	584c	28	x		293

No.	Page ref.	Chapter	Insight	Power	C
69	585b	28	x		295
70	585b	28	x		295
71	585b	28	x		295
72	585b	28	x		295
73	585b	28	x		296

It will be observed that over half of the above cases link the term *fang-pien* with the idea of the perfection of insight, which supports the stress on this link noted in the discussion above. 'Power of skilful means' represents just under a quarter of the cases, and it seems to be little other than a variant of skilful means as far as Kumārajīva was concerned.

The Great Prajñā-pāramitā Sutra, T223, contains 225 cases of the term *fang-pien*, as follows.

Chapter I: 219b, 220a, 220a
Chapter II: 221b, 221b, 221b
Chapter III: none
Chapter IV: 225b, 225b, 225b, 225c, 225c, 225c, 225c, 226a, 226a, 227c
Chapter V: none
Chapter VI: none
Chapter VII: none
Chapter VIII: 233b, 233b
Chapter IX: 235c, 235c
Chapter X: 237a, 237a, 237b, 237b, 237b, 237b, 239a
Chapter XI: 240a, 240a, 240a, 240a, 240b, 241a, 241a
Chapter XII: 242c
Chapter XIII: none
Chapter XIV: 244b, 244b
Chapter XV: 246c
Chapter XVI: none
Chapter XVII: none
Chapter XVIII: 250a
Chapters XIX-XXX: none
Chapter XXXI: 280c, 280c, 281a, 282c, 282c, 282c, 282c, 282c
Chapter XXXII: none
Chapter XXXIII: none
Chapter XXXIV: 286c, 286c
Chapters XXXV-XXXVIII: none
Chapter XXXIX: 299b, 301a, 301a, 301a, 301a, 301a, 302a, 302a
Chapter XL: none
Chapter XLI: 304b
Chapter XLII: 307c, 307c, 307c, 307c
Chapter XLIII: none
Chapter XLIV: none
Chapter XLV: 315c

Chapter XLVI: 320a, 320a, 320b, 320b, 320b

Chapter XLVII: 321a, 321a, 321a, 321a, 322a, 322a, 322b

Chapters XLVIII-L: none

Chapter LI: 330a, 330a, 330a, 330a, 330b, 330b, 330b, 330b, 330b, 330c, 330c, 331a, 331a, 331a, 331b

Chapter LII: none

Chapter LIII: none

Chapter LIV: 336b, 336b, 336b, 336b, 336b, 336b, 336b, 336c, 336c, 336c, 336c, 336c, 337a, 337a, 337a, 337a, 338c

Chapter LV: none

Chapter LVI: 342a, 343a

Chapter LVII: 344a, 344a, 345a, 345b, 345c, 345c, 345c, 345c, 346c, 346c, 346c, 346c

Chapter LVIII: none

Chapter LIX: none

Chapter LX: 350c, 351a, 351a, 351a, 351b

Chapter LXI: 352b, 352b, 352b, 353a, 353a, 353b

Chapter LXII: 356a

Chapter LXIII: 357b, 357b, 357b, 357c

Chapters LXIV-LXVI: none

Chapter LXVII: 364c, 364c

Chapter LXVIII: none

Chapter LXIX: 368c, 368c, 368c, 368c, 368c, 368c, 368c, 368c, 368c, 369b, 372a, 372b, 373a

Chapter LXX: none

Chapter LXXI: 378b, 378b, 378b

Chapter LXXII: none

Chapter LXXIII: 380a, 380a, 380a, 380a, 380a, 380a, 380a, 380b

Chapter LXXIV: none

Chapter LXXV: 385b

Chapter LXXVI: 387c, 387c, 388b

Chapter LXXVII: none

Chapter LXXVIII: 392c, 394b, 394b, 394c

Chapter LXXIX: 398b, 398b, 398c, 400b, 400c

Chapter LXXX: 401a, 401a, 401a, 401a, 401a, 401b, 401c, 401c, 401c, 402a, 402a, 402b

Chapter LXXXI: 404b, 404b, 404b, 404b, 404b, 404c, 404c, 405a, 405a

Chapter LXXXII: 407c

Chapter LXXXIII: 409c, 410a, 410a, 410a, 410b

Chapter LXXXIV: 412b

Chapter LXXXV: 412c, 412c

Chapter LXXXVI: 414b

Chapter LXXXVII: none

Chapter LXXXVIII: 416c, 416c, 418a, 418b, 418b, 418b, 418c, 419a, 419a, 420a, 421a, 421b

Chapter LXXXIX: 422b, 422b, 422b, 422c, 422c, 422c
Chapter XC: none

The usage in this sutra closely reflects that of the shorter sutra (T227), and no attempt has been made to correlate them in detail. However, each case has been examined and there is no doubt that the main themes are entirely consistent. The close association between skilful means and the perfection of insight is equally striking in the longer sutra, while it is not possible to document a similarly close connection with 'compassion'. Of course skilful means is analogous to compassion in so far as it is directed towards the salvation of living beings. Among the large number of cases listed above, one case (410b) makes supernatural powers 神通 dependent upon the power of skilful means 方便 (as is also sometimes found in texts not presently under close study, e.g. in T245 at T VIII 827a). One other case in the list links skilful means with spells (*dhāraṇī*), but only in so far as both issue from the perfection of insight (T VIII 418b: 常行般若波羅蜜得大方便 力及得諸陀羅尼). Thus special powers and magic spells contribute little to the basic definition of skilful means. As in the shorter sutra, skilful means entails not practising with respect to characteristics (237a-237b), that is, e.g. practising *dhyāna* (*ch'an* or *zen*) without being reborn accordingly (225b-225c), yet getting others to enter *dhyāna* (250a). It means not suffering from conceit (282c), and again and again it means bringing across living beings while practising that insight into the voidness of all things which subverts the necessity of so doing.

The occurrences of the term *fang-pien* in the three treatises referred to in the discussion in Chapter Six are as follows:

The Middle Treatise (T1564), T XXX 25a.
The Twelve Topic Treatise (T1568), T XXX 166b, 167b, 167b.
The Hundred Treatise (T1569), T XXX 168c, 170c, 180c, 180c, 180c.

APPENDIX F
SKILFUL MEANS IN THE
ŚŪRAMGAMASAMĀDHI SUTRA

Only fragments of this sutra exist in Sanskrit, but it was among the earliest Mahayana sutras to be translated into Chinese. The first translation of A.D. 186 is now lost, but various others remain, notably that of Kumāra-jīva entitled *Shou-leng-yen san-mei-ching* 首楞嚴三昧經 J. *Shuryōgon-zanmai-kyō*).

The sutra and version in question is No. 642 in the *Taishō Shinshū Daizōkyō* and should not be confused with an eighth century *Śūramgama-sūtra* (T945) which has been widely used in East Asia and also translated into English. Kumārajīva's version of the sutra, T642, with which we are here concerned, has been translated into French by Étienne Lamotte in *La Concentration de la Marche Héroique*, Volume XIII in the series *Mélanges Chinois et Bouddhiques*, 1965 Brussels (Institut Belge des Hautes Études Chinoises).

The term *fang-pien* appears ten times in the sutra and Lamotte regularly translates it as *moyen(s) salvifique(s)*, except on one occasion (Lamotte 177) where he has *artifice salvifique*. In one case he supplies the term *l'habilité* and glosses his translation from the Chinese with the term *upāyakauśalya*, even though there is no full equivalent to this in the text itself (Lamotte 160, T XV 634a). Kumārajīva sometimes translates *upayakauśalya* as fang-pien-li (方便力), and this term does in fact appear in two of the other contexts in question. On each of these occasions however Lamotte simply glosses with the term *upāya*. The first time he translates 'par la force des moyens sal-vifiques' (Lamotte 123, T XV 630a), following the parallel phrases in the context which also contain 力 (*force*). The second time (Lamotte 199, T XV 638a) he translates 'recourant à un moyen salvifique', this time obscuring the 力. On each of these occasions the complete phrase is 以方便力 which could perhaps best be rendered as 'by the power of his (their) skilful means', though of course Lamotte's varied treatment (though not the varied glosses) may be said to be justified by the contexts.

A brief note on each of the ten occurrences follows.

(i) (T XV 629b, cf. Lamotte 118) Here 'a good knowledge' of *fang-pien* is one of the many excellent qualities of the *bodhisattva-mahāsattvas*. It is closely associated (indeed more closely than the translation suggests) with a knowledge of all languages, the phrase running 善知一切言辭方便 (cf. also (iii) below).

(ii) (T XV 630a cf. Lamotte 123) Here four bases of manifestation (現) are listed, namely: the power of deep wisdom (深慧力) which manifests the

194

turning of the wheel of the Dharma, the power of skilful means (方便力) which manifests the entry into nirvana, the power of *samādhi* (三昧力) which manifests the division of relics, and the power of the original vow (本願力) which manifests the disappearance of the Dharma. The parallelism implies that all of these are closely associated, and it will not go unnoticed that they are to do with the foundation of the workings of Buddhism as a religion.

(iii) (T XV 631b, cf. Lamotte 136) Knowledge of 'all means' is again stressed here as in (i) above, but so too is ability or skill (善能) an aspect which seems to have been omitted altogether in Lamotte's translation (the complete phrase runs 善能了知一切方便). The last half of this phrase suggests, incidentally, that in the case of (i) above the 一切 should be taken with the 方便 as well as with the 言辭.

(iv) (T XV 631c, cf. Lamotte 138) The phrase is 善知一切方便迴向 in which comprehensive knowledge is again a keynote (cf. (i) and (iii) above). Lamotte rather opaquely translates 'Bien connaitre toutes les applications des moyens salvifiques'. It may be however that 方便 is here qualifying 迴向 (cf. Lamotte's own gloss *upāyapariṇāmana*) which should then be translated 'expedient transfers [of merit]'. This would indicate the appropriate use of the incalculable amounts of merit referred to in the previous sentence.

(v) (T XV 634a, cf. Lamotte 160) This case also includes the notion of ability (能) and makes the knowledge of *fang-pien* the continuation of a bodhisattva's development after he has completed the six perfections. This is no doubt the reason why Lamotte glossed it as *upāyakauśalya* as noted above.

(vi) (T XV 634a, cf. Lamotte 160) cf. (v) above.

(vii) (T XV 635a, cf. Lamotte 177) A certain Brahmarāja is said not to appreciate the skilful means used by a bodhisattva (不解菩薩所行方便) Cf. the following.

(viii) (T XV 635a, cf. Lamotte 177) This picks up the preceding phrase and refers to the other Brahmarājas (i.e. *all* the others, 餘諸梵王) who *do* understand. What they understand is 'the wisdom-and-means of a bodhisattva' (菩薩智慧方便). This is a clear association of this pair of qualities.

(ix) (T XV 638a, cf. Lamotte 199) One of the cases of 方便力 discussed above. The wider context of this case is discussed further below.

(x) (T XV 645a, cf. Lamotte 272) Here 'the inconceivable [virtue] of skilful means' (方便不可思議) is listed as one of twenty inconceivable virtues (二十不可思議功德). It is noteworthy that *fang-pien* in this list is closely associated with other important virtues such as merit, knowledge, wisdom and eloquence (cf. the above cases).

The basic position of this sutra, if it is 'a position', is the same as that of all the sutras discussed above. That is to say, it is fundamentally concerned with the bodhisattva's insight into the voidness and thus the identity of all dharmas, coupled with his activity of differentiating these same dharmas for the sake of aiding beings attached to this or that point. The sutra contains a variety of dialogues and itemised lists and lays special stress on the *samādhi* referred to in the title, which is however neither more nor less than the state of concentration maintained by buddhas and bodhisattvas. Of the ten occurrences of the term *fang-pien* in Kumārajīva's version, seven are in lists (see above). The other occurrences are in two narrative contexts which merit brief attention here.

The first (containing cases vii and viii above) is a story of a previous existence of the Buddha Śākyamuni, then still a bodhisattva. He is in his palace surrounded by his harem when he is visited by numerous heavenly beings. One of these, who is said not to have grasped the principle of *fang-pien*, asks why the bodhisattva is so wise yet continues to be attached to his royal status and to his pleasures. The answer is given by others of the heavenly beings who by contrast *have* understood the wisdom or insight and the *fang-pien* of the buddhas. They explain that he is in reality not attached to his royal status and his pleasures, but that he appears as a lay figure in order to educate beings and bring them to maturity. He appears as a bod-hisattva, yet all the while he has already attained buddha-hood in other realms where he is proclaiming the Dharma. The ignorant inquirer then asks what *samādhi* it is which makes it possible for him to perform these feats, and the answer is of course that it is the *Śūraṃgama-samādhi* (Lamotte 178; T XV 635a).

This identification is important because it indicates that the dual basis of insight and means is fundamentally associated with the *samādhi* so generally praised in this sutra. Other lengthy sections extol the bodhisattva's ability to do two things at once as a result of this *samādhi* (E.g. Lamotte 124ff, 131ff, 141ff, 242ff, 245ff). The principle is that he conforms himself to the things of the world without being sullied by them. (Lamotte 138; 'Se conformer aux choses du monde, sans en contracter la souillure', T XV 631c 順諸世法而不染汚). An example of the application of the principle is his ability to demonstrate experience of pleasure in the company of musicians without losing within himself the concentration (*samādhi*) of the recollection of the Buddha (Lamotte 139; T XV 631c於衆伎樂現自娛樂而內不捨念佛三昧; the term 現 seems to be slightly obscured in Lamotte's translation, for the point must be that the bodhisattva is able to manifest or make a show of enjoy-ment in order to effect a solidarity with those attached to enjoyment. In the same way he can manifest various infirmities, making himself lame, deaf, blind or dumb, in order to bring beings to maturity. (Lamotte 139. T XV 631c示現種種癃殘跛蹇聾盲瘖瘂以化衆生.) Some of the occurrences of the term *fang-pien* occur within lists of these abilities, which suggests that *fang-pien* itself is just one accomplishment among many. However, when the term emerges to centrality as in the narrative considered above, it seems to be a way of referring to all such abilities or activities in principle. The similarity of this line of thought with that of The Teaching of Vimalakīrti, and the Avalokiteśvara chapter of The Lotus Sutra, is quite evident.

It was also noted in the above case that *fang-pien* was related to the wisdom or insight of the bodhisattva. The second narrative context con-taining the term in this sutra (case ix above) illustrates this fundamental relationship rather deftly. The story is a battle of wits between Māra (the devil) and some *devas* who encourage him to raise the thought of supreme perfect enlightenment, that is to say, to enter on the path of bodhisattva-hood. (Lamotte 199; T XV 638a). Māra attempts to trick the *devas* by offering to do so on condition that they in turn renounce the thought of enlightenment, which under the circumstances would seem to be an appropriate *quid pro quo*. The *devas* call his bluff, and by their power of skilful means declare that they have renounced the thought of enlightenment. Māra in turn then has to produce the thought of enlightenment, but is thereby defeated because in so far as one being produces the thought of enlightenment all others do so equally. The identification arises because the thought of enlightenment is without differentiation. (T XV 638a 若一菩薩發菩提心。一切菩薩亦同是心。所以者何。心無差別。於諸衆生心皆平等; Lamotte (199) translates 菩提心 as *bodhicitta* and 心 as *citta*). In this way Māra's ruse unwittingly brings about its own defeat, but it is through *fang-pien* or skilful means that this result is realised. The logic of the skilful means is that the *devas* begin by accepting the differentiation in terms of which Māra's threat is real, but they use the situation which seems to be produced thereby in order to move to non-differentiation, in terms of which Māra's threat is no threat at all.

BIBLIOGRAPHY

This bibliography lists works cited above, except for ordinary Japanese dictionaries etc. referred to in Chapter Eight and pieces by the present writer referred to in General Observations, note 1.

Baruch, W., *Beiträge zum Saddharmapuṇḍarīkasūtra*, Leiden, 1938.
Basak, R. (ed.), *Mahāvastu Avadāna*, 3 Vols., Calcutta, 1963 ff.
Böhtlingk and Roth, *Sanskrit-Wörterbuch*, St. Petersburg, 1855.
Burnouf, M. E., *Le Lotus de la Bonne Loi*, 2 Vols., Paris, 1852, 2nd ed., 1925.

Ch'en, K. K. S., *Buddhism in China, A Historical Survey*, Princeton, 1964.
Conze, Edward (trans.), *Selected Sayings from the Perfection of Wisdom*, London, 1955.
Conze, Edward (ed. and trans.), *Vajracchedika Prajñāpāramitā*(Serie Orientale Roma XIII), Rome, 1957.
Conze, Edward, *Buddhist Wisdom Books*, London, 1958.
Conze, Edward, *The Prajñā-pāramitā Literature* (Indo-Iranian Monographs, No. 6), 'S-Gravenhage, 1960.
Conze, Edward (trans.), *The Large Sutra on Perfect Wisdom, with the divisions of the Abhisamayālaṅkāra*, Part I, London, 1961.
Conze, Edward (ed. and trans.), *The Gilgit Manuscript of the Aṣṭādaśasāhasrikā Prajñāpāramitā. Chapters 55-70 corresponding to the 5th abhisamaya.* (Serie Orientale Roma XXVI), Rome, 1962.
Conze, Edward, *Buddhist Thought in India*, London, 1962.
Conze, Edward, *Thirty Years of Buddhist Studies*, London, 1967.
Conze, Edward, *The Short Prajñāpāramitā Texts*, London, 1973.
Conze, Edward, *The Perfection of Wisdom in Eight Thousand Lines and its Verse Summary*, Bolinas, 1973.
Cowell, Müller and Takakusu (trans.), *Buddhist Mahayana Sutras* (Sacred Books of the East Vol. XLIX), Oxford, 1894.

Davidson, J. Leroy, *The Lotus Sutra in Chinese Art*, New Haven, U.S.A., 1954.
Demiéville, P., 'Vimalakīrti en Chine', in Lamotte's *L'Enseignement de Vimalakīrti*.
Demiéville, P. et al., *Hōbōgirin, Dictionnaire Encyclopédique du Bouddhisme d'après les sources Chinoises et Japonaises*, Paris and Tokyo, 1929 ff.
Demiéville, P. et al., *Hōbōgirin, Fascicule Annexe* (Appendix to previous).
de la Vallée Poussin, L., 'Lotus of the True Law', in J. Hastings, *Encyclopedia of Religion and Ethics* VIII.
de Lubac, Henri, *Amida*, Paris, 1955.

de Mallmann, Marie-Thérèse, *Introduction à l'Étude d'Avalokiteçvara*, Paris, 1967.

de Visser, M. W., *Ancient Buddhism in Japan*, 2 vols., Paris, 1928.

Dutt, N., *Saddharmapuṇḍarīkasūtram with N. D. Mironov's Readings from Central Asia*, Calcutta, 1953.

Edgerton, Franklin, *Buddhist Hybrid Sanskrit Dictionary and Grammar*, 2 vols., New Haven, U.S.A., 1953.

Eliot, Sir Charles, *Japanese Buddhism*, London, 1935.

Frauwallner, Erich, *Die Philosophie des Buddhismus*, Berlin, 1956.

Fujimoto, R., Inagaki, H., and Kawamura, L. S. (trans.), *The Jōdo Wasan*, (Ryūkoku Translation Series IV), Kyōto, 1965.

Fukaura Masabumi (trans.), 'Yuimakisshosekkyō' in *Kokuyaku Issaikyō* Sutra Section VI, Tokyo, 1933. 深浦正文, 維摩詰所説経, 国訳一切経

Fuse Kōgaku, *Hokekyō Seiritsu Shi*, Tokyo, 1934. 布施浩岳, 法華經成立史。

Fuse Kōgaku, 'Hokekyō Seiritsu no Rekishi', in Kubota Masabumi (ed.) *Hokkekyōnyūmon*, Tokyo, 1966. 布施浩岳, 法華経成立の歴史（久保田正文, 法華経入門）。

Giles, H. A., *Chinese-English Dictionary*, London, 1892.

Glasenapp, H. von, "Der Buddha des 'Lotus des guten Gesetzes'", *Jahrbuch des Lindenmuseums* Heidelberg 1951.

Grassmann H., *Wörterbuch zum Rig-veda*, Leipzig, 1873.

Hakeda, Y. S. (trans.), *The Awakening of Faith*, New York and London, 1967.

Hakeda, Y. S., *Kūkai, Major Works*, New York and London, 1972.

Hashimoto Hōkei *Yuimakyō no Shisōteki Kenkyū*, Kyōto, 1967. 橋本芳契, 維摩経の思想的研究。

Hurvitz, L., Chih-I (538-597) *An Introduction to the Life and Ideas of a Chinese Buddhist Monk* (Mélanges Chinois et Bouddhiques XII 1960-62), Brussels, 1962.

Idzumi Hōkei, 'Vimalakīrti's Discourse on Emancipation (Vimalakīrti-Sutra)', *Eastern Buddhist* II-IV (1922-28, serially).

Inada and Funabashi, *Jōdo Shinshū*, Kyōto 1961.

Inagaki, H., Yukakawa, K., and Okano T. R. (trans.), *The Kyō Gyō Shin Shō*, (Ryūkoku Translation Series V). Kyōto, 1966.

Iwano Masao (ed.) *Kokuyaku Issaikyō*, various dates. 岩野眞雄, 國譯一切經。

Jacobi (H.) trans., *Gaina Sutras* (Sacred Books of the East, vol. XXII), Oxford, 1884.

Johnson, Francis, *Hitopadeśa: The Sanskrit Text, with a Grammatical Analysis, Alphabetically Arranged*, London, 1884.

Jones, J. J. (trans.), *The Mahāvastu*, 3 vols., (Pali Text Society), London, 1949 ff.

Julien, Stanislas, *Méthode pour Déchiffrer et Transcrire les Noms Sanscrits qui se Rencontrent dans les Livres Chinois*, Paris, 1861.

Kato, B., Soothill, W. E. and Schiffer, W., *Myōhō-Renge-Kyō, The Sutra of the Lotus Flower of the Wonderful Law*, Tokyo, 1971.

Kern, H., *Saddharma-Puṇḍarīka or The Lotus of the True Law*, Oxford, 1884, (Max Müller, ed., Sacred Books of the East, Vol. XXI), reprinted New York, 1963.

Kern, H. and Nanjio, B. (eds.), *Saddharmapuṇḍarīka*, St. Petersburg, 1908-1912.

Kumoi Shōzen, 'Hōben to Shinjitsu' in Ōchō Keinichi (ed.) *Hokkeshisō*, Kyōto, 1969. 雲井昭善，方便と真実；横超慧日，法華思想。

Lamotte, Étienne, *L'Enseignement de Vimalakīrti (Vimalakīrtinirdeśa)*, Louvain, 1962.

Lamotte, Étienne, *La Concentration de la Marche Héroïque (Śūraṃgama samādhisūtra)*, (Mélanges Chinois et Bouddhiques, XIII) Brussels, 1965.

Lancaster, Lewis, *An Analysis of the Aṣṭasāhasrikā-prajñāpāramitā-sūtra from the Chinese translations.* Diss. Univ. of Wisconsin, 1968.

Luk, Charles, *The Vimalakirti Nirdesa Sutra*, Berkeley, California, 1972.

Masuda, Hideo, "Hannyakyō ni okeru 'hōben' no imi ni tsuite", *Indogaku Bukkyōgaku Kenkyū* 23 (1964). 増田英男，般若經における［方便］の意味について，印度學佛教學研究十二ノー（23）。

Matsunaga, Alicia, *The Buddhist Philosophy of Assimilation, The Historical Development of the Honji Suijaku Theory*, Tokyo, 1969.

Matsunaga, Alicia and Daigan, 'The Concept of Upāya 方便 in Mahayana Buddhist Philosophy', *Japanese Journal of Religious Studies* I, 1 (1974).

Mathews, R. H., *Chinese-English Dictionary*, Shanghai, 1931, (Revised American Edition, Cambridge, Mass., 1943).

May, Jacques, (trans.), *Candrakīrti: Prasanna-padā Madhyamaka-vṛtti, Douze chapitres traduits du sanscrit et du tibétain*, Paris, 1959.

Mironov, N. D., 'Buddhist Miscellanea II: Central Asian Recensions of the Saddharmapuṇḍarīka', *Journal of the Royal Asiatic Society*, 1927.

Mochizuki Kankō (ed.), *Kindai Nihon no Hokke Bukkyō*, Kyoto, 1968. 望月歓厚，近代日本の法華仏教。

Monier-Williams, Sir M., *Sanskrit-English Dictionary*, Oxford, 1899.

Nakamura Hajime and Kino Kazuyoshi (eds.), *Hannya-shingyō Kongō-hannya-kyō*, Tokyo, 1961. 中村元・紀野一義，般若心経金剛般若経。

Nanjiō, Bunyū, *Catalogue of the Chinese Translation of the Buddhist Tripi-taka*, Oxford, 1883, Tokyo, 1929.

Niwano Nikkyō, *Hokkekyō no Atarashii Kaishaku*, Tokyo, 1966. 庭野日教，法華経の新しい解釈。

Nobel, J., *Suvarṇaprabhāsottama-sūtra, Das Goldglanz-sūtra, ein Sans-krittext des Mahayana-Buddhismus*, 2 vols., Leiden, 1958.

Ōchō Keinichi, *Hokke Shisō*, Kyōto, 1969. 横超慧日，法華思想。

Ōchō Keinichi, *Hokekyō Josetsu*, Kyōto, 1962, 1972. 横超慧日，法華経序説。

Oda Tokunō, et al., *Bukkyō Daijiten*, Tokyo, 1954, 1972. 織田得能，佛教大辭典。

Puini, Carlo, *Avalokiteçvara Sutra, Traduction Italienne de la Version Chinoise avec Introduction et Notes* (Atsume Gusa, Textes 6), Paris and London, 1873).

Pye, Michael, 'Assimilation and Skilful Means', *Religion, Journal of Religion and Religions*, I, 2 (1971).

Pye, Michael, Various, see General Observations, note 1.

Rawlinson, A., *Studies in the Lotus Sutra (Saddharmapuṇḍarīka)*, 2 vols., Ph.D. thesis, Lancaster, 1972.

Renondeau, G. (trans.), "Le 'Traité sur l'État' de Nichiren", *T'oung Pao* vol. XL, 1-3.

Renondeau, G., *La Doctrine de Nichiren*, Paris, 1953.

Rhys Davids, T. W. and C. A. F., *Dialogues of the Buddha* III Parts, (Sacred Books of the Buddhists vols. II-IV, Pali Text Society, 1899, 1910, and 1921 respectively).

Risshō Kōsei-kai (ed.), *Muryōgikyō, The Sutra of Innumerable Meanings*, and *Kanfugen-gyō, The Sutra of Meditation on the Bodhisattva Universal Virtue*, (translations by various hands) Tokyo, 1974.

Robinson, R. H., *Early Mādhyamika in India and China*, Madison, Mil-waukee and London, 1967.

Ryūkoku Translation Series, Jōdo Wasan (IV) and *Kyō Gyō Shin Shō* (V), see Inagaki, and Fujimoto.

Sakamoto Yukio and Iwamoto Yutaka, *Hokekyō*, 3 vols., Tokyo, 1962-1967. 坂本幸男・岩本裕，法華経。

Sansom, G. B., 'Nichiren', chapter in Sir Charles Eliot's *Japanese Buddhism*, London, 1935.

Sawada Kenshō, 'Bukkyō ni okeru hōben no shisō ni tsuite', *Bukkyō Bunka Kenkyū* 12 (1963) 沢田謙照，仏教における[方便]の思想について，仏教文化研究。

Sekiguchi Shindai (ed.), *Makashikan* 2 vols. Tokyo, 1966. 関口真大，摩訶止観。

Shimizudani Zenshō
  Saikoku Junrei Annaiki, Fujii, (Ōsaka-fu) 1933 onwards. 清水谷善照,
  西国巡禮案内記。
Shōtokujinai Shōtokunichiyōgakkō, *Eiri Ishaku Kannon Seiten*, Hakodate,
  1958. 聖德寺内聖德日曜学校, 絵入意譯觀音聖典。
Spae, Joseph J., *Christian Corridors to Japan*, Tokyo, 1965.
Stcherbatsky, Th., *The Central Conception of Buddhism*, London, 1923.
Stcherbatsky, Th., *The Conception of Buddhist Nirvāna*, Leningrad, 1927,
  and The Hague, 1965.
Suzuki, D. T., *Outlines of Mahayana Buddhism*, London, 1907, (reprinted
  with Prefatory Essay by Alan Watts, New York, 1963).
Suzuki, D. T., *Essays in Zen Buddhism*, Series I-III, London, 1927-34.
Suzuki, D. T., *Studies in the Lankavatara Sutra*, London, 1930.
Suzuki, D. T. (trans.), *The Lankavatara Sutra*, London, 1932.
Suzuki, D. T., *Zen Buddhism and its Influence on Japanese Culture*, (The
  Ataka Buddhist Library IX), Kyōto, 1938.

Taishō Shinshū Daizōkyō Kankōkai (Society for Publication of Taishō
  Shinshū Daizōkyō), *Taishō Shinshū Daizōkyō Mokuroku*, Tokyo, 1969.
  大正新修大藏經, へへ目錄。
Tajima Ryūjun, *Les Deux Grands Mandalas et la Doctrine de l'Ésotérisme
  Shingon*, (Bulletin de la Maison Franco-Japonaise, Nouvelle Série, Tome
  VI), Tokyo and Paris, 1959.
Takakusu, J. and Watanabe, K., *Taishō Shinshū Daizōkyō* (*The Tripitaka
  in Chinese*), 85 vols., Tokyo 1927 and 1960. 高楠順次郎・渡邊海旭, 大
  正新修大藏經。
Tucci, G., *Minor Buddhist Texts I*, (Serie Orientale Roma IX), Rome 1956.

Ui Hakuju, *Bukkyō Jiten*, Tokyo, 1965. 宇井伯壽, 佛教辭典。
Ui Hakuju, *Ui Hakuju Chosaku Senshū*, 7 vols., Tokyo, 1968. 宇井伯壽著
  作選集。

Watanabe Shōkō, *Nihon no Bukkyō*, Tokyo, 1958. 渡辺照宏, 日本の仏教。
Weller, F., *Orientalistische Literaturzeitung* No. 2, 1937, pp. 118-125, (review
  of Wogihara and Tsuchida).
Wilkins, Charles, *Fables and Proverbs from the Sanskrit, being the Hitopadesa*,
  London, 1885.
Windisch, E., *Die Komposition des Mahāvastu* (Abhandlungen der philo-
  logisch-historischen Klasse d. k. sächsischen Gesellschaft der Wissen-
  chaften, Bd. XXIV, No. XIV), 1909.
Wogihara, U. and Tsuchida, C., *Saddharmapuṇḍarīka-sūtram, Romanised
  and Revised Text of the Bibliotheca Buddhica Publication*, Tokyo, 1934.

Xīnhuá Zìdiǎn, Peking, 1971. 新华字典。

Yampolsky, Philip B., *The Platform Sutra of the Sixth Patriarch*, New York
  and London, 1967.

INDEX